ATLANTA

Thank you for being awesome!

... And coaching us through the stages in which we were still referred to as babies, children, and the young'uns.

We love you,

Cassie, Julian, , Mike

The golden dome of the
Georgia Capitol shines brightly

FIRST EDITION

ATLANTA

Carol & Dan Thalimer

The Countryman Press
Woodstock, Vermont

To Maizie Hale, Liz Lapidus, and Melissa Libby, who've been keeping us current on the Atlanta restaurant scene for years—as well as keeping us well fed.

We welcome your comments and suggestions. Please contact Great Destinations Guide Editor, The Countryman Press, P.O. Box 748, Woodstock, VT 05091, or e-mail countrymanpress@wwnorton.com.

ISBN 978-1-58157-086-1

Cover photo © isifa Image Service s.r.o/Alamy
Interior photos by the author unless otherwise specified
Book design Bodenweber Design
Page composition by Susan McClellan
Maps by Mapping Specialists, Ltd., Madison, WI © The Countryman Press

Published by The Countryman Press, P.O. Box 748, Woodstock, Vermont 05091

Distributed by W. W. Norton & Company, Inc., 500 Fifth Ave., New York, NY 10110

Printed in the United States of America

10 9 8 7 6 5 4 3 2 1

OVERALL MAP

Contents

Introduction   10

What's Where in Metropolitan Atlanta   13

1

Atlanta/Downtown

47

2

Atlanta/Midtown

81

3

Atlanta/Buckhead and Vinings

115

4

Decatur

145

5

Stone Mountain Village, Stone Mountain Park, and Beyond

171

6

Atlanta's Playground: Lake Lanier

193

7

Hospitality Highway: Sandy Springs, Roswell, Alpharetta, Cumming, and Points North

211

8

MARIETTA

243

9

WESTSIDE

265

10

THE SOUTHERN CRESCENT

277

11

McDONOUGH, HAMPTON, LOVEJOY, AND LOCUST GROVE

296

12

NEWNAN

307

INDEX   322

ACKNOWLEDGMENTS

Although we've written 15 other books about Georgia and the South, this one was one of the most pleasurable because this time we've been writing specifically about our hometown of almost 30 years.

We'd especially like to thank our editors at The Countryman Press: Kermit Hummel, Jennifer Thompson, and Kathryn Flynn for their guidance, suggestions, and infinite patience.

No matter how long we've lived in the Atlanta metro area or how much traveling we've done throughout the state, we could never keep up-to-date with all the latest activities, attractions, lodgings, restaurants, shopping, and events without the assistance of the state regional representatives at the Georgia Department of Economic Development's Tourism Division. For this book we are particularly grateful to Brittney Warnock, the Atlanta Metro representative, and Alison Tyrer.

We've had assistance from the staffs at almost every convention and visitors bureau, chamber of commerce, welcome center, and travel association in the area. Just a few of them include: Alpharetta CVB—Candice Cocco and Brooke Atha; Atlanta CVB—Amanda Dyson and Lauren Jarrell; Cobb County CVB—Judy Renfroe; DeKalb CVB—Jeff Mills; Gwinnett CVB—Cricket Elliott and Gay VanOrt; Henry County Chamber of Commerce/CVB—Sarah Robbins and Michelle Lassiter; Historic Roswell CVB—Marsha Saum; Marietta Welcome Center and Visitors Bureau—Christy Duffner and Theresa Jenkins. These and many others too numerous to list can be found in the *Guidance* section of each chapter. We're sure these professionals will be as helpful to you as they have been to us.

The restaurant scene in the metro area is in constant flux. It would be impossible to keep up with all the changes without the assistance of Maizie Hale of Maizie Hale Public Relations, Liz Lapidus of Liz Lapidus Public Relations, and Melissa Libby of Melissa Libby and Associates, among others.

To the countless others at specific activities, attractions, lodgings, restaurants, shopping venues, and events—thank you.

INTRODUCTION

When we moved to Atlanta in 1979, we were as guilty as many others in saying, "Atlanta is a fantastic place to live, but I wouldn't want to visit there." Now we have to admit our own ignorance about the number and quality of the attractions that awaited if only we had taken the time to search them out. But we were smug in thinking that our chosen city was no New York City, no San Francisco, no Los Angeles, no Washington, D.C., or the like. Of course, the fact that Atlanta was not one of these supercities was one of the very reasons we had decided to live here.

For seven years we owned three travel agencies and jetted all over the world. When people asked us about where to go or what to see in Atlanta, we'd glibly reply, "The only place we know how to get to is the airport." But when we started writing about travel we finally started investigating what was in our own back yard, and we were amazed at the variety of attractions. Sure, maybe they're not as well known as the Statue of Liberty, Fisherman's Wharf, Disneyland, or the Washington Monument, but they're worth seeing nonetheless.

Over the intervening years Atlanta has truly become a world-class city, hosting, for example, the 1996 Centennial Olympic Summer Games. Numerous attractions have been added, such as the New World of Coca-Cola and most recently the Georgia Aquarium, and the city's lodgings, restaurants, shopping opportunities, and activities make Atlanta an even more attractive tourist destination.

Metropolitan Atlanta is impossible to describe in one chapter because of its sprawling size and its wealth of attractions. In addition, there are several well-defined areas of the city, each with a unique personality, so we've created individual chapters for several of these sections.

With no natural boundaries to inhibit its growth, the metropolitan area has grown unabated in all directions. The metropolitan Atlanta area now consists of 28 counties, more than 140 municipalities, and a population of more than 5 million people. Everything within an hour's drive or even more of downtown is considered part of the metro area and, in fact, many of these towns have become bedroom communities for Atlanta residents. Despite their inclusion in the metro area, many of these municipalities have retained their small-town charm and have numerous attractions, lodgings, and restaurants of their own to attract tourists. We've grouped some of these small towns within close proximity to each other into chapters as well.

To many people from all over the world, Atlanta exists in a time warp revolving around the Civil War and the most famous story about its past, *Gone with the Wind*. Its history, however, predates the Civil War, Scarlett O'Hara, and Rhett Butler. In 1782 a thriving Creek Indian village and trading post called Standing Peach Tree (some say it was actually Pitch Tree) existed along what is now called Peachtree Creek where it empties into the Chattahoochee River. Historians theorize that there was either a single peach tree or a pine (pitch) tree on the spot. From these humble beginnings grew what is now the capital of the South and a plethora of things named Peachtree.

Atlanta began taking shape in 1837, when the Western and Atlantic Railroad decided to make the area the southern end of its operations. (The honor had been offered to nearby Decatur, which turned it down; otherwise, there might never have been an Atlanta at all.) The town was originally called Terminus because that's what it was—the end of the line. In

1843, it was renamed Marthasville for the daughter of Governor Wilson Lumpkin. (The aforementioned Martha Lumpkin is buried in Oakland Cemetery; see the Downtown chapter.) In 1847, the town was renamed once again; this time it was called Atlanta—probably a feminine form of Atlantic (as in Western and Atlantic), and the name finally stuck.

By the beginning of the Civil War in 1861, Atlanta was a major rail hub, a manufacturing center, and a supply depot, so it's no wonder that the city was a target of destruction by Union forces under General William Tecumseh Sherman. When the Union forces finally took Atlanta in 1864, all of the railroad facilities, almost every business, and more than two-thirds of the city's homes were destroyed—making Atlanta the only major American city ever destroyed by war.

But the city wasn't held down for long, giving rise to the city's association with the Egyptian legend of the phoenix rising from the ashes. In 1868, the Georgia capital was moved from Milledgeville to Atlanta—making the city the fifth and last state capital. Newspaperman Henry Grady almost single-handedly created the image of the reconciled "New South" where business opportunities were rife. Colleges and universities opened, telephones and trolleys were introduced, and the 1895 Cotton States Exposition introduced 800,000 visitors to the vibrant city, all of which began a long upward economic surge that lasts to this day.

"The city too busy to hate" took the lead in peacefully strengthening minority rights in the Southeast during the 1950s and 1960s. In 1963, Mayor Ivan Allen Jr. was the only white Southern mayor to testify before Congress in support of the pending Civil Rights Bill. When native son Martin Luther King Jr. was assassinated in 1968, it was the same Mayor Allen who pleaded for calm and who was rewarded with peaceful mourning.

Ever optimistic, the city decided to build a stadium when it didn't even have a professional team to play there. That optimism paid off when major league baseball's Braves moved from Milwaukee to Atlanta and the city was awarded the Falcons expansion football team. Today the city boasts not only baseball and football franchises, but also basketball, hockey, and arena football teams.

Now a world-class city, top leisure destination, and competitive meetings and conventions market, Atlanta has one of the nation's busiest airports, an efficient public transportation system, convention facilities that have made it second in the nation in convention business, the Underground Atlanta shopping and entertainment complex, a new stadium, a sports dome, a sports and entertainment arena, and a new from-the-ground-up live/work/play neighborhood. The city has hosted the 1988 Democratic National Convention, Super Bowls in 1994 and 2000, the NCAA Men's and Women's Basketball Final Four, and the NBA All-Star Game, among other top-notch events.

Another jewel in the city's crown was added when the 1996 Centennial Olympic Summer Games were awarded to Atlanta and 2 million people visited the city during the two-week event. The Olympics served as an impetus for a resurgence of downtown, with more than $2 billion in construction projects and other changes, the major legacy of which is Centennial Olympic Park (see *Nature Preserves and Parks* in the Downtown chapter). The predominance of the park has led to the construction of new hotels, the Georgia Aquarium, and the New World of Coca-Cola.

Sometimes it's hard to say you were wrong. Loving Atlanta and all it has to offer both the resident and the visitor makes it easy for us to say, "Atlanta's a great place to live and a great place to visit."

What's Where in Metropolitan Atlanta

This section offers some general information that is helpful to travelers, some of which would be too repetitive to include in each individual chapter—information about airports and airlines, car rentals, mass transit, bus and train travel, and the like. In addition, in this section we offer information about some of Atlanta's most outstanding attractions, fairs and festivals, activities, and lodgings to spur your curiosity. These brief mentions will be more fully described in the pertinent chapters. In this chapter, we merely reference these without contact information; in the separate chapters, for each entry we give you the telephone number(s), Web site if there is one, address, hours of operation, and admission, lodging, or meal price. In this chapter, we also give you some information about associations and councils that might be helpful, references to other books or Web sites, and regulations such as those for fishing, hunting, smoking, building fires, and littering.

African American Sites

In a state where a major part of the economy was once based on slave labor, where the Civil War often intruded, and where there were numerous events connected with the Civil Rights Movement of the 1960s, it's not surprising that there are many significant historical sites related to the lives and history of African Americans. The most significant of these sites and one of the most-visited attractions in the state is the **Martin Luther King Jr. National Historic Site** on Auburn Avenue in Atlanta. The site contains the birthplace of Dr. King. Adjacent to the historic site is the **King Center for Non-Violent Social Change.** Also in Atlanta is a collection of six prestigious black colleges, known collectively as **Atlanta University,** and several African American–inspired museums such as **APEX, Hammonds House,** and the **Herndon Home.** Numerous festivals such as the **Atlanta Black Arts Festival** celebrate African American heritage and culture. Numerous restaurants serve traditional soul food.

Agricultural Fairs

Despite the fact that metro Atlanta is largely urban and suburban, there are rural regions included in the metro area, and you can find a few fairs such as the **Forsyth County Fair** in Cumming and the **North Georgia State Fair** in Marietta. Although these fairs don't exhibit farm animals, they do have exhibits of award-winning fruits, vegetables, and flowers. In addition they offer midway carnival rides, arts and crafts shows, stunt shows, and entertainment. For more information about fairs, contact the **Georgia Association of Agricultural Fairs** (478-477-2334).

Airport and Airlines

Atlanta is the major hub in the Southeast. In fact, so many people pass through the city's airport, there used to be a T-shirt on sale in the airport shops that read, I DIED AND WENT TO HEAVEN, BUT I HAD TO CHANGE PLANES IN ATLANTA. Fortunately, visitors to the metro Atlanta area won't have to change planes when they arrive. To avoid repetition in the various chapters, we will give the specific contact information about the airport, the airlines that fly into it, and on-site car rental firms and shuttle information only once and will simply reference What's Where in the individual chapters.

The primary airport, which serves metro

Atlanta and much of Georgia from all over the world, is **Hartsfield-Jackson Atlanta International Airport** (1-800-897-1910; www.atlanta-airport.com), 6000 North Terminal Parkway, Suite 435, Atlanta 30320. One of the busiest airports in the world, it is served by 23 airlines. The primary airlines are **Delta** (1-800-221-1212; www.delta.com) and **AirTran** (1-800-247-8726; www.airtran.com), but the entire list includes **Air Canada** (1-888-247-2262; www.aircanada.com), **Aeromexico** (1-800-237-6639; www.aeromexico.com), **Air France** (1-800-237-2747; www.airfrance.com), **Air Jamaica** (1-800-523-5585; airjamaica.com), **Atlantic Southeast Airlines** (1-800-325-1999; www.flyasa.com), **American** (1-800-433-7300; www.aa.com), **America West** (1-800-327-7810; www.americawest.com), **British Airways** (1-800-247-9297; www.britishairways.com), **Comair** (1-800-325-1999; www.comair.com), **Continental** (1-800-231-0856; www.continental.com), **Continental Express** (1-800-525-0280; www.continental.com), **Corporate** (1-800-555-6565; corporate-airways.com), **Frontier** (1-800-432-1359; www.frontierairlines.com), **Independence Air** (1-800-359-3594; www.flyi.com), **Korean Air** (1-800-438-5000; www.koreanair.com), **Lufthansa** (1-800-645-3880; www.lufthansa.com), **Midwest** (1-800-452-2022; midwestairlines.com), **Northwest** (1-800-225-2525; www.nwa.com), **South African Airways** (1-800-722-9675; www.flyssa.com), **United** (1-800-241-6522; www.united.com), and **US Airways** (1-800-428-4322; www.usair.com). Transportation into the city is available from the airport by taxi (see *Taxis*), MARTA rail (see *Bus/Rail Services*), limousine, shuttle, and rental car (see *Car Rentals*).

Air Tours

An exciting way to see the metro area is from above. You can relive the romantic days of early flight by taking one of the tours offered by **Biplane Rides Over Atlanta,** which provides tours over the city and Stone Mountain as well as more distant trips over Lake Lanier and even to the north Georgia mountains.

Amtrak

Amtrak (1-800-USA-RAIL; www.amtrak.com) makes only five stops in Georgia and only one in the metro area. The Crescent route, which runs from New York to New Orleans, stops in Atlanta as well as in Toccoa and Gainesville. Because the Atlanta station (404-881-3067; 1-800-USA-RAIL; www.amtrak.com), 1688 Peachtree Street Northwest, is the only station to serve the metro area, we will give that information only here and not list it in each chapter—simply referencing What's Where.

Amusement Parks

No matter what your age, you can indulge the kid in you at Atlanta's amusement parks—some large, others small. All have rides; some have entertainment. The granddaddy of theme parks is **Six Flags over Georgia** in Austell just outside Atlanta. Six Flags also operates two sibling parks in Georgia: **Six Flags American Adventures** (geared toward young children) and **Six Flags White Water** (a water park), both in Marietta just outside Atlanta. Some other amusement parks in the metro area include **Dixieland Fun Park** in Fayetteville, **Fun Town of Henry County** in McDonough, **Lake Lanier Islands Beach and Water Park** in Buford, **Malibu Grand Prix Family Entertainment Center** in Norcross, **Mountasia Family Fun Center** in Marietta, **StarTime Entertainment Complex** in Roswell, and **U.S. Play** in Kennesaw. Not an amusement park in the pure sense, **Stone Mountain Park** offers a train ride, aerial tram ride, numerous games, and many other museums and attractions. And although it is not actually an amusement park, the **Beach at Clayton County International Park** in Jonesboro also offers multiple activities.

Antiquarian Books

C. Dickens in the Buckhead section of Atlanta sells fine, rare, and collectible books, as well as maps, historical documents, autographs, and manuscripts.

Antiques

For information about antiques shops in Georgia, consult the Web site www.antiqueshopsa2z.com/ga-city.htm. In the Atlanta metro area, contact the **Antique Dealers Association of Marietta** (www.antiquesofmarietta.com) and the **Chamblee Antique Dealers Association** (www.antiquerow.com). **Georgia's Antiques Trail** (www.historicgeorgia .org/trails) stretches 200 miles from Conyers to McDonough and consists of 200 shops and dealers.

Aquariums

Opened in November 2005, the **Georgia Aquarium** is the largest aquarium in the world. Expectations were that the aquarium would attract 2 million visitors in the first year, but with an average daily attendance of 10,000, the 2 million mark was passed in only six months. At the 6?-month mark, there had been 5 million guests. Visitors are particularly entranced with the beluga whales and the whale sharks. Tickets are for specified days and times, so be sure to make your reservations well in advance to avoid disappointment.

Area Codes

The Atlanta metropolitan area alone has three (soon to be four) area codes, making it necessary to dial all 10 digits whenever you make a call. It is not unheard of for a business with more than one phone line to have two different area codes, although

The Georgia Aquarium, which opened in 2005, is the largest aquarium in the world.

there is generally a primary line that rolls over to the other numbers. In general, the area of the metropolitan region inside the I-285 perimeter highway that circles Atlanta uses the 404 area code, while the areas outside I-285 use 678 and 770. There are exceptions, however, so be sure to check the number. This 404, 678, 770 area is one of the largest toll-free calling areas in the country, stretching all the way from the Georgia/Alabama line on the west side of the metropolis to Monroe, Social Circle, and Covington to the east; from Barnesville considerably south of the metro area to Clermont considerably north. Some places close to the Atlanta metro area use 706 and 762.

Art Associations and Councils

The Atlanta metro area is home to numerous arts associations and local arts groups as well as several symphony orchestras, major art museums, and community theaters. For the most complete information about arts in Georgia, contact the **Georgia Council for the Arts** (404-685-2787; www.gaarts.org).

Art Museums

The **High Museum of Art** in Atlanta is the state's premier art museum. Not only are the collections impressive, but the structure is an outstanding work of art itself. The striking primary building was designed by Richard Meier, and a recently opened addition was designed by Renzo Piano. Currently, the museum is operating three years of major exhibitions in partnership with the Louvre in Paris. Some other important art museums in the area include the **Marietta/Cobb Museum of Art** in Marietta, the **Michael C. Carlos Museum of Emory University** in Decatur, and the **Museum of Contemporary Art of Georgia**. For more information consult the **Georgia Association of Museums and Galleries** (www.gamg.org) or these Web sites: www.georgia.worldweb.com/Sights Attractions/Museums or www.artcyclopedia .com/museums/art-museums-in-usa -georgia.html.

The striking High Museum of Art was designed by architect Richard Meier.

Atlanta Metropolitan Area Defined

The Atlanta Metropolitan Statistical Area (MSA) as defined by the federal government encompasses 28 counties and 140 cities, towns, and other municipalities with a total population of approximately 5.1 million. Between April 1, 2000, and July 1, 2006, the Atlanta MSA was ranked number one among the country's 361 MSAs in growth with 890,000 new residents, although Atlanta ranks ninth in size among U.S. cities. For the purposes of this book, however, we will stick pretty close to the definition of the Metro Atlanta tourism region as defined by the Georgia Department of Economic Development's Tourism Division. This area includes not only the area within the city limits of Atlanta, but also Fulton and DeKalb Counties, which contain parts of the city, and Clayton, Cobb, Coweta, Douglas, Fayette, Gwinnett, Henry, and Rockdale counties. This area stretches from Alpharetta and Buford in the north to Grantville, Moreland, and Senoia in the south; from Douglasville in the west to Lawrenceville in the east. Because of their proximity to this area, the ease with which they are accessed, their use as bedroom communities, and their natural inclusion in the metro area, we've extended the area slightly to include some towns and attractions in parts of Carroll, Cherokee, Forsyth, and Hall counties.

Attraction/Restaurant/Shop Hours

We list the days of the week and the hours that attractions, as well as restaurants and shops, are open as of publication time. Obviously many of these will change in the future. In general, museums, some other attractions, and many restaurants are closed on Monday, and almost all attractions and many restaurants are closed on Christmas and some other holidays. It would make the individual entries about these attractions, restaurants, and shops too unwieldy to list all the days they are closed. To avoid disappointment, please check ahead if you're traveling on major holidays such as New Year's Day, Martin Luther King Day, Easter, Memorial Day, Labor Day, and Thanksgiving. Many of Georgia's state parks and historic sites also are closed on Monday—except when a major holiday falls on a Monday. Always check the appropriate Web sites or call before you travel to get the most up-to-date times of operation.

Auto Racing

Auto racing is an extremely popular sport in Georgia, and the Atlanta metro area is no exception. The **Atlanta Motor Speedway** in Hampton is world renowned and its races attract the largest single-day attendance of any sport in Georgia. Other racetracks include **Lanier National Raceway** and **Road Atlanta and Panoz Racing School**, both in Braselton.

Ballooning

There's an exciting and romantic way to get a bird's-eye view of parts of Georgia: a ride in a hot-air balloon. **Adventures Aloft** in Lawrenceville and **Balloons Over Georgia** offer these rides in the Atlanta metro area. In general, rides are offered in the early morning or before dusk and are highly dependent on the weather, so check ahead.

Beaches

Because Atlanta is landlocked, it does not boast any natural beaches. Several parks and other attractions feature man-made beaches, including the **Beach at Clayton County International Park** in Jonesboro and **Lake Lanier Islands Beach and Water Park** in Buford.

Bed and Breakfasts

Many travelers prefer accommodations in small historic properties with breakfast included. Metro Atlanta offers several such properties—primarily in Victorian-era "Painted Ladies." Prices vary from $50–650, but average $150–200 per night.

The upside of a stay in a bed and breakfast is personal attention, recommendations about attractions and restaurants from your host, and the greater likelihood that guests will interact with each other than if you stayed in impersonal hotels. If you think you'd like to try a B&B, keep in mind that bed and breakfasts are usually in someone's home and that there are often strict rules about pets, children, and smoking, as well as deposit and cancellation policies that are more stringent than other types of accommodations. B&Bs may not be wheelchair accessible and certainly don't have all the amenities of a large hotel. A stay in a B&B is usually by reservation only with no walk-ins. The prices we quote are for one night for one or two people; there is almost always an additional charge for more than two guests. In addition to our suggestions, some other places to get recommendations include www .abba.com, www.georgiabedand breakfasts.com, www.usinns.com/html/ regions/GA, and www.bnblist.com/ga/ ga.htm.

Bicycling

Every biker, from the occasional weekend recreational rider to the serious cycler, can find what he's looking for in and around Atlanta, although he'll have to head north to the mountains for rigorous mountain biking. For information on biking in Georgia, consult the state's travel Web site, www.georgia.org, and choose the "Adventure" link. Also consult the Web site www.dirtworld.com.

Readers also might like to contact the following organizations about bicycling in the state: **Atlanta Bicycle Campaign** (404-881-1112; www.atlanta.bike.org), a bicycle advocacy group in the Atlanta metro area; **Georgia Bicycle Federation** (www.bicycle

georgia.com), which is dedicated to making Georgia a friendlier place to ride; and **Georgia Bikes** (404-634-6745; www.georgia bikes.org), a nonprofit organization dedicated to improving bicycling conditions and promoting cycling.

Bird-Watching

The **Audubon Society** (www.audubon.org/states) has several chapters in Georgia. Contact the **Atlanta Audubon Society** at 770-913-0511 or at its Web site: www.atlantaaudubon.org. The society has designated 29 regions of Georgia as Important Bird Areas. Several birding trails attract casual and serious bird-watchers. Avid birders would probably like to consult "Birds of Georgia," the Georgia Wildlife Federation's species list (www.gwf.org/resources/georgiawildlife/ birdindex.html). Another source of information is the Web site www.georgianature .org/member_spotlight/index.html. Some excellent book resources include *Birding Georgia* by Giff Beaton; *Birds of Georgia Field Guide* by Stan Tekiela; *Georgia Birds* by James Kavanagh; and *Georgia Bird Watching: A Year-Round Guide* by Bill Thompson III.

Boating on the Chattahoochee River

The river is open for boating from 30 minutes before sunrise to 30 minutes after sunset. Night boating is not allowed. Jet Skis are not permitted. No boats or rafts are rented by the various units of the Chattahoochee River National Recreation Area, but there are authorized outfitters, instructors, and guides available nearby for hire (check the park's Web site, www.nps.gov/chat). Approximate float times with distances for seven possible canoe trips also can be found on the park's Web site. U.S. Coast Guard-approved personal flotation devices must be carried on board all vessels for each person. All children younger than 10 must wear such a device when a vessel is underway. All

Georgia Department of Natural Resources boating regulations apply and all motorized boats must be registered. The river remains at about 50 to 55 degrees year-round, so hypothermia is an issue not to be taken lightly. A $3 daily use parking fee or a $25 annual park pass is required.

Boat Excursions

See *Canoeing, Kayaking, Tubing, White-Water Rafting*; and *Cruises*.

Books

Visitors can get the flavor of Atlanta's past by reading fictional and nonfictional accounts set in the city or state—many by Atlantans or Georgians. Still the second-best-selling book in the world after the Bible, *Gone with the Wind* by Margaret Mitchell paints the stereotypical portrait of the Old South. *Peachtree Road* by Anne Rivers Siddons and *A Man in Full* by Tom Wolfe put the old and new moneyed classes of Atlanta at the end of the 20th century under the microscope. Mystery lovers might enjoy the works of Kathy Hogan Trochek and Patricia Sprinkle that are set in Atlanta.

In the humor genre, the late Lewis Grizzard comes to mind. Some of Grizzard's books include *If I Ever Get Back to Georgia, I'm Gonna Nail My Feet to the Ground; Chili Dawgs Always Bark at Night*; and *When My Love Returns from the Ladies Room, Will I Be Too Old to Care?*

And the Dead Shall Rise: The Murder of Mary Phagan and the Lynching of Leo Frank by Steve Oney is a shocking true case of anti-Semitism in Atlanta at the turn of the 20th century. In the children's book category, Joel Chandler Harris is famous for the Negro tales he incorporated into the Uncle Remus stories in the late 19th century. Written in the late 20th century and told from a child's point of view, *Turn Homeward, Hannalee* by Patricia Beatty is a fictionalized version of the true story of the women and children taken from Roswell during the Civil War, charged with treason, and sent north to be imprisoned or placed in servitude. A fictionalized version from an adult's point of view is *The Roswell Woman* by Frances Patton Stratham. Some other travel guides you might want to consult include three of our other guides: *Georgia: An Explorer's Guide*—everything you ever wanted to know about traveling in Georgia; *Fun with the Family: Georgia*, a collection of activities, attractions, festivals, lodgings, and restaurants specifically of interest to families with young children; and *Romantic Days and Nights in Atlanta*, themed getaways for long weekends created for couples with romance in mind.

Within the various categories of this What's Where section of the book, you'll find numerous suggestions for books under the categories *Bicycling, Bird-Watching, Camping, Hiking*, and *Mountain Biking*.

Bus/Rail Service

The **Greyhound Bus Lines** (404-584-1738; www.greyhound.com) station at 232 Forsyth Street, Atlanta, is open 24 hours a day and is the eighth-busiest station in the country. Because the Atlanta station is the closest one to most of the areas of the city, suburbs, and towns described in many other chapters, we will simply reference What's Where rather than repeat the information.

Atlanta offers the best **mass transit** in the state. Not only does the city have a comprehensive mass transit system, those of several nearby counties connect to it, creating a vast network. In order to avoid repetitive material, we will describe the various mass transit systems that serve the metro area here and simply reference What's Where in the individual chapters.

The Atlanta metro area is served by the **Metropolitan Atlanta Rapid Transit Authority**, known locally as **MARTA; BUC (Buckhead's Uptown Connection); Georgia Tech Technology Square Trolley;**

Cobb Community Transit; Gwinnett County Transit; and **Xpress.**

MARTA (404-848-4711; www.its marta.com), 2424 Piedmont Road Northeast, Atlanta 30324, the city's bus/rail system, is the most cost-effective and convenient way to get around the Atlanta area (specifically Fulton and Dekalb Counties), with a variety of routes and pass options available. A station at the airport makes access to the city and suburbs easy. The regular fare is $1.75 one-way, and transfers are available between buses or between buses and trains. Exact change or fare cards (available at all station entrances) can be used. Visitor passes are available beginning at $7 for one day unlimited use up to $13 for a seven-day pass. Buses generally run between 5 AM and 1 AM weekdays, and between 6 AM and 1 AM on weekends and holidays. Trains run 5 AM to 1 AM daily. MARTA allows bicycles on all its trains, and there are bike racks on the front of some buses (the racks handle only two bikes at a time). Many MARTA stations have bike racks for commuters who wish to bike to the train. Transfers are free between MARTA and Cobb Community Transit (CCT), Gwinnett County Transit (GCT), and Xpress.

While in the Buckhead area of Atlanta, take advantage of the free **BUC (Buckhead's Uptown Connection)** shuttle, which connects the Lenox Square and Buckhead MARTA rail stations with major hotels, dining locations, retail centers including Lenox Square and Phipps Plaza, and key office buildings. The BUC operates 7 AM to 10 PM weekdays. For information, contact the Buckhead Area Transportation Management Association (404-842-2682; www.batma.org; www.bucride.com).

Another option for getting around a limited area of the city is the free **Georgia Tech Technology Square Trolley** (404-894-9645). These rubber-tired, alternative-fuel vehicles, designed to look like old-fashioned trolleys, provide service from the center of the campus to Technology Square to the Midtown MARTA station. This means out-of-town visitors can take MARTA rail from the airport to the Midtown station, and then transfer to the trolley to reach the campus and the Georgia Tech Hotel and Conference Center. The free Tech Trolley runs every four minutes and is available to students, faculty, staff, and visitors.

In the nearby suburbs of Marietta and Cobb County, mass transit is provided by **Cobb Community Transit** (770-427-4444; www.cobbdot.org/cct.htm), 463 Commerce Park Drive, Suite 114, Marietta 30060. Information line available 4 AM to midnight Monday through Saturday. Fares are $1.25 one-way for adults, 80¢ for youth 18 and younger, 60¢ for seniors and disabled; 10- and 20-ride tickets are available. The transit authority provides bus service throughout the county and connecting service to MARTA at the Arts Center station in Midtown.

For mass transit transportation in Gwinnett County, **Gwinnett County Transit** (770-822-5010) provides express, local, and paratransit services. Express buses to and from Atlanta operate weekdays and include six routes using the HOV lanes on I-85. Free park-and-ride lots are located at I-985, Discover Mills shopping mall, and Indian Trail. Local bus service within Gwinnett County operates five routes Monday through Saturday, connecting neighborhoods and businesses to cultural, shopping, and educational opportunities.

Xpress (404-463-4782; www.xpress ga.com) is metro Atlanta's newest public transit service. Fares are $3 one-way, $5 round-trip. Routes operate 5:30 AM to 9:30 PM weekdays. Operated in partnership with the Georgia Regional Transportation Authority and 11 counties, the service provides an easy-to-use connection from Cumming, Fairburn, Jonesboro, and Morrow to downtown Atlanta, where passengers can transfer to the MARTA bus/rail system.

Camping

One wouldn't necessarily expect to find camping opportunities in a metropolitan area, and indeed camping facilities are extremely limited in the Atlanta area. There are, however, camping facilities near **Six Flags over Georgia** in Austell, near Lake Allatoona close to Acworth, near Lake Lanier in several locations, at **Stone Mountain Park** near Marietta, and south of the city near McDonough. These camping facilities will be described in the appropriate chapters. Camping is not allowed in the Chattahoochee River National Recreation Area. An excellent resource for information about camping in Georgia is *Camping Georgia* by Alex Nutt, and there are dozens of camping Web sites, of which avid campers are probably already aware. See also the next entry, *Camping in State Parks*.

Camping in State Parks

The only two state parks (Sweetwater Creek State Conservation Park and Panola Mountain State Conservation Park) specifically in the Atlanta metro area as defined by the Georgia Department of Economic Development's Tourism Division do not have overnight camping facilities. Because we have slightly extended the area we're describing as the metro area, we have described **Fort Yargo State Park** in Winder, which does offer camping facilities. At state park campgrounds, a two-night minimum stay is required for most reservations, except a three-night minimum is required for Memorial Day, Labor Day, and Independence Day weekends. RV and most other campsites offer electric and water hookups, grills or fire rings, and picnic tables. Comfort stations with hot showers, flush toilets, and electrical hookups are conveniently located. All campgrounds have a dump station and some offer cable

TV hookups. Campers younger than 18 must be accompanied by an adult. Pets are welcome if kept on a 6-foot leash and attended at all times. Separate group camps and pioneer camps are available. A deposit is required and there are cancellation penalties. To find out about camping at specific state parks, consult the Web site www.gastateparks.org.

Canoeing, Kayaking, Tubing, White-Water Rafting

Canoeing, kayaking, and tubing can be good ways to see Atlanta's wildlife. Families with small children might enjoy floating down a placid river in an inner tube or gliding along in a canoe or kayak. Tubing is popular in the Chattahoochee River National Recreation Area, which runs from Lake Lanier through the metro Atlanta area. **Chattahoochee River Outfitters** in Roswell is a local outfitter. (See *Boating on the Chattahoochee River*.)

Car Rentals

All the major car rental companies have numerous locations throughout the metro Atlanta area, although all of them are not found everywhere. Rather than give car rental contact information in every chapter, we will list that information here and simply reference What's Where. These car rental firms include **Alamo** (1-800-462-5266; www.alamo.com), **Avis** (1-800-331-1212; www.avis.com), **Budget** (1-800-527-0700; www.budget.com), **Dollar** (1-866-434-2226; www.dollar.com), **Enterprise** (1-800-261-7331; www .enterprise.com), **Hertz** (1-800-654-3131; www.hertz.com), **National** (1-800-CAR-RENT; www.national.com), and **Thrifty** (1-800-847-4389; www .thrifty.com).

Car rentals are available on-site at Hartsfield-Jackson Atlanta International Airport from **Avis, Budget, Dollar, Enterprise, Hertz, National/Alamo,** and

Thrifty. Off-site car rentals include **Airport Rent A Car of Atlanta** (1-800-905-4997), **EZ Rent A Car** (404-761-4999), and **Payless Car Rental** (404-766-5034).

Carriage Tours

A particularly romantic way to see an area is to take a leisurely carriage ride of a small section of the city. **Amen Carriage Tours** offers rides in downtown Atlanta and **Yellow Rose Carriage Services** offers them around the square in Marietta.

Cemeteries

We have a fascination with old cemeteries. They are fonts of historical data and poignant personal stories, and often boast ornate and unusual headstones and mausoleums. The most important cemetery in the Atlanta metro area is **Historic Oakland Cemetery**, but others include **Westview Cemetery**, the **Marietta Confederate Cemetery**, the **Marietta National Cemetery**, and the **Patrick Cleburne Confederate Memorial Cemetery**. In addition to these, we also describe several other small historic cemeteries.

Chapter Headings

Chapters are divided among the three principal areas of the city—Downtown, Midtown, and Buckhead—as well as numerous suburbs and surrounding towns, including Buford and Lake Lanier, Decatur, the Hospitality Highway, Marietta, McDonough, Newnan, Southside, Stone Mountain, and Westside. Rather than put the three chapters about the city proper in alphabetical order, we've described Downtown first and have worked our way north to Midtown and then to Buckhead. In order to keep the chapter titles from getting too long, we have listed only the main town or towns in the heading. Each chapter, however, also will contain information about attractions in nearby towns.

Chattahoochee River

The Chattahoochee, which is the Cherokee word for "River of the Painted Rock," emerges as Chattahoochee Spring in the northeast Georgia mountains near the White/Union County line and wends its way to Lake Seminole at the Georgia/Florida border. As part of its course it creates the southern half of the border between Georgia and Alabama, as well as being impounded to create several significant lakes. The river offers opportunities for fishing, hiking, picnicking, canoeing, and rafting. Visitors may see wildflowers, waterfowl, and wildlife such as muskrats and beavers. Island Ford, the headquarters unit of the Chattahoochee River National Recreation Area (see *Recreation Areas* in the Decatur chapter), is in Dunwoody.

Children, Especially for

Throughout this book, attractions, restaurants, and lodgings that are of special interest to families with children or are particularly child-friendly are indicated with the ✐ icon.

Children's Museums

Youngsters aren't neglected when it comes to metro Atlanta's museums. There are several museums geared specifically to the small-fry, including **Imagine It! The Children's Museum of Atlanta**. Several important museums aren't just for adults, but offer interactive children's rooms in their facilities, including the **High Museum of Art** in Atlanta. The **Center for Puppetry Arts** in Atlanta is of special interest to both adults and children.

CityPass

Created by the Atlanta Convention and Visitors Bureau, the CityPass allows nine days to see the Georgia Aquarium, World of Coca-Cola, High Museum of Art, Inside CNN Atlanta Studio Tour, Fernbank Museum of Natural History or Atlanta

Civil War graves in the historic Oakland Cemetary are watched over by the Confederate Lion.

Botanical Garden, and Zoo Atlanta or Atlanta History Center at a savings of almost 50 percent. Passes can be purchased at the individual attractions listed or online at www.atlanta.net/citypass. Adults $64, children $45.

Civil War Sites

Georgia has significant Civil War history. As Union troops pushed into the state from Chattanooga, the Confederacy had an important victory at Chickamauga in north-west Georgia (now a national battlefield park), but couldn't stop the relentless advance toward Atlanta, which was targeted because it was a rail center and supply distribution point for the Confederacy. After taking Atlanta, Union General William Tecumseh Sherman's March to the Sea headed across central Georgia to Savannah, destroying just about everything in his path. When in Georgia, don't be surprised to hear the Civil War described as "The War" as if there were no other. You'll also hear it referred to as "The War of Northern Aggression" and our favorite, "The Recent Unpleasantness." Sherman is snidely referred to as "That Pyromaniac from the North." Numerous battle re-enactments, living history camps, and other activities occur throughout the year and are described in the *Special Events* section of individual chapters. The most significant Civil War site in the Atlanta metro area is **Kennesaw Mountain National Battlefield Park** in Kennesaw, but there are several others, all of which are described more fully in the appropriate chapter. See also *Re-enactments.*

Cottage Rentals

Cottage rentals are a popular and usually reasonably priced lodging alternative for stays of a week or more at a lake or state park. Naturally, cottage rentals are limited in the metro Atlanta area with the exception of some on Lake Lanier and those at **Fort Yargo State Park.** Another source of information about cottage rentals is a local chamber of commerce—many of these are listed in the *Guidance* section of each chapter.

Cottage Rentals in State Parks

Fort Yargo State Park in Winder is the only state park in the Atlanta metro area with cottages. In general, state parks require a two-night minimum stay (three nights on Memorial Day, Independence Day, and Labor Day weekends), although some require a five- or seven-night minimum in the summer. Shorter stays may be available at the last minute. There is a maximum 14-night stay, although if you have vacated the cottage for four nights, you may return. Youth younger than 18 must be accompanied by an adult. After a successful experiment allowing pets in cottages at three state parks in 2005, all state parks now welcome pets in selected cottages. Prior arrangements are required, though, so don't just show up with your pet. Deposits are required and there are cancellation penalties. To learn more about state park cottages, consult the Web site at www.ga stateparks.org.

Counties

Georgia has 159 counties—most of them are very small—and many have only one municipality. Years ago the thinking was that a county shouldn't be any larger than the distance a person could travel by horseback from his farm to the county seat, transact his business, and return home in the same day. An exception is Fulton County, of which Atlanta is the county seat. Fulton County, which was created by combining three counties, is 48 miles long and stretches from Alpharetta in the north to Palmetto in the south. The remainder of what is considered the metropolitan Atlanta area consists of nine other counties.

Covered Bridges

Georgia once had more than 200 covered bridges. Today there are only 16, and not all of them are historic. Only three have survived in the metro Atlanta area: **Concord** near Smyrna, **Haralson Mill** in Conyers, and **Poole's Mill** near Cumming. For more information about these and other Georgia covered bridges, consult the Georgia Department of Transportation's Web site, www.dot.state.ga.us/specialsubjects/ specialinterest/covered.

Crafts

If you have an interest in a particular craft and want to find the best locations to purchase examples, there are dozens of craft guilds such as the **Chattahoochee Handweavers Guild** (www.chgweb.com), the **Georgia Basketry Association** (www.geocities.com/ga_basketry_assoc), and the **Peachtree Arts and Crafts Association** (770-457-5510). To find contact information for other guilds, check out the Crafts Report Online at www.crafts report.com/resources/south/georgia.html.

Cruises

The term *cruise* can cover a lot of territory, but in the context of this guide it generally means a boat ride or excursion of fairly short duration that might be focused on sight-seeing, wildlife observation, or fishing. Because Atlanta is landlocked and the Chattahoochee River is not navigable this far north, there are precious few opportunities for cruises. The two that come immediately to mind are the *Scarlett O'Hara*, a replica paddle wheeler, and the **DUKW** amphibious vehicles, both of which operate on the lake at Stone Mountain Park.

Cultural Events/How to Find

The best places to find current information about theatrical and musical events occurring in the city are the Web sites atlanta.citysearch.com and www.atlanta

performs.com as well as the Thursday Access Atlanta section of *The Atlanta Journal-Constitution*, *Creative Loafing*, or *The Sunday Paper*. Also check the Web sites of series such as www.BroadwayAcrossAmerica.com and specific venues described in the individual chapters.

Cultural Organizations

The world-renowned **Atlanta Symphony Orchestra** offers classical and pops series. In the metro area, there are also the DeKalb, Gwinnett, and Southern Crescent symphonies. Atlanta also offers the **Atlanta Ballet**, the **Atlanta Opera**, and the **Capital City Opera**. Theater of all kinds proliferates in the metro area (see *Theaters/Summer* and *Theaters/Year-Round*). See also *Art Museums*.

Cultural/Theater Tickets

Check out **AtlanTIX** (678-318-1400) at the Atlanta Convention and Visitors Bureau Underground Atlanta Visitors Center, 65 Upper Alabama Street, or the location at the Simon Guest Services Booth inside Lenox Square Mall, Peachtree Road and Lenox Road. Atlanta's same-day, half-price outlet offers tickets to a wide variety of theater, dance, and musical performances as well as half-price same-day and day-after tickets to Zoo Atlanta, the Atlanta History Center, the High Museum of Art, the Margaret Mitchell House and Museum, and other attractions. AtlanTIX is open 11–6 Tuesday through Saturday, noon–4 Sunday.

Curiosities

Part of the fun of traveling around any state is finding the offbeat attraction. Atlanta, with several oddities, is no exception. The primary one is the **Big Chicken** in Marietta—part of an unusual Kentucky Fried Chicken restaurant. You'll find others in the individual chapters and may discover some we haven't listed on your travels.

Dining and Eating Out

The prices we list for your guidance are for entrées only. You could easily more than double the price of a meal by adding appetizers, soup, salad, side dishes, dessert, and cold beverages, tea, or coffee. Certainly the meal price would be greatly increased by adding alcoholic beverages. The *Dining Out* category is considered to be fine dining in a more formal setting. This category is usually also more expensive—in general, we've listed restaurants here when entrées are $20 or higher. The *Eating Out* category is much more casual and also more affordable, with entrées less than $20. Some restaurants were hard to categorize. Perhaps, for example, a restaurant's entrées are less than $20, but the ambience is formal, with linen tablecloths and napkins, mood lighting, candlelight, soft music, and flowers. In that case, we've listed it with fine dining. Although we've tried to put each restaurant in the category in which we think it fits best, it might also fit into the other category, so we hope the description of it makes it possible for you to make a decision about whether this is what you're looking for or not. Also be aware that prices will almost inevitably have changed by the time you travel.

Driving Tours

Georgia boasts many state-designated trails, some of which have sites included in the metro area. For example, the **Blue and Gray Trail** (www.blueandgraytrail.com), which stretches from Chattanooga to Dallas and includes Kennesaw and Marietta, has significant Civil War sites. The **March to the Sea Heritage Trail** (www.gcwht.org) follows the 350-mile route of General Sherman from Atlanta to the coast and includes several sites in the metro area. The **Old Dixie Highway** (www.dixiehighway.org), which was the nation's first planned roadway, was a major north/south route to Florida before the advent of interstate highways. It stretches 90 miles from north Georgia to Marietta and also includes Acworth and Kennesaw. The newest is the **Hospitality Highway** (www.hospitality highway.com), which stretches north from Sandy Springs to Dahlonega (see the Hospitality Highway chapter).

Atlanta and many of the surrounding cities and towns have devised driving tours of historic neighborhoods. Just a few of these include the **Gone with the Wind Driving Tour of Homes** in Jonesboro, the **Cannonball Trail** in Marietta, **Senoia Driving Tour of Homes, Historic Grantville Driving Tour**, and others.

Emergencies (Medical)

The Atlanta metro area is universally covered by 911 services for life-threatening situations. In each chapter, we also list nearby hospitals for situations that are not life threatening.

Events

We've listed outstanding and often highly unusual annual events within each chapter. Some of the most-anticipated large festivals include the **Atlanta Dogwood Festival, Atlanta Jazz Festival, Children's Health Care of Atlanta Children's Christmas Parade, National Black Arts Festival**, and the **Southeastern Flower Show**—all in Atlanta—and the **Renaissance Festival** in Fairburn. We give a brief description, contact information, and an admission price if there is one. Space prohibited us from describing more events in detail, so find others by checking the Web sites of convention and visitor's bureaus and chambers of commerce, which are listed in the *Guidance* section of each chapter. Other listings can be found at the state's travel Web site, www.georgia.org. Even more information can be obtained from the **International Association of Fairs and Expositions** (www.fairsand expos.com).

Extravaganzas

Excess and pageantry excite many visitors. The **Medieval Times Dinner and Tournament** in Lawrenceville and the **Laser Show Spectacular** at Stone Mountain Park provide plenty of thrills for all ages.

Factory Outlets

Georgia has clusters of outlet stores scattered throughout the state, primarily along I-75 and I-85 north and south of the Atlanta metro area. Although all but one of these (**Tanger Outlet Center** in Locust Grove) are technically outside the area covered by this book, you may be driving by them on the way to or from Atlanta, or may decide that they are worth a side trip. Some of these outlet centers, which offer a variety of merchandise, include **Commerce Factory Stores** in Commerce, **North Georgia Premium Outlets** in Dawsonville, **Peach Festival Outlet Shops** in Byron, and **Tanger Outlets of Commerce.** Many individual off-price shops can be found throughout the metro area. Atlantans were particularly happy when the famous **Filene's Basement** opened in Buckhead.

Fall Foliage

Colors are usually at their most brilliant in north Georgia during the last week in October and the first week in November. The air is usually clear and crisp, making travel especially appealing. The downside is that roads are often clogged with sightseers. North of Atlanta, restaurants and shops are crowded and it's essential to have made overnight reservations far in advance. Unlike some other states, where leaf season is considered off-season with reduced prices, in Georgia fall is still high season. In fact, hostelries may require three-night minimum stays and full nonrefundable payment in advance. Some Web sites to consult about fall foliage as the season approaches include www.forestry.about.com, www.atlanta.city

search.com, www.tripspot.com/foliage feature.htm, www.fs.fed.us/conf/fall/falcolor.htm, www.11alive.com, www.ajc.com, and www.trails.com.

Farm B&Bs

Farm B&Bs offer a complete change of pace for city dwellers—lots of wide-open spaces, farm animals, hearty breakfasts, and a casual atmosphere. Some are on working farms, some are not. One of the most outstanding is **The Inn at Serenbe**, located in Palmetto just south of Atlanta. Accommodations exude casual elegance; meals are gourmet delights. In addition to farm animals to feed or pet, guests enjoy a restaurant, a collection of folk art, swimming pool, hiking trails, and a waterfall. See *Bed and Breakfasts* for a list of B&B resources.

Farmer's Markets

The best source of fresh fruit, produce, and many other food and plant items is one of the state's numerous farmer's markets. The largest is the **Atlanta State Farmer's Market** in Forest Park just south of the city, which even offers a trolley tour of the huge site. Other popular farmer's markets include **Buford Highway Farmer's Market** in Atlanta, **Harry's Farmer's Market** in Roswell, **International Farmer's Market** in Chamblee, and **Your DeKalb Farmer's Market** in Doraville—all of which are in the metro Atlanta area. For more information about farmer's markets, consult the Web site www.n-georgia.com and click on "Farmers Markets."

Film

Since the inception of the **Georgia Film, Video & Music Office** (404-962-4052; www.filmgeorgia.org) in 1973, 500 major motion pictures and TV programs have been filmed in Georgia, including *Midnight in the Garden of Good and Evil, Forrest Gump, The Legend of Bagger Vance, Glory, Sweet Home Alabama, Fried Green Tomatoes, The Fighting Temptations, In the Heat of the Night,* and the Emmy-winning HBO film "Warm Springs." Several film festivals occur annually. Probably the most famous movie made in and about Atlanta (other than *Gone with the Wind,* which wasn't made here) is *Driving Miss Daisy.*

Fire Permits

Permits are not usually required for camp fires, but campers are responsible for any damage caused by their fire, which may include the cost of fighting the fire and the cost of timber destroyed, so exercise extreme caution. In extreme drought conditions, camp fires may be prohibited, so be sure to keep up with advisories. Only dead or downed wood can be used. Better yet, use a portable stove fueled by propane gas or Sterno®. Permits are required for all other outdoor burning. You must contact the local Georgia Forestry Commission office (1-800-GA-TREES; www.gfc.state.ga.us) to obtain a permit before you proceed with any other outdoor burning.

Fishing

Licenses are required for both fresh and saltwater fishing. Call 1-800-ASK-FISH for detailed information about fishing in Georgia. In addition to fishing regulations and license information, the recording gives a weekly update on fishing conditions, locations of boat ramps, and the answers to commonly asked questions. Alabama, Florida, and South Carolina have reciprocal freshwater fishing agreements with Georgia, so residents of those states don't have to get a Georgia license if they already have a valid one. There may be differences between the states, however, in the number or size of fish caught, so be sure to check local regulations. Licenses can be purchased at most sporting goods stores, most bait and tackle stores, and at large stores such as Wal-Mart that have a sporting goods department. You also can get a license by going to www.permit.com. A complete list of fishing regulations is available in the Georgia Department of Natural Resources/Wildlife Resources Division brochure, "Georgia Sport Fishing Regulations." A downloadable version of the brochure can be found on the Web site at www.gofishgeorgia.com.

Fishing Guide Services

Lake Lanier is a prime fishing lake for bass and striper, and several guide services are available, including Fishing Lanier with Bill Vanderford, Harold Nash Lake Lanier Striper and Bass Fishing Guide Service, Larry's Lanier Guide Services, and Tight Line Charters. There are also several guide services for fishing on the Chattahoochee River.

Frights

Halloween is a fright-filled holiday in the metro area with dozens of haunted houses and other spine-tingling events, the most-popular of which is the **Tour of Southern Ghosts**—blood-curdling tales told at the plantation at Stone Mountain Park. Visitors might want to see if they are brave enough to try the **Halloween Hayride and Family Festival** in Palmetto or the **Horror Hill Haunted Trail and Vertigo Haunted Trail** in Newnan.

Fruit and Berry Picking

If you want the freshest and most succulent fruits and berries, you might like to pick your own. And although it may be hard to believe, there are several places not too far from the metropolis where you can do that. The activity also can provide a pleasant couple hours of entertainment for the whole family. We describe a few of them in various chapters. For more information about pick-your-own facilities, consult the Web site www.pickyourown.org/GA.htm.

Gardens

Georgia's ideal climate makes gardens possible year-round in all but the most mountainous areas of north Georgia. In Atlanta the most significant gardens are those at **Antebellum Brumby Hall and Gardens** in Marietta, the **Atlanta Botanical Garden**, gardens at the **Atlanta History Center**, **Dunaway Gardens** near Newnan, **Georgia Perimeter Native Plant Garden and Wildflower Center of Georgia** in Decatur, the **Japanese Garden** at the **Jimmy Carter Presidential Library and Museum**, **Robert L. Stanton Rose Garden** at Fernbank, the **Vines Botanical Gardens** in Loganville, and the small but picture-perfect **Lewis-Vaughn Botanical Garden** in Conyers. Some of these gardens offer classes, talks, and demonstrations as well as special events and festivals.

Georgia Grown

Georgia leads all other states in the production of poultry, pecans, peanuts, eggs, and rye, and is in second place in cotton production. The Peach State actually ranks behind California and South Carolina in peach production, although its numbers are still significant. Other important food crops include tomatoes, watermelon, and Vidalia onions. While you're visiting the state you might want to sample the Georgia-grown products, many of which can be purchased at the Atlanta State Farmer's Market in Forest Park. Be on the lookout for farms and orchards that offer pick-your-own fruits, nuts, or vegetables.

Georgia/Atlanta Made

Atlanta artists and craftspeople create some other famous products, including rocking chairs produced by the **Brumby Chair Company** in Marietta, which were used in the White House during Jimmy Carter's presidency. **Frabel Art Glass** in Buckhead, created by Hans Godo Frabel, has been presented to U.S. presidents such as Gerald

The Robert L. Stanton Rose Garden at the Fernbank Museum of Natural History is home to more than 1,000 rosebushes.

Ford and Jimmy Carter, as well as to royalty such as Queen Elizabeth II. Frabel's art glass works include abstracts, color abstracts, animals, flowers, fruits, hearts, and much more. The studio also produces crystal. Many of the works are used for awards. Frabel recently displayed a large installation of pieces at the Atlanta Botanical Garden.

Georgia Public Broadcasting

There's almost nowhere you can go in Georgia where you'd be out of range of a Georgia Public Broadcasting radio or TV station (in Atlanta WGTV, Channel 8). Keep in mind that depending on the cable company that represents a specific area, these channel numbers may be different. For information in Atlanta, call (404) 685-4788 or consult the Web site www.gpb.org. Atlanta also has public television (WABE, Channel 30) and radio (WPBA, 90.1) stations operated by the Atlanta Board of

Education. Call 678-363-7425 for the television station or 404-892-2962 for the radio station.

Ghost Tours

A city and state with so much history is bound to have a few ghosts. Several options for ghost tours include the **Tour of Southern Ghosts** held at the plantation at Stone Mountain Park in October and **Roswell Ghost Tours,** which are held year-round.

Golf

It might surprise you to know that there are several public golf courses within the city limits of Atlanta, each described in the appropriate chapters: **Candler Park Golf Course** Downtown, **Bobby Jones Golf Course** at Atlanta Memorial Park in Midtown, and **North Fulton Golf Course** at Chastain Memorial Park in Buckhead. We also have described some resort courses in the appropriate chapters, including

Chateau Elan Winery and Resort in Braselton and **Emerald Pointe Resort** at Lake Lanier Islands (see the Atlanta's Playground chapter) and two courses at Stone Mountain Park (see the Stone Mountain chapter). In addition, there are dozens and dozens of public and semiprivate courses in the metro area, but they are too numerous to describe here. For information about all the golf courses in Georgia, consult the Web site, www.golflink.com/golf-courses/state.asp?state=GA. More information can be obtained from the Georgia State Golf Association (770-955-4272; 1-800-949-4742; www.gsga.org).

Guidance

In order to avoid repetitive information in multiple chapters, we will describe the major tourist contacts here and then refer to What's Where in the individual chapters. To plan a trip to Atlanta, contact the **Atlanta Convention and Visitors Bureau** (404-521-6600; www.acvb.com), 233 Peachtree Street, Suite 100, Atlanta 30303. Also consult the Web site www.atlanta.net for up-to-date information on hotel and restaurant reservations, directions, guidebooks, maps, and help in creating an itinerary.

There are several visitor's centers at various locations around the city. The visitor's center at **Atlanta Hartsfield-Jackson International Airport**, 6000 North Terminal Parkway, Suite 435, Atlanta 30320, is open 9–9 weekdays, 9–6 Saturday, and 12:30–6 Sunday. There are two visitor's centers downtown at the Georgia World Congress Center and at Underground Atlanta (see the Downtown chapter), and one in Buckhead at Lenox Square mall (see the Buckhead chapter).

Guide Services

See *Canoeing, Kayaking, Tubing, White-Water Rafting* and *Fishing Guide Services.* Numerous guide services are described in individual chapters.

Guided Tours

When we travel to a new place, we like to take a guided tour first to get the flavor of the area so we'll know which attractions we'd like to see in more detail. Several companies offer guided tours—some walking, some by bus or horse-drawn carriage or even Segway personal transporter. In Atlanta tours are offered by **American Sightseeing Tours, Atlanta Preservation Center Tours, City Segway Tours Atlanta, Georgia Institute of Technology Campus Tours, Gray Line Tours, Landmarks Through History Tours, Amen Carriage Tours**, and **Yellow Rose Carriage Services**.

Handicapped Access

Attractions, lodgings, and restaurants that are at least partially handicapped accessible are identified with the & icon. Keep in mind, however, that just because an entry is listed as wheelchair accessible doesn't mean it is fully accessible. A multistory attraction such as a historic home may have a ramp to allow access to the first floor, but other floors may not be accessible at all. A hotel or other lodging may have wheelchair access to guest rooms on the first floor or access to rooms on other floors via an elevator, but bathrooms don't necessarily have full accessibility with roll-in showers, handrails, or other modifications. Likewise, restaurants may have access to rooms on the first floor only and restrooms may have limited wheelchair accessibility. We try to indicate the true conditions in each entry if we think the distinction needs to be made, but it's probably best to call ahead.

Hiking

Just outside the city proper are hidden areas of undeveloped land conducive to both easy and challenging hiking. Even the big city has parks and other areas that provide hiking opportunities. The **PATH Foundation** (404-875-7284; www.path foundation.org) is a nonprofit organization working to build and maintain greenway trails throughout metro Atlanta and Georgia. Thus far the organization has helped develop 100 miles of urban trails, including the **Silver Comet, Stone Mountain, Lionel Hampton, Westside, Arabia Mountain, Chastain Park, South Decatur Trolley, Northwest Atlanta**, and **Freedom Park Trails.**

Some books that would be particularly helpful to hikers are *Atlanta Walks* by Ren and Helen Davis, 45 self-guided tours in the metro area along with walking, running, and bicycling information; *Georgia Walks,* also by Ren and Helen Davis, which details 50 tours; and *60 Hikes within 60 Miles of Atlanta* by Randy and Pam Golden.

Historic Homes and Sites

Because the city was virtually destroyed during the Civil War and because there seems to be a never-ending penchant for tearing down the old to build something new, Atlanta has few historic treasures. Most of those that survive are from the mid to late 19th and early 20th centuries. Fortunately, some of them are open for public tours: **Fox Theatre, Georgia State Capitol, Governor's Mansion, Historic Oakland Cemetery, Margaret Mitchell House and Museum**, and **Rhodes Hall**, all in Atlanta; **Bulloch Hall, Barrington Hall**, and the **Smith Plantation Home** in Roswell; **Historic Complex of the DeKalb Historical Society** in Decatur; **Antebellum Brumby Hall and Gardens** and **The Root House Museum**, both in Marietta; and the **Williams-Payne House** in Sandy Springs. In every chapter you'll find historic homes that are open for tours either because of the importance of the people who lived there or because of the architectural significance of the structure itself or both. See also *African American Sites, Bed and Breakfasts, Civil War Sites, Covered Bridges, Railroad Excursions and Museums,* and *Theaters.*

Historic homes like this one in Newnan can be hard to find in Atlanta, which was nearly destroyed in the Civil War but there are some in Inman Park and other historic neighborhoods.

History

See also *African American Sites, Civil War Sites,* and *Historic Homes and Sites.*

Horseback Riding

Horseback riding is a popular activity in Georgia but is not easily found in the metro area. For several years, companies offering horseback riding declined precipitously because of liability issues. The Georgia legislature, however, passed a law that requires participants to sign a waiver releasing the company from liability. Since then, many companies have begun offering horseback riding again. Options for horseback riding can be found in several chapters. One of the most outstanding is **Lake Lanier Islands Equestrian Center** near Buford (see the Atlanta's Playground chapter).

Horse Racing

Horse racing is not a widely available activity in Georgia, which makes the racing there that much more special. Two highly anticipated and well-attended annual events include the **Atlanta Steeplechase** in Kingston and the **Steeplechase at Callaway** in Pine Mountain. These events including tailgating, special food tents, terrier races, and, of course, fancy hats for the ladies.

There are a few other horse races and events. Contact the **Georgia Thoroughbred Owners and Breeders Association** (1-866-66-GTOBA; www.gtoba.com) for information about races. Contact the **National Barrel Horse Association** (706-823-3728; www.nbha.com) for information about shows and events.

Hours of Operation

The hours listed here for attractions, restaurants, shops, and so on are the most up-to-date we could get at publication time. Hours will undoubtedly change, however, so call ahead or consult an attraction's or restaurant's Web site before traveling to avoid disappointment. Although we don't mention it when listing the hours for each entry, it should be understood that most attractions and many restaurants are closed on major holidays such as Thanksgiving, Christmas, New Year's Day, and some other holidays. Assume attractions are closed on holidays or check ahead when in doubt.

Hunting

Hunting is permitted in the national forests and most wildlife management areas throughout the state, some of which are found in the far reaches of the metro area. Hunting regulations for all types of birds and animals can be found at the Georgia Department of Natural Resources Web site, georgiawildlife.dnr.state.ga.us. Some sources for more hunting information, including guide services, are www.gunnersden.com, www.huntfind.com, and www.huntingsociety.org/Georgia.html.

Information (Official) about Atlanta and Georgia

Atlanta contact information is listed under *Guidance.*

For more information about traveling in Georgia, contact the **Georgia Department of Economic Development's Tourism Division** (1-800-847-4842; www.georgia.org/Travel). You can request a free Georgia road map and a free Georgia travel guide. The state also publishes a guide to African American–related attractions, a calendar of events, and a golf guide. You can also request or download brochures using the Web site www.georgia.org/Travel/InfoDownloads/Brochures.htm. The state operates 11 welcome centers, most of which are at primary interstate highway access points into Georgia from other states: on I-20 westbound in Augusta, US 185 in Columbus, I-95 northbound in Kingsland, I-85 southbound in Lavonia, US 280 in Plains, I-75 southbound in Ringgold, I-95 southbound in Savannah,

US 301 in Sylvania, I-20 eastbound in Tallapoosa, I-75 northbound in Valdosta, and I-85 northbound in West Point. These staffed centers can provide you with maps, the state travel guide, brochures on attractions and lodgings, and advice. Other sources of information include the **Georgia Department of Transportation** (404-656-5269) and the **Georgia Department of Natural Resources, Environmental Protection Division** (404-656-0099; 404-656-0069).

Inns

Over almost 30 years of traveling in and writing about Georgia, we have personally stayed in and inspected hundreds of accommodations throughout metro area and the state. It's hard to keep up, however, and we've also relied on recommendations from travel professionals and others. No lodging has paid to be in this book.

Kayaking

See *Canoeing, Kayaking, Tubing, White-Water Rafting*.

Lakes

The most significant lakes in the Atlanta metro area are **Lake Lanier** and **Lake Allatoona.** These lakes and the lands surrounding them provide innumerable opportunities for water sports, hiking, camping, and other outdoor pursuits. They are described more fully in the appropriate chapters.

Litter

There are 11 litter control laws in Georgia. Fines for littering may range from $200 to $1,200. Contact local law enforcement agencies to report violations. For more information, contact **Keep Georgia Beautiful** (404-679-4910; www.keepgeorgia beautiful.org).

Lodgings

Atlanta's current hotel room inventory is more than 92,000 rooms. One thousand new rooms are being added in 2007 and 2008—primarily through several new boutique hotels located in landmark buildings. For the most part, we describe bed and breakfasts, small inns, boutique hotels, other one-of-a-kind properties, resorts, and upscale lodgings because visitors are already familiar with chain hotels and motels. As with restaurants and shops, lodgings come and go, so one that we've described may no longer be available when you're ready to travel.

Maps

Sources for Georgia maps include the **Georgia Atlas and Gazetteer,** which is available from Amazon, REI, and other sources. It provides DeLorme topographic maps that show highways and back roads as well as information on campgrounds, scenic routes, and natural features. The **Georgia Department of Economic Development's Tourism Division** (www.georgia.org) can provide a state road map. **Georgia Department of Transportation** (www.dot.state.ga.us) maps include the Georgia Bicycle Map, State Highway Transportation Map, city and county maps, and online maps. The **Chattahoochee-Oconee National Forests** (www.fs.fed.us/conf) can provide maps of the forests.

Marinas

The metro area's two big lakes—Lake Lanier and Lake Allatoona—offer innumerable opportunities for water-based recreation. Several marinas offer rentals, gas, supplies, and repairs, and some even rent houseboats: **Aqualand Marina, Harbor Landing Marina, Holiday Marina on Lake Lanier**—all on Lake Lanier—and **Holiday Harbor Marina** on Lake Allatoona, among others.

Mountain Biking

The best source of information about mountain biking in north Georgia is the U.S. Forest Service (770-297-3000), which maintains many of the trails and can give you maps and advice. Places to ride are described in many chapters. Currently biking is allowed only in the Sope Creek, Columns Drive, and Interstate North units of the **Chattahoochee River National Recreation Area.**

Some books that will be helpful to mountain bikers include *Mountain Biking Georgia: A Guide to Atlanta and Northern Georgia's Greatest Off-Road Bicycle Rides* by Alex Nutt; *Mountain Biking Georgia,* also by Alex Nutt; and *Off the Beaten Track: Guide to Mountain Biking in Georgia* by Jim Parham. See also *Bicycling* for information about bicycling organizations and other references.

Mountains

Georgia's Appalachian and Blue Ridge mountains are ancient and worn down and sometimes ridiculed by travelers from the western United States to whom Georgia's "mountains" are little more than bumps or hills. Atlanta sits just in the foothills of these mountains. **Kennesaw Mountain** north of Atlanta was the scene of fierce fighting during the Civil War. A climb to the top rewards hikers with an excellent view of Atlanta on a clear day. **Stone Mountain** is the world's largest exposed granite monadnock and the centerpiece of a recreational park. A carving of Confederate generals on its side was begun by the same sculptor who created Mount Rushmore. Visitors can hike to the top or take a cable car. Once at the top, they have excellent views of Atlanta. **Sawnee Mountain** in Cumming offers hiking and panoramic views from the Indians Seats rock formation at the summit. The entire northern part of Georgia is mountainous.

Museums

We've mentioned many different types of museums under the headings *Art Museums, Children's Museums,* and *Railroad Excursions and Museums.* Just a few other museums include the **African American Panoramic Experience, Atlanta Cyclorama and Civil War Museum, Atlanta History Center, Fernbank Museum of Natural History, Jimmy Carter Presidential Library and Museum, National Museum of Patriotism, William Bremen Jewish Heritage Museum, World of Coca-Cola,** and **Wren's Nest House Museum.**

Music Concert Series

The Atlanta metro area boasts not only the acclaimed **Atlanta Symphony Orchestra,** but several other symphonies, not counting several college and university orchestras. The ASO offers a classical series, a pops series, family concerts, and free summer concerts in metro area parks. All the other symphonies also have concert series, which are described in the appropriate chapters. A pleasant spring-though-fall evening diversion in Atlanta is to attend an outdoor concert. One of the most famous venues is **Chastain Park Amphitheater** in Atlanta, which hosts two different series of musical acts, including one with the Atlanta Symphony Orchestra. Two other outdoor venues in the Atlanta metro area are the **HIFI Buys Amphitheater** south of Atlanta and the **Villages Amphitheater** in Fayetteville. Many individual chapters list concert series, many of them performed outdoors (see *Entertainment* in each chapter). Just a few of these are the **Chateau Elan Summer Concert Series** in Braselton, **Moonlight and Music Concert Series** in Lawrenceville, **Glover Park Concert Series** in Marietta, **Music on the Square Concert Series** in McDonough, **Riverside Sounds Concert Series** in Roswell, the **Sun Trust Lunch on Broad Concert Series** in downtown Atlanta, and the **Summer Concert**

Series at the Depot in Kennesaw. Numerous music festivals vary in length from a day to a week or more. One of the best known festivals is the **Atlanta Jazz Festival.**

Native American Sites

Before European explorers and settlers came to Georgia, Native Americans inhabited the region—primarily Cherokees in the north and Creeks and Seminoles in the south. The discovery of gold in the mountains near Dahlonega led to the seizure of the Native Americans' land and their expulsion via the Trail of Tears. Then all the land in north Georgia was opened to white settlers by way of a land lottery. The only Native American sites open to the public are located just north of the metro area covered in this book, but there are several worth driving to, including the **Chieftans Museum and Major Ridge Home** in Rome, **Chief Vann House Historic Site** and **Fort Mountain State Park** in Chatsworth, **Etowah Indian Mounds Historic Site** in Cartersville, the **Funk Heritage Center and Appalachian Settlement** in Waleska, and the **New Echota Cherokee Capital Historic Site** in Calhoun.

Nature Preserves

Despite the preconception of many out-of-state potential visitors, the entire metro Atlanta area is not solid concrete and high rises. Green space has been preserved within all the towns and cities, and immense green spaces are still protected in the outlying areas. The **Chattahoochee-Oconee National Forests** cover a vast area of north and central Georgia, providing endless opportunities for hiking, bird-watching, camping, and other outdoor pursuits. Some other important nature preserves in the metro area include the **Chattahoochee Nature Center** in Roswell; **Chattahoochee River National Recreation Area;** the **Cubihatcha Outdoor**

Center/Towaliga River Preserve in Locust Grove; **Davidson-Arabia Mountain Nature Preserve and Heritage Area** in Lithonia; the **Newman Wetlands Center** in Hampton; **Panola Mountain State Conservation Park** in Stockbridge; and the **Sawnee Mountain Preserve** in Cumming.

Outdoor Venues

Chastain Park Amphitheater, a horse-shoe-shaped venue developed as a government works project in the 1930s, remains beloved by Atlantans who bring gourmet dinners, fancy table settings, candles, and floral arrangements to enhance their concert experience. More casual are the **HIFI Buys Amphitheater** south of Atlanta, the **Mable House Barnes Amphitheatre** in Mableton, and the **Villages Amphitheater** in Fayetteville. Many individual chapters list outdoor concerts or series that may take place in a park or on the courthouse square (see *Entertainment* or *Special Events*). See also *Music Concert Series.*

Parking

You'll be hard-pressed to find free on-street parking in Atlanta during the day, although there is often free parking after 6 PM and on Sunday. On the other hand, you can find some free parking in the smaller towns and suburbs around Atlanta. In the various chapters, we give details about the parking situation, including metered parking, parking lots and garages, and special event parking. In Atlanta, for example, you may pay up to $20 for special event parking. Many attractions have free parking.

Parking at State Parks

The parking fee at state parks is $3 daily, but overnight guests in lodges or camp-grounds pay the fee only once for the duration of their stay. If you are a frequent visitor to Georgia State Parks, save money by purchasing the annual **ParkPass** for $30. Seniors age 62 and older can purchase the

ParkPass for $15. Seniors are also eligible for discounts of 20 percent on camping fees, lodge room rates, and golf fees. Also available is the **Historic Site Annual Pass**, which costs $35 for a family, $20 for adults, and $15 for children. In addition the daily parking fee, state historic sites charge an additional entrance fee of $1.50–$7.

Parks and Forests
See *Nature Preserves*.

Parks/City
Within the city of Atlanta, there are an amazing number of significant parks, including the largest of them all—**Piedmont Park** in Midtown, as well as **Atlanta Memorial Park** in Midtown, **Centennial Olympic Park** downtown, **Chastain Park** in Buckhead, **Grant Park** in the neighborhood of Grant Park, and many others.

Parks/State
Georgia State Parks celebrated their 75th anniversary in 2006. The entire statewide system includes 48 state parks and 18 historic sites. Although every park doesn't have every feature, combined the state parks offer accommodations in cabins, campgrounds, lodges, and even yurts; beaches; covered bridges; golf; hiking; historic homes and other structures; horseback riding; flying model airplanes; forts; miniature golf; museums; Native American sites; waterfalls; water sports; and wildlife observation. Consult the Web site www.ga stateparks.org for more ideas about events and outdoor activities. See also *Camping in State Parks* and *Parking at State Parks*. In the Atlanta metro area there are only two state parks: Sweetwater Creek State Conservation Park in Lithia Springs and Panola Mountain State Conservation Park in Stockbridge. In the extended area we describe is Fort Yargo State Park in Winder. See separate descriptions in the appropriate chapters.

Parks/National
Georgia boasts several national parks. In the metro Atlanta area, you'll find the **Chattahoochee River National Recreation Area, Kennesaw Mountain National Battlefield Park** in Kennesaw, and the **Martin Luther King Jr. National Historic Site**. Each is described with its contact information in the appropriate chapter. For more information, consult the Web site www.nps.gov.

PATH Foundation
The PATH Foundation (404-875-7284; www.pathfoundation.org), mailing address P.O. Box 14327, Atlanta 30324, has been instrumental in developing 18 miles of greenway bike paths and 22 miles of on-street bike routes in the metropolitan area, as well as bike routes throughout the rest of Georgia. Call or consult the Web site for maps.

Pets
Unless you're traveling in the winter or driving directly to and from your destination, traveling with your dog can be problematic. We tried touring the state with one of our five dogs in an RV and ran into problems we didn't anticipate. Although Nero was perfectly comfortable while on the road with the air-conditioning running (in fact, he was often sitting regally in the passenger seat while one of us was working on the computer at the kitchen table), what to do when we stopped at a restaurant or attraction? We couldn't leave him in the RV unless we left the a/c running, and with today's gasoline prices that wasn't a very attractive option. We couldn't leave him tied outside the RV because it was too hot and we were concerned with his safety or the risk of him being stolen. We ended up running the RV so the air conditioner would be on and just watched the dollar signs mounting. Although pets are welcome in state park campgrounds and selected

state park cottages, they must be leashed at all times. Uncivilized though it may be, dogs are not welcome on Georgia's beaches. Knowing that many of our readers won't be happy leaving their best friend at home, however, we've indicated with the icon those lodgings, parks, hotels, and the like that are pet-friendly. For more information about travel with pets, consult the **Pet Friendly Travel** Web site, www.petfriendly travel.com/locations/US/Georgia/GA, which primarily lists cabins and cottages.

Population

The 2000 census reported Georgia's population as 8,186,453 and the Atlanta metro area's population as 4,708,000. Today the latter is estimated to be 5.1 million. Projections for 2010 are 9 million for Georgia and 6 million for the metro Atlanta area.

Public Restrooms

In general, visitors can find public restrooms at welcome/visitor's centers; government buildings such as city halls and courthouses; office buildings; restaurants; large shopping centers; major attractions; city and state parks; and convenience stores.

Rail Service

See *Amtrak* for interstate rail transportation and see MARTA under *Bus/Rail Service* for a description of Atlanta's rapid rail service.

Railroad Excursions and Museums

Atlanta's existence was based on it being a railroad terminus and later a major rail hub. Rail traffic continues to play a significant role in the city's economy. Although Atlanta's magnificent railroad terminal was torn down in the name of progress, many quaint, once-abandoned railroad depots enjoy new lives as museums, offices, restaurants, art galleries, and other uses. Several rail beds have been converted to

Rails-to-Trails paths used by walkers, joggers, cyclists, and skaters.

Museums range from large facilities with rolling stock such as the **Southeastern Railway Museum** in Duluth to smaller facilities with model trains. The **Southern Museum of Civil War and Locomotive History** in Kennesaw contains *The General,* the famous locomotive that was stolen during the Civil War and resulted in the Great Locomotive Chase.

Rates

The prices listed in all categories were the most up-to-date we could find at press time, but undoubtedly rates will change, so check ahead before you travel. The prices listed are merely a guideline so you can tell whether something is economical, moderate, or expensive. We've marked some entries with a 🎖 icon to indicate that it's an especially good value. In order to categorize an attraction, restaurant, or lodging as economical, we've decided that an attraction should have an admission fee of $10 or less, a restaurant should offer entrées at $20 or less, and lodgings should have room rates of $100 or less. This system isn't foolproof, however. An attraction such as a theme park, for example, may have an admission fee of considerably more than $10, but have so much to offer that it's actually economical.

Reenactments

Many Georgians have not forgotten the Civil War. The Sons of the Confederacy and other organizations reenact some of the battles that occurred in the state, including the **Battle of Jonesboro,** which occurred south of Atlanta. Reenactments consist of costumed soldiers, firing of weapons, and camps set up to reflect the life of the soldier. Sutlers often sell replica period clothing, weapons, and other wares. More detailed descriptions are given in the *Special Events* section of the pertinent chapters. See also *Civil War Sites.*

Reenactors bring the Civil War to life for visitors.

Resorts

We define resorts as properties with lodging, restaurants, and activities such as boating, children's programs, golf, horseback riding, tennis, spas, and the like. The Atlanta metro area boasts several properties that fit this definition. Among them are **Chateau Elan Winery and Resort** in Braselton, **Emerald Pointe Resort** at Lake Lanier Islands near Buford, the **Marietta Conference Center and Resort** in Marietta, and **Stone Mountain Park**.

Restaurants

A few restaurants enjoy a multidecade life, while unfortunately most others turn over quickly. Even though they may not be the current trendiest restaurants in town, we've tried to suggest eateries that have shown some staying power. Of course, even some of those may be closed when you visit a particular locale, so it's best to call ahead to avoid disappointment. For the most part, we describe one-of-a-kind eateries because visitors will already be familiar with chain restaurants. In the event that a restaurant you particularly wanted to visit has closed, consult our other suggestions, ask your concierge for help, or check with the welcome/visitor's center. Ask about the current hot spot when you get to an area and you may be in for a taste sensation, too. Cuisine ranges from the sublime to the ridiculous, from gourmet to take-out. As you read the individual chapters, you'll find that barbecue and down-home cookin' restaurants are prominently featured throughout the area. Fresh seafood is the top choice on the coast and islands, but

good seafood can be found almost anywhere.

Rivers

Georgia is laced with rivers and streams—
some of them dammed into lakes. You'll
notice that practically all of them still bear
their Indian names. The major rivers in the
Atlanta metro area include the **Chattahoochee,** which flows all the way from Lake
Lanier north of Atlanta to the Florida border and creates the border between Georgia
and Alabama, and the **Flint,** which flows
from the Atlanta metro area along the western border of the state and provides some
white-water rapids.

It was due to two strange bedfellows—
former President Jimmy Carter and former
House Speaker Newt Gingrich, two
Georgians whose politics could hardly be
more different— that a 48-mile section of
the river was designated as the **Chattahoochee River National Recreation Area**

(CRNRA). Now celebrating its 27th
anniversary, the 6,500-acre, 14-park
recreation area is owned and maintained by
the National Park Service. With more than 3
million visitors annually, the CRNRA is the
most popular of Georgia's 10 National Park
Service units and is home to more than 900
species of plants, old- and new-growth
hardwood forests, 20 species of fish, and
numerous animal species. Human presence
in the river corridor began as early as
10,000 B.C. and was well established by
5,000 B.C. Evidence of human habitation
ranges from remnants of Native American
settlements to the ruins of the Roswell cotton mills to significant Civil War sites.

For those who know about the CRNRA,
the river and its surrounding lands are
popular escapes from the city for hiking,
fishing, boating, and other outdoor pursuits. One of the most popular activities is
"shooting the 'Hooch"—floating down the
river on a raft on a hot summer day.

*"Shooting the 'Hooch," floating down the Chattahoochee River on a hot summer day, is a favorite Atlanta
pastime.*

Sailing

Georgia's many lakes are meccas for sailors. **Lanier Sailing Academy** on Lake Lanier north of Atlanta offers sailing classes and rentals. Numerous sailing companies, marinas, and boat ramps are described in the individual chapters.

Shops

Shops have the same problem as eateries in regard to staying power or lack thereof (see *Restaurants*). We've tried to pick not the hottest flash-in-the-pan shops, but those that have been around for a while. As with restaurants, in the event that a store you wanted to visit has closed, consider our other suggestions, ask your concierge, or check with the welcome/visitor's center. These travel professionals also will be the best source of advice about the newest up-and-coming shops.

Shuttles/Limousines

A few shuttle/limousine services in the Atlanta metro area include **Atlantic Limousine Service** (1-888-667-9300; www.atlanticlimo-ga.net), 2679 Peachtree Square; **Executive Priority Limousine Service** (404-881-9770), 265 Ponce De Leon Avenue Northeast; and **White Glove Limousine** (404-255-3955), 175 West Wieuca Road Northeast. Others will be described in individual chapters.

Smoking

On July 1, 2005, Georgia enacted a ban on smoking in any buildings open to the public—much to the joy of nonsmokers. That should have meant that we could simply list all hotels, lodgings, and so forth as non-smoking. Nothing's ever that simple, however. As with most laws, there are still many loopholes and exceptions. Establishments such as bars and nightclubs that don't admit anyone younger than 18 can still allow smoking. Many restaurants still allow smoking in their bars and on patios and decks, so these areas may be even more packed with smokers than before. Some establishments have a no-smoking policy until late at night and then permit smoking. Few bed and breakfasts, which are often housed in historic homes, allow smoking indoors, but may allow it on porches or decks. Insurance companies, however, may decree that bed and breakfasts not allow smoking even on the porches because of the possibility of fire. We have, therefore, still tried to indicate whether an establishment allows smoking or not, and if they do, where.

Special Lodgings

Atlanta currently boasts only one five-star property: the **Four Seasons**, but has a plethora of four-star hostelries. In addition there are some very special B&Bs.

Sports Teams

Atlanta has "America's Team"—the last-to-first **Braves** baseball team, as well as the **Falcons** football team, **Hawks** basketball team, **Thrashers** hockey team, and **Georgia Force** arena football team. Other teams include the Atlanta **Silverbacks** soccer team and the Gwinnett **Gladiators** hockey team.

Taxis

Sometimes getting around Atlanta is best via taxi. Atlanta's professional taxi cab drivers know the city's streets like the back of their hands and are used to the massive traffic jams. What's more, Atlanta has more than 1,500 taxis available to take you between accommodations and attractions. With preset rates for trips to and from the airport, downtown, and Buckhead, taxis provide an economical mode of transportation in Atlanta. Ask the concierge at your hotel for a list of taxi services in the area or simply flag down an on-duty cab. All cab companies are regulated under the same rate schedule, so it seldom makes any difference which taxi you take. From the airport the following flat rates apply:

Flat Rate Zone from Hartsfield

	One Person	Two People	Three People	Four or more
To Downtown				
	$25	$26 ($13 each)	$30 ($10 each)	$40 ($10 each)*
To Buckhead				
	$35	$36 ($18 each)	$39 ($13 each)	$45 ($11.25 each)*
To Midtown				
	$28	$30 ($15 each)	$35 ($11.66 each)	$40 ($10 each)*

* An additional $2 charge for each person beyond the fourth.
Rates to areas outside the Central Business District are computed by a meter. Standard charges are: $2 for the first $1/7$ mile; 25¢ for each additional $1/7$ mile; $18 per hour wait time.

Tennis

Metro Atlanta is a mecca for tennis players. ALTA, the Atlanta Lawn Tennis Association, has one of the largest groups of tennis players in the nation. Among the premier tennis facilities are the **Bitsy Grant Tennis Center** at Atlanta Memorial Park in Midtown, the **Blackburn Tennis Center and Park** in Sandy Springs, **the Chastain Memorial Park Tennis Center** in Buckhead, the **North Fulton Tennis Center** in Sandy Springs, the **Peachtree City Tennis Center** in Peachtree City, and the **South Fulton Tennis Center** in College Park. Outside the city, one of the most outstanding facilities is the **Stan Smith Tennis Center** at Chateau Elan Winery and Resort in Braselton.

Theaters/Summer

Most theater in Atlanta is offered during a September-to-May season, but theater lovers don't have to be bereft the rest of the year. During summer, six Broadway musicals are brought to Atlanta by **Theater of the Stars** and performed at the Fox Theatre. The **Georgia Shakespeare Festival** performs the Bard's plays as well as those of other playwrights on the campus of Oglethorpe University in the Buckhead section of Atlanta.

Theaters/Year-Round

Professional and amateur theater is alive and well in Georgia. The Atlanta metro area alone has dozens of theater groups ranging from the renowned **Alliance Theater** at the Woodruff Arts Center to the **Theatre in the Square** in Marietta. Theater-goers also flock to **Agatha's—A Taste of Mystery,** the **Jewish Theater of the South**, and the **New American Shakespeare Tavern**. Large-cast traveling Broadway shows often perform at Atlanta's **Fox Theatre** or the **Boisfeuillet Jones Atlanta Civic Center.** Some historic theater structures, which are worth seeing in their own right, include the Egyptian/Moorish-style **Fox Theatre** on Peachtree Street in Atlanta. **Broadway in Atlanta** and **Theatre of the Stars** bring Broadway shows to the city.

Traffic and Highway Tips

One of the things the Atlanta metro area is most infamously known for is horrendous traffic. With I-75, I-85, and I-20 meeting in downtown Atlanta, it's no wonder that traffic is a problem—especially during the morning and evening rush hours. The I-285 perimeter highway around Atlanta does little to speed you on your way. GA 400, a toll road that stretches north from Atlanta to Dahlonega, is one of the most

The area where I-85 meets I-285 is known as Spaghetti Junction.

congested roads in the state. In the Atlanta metro area, getting off the major highways and using surface roads and streets gains you little except perhaps being easier on the nerves. To make matters worse, the Atlanta metro area now stretches practically from Macon south of Atlanta to the Tennessee border on the north, and from the Alabama line in the west to past Covington on the east. Friday nights and Sunday nights are particularly heavily traveled as folks try to get away for the weekend or return home. Not that any of our readers would ever run a red light, but be forewarned that some municipalities are using photo enforcement at traffic lights.

Trails
See *Driving Tours, Hiking, and Walking Trails.*

Trolleys
Seeing the sights via a nostalgic trolley is a popular choice for travelers. The **Express** Trolley Tour at the Atlanta State Farmer's Market in Forest Park is an interesting way to see the giant fresh market.

Walking Tours
Both guided (see *Guided Tours*) and self-guided walking tours are available throughout metro Atlanta and some of the small towns surrounding it. Many small towns such as Marietta and Roswell and historic neighborhoods with structures from the turn of the 20th century are particularly conducive to walking tours. Just some of these are **City of Decatur Walking Tours, Midtown Art Walking Tour,** and the **Walking Tour of Emory University Campus.**

Walking Trails
Less strenuous than hiking trails in the mountains and national forests, many trails are more conducive to walking, jogging, bicycling, and inline skating. Some of them

are also stroller and wheelchair accessible. In the metro area, the **Silver Comet Trail** stretches from northwest Georgia to the Alabama line, and the **Wild Horse Creek Trail** in Powder Springs connects with the Silver Comet Trail. The **Roswell Trail System and River Walk** permits strolls along the Chattahoochee River.

Waterfalls

North Georgia's mountains are conducive to sudden changes in elevation—creating waterfalls along rivers and streams. Because the Atlanta metro area is in the foothills of the mountains, changes in elevation aren't as significant there. The only interesting waterfall is that along Vickery Creek in the Vickery Creek unit of the Chattahoochee River National Recreation Area in Roswell. It was manmade in the 1880s by damming the creek to provide power for a textile mill. A hike to the falls provides a couple of hours of solitude in the great outdoors. For information on other waterfalls in Georgia, visit any of the following Web sites: www.waterfalls-guide.com/ga_waterfalls-guide.htm, www.n-georgia.com/waterfal.htm, and www.georgiatrails.com/waterfalls.html.

Web Sites

The intent of our descriptions of individual attractions, activities, lodgings, restaurants, special events, and the like is only to whet your appetite. With the entries that particularly strike your fancy, we assume you'll want to know much more. Whenever they are available, therefore, we've included Web sites with the contact information for each entry. Accessing the Web site enables you to learn more about an entry we've described, see numerous color pictures—perhaps even a live Web cam—and check for the latest hours and prices before you travel. We've listed many Web sites under specific entries and appropriate categories,

but in order to reduce repetition, we'll list a few here that would be found under several categories. You can access lists of Georgia ATV trails, bike trails, hiking clubs, hiking trails, horse trails, and waterfalls at the Web site www.mountaintravelguide.com/georgia/georgia.htm. The e-library of the Georgia Wildlife Federation (www.gwf.org/resources/georgiawildlife/wildlifeindex.html) includes lists of amphibians, mammals, reptiles, and other categories. The Web site of the Georgia Nature-Based Tourism Association is www.georgianature.org.

When to Go

Atlanta is blessed with a moderate climate year-round and doesn't really have a high season and low season as some cities do. Springs and falls are long, pleasant, and colorful, with flamboyant flowers or leaves. Winters are mild, although freezing temperatures and snow and ice are not unheard of. These occasional cold snaps, snowstorms, or ice storms are rare and short-lived. Winter daytime temperatures average 55 degrees, so a blazer or lightweight coat is usually sufficient for being outdoors. Winter nights can drop down to the 40s, 30s, or even 20s, so a warmer coat, gloves, and a hat may be necessary then. Summers, on the other hand, can be quite hot, with daytime temperatures around 95 degrees for prolonged periods and sometimes even breaking 100 degrees for several days. Humidity can be high as well. Traveling in the autumn is ideal because temperatures have abated and the area is less crowded once children go back to school. (In Georgia, most schools start very early in August, so you don't even have to wait for Labor Day to reap the benefits of fewer crowds, although it is still quite hot.) Very warm temperatures can extend well into October. We also give some information in the *When to Go* section of the individual

Atlanta winters are usually mild, but the area occasionally gets enough snow to make a decent snowman.

chapters about times when it might be better NOT to visit an area because of special events or other reasons that make the area crowded and lodging hard to get. The very things like fall foliage that make folks want to visit an area also make it the most crowded.

Wineries

Climate, topography, elevation, and soil conditions make wine production in Georgia viable, although the industry is still in its infancy. Most of the wineries and the widest variety of grapes are found in the northern part of the state—an easy drive from Atlanta. The **Georgia Wine Highway** stretches from Clayton to Braselton and includes eight wineries. Some of the primary wineries in this area include **Chateau Elan Winery and Resort** in Braselton, **Frogtown Cellars** in Dahlonega, **Three Sisters Vineyards and Winery** in Dahlonega, and **Wolf Mountain Vineyards and Winery** in Dahlonega. Some of the wineries have free tours and tastings; others charge a small fee. Several also offer a restaurant and/or shop.

For more information, contact the **Wine Growers Association of Georgia** (706-878-9463; www.georgiawine.com). Other sources of information are **Georgia Wine Country** (www.georgiawinecountry.com) and the **Georgia Wine Council** (www.georgiawinecouncil.org).

Worth Driving For

In a few instances we describe an attraction that's not in the metro Atlanta area as we've defined it, but close to the farthest attraction in a chapter. For example, not far from Cumming in the Hospitality Highway chapter and Lake Lanier in the Atlanta's Playground chapter is the **Kangaroo Conservation Center** in Dawsonville, which has the largest concentration of kangaroos outside Australia. In such cases, we've added the heading "Worth Driving For," so you can decide whether you'd like

Visitors to Zoo Atlanta make sure to stop by its giant panda exhibit.

to venture a little farther to explore something special.

Zoos/Animal Preserves

You don't have to travel to exotic foreign countries to see wild animals that aren't native to America or Georgia. Several zoos throughout the area showcase a variety of these creatures. Others may have more docile farm animals just right for petting. **Zoo Atlanta** is the most prestigious of Georgia's zoos. It is one of only a few zoos in America to have an adorable pair of giant pandas on loan from China. Their baby Mei Lan, the darling of all Atlantans, has just begun to come outside to play in full view of visitors. Zoo Atlanta also boasts an exceptional primate collection as well as other wild and tame animals. Most travelers will be surprised to find that the largest collection of kangaroos outside Australia is just north of Atlanta at the **Kangaroo Conservation Center** in Dawsonville. Some other organizations with wild and tame animals are **Noah's Ark Animal Rehabilitation Center** in Locust Grove and the **Yellow River Game Ranch** in Lilburn.

The Atlanta Skyline as seen from Centennial Olympic Park.

Atlanta/Downtown

Downtown proper is bounded by North Avenue on the north, Turner Field on the south, Boulevard on the east, and Northside Drive on the west. The area is undergoing a vibrant renaissance and is now the site of convention facilities, major attractions, cultural venues, sports venues and events, sophisticated hotels, world-class restaurants, and abundant nightlife. Access is easy from the airport via taxi or rail, and getting around downtown is easy on foot or by taxi, bus, or rail. In fact, this is the one region of the metro area where you can easily get around without a car. Among the bus and walking tours available is one you can take using the Segway personal transporter.

In 1996, Downtown was the host of the Centennial Olympic Summer Games, the major legacies of which were the Olympic Stadium (now Turner Field) and Centennial Olympic Park. The rebirth of the area around the park has seen the construction of new hotels and several important new attractions, including the Georgia Aquarium (the largest in the world) and the New World of Coca-Cola. CNN, whose world headquarters is next to the park, is another major contributor to Downtown's vitality.

Sports venues include the Georgia Dome, where Atlanta Falcons football is played; Turner Field, where Atlanta Braves baseball is played; and Philips Arena, where Atlanta Hawks basketball and Atlanta Thrashers hockey are played.

Historic attractions include the Atlanta Cyclorama and Civil War Museum, the Herndon Home, Historic Oakland Cemetery, the Martin Luther King Jr. National Historic Site, Wren's Nest House Museum, and others.

Museums include the African American Panoramic Experience, Georgia Capitol Museum, and the Jimmy Carter Presidential Library and Museum, among others.

One of the most unusual areas in Downtown is Underground Atlanta, a region of shops, restaurants, and nightspots created when viaducts were built over railroad tracks. And no visit to Downtown would be complete without a trip to Zoo Atlanta to see the two giant pandas on loan from China and their adorable baby daughter as well as an outstanding primate collection.

In addition to the commercial district where the big hotels are located, Downtown has many interesting historic neighborhoods (some residential, some commercial), including Cabbagetown, Candler Park, Fairlie-Poplar, Grant Park, Inman Park, Little Five Points, Sweet Auburn, and West End. Many attractions are found in these neighborhoods and they often offer bed and breakfast accommodations, quaint or quirky boutiques, and popular eateries.

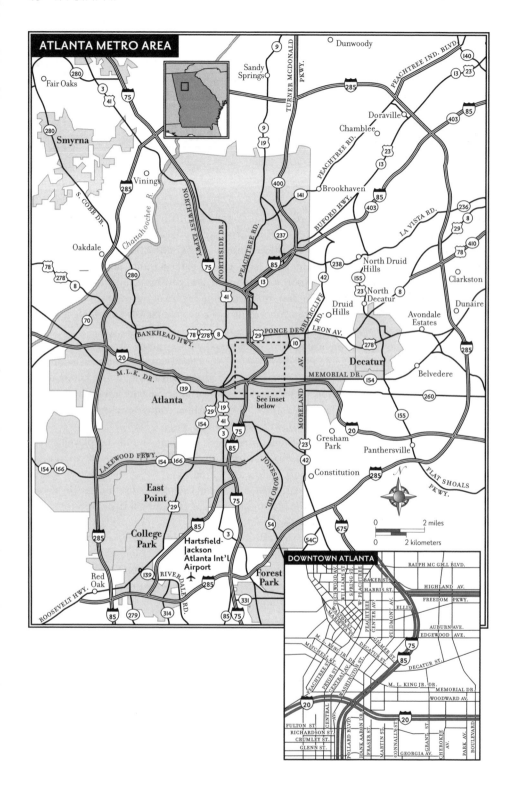

GUIDANCE

To plan a trip to Atlanta, contact the **Atlanta Convention and Visitors Bureau** (404-521-6688; 1-800-ATLANTA; www.acvb.com), 233 Peachtree Street Northeast, Suite 100, Atlanta 30303. Open 8:30–5:30 weekdays. Also consult the Web site www.atlanta.net for up-to-date information on hotel and restaurant reservations, directions, guidebooks, maps, and help in creating an itinerary. There are several Atlanta CVB Visitor Centers at various locations around the city to aid visitors. The **Visitor Center at Hartsfield-Jackson Atlanta International Airport**, 6000 North Terminal Parkway, Suite 435, Atlanta 30320, is open 9–9 weekdays, 9–6 Saturday, 12:30–6 Sunday. Downtown, the **Visitor Center at the Georgia World Congress Center**, 285 International Boulevard, Atlanta 30303, is open only during Georgia World Congress Center events, but the **Visitor Center at Underground Atlanta**, 65 Upper Peachtree Road, Atlanta 30303, is open 10–6 Monday through Saturday, noon–6 Sunday. In Buckhead there is also a **Visitor Center at Lenox Square Mall** (see the Buckhead chapter).

> **Atlanta Ambassador Force**
>
> Begun during the 1996 Centennial Olympic Summer Games to aid the vast number of visitors from around the world, the 60-person Atlanta Ambassador Force was such a success it's still around to help present-day visitors. The friendly ambassadors patrol a 190-square-block area from 7 AM to 10:30 PM daily. Just look for their turquoise jackets and white pith helmets. Ambassadors don't carry weapons, but they do have portable radios. They keep an eye out for anyone who looks lost and can also give directions, suggest attractions and restaurants, and relate history. Best of all, the services of these street concierges are free. For other information about the ambassadors, contact the Atlanta Downtown Improvement District at 404-215-9600.

Check out **AtlanTIX** (678-318-1400) at the Atlanta Convention and Visitors Bureau Underground Atlanta Visitor Center or at Lenox Square Mall. Atlanta's same-day, half-price outlet offers tickets to a wide variety of theater, dance, and musical performances as well as half-price tickets to other attractions (see What's Where). AtlanTIX outlets are open 11–6 Tuesday through Saturday and noon–4 Sunday. Also check out **CityPass** (see What's Where), which allows nine days to see six major attractions at a discount of almost 50 percent. Passes can be purchased at www.atlanta.net/citypass.

Getting There

By air: See What's Where.
By bus: See What's Where.
By car: Access to Atlanta is easy with I-75 and I-85 running north/south, and I-20 running east/west. All of them meet in downtown Atlanta.
By train: See What's Where.

Getting Around

For car rental companies, see What's Where.
Sometimes getting around Atlanta is best via taxi (see What's Where). Transportation via limousine service is available from an ever-increasing number of companies (see What's Where). For other taxi or limousine services, check the Yellow Pages.

Another easy and economical alternative is to use mass transit (see What's Where).

MARTA also operates the **Braves Stadium Shuttle.** On days when the Atlanta Braves are playing at Turner Field (known locally as "The Ted"), MARTA offers easy bus/rail service to the stadium from downtown. The Braves Stadium Shuttle provides bus service from the Five Points rail station—proceed from the station through Underground Atlanta to the shuttle buses waiting at the plaza. Golf cart transportation from the rail station to the bus is available for elderly or disabled game-goers. The shuttle begins service 90 minutes before game time and continues until the stadium is empty. Each passenger needs a rail-to-bus or bus-to-bus transfer or a regular fare to ride the shuttle.

Parking

There is little on-street parking downtown. For the most part, what on-street parking exists is metered but free during evenings and on Sunday. You probably wouldn't want to park on the street in such a congested area anyway. There are, however, plentiful for-fee parking lots and parking decks. Some of the attractions described in this chapter have free parking.

Public Restrooms

There are public restroom facilities at the Visitor Center in Centennial Olympic Park, at the Georgia Dome, in various buildings on the Georgia State University campus, at the Omni/CNN center, at Philips Arena, the Georgia Capitol, Georgia World Congress Center, and Underground Atlanta, as well as at major attractions.

When to Go

There's almost never a bad time to visit Atlanta (see What's Where). Some times to avoid, however, might include the Chick-fil-A Bowl/Big Peach Drop on New Year's Eve or other major events that draw big crowds. It might be best to call the CVB before planning a trip to find out what events are happening during your visit.

Medical Emergency

For life-threatening situations, call 911. In less urgent cases, immediate care is available at **Grady Memorial Hospital** (404-616-6200; www.gradyhealthsystem.org), 80 Jesse Hill Jr. Drive Southeast, and its associated **Hughes Spalding Children's Hospital** (404-616-6600; www.gradyhealthsytem.org), 35 Jesse Hill Jr. Drive Southeast. Immediate care is also available at **Emory Crawford Long Hospital** (404-686-4411; www.emoryhealthcare.org), 550 Peachtree Street Northeast.

Villages/Neighborhoods

Atlanta was almost completely destroyed during the Civil War and also has been accused of tearing down everything more than a few decades old to build something new, so there are not as many historic buildings as might be found in a city of comparable age and size. There are, however, several historic neighborhoods dating from the late 1800s and early 1900s.

Cabbagetown. This neighborhood, which is south of Inman Park, east of Oakland Cemetery, north of Grant Park, and west of Reynoldstown, is the oldest industrial settlement in Atlanta, dating from after the Civil War. The area was originally the home of the Atlanta Rolling Mill, which was burned during the Atlanta Campaign. In 1885 the Fulton

Bag and Cotton Mill was built to replace it and a mill town grew up around it with one- and two-story shotgun houses and cottages along narrow streets. When the mill closed in 1977, the neighborhood went into a rapid decline, which was only halted and reversed by the intown renaissance of the mid-1990s. The mill has been converted into the nation's largest residential loft community, and the neighborhood has attracted artists and musicians as well as families.

Candler Park. This historic neighborhood, which is listed on the National Register of Historic Places, was a large residential neighborhood dating from the late 19th and early 20th centuries. It actually began as a separate town called Edgewood, which became an in-town streetcar suburb of Atlanta. Bounded by Clifton Avenue on the east, DeKalb Avenue on the south, Moreland Avenue on the west, and North Avenue on the north, Candler Park is characterized by late-Victorian and bungalow/Craftsman architecture. The Victorian era is represented by small, unadorned cottages and large homes with considerable detailing and trim. Some houses representing the period from 1910 to 1930 are Greek Revival, Tudor, and other styles. In the 1970s and 1980s, gays began buying and restoring the homes, and now Candler Park is one of the most gay-friendly areas of the metropolis.

Fairlie-Poplar Historic District. A short walk from major downtown attractions and hotels, this vibrant area is a National Register Historic District characterized by classic examples of commercial architecture largely developed in the early 20th century. The district is also a visual illustration of Atlanta's transition from the Victorian era to the modern era. The city's first and oldest high-rises sit side-by-side with three- and four-story buildings from the 19th century. Newly improved with brick sidewalks, trees, public art, and streetscapes, the neighborhood has a pedestrian-oriented ambience unique to Atlanta. Restaurants and boutiques occupy the street level of many of these buildings, and the district is the site of several popular events such as the Lunch on Broad concert series (see *Special Events*).

Grant Park Historic District. Bounded by Glenwood and Atlanta Avenues and Kelly and Eloise Streets, this is one of Atlanta's oldest neighborhoods. Centered on Grant Park (see *Nature Preserves and Parks*), the majority of the district's structures are residences built between the late 1800s and early 1900s. Large two-story mansions face the park while more modest, modified Queen Anne frame dwellings radiate from the park on surrounding streets. One-story cottages and Craftsman bungalows predominate east of the park. A section of the main line of Civil War earthen breastworks and a battery known as Fort Walker are preserved in the southeast corner of the park. Grant Park is also home to the Atlanta Cyclorama and Civil War Museum (see *Museums*) and Zoo Atlanta (see *For Families*).

Inman Park. Once trolley transportation was available, Atlanta's well-to-do moved away from downtown. Begun in 1889, Inman Park was Atlanta's first suburb. Elegant Victorian-era Painted Lady homes with turrets, verandas, and elaborate gingerbread were

> **How Did Cabbagetown Get Its Name?**
> One story is that the poor Appalachians who worked the mill grew cabbages in their front yards and, of course, cooked them quite frequently. Another story is that a train carrying cabbages derailed and spilled cabbages all over the neighborhood. Another version of this story is that it was a model T Ford truck that overturned, dumping the cabbages. In either of these versions, residents rushed out of their homes to gather up the free cabbages. An alternate story is that cab drivers nicknamed the various neighborhoods in Atlanta and they are the ones who called this area Cabbagetown because of the pervasive odor of cabbages.

built here by such wealthy magnates as Coca-Cola's Asa Candler and Ernest Woodruff. Other homes include mail-order Craftsman bungalows. The neighborhood is nationally renowned for its preservation efforts. Numerous mansions in this neighborhood operate as bed and breakfasts (see *Lodging*). Some of these homes are open to the public during the annual Inman Park Festival and Tour of Homes (see *Special Events*).

Little Five Points. Located adjacent to the residential Inman Park neighborhood, Little Five Points (affectionately known as L5P) is a dining, entertainment, and shopping mecca for Atlanta's youthful consumers. The funky commercial district attracts hippies, yuppies, bikers, New Age flower children, aging flower children, Rastafarians, punks, freaks, stoners, and just about everyone else. Atlanta's Greenwich Village- or Haight-Ashbury-like Little Five Points is the "in" place to go, with numerous offbeat restaurants, clubs, shops, and theaters—all with their own peculiar twist.

Sweet Auburn. Auburn Avenue was the epicenter of African American enterprise from the 1890s to the 1940s, when it was hailed as the richest black street in America. An object of pride in the black community, it became known as Sweet Auburn. But once Civil Rights laws were passed and blacks were free to shop anywhere, Auburn Avenue began to decline and, in fact, became quite seedy. Today, with sites to see including the Martin Luther King Jr. National Historic Site and the African American Panoramic Experience Museum (APEX), the district is undergoing a renaissance. "Sweet Auburn: Where the Dream Began," an exhibit at the Martin Luther King Jr. historic site's visitor's center, chronicles the achievements of Atlanta's African Americans in the early 1900s. Sweet Auburn is also home to the Southern Christian Leadership Conference.

West End. This neighborhood, which pre-dates Atlanta by several years, was founded around the Whitehall Tavern, a stop on the Lawrenceville-to-Newnan post route. Development of the railroads pushed Atlanta out to and beyond West End by 1884, and West End petitioned for annexation. Around the turn of the 20th century, Atlanta's most affluent African Americans began to build or buy impressive homes in West End. By the 1960s, West End's star had waned and it was threatened with the loss of most of its historic architectural treasures to commercial development. In the 1970s, however, preservationists began restoring the remaining homes, and today the neighborhood is socially diverse and culturally rich. In addition to the tree-lined streets and outstanding architecture, sights to see in West End include the Wren's Nest, home of Joel Chandler Harris, creator of the Uncle Remus tales; the opulent Victorian-era Westview Cemetery; the Herndon Home; Hammonds House Galleries and Resource Center; and the Atlanta University Center complex of six historic black colleges and universities.

TO SEE

Cultural Sites

🌱 ⛫ **Clark Atlanta University Art Galleries** (404-880-8000; www.cau.edu), 223 James P. Brawley Drive Southwest. Open 11–4 Tuesday through Friday, noon–4 Saturday. Located on the campus of one of the city's oldest black universities, the galleries feature 640 contemporary African and African American artworks, including paintings, sculpture, the *Art of the Negro* murals by Hale Woodruff, paper works, and ethnographic artifacts. Among the artists represented are Romare Bearden and Henry Ossawa Tanner. Donations accepted.

✒ ✿ ⅃ **Folk Art Park,** Baker Street and Piedmont Road. Open daily. A permanent outdoor tribute to Southern folk art, the exuberant installation contains whimsical designs created by or in homage to some of the South's finest outdoor artists. *Homage to Reverend Howard Finster* was fashioned by the renowned artist's grandson using found objects, concrete, metal, glass, and marble to create a piece similar to those found in Finster's Paradise Gardens in Summerville. *Homage to St. EOM's Pasaquan* replicates the visionary environment in which the late artist Eddie Owens Martin, who called himself St. EOM (his initials), lived in southwest Georgia near Columbus. *Quilt Traditions* is a series of quilt-pattern motifs cut out of the stainless steel roof of a sunshade structure. The steel and plastic gourds of *Gourd Tree* house purple martins, while the painted steel pieces of *Windmills* gyrate cheerfully in the breeze. *Rolling Hills of Georgia* is rendered in concrete, glass marbles, and painted steel. Free.

✿ ⅃ **Johnny Mercer Collection/Georgia State University** (404-651-2477), Library South Building, 103 Decatur Street. Collection open 9–5 weekdays; exhibit open during regular library hours. Many familiar songs such as "Moon River," "The Days of Wine and Roses," and "I'm an Old Cow Hand" were penned by Savannah native Johnny Mercer, who wrote the lyrics for more than 1,000 songs between 1930 and 1976. Mercer also wrote the music for 55 of those songs although, amazingly, he neither read music nor played an instrument. Memorabilia such as correspondence, photographs, handwritten manuscripts of songs, sound recordings and tapes, and sheet music are displayed at the university and/or available for research. Free.

✿ ⅃ **Spelman College Museum of Fine Arts** (404-681-3643; museum.spelman.edu/museum/current.shtml), 350 Spelman Lane. Open 10–4 Tuesday through Friday, noon–4 Saturday. Closed Sunday, Monday, holidays, and Spelman College breaks. The museum focuses on culture, gender, and race, which are explored through photography, narrative, and video. Works by and about women of the African Diaspora are displayed. Admission $3; parking $3.

For Families

✒ ⅃ **Georgia Aquarium** (404-581-4000; www.georgiaaquarium.org), 225 Baker Street. Open 10–5 Monday through Thursday, 9–6 Friday through Sunday; hours extended one hour in the summer; other extended hours during holiday periods such as spring break. Tickets are for a specific time, and the last admission is one hour prior to closing. The aquarium, which resembles a huge ship (some have called it a modern-day Noah's Ark), is one of the largest aquariums in the world, with 5 million gallons of water containing more than 55,000 animals from 500 species. Conveniently located near Centennial Olympic Park and the Georgia World Congress Center, the aquarium uses innovative technologies and interactive and interdisciplinary techniques to educate and entertain visitors. The space is divided into five sections. The Tropical Diver area includes an Indo-Pacific reef with appropriate sea life, while the Ocean Voyager section contains a 2-million-gallon tank bisected by a glass tunnel through which visitors can walk for optimum viewing. Another huge tank and five smaller tanks surrounded by live vegetation make up the Cold Water Quest area. A 50-foot interactive fishing trawler, lighthouse, and boat house create a big playroom for kids of all ages in the Georgia Explorer area, which also contains examples of sea life representative of Georgia's coastal estuaries and near-shore ocean areas. The highlights of the river-based River Scout section include a see-through tunnel and a play wall for children. Sea life ranges from ferocious to snuggly, flamboyant to plain, scarce to common, and represents aquatic ecosystems from around the globe. Reptiles, amphibians, and invertebrates are also represented. But the sea life exhibited here isn't just to look at; it's meant to educate the public and impress upon them the need for protection and preservation. Other attractions include a 4-D Theater, behind-the-scenes tours, Deepo's Undersea 3-D Show, and Café Aquaria. The facility, which opened in the fall of 2005, was begun with a $200 million gift from Bernie Marcus, co-founder of Home Depot, based right here in Atlanta. Guided tours are available. Admission to the aquarium is included in the CityPass (see What's Where). General admission: adults $24, seniors $20, children 3–12 $18; admission and 4-D Theater: adults $29.50, seniors $25.50, children $22; admission and behind-the-scenes tour: adults $69, seniors $65, children $62; Deepo Pass: adults $45, children $35. Parking $10.

✄ ✤ ⚷ **Imagine It! The Children's Museum of Atlanta** (404-659-KIDS; www.imagineit-cma.org), 275 Centennial Olympic Park Drive Northwest. Open 10–4 weekdays, 10–5 weekends. This is one place youngsters will never hear "Don't touch!" Instead, everything is designed to be touched. Geared for ages 3 to 8, the museum's high-energy, hands-on, larger-than-life, out-of-the-ordinary interactive displays encourage the small-fry to explore and discover through exhibits like "Fundamentally Food," "Let Your Creativity Flow," "Tools for Solutions," "Leaping into Learning," and the Morph Gallery. Anyone age 3 or older $11.

Guided Tours

✤ **Atlanta Preservation Center Tours** (404-688-3353; www.preserveatlanta.com), 327 St. Paul Avenue. Office open 9–5 weekdays. Call or consult the Web site for tour schedules, which, with the exception of the Fox Theatre, are offered April through November. Fox Theatre tours are offered year-round. Reservations are not required. Tours last one to two hours and are canceled in the event of rain, except for the **Fox Theatre** tour. The organization offers separate guided walking tours showcasing the Fox Theatre (see the Midtown chapter), **Historic Downtown, Sweet Auburn/MLK Jr. Historic District, Inman Park, Druid Hills, Grant Park**, and **Ansley Park** (see the Midtown chapter). Guides are experts in architecture, history, and preservation. Adults $10, seniors and students $5.

City Segway Tours-Atlanta (404-588-2274; 1-877-734-8687; www.citysegwaytours.com/atlanta), 50 Upper Alabama Street, Suite 256 (on the upper level of Underground Atlanta). Tours at 10 and 2 daily, February 15 through December 30; reservations required with payment in advance (refundable if cancellation is made at least 72 hours prior to the tour). The two-wheeled Segway Human Transporter, a self-balancing personal transportation device, is perfect for a guided tour of downtown Atlanta because you can cover more territory than you could on foot. After a brief training session, the three-hour tour includes Atlanta's highlights: Underground Atlanta, the Georgia State Capitol, Sweet Auburn district including the Martin Luther King Jr. National Historic Site and Ebenezer Baptist Church, Centennial Olympic Park, Georgia Aquarium, New World of Coca-Cola, and the CNN Center. Imagine the looks you'll get from passersby as you cruise past. Tours operate rain or shine (ponchos are provided for inclement weather). Everyone must sign a liability waiver (an adult must sign for those younger than 18), and each party must sign a damage waiver that includes a deposit of $500 on a credit card (the deposit is canceled at the end of the tour and does not appear on your statement). All riders must be at least 12 years old; pregnant women are not permitted. $70.

🐚 **From Civil War to Civil Rights** tours are given from **Underground Atlanta** (404-523-2311; 1-866-494-6187, Ext. 1494; www.underground-atlanta.com), 50 Upper Alabama Street. Tours at 11, 1, and 3 Friday and Saturday; 1 and 3 Sunday. The tour includes Underground Atlanta, the Union Depot site, the Connelly Building and the viaducts, and describes the history of the unique attractions. Adults $7, seniors $5, students $4.

🐚 ♿ **Georgia Dome** (404-223-TOUR; www.gadome.com), One Georgia Dome Drive Northwest. Tours are offered on the hour between 10 and 3 Tuesday through Saturday. Tours of the world's largest cable-supported dome are truly awe-inspiring. The 70,000-seat facility is not only the home of the Atlanta Falcons football team and the Chick-fil-A Bowl, but the complex also hosted the 1996 Centennial Olympic Summer Games gymnastics and basketball events, the 1994 and 2000 Super Bowls, the 2002, 2005, and 2007 NCAA Men's Final Four, the 2002 and 2003 NCAA Women's Final Four, the U.S. Hot Rod Association's Monster Jam, and more. The tour begins at the Dome Administration Entrance between Gates B and C. Guests visit the observation level, press box, the exclusive Dome suites, and the locker room before ending on the field, where they can toss a football. To commemorate annual college rivalries, a section of the floor level is dedicated to mini museums highlighting SEC football and basketball championships, the Chick-fil-A Bowl, and the Bank of America Atlanta Football Classic. The museums (they're showcases, really) are located near the Gate E entrance. An Atlanta Falcons museum has recently been added in this area as well. Adults $6, seniors and students $4 ($1 discount with a Falcons ticket stub, CNN tour stub, or Turner Field tour stub).

Gray Line of Atlanta (404-767-0594; 1-800-965-6665; www.grayline.com). The tour company offers three options. Tour 1, "Georgia's Great," is a morning tour and includes entrance to the New World of Coca-Cola, the Jimmy Carter Library, and the Martin Luther King Jr. National Historic Site. The three-hour tour departs from Underground Atlanta at 9 AM Tuesday through Saturday and costs $48 for adults, $38 for children 6–12. Tour 2, "All Around Atlanta," includes admission to the Atlanta Cyclorama, the Margaret Mitchell House, and the Georgia Aquarium. The four-hour tour departs from Underground Atlanta at 1 PM Tuesday and Thursday and costs $55 for adults, $47 for children. Tour 3, the "Atlanta Grand" tour, is another afternoon tour and includes entrance to the Atlanta Cyclorama, Atlanta History Center, and Swan House. The four-hour tour departs from Underground Atlanta at 1 PM Wednesday, Friday, and Saturday and is also $55 for adults and $47 for children. Tour 4, the combination tour, includes both the morning and afternoon tours with time out for lunch on your own. Tour 4 costs $82 for adults and $74 for children.

🐚 ♿ **Inside CNN Atlanta Studio Tour** (404-827-2300; 1-800-426-6868; www.cnn.com/studiotour), One CNN Center (Marietta Street at Centennial Olympic Park Drive). Open 8:30–5 daily; tours begin every 20 minutes. Reservations for a specific time are required a day in advance, but same-day tickets will be sold if available. Tours of the high-tech, fast-paced, 24/7 news network show visitors behind-the-scenes action of the actual on-the-air newsrooms via glass-enclosed overhead walkways. The tour begins with an overview of the network in the Control Room Theater. A special, longer VIP tour is also available for an additional fee. Adults $10, seniors $8, children $7 (children younger than 6 are not admitted). Included as an attraction in the **Atlanta CityPass** (see What's Where).

🐚 **Turner Field Tours** (404-614-2311; www.bravesmuseum.com), 755 Hank Aaron Drive, Atlanta. Tours leave on the hour between 10 and 2 Monday through Saturday, October through March. During the April through September baseball season, the museum

Tours of Turner Field include a stop alongside this statue of Hank Aaron.

and tours are available 9–3 Monday through Saturday, 1–3 Sunday. On game days, the last tour leaves at noon. No tours are offered on the day of any Sunday or afternoon home game. Tours begin at the Braves Museum and include Coca-Cola Sky Field, a luxury suite, the press box, broadcast booth, locker room, dugout, Scouts Alley, and the Braves Clubhouse Store. Among the sights to see at the stadium are the **Hank Aaron statue**, a tribute to the home-run king; the **Ivan Allen Jr. Braves Museum and Hall of Fame** (see *Museums*); the **Braves Clubhouse Store**, purveyor of all things with the Braves logo; and **Scouts Alley**, where wannabes can test their skills. Eating out at the stadium is easy with several fast food outlets as well as the **Braves Chop House**, where diners can order chicken wings, burgers, and barbecue while overlooking the field, and the **755 Club** (named for Hank Aaron's 755 career home runs), also overlooking the field. **Turner Beach**, which is located in right field, opens two hours before game time and features hospitality "lifeguards," tropical palm trees, a cabana bar, food concessions, a picnic area, and lounge chairs. Adults $10, children $5; admission to museum only during games is $2. Free parking in the North Lot.

Historic Homes and Sites

Atlanta Cyclorama and Civil War Museum (404-624-1071; 404-658-7625; www.bcaatlanta.com), Grant Park, 800-C Cherokee Avenue Southeast. Open 9:30–4:30 Tuesday through Sunday, until 5:30 in summer. Before there were movies and television, there were cycloramas—huge, larger-than-life-size, wraparound paintings that could keep viewers occupied for hours. A major attraction since 1887, this cyclorama is the longest running show in the country. Depicting the July 22, 1864, Battle of Atlanta, it measures 358 feet long (that's longer than a football field) by 42 feet high, covering 15,000 square feet. The 9,000-pound heavy-gauge cotton duck treasure was originally even bigger, measuring 400 feet by 50 feet, but after damage caused by numerous relocations, it shrunk to its current size. In 1885, 10 German artists came to Atlanta to study the terrain of the battle, and then began the painting. It was first displayed in Detroit, then toured major cities in America before being given to Atlanta in 1887. The marble and granite building that houses the painting was constructed in 1921. Between 1934 and 1936, the Works Progress Administration created the 3-D foreground to the painting. There are very few of these paintings left in the world (only one other in America), and none as high-tech as this one has become. Revolving stadium seating has been introduced into the circle created by the painting, and the addition of narration, dramatic lighting, sound effects, and the 3-D dio-

The Atlanta Cyclorama has been a major attraction in the city for more than 120 years.

rama put viewers right into the action. Before viewing the painting, watch the introductory film *The Atlanta Campaign.* Also displayed at the museum are period photos, weapons, and uniforms, but another star shares the spotlight with the cyclorama painting: the locomotive *Texas,* which figured prominently in the Civil War episode known as the Great Locomotive Chase (see the Marietta chapter for more information). It was the *Texas,* running backwards at that, which finally caught up with the stolen *General*, which had been kidnapped by Yankee raiders. Adults $6, seniors $5, children 6–12 $4.

🍴 ⚒ **Georgia State Capitol** (404-656-2844; www.sos.state.ga.us), Capitol Avenue and Martin Luther King Jr. Drive. Open 8–5:30 weekdays. September through May, guided tours available at 10, 10:30, 11, 1, 1:30, and 2; in the summer, tours at 10, 11, 1, and 2. Last in a series of Georgia's five capital cities, Atlanta has been the state capital since 1868. The imposing Atlanta capitol was completed in 1889 in the Renaissance Revival style with strong Victorian influences. Its gleaming dome rises 37 feet from the floor and is plated in 23-karat gold mined in the north Georgia mountains and brought to the city by wagon train. The capitol recently has undergone extensive renovations. The tour includes a short film and showcases paintings and sculptures of prominent Georgians such as Benjamin Harvey Hill, James Oglethorpe, and Robert Toombs, along with several who were prominent in Georgia history like the Marquis de Lafayette. Marble busts honor Button Gwinnett, George Walton, and Lyman Hall, Georgia's three signers of the Declaration of Independence. Stop to see the **Georgia Capitol Museum** (see *Museums*). Outside, stroll the grounds and admire the statues and monuments dedicated to prominent Georgians such as Jimmy Carter, former Georgia governor and 39th president of the United States. Free.

🍴 **Herndon Home** (404-581-9813; www.herndonhome.org), 587 University Place Northwest. Open 10–4 Tuesday and Thursday with tours on the hour. Designed and built in 1910 by Alonzo and Adrienne Herndon using African American craftsmen, this 15-room,

6,000-square-foot Beaux-Arts National Register of Historic Places home tells the couple's story. Mr. Herndon was born into slavery in Social Circle, Georgia, in 1858, and when freed after the Civil War became a successful barber. Later he became wealthy after acquiring the Atlanta Life Insurance Company, which became the largest African American insurance company in the nation (it is still in business today). In fact, by 1895, Herndon was a millionaire and the richest African American in Atlanta. He went on to become one of the most successful black businessmen in America as well as a leading philanthropist. Mrs. Herndon was a Shakespearean actress who had traveled the world and also taught drama at Atlanta University. Together they determined to fill their new home with magnificent furnishings and art purchased on their world travels. Sadly, after supervising the construction of the mansion, Mrs. Herndon never got to enjoy it; she died of Addison's disease only days after they moved in. On display are original Herndon family belongings such as period furnishings, elaborate Persian carpets, Venetian and Roman glass dating to 200 B.C., and artwork. The couple's son, who was a successful businessman in his own right, bequeathed the home to become a museum. Adults $5, students $3.

🐾 ♿ **Historic Oakland Cemetery** (404-688-2107; www.oaklandcemetery.com), 248 Oakland Avenue Southeast. Cemetery open dawn to dusk daily; visitor's center, where guests can get the brochure for a self-guided walking tour, open weekdays. Guided tours are available weekends, April through November, at 10, 2, and 6:30 Saturday, and 2 and 6:30 Sunday. A stroll through this cemetery, opened in 1850, is like an Atlanta history lesson with 70,000 stories to tell. The 88-acre burial ground is filled with excessive funerary statuary, opulent Gothic-Revival and Neoclassical mausoleums, some as big as houses, and beautiful gardens. This is reputedly the only cemetery in the country where Confederate and Union soldiers—6,900 Confederates and 16 Unions—are buried intermingled rather than in separate sections. The Civil War graves, among them those of 3,000 unknowns, are

Unique headstones and impressive mausoleums can be found at every turn in Oakland Cemetery.

Sunday in the Park at Oakland Cemetery

Historic Oakland Cemetery sponsors guided tours, exhibits, storytelling by costumed guides, entertainment, and refreshments. The celebration revives the Victorian tradition of making a day's outing from a visit to loved ones' graves and spending the rest of the day picnicking, reading, visiting with relatives and friends, or strolling through the cemetery. Oakland Cemetery, in particular, lends itself to this custom—after Piedmont Park and Grant Park, it is the third-largest green space in the city. During this shindig, graves and mausoleums are extravagantly decorated in the Victorian manner, with elaborate arrangements of florals and greens. Just another piece of trivia: Readers of *The Atlanta Journal-Constitution* voted the cemetery one of the Top Ten Places in Atlanta to Smooch.

watched over by the magnificent statue of the **Confederate Lion**, modeled after the Swiss Lion of Lucerne. It's hard to tell whether he's sleeping or crying. Among the other Civil War notables are three generals and Capt. William Fuller, Engineer Jeff Cain, and Anthony Murphy, who chased—and two of whom eventually caught—the locomotive *The General,* which had been hijacked by Union spies during the famous Great Locomotive Chase (see the Marietta chapter). Luminaries buried here include Margaret Mitchell Marsh, author of *Gone with the Wind,* golfing great Bobby Jones, several Georgia governors, and many Atlanta mayors. A poignant Potter's Field is the final resting place of many of Atlanta's poor. When slavery still existed, African Americans were buried in a separate section, and there are Jewish sections as well. Guided tours cover numerous topics and explore many facets and areas of the cemetery, including history, art and architecture, symbolism, the Civil War, women, Jews, African Americans, and gardens. Numerous special events occur at the cemetery throughout the year, including Sunday in the Park on the first Sunday in October, and Halloween tours on Friday and Saturday evenings prior to Halloween. An unexpected benefit to visiting Oakland Cemetery is a splendid view of the downtown skyline. After visiting the cemetery, you may want to grab a bite at **Six Feet Under** nearby (see *Eating Out*). Cemetery free; self-guided walking tour map $2; guided tours: adults $10, children $5, seniors $3.

🐾 ♿ **Martin Luther King Jr. National Historic Site** (404-331-5190 for the visitor's center; 404-331-6922 for recorded information; www.nps.gov/malu), 450 Auburn Avenue Northeast. Open 9–5 daily; hours extended to 6 between June 15 and August 15. Guided tours are offered on the hour between 10 and 5 most of the year and on the half-hour in the summer. A memorial to the revered civil rights leader, the site consists of King's birthplace and home; historic Ebenezer Baptist Church; and an interpretive center. The King Center for Non-Violent Social Change actually owns the birthplace home, but it is operated and maintained by the National Park Service. The Gothic Revival–style Ebenezer Baptist Church, where King was baptized and preached as co-pastor with his father, was also where the Southern Christian Leadership Conference was formed, where King's funeral service was held after his 1968 assassination, and where his mother was shot. Until recently the church was used by the active congregation, but they finally outgrew the sanctuary, so just a few years ago a striking new church was built across the street. The original church is now used as a museum and a place for special services. Be sure to spend some time in Peace Plaza outside the visitor's center. It contains the International World Peace Rose Garden, a flowing fountain, and the statue *Behold.* Free, but tickets for the birthplace

The Martin Luther King Jr. National Historic Site pays tribute to the civil rights leader.

tour are required for scheduling purposes. They can be picked up at the visitor's center. Adjacent to the historic site is the **King Center for Non-Violent Social Change** (404-526-8900; www.thekingcenter.org), 449 Auburn Avenue Northeast. Also open 9–5 daily, until 6 in the summer. The center, founded by Coretta Scott King in 1968, is the official living memorial to Dr. King. The center serves as the international clearinghouse of official King programs, public information, and educational materials, but most of the 650,000 annual visitors come to pay homage to Dr. and Mrs. King at their crypt set amid a reflecting pool. Free.

✿ 🐾 ♿ **Underground Atlanta** (404-523-2311; 1-866-494-6187, Ext. 1494; www.underground-atlanta.com), 50 Upper Alabama Street Southwest. Shops are generally open 10–9 Monday through Saturday, 11–6 Sunday; restaurants and night spots are open later. Atlanta, as will come as no surprise to anyone who's ever tried to drive here, is no stranger to paralyzing traffic jams. What may be surprising, however, is the fact that when Atlanta was a youngster in the mid-1880s, trains and horse-drawn buggies created the first traffic jams where streets crossed railroad tracks. At that time, the solution was to build viaducts over the tracks, but that left adjacent business owners with their entrances below street level. They responded by opening new entrances on the second floor at the new street level. That's why Atlanta has Upper and Lower Alabama Streets and Upper and Lower Pryor Streets. Long forgotten, the lower level got a new lease on life as a shopping/entertainment mecca. Six blocks encompassing 12 acres are crammed with 100 shops, 14 restaurants and night spots, street vendors' carts, and sculptures that line both levels and create an urban playground for all ages. Street performers often keep visitors entertained. Visitors roam at will, but those who desire a guided tour should see the write-up for the **"From Civil War to Civil Rights"** tour under *Guided Tours*. Free.

🐾 ♿ **Westview Cemetery** (404-755-6611), 1680 Westview Drive. Open daily during daylight hours. Begun in 1884 at the height of the rural cemetery movement, Westview contains ornate gravestones, mausoleums, and funerary memorial art. The Westview Mausoleum, one of the South's most famous shrines, contains 27 stained-glass windows depicting the life of Christ and a mural called *Faith, Hope, and Charity*. Famous Atlantans buried here include Asa Candler and Robert W. Woodruff, the first two owners of the Coca-Cola Company; newspapermen Henry Grady and Joel Chandler Harris; former mayor William B. Hartsfield (after whom the Atlanta airport and Zoo Atlanta's beloved late gorilla Willie B. were named), and philanthropists whose names you'll see all over Atlanta:

Henrietta Egleston (Egleston Children's Hospital), Hyatt M. Patterson (Patterson Funeral Homes), Joseph M. High (High Museum of Art), and Richard B. Rich (Rich's department stores). Free.

🍃 🐌 **Wren's Nest House Museum** (404-753-7735), 1050 Ralph David Abernathy Boulevard Southwest. Open 10–2:30 Tuesday through Saturday. This turn-of-the-20th-century building, Atlanta's oldest house museum, was the home of Joel Chandler Harris, a newspaperman, folklorist, novelist, and poet who preserved in print the folksy Uncle Remus tales he had heard from slaves as a child. Harris lived here from 1881 to 1908; Mrs. Harris stayed on until 1913, leaving her husband's room the way it was the day he died. When she left and the city purchased the home to use as a museum dedicated to Harris, she decreed that his room remain in that condition. That's why it looks as though he had just stepped out. The "briar patch" is furnished with original family pieces and Uncle Remus memorabilia such as a diorama built by the Disney Studios when it produced the movie *Song of the South*, which is based on the Uncle Remus tales. Interesting in and of itself, the house was constructed in 1870 as a three-room shotgun house. Harris had extensive renovations done in 1883 and 1884, with an addition wrapping around the original house resulting in the large Queen Anne/Eastlake-style residence visitors see today. Some of the outstanding architectural features include wooden fish-scale tiles on the second-floor porch gables and on the second story of the center section, wooden latticework arches under the porch eaves, and low pointed-arch panels that form the porch railings. Harris originally called the property Snap Bean Farm, but changed it to Wren's Nest when a family of wrens built its home in the family's mailbox. The museum hosts quarterly storytelling events. Adults $3, seniors and teens $2, children 4–12 $1.

Museums

🐌 🐌 **African American Panoramic Experience** (404-523-2739; www.apexmuseum.org), 135 Auburn Avenue. Open 10–5 Tuesday through Saturday; also open 1–5 Sunday in February and June through August. Known as APEX for short, the museum is dedicated to presenting and preserving the culture, history, and traditions of people of African descent by tracing the details of that history and documenting the stories of Atlanta's African American pioneers, inventors, and storekeepers. The museum presents a visual journey through the historic Sweet Auburn district, known in its heyday as the Street of Pride. One of the displays is a model of Atlanta's first black-owned drugstore. The Trolley Theater, which occupies an actual trolley, presents several documentary films. Adults $4, seniors and children $3.

🍃 🐌 🐌 **Georgia Capitol Museum** (404-651-6996; www.sos.state.ga.us/museum), 206 Washington Street. Open 8–5:30 weekdays. Located inside the state capitol, this modest museum preserves and interprets the history of the building and the state through memorabilia, artwork, Native American artifacts, fossils and minerals, scenes from Georgia's five diverse geographic regions, and 1939 World's Fair dioramas depicting Georgia industry, state symbols, and a replica of *Miss Freedom*, the statue that adorns the top of the Georgia Capitol. Free.

🐌 **Hammonds House Galleries and Resource Center for African American Art** (404-612-0500; www.hammondshouse.org), 503 Peeples Street. Open 10–6 Tuesday through Friday, 1–5 Saturday and Sunday. The 1857 Eastlake-style residence in the West End, which was the home of African American physician and art patron Otis Thrash Hammonds until his death in 1988, houses Georgia's only exclusively African American fine art museum.

The mission of the museum is to display the art of people of African descent and to disseminate an understanding of art from the African Diaspora. Collections include Haitian art and works by Romare Bearden, Bill Taylor, and 200 others representing the time period 1841 to the present. Be sure to admire the 14-room house itself—one of the oldest in the West End—including its seven fireplaces and its lighting fixtures made of brass and hand-blown glass. Adults $2, seniors and students $1.

♦♠ & **Jimmy Carter Presidential Library and Museum** (404-865-7101), 441 Freedom Parkway. Open 9–4:45 Monday through Saturday, noon–4:45 Sunday. One of 10 presiden-

tial libraries administered by the National Archives and Records Administration and the only presidential library in the Southeast, this facility chronicles the life and career of Jimmy Carter, the former peanut farmer who became governor of Georgia and president of the United States. See a life-size re-creation of part of the Oval Office as it looked during the Carter administration and view state gifts from heads of foreign governments received during Carter's tenure as president, reproductions of first lady Rosalynn Carter's inaugural gowns, a formal White House dinner setting, and memorabilia from the 1976 campaign. Take time to stroll the rose garden and the beautiful and serene Japanese garden, where visitors can admire an unobstructed view of the Atlanta skyline (see *Gardens*). Books written by President and Mrs. Carter as well as copies of White House china are for sale in the museum shop. Adults $8, seniors $6, children younger than 16 free.

The Jimmy Carter Presidential Library and Museum details the life and times of the nation's 39th president.

♠ & **Museum of Design** (404-688-2467; www.museumofdesign.org), Marquis II Tower (Lobby and Garden Levels), 285 Peachtree Center Avenue. Open 11–5 Tuesday through Saturday with extended hours during exhibit opening receptions and First Thursday Art Walks. Gift shop open 10–6 weekdays. Dedicated to the study of design and its impact on daily life, this Smithsonian-affiliated museum's exhibits explore the uses, effects, and meaning of design, which might include textiles, furniture, or other media. In conjunction with the Smithsonian, the museum will be able to bring more prestigious collections—such as those of the Cooper-Hewitt National Design Museum—to Atlanta. Turner First Thursday Art Walks include leisurely strolls through the museum and neighboring galleries. A map and refreshments are available at SunTrust Plaza. Free, but donations are greatly appreciated. Guided tours, gallery talks, and lectures are also free.

♦♠ & **New World of Coca-Cola** (404-676-5151; 1-800-676-COKE; www.worldofcoca -cola.com), 121 Baker Street. Open 9–5 daily (8–6 June through August). Last admission one hour prior to closing. Advance reservations strongly recommended. Atlanta is the home and world headquarters of the world's most popular soft drink, so where else would be a more natural spot for a museum dedicated to it? The story of Coca-Cola—from its development as an 1886 drugstore drink to its current position as a worldwide phenomenon—is told at the New World of Coca-Cola, which is twice the size of the old museum. You'll learn about Coca-Cola through a film in the Happiness Factory Theater, a real bottling line, and exhibits of 1,000 items of memorabilia in the Coca-Cola Loft and Milestones of Refreshment areas. You can embark on a cinematic journey around the world at the 4-D theater (be prepared for a bumpy ride). Coca-Cola and everyday people are interpreted through art in the Pop Culture Gallery, and iconic Coca-Cola ads are shown in the Perfect Pauses Theater. Visitors can meet the Coca-Cola polar bear in the Hub area, taste experimental flavors and 22 flavors from around the world that are not available in this country in Taste It!, and shop for souvenirs in the Coca-Cola Store. Note: For previous visitors, the attraction has moved from the plaza at Underground Atlanta to this new location near the Georgia Aquarium and Centennial Olympic Park. Parking available in the Pemberton Place garage for $10, or easily access the site via MARTA rail or bus. Adults $15, seniors $13, children 5–12 $9; $1 off when tickets are purchased online. Included as an attraction in the Atlanta CityPass (see What's Where).

To Do

Bicycling

It's essential to have your own bike, because there are no rentals downtown.
MARTA: See What's Where.
PATH Foundation: See What's Where. The Atlanta/DeKalb Greenway Trail System includes the **Freedom Parkway Trail** on the way to the Jimmy Carter Presidential Library and Museum. The east/west section, with its switchbacks and straightaways, was an immediate hit with cyclists, joggers, in-line skaters, and strollers. The north/south section is being created and will include a section that ends at the Inman Park MARTA station. Free.

Carriage Rides

Amen Carriage Company (404-653-0202), office at 290 Martin Luther King Jr. Drive, Unit 7A; carriage stands at Peachtree Street and International Boulevard, and Centennial Olympic Park and International Boulevard. Available 6 PM–1 AM weekday evenings, noon–1 AM weekends, except during exceptionally hot weather when it is dangerous for the horses to be out. These romantic 15- and 30-minute carriage rides cover most of historical downtown and Centennial Olympic Park. Adults $25, children $10 for 15-minute rides; double for 30-minute rides.

For Families

♂ 🐾 ♿ **Turner Field/Ivan Allen Jr. Braves Museum and Hall of Fame** (404-614-2311; www.bravesmuseum.com), 755 Hank Aaron Drive. Open 9–3 Monday through Saturday, 1–3 Sunday; open 9–noon on game days. No tours on the afternoons of home games. Located at Turner Field and named for a former mayor rather than a baseball player, the museum contains 500 Braves artifacts, such as the bat with which Hank Aaron hit his record-breaking 715th home run (he went on to hit 755 home runs in his major league career), and photographs that trace the team's 130-year-plus history from its beginning in Boston (1871–1952) to Milwaukee (1953–1965) to Atlanta (1966–present). The Hall of Fame honors the careers of an ever increasing number of Braves legends. Included in the tour of the stadium are stops at a luxury suite, the terrace and service levels, and the press box and broadcast booth (see Turner Field Tours under *Guided Tours*). Tour price: adults $10, children $5.

♂ ♿ **Zoo Atlanta** (404-624-5600; 1-888-945-5432; www.zooatlanta.org), 800 Cherokee Avenue Southeast. Open 9:30–4:30 daily; open until 5:30 on weekends during daylight-saving time. Gates close one hour prior to the zoo closing. Zoo Atlanta, one of the 10 oldest, continuously operating zoos in the nation, is located in the historic Grant Park neighborhood. This location does limit the size of the zoo, and at one time it had the dubious distinction of being one of the worst in the country. Visionary leadership and community support, however, transformed it into one of the best. More than 700 animals representing 200 species from all over the world roam freely in habitats such as an Asian rain forest and an African savannah. The most popular stars right now are Lun Lun and Yang Yang, adorable giant pandas on loan from China, along with their daughter Mei Lan, who was born at Zoo Atlanta in late 2006. In fact, Zoo Atlanta is one of only four U.S. zoos to exhibit giant pandas. (Note: In order to limit visitors to the panda viewing area to 50 at a time, specific 15-minute tickets are required for panda viewing. The last session begins at 2:45. These tickets are free with admission to the zoo, but to avoid long lines, they can be reserved online for a convenience fee of $2.50 for members and $5 for nonmembers.) Not to be upstaged, however, is the outstanding primate collection, the largest in the country, which includes gorillas and orangutans. The newest additions to the zoo are red kangaroos. Warthogs and meerkat exhibits were opened in June 2007. Whether your particular pas-

Lun Lun and Yang Yang, giant pandas on loan from China, are one of Zoo Atlanta's biggest attractions.

Golf
🐾 **Candler Park Golf Course** (404-371-1260), 585 Candler Park Drive. Open 8–6:30. Golf in downtown Atlanta? Who would have thought it was possible? The nine-hole, 2,064-yard, par 31 course provides a rare opportunity for in-town golfing. Built in 1928, it was once the private course of Coca-Cola founder Asa Candler and was where he entertained business associates. Candler eventually gave the course to the City of Atlanta, which continues to maintain it. A forest of pine and oak bisects the course, and the terrain varies from flat to hilly, which creates challenges for all levels of players. Weekends $10 for Atlanta residents, $13 for nonresidents; weekdays $7 residents, $10 nonresidents.

sion is exotic animals from foreign shores such as African lions or Sumatran tigers, or whether it's birds, reptiles, or gentle farm animals at the petting zoo, you'll find plenty at the zoo. What you won't see are polar bears and other animals that can't tolerate Atlanta's torrid summer temperatures. A miniature train takes small-fry on a short trip around the property. Visitors also can ride the Endangered Species Carousel and play in the KIDZone. Keeper talks, training demonstrations, wildlife shows, and animal feedings are other popular activities. Adults $17.99, seniors $13.99, children $12.99. Included as an attraction in the Atlanta CityPass (see What's Where).

GREEN SPACE

Gardens
✎ 🐾 ♿ **Jimmy Carter Presidential Library and Museum** (404-865-7101), 441 Freedom Parkway. Open 9–4:45 Monday through Saturday, noon–4:45 Sunday. Outside the facility (see *Museums*) there is a 2,500-square-foot rose garden with 80 varieties, a wildflower meadow, and a tranquil Japanese garden with two waterfalls—the larger one represents Mr. Carter, the smaller one his wife, Rosalynn. Cherry trees blossom in the spring. Adults $9, seniors $6, children younger than 16 free.

Nature Preserves and Parks
✎ 🐾 ♿ **Centennial Olympic Park** (404-223-4412; 404-222-PARK for a recorded informational message; www.centennialolympicpark.com), 265 Park Avenue West Northwest. Open 7–11. This 21-acre park is the living legacy of the 1996 Centennial Olympic Summer Games. Deteriorating warehouses and businesses were torn down to make room for the park, where 2 million visitors gathered during the two-week games. Features of the park include gigantic lighted columns, Quilt Plaza, Centennial Plaza, the visitor's center, water gardens, sculptures, lawns, and playgrounds, but few trees—all connected by walkways laid with bricks donated by local citizens to help pay for the park. The highlight of the park is the gigantic Fountain of Rings, the largest interactive depiction of the Olympic logo in the world. During the warm-weather months, different heights of water spurt out of 250 jets in the ground and invite the young and young-at-heart to jump in and get wet. An hourly dancing water show is set to music. The park is also the site of a variety of free events and concerts throughout the year, including Music at Noon, Wednesday Wind Down, a Fourth of July celebration with fireworks, and the Fourth Saturday Family-Fun Days held April

Centennial Olympic Park Trivia

• 800,000 bricks were used in the park. Laid end to end, they would stretch 100 miles, from Turner Field to Columbus, Georgia.

• The underground conduit for power distribution stretches 4.5 miles; for lighting, 8 miles.

• There are more than 11 miles of underground irrigation.

• The man-hours required to complete the park are equivalent to one man working full time for 100 years.

• Granite from each of the five continents represented by the Olympic Games was used in the park.

• Each of the five Olympic rings in the fountain is 25 feet in diameter—large enough to park two cars side by side.

Fun in the Fountain of Rings at Centennial Olympic Park

through September. Even in balmy Atlanta, modern technology makes it possible to have an outdoor ice-skating rink at Christmastime, when the park is aglitter with a holiday lights display (see **Holiday in Lights** under *Special Events*). Free access to the park; admission to some activities.

✄ 🎭 ♿ **Grant Park.** The 131-acre green space and recreational area in the center of the Grant Park Historic District was a gift to the city from Colonel Lemuel P. Grant, the district's earliest settler. He was instrumental in the construction of the Georgia Railroad when Atlanta was founded in 1840, and designed and constructed defensive fortifications around the city during the Civil War. His antebellum home survives. In 1883, Grant donated 100 acres of his vast estate to the city for use as a park. The city purchased additional property in 1890, and in 1909 the Olmstead brothers—sons of Frederick Law Olmstead, pioneer landscape architect of New York's Central Park, Atlanta's Piedmont Park, and the Biltmore Estate in Asheville, North Carolina—made numerous improvements to the park. Today the park boasts a beautiful lake, numerous springs, playgrounds, picnic facilities, the Atlanta Cyclorama and Civil War Museum (see *Museums*), and Zoo Atlanta (see *For Families*). Free access to the park; admission to the museum and zoo.

✄ 🎭 ♿ **Springvale Park.** Located on either side of Euclid Avenue along Waverly Way, the park was established in 1889 by Joel Hurt, the developer of the Inman Park neighborhood. He was also the first developer to introduce evergreen planting to Atlanta, a legacy that endures to this day. The landscape architects, the Olmstead brothers, were hired to embellish the park. Note the 1889 stone wall and the gigantic live oak planted by Joel Hurt more than 100 years ago. The park is undergoing a major restoration thanks to the National

Trust for Historic Preservation, the State Historic Preservation Office, a federal grant, and the monetary and physical contributions of residents. Free.

🌭 ♿ **Woodruff Park**, 65 Park Place. This small downtown oasis is named for the late Robert W. Woodruff, a Coca-Cola executive and philanthropist. A waterfall, fountain, and amphitheater-like seating make this park a perfect place to enjoy a sandwich, read a book, or people-watch. The park is sometimes the site of entertainment, too. The park's bronze sculpture, *Phoenix Rising from the Ashes,* a statue of a woman and a phoenix, represents Atlanta's reincarnation after the Civil War. A representation of the sculpture is often used as Atlanta's logo. Free.

LODGING

Bed and Breakfasts

In Inman Park

1890 King-Keith House Bed and Breakfast (404-688-7330; 1-800-728-3879; www.kingkeith.com), 889 Edgewood Avenue Northeast. The opulent Queen Anne-style King-Keith House is one of the most photographed houses in Atlanta. The mansion is characterized by 12-foot ceilings, carved fireplaces, spacious rooms, stained glass windows, and period antiques. Accommodations include rooms, suites, and a private cottage with a Jacuzzi tub for two. Guests enjoy elegant public spaces, private gardens, complimentary snacks and beverages, and a full gourmet breakfast. This is a nonsmoking property; smokers may indulge on the porch. There is one first-floor room that is wheelchair accessible, but the inn isn't really ideal for those in a wheelchair. $120–210.

🌭 **Heartfield Manor** (404-523-8633; www.inmanpark.org/heart.html), 1882 Elizabeth Street Northeast. This 1903

Craftsman cottage features a two-story entrance with a grand balcony, stained glass windows, and wainscoting. All rooms and suites are furnished with period pieces. Some guest accommodations offer a full kitchen; some have a small refrigerator and microwave. No smoking. Not wheelchair accessible. $80–115 plus tax.

Sugar Magnolia Bed and Breakfast (404-222-0226; www.sugarmagnoliabb.com), 804 Edgewood Avenue Northeast. Accommodations are offered in a magnificent, well-preserved Queen Anne-Victorian mansion. Built in 1892, the house is embellished with gables, ornate chimneys, whimsical turrets, and an inviting wraparound porch. The inside is characterized by 12-foot ceilings, a grand staircase, six fireplaces, beveled glass, and hand-painted plasterwork. Luxurious accommodations are offered in the Royal Suite, the Cottage Suite, the Garden Room, and the Aviary. Smoking outdoors only. Not wheelchair accessible. $110–150.

Inns and Hotels

Downtown

♿ **The Ellis Hotel** (404-523-5155), 176 Peachtree Street. The new luxury boutique hotel occupies the former 1913 Winecoff Hotel at Peachtree and Ellis Streets. Although the exterior has been meticulously preserved, the interior has been created anew with a completely fresh design. Fifteen stories contain 126 rooms and one suite with four-star amenities and the latest in in-room technology, a ground-floor patio café, a second-story restaurant and lounge with a balcony overlooking Peachtree Street, and a fitness center. No smoking. Wheelchair accessible. $140–330.

♿ **The Glenn Hotel** (404-521-2250; 1-866-40GLENN; www.glennhotel.com), 110 Marietta Street Northwest. Downtown Atlanta's first boutique hotel, the Glenn

Hotel occupies the historic Glenn building, which was constructed in 1923 as an office building named for then-mayor John T. Glenn. Accommodations include 93 rooms, 16 suites, and the Jezebel Penthouse Suite—all of which exude what the management likes to call "Manhattan sophistication, South Beach sex appeal, and Atlanta Southern charm." Rooms feature such amenities as rain-flowing showers, plasma televisions, and bath amenities by Gilchrist and Soames. Public spaces include the Glenn Hotel Restaurant and Bar (see *Dining Out*), the Lobby Bar, and the Rooftop Bar, which affords fantastic views of Atlanta's skyline. The hotel is conveniently located within walking distance of the CNN Center, Philips Arena, the Georgia Dome, the Georgia World Congress Center, Centennial Olympic Park, the Georgia Aquarium, and the New World of Coca-Cola. No smoking. Wheelchair accessible. $179–259.

✍ ♿ **Omni Hotel at CNN Center** (404-659-0000; 1-800-843-6664; www.omnicnn.com), 100 CNN Center. The AAA four-diamond hotel's downtown location and easy accessibility to the MARTA rail system make it a popular base of operations when visiting the city. Attached to the CNN Center, the recently renovated hotel has the advantage of its restaurants, bars, shops, and movie theaters. The hotel is adjacent to Philips Arena, where scores of sporting events and concerts occur, and across from the Georgia World Congress Center, Georgia Dome, and Centennial Olympic Park. Nonsmoking and smoking rooms available. Wheelchair accessible. $189 and up.

✍ ♿ **The Ritz-Carlton, Atlanta** (404-659-0400; 1-888-241-3333; www.ritz-carlton.com), 181 Peachtree Street Northeast. Ritz-Carltons are world-renowned for their not-to-be-topped personal service, flawless facilities, and superior dining. This AAA four-diamond downtown Atlanta property is no exception.

The 25-story, 444-room hotel is situated in the heart of downtown's business, finance, and government district within walking distance of many attractions, bars, restaurants, shops, and a MARTA station. Gracious guest rooms and suites have bay-window views of the downtown skyline. Exquisite dining is available at the Atlanta Grill (see *Dining Out*). Nonsmoking and smoking rooms available. Wheelchair accessible. $400 and up.

♿ **TWELVE Centennial Park** (404-418-1212; www.twelvehotels.com/CentennialPark/HotelHome.do), 400 West Peachtree. An exciting new hotel in downtown Atlanta, TWELVE Centennial Park joins its trendy sister hotel in Atlantic Station (see the Midtown chapter). With panoramic skyline views, the hotel is within easy walking distance of the Georgia Aquarium, the New World of Coca-Cola, Philips Arena, the Georgia Dome, and other attractions. Its 102 one- and two-bedroom suites offer superb amenities. Other attractions at the hotel include an outdoor pool, business, center, fitness center, and Room at TWELVE Centennial Park restaurant. No smoking. Wheelchair accessible. $205–225.

✍ ♿ **Westin Peachtree Plaza** (404-659-1400; www.westin.com), 210 Peachtree Street Northwest. For many years the tallest building in Atlanta, the cylindrical-shaped hotel's title has been usurped by loftier structures in recent years. It does, however, still reign as the best publicly accessible place to get a spectacular view of Atlanta, not only from guest rooms, but also from its revolving 73rd-floor Sun Dial Restaurant, Bar, and View (see *Dining Out*). The hotel's 1,000 recently renovated rooms are furnished with Westin's signature Heavenly Beds and Heavenly Baths. Amenities include a swimming pool, shops, a fitness center, 24-hour room service, and high-speed Internet access in all rooms. Nonsmoking and smoking rooms available. Wheelchair accessible. $295–500.

WHERE TO EAT

Dining Out

Downtown

&. **Atlanta Grill** (404-659-0400), 181 Peachtree Street Northeast. Open 6:30–midnight daily. Located in the Ritz-Carlton, this upscale AAA four-diamond restaurant offers Southern-inspired cuisine in a clublike atmosphere. Seasonal outdoor seating is available on the veranda overlooking Peachtree Street. No smoking. Wheelchair accessible. Dinner entrées $15–45.

&. **City Grill** (404-524-2489; www.citygrill atlanta.com), 50 Hurt Plaza at Edgewood Avenue. Open for lunch 11:30–2 weekdays, for dinner 5–10 Monday through Saturday, and for a preshow menu 5–6:30 Monday through Saturday. This beautiful classical building was once a bank, and diners may feel as though they need to take out a loan to pay for the $60–90 dinner, so save this swanky, sophisticated restaurant for a special occasion. On the exterior, this is one of the most architecturally striking buildings in downtown Atlanta; the interior is just as elegant. Diners enter a glass-enclosed atrium, and then climb a graceful marble staircase to the dining room. Vast open space showcases towering ceilings supported by classical columns, ornate plasterwork, marble, crystal chandeliers, murals, plush fabrics, and subdued colors—all of which produce a rarefied ambience. The imaginative Southern cuisine might feature sweetbreads, escargot, quail, seafood, lamb, veal, duck, beef, or pork with suitable accompaniments. No smoking. Wheelchair accessible. Reservations strongly suggested. Gentlemen should wear a coat and ladies should dress appropriately. $9–19 for lunch, $21–38 for dinner; preshow menu is $25 for two courses, $30 for three courses.

The Glenn Hotel Restaurant and Bar (404-521-2250; 1-866-40Glenn; www.glennhotel.com), 110 Marietta Street Northwest. Open 7–10 for breakfast and 6–10 for dinner daily. The cuisine is described as eclectic/fusion and American. Dinner entrées might include Chilean bass, trout, seafood bouillabaisse, lobster, filet mignon, lamb, duck, short ribs, pork, and chicken. No smoking. Wheelchair accessible. $18–30.

&. **Nikolai's Roof** (404-221-6362; www.nikolaisroof.com), 255 Courtland Street Northeast. Open 5:30–11 PM Tuesday through Saturday. Located atop the Atlanta Hilton, this restaurant is the Fabergé jewel among the city's restaurants, being the first eatery downtown to earn a four-star rating. Russian influences are seen in the depictions of Fabergé eggs that adorn the gold-rimmed service plates, the waiters dressed in red Imperial Russian uniforms, the ambience, and in twists to the French/Continental menu. Diners can begin their feast with hors d'oeuvres such as caviar accompanied by ice-cold flavored vodkas. Entrées include beef, seafood, duck, and even wild boar. The extensive wine list features more than 400 wine labels. Service is especially attentive. No smoking. The restaurant is wheelchair accessible; restrooms are not. Reservations are required, as are a jacket and tie for gentlemen. $45–86.

&. **Pittypat's Porch** (404-525-8228; www.yp.bellsouth.com/sites/pittypats porch), 25 International Boulevard Northwest. Open 5–9 Sunday through Thursday, 5–10 Friday and Saturday. Fans of *Gone with the Wind* will remember Scarlett's flighty Aunt Pittypat with whom she stayed while in Atlanta. For more than 30 years this upscale restaurant has paid homage to Aunt Pittypat and has been visited by scores of celebrities. The first level of the restaurant has been cleverly arranged to resemble a Southern veranda overlooking the dining room, which is one level below. Sit awhile in one of the rockers and sip a mint julep or other libation before dining. In the plush surroundings of the formal dining room, which exudes Old South charm, tuxedo-clad waiters serve gourmet Southern cuisine with such dishes as venison, crab cakes, or Old South barbecue. Follow it all with a traditional dessert such as bread pudding or cobbler. No smoking. Wheelchair accessible. $18–24.

♭ **Prime Meridian** (404-818-4450), 100 CNN Center. Open 5:30 PM–10:30 PM daily. The restaurant's location in the Omni Hotel at CNN Center provides views of Centennial Olympic Park and the downtown skyline. Fine Continental cuisine is blended with local and regional specialties. Diners enjoy the open kitchen, exhibition grill, and floor-to-ceiling wine rack. You can watch your dinner being prepared by reserving one of the chef's tables. No smoking. Wheelchair accessible. Average dinner entrée $24.

♭ **Room at TWELVE Centennial Park** (404-418-1212; www.twelvehotels.com/CentennialPark/HotelHome.do), 400 West Peachtree. Open for breakfast 6:30–10 weekdays, 7:30–10:30 weekends; for lunch 11:30–2:30 weekdays, 10:30–2:30 weekends; for dinner 5:30–10 Sunday, 5:30–11 Monday through Thursday, 5:30–midnight Friday and Saturday. The hotel's restaurant, Room at TWELVE Centennial Park, is an American steakhouse serving meat, fish, sushi, and skewered dishes from the Tandoori Oven. Indoor and outdoor dining are available for breakfast, lunch, and dinner. No smoking. Wheelchair accessible. $5–12 for breakfast, $7–13 for lunch, $9–24 for dinner.

♭ **Ruth's Chris Steak House** (404-223-6500; 1-800-544-0808; www.ruthschrisdowntown.citysearch.com), 267 Marietta Street/Centennial Park. Open 11–11. Located in the Embassy Suites Hotel overlooking Centennial Olympic Park, the Atlanta incarnation of the world-famous restaurant chain serves aged USDA prime steaks as well as seafood and other favorites accompanied by an exceptional wine list and classic desserts. No smoking. Wheelchair accessible. $41–80.

♭ **The Sun Dial Restaurant, Bar, and View** (404-589-7506; www.sundialrestaurant.com), 210 Peachtree Street Northwest. Open for lunch 11:30–2:30 daily; for dinner 6–11 Sunday through Thursday, 6–11:30 Friday, 5:30–11:30 Saturday. This trilevel, revolving complex atop the Westin Peachtree Plaza hotel offers superb views of downtown as well as exquisite cuisine in the restaurant and wonderful jazz by the Mose Davis Trio in the bar. The facility makes a 360-degree circuit each half-hour. Visitors who are not customers of the restaurant or lounge may ride the glass elevators to The View level for $5. No smoking. Wheelchair accessible. $10–17 for lunch, $26–36 for dinner.

♭ **Trader Vic's** (404-221-6339; www.hilton.com), 255 Courtland Street Northeast. Open for dinner 5–11 Monday through Saturday. Located on the lower lobby level of the Hilton Atlanta, the restaurant whisks diners away to the South Seas with palm trees, tiki torches, and Polynesian wood carvings. Trader Vic's invented the famous Mai Tai cocktail, so begin with one of those and then enjoy cuisine prepared in giant Chinese smoke ovens. No smoking. Wheelchair accessible. $19–34.

Eating Out

In Cabbagetown

♭ **Agave** (404-588-0006; www.agaverestaurant.com), 242 Boulevard Southeast. Open 5–10 Sunday through Thursday, 5–11 Friday and Saturday. The specialties here are Southwestern cuisine and tequila. Entrées might include enchiladas or burritos as well as meat loaf, seafood, chicken, pork, steak, and lamb—all with a

Southwestern twist. No smoking. Wheelchair accessible. $14–24.

  Ⴀ **Six Feet Under** (404-523-6664; www.sixfeetunderatlanta.com), 415 Memorial Drive, Southeast. Open 11 AM–midnight Sunday, 11 AM–1 AM Monday through Thursday, 11 AM–2 AM Friday and Saturday. Just from looking at the bedraggled, dated exterior of this eatery directly across the street from historic Oakland Cemetery (see *Historic Homes and Sites*), you'd never guess that folks were "just dying to get in" to feast on a wide range of seafood, burgers, and fried green tomatoes, and to sip some of the 21 kinds of beer. Many folks enjoy sitting on the rooftop-covered patio to enjoy the view of the cemetery. Smoking allowed after 10 PM in the bar area only. Wheelchair accessible. $9–31 (but most under $20).

In Candler Park
Ⴀ **Flying Biscuit Café** (404-687-8888; www.flyingbiscuit.com), 1655 McLendon Avenue. Open 7 AM–10 PM Sunday through Thursday, 7 AM–10:30 PM Friday and Saturday. Located in a cheerful and eclectically decorated Craftsman bungalow in the historic Candler Park neighborhood, the Flying Biscuit Café is the home of nonstop breakfast, but the eatery also serves lunch and dinner. Breakfast includes everything from eggs to smoked salmon to tofu, and dishes are always accompanied by the famous biscuits. Lunch items include salads, sandwiches, burgers, burritos, quesadillas, meat loaf, and specialties such as Love Cakes, which are made from black beans and cornmeal. Dinner choices include salmon, chicken, catfish, and pasta. At the bakery next door, diners can purchase biscuits to go. No smoking. Wheelchair accessible. $4.95–8.95 for breakfast, $6.95–8.95 for lunch, $8.95–13.95 for dinner.

Downtown
Busy Bee Cafe (404-525-9212; www.thebusybeecafe.com), 810 Martin Luther King Jr. Drive Southwest. Open 11–7 Sunday through Friday. Closed Saturday. For more than 50 years, local office workers, police officers, and politicians have flocked to this soul-food café for the "bee-licious" fried chicken, beef stew, and even chitlins, giblets, ham hocks, and neck bones accompanied by traditional side items such as broccoli-cheese casserole or candied yams. Wash it down with fresh-squeezed lemonade and top it off with old-fashioned banana pudding or red velvet cake. No smoking. Not wheelchair accessible. $7–9.

Hard Rock Café (404-688-7625), 215 Peachtree Street Northeast. Open 11 AM–midnight Sunday through Thursday, 11 AM–2 AM Friday and Saturday. Memorabilia from legendary rock and roll bands and entertainers adorns the walls of this popular eatery. Wide-screen televisions play music videos. And, oh yes—there's food, too. No smoking. Wheelchair accessible. $8–20.

Mary Mac's Tea Room (404-876-1800; www.marymacs.com), 224 Ponce de Leon Avenue Northeast. Open 11–9 daily. A local favorite for more than 50 years, Mary Mac's is big on Southern hospitality and heaping helpings of comfort food. The popular eatery was opened in 1945 by Mary MacKenzie. Calling it a "tea room" was an attempt to add a touch of class in the days after World War II. The restaurant was then ably operated by renowned restaurateur Margaret Lupo from 1962 to 1994. Today, John Ferrell, Mrs. Lupo's handpicked successor, continues the tradition. Diners pig out on fried chicken, chicken and dumplings, country-fried steak and gravy, fried catfish, meat loaf, turnip and other greens, fried green tomatoes, sweet potato soufflé, home-baked breads, banana pudding, bread pudding with wine sauce, and peach cobbler served with the table wine of the South (sweet tea). If it's your first visit, be sure to ask for your complimentary cup of turnip green pot likker and corn bread. No smoking. Wheelchair accessible. $2–5.50 for lunch, $7.50–16.50 for dinner.

In Little Five Points

♪ ☻ ♿ **Front Page News** (404-475-7777; www.fpnnews.com), 351 Moreland Avenue Northeast. Open 11 AM–midnight Sunday through Wednesday, 11 AM–1 AM Thursday, 11 AM –2 AM Friday and Saturday. If you're looking for Cajun flavor and drinks galore, this is the place to come. Walls are covered with front-page newspaper clippings, but the ambience is more New Orleans-like. Many people come here strictly for the cocktails—there's even a make-your-own Bloody Mary bar. Try the "Blanche" martini, a saucy homage to *A Streetcar Named Desire.* Front Page News even has its own covered parking—a rarity in Little Five Points. No smoking before 10 PM; smoking allowed after that. Wheelchair accessible. Entrées $10–23.

☻ ♿ **The Vortex Bar and Grill** (404-688-1828; www.thevortexbarandgrill.com), 438 Moreland Avenue Northeast. Open 11 AM–midnight Sunday through Wednesday, 11 AM–3 AM Thursday through Saturday. The first hint a visitor has that this might not be a traditional restaurant is the giant skull with bulging eyes that creates the front of the building. Diners actually enter through the mouth of the skull. Once inside, they'll discover that this Atlanta institution serves high-quality pub food and a wide variety of alcoholic beverages. The Vortex consistently wins the Best Burger in Atlanta award from local and national publications. Other kudos from *Creative Loafing* and *Atlanta Magazine* include Best Veggie Burger, Best Beer Selection, Best Neighborhood Bar, and One of the Top 50 Restaurants in Atlanta. Political correctness has no place here, and the eatery also enforces a "No Idiot Policy" by which anyone who acts like an idiot will be asked to leave. Smoking allowed (no one under the age of 18 is admitted). Wheelchair accessible. $9–12 depending on just how carried away you get with your burger.

Coffeehouses

With the current popularity of coffeehouses, there's a Starbucks on practically every corner and numerous other coffeehouses scattered around town.

ENTERTAINMENT

Music

☻ **SunTrust Lunch on Broad Concert Series** (404-658-1877; www.centralatlanta progress.org/HavingFun_LunchBroad.asp). Held 11–2:30 every Friday, mid-April/early May through the end of September, in the historic Fairlie-Poplar District between Walton and Luckie Streets. The free weekly series, the longest running event of its kind in the United States, features live jazz, soft rock, and other musical genres as well as the tastes and smells of international gourmet foods at eight nearby restaurants. Streets are cleared and closed off so patio tables and chairs can be set up to create a casual street café ambience. Bring your own lunch or purchase something from one of the restaurants, and then settle back to enjoy the music.

Tabernacle (TicketMaster 404-659-9022; www.ticketmaster.com), 152 Luckie Street Northwest. Voted Best Venue by INsite *Atlanta* and *Creative Loafing,* and recently named Best Live Music Venue in Atlanta by *Rolling Stone*, this historical landmark is a must-see entertainment complex. Local and regional artists have painted original designs in every corner of the former Baptist church. Exotic fabrics, elegant antiques, and Oriental rugs complement the eclectic outsider art and sculpture. The sanctuary is the main performance room where acts such as Lenny Kravitz, The Smashing Pumpkins, Kid Rock, Lynyrd Skynyrd, Elvis Costello, and Willie Nelson have performed. Call for a schedule of performances and ticket prices (usually in the $25–45 range). Tickets are available through TicketMaster at 404-249-6400 and at all TicketMaster locations. The box office sells tickets only on the night of a performance, which might lead to disappointment in the event of a sold-out show.

Nightlife

& ♞ **Euclid Avenue Yacht Club** (404-688-2582), 1136 Euclid Avenue Northeast. Open from 3 PM to the wee hours of the morning Monday through Thursday, from noon Friday and Saturday. This Little Five Points neighborhood bar is always packed to the rafters with students, regulars, bikers, and visitors. This is a smoking bar. Wheelchair accessible. No cover charge.

& **Kenny's Alley at Underground Atlanta** (404-523-2311; www.underground-atlanta.com/HTML32.phtml). Occupying a wing at Underground Atlanta, Kenny's Alley features several clubs that offer high-energy dance music, rock and roll, Latin-influenced music and dance, reggae, karaoke, and music with an Irish flair. Current clubs include the Irish Bred Pub, Island Oasis, Jamaica Jamaica, Sugar Hill, Motion, and The House. This is the only place in Atlanta where patrons can carry a drink from bar to bar until 4 AM. Patrons must be 21 years of age or older to gain entry after 9 PM. $3 valet parking is available Thursday through Saturday nights in the plaza on the east side of Underground Atlanta at 75 Martin Luther King Jr. Boulevard.

& **Masquerade** (Call the business office at 404-577-8178 between 10 and 7; www.masquerade atlanta.com), 695 North Avenue Northeast. Open Wednesday through Saturday nights until 3:30 or 4 AM. The trilevel club (the levels are Heaven, Hell, and Purgatory) is located in an old warehouse in Little Five Points. Entertainment runs to heavy metal and punk bands. Smoking allowed. Wheelchair accessible, but crowding could make it very difficult to navigate. Show charges range from $5–8 in Hell and Purgatory, $5–20 in Heaven. For multiday events, special two- and three-day passes are available.

& **Star Community Bar** (404-681-9018), 437 Moreland Avenue in Little Five Points. Open from 4 PM Tuesday through Sunday; shows start at 9:30 or 10 weekdays, 10:30 weekends. Acts run the gamut from country to swing to rockabilly to blues. Monday is karaoke night. Admission is for those 21 years of age and older at all times. Smoking allowed. Wheelchair accessible. Cover charge usually $3–8.

& **Variety Playhouse** (404-521-1786; www.variety-playhouse.com), 1099 Euclid Avenue. Located in Little Five Points, Variety Playhouse is a combination theater and nightclub with a mixture of theater seating, tables and chairs, and dancing and standing areas, and it therefore presents a wide variety of entertainment—primarily live concerts. Bands play rock, indie, jazz, folk, and many other genres of music. Smoking limited to the Smoking Alley, a designated outdoor area. Wheelchair accessible. Call for a schedule of events and ticket prices. All shows are general admission; some tickets can be purchased at a discount in advance.

Professional Sports

✂ & **Atlanta Braves** (404-249-6400; 404-522-7630; 1-800-326-4000; www.atlanta.braves.mlb.com), 755 Hank Aaron Drive. The Major League Atlanta Braves baseball team plays at Turner Field (see *Guided Tours*). For transportation to the stadium, see the Braves Stadium Shuttle described in *Getting Around*. There are 178 "skyline" (we translate this as "nosebleed") seats along the far ends of the upper deck. Those adventurous enough to take a chance on same-day tickets might snare one of them for $1. Be forewarned, though: Some spectators in these seats report that they have to duck to avoid being hit by the blimps broadcasting the game. Call for a schedule of games and ticket prices.

✍ ♿ **Atlanta Falcons** (404-223-8000; 404-249-6400; 1-800-326-4000; www.atlanta falcons.com), One Georgia Dome Drive. The National Football League's Atlanta Falcons play at the Georgia Dome (see *Guided Tours*). Located in Atlanta since 1966, the team played in Super Bowl XXXIII in 1998. Call for a schedule of games and ticket prices.

✍ ♿ **Atlanta Hawks** (office 404-878-3800; tickets 1-866-715-1500; www.nba.com/hawks), One Philips Drive. The National Basketball Association's Atlanta Hawks play at Philips Arena. The team came to Atlanta in 1968, reached the division finals the very next year, and has enjoyed an illustrious reputation ever since. Call for a schedule of games and ticket prices.

✍ ♿ **Atlanta Thrashers** (404-878-3300; www.atlantathrashers.com), One Philips Drive. The NHL's Atlanta Thrashers play at Philips Arena. One of Atlanta's newest teams, the Thrashers have finished second in the Southeast Conference, but have not yet reached the playoffs.

✍ ♿ **Georgia Force** (office 404-965-4344; tickets 404-222-5770; www.georgiaforce.com), ticket office at One Georgia Dome Drive. The Force plays arena football at Philips Arena, and Atlanta's newest team has an impressive record as playoff contenders. Call for a schedule of games and ticket prices.

Theater

♿ **Agatha's—A Taste of Mystery** (404-584-2255; 404-584-2211; www.agathas.com), 161 Peachtree Center Avenue. Shows at 7:30 Monday through Saturday, 6 Sunday. Participants are asked to arrive 15 to 30 minutes early. Reservations must be made by phone. Named for—who else?—Agatha Christie, the queen of mystery writers, this campy interactive dinner theater unfolds a mystery during a five-course dinner consisting of hors d'oeuvres, soup, salad, a choice of five main courses, dessert, wine, and coffee. Always a farce with humor ranging from lowbrow to literate, the performance is presented by several actors with help from audience members who have permission to be silly. Rest assured that one of the professional cast members will die early on. Almost everyone in the audience is given a few lines to say before the murderer is unmasked. It might even be you. There is no stage and the actors move around among the diners, so you can see and hear from all seats. Shows run for 13 weeks, so you could go back numerous times throughout the year and see different shows. No smoking. Wheelchair accessible. $52.50 Monday through Thursday (cocktails extra), $62.50 Friday through Sunday as well as December and holidays. A $20 deposit is required per person; checks are preferred to credit cards.

Horizon Theater (404-584-7450; www.horizontheatre.com), Euclid and Austin avenues. For more than 20 years, this Little Five Points theater company has been presenting area and world premieres of contemporary plays. In addition to the five- or six-play mainstage season, the company develops new plays through workshops, readings, and the annual New South Play Festival, which is dedicated to plays from, for, or about the South. Another popular series is the New Horizons Off-Night Series, which offers offbeat and challenging plays by new writers. Call for a schedule of performances and ticket prices.

King Plow Arts Center/Actors' Express Theatre Company (404-607-7469; www.actorsexpress.com), 887 West Marietta Street Northwest, Suite J-107. Office open 10–6 weekdays. The troupe produces six main-stage shows each year, often reflecting original works and perspectives particular to Atlanta. The theater is housed in an award-winning, artfully restored, nearly 100-year-old factory where plows and other agricultural equipment were manufactured. Call for a schedule of performances and ticket prices.

Rialto Center for the Performing Arts at Georgia State University (404-651-4727; www.rialtocenter.org), 80 Forsyth Street. Box office open 10–4:30 weekdays; for weekday performances, open until a half-hour past curtain time; for weekend performances, open two hours prior to performance time until a half-hour after curtain time. This lovely historic movie theater in the Fairlie-Poplar district has been fully restored and hosts international musical artists as well as theatrical and dance performances. The center is well known for its Signature Series featuring music and dance, as well as for its two-level gallery space in the lobby. The Rialto is partnering with Hilton Atlanta and Nikolai's Roof to offer dinner/show and dinner/show/overnight packages. Call for a schedule of events and ticket prices.

Seven Stages Theater (office 404-522-0911; tickets 404-523-7647; www.7stages.org), 1105 Euclid Avenue. This avant-garde, cutting-edge theater in Little Five Points presents plays that delve into the social, political, and spiritual values of contemporary issues. Seven Stages, which occupies the Euclid Avenue Arts Center located in a restored 1920s movie theater, sports a proscenium main stage and a flexible-seating black box theater. In addition to modern classics and the works of new playwrights, the theater has produced several plays in conjunction with international theater companies from other countries. Call for a schedule of performances and ticket prices.

Theatrical Outfit (678-528-1500; www.TheatricalOutfit.org), 84 Luckie Street. The long-time Atlanta theatrical organization got a new home in 2004, the intimate 200-seat Balzer Theater located in the old Herren's restaurant space next door to the Rialto. Productions run the gamut from comedy to drama to musicals to one-person shows. Theatrical Outfit is partnering with Hilton Atlanta and Nikolai's Roof to offer dinner/show and dinner/show/overnight packages. Call for a schedule of performances and ticket prices.

SELECTIVE SHOPPING

Art Galleries

Lynne Farris Gallery (404-892-8436; www.lynnefarris.com), Hurt Building Grand Lobby, 50 Hurt Plaza. Open by appointment only. The gallery features contemporary works by local and regional artists in a delightful environment.

Body Art and Piercings

Piercing Experience (404-378-9100; www.piercing.org), 1654 McLendon Avenue. Open 1–7 Tuesday through Thursday and Sunday, noon–9 Friday and Saturday. Get everything here, from an ear or tongue piercing to a belly-button or nipple ring. The Candler Park shop offers a wide variety of body jewelry, including bone, stone, glass, wood, and titanium.

Sacred Heart Tattoo Parlor (404-222-8385), 483 Moreland Avenue in Little Five Points. Open noon–9 Sunday through Thursday, noon–10 Friday and Saturday. From the smallest, most discrete tattoo to full-body art, there's an artist here to meet your needs.

Books

A Cappella Books (404-681-5128; 1-866-681-5128; www.acappellabooks.com), 484-C Moreland Avenue Northeast. Open 11–9 Monday through Thursday, 11–10 Friday and Saturday, noon–8 Sunday. Shop here for new, used, and out-of-print books, including Beat literature, progressive and counterculture subjects, and books about music. Located in the Little Five Points neighborhood.

Clothing, Vintage

Frock of Ages (404-370-1006), 1653 McLendon Avenue. Open noon–6 Wednesday through Saturday, noon–4 Sunday. The vintage clothing store in Candler Park carries men's, women's, and children's clothing as well as accessories.

Psycho Sisters (404-523-0100), 428 Moreland Avenue. Open 10–10 Monday through Saturday, 11–8 Sunday. This consignment shop in Little Five Points specializes in '60s hippie, '70s disco, and '80s rocker threads. The store buys, sells, and trades "cool clothes for cool people."

Stefan's Vintage Clothing (404-688-4929), 1160 Euclid Avenue. Open 11–7 Monday through Saturday, noon–6 Sunday. This Little Five Points vintage clothing store carries clothing and accessories from the 1900s to the 1960s.

Food

Sweet Auburn Curb Market (404-659-1665; www.terminalmarkets.com/sweet auburn.htm), 209 Edgewood Avenue Southeast. Open 8–6 Monday through Saturday. Built as an outdoor marketplace in 1918, the market moved indoors in 1924. It originally had live animals that could be butchered on the spot and, although the market is in a traditionally African American neighborhood, whites could come inside, but blacks had to make purchases from the curb. Today you can buy not only fresh meat, fish, and produce from local and organic farms, but also African and Caribbean foods, African clothing, cell phones, flowers, hair-care products, and prescription drugs. You can even register to vote here.

Health Food

Arden's Gardens (404-827-0424), 1117 Euclid Avenue. Open 10–8 Sunday through Friday, 9–8 Saturday. More than 10 years ago, Arden Zinn began making fresh juices for herself, her family, and her friends. That small undertaking has blossomed into Atlanta's premier fresh juice manufacturer. From the company's East Point processing plant, 20 different kinds of fresh juices are created six days a week and sent all over the city to Arden's Gardens outlets, grocery stores, coffee and bagel shops, health food stores, restaurants, and health clubs. All juices and smoothies use only fresh fruits and vegetables; no preservatives, sweeteners, concentrates, purees, dairy products, ice, or even water are added. Stop by this Little Five Points outlet for a quick pick-me-up of fresh juice or a smoothie. Take some with you, but not too many. The juices are so fresh, they don't have a very long shelf life.

Sevananda (404-681-2831), 467 Moreland Avenue. Open 9–10 daily. Shop here for organic food and supplements, Bach flower extracts, and Naturade products. Sevananda features a grocery, bakery, deli and salad bar, and carries all major herbs in pill, powder, and liquid form. This is where Little Five Points residents and those from surrounding neighborhoods shop.

Records and Compact Discs

Criminal Records (404-215-9511; www.criminal.com), 466 Moreland Avenue. Open 10–9 Monday through Thursday, 10–10 Friday and Saturday, noon–7 Sunday. This record/CD store in Little Five Points carries a wide variety of merchandise, including alternative music and independent publications. Check the calendar of in-store events.

Special Shops

Junkman's Daughter (404-577-3188), 464 Moreland Avenue. Open 11–7 Monday through Thursday, 11–8 Friday, 11–9 Saturday, noon–7 Sunday. Located in the heart of Little Five Points, this fun, funky alternative shop carries inexpensive club clothing—often leather and often embellished with chains and studs—and other off-the-wall and utterly tacky items. Readers get the idea from some titles the store has won: Best Slut Gear and Best Store That Claims Not to be a Head Shop. The stairway to the mezzanine shoe department is appropriately encased within a 20-foot-tall red high-heel shoe. Some shoppers are serious about shopping here; others come just for the fun of looking around or to find a costume.

SPECIAL EVENTS

Monthly: **Turner First Thursday Art Walks** (404-658-1877; www.atlantadowntown.com/HavingFun_FirstThursdays.asp). From 5–8 on the first Thursday of each month, art lovers can view the arts, tour the historic districts of downtown, and enjoy discounts at select restaurants. New programs and additional venues attract singles, couples, businesspeople after work, and visitors. The self-guided tour of galleries has no beginning or ending point, so participants can proceed at their own pace. Participating galleries include the Museum of Contemporary Art of Georgia, Museum of Design Atlanta, GSU School of Art and Design Gallery, Arts for All Gallery at VSA Arts of Georgia, Rialto Center for the Performing Arts at Georgia State University, Paige Harvey Art Studio, (context), and the Atlanta/Fulton County Library Gallery at Central Library. Validated parking is available at the Museum of Contemporary Art of Georgia at SunTrust Plaza. Free.

January: **King Week** (404-524-1956; www.kingcenter.org). Call for a schedule of events and prices. The weeklong event, sponsored by the King Center for Non-Violent Social Change, produces live performances, religious and inspirational concerts, and educational seminars to honor Nobel Laureate Martin Luther King Jr.

February: **Southeastern Flower Show** (404-351-1074; www.flowershow.org). Open 10–9 Wednesday through Friday, 9–9 Saturday, 9–6 Sunday. The area's premier horticultural event, held at the Georgia World Congress Center, is a five-day extravaganza featuring 4 acres of landscape and floral exhibitions, garden-related merchandise displayed by more than 100 vendors, a photography exhibit, seminars and demonstrations by local and nationally known speakers, and more. During the day, take tea in the elegant Tea Garden, which transforms into a pub at 5 PM. Adults $18, children 5–15 $6.

March: **St. Patrick's Day Family Festival** (404-523-2311; www.stpatsatlanta.com). The event, which takes place over three days at Underground Atlanta, features live traditional Irish music and performances by Celtic Irish rock bands, Irish dance contests, children's activities, Irish food and beverages, and unique Irish vendors. The festival ends with the **St. Patrick's Day Parade,** celebrating its 126th year in 2007, which features local and national bands, Irish societies, festive floats, bagpipe and drum corps, Irish dancers and musicians, military units, police units, high-tech firefighting equipment, drill teams, dogs, horses, antique cars, and clowns. Wear green or be pinched. Free.

Mid-April through mid-May: **Atlanta Jazz Festival** (404-817-6999; www.atlanta.net/visitors/atlanta-jazz-festival.html). An international roster of artists performs in numerous venues around the city. All events are free except the Soulful Sounds of the City concert series at Chastain Park. (For details, see *Special Events* in the Midtown chapter).

Late April: **Inman Park Festival and Tour of Homes** (770-242-4895; www.inmanpark.org/festival.php). The last full weekend in April sees this much-anticipated neighborhood festival, considered one of Atlanta's most spirited and eclectic. It consists of the city's largest street market; a juried arts and crafts show featuring some of the South's finest artists; a tour of homes that includes Victorian-era "Painted Ladies," Craftsman bungalows, contemporaries, and loft conversions; live entertainment featuring many genres of music; a dance festival showcasing ballet and modern dance companies; children's activities; a flea market; and a wide variety of food and beverages. The highlight of the festival, however, is the parade, which features the Inman Park Butterfly, floats, bands, art cars, politicians, drill teams, the inimitable Kelly's Seed and Feed Marching Abominable Band, clowns, jugglers, and the Inman Park Trash Monarch, who sits in a throne atop a street sweeper. Most activities free; fee for tour of homes.

Early May: **Sweet Auburn SpringFest** (404-886-4469; sweetauburn.com/springfest2005). Hours are 11–10 Saturday, 2–9 Sunday. The largest multicultural street festival in the Southeast attracts more than 500,000 visitors with music, art, film, health, sports, and food. Events include live performances on seven stages, the Family Fun Zone for kids, the International Film Festival, and more. Free.

May through August: **Sunset Safaris at Zoo Atlanta** (404-624-5600; 1-888-945-5432; www.zooatlanta.org). From 6:30–9 one Saturday each summer month, families who visit the zoo in Grant Park can take a safari to an exotic continent without ever leaving Atlanta. Each month spotlights a different continent and showcases animals and activities related to that continent. The African Sunset Safari, for example, might include learning about animals indigenous to Africa that live at the zoo, storytelling at the Elder's Tree, native music and dance, crafts, and food. Call for specific dates, prices, and the continent being highlighted.

July: **National Black Arts Festival** (404-730-7315; www.nbaf.org). The 10-day festival celebrates the creative contributions of people of African descent through visual arts, music, theater, and dance in venues all over the city. Call for a schedule of events and ticket prices.

October: **Sunday in the Park** (404-688-2107; www.oaklandcemetery.com), Oakland Cemetery, 248 Oakland Avenue Southeast. This annual old-fashioned street party and picnic features traditional craftspeople and artists, musical entertainment, interactive children's activities, and refreshments. The event also includes a photography contest and a Victorian Hat and Costume Contest. Free.

Mid-November: **Holiday in Lights** (404-222-PARK; www.centennialolympicpark.org). From mid-November through early January, Centennial Olympic Park is decked out with millions of lights that create lighted scenes. As an extra special treat, an outdoor ice skating rink provides hours of entertainment for Southerners not used to this activity. Skating is $6 for 90 minutes; rental skates $2. Free.

December: **Children's Health Care of Atlanta Children's Christmas Parade** (404-785-NOEL for recorded information; www.choa.org). Festival hours are 10–9 weekdays, 10–5 Saturday, noon–5 Sunday. The festival, Atlanta's premier holiday event, kicks off on the first Saturday in December with the popular **Children's Christmas Parade.** The parade consists of marching bands, costumed dogs, antique cars, dance groups, holiday-themed floats, giant helium balloon characters, specialty groups, clowns, and the grand finale—the arrival of Santa and Mrs. Claus (who, coincidentally, are portrayed by your authors). The parade begins at Peachtree Street near Baker Street, follows Peachtree, turns right on Marietta Street, then left, ending at Centennial Olympic Park. Hints for parade watching: Leave your car at home and access the parade route from the Five Points, Peachtree Center, or Georgia World Congress Center MARTA stations. Seats are available in the grandstand for $10. Wheelchair accessible. Parade free; festival: adults $12, seniors and children 2–12 $6.

Chick-fil-A Bowl Parade/Chick-fil-A Bowl (tickets 404-586-8499; www.chick-fil-abowl.com). Prior to the bowl game, more than 30 bands; classic cars; giant helium balloons; floats; participating team presidents, bands, cheerleaders, and mascots; and the Chick-fil-A cows parade down Peachtree Street to International Boulevard, and then through Centennial Olympic Park to the Georgia World Congress Center. After the parade, the NCAA football bowl game, the only one that guarantees a matchup between an ACC team and an SEC team, begins at the Georgia Dome. Thirty activities connected with the game occur the week prior, including two basketball doubleheaders and the popular FanFest. The annual event sells out before the teams are even selected, so book early to avoid disappointment.

New Year's Eve Peach Drop (404-523-2311; www.underground-atlanta.com). Held at Underground Atlanta, the annual midnight drop of the 800-pound peach is preceded by entertainment and activities, and followed by a fireworks display and more live performances. Family-oriented activities begin at noon. Free.

The Fox Theatre is one of Midtown's most famous landmarks.

2

ATLANTA/MIDTOWN

Midtown is a 9-square-mile district situated between Downtown and Buckhead. Once known as Uptown, the official designation of this tiny section of the city is that it is bounded by Monroe Drive on the east, Northside Drive on the west, the Brookwood Amtrak Station on the north, and Ralph McGill Boulevard on the south. For the purposes of this chapter, however, we have elected to make Ponce de Leon Avenue the southern boundary.

Midtown was developed in the 1870s as a streetcar suburb. It grew and prospered until the 1960s, when suburban growth moved even farther from the city. During the next decades, Midtown became much more commercial and much less residential. In the 1980s, however, the Midtown Alliance and renewed interest in in-town living sparked a renaissance in Midtown that continues to this day. Neighborhoods within Midtown include Ansley Park, Atlantic Station, Morningside, Poncey-Highland, and Virginia-Highland.

Midtown's principal claim to fame is that it is Atlanta's arts district and the home of the city's most revered cultural institutions—the Atlanta Symphony Orchestra, the Alliance Theater, the High Museum of Art, the Atlanta College of Art, and the Atlanta Botanical Garden—as well as several other museums, swanky hotels, trendy restaurants, and the city's largest park. Midtown is known for its residential diversity and its energetic business district where bungalows coexist with skyscrapers, restaurants, and churches. (For more information about Atlanta's history, see the Downtown chapter.)

GUIDANCE
See What's Where.

Getting There
By air: See What's Where. Numerous transportation options are available from the airport to Midtown, including rental cars, taxis, shuttles, limousines, and MARTA rail (see What's Where). The **Atlanta Link** (404-524-3400) offers shuttle service to Midtown.
By bus: See What's Where. The station is located downtown, so transportation to Midtown would have to be arranged by taxi, shuttle, or limousine.
By car: See What's Where. Exits at North Avenue, 10th, 14th, and 17th Streets off the I-75/85 Connector provide access to Midtown. The principal artery within Midtown is Peachtree Street, which runs north/south.
By train: See What's Where.

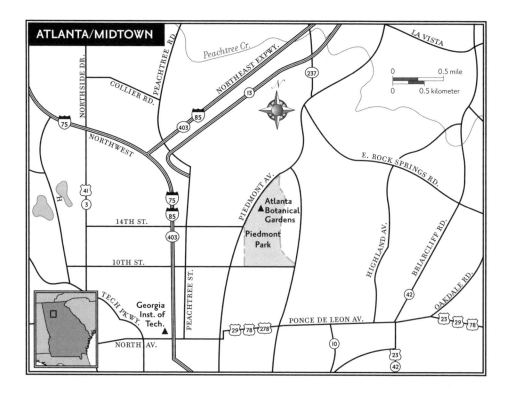

Getting Around

See What's Where. In addition to the MARTA mass transit system, another option for getting around is the free **Georgia Tech Technology Square Trolley** (see What's Where), available only in Midtown.

Parking

There is minimal on-street parking in the commercial areas of Midtown, and most of that is metered (free in the evening and on Sunday). There are a few free parking lots and decks at businesses, but all other parking is in for-fee lots and decks. There is plentiful free on-street parking in the residential neighborhoods. You can, for example, park in the neighborhood across from the Atlanta Botanical Garden and walk a block or two to the garden. When visiting Piedmont Park, you will almost surely have to find alternative parking in nearby neighborhoods because there is almost no parking at the park or on its bordering streets.

Public Restrooms

Public facilities can be found at the Woodruff Arts Center, the W Hotel Colony Square hotel and its associated shopping mall, Piedmont Park, the visitor's center at the Margaret Mitchell House, and all other major attractions.

Medical Emergency

For life-threatening situations, call 911. For less severe but still immediate-care needs, go to Atlanta's **Piedmont Hospital** (404-605-5000), 1968 Peachtree Road.

Villages/Neighborhoods

Ansley Park was built more than a century ago to attract Atlanta's wealthiest and most prestigious families. While Downtown's Inman Park (see the Downtown chapter) was the city's first trolley suburb, Ansley Park was its first driving suburb. Today Ansley Park contains gracious residences and grand estates, tree-lined streets, broad lawns, and bucolic parks. The entire neighborhood is a National Register Historic District. It boasts an elegant inn and is within walking distance of the Woodruff Arts Center, Piedmont Park, and the Atlanta Botanical Garden as well as numerous shops and restaurants.

Atlantic Station, Atlanta's newest, from-the-ground-up neighborhood, was built on the site of the old Atlantic Steel Mill manufacturing complex, a long-abandoned eyesore along the I-75/I-85 corridor at 17th Street. The site is rapidly becoming an upscale mixed-use live/work/play neighborhood with the swanky new TWELVE hotel and numerous shops, restaurants, night spots, and a 16-screen Regal theater. Shops include IKEA, Banana Republic, GAP, West Elm, Taste Clothing Boutique, and Bath & Body Works, among others. Eateries range from snacks to gourmet dining and include Atlantic Grill, Au Bon Pain, Bonehead's Fish and Piri-Piri Chicken, California Pizza Kitchen, Cold Stone Creamery, Copeland's Cheesecake Bistro, Doc Green's, Dolce, FOX Sports Grill, The Grape, Moe's Southwest Grill, PJ's Coffee and Lounge, Rosa Mexicano, Strip Steaks and Sushi, Tahitian Moni Café, and Ten Pin Alley, an ultra bowling alley/lounge/eatery (see *Entertainment*).

Morningside/Lenox Park is identified by the handsome urn-and-column markers at the major entrances. When Lenox Park was being developed in the 1920s, the architects placed columns throughout the neighborhood. In 1989, only four of them remained, and they were in disrepair. So one survivor was disassembled and copied, and 11 new markers soon joined the four refurbished ones to create a strong visual identity for Morningside. The neighborhood had been developed in 1923 as a new kind of suburb where commuters could live and travel into the city by streetcar or automobile. The new development prospered after the city annexed it in 1925. In 1934, the Morningside Civic League beautified the area by planting crepe myrtles and dogwood. In the 1960s, the close-knit neighborhood was threatened with the construction of an interstate highway, but it was successfully defeated.

Poncey-Highland centers, naturally enough, on the intersection of Ponce de Leon and Highland Avenues, and blends almost imperceptibly into Virginia-Highland. Businesses, shops, restaurants, and music venues make this a great place to walk and hang out.

Virginia-Highland is a trendy neighborhood, one of Atlanta's most popular for shopping, dining, and nightlife. The name derives from the intersection of Virginia and Highland Avenues, and its history is traced to its initial settlement by farmers in the early 1800s. When the Atlanta Street Railway Company opened the area to development in the 1890s, the farms were subdivided into building lots for residential and commercial use. One of the earliest neighborhoods was Atkins Park at Highland and Ponce de Leon avenues, and the bungalow was the predominant style of architecture here through the 1920s. Businesses quickly followed homes, and the prime area for commercial development became the intersection of Virginia and Highland. Atkins Park restaurant opened in 1927 and is said to have the oldest liquor license in the city of Atlanta. Virginia-Highland thrived into the 1960s, but like many other in-town neighborhoods, suffered deterioration and a loss of population soon thereafter. In the '70s, however, a few families moved into the neighborhood and began rehabilitation of homes and businesses. Today,

Virginia-Highland is one of Atlanta's most desirable neighborhoods. Visitors enjoy numerous restaurants, night spots, and shops. A special shopping area in Virginia-Highland is **Amsterdam Walk** (see *Selective Shopping*) on Amsterdam Avenue off Monroe Drive near Piedmont Park, an area of trendy shops, restaurants, and night spots.

To See

Cultural Sites
& **Robert W. Woodruff Arts Center** (404-733-5000; www.woodruffcenter.org), 1280 Peachtree Street. Open daily. The Woodruff, the fourth-largest arts center in the country, offers the finest in visual and performing arts in the Southeast. The center encompasses the Alliance Theatre, the Savannah College of Art and Design Gallery, and the Atlanta Symphony Orchestra under one roof, the **High Museum of Art** on the same campus (see separate entries under *Museums* and *Entertainment*), and the 14th Street Playhouse nearby. Free access to the center, gift shop, and College of Art galleries; admission charged for the museum, plays, concerts, and events.

Guided Tours
🌿 **Atlanta Preservation Center Tours** (404-688-3353; www.preserveatlanta.com), 327 St. Paul Avenue. Call or consult the Web site for tour schedules. The organization offers separate guided walking tours showcasing Ansley Park. (For other tours offered by the organization, see the Downtown chapter.) Adults $10, seniors and students $5.
🌿 **Georgia Institute of Technology Campus Tours** (404-894-2691; www.visits.gatech.edu), general college address 225 North Avenue. Georgia Tech is a 400-acre oasis in the middle of bustling Midtown and within sight of Downtown. The university offers several guided tours of the campus every weekday. These are heavily slanted toward prospective students and parents, however, and may have too much emphasis on residence halls, dining halls, classrooms, and the like for the general public. Visitors who would simply enjoy a look at the beautiful parklike campus and several of its historic and unusual contemporary buildings might be better served by taking the self-guided tour so they can pick and choose how much they want to see. If that's the case, go to the Web site at www.visits.gatech.edu/weekend and print out the walking/driving tour map and accompanying description. Among the 160 buildings on campus, visitors will see everything from Gothic-style residence halls designed by Georgia Tech professors in the 1920s to modernistic buildings designed by alumni. In addition to those old residence halls, other historic buildings include the Administration Building, which is known as **Tech Tower** because large letters on the tower spell out T-E-C-H. This National Register of Historic Places structure was built in 1888 and is one of two original buildings on campus. The **Carnegie Building**, the college's first library, was built with funds from philanthropist Andrew Carnegie in 1906. The **President's Home,** located on the highest spot on campus, was built in 1949 on the site of a Confederate outpost burned by Union troops. Among the modern structures you'll find the **Boggs Building**, the sides of which resemble the Periodic Table; the **Manufacturing Research Center,** the sides of which resemble conveyor belts; and the **Manufacturing Related Disciplines Complex I,** which was designed to look like a four-cylinder engine from above. The **Kessler Campanile** in Georgia Tech Plaza is an 80-foot stainless steel

tower lit from within and programmed to play a carillon version of "Ramblin' Wreck." Athletic facilities include **Bobby Dodd Stadium/Grant Field**, the oldest on-site campus stadium in NCAA Division 1-A and home of Georgia Tech football since 1913; the **Aquatic Center**, where the 1996 Olympic swimming and diving competitions were held; **Russell Chandler Baseball Stadium**; the **Bill Moore Tennis Center; Alexander Memorial Coliseum**, also known as the Thrillerdome and the site of Yellow Jacket home basketball games; **O'Keefe Gymnasium**, home of volleyball and gymnastics; and the **Bud Shaw Sports Complex**. Most of Tech's 32 fraternities and nine sororities are located in houses bounded by Fowler Street, Techwood Drive, Bobby Dodd Way, and Sixth Street. Another interesting stop is the **Smithgall Student Services Building**, where the flags of every nation represented in the student body are flown in the atrium area. Musical and dramatic performances are offered in the **Ferst Center for the Arts** (see *Entertainment*). Before leaving the campus, you might want to stop at the **Houston Bookstore and Mall** to purchase Tech souvenirs. You can get to the campus by car and park in the visitor's center lot, other visitor-designated lots, or at meters throughout the campus. Or take the Georgia Tech Technology Square Trolley from Midtown to the campus (see *Getting Around*). Free.

Historic Homes and Sites

& **Margaret Mitchell House and Museum** (404-249-7015; www.gwtw.org), 990 Peachtree Street Northeast. Open 9:30–5 daily; museum shop 10–6. Within this turn-of-the-20th-century Tudor Revival residence called the Crescent Apartments was the small, cramped flat of Margaret Mitchell and her husband John Marsh. They lived there from 1925 to 1932, and it's where she wrote most of *Gone with the Wind,* which still sells a copy every two minutes. The house had been built as a fashionable single-family home in 1899, but was converted to a 10-unit apartment building in 1919. The Marshes lived in #1 on the lower level, which she dubbed "The Dump." Although tiny, their apartment became a literary salon for bohemian Atlanta and a gathering place for aspiring writers and journalists. Restored after two fires, the house and the apartment, as well as an adjacent visitor's center and a museum, are open for one-hour docent-led tours. The tour starts in the visitor's center with "Before Scarlett: The Writings of Margaret Mitchell," an exhibit which includes some of her childhood drawings, an introductory movie called *It May Not Be Tara,* and changing displays. An exhibition of never-before-seen letters written by Mitchell and her husband to his family document how dramatically their lives changed after the publication of the book. In the apartment, visitors can see original Mitchell pieces such as her typewriter and her 1937 Pulitzer Prize, appropriate period furnishings, and other treasures such as the famous leaded-glass window out of which Mitchell looked while writing the book. After touring the apartment, guests proceed to the *Gone with the Wind* Movie Museum, where they can see exhibits about the making of the movie and the Atlanta premiere, film footage, movie scripts, and set design sketches, as well as the doorway of Tara from the movie set and the famous portrait of Scarlett, still liquor-stained after Clark Gable's Rhett Butler threw a drink at it. Memorabilia from the Herb Bridges collection, considered to be the largest *GWTW* collection in the world, includes posters, dolls, games, plates, jewelry, and costumes. The museum shop (404-249-7117) boasts a wide variety of *GWTW* collectibles. Adults $12, seniors and students $9, youth 6–17 $5. Free parking is available adjacent to the property, and the Midtown MARTA station is only one block away.

The castlelike Rhodes Hall was built in 1904

🐚 **Rhodes Hall** (404-885-7800; www.rhodeshall.org), 1516 Peachtree Street Northwest. Open 11–4 weekdays, noon–3 Sunday (closed Saturday). Along with the Margaret Mitchell House, this is one of the few grand homes left along what was once a fashionable residential street. In 1904, furniture magnate Amos Rhodes had the Romanesque-Revival, castlelike house built of Stone Mountain granite to resemble several Rhine Valley castles he'd seen in Europe. He called it *Le Reve (The Dream)*, and it was one of the first houses in Atlanta to have electricity. Among the interior features are fine woodwork, a mahogany spiral staircase, mosaic tile fireplaces, and decorative finishes. Nine stained glass windows depict the story of *The Rise and Fall of the Confederacy*. Headquartered at Rhodes Hall is the Georgia Trust for Historic Preservation (www.georgiatrust.org), the largest statewide, nonprofit preservation organization in the country. Get information here on other trust properties. $5.

Museums

🐚 ♿ **American Museum of Papermaking** (404-894-7840; www.ipst.edu/amp), IPST Building at Georgia Tech, 500 10th Street Northwest. Open 9–5 weekdays. The museum traces the history of papermaking from 4,000 B.C. to the present, and displays the works of contemporary paper artists as well. The premier collection includes artifacts from around the world, including palm leaf books, parchment scrolls, early experiments in fiber, and beautiful watermarks. Free, but a suggested donation of $3 is accepted.

✂ 🐚 ♿ **Center for Puppetry Arts** (404-873-3391; www.puppet.org), 1404 Spring Street Northwest. Museum open 9–5 Tuesday through Saturday, 11–5 Sunday. Call for a schedule of performances. The center, dedicated to exploring the dazzling art of puppetry as an ancient, international, and popular art form, was opened in 1978 by Kermit the Frog and his creator, Jim Henson. The first puppetry center in the country and still the largest American organization solely dedicated to the art of puppet theater, the center boasts an astounding collection of 350 one-of-a-kind puppets from different time periods and different countries—the largest permanent collection in the country. Among the biggest puppets at the center are the two-story-tall puppets seen around the world in the opening ceremonies of the 1996 Centennial Summer Olympic Games. Other famous puppets in residence include Pigs in Space from *The Muppet Show;* Madame, the saucy, naughty octogenarian puppet who used to appear on *The Ed Sullivan Show;* and masks from *The Lion King.* "Puppets: The Power of Wonder" is a permanent interactive exhibit of puppets, books, posters, and videos that show how puppetry has influenced religion, people, and

The Story Behind Gone with the Wind

Although Margaret Mitchell was somewhat of a tomboy, she was unfortunately also fragile. A series of accidents and arthritis caused high-spirited "Miss Peggy" to resign her job as a reporter at *The Atlanta Journal* in 1926 at the young age of 26 to convalesce at "The Dump." At first she devoured every book her husband could bring her from the library, and when she exhausted that resource he suggested that she write a book herself. He bought her a Remington typewriter and presented it to her with this salute: "Madam, I greet you on the beginning of a new career." Somewhat on a lark, she asked him what she should write about. He counseled her to write about what she knew, so she began her opus by fictionalizing the stories told by her family and Civil War veterans. Her writing was kept a total secret, and only her husband was allowed to read what she had written. Whenever their eclectic group of friends came over, she hid the manuscript anywhere she could around the apartment, but rumors were rife that she was writing something.

When Harold Latham with Macmillan Publishing was in Atlanta looking for new Southern authors, he asked her about her alleged book, but she continued to deny its existence. When one of her friends taunted her that she didn't think Mitchell had it in her to write a successful book because she didn't take life seriously enough, Mitchell took the manuscript (all 60 manila envelopes of it packed into a suitcase) to Latham at the Georgian Terrace Hotel, where she told him, "Take it before I change my mind."

Interestingly, the novel was about a young woman named Pansy O'Hara and it had no first chapter, as Mitchell had written the last chapter first. With Latham's encouragement, she changed the heroine's name to Scarlett, and the rest is history. The book won a Pulitzer Prize, has been translated into many languages, and is the second-best-selling book of all time, surpassed only by the Bible.

politics throughout the ages and around the world. Fun-filled workshops in which children create and take home their own puppets are available for youngsters age 5 and older. The center also produces daytime shows for children and families as well as cutting-edge evening shows for adults in the New Directions Series and **Xperimental Puppetry Theater** (see *Theater*). Museum admission: adults $8, seniors and students $7, children $6. Shows $12; behind-the-scenes tours are $5 with a single-show ticket, $4 for members and Flex Pass holders.

🐾 ♿ **Federal Reserve Bank of Atlanta Visitors Center and Monetary Museum** (404-498-8764; www.frbatlanta.org), 1000 Peachtree Street Northeast. Open 9–4 weekdays. The self-guided tour is most appropriate for those 13 and older. The history of money and the Federal Reserve's role in the economy are described through interactive multimedia exhibits. Among the fascinating displays are early forms of legal tender such as wampum, arrowheads, and currency of wildcat banks; gold bars; gold coins minted in Dahlonega, Georgia, when it was a U.S. Mint; and other rare coins such as the beautiful Saint-Gaudens $20 gold coin featuring Lady Liberty lighting the way to freedom. Overlooks allow a peek at the cash and check operations, the bank's automated vault, and the cash-processing areas. Visitors can watch as $10 million worth of currency notes is shredded daily, or see a rare sheet of $100,000 gold certificates and other large denominations no longer in print. Free.

🐾 ♿ **High Museum of Art** (404-733-HIGH; 404-733-4400; www.high.org), 1280 Peachtree Street Northeast. Open 10–5 Tuesday through Saturday, noon–5 Sunday; extended hours until 8 on Thursday, until 10 on the third Friday for Jazz Fridays. Guided

Not all of the impressive art at the High Museum is indoors

highlights tours at 1 Tuesday, Wednesday, and Friday through Sunday; at 1 and 6:30 Thursday. Family tours at 2 on weekends. Located in the heart of Midtown as an integral part of the Woodruff Arts Center complex, the High Museum of Art was already Atlanta's largest museum, but has recently added another 177,000 square feet designed by famed architect Renzo Piano, which includes new gallery space, special exhibition halls, a coffee bar, and a pedestrian-friendly "village of the arts." Upon arrival, admire the striking architecture of the sleek, white, contemporary building and the huge outdoor sculptures. The American Institute of Architects called the original Richard Meier-designed building one of the Top Ten Buildings of the 1980s. *The New York Times* extolled it as "among the best museum structures any city has built in the last generation." Inside, a several-story atrium is surrounded by a spiral ramp from top to bottom. Among the museum's collections are 19th- and 20th-century European and American paintings, art, and furniture; English ceramics; prints by French and German Impressionists; sub-Saharan African pieces; decorative and folk art; modern and contemporary works; and photography. The critically acclaimed Virginia Carroll Crawford Collection of American Decorative Arts chronicles styles from 1825 to the early 20th century. The Samuel H. Kress Foundation collection includes Italian paintings and sculpture representing the 14th through the 18th centuries. The newest coup for the museum is a three-year partnership with the Louvre for rotating exhibits from the Paris museum to be displayed in Atlanta. Tours of Louvre Atlanta are by timed entry tickets. Linger for a snack or a gourmet meal at **Table 1280** (see *Dining Out*). The museum is easily accessible from the MARTA Arts Center Station just across the street. Adults $15, seniors and students with ID $12, children 6–17 $10; free to Fulton County residents on the first Saturday of each month. Included as an attraction in the **Atlanta CityPass** (see What's Where).

🐾 ♿ **The Museum of Contemporary Art of Georgia** (404-881-1109; www.mocaga.org), 1447 Peachtree Street. Open 10–5 Tuesday through Saturday. The museum owns more than 500 works in a variety of media by 110 artists who were born, lived, or did a significant amount of their work in Georgia. These works include paintings, prints, sculpture, photographs, computer-generated images, and installation pieces. Parking is available under the building. Wheelchair accessible. Adults $3, students $1, members free.

🍴 🐾 ♿ **The National Museum of Patriotism** (404-875-0691; 1-877-276-1692; www.museumofpatriotism.org), 1405 Spring Street Northwest. Open 10–4 Tuesday through Friday, 10–5 Saturday, noon–5 Sunday. The museum is two blocks from the Arts Center MARTA station. A five-minute film in the America Room Theater sets the stage for exploring the meaning of patriotism with scenes as diverse as July Fourth parades, flag burnings, and anti-American demonstrations. Exhibits include "Symbols of America," "The Immigrant Experience," "United We Stand," "Sweetheart Jewelry and Collectibles," "Hall of Patriots," "The U.S. Military," and more. Adults $6, seniors $4, children younger than 6 and active military free. Free parking.

🍴 🐾 ♿ **The William Breman Jewish Heritage Museum** (404-873-1661; www.the breman.org), 1440 Spring Street. Open 10–5 weekdays, 1–5 Sunday; closed Saturday and most Jewish and many secular holidays. The largest museum of its kind in the Southeast, this repository explores Atlanta's Jewish history from 1845 to the present through exhibits of everyday items. Videos examine two tragic events in Atlanta: the murder of 13-year-old factory worker Mary Phagan, which was blamed on a Jew and resulted in his lynching; and the 1958 bombing of Atlanta's Reform Jewish temple. There is also an exhibit on the Holocaust and survivors who live in Georgia, a hands-on Discovery Center for children, educational programs, and genealogical archives. "Fabulous Fridays: Music and Me" programs occur during the summer. Adults $10, seniors $6, children 3–6 $2.

Places to View Downtown and Midtown

These locations afford excellent views and photo ops—some can be seen from your car, others require you to get out and walk. The **Fifth Street Bridge** and the **17th Street Bridge** as they cross the I-75/I-85 Downtown Connector provide stunning views of Downtown and Midtown. Although you can glance at the view as you drive across the bridge, you'd be taking your life in your hands to stop in traffic. Park somewhere nearby and walk. Then you can linger as long as you'd like and perhaps get some good photos. After you've enjoyed the Downtown view from the Fifth Street Bridge, turn around and look the other way for a good view of Midtown's skyscrapers. **Piedmont Park** also provides wonderful panoramas of Midtown architecture.

Scenic Drives

Not scenic in the traditional sense of unobstructed natural scenery, a drive along **Peachtree Street** from Downtown through Midtown, which changes to Peachtree Road at the Brookwood Amtrak station in Buckhead, is a fascinating ride nonetheless. This is the most prestigious street in Atlanta. It was once full of mansions, but now contains many striking skyscrapers and noteworthy businesses. You can start downtown and drive way out beyond Lenox Square mall in Buckhead. In the Midtown section of Peachtree Street, you'll see the fabulous Fox Theatre and the historic Georgian Terrace Hotel just across from it, the historic Margaret Mitchell House and Museum, the magnificent new Federal Reserve Bank of Atlanta and Monetary Museum, the Robert W. Woodruff Arts Center and the High

There are many places in Midtown that provide ideal views of the city's skyline. This one is from Piedmont Park.

Museum of Art on the same property, historic Rhodes Hall, many imposing churches and synagogues, and much of the public art described in *Walking Tours*.

To Do

Many of the activities listed below are available at **Piedmont Park** (404-875-7275; www.piedmontpark.org), Fourteenth Street and Piedmont Road. Open 6 AM–11 PM daily. Entrances at Park Drive Bridge, Charles Allen Drive Gate, 12th Street Gate, and 14th Street Gate. Free.

Bicycling
MARTA (see What's Where) allows bicycles on all its trains and some buses.
PATH Foundation: See What's Where; also see *Skating* for bicycle rentals.

Fishing
Lake Clara Meer at Piedmont Park attracts anglers of all ages because it is regularly

Bird-Watching
Despite its urban location, **Piedmont Park** is a mecca for bird-watchers. More than 175 species have been sighted. Open lawns, forested areas, and the lake attract water birds, songbirds, and raptors. It's not uncommon to see the great blue heron, Cooper's hawk, killdeer, red-headed woodpecker, black-crowned night heron, rose-breasted grosbeak, red-breasted nuthatch, or the brown thrasher—Georgia's state bird.

Lake Clara Meer at Piedmont Park is an angler's delight.

stocked with fish, including largemouth bass, crappie, bream, and catfish. Three new fishing piers and a dock make it easy to find just the right spot.

Golf

The very prestigious golf clubs in Midtown are all private. Two, however—the Cherokee Town and Country Club South and the Ansley Golf Club—have reciprocal arrangements with other clubs around the country, so you may want to check to see if yours is one of them. Don't despair if your club doesn't have a reciprocal agreement with these clubs. Golf is available nearby at the **Candler Park Golf Course** (see the Downtown chapter) and at the **Bobby Jones Golf Course at Atlanta Memorial Park** (see the Buckhead chapter).

> **Events for Families**
> The best source of current events for children and families is the Web site www.atlantakids.net.

Running/Walking

♂ ♞ **Piedmont Park**, the finish of the world-famous Peachtree Road Race, offers the only off-road urban running in the Midtown area. The park features several miles of paths and has water fountains scattered along the routes. The 0.7-mile Active Oval circles the ball fields and has a moderate grade. The mostly level 0.96-mile Lake Loop circles Lake Clara Meer. Combining the Lake and Active Oval routes results in a 1.15-mile circuit. The 1.68-mile Park Loop is the longest trail and has the greatest change in elevation. It loops around a meadow and joins the Active Oval. Finally, you can circle the entire park for a total of 2.75 miles.

Runners can trace the path of the 10K Peachtree Classic without entering the race.

Depart from Lenox Square mall (see the Buckhead chapter) and go south on Peachtree Road, following the peach logos in the sidewalk. Turn left at 14th Street and finish at Piedmont Park.

Skating

✍ 🐾 The best place for skating, in-line skating, and skateboarding is **Piedmont Park**. These activities are allowed on the main roadway (closed to vehicular traffic) and the 10th Street Meadow paths, but not on the pedestrian-only paths, stairways, lake bridge, grass, or seating areas.

✍ 🐾 **Skate Escape** (404-892-1292; www.skateescape.com), 1086 Piedmont Avenue Northeast at 12th Street. Open daily, noon–6 in the winter and 11–7 in the summer. Located across the street from Piedmont Park, the company rents bikes, in-line skates, or roller skates that can be enjoyed in the park. Conventional or in-line skates can be rented for $6 per hour. Single-speed and children's bikes can be rented for $6 per hour, $40 per 24-hour period.

Swimming

✍ 🐾 **Piedmont Park Swimming Pool** (404-892-0117). Open Memorial Day through Labor Day. Free swimming available 1:30–4:15 weekdays; pay swimming 4:30–7:30 weekdays. On Saturday and Sunday, the pool is open noon–7:30 for pay swimming.

Tennis

✍ 🐾 **Piedmont Park Tennis Center** (404-853-3461). Open 10–9 weekdays, 10–6 weekends. The park has a long tradition of welcoming tennis players. Seven clay courts were built in 1913 and eight more added in 1914. Today, the City of Atlanta Bureau of Parks operates 12 courts at Piedmont. Court rental $2.50 per hour; night play $3 per hour.

GREEN SPACE

Gardens

✍ 🐾 ♿ **The Atlanta Botanical Garden** (404-876-5859; www.atlantabotanicalgarden.org), 1345 Piedmont Avenue Northeast. Open 9–7 Tuesday through Sunday, April through September; 9–6 Tuesday through Sunday, October through March. This tranquil 30-acre oasis bordering Piedmont Park (see *Nature Preserves and Parks*) has something blooming year-round in annual, dwarf conifer, fragrance, herb, ornamental grass, perennial, rose, spring and summer bulb, vegetable, and vine arbor gardens. Fountains and sculptures complement the various gardens.

Amble through Storza Woods, a 15-acre urban forest with a one-mile nature trail, a wildflower trail, and an overlook. The centerpiece of the Woodland Shade Garden is a stream and fern glade, while a diminutive but picture-perfect Japanese Garden is entered through a moon gate. The Children's Health Care of Atlanta Children's Garden, aimed at ages 4 to 11, features a Laugh Garden where youngsters wind through a maze of evolution, beginning at a caterpillar's mouth and ending in the Butterfly Garden. Kids also can dig for "fossils" at the Dinosaur Garden, learn about carnivorous plants at the Soggy Bog, and experience the singing stone at Rocky Pointe.

Tropical plants take center stage at the Atlanta Botanical Garden's Dorothy Chapman Fuqua Conservatory.

The Dorothy Chapman Fuqua Conservatory and Fuqua Orchid Center overflows with exotic tropical plants, including lowland orchids, while Desert House showcases endangered succulents. Of particular interest at the garden are the carnivorous plants, poison-dart frogs, and rare mountaintop plants never displayed before in the Southeast. Visitors also can peek in the windows of the Center for Conservation and Education to see the culture lab where threatened plants are propagated. Throughout the year, the garden sponsors festivals, flower and plant shows, demonstrations, plant sales, and social events such as "Cocktails in the Garden" and concerts on the lawn.

Over the past several years there have been major installations by glass artists Chihouly, Frabel, and Nikki. Adults $12, seniors and children 3–17 $9. Included as an attraction in the **Atlanta CityPass** (see What's Where).

Lakes
See Lake Clara Meer at **Piedmont Park** under *Nature Preserves and Parks.*

Nature Preserves and Parks
✦ ✿ ♥ & **John Howell Park**, Virginia Avenue. Open daily. This small Virginia-Highland neighborhood park provides opportunities for active recreation and quiet relaxation. The naturalistic design includes significant plantings, winding pathways, and alternating open spaces and shady sitting areas. The cushy, futuristic Cunard Memorial Playground—created along with a garden to honor a mother and her two sons who were killed when a tree fell on their car during a storm—was built using community labor. Volleyball, Frisbee, and in-line skating are popular activities. Leashed dogs are welcome. Free.

✦ ✿ ♥ & **Orme Park**, 795 Brookridge Drive. Open daily. Maintained by the City of Atlanta

Piedmont Park, Atlanta's most popular park

Parks Department, the 6.6-acre Virginia-Highland neighborhood park features mature trees and plantings, open spaces, a winding pathway, a stream, and a playscape. The Friends of Orme Park and others are working to restore the park. Leashed dogs are welcome. Free. 🐾 🐶 ☀ ♿ **Piedmont Park** (404-875-7275; www.piedmontpark.org), Fourteenth Street and Piedmont Road. Open 6 AM–11 PM daily. Entrances at Park Drive Bridge, Charles Allen Drive Gate, 12th Street Gate, and 14th Street Gate. Known and utilized as Atlanta's backyard for more than 100 years, Piedmont Park was created for the 1895 Cotton States and International Exposition by Frederick Law Olmstead, architect of New York's Central Park and creator of the grounds at the Biltmore House in Asheville, North Carolina. This World's Fair ran for 100 days, featured 6,000 exhibits, and attracted 800,000 visitors. The Midtown park also served as the driving ground and racetrack (for horses and buggies, not cars) of the Gentleman's Driving Club. The first intercollegiate football rivalry in the South, between the University of Georgia and Auburn University, was played here. From 1902 to 1904, the Crackers, Atlanta's original professional baseball team, played here as well.

Piedmont Park became a city park in 1904, when the city of Atlanta extended the city limits north to encompass the park. Today, the 180-acre park with tiny Lake Clara Meer attracts cyclists, joggers, picnickers, rollerskaters, and walkers. In addition, the park features tennis courts, softball fields, a swim center, playgrounds, 0.7–1.7-mile walking loops, a community garden, and a farmer's market spring through fall (see *Selective Shopping—Food*). There's no definitive answer for why the lake was named Clara Meer. Speculation is that it might just be an archaic form of "clear lake," or that it was named for the daughter of John Fitz, who farmed the land that later became the park. No matter—it's a great place to fish for largemouth bass and catfish, or to feed the ducks.

Overlooking the newly restored Clara Meer dock near the 12th Street entrance, the

Piedmont Park Visitor Center was built in 1910 as a comfort station. Now restored, it features a ceiling mural called *A Day in the Park* by local artist Ralph Gilbert. Within the park are several significant pieces of public art, including *Free Nelson Mandela,* made from a granite boulder, barbed wire, and steel pipe; *Peace Monument,* a bronze angel standing over a fallen soldier; and *The Last Meter,* which commemorates the Peachtree Road Race. Playscapes, a sheet metal and steel pipe playground located in the southeast corner of the park, is easy enough for younger children but interesting enough to satisfy older ones. Leashed dogs are welcome in the park, but dog lovers also appreciate the off-leash, fenced-in dog park within the park. In fact, Piedmont Park had Atlanta's first dog park, and dog Frisbee competitions and championships are held here frequently.

The Piedmont Park Conservancy has raised nearly $20 million of mostly private funds and is halfway through an ambitious restoration of the park to Olmstead's original design. About 600 trees have been planted, and benches, swings, water fountains, additional lighting, and grills added.

The city's most popular park often hosts festivals and special events. During the year the park is the scene of the **Atlanta Dogwood Festival** (see *Special Events*), **Screen on the Green film festival, Atlanta Jazz Festival** (see *Special Events*), **Atlanta Pride Festival,** and **Peachtree Road Race** (see the Buckhead chapter).

The **Park Tavern Brewery and Eatery** (404-249-0001; www.parktavern.com), 500 10th Street Northeast, and **Willy's Mexicana Grill** (404-249-9054; www.willsmexicanagrill.com), 1071 Piedmont Road, anchor the two ends of the park. Adjacent to the park is the **Atlanta Botanical Garden** (see *Gardens*). All entrances and most areas are wheelchair accessible. With all of these attractions, there is one drawback: The park has very little parking. Free.

Walks

🐾 **Midtown Art Walking Tour.** Begin at the **Margaret Mitchell House** (see *Museums*) and walk north on Peachtree Street. See *Tai Chi,* an abstract bronze, and *Forgotten Alchemy,* a blue-patina bronze square balanced on a sphere, in front of the First Union Plaza building. In front of Colony Square at 14th Street is *Sabine Women,* a geometric steel piece. At the next corner, 15th Street, see *Trilon,* a three-sided, copper-clad concrete abstract with a pool and fountain. Just past it is *Teatro XIX,* an arrangement of bronze architectural elements. Cross Peachtree Street and take a detour through the colonnade of the AT&T Promenade building to the courtyard to see *Olympia,* a colorful abstract of painted metal. Return to 15th Street and cross to the south side of the Woodruff Arts Center to see *World Events,* a 25-foot, four-ton youth holding a sphere. Upon closer examination, the sculpture proves to be entirely created from interlinked human figures. Return to Peachtree Street and turn north. In the lawns of the High Museum are *Three Up Two Down,* a colorful stabile; *Red,* a large, red, stainless-steel rectangular shape; *Lichtenstein House,* a whimsical 3-D house; a bronze statue of Robert W. Woodruff, Coca-Cola executive and major philanthropist after whom the Woodruff Arts Center is named; and *L'Ombre,* a bronze casting by Rodin that was given by the French government in memory of 122 Atlanta art patrons and civic leaders who were killed in a 1962 Paris plane crash while on an art tour of Europe. Continue walking north to 19th Street to see *Athletes Monument,* five athletes representing the five Olympic rings supporting a globe. The piece was commissioned by Prince Charles and the Prince of Wales Institute of Architecture, and presented to Atlanta during the 1996 Centennial Olympic Summer Games. Free.

LODGING

Bed and Breakfasts

In Ansley Park

&. **Ansley Inn Bed and Breakfast** (404-872-9000; 1-800-446-5416; www.ansley inn.com), 253 15th Street Northeast. Conveniently located in the tony Ansley Park neighborhood, this boutique hostelry is an elegant and beautifully restored English Tudor mansion with exquisite furnishings and decorative accents. It was built in 1907 as the home of George Muse of Muse's Department Stores. The inn has taken this wonderful home and created a residential flavor with the luxury and service of top-class hotels, earning it several awards and mention in many national publications. Interior features include massive fireplaces, crystal chandeliers, Oriental carpets, and period Chippendale, Empire, and Queen Anne furnishings. Each sumptuous guest room features a whirlpool tub, and some boast a gas-log fireplace. A full Southern breakfast is served from 7 AM –10 AM each weekday morning and from 8 AM–11 AM on weekends. Complimentary refreshments are served in the late afternoon. The front desk is staffed 7 AM–11 PM daily. A real plus in Midtown is free off-street parking, so you can leave your car here and walk to many Midtown attractions such as the Woodruff Arts Center, the Atlanta Botanical Gardens, and Piedmont Park. Smoking outdoors only. Wheelchair accessible in one room on the first floor. $160–250 in the main house; $120–175 in the annex. Ask about the $99 weekday special offered Sunday through Thursday nights.

Shellmont Inn (404-872-9290; www.shellmont.com), 821 Piedmont Avenue Northeast. A member of the prestigious Select Registry, Distinguished Inns of North America and the winner of several restoration awards, the Shellmont is an exquisitely restored 1891 National Register mansion. Outstanding architectural features include stained, beveled, and leaded glass; curved and bow windows; intricately carved woodwork; coved ceilings; and hand-painted stenciling. Public areas and guest rooms are furnished with antiques, Oriental carpets, and period wall treatments. Wicker-filled verandas overlook lawns, gardens, and a Victorian fish pond. Breakfast is a special occasion and features a variety of juices, coffees, teas, cereals, granolas, fruits, breads, a hot entrée, and specialties of the house. Breakfast is served at 7:30 and 8:30 on weekdays, and 8:30 and 9:30 on weekends. Smoking outdoors only. Not wheelchair accessible. $170–300.

In Virginia-Highland

Gaslight Inn Bed & Breakfast (404-875-1001; www.gaslightinn.com), 1001 St. Charles Avenue Northeast. Built in 1913, this Craftsman home has been seen on CNN, the Discovery Channel, and the Travel Channel, as well as in many national and international publications. It was even featured in a question on *Jeopardy*. The elegant, sophisticated inn actually has some flickering gaslight fixtures. A variety of accommodations—located in the Primary Residence, the Carriage House, and the Victorian Cottage—range from affordable guest rooms to luxurious suites. Some rooms and suites feature a fireplace, double whirlpool tub, or private garden. Some even boast a kitchen, which makes them perfect for long-term stays. Guests enjoy several indoor and outdoor public spaces as well as private areas, nooks, and alcoves. The sumptuous continental-plus breakfast can be enjoyed in the formal dining room, in the garden, or on the front porch. Another plus to staying at this B&B is that it's within easy walking distance of the shops and restaurants of Virginia-Highland. Smoking is permitted only outdoors. Not wheelchair accessible. $115–215;

ask about numerous packages. A two-night minimum is required on weekends.

Virginia-Highland Bed and Breakfast (404-892-2735; 1-877-870-4485; www.gaslightinn.com), 630 Orme Circle Northeast. This restored 1920s Craftsman bungalow is nestled within a cottage garden, creating a true urban retreat. In fact, owner Adele Northrup is an avid gardener and the house is filled with fresh flowers. The interior is decorated with eclectic antiques and collectibles. Guest rooms feature a queen- or king-size bed, and some boast a whirlpool tub or a private entrance. Attentive, informal service ensures a relaxing and enjoyable stay. A full breakfast is served in the sunny kitchen or in the formal dining room. The B&B is within walking distance of Highland Avenue shopping, dining, and entertainment. Also geared to the business traveler, Virginia-Highland offers high-speed wireless Internet access and a printer/copier/fax. No smoking on the property. Not wheelchair accessible. $139 and up.

Inns and Hotels

In Midtown

& **Best Western Granada Suites** (404-876-6100), 1302 West Peachtree Street. This boutique hotel with a Spanish hacienda feel occupies a historic property that began life in 1922 as an apartment building. Today it offers guest rooms, suites, and a penthouse suite. In keeping with the Spanish architecture, the intimate inn wraps around a courtyard with a bubbling fountain. The lobby is decorated with Spanish art and opulent Victorian-era antiques. Smoking and nonsmoking rooms available. Wheelchair accessible. $116–199.

✒ & **Four Seasons Hotel Atlanta** (404-881-9898; www.fourseasons.com/atlanta), 75 14th Street Northeast. All Four Seasons Hotels are renowned for incomparable personal service, outstanding amenities, elegant rooms and suites, and wonderful restaurants. The swanky five-star, five-diamond Four Seasons Atlanta meets each of these standards. For a room with a view of both Downtown and Midtown, ask for an upper-level corner Premier Room. Among the recently renovated hotel's luxurious amenities, the palatial Romanesque indoor pool is Atlanta's only saltwater pool. The **Park 75** restaurant offers gourmet meals (see *Dining Out*), and afternoon interludes might include high tea or a drink in the lounge. The newest addition is the Spa and Health Club. The hotel is located in the heart of Midtown's arts district and offers special packages in conjunction with the High Museum, the Atlanta Symphony Orchestra, and other cultural institutions. Smoking and nonsmoking rooms available. Wheelchair accessible. Weekend room rates start at $230.

✒ & **Georgian Terrace Hotel** (404-897-1991; 1-800-651-2316; www.thegeorgian terrace.com), 659 Peachtree Street Northeast. Known as the Grand Dame of Peachtree Street, this stately 1911 hotel has numerous connections with *Gone with the Wind*. Margaret Mitchell met Harold Latham of Macmillan Publishing in the dining room to deliver her manuscript, which filled 60 manila envelopes and until then had been seen by no one except her husband. In 1939, when the movie premiered in Atlanta, the stars of the film stayed here and attended gala parties. Many other luminaries such as Calvin Coolidge, Warren G. Harding, Charles Lindbergh, F. Scott Fitzgerald, Tallulah Bankhead, and Rudolph Valentino also have stayed here. Today the hotel consists of the original 10-story building with marble floors, Palladian and French windows, spiral staircases, stained-glass skylights, intricate plaster moldings, crystal chandeliers, elegant latticework, and large murals. A stunning atrium connects a modern 19-story wing to the original building. Accommodations, which are offered in standard rooms and junior, one-, two-, and three-bedroom suites, feature antique-style furnishings, "dream" beds with European-style duvet covers, and large bathrooms. Suites boast a living/dining area, a fully appointed kitchen, and even a washer and dryer, making the hotel an excellent choice for a family or for an extended stay. Other amenities include the elegant **Savoy Bar and Grill** (see *Dining Out*) and a fitness center. On the roof is a Junior Olympic-sized pool with a sweeping view of downtown Atlanta. The hotel is located directly across the street from the **Fox Theatre** (see *Theater*) and a block from the North Avenue MARTA rail station. Several restaurants are within walking distance. Smoking and nonsmoking rooms available. Wheelchair accessible. Getaway packages start at $154.

& **Georgia Tech Hotel and Conference Center** (404-347-9440; www.gatechotel.com), 800 Spring Street. Located in the university's new Technology Square complex, which encompasses three blocks in the heart of Midtown, this high-tech, upscale, 252-room hotel offers accommodations to university visitors, families of students, conference-goers, and those traveling for both business and pleasure. Each comfortable deluxe guest room features a flat-screen television, marble bath with upgraded amenities, and cutting-edge technology such as a laptop-ready desk and hard-wired and wireless Internet access. The hotel also offers a full-service club lounge with limited menu service from 3 PM to midnight, a lobby bar, advanced fitness center, indoor swimming pool, and concierge service. Technology Square features retail stores, restaurants, a day spa, and restaurants. Smoking and nonsmoking rooms available. Wheelchair accessible. $159–209.

✍ 🐾 & **Hotel Indigo-Atlanta Midtown** (404-874-9200; www.ichotelsgroup.com),

683 Peachtree Street Northeast. This trendy boutique hotel is located in a historic building across the street from the Fox Theatre. A member of Inter-Continental Hotels Group, it's a complete change from the "cookie cutter" approach. Plush bedding, area rugs on hardwood floors, spa-inspired baths, and a seashore theme make it a standout. High-speed Internet access is available in the lobby and each guest room. The hotel also features the Golden Bean bar and restaurant, self-service laundry facilities, and a health and fitness center. Pets are allowed. In fact, from 5–8 on Tuesday, guests and locals can have cocktails with their dogs (poochy gets a bowl of ice water). A dollar from each cocktail goes to the Piedmont Park dog park (see **Piedmont Park** under *Nature Preserves and Parks*) or to the Atlanta Humane Society. Smoking and nonsmoking rooms available. Wheelchair accessible. $119–200.

✍ 🐾 & **Sheraton Colony Square Hotel** (404-892-6000; 1-800-422-7895; www.sheratoncolonysquare.com), 188 14th Street Northeast. Location, location, location—this hotel is across from the High Museum of Art and the Woodruff Arts Center, home of the Atlanta Symphony Orchestra and the Alliance Theatre. It's also within very easy walking distance of Piedmont Park, the Atlanta Botanical Garden, and the Arts Center MARTA rail station. Guest rooms feature the plush Sheraton Sweet Sleeper Bed (the hotel even has comparable cribs for babies and beds for dogs), rain forest showerheads, and high-speed Internet access. Extra luxuries are available in Club Level rooms. The multiuse building contains not only the hotel but restaurants, shops, and offices. Hotel amenities include the 14th Street Bar and Grill, a Starbucks Coffee kiosk, the Lobby Lounge, an outdoor pool (open seasonally), and a fitness center. Smoking and nonsmoking rooms available. Wheelchair accessible. (Note: Travelers should be aware that this hotel is scheduled to become a W Hotel in February 2008. The telephone numbers will remain the same, but the Web site will be www.starwoodhotels.com/whotels.) $139–304.

🎣 ♿ **TWELVE Hotel and Residences Atlantic Station** (404-961-1212; www.twelvehotels.com/AtlanticStation), 361 17th Street. Located in the new live/work/play Atlantic Station neighborhood, this boutique hotel, which also features condominiums, has recently been named one of the hottest new hotels in the world by *Conde Nast Traveler*. The chic contemporary decor combines with unsurpassed amenities to create an exceptional experience. The hotel boasts 101 one- and two-bedroom suites with a full kitchen as well as amenities such as a flat-panel television, DVD player, Wi-Fi access, and the GHOST desktop application, which permits guests to access all kinds of services online. Other features of the hotel include a restaurant (see *Dining Out*), a private guest lounge, an outdoor pool, and a fitness center. No smoking. Wheelchair accessible. $200 for a one-bedroom suite; $225 for a two-bedroom suite.

In Poncey-Highland

🎣 ♠ ♥ **The Highland Inn** (404-874-5756; www.thehighlandinn.com), 644 North Highland Avenue. This quaint hotel was built in the 1920s as the Wynne Hotel and Tea Room. Today it offers simple, affordable rooms and suites with Old World charm. In addition to being pet-friendly, the hotel has laundry facilities and offers continental breakfast. More than 60 restaurants are within walking distance. No smoking. Not wheelchair accessible. $94–122.

WHERE TO EAT

Dining Out

In Midtown

♿ **Bacchanalia/Quinones at Bacchanalia** (404-365-0410; www.starprovisions.com), 1198 Howell Mill Road Northwest. Open from 6 Monday through Saturday; Quinones at Bacchanalia open from 6 Tuesday through Saturday. Bacchanalia is one of the top restaurants in the city (in fact, it is one of only two four-star restaurants in the state), and is certainly one of the most romantic. Suave glamour is achieved in an old warehouse space where chef/spouses Clifford Harrison and Anne Quatrano blend cultural traditions as diverse as Californian nouvelle cuisine and continental European dishes for their four-course dinners. The resulting menu includes selections such as smoked trout amuse, asparagus with truffled morels, sake halibut with Japanese barbecue sauce, black grouper sashimi, crab fritters, and lobster poached in butter. The menu changes daily and the restaurant maintains a superb wine list. A restaurant-within-a-restaurant, **Quinones at Bacchanalia** serves a prix fixe Southern nine-course tasting dinner—often using fresh ingredients from Summerland Farm, where the owners live. No smoking. Wheelchair accessible. Bacchanalia $72 for dinner, $115 with pairing wines; Quinones $95 for dinner, $165 with pairing wines.

♿ **Einstein's** (404-876-7925; www.einsteins atlanta.com), 1077 Juniper Street Northeast. Open 11–11 Monday through Thursday, 11–midnight Friday, 10–midnight Saturday, 10–11 Sunday; bar open one hour past closing. Einstein's occupies two bungalows just a few blocks from the arts district. Lunch and dinner choices range from salads and special sandwiches such as the jerk chicken or portobello and Brie melt to salads and hearty fare such as steaks and chops. Brunch runs the gamut from French toast to steak and eggs. In good weather, dine outside on the tree-shaded patio, which has earned the restaurant the Best Outdoor Dining Experience in Atlanta designation from *Creative Loafing*. No smoking. Wheelchair accessible. $4–17 for lunch, $7–18 for dinner, $8–14 for brunch.

♪ & **The Lobby at TWELVE** (404-961-7370; www.lobbyattwelve.com/home.html), 361 17th Street, Atlanta. Open for breakfast 6:30–10 weekdays, 7:30–10:30 weekends; for lunch 11:30–2:30 weekdays, 10:30–2:30 weekends; for dinner 5:30–10 Sunday, 5:30–11 Monday through Thursday, 5:30–midnight Friday and Saturday. Traditional American cuisine with a contemporary twist is served in the trendy restaurant at the TWELVE Hotel and Residences Atlantic Station (see *Lodging*). Patrons enjoy the open kitchen surrounded by two dining areas and the wood-burning pizza oven which serves as a backdrop to the bar. Breakfast, lunch, and dinner are served. Complimentary valet parking is available for dinner guests, as is pay parking in the lot underneath the hotel. No smoking. Wheelchair accessible. $5–12 for breakfast, $7–13 for lunch, $9–24 for dinner.

& **NAM** (404-541-9997; www.nam restaurant.com), 931 Monroe Drive/ Midtown Promenade. Open lunch 11:30–2:30 weekdays; dinner 5:30–9:30 Monday through Thursday, 5:30–10:30 Friday and Saturday. This Vietnamese restaurant is a successful mixture of tradition and glamour. Run by Alex and Chris Kinjo and their mother, Ann Hoang, the eatery focuses on dishes that reflect contrasting flavors, varied textures, and exotic ingredients prepared with traditional Vietnamese cooking techniques. Selections include delicate snacks and dishes that range from banh beo (rice cakes with ground shrimp and scallions) to whole striped bass inside an opo squash wrapped in banana leaves. Boutique wines

are also served. No smoking. Wheelchair accessible. $13–50.

& **Nan Thai Fine Dining** (404-870-9933; www.nanfinedining.com), 1350 Spring Street. Open 11:30–2:30 weekdays; 5:30–10 Monday through Thursday, 5:30–11 Friday, 5–11 Saturday, 5–10 Sunday. The decor in the soaring dining room follows the Thai zodiac. Cream banquettes, silk pillows in cream and mocha, and neutral carpet serve as a background for soaring red columns— and all of it combines to create a bold yet still understated look. Fancy ingredients such as lobster tail or lamb come in intricate presentations. The curries are especially noteworthy, and a chef's table at the exhibition kitchen provides a glimpse of culinary artistry. No smoking. Wheelchair accessible. $15–31.

& **Park 75 Restaurant** (404-253-3840; www.fourseasons.com/atlanta), 75 14th Street Northeast. Open 6:30–11 AM Monday through Saturday, 7–10 AM Sunday; 11:30 AM–2 PM Monday through Saturday; 5:30–10:30 PM Monday through Saturday; Sunday brunch 11–2; afternoon tea 2–4 (reservations for tea required 24 hours in advance). Located in the luxurious **Four Seasons Hotel** (see *Lodging*), the restaurant's ambience is a rich combination of styles and textures. What's more, it was described as "an opulent oasis and the best place in the world for Sunday brunch" by the Zagat restaurant survey. Park 75 is one of only two restaurants in Georgia to receive a *Mobil Travel Guide* four-star rating. The New American cuisine is considered culinary art, from the sea scallops Rockefeller to the rack of spring meadow lamb. Tasting menus are highlighted at dinner, and the extensive wine list features American and international selections. Up to eight guests can be accommodated at the Chef's Table in the heart of the kitchen, where diners can learn about the spectacular nine-course dinner and enjoy wine pairings. No smoking. Wheelchair accessible. Reservations suggested for all meals. $15–30 for breakfast, $15–40 for lunch, $28–60 for dinner, $42 for brunch, $21 for afternoon tea.

&. **The Savoy Bar & Grill** (404-898-8350), 659 Peachtree Street Northwest. Open 6:30–10 AM daily for breakfast; 11:30–5:30 daily for lunch (brunch on Saturday and Sunday); 5:30–10 for dinner Monday through Saturday (and Sunday on nights of Fox Theatre performances); light fare 2–11. Located off the lobby of the historic Georgian Terrace Hotel (see *Lodging*), the upscale restaurant offers American Continental cuisine with a Southern twist. Tempting menu selections might include vegetable ravioli, grilled veal T-bone, or seared halibut. Make sure to get the Vidalia onion tart as a side dish; the pastry crust conceals goat cheese and the famous Georgia onions. A sumptuous brunch is served on weekends, and casual alfresco dining is offered on the terrace. The Savoy is also an excellent place to eat before a show at the Fox Theatre (see *Entertainment*). In fact, there is a special prix fixe menu with wine, salad, entrée, and dessert any night there is a performance at the Fox (patrons must have tickets to the show and reservations are required). Smoking in the bar and on the terrace only. Wheelchair accessible through the main entrance of the hotel, but the wheelchair has to be collapsed to go through the revolving door. $11–15 for breakfast, $6–15 for lunch, $10–35 for dinner, $39.95 for prix fixe preshow dinner.

&. **South City Kitchen** (404-873-7358; www.southcitykitchen.com), 1144 Crescent Avenue Northeast. Open 11–3:30 daily; 5–11 Monday through Thursday, 5–midnight Friday and Saturday, 5–10 Sunday. The restaurant is located in a renovated historic home near the Woodruff Arts Center and High Museum of Art. Not a faithful restoration, this remodeling involved gutting and opening up the interior to result in a sleek, steel-and-glass look with an open kitchen and a long, snazzy bar. Billed as "where the low country meets the high-rises," the South City Kitchen serves imaginative, nouvelle Southern cuisine with low-country and Southwestern influences. Some specialties include Charleston she-crab soup, buttermilk fried chicken, and grilled Georgia mountain trout. When the weather's warm and breezy, outdoor dining is popular. No smoking. Wheelchair accessible on the patio and ground floor; rest-rooms not wheelchair accessible. $6–15 for lunch, $8–15 for brunch, $14–25 for dinner.

&. **Spice** (404-875-4242; www.spice restaurant.com), 793 Juniper Street. Open 5–11 Monday through Thursday, 5–midnight Friday and Saturday, 5–10 Sunday; Sunday brunch 11–3. Located in an updated 19th-century home, this hot Midtown restaurant features bold and sassy neoclassical American cuisine featuring such dishes as pomme soufflés, fried lobster tail, and stuffed quail. The over-the-top decor and lively bar scene pull in large weekend crowds. Smoking in the bar only. Wheelchair accessible. $16–35 for dinner, $16–25 for brunch.

&. **Table 1280 Restaurant and Tapas Lounge** (404-897-1280; www.table 1280.com), 1280 Peachtree Street. Open 11–2 Tuesday through Saturday for lunch, 5–9 for dinner, 11–10 lounge; 11–3 Sunday for brunch, 3–6 lounge. The on-site restaurant overlooking the Piazza at the Woodruff Arts Center, Table 1280 is an American brasserie serving full dinners or lighter fare. Dinners might feature duck, lamb, seafood, beef, or pork. Brunch features Belgian waffles, pancakes, egg dishes, crab cakes, sandwiches, and burgers. A Louvre-inspired prix fixe lunch of soup, quiche, and dessert is available as well as a two- or three-course prix fixe dinner (5–6:30). No smoking. Wheelchair accessible. $12–16 for lunch ($24 for prix fixe lunch); $20–30 for dinner ($28 for two-course prix fixe or $35 for three-course prix fixe dinner); $7–16 for brunch; $6 each or three for $16 for tapas.

&. **Tierra** (404-874-5951; www.tierra restaurant.com), 1425-B Piedmont Avenue. Open 6–10 Tuesday through Saturday. Reservations suggested. This tiny bistro's menu offers a gourmet slant to Hispanic New World cuisines. Each quarter spotlights a different country, with a core menu of exciting specialties such as pio-nonus (plantains wrapped around spiced ground beef), pupusas (Salvadoran grilled corn cakes), and cajeta pudding made with goat's milk and sugar. Ask about the schedule for National Day, when a country is highlighted with a prix fixe menu in the $22.50–25 range. The secluded patio is appealing in good weather. Tango night, when dancers perform, is held at 8 PM on the second and fourth Wednesday of each month. No smoking. Wheelchair accessible. $14–22.

&. **Veni Vidi Vici** (404-875-8424; www.buckheadrestaurants.com), 41 14th Street. Open 11:30–11 weekdays, 5–11 Saturday, 5–10 Sunday. Reservations recommended. This northern Italian restaurant is the only fine-dining establishment we know of that's located in a parking garage. The restaurant, situated on the ground floor with a small outdoor area, is convenient to many of Midtown's soaring skyscrapers as well as to the Robert W. Woodruff Arts Center, making it perfect for preperformance dining. Sleek and sophisticated inside, Veni Vidi Vici serves appetizers such as grilled eggplant rolls with goat cheese, grilled octopus on polenta, and gnocchi with Gorgonzola and smoked prosciutto. Antipasti, salads, sliced Italian meats and cheeses, paninis, and a wide array of pastas and risotto are joined on the menu by entrées such as calves' liver, salmon, lamb, veal, and rotisserie specialties such as suckling pig and roasted young rabbit. Outdoor seating is available in good weather. No smoking. Wheelchair accessible. Entrées $17–29; a full meal would run about $48.

&. **Woodfire Grill** (404-347-9055; www.woodfiregrill.com), 1782 Cheshire Bridge Road. Open 5:30–10 Tuesday through Thursday, 5:30–11 Friday and Saturday, 5:30–9:30 Sunday. Chef Michael Tuohy creates innovative northern California cuisine by using seasonally influenced ingredients, organic meats, and local produce. Foods are wood-fire roasted and grilled; in fact, the grill, rotisserie, and oven are in the center dining area and have a Chef's Table next to them. The menu features appetizers (called tastes), small plates, main courses, and platters for sharing. From pizza to cheese, homemade breads to desserts, seafood to beef, everything is simple and deeply satisfying. The Front Room is an ideal place to wait for friends, or you can sit at the Communal Table and make new friends. Monthly Cheese Club events are held in the Front Room as well. In addition to the artistry created by the cuisine, the eatery features the works of local artisans. No smoking. Wheelchair accessible. $17–30.

In Virginia-Highland

&. **Babette's** (404-523-9121; www.babettes cafe.com), 573 North Highland Avenue. Open 5:50–10 Tuesday through Saturday, 5–9 Sunday; Sunday brunch 10:30–2. Babette's is a combination farmhouse and bistro located between Inman Park and Poncey-Highland. Chef/owner Marla Adams creates dishes according to the seasons. The cuisine is a little French, Italian, Spanish, and Mediterranean. Marla describes it as "natural, simple, rustic, and earthy." Parking at the café is valet only, or you can park on nearby Williams Street. No smoking. Wheelchair accessible from a ramp on the side. Dinner entrées $14.50–24.75; brunch $5.75–13.50.

Sotto Sotto (404-523-6678; www.sotto sottorestaurant.com), 313 North Highland Avenue. Open 5:30–11 Monday through Thursday, 5:30–midnight Friday and Saturday, 5:30–10 Sunday. This smashing Italian restaurant attracts a high-profile crowd to dine on a wide variety of antipasti and pasta. Original dishes such as Tortelli di Michelangelo, Tagliatelle ai Funghi, and Risotto Mantecato are served in the intimate space with rough-hewn cream and mint walls and wooden tables and chairs. Check to see if one of the monthly Tour of Italy dinners or wine pairings is scheduled during your Atlanta visit. Valet and street parking available. Nonsmoking area. Limited wheelchair accessibility. À la carte entrées $14–24; Chef's Choice three-, four-, or five-course dinners $40–55 per person.

Eating Out

In Midtown

🍴 ♿ **Atmosphere** (678-702-1620; www.atmospherebistro.com), 1620 Piedmont Avenue. Open 11:30–2 Friday, 11:30–2:30; 6–10 Tuesday through Thursday, 6–10:30 Friday and Saturday, 6–9:30 Sunday. Reservations recommended on weekends. Located in a cottage near Ansley Mall, the French restaurant does bistro classics such as duck confit, escargot with white wine, rack of lamb, and salmon tartar, but don't decide what to order until you check out the elegant specials. Each stylish dining room features soft lighting, warm tones, textural contrasts, and romantic music. Many of the wine selections are French. Save room for decadent chocolates, heavenly desserts, and a perfect café au lait. Dining on the charming patio is a pleasant option in good weather. No smoking. Wheelchair accessible. $14–20.

🍴 ♿ **Baraonda Café Italiano** (404-879-9962; www.baraondaatlanta.com), 710 Peachtree Street. Open 11–10:30 Monday through Thursday, 11–midnight Friday, 5–midnight Saturday, noon–10 Sunday. The name refers to creative chaos from which good things will emerge, and the house specialty is thin Euro-style pizzas baked in an authentic wood-brick oven. In addition to pizzas, the eatery serves antipasti, insalate, calzone, pasta, and secondi; substantial entrées include lamb chops, veal scaloppini, and fish of the day. On Monday nights, "Fifteen for $15" offers a selection of 15 wines for $15. A pleasant covered patio with heaters makes outdoor dining possible in almost all weather. A plus to dining here is that the restaurant is within walking distance of the Fox Theatre. Free parking available at the Georgian Terrace. Smoking in the bar only. Wheelchair accessible. $8–17 for dinner, $4–8.50 for lunch.

🍴 🍴 ♿ **Front Page News** (404-897-3500; www.fpnnews.com), 1104 Crescent Avenue. The presses start rolling at 11 AM for lunch or weekend brunch; the dinner edition goes until 11 PM, until 2 AM on Friday and Saturday. Atlanta's Best Outdoor Dining, Best Patio, Best Brunch, Best Cajun Food, Best Burger, Best After-Work Hangout, and Best All-Over Restaurant are all kudos heaped on this popular restaurant by *Atlanta Magazine* and *Creative Loafing*. With its brick courtyard, 12-foot-tall cast-iron fountains, flickering gaslights, and lush foliage, it's very reminiscent of New Orleans French Quarter eateries. FPN serves newsworthy Cajun- and Creole-influenced food as well as burgers, po'boys, sandwiches, salads, and fish accompanied by microbrews, martinis, New Orleans-style hurricanes, and other libations. In fact, the restaurant has a 100-item build-your-own Bloody Mary bar. During colder weather, FPN fires up the outdoor heaters and the fireplace so the good times can keep on rolling. Smoking is permitted only in the bar areas and outside on the patio downstairs. Wheelchair accessible. $7–11 for lunch, $10–22 for dinner, $8–16 for brunch.

✎ ☏ ♿ **Gladys Knight and Ron Winans' Chicken and Waffles** (404-874-9393; www.gladysandron.com), 529 Peachtree Street Northwest. Open 11–11 Monday through Thursday, 11–4 AM Friday and Saturday, 11–8 Sunday. In the 1930s, Harlem celebrities who came to Wells Restaurant in the early hours of the morning couldn't decide whether they wanted dinner or breakfast, and the strange-but-delicious combination of fried chicken and waffles was born. Singer and Atlanta native Gladys Knight has re-created the tradition in Midtown Atlanta. Menu items include smothered chicken, fried chicken, brown-sugar salmon, baked chicken, barbecue turkey wings, and Veggie Soul (four vegetables and a corn bread muffin). No smoking. Wheelchair accessible. $7–15.

☏ ♿ **Green Sprout** (404-874-7373; www.greensproutga.com), 1529 Piedmont Avenue, Suite D. Open 11:30–10 Monday through Thursday, 11:30–11:30 Friday and Saturday, 11:30–10:30 Sunday. Not your run-of-the-mill vegetarian restaurant, this casual eatery serves a pure vegan menu specializing in a type of Chinese cuisine that uses soy protein and wheat gluten as substitutes for duck, chicken, beef, ham, and shrimp. Menu choices include such items as stuffed eggplant with black bean sauce, Shanghai-style "noodles" made of Yukon Gold potatoes with pickled Chinese vegetables, and other unusual and delicious specials. Some dishes including eggs can be ordered. No smoking. Wheelchair accessible. $5.95–7.25 for lunch, $6–9 for dinner.

☏ ♿ **Joe's on Juniper** (404-875-6634; www.joesatlanta.com), 1049 Juniper Street Northeast. Open 11 AM–2 AM Monday through Saturday, 11–midnight Sunday; brunch until 3 PM on Saturday and Sunday. A renovated historic cottage provides a home for Joe's, which purveys burgers, hot dogs, chili, soup, wings, munchies, salads, sandwiches, and desserts. The restaurant also serves brunch on weekends—here it is known as "blunch" and consists of eggs Benedict, omelettes, French toast, and other goodies. Joe's has an extensive variety of beers, too. Diners enjoy the porch and patio in good weather. No smoking until 5 PM; after 5, only adults are admitted and smoking is permitted. Wheelchair accessible. $6.95–12.95; brunch $5.95.

☏ ♿ **ONE.midtown kitchen** (404-892-4111; www.onemidtownkitchen.com/home.html), 559 Dutch Valley Road. Open 5:30 PM–11 Monday through Thursday, 5:30–midnight Friday and Saturday, 5:30–10 Sunday. This hip eatery overlooking Piedmont Park attracts beautiful people, while the innovative and no-hype food focuses on the freshest ingredients and local products. Just a few menu highlights include a hanger steak on Parmesan-herb fries or lamb ribs baked in honey, chipotle, and soy sauce. The more-than-75-bottle wine list, which changes regularly, is available by the glass or bottle priced in tiers at $20, $30, $40, $50, and $60, and there is a reserve list that goes as high as $365. No smoking. Wheelchair accessible. All menu items less than $29.

☏ ♿ **Toast** (404-815-9243; www.toastrestaurant.com), 817 West Peachtree Street, Suite E-125. Open 10:30 AM–3 PM Monday, 11:30–10 Tuesday through Friday, 5–11 Saturday, 10:30–3 for Sunday brunch. This casual, unpretentious café features such light specialties as sweet corn and mascarpone agnolotti with chanterelles, slow-cooked rib eye, or the signature sandwich called the Toasty. Pasta, pastries, and breads are made fresh daily. Desserts are on the rich side, but you can justify it if you've had a light meal. The eatery has a short but pleasing wine list with wines by the glass at affordable prices. There are beer tastings on Wednesday. Smoking outdoors only. Wheelchair accessible. $7–12 for lunch, $7–20 for dinner, $6–10 for brunch.

✏ 🍸 ⛐ **The Varsity** (404-881-1706;
www.thevarsity.com), 61 North Avenue
Northwest. Open 10–11:30 Sunday through
Thursday, until 12:30 AM Friday and
Saturday. The Varsity started out in 1928 as
a hangout for Georgia Tech students, but
grew to become the world's largest drive-in
restaurant. The menu is topped with chili
dogs, onion rings, fried pies, and the
eatery's famous Frosted Orange drink, but
also includes burgers, barbecue, chicken
salad, ham salad, fries, and coleslaw.
Diners can enjoy the luxury of curb service
or go inside, but know what you want—car
hops and counter workers don't brook any
lollygagging when ordering. After all, they
have to keep things moving to dispense 2
miles of franks, 300 gallons of chili, 2,000
pounds of onions, and fried pies to 12,000
to 15,000 customers each day. Be sure to
peruse the memorabilia and photos of all
the famous people who've eaten here. No
smoking. Wheelchair accessible downstairs. Under $5.

🍸 ⛐ **Vickery's Crescent Avenue Bar and
Grill** (404-881-1106; www.vickerys
barandgrill.com), 1106 Crescent Avenue
Northeast. Open 11 AM–1:30 AM weekdays, 5
PM–1:30 AM Saturday (bar open until 2:30
AM), 11 AM–12:30 AM Sunday (bar open until
midnight). Vickery's was opened in 1983 by
three guys and their dog as a place to get a
stiff drink and a cheeseburger. The old
house in which the restaurant is located
once belonged to Margaret Vickery, who
was said to have been visited often by
Margaret Mitchell, who lived up the street.
Today the casual eatery serves a wide variety
of appetizers, soups, salads, sandwiches,
burgers, and substantial entrées such as
salmon, ravioli, tenderloin medallions,
pork chops, and seafood. Brunch includes
stratas, French toast, pancakes, crepes, and
many egg dishes. There are smoking areas
indoors and out. Wheelchair accessible
through the front gate. Dinner entrées
$15–21; brunch $4.25–11.

In Virginia-Highland

🍸 ⛐ **Atkins Park Tavern** (404-876-7249;
www.atkinspark.com), 794 North Highland
Avenue. Open 11 AM–3 AM Monday through
Saturday, 11 AM–midnight Sunday. Atlanta's
oldest continuously licensed restaurant/
bar, Atkins Park has been serving food
and drink since 1922. The Creole-
influenced menu features gumbo, jambalaya, and po'boys. Although bar
grub—including ample appetizers and
bulging sandwiches—is served until the wee
hours, full dinner service ends at 11 on
weeknights and midnight on weekends.
Every May, Atkins Park holds a massive
crawfish boil that's one of the area's favorite
events. Smoking permitted at the bar
(which is in a separate room). Wheelchair
accessible. $9–10 for lunch, $12–20 for
dinner.

✏ 🍸 ⛐ **Belly General Store** (404-872-
1003; www.bellystore.com), 772 North
Highland Avenue Northeast. Open 7–5
Sunday through Thursday, 7–7 Friday and
Saturday. Located inside a gift shop that
used to house a pharmacy, the eatery features a counter and a rustic community
table. Snack on homemade olive oil bagels,
breakfast wraps, paninis, soups, salads,
sandwiches, and the best cupcakes in town.
Most folks get their food to go because of
the limited seating. No smoking.
Wheelchair accessible. $1.50–7.

✏ 🍸 ⛐ **Fritti Restaurant** (404-880-9559;
www.frittirestaurant.com), 309 North
Highland Avenue. Open 11:30–3 weekdays;
5:30–11 Monday through Thursday,
5:30–midnight Friday, 11:30–midnight
Saturday, 1–10 Sunday. A sister to **Sotto
Sotto** (see *Dining Out*), this casual eatery
serves Italian-style fried snacks such as
smelts, mushrooms with truffle oil, and
calamari, as well as Eurocentric specialty
pizzas baked in an Italian-made wood oven.
The bar and the classy patio are popular
seating options. No smoking. Wheelchair
accessible. $13–24.

& George's Bar and Restaurant (404-892-3648), 1041 North Highland Avenue Northeast. Open 11:30–11 Monday through Saturday, noon–9 Sunday. Located here since 1961, the down-home neighborhood pub serves burgers, hot dogs, and finger foods such as chicken fingers. The decor features 1960s-era booths, sports memorabilia, and video games. Adults only, so smoking allowed. Restaurant wheelchair accessible, but not restrooms. $5–7.50.

& Manuel's Tavern (404-525-3447; www.manuelstavern.com), 602 North Highland Avenue. Open 11 AM–2 AM Monday through Saturday, 11 AM–midnight Sunday; brunch until 3 PM Saturday and Sunday. *New York Times Magazine* calls it Atlanta's quintessential neighborhood bar, *Atlanta Magazine* calls it the Best Bar in Atlanta, and *Creative Loafing* calls it the Best Neighborhood Bar. This venerable Atlanta institution was founded in 1956 by the late Manuel Maloof and is now run by his family. A staunch Democrat, Manuel attracted politicians, journalists, law enforcement officers, celebrities, and others. Although Manuel is gone, these types still frequent the tavern, where they mingle in a warren of oddly laid-out rooms with large booths and wooden tables. Above-average bar fare includes wings, hot dogs, burgers, and other simple grub. Wide-screen televisions allow diners to watch the Atlanta Braves, other favorite sports teams, and CNN. Manuel's also hosts Atlanta's longest-running improvisational group, Laughing Matters, the first Saturday of each month. Video golf, pinball, and Sunday evening trivia contests are other diversions. There is a large designated nonsmoking area in a separate room. Wheelchair accessible. $6.50–22.

 Murphy's (404-872-0904; www.murphys vh.com), 997 Virginia Avenue. Open 11 AM–10 PM Monday through Thursday, 11 AM–midnight Friday, 8 AM–midnight Saturday, 8 AM–10 PM Sunday; brunch served until 4 Saturday and Sunday. Limited reservations accepted; call-ahead seating available for dinner only. Complimentary valet parking offered every evening after 5. A perennial favorite in the epicenter of the Virginia-Highland shopping and nightlife district, Murphy's has a jazzy new design and an ambitious menu. The community bistro is the ideal amalgamation of upscale comfort food, unassuming service, an inviting high-energy ambience, and good prices. The contemporary American cuisine features everything from heirloom tomato and goat cheese bruschetta to burgers with avocado mayonnaise and apple wood-smoked bacon. The recent renovation made room for a sophisticated martini and wine bar and a retail wine shop where weekly wine tastings and seminars are held. No smoking. Limited wheelchair accessibility. $4.50–15 for lunch, $4.95–23.95 for dinner, $4.50–14 for brunch.

Snacks

In Virginia-Highland

 & Paolo's Gelato Italiano (404-607-0055; www.paolosgelato.com), 1025 Virginia Avenue. Open noon–10 Tuesday through Saturday, noon–9 Sunday. Paolo's, identified by the giant ice-cream cone outside, offers more than 60 handcrafted Italian gelato flavors, including limoncello, almond, and panna cotta. In addition, Paolo's carries imported candies, chocolates, and coffees. No smoking. Wheelchair accessible. $1–10.

 & Pura Vida (404-870-9797; www.puravidatapas.com), 656 North Highland Avenue. Open 5:30–10 Sunday through Thursday, 5:30–11:30 Friday and Saturday. Sophisticated tapas include small napoleons of duck and ripe plantains, homemade malanga chips with cremini mushroom dip, Puerto Rican monfongo, and saffron flan with vanilla coconut cream. These delicacies go well with sangria. No smoking. Wheelchair accessible. Tapas $10 each.

Coffeehouses

🦐 ♿ **Java Vino** (404-577-8673; www.java vino.com), 579 North Highland Avenue. Open 6:30 AM–11 AM Monday, 6:30 AM–10 PM Tuesday through Thursday, 6:30 AM–midnight Friday, 8 AM–midnight

Saturday, 8–8 Sunday. This Poncey-Highland coffee and wine house offers a comfortable environment for drinking and eating. The owners want to educate Atlantans about coffee and its impact on the world's environment and social conditions. The wine list features more than 100 wines and the business sponsors Sunday afternoon wine tastings twice a month. No smoking. Wheelchair accessible. $5–10.

ENTERTAINMENT

Dance

Atlanta Ballet/Atlanta Ballet Centre for Dance Education (404-873-5811; www.atlanta ballet.com), office: 1400 West Peachtree Street. Call for a schedule of performances and ticket prices. Founded in 1929, the Atlanta Ballet is the oldest continuously running dance company in the nation. What began as a small dance troupe that practiced in a garage is now one of the country's premier professional ballet companies, recognized for the artistry of its dancers and its innovative programming. The company performs classic works, children's stories, and an annual *Nutcracker* at the Fox Theatre.

Music

Atlanta Opera (404-881-8801; www.atlantaopera.org), office: 728 West Peachtree Street Northwest. Office open 9–5 weekdays. Call for a schedule of performances and ticket prices. The group produces four fully staged operas annually at the **Cobb Energy Performing Arts Center** (see the Marietta chapter).

Atlanta Symphony Orchestra (404-733-5000; 404-733-4900; www.atlanta symphony.org), 1280 Peachtree Street Northeast. Call for a schedule of performances and ticket prices. At 60 years old, the symphony is relatively young to have achieved such international prominence under the batons of maestros Robert Shaw, Yoel Levi, and now Robert Spano. The symphony performs more than 250 times each year, including a classical season of 30-plus concerts of concertos and epic symphonies, a pops series of six lighter concerts, several family and holiday concerts, and 15 performances by the Atlanta Youth Orchestra, all in the Woodruff Arts Center's Symphony Hall. The symphony also performs an outdoor summer series at **Chastain Park Amphitheater** (see the Buckhead chapter) and several free community concerts around Atlanta.

Center Stage Atlanta (404-885-1365; www.centerstage-atlanta.com), 1374 West Peachtree Street. This venue with stadium-style seating and general admission standing room presents the very latest in musical acts, with particular emphasis on rock/pop and R&B/hip-hop. Call for a schedule of performances and ticket prices. Parking is available in the lot underneath for $10 per car and in three nearby lots for $5 per car.

Nightlife

♿ 🦐 **Blind Willie's** (404-873-2583), 828 North Highland Avenue. Open 8 PM–1 AM Sunday through Thursday, until 2 AM Friday and Saturday. Named for Thomson, Georgia, native

"Blind Willie" McTell, whose "Statesboro Blues" was made popular by the Allman Brothers Band, this world-renowned bar showcases New Orleans- and Chicago-style blues. A diverse group of fans flocks here for Atlanta's best live blues with featured artists like Francine Reed, Lotsa Poppa, and House Rocker Johnson. Cajun and zydeco are sometimes featured, and Cajun-style bar food is served. Dark mood lighting and posters of old bluesmen set the tone. Parking can cost up to $10, so try to find a place on Greenwood, Drewry, or Briarcliff Place. Smoking permitted. Wheelchair accessible. Cover charge $10.

🍴 ♿ **Churchill Grounds** (404-876-3030; www.churchillgrounds.com), 660 Peachtree Street Northeast. Tuesday through Sunday, the doors to the club's Whisper Room open at 9 PM for shows at 9:30 and 11:30. This intimate and sophisticated coffee shop offers much more than coffee. In fact, it's considered one of Atlanta's premier jazz clubs. At Churchill Grounds, the management seeks dedicated and talented jazz musicians such as Russell Gunn, Cedar Walton, Freddie Cole, Loston Harris, and others to promote and preserve the art form. Those with a hunger for more than music can satisfy those cravings with salads, sandwiches, pasta, espresso, cappuccino, and desserts. Smoking is allowed only in a very small area in the back of the performance room. Wheelchair accessible. Cover charge minimum $10.

🍴 ♿ **Limerick Junction** (404-874-7147; www.limerickjunction.com), 822 North Highland Avenue. Entertainment 5 PM–1 AM Monday through Wednesday, until 2 AM Thursday through Saturday, until midnight Sunday. Named after a train station in the small Irish city, Atlanta's oldest Irish pub features traditional Irish music nightly in a rollicking, good-time atmosphere. Guinness and Harp are on tap, and hearty pub food such as Irish stew, fish and chips, shepherd's pie, Irish soda bread, and corned beef sandwiches is served. Munchies, burgers, hot dogs, and the like are also on the menu. Monday night has been Open Mic Night here since 1988, making Limerick Junction the longest running show of its kind in Atlanta. Parking is a big problem, so you might want to take a taxi. Smoking permitted. Wheelchair accessible. Cover charge $3 Friday and Saturday only.

♿ **Ten Pin Alley** (404-872-3364), 261 19th Street Northwest. Open 7 PM–1 AM Sunday through Thursday, 6 PM–2 AM Friday and Saturday. This adult playground, owned by Ashton Kutcher and Wilmer Vanderrama, is a three-level multiplex with a sophisticated bowling alley, an ultra-exclusive lounge, and an American-themed eatery. Twelve bowling lanes, three billiards rooms, and DJ-presented music guarantees fun for the 21+ crowd. No smoking. Wheelchair accessible (except for third floor). Food $7–14; bowling $40 per hour Monday through Thursday, $80 per hour Friday and Saturday; billiards $40–60 per hour; no cover charge for music and dancing.

Theater

♿ **Alliance Theatre Company** (404-733-5000; www.alliancetheatre.org), Woodruff Arts Center, 1280 Peachtree Street. Call for a schedule of performances and ticket prices. The Southeast's premier professional theater and one of the largest regional theater companies in the nation presents 10 productions yearly, including classic dramas, comedies, contemporary plays, and regional and world premieres. All are performed in its main theater or its more intimate Hertz Stage, while Theatre for Young Audiences shows are presented in the nearby 14th Street Playhouse. The Alliance has produced many world premieres, including Tennessee Williams' *Tiger Tail,* Pearl Cleage's *Blues for an Alabama Sky,* Sandra Deer's *So Long on Lonely Street,* Alfred Uhry's *The Last Night of Ballyhoo,* Elton John and Tim

Rice's *Elaborate Lives: The Legend of Aida,* and several others. Wheelchair accessible.

♿ **Ansley Park Playhouse** (404-875-1193; www.ansleyparkplayhouse.com), 1545 Peachtree Street. Shows at 8 Thursday through Saturday, 3 Sunday. Atlanta's longest running production, *Peachtree Battle,* has been playing here for more than five years of sold-out performances. In 2003, the play surpassed the record of *Driving Miss Daisy* (which played 1988–1990), and it's still running. The comedy/drama centers on a blueblood Buckhead family about to embark on the wedding of the younger son to a Hooters girl. Mix in an alcoholic grandmother, a cheating husband, an anorexic daughter, a gay son, and a maid from a battered women's shelter, and you have all the ingredients for broad farce. The topical parody of Atlanta's upper crust is fall-on-the-floor-laughing hysterical to metro residents who catch on to all the "in" jokes, but it's hilarious to out-of-towners as well. Previously shown at the Peachtree Playhouse, it is now running at the Ansley Park Playhouse, Atlanta's uptown theater housed on the street level of the Peachtree Point Building. Tickets $26.50 general admission. Advance tickets are a must—the production is often sold out six weeks in advance.

♿ **Boisfeuillet Jones Atlanta Civic Center** (404-523-6275; www.atlantaciviccenter.com), 395 Piedmont Avenue Northeast. Call for a schedule of events and ticket prices. Named for a prominent Atlanta philanthropist, the civic center hosts many diverse productions, including some traveling Broadway shows. The stage is the largest in the Southeast and therefore attracts big productions such as *Miss Saigon.*

✎ ♿ **Center for Puppetry Arts** (office: 404-873-3089; tickets: 404-873-3391; www.puppet. org), 1404 Spring Street Northwest. Open 9–5 Tuesday through Saturday, 11–5 Sunday. During the school year, performances are at 10 and 11:30 weekdays, and at 11, 1, and 3 Saturdays. Call for a schedule of performances. The center (see *Museums*) produces numerous children's and adult shows throughout the year. $12.

♿ **Ferst Center for the Arts at Georgia Tech** (box office: 404-894-9600; www.ferstcenter. org), 349 Ferst Drive Northwest. Box office open 9–7 weekdays, 10–5 Saturday. Call for a schedule of performances and ticket prices. This venue features an outstanding selection of concerts, recitals, dance, film, opera, music, and theater from September through May. The center is also the performance venue for **Atlantic Lyric Theatre, Ballethnic Dance Company,** the **Atlanta Gay Men's Chorus,** and numerous one-time events. The center has hosted performances as diverse as those by Itzhak Perlman, Marcel Marceau, and Wynton Marsalis, as well as events such as the 1992 vice presidential debates and the secretaries of defense roundtable. In addition, the facility houses the **Richards and Westbrook Galleries,** which display visual arts by a wide spectrum of artists. Wheelchair accessible.

✎ ♿ **Fox Theatre** (404-881-2013; www.foxtheatre.org), 660 Peachtree Street Northeast. Call for a schedule of performances and ticket prices. Originally planned to be the Yaarab Temple Shrine Mosque, the theater was lavishly designed with Moorish, Egyptian, and Art Deco influences to reflect the then-recent discovery of King Tut's tomb in 1922. Onion domes and minarets ornament the outside. The interior, designed to resemble the outdoor courtyard of an Arabian fortress, is also a visual treat. Trompe l'oeil, false beams, false balconies, false tents, and ornate grillwork hide virtually every practical feature, including heating and air-conditioning ducts. The "sky" has twinkling stars and moving clouds. The theater's detailing and furnishings are equally ornate. A gargantuan and ornate Moller organ, affectionately known as Mighty Mo, rises magically from beneath the floor of the orchestra pit. Even the restrooms are unbelievably opulent. With all this excess, it's no wonder that funding problems during construction caused the Shriners to go into partnership

The restored Fox Theatre, now known as the Fabulous Fox, hosts a wide variety of events.

with the William Fox theater group, so when the edifice opened in 1929, it served dual purposes as a meeting place and a movie theater. The threat of demolition in the 1970s to make room for a parking deck galvanized the local citizenry to form Landmarks Inc., which saved and restored the theater, now known affectionately as the Fabulous Fox. To date more than $20 million has been spent on the restoration. Today the magnificent 4,500-seat performance venue, which is designated a National Historic Landmark and a Georgia Museum Building, hosts a wide variety of events, from movies to traveling Broadway shows, ballet to rock concerts. Mighty Mo, which sports four keyboards and 4,000 pipes, has delighted audiences for 75 years and is often played before performances. A tribute to the Fox's movie-palace heritage is the **Summer Film Festival**, a popular series of classic and contemporary films. For a more in-depth look, the Atlanta Preservation Society offers tours of the theater on Monday and Thursday mornings and twice on Saturday (see *Guided Tours*). Smoking outdoors only. Wheelchair accessible.

&. **The New American Shakespeare Tavern** (404-874-5299; www.shakespeare tavern.com), 499 Peachtree Street Northeast. Box office open 1–6 Tuesday through Saturday, 3–6 Sunday. Performances at 7:30 Thursday through Saturday, 6:30 Sunday. Dinner is available from one hour and 15 minutes before the show until 10 minutes before the show. *Atlanta Magazine* calls the tavern the Best Place for the Bard and a Brewski. Designed to resemble a Globe-like tavern of the Elizabethan period, the pub produces a different show each month. After dining on British pub food such as Cornish Pasty, Cornish Gobble, the King's Supper, or shepherd's pie accompanied by Irish ales and premium wines, enjoy the Elizabethan scenery, Renaissance and medieval costumes, and live acoustic music, all of which enhance the boisterous action of one of the Bard's plays. The tavern also performs original works, variety shows, and classics by other playwrights. Smoking outdoors only. Wheelchair accessible from the entrance behind the building. $10–32 depending on seat location and night of the week. Ask about discounts and special programs. Dinner prices ($3.75–8.75) are in addition to tickets for the play, so it's possible to purchase tickets to the play only. Seating is on a first-come, first-served basis based on seating location purchased. Table seating is limited, but all seats can accommodate food and beverages. Main floor and box seating feature tables and chairs—balconies chairs only.

SELECTIVE SHOPPING

The funky Virginia-Highland/Morningside shopping area called **Amsterdam Walk,** which is themed around individuality, especially in apparel and furniture, backs up to the dog park at Piedmont Park. Old warehouses contain trendy shops such as Shoemaker's Warehouse, Cook's Warehouse, Flora Dora, Bed Down, Gado Gado, Piedmont Bark, Straight from the Apple Men's Wear, and Intaglia furniture. Other attractions include the Fitness Factory gym, Little Jumping Bean (an inflatable indoor playground for children), Salon Me and Medspa, Simply Sun Tanning Salon, and the popular Bread Garden bakery. Eateries and night spots include the bluegrass-focused Right Light Café, Amsterdam Café, and Miss Q's gay sports bar.

Antiques

Paris on Ponce (404-249-9965; www.parisonponce.com), 716 Ponce de Leon. Open 11–6 Wednesday through Saturday, noon–6 Sunday. This vast three-building warehouse complex with its warren of rooms is quirky and eccentric. The first hint that you're in for an unusual experience is the mural of French storefronts at the entrance. Inside, mannequins are decked out in gold lamé, red cellophane, and other fanciful garb. But now down to the serious shopping. The store sells everything from 18th-century antiques to new design furniture to unique gifts and everything in between at less-than-wholesale prices. If you can think of it, the emporium probably has it.

Books

Atlanta Book Exchange (404-872-2665), 1000 North Highland Avenue. Open 10–10 Monday through Saturday, noon–8 Sunday. In this day of large chain bookstores, this independent one is a rarity and a pleasant one at that. Located in an old house, this no-frills bookstore is packed to the rafters with new books priced 5 percent to 40 percent off, as well as used, out-of-print, and remainder books. There is a method in the seeming madness—shelves are marked with small tabs identifying the subject. There is parking in front and back.

Clothing

fab'rik (404-881-8223; www.fabrikstyle.com), 1114 West Peachtree Street. Open 11–7 Monday through Saturday, noon–5 Sunday. This hip fashion boutique offers adorable clothes at affordable prices. There's little that costs more than $100 among the women's jeans and T-shirts, skirts, and dresses or the men's slacks and shirts. Jewelry includes semiprecious necklaces, leather bracelets, and copper-wire earrings. Shoes are the best bargain. Although the ambience of the store is minimalist, fab'rik hangs contemporary art by local artists. A nice touch is that the store offers carbonated, oxygenated, still, and flavored waters from Iceland and Canada at the water bar (samples are free with a purchase).

Crafts

Ten Thousand Villages (404-892-5307; www.tenthousandvillages.com), 1056 St. Charles Avenue Northeast. Open 11–6 Tuesday through Saturday, 1–5 Sunday. This nonprofit cooperative store works with 70 other stores across the country on a fair-trade model, paying artisans a percentage of the sales of the handicrafts from around the world. One room features home accessories such as statues and candlesticks; the other room displays clothing and jewelry. You'll find everything—saris and wooden animals from Kenya, pottery from Peru, figurines and wooden boxes from Haiti and Bangladesh—at extremely reasonable prices. The helpful members of the sales staff are volunteers. You'll go home with treasures for yourself or others, and you'll feel good for helping citizens of Third World countries.

Food

Green Market at Piedmont Park (404-875-7275; www.piedmontpark.org), Fourteenth Street and Piedmont Road. Market open 9–1 Saturday, May through October. This popular event features fruits, vegetables, flowers, plants, and shrubs grown in the fields in the surrounding countryside. It's more than just a farmer's market, however. Visitors may hear the strains of sultry jazz performed by a saxophonist and watch local chefs prepare gourmet meals using ingredients from the market (the best part is that watchers get to taste, too). You also can buy a cup of coffee from Illy's coffee, purchase dog treats from Taj Ma-Hound, or pick up something one-of-a-kind from a local artist—all while enjoying the park.

Star Provisions (404-365-0410; www.starprovisions.com), 1198 Howell Mill Road. Open 10–10 Monday through Saturday. This cook's market is owned by the masterminds behind **Bacchanalia**—one of Atlanta's two five-star restaurants (see *Dining Out*)—and **Floataway Café** (see the Decatur chapter). You'll find everything here, from restaurant-quality cookware and gadgets to seasonal tableware and linens. Gourmet food products such as A-grade foie gras, $100 bottles of vinegar, ahi tuna, and 200 varieties of cheese (most of which are available to taste) also are available. There are formal wine tastings on Friday evening. Bacchanalia uses ingredients obtained here for its stellar meals.

Furniture, Lighting, and Accessories

Space (404-228-4600), 800 Peachtree Street Northeast. Open 10–7 weekdays, 10–6 Saturday, by appointment Sunday. Modernists love the sleek European contemporary furniture and accessories. The stark setting makes the streamlined furniture stand out even more. Ultrasophisticated accessories include items like milky-white vessels, illuminated plastic panels, and sleek black leather boxes.

Gifts

Twelve (404-541-2357), 1000 Piedmont Avenue, Suite D. Open 9:30–7:30 weekdays, 10–5:30 Saturday. This shop purveys uncommon gifts, handcrafted jewelry, art, flowers, vases, designer handbags, and throw pillows. Twelve creates customized floral arrangements, too. Free parking in the lot behind the store is a rarity in Midtown.

Other Goods

Highland Woodworking (404-872-4466; www.highlandwoodworking.com), 1045 North Highland Avenue. Open 9:30–6 weekdays, 8:30–6 Saturday, noon–5 Sunday. This was one of the first home renovation specialty hardware stores in Atlanta. If you need any kind of fine woodworking tools, this is the place to come. The staff is very knowledgeable. Check out the book selection, too.

Wired & Fired (404-885-1024; www.wiredfired.com), 994 Virginia Avenue. Open 11–10

Monday through Thursday, 11–midnight Friday and Saturday, 11–9 Sunday. At this quaint paint-your-own pottery, you can create your own masterpiece with paint, glitter, and ribbon. If you don't have the time or the inspiration, there are also many already-finished pieces from which to choose. Coffee and juice are served.

Special Stores

Belly General Store (404-872-1003; www.bellygeneralstore.com), 772 North Highland Avenue Northeast. Open 7–5 Sunday through Thursday, 7–7 Friday and Saturday. At this upscale neighborhood bodega, visitors can shop for gifts and gourmet food items or enjoy a quick bite (see *Eating Out*). The campy store specializes in fresh and gourmet foods, locally grown produce, artisan cheeses, Parisian bread, and imported chocolates as well as home accessories, colorful glassware, vintage enamelware, and beeswax candles.

SPECIAL EVENTS

April: **Atlanta Dogwood Festival** (404-817-6642; www.dogwood.org). Spring in Atlanta is heralded with a three-day art and music festival in Piedmont Park. Fun activities for the entire family include a dog Frisbee competition, kid's village activities, rock-climbing wall, and an artist's market featuring 250 exhibitors. The ever-popular U.S. Disc Dog Southern Nationals, hosted by the Greater Atlanta Dog and Disc Club, features demonstrations on Friday afternoon and competitions all day Saturday and Sunday. The juried arts festival features the country's top painters, sculptors, photographers, jewelry craftsmen, and glassblowers. (Note: Despite the fact that one of the main events involves dogs and the fact that the park is dog-friendly, pets are not permitted at the festival.) Free.
May: **Atlanta Jazz Festival** (404-817-6999; www.atlanta.net/visitors/atlanta-jazz-festival. html). The monthlong festival is the largest free jazz festival in America. Internationally renowned jazz artists perform at various venues throughout the city. The activities culminate with a three-day festival at Piedmont Park. Several series dot the schedule, including the "Nightlife Series," "Dinner and Jazz Series," "Have a Little Jazz with Lunch," and "For Late Night Jazz Jam Lovers." There are also numerous special feature jazz events such as "An Evening at Chastain Park." Festival-goers are encouraged to use MARTA because many of the venues have limited parking. The majority of events are free and open to the public.
Virginia-Highland Summerfest (SummerfestInfo@vahi.org). The beginning of summer is celebrated at this family-oriented event with diverse arts, great food, live musical performances, and more. The festival, which has been voted Best Neighborhood Festival by *Creative Loafing,* is one of the best artists' markets in the Southeast. Free, but donations greatly appreciated.
July: **National Black Arts Festival** (404-730-7315; www.nbaf.org). Events occur all over the city. (For more detailed information, see the Downtown chapter.) Events free to $45.
December: **Virginia-Highland Tour of Homes** (leave a message at 404-467-9922, Ext. 301, and your call will be returned; tour@vahi.org). The two-day event features entrance to several private homes in the neighborhood as well as spectacular food tastings and chef demonstrations. $20 in advance; $25 days of event.

The elegant Swan House on the grounds of the Atlanta History Center

SWAN HOUSE

3

ATLANTA/BUCKHEAD AND VININGS

Glitzy Buckhead, Atlanta's Beverly Hills, is a 28-square-mile district 4 miles north of Downtown and immediately north of Midtown (see separate chapters). Buckhead has been called "Where old money lives and new money parties" by *The Atlanta Journal-Constitution*, and the *Robb Report* rates the area as one of America's Top Ten Affluent Communities. And anyone who has read Tom Wolfe's *A Man in Full* or Anne Rivers Siddons' *Peachtree Road* has gotten quite a picture of the jewel of Atlanta.

The tony district of high-rises, exclusive town houses, homes from the turn-of-the-20th century through the 1960s, and new loft condos is bounded by the Chattahoochee River to the west, Buford Highway and Sidney Marcus Boulevard to the east, the Brookwood Amtrak Station to the south, and Roswell and Wieuca roads to the north. But Buckhead is much more than just a physical area of Atlanta—it has the most beautiful and expensive neighborhoods, the finest restaurants, the most luxurious hotels, the best shopping, and the hottest nightlife. It's *the* place to see and be seen.

Yet with all these accolades, Buckhead's not at all snobby. The area is so electric and eclectic, tattoo parlors co-exist with haute couture fashion boutiques, upscale home-design shops, museum-quality antiques shops and art galleries, and everything in between.

Buckhead began much more humbly, of course. In fact, the first population center in what is now Atlanta was a Creek Indian village located where Peachtree Creek empties into the Chattahoochee River in present-day Buckhead. A network of trails led to the village, an important trading center, and **Fort Peachtree** (see *Historic Homes and Sites*) was built here during the War of 1812. The Creeks were driven from their ancestral lands by 1823 and the land became the property of the state of Georgia, which distributed plots to white settlers by lottery. In the 1950s, Creek meal-grinding pits worn into granite boulders were discovered during grading for Lenox Square Mall, reminding current residents of the area's first inhabitants.

It's a joke around Atlanta that all roads are called Peachtree. Of course, that's a slight exaggeration, but in Buckhead there are 12 Peachtree Circles, Drives, Roads, and Streets. The majority of streets, however, are actually named for early settlers, mills, ferries, and farms: Collier, Paces Ferry, Moores Mill, and Irby Avenue are some examples.

The land on which Piedmont Hospital now stands in the Brookwood Hills district was known as Deerland Park and was very rural, even into the 1920s. In fact, it remained a farm until the 1940s. When the family that lived there traveled, their luggage was taken to the Brookwood Station (which now serves Amtrak) by mule-drawn wagon.

Irbyville/Buckhead

In the mid-1800s, Buckhead might have been named Irbyville after Henry Irby, but the area ended up being named for a buck's head that hung outside Irby's Tavern at what is now West Paces Ferry and Roswell roads. In honor of the name "Buckhead," a whimsical sculpture was designed by artist Frank Fleming in 1998. Located in Buckhead Triangle Park, which was the site of Irby's Tavern, the sculpture is called *The Storyteller* (also affectionately known as "The Buck Man"). The design of the tableau consists of a buck seated in a chair telling stories to small woodland creatures.

Buckhead, sometimes called "Jesus Junction," is home to 48 houses of worship—some of them very grand, including the Episcopal Cathedral of St. Philip and the Catholic Cathedral of Christ the King. Peachtree Presbyterian has the country's largest Presbyterian population, while St. Philip has the largest Episcopal congregation. Second Ponce de Leon Baptist and Wieuca Road Baptist have two of the country's largest Southern Baptist congregations, and Ahavath Achim Synagogue has the third-largest Conservative Jewish congregation in the United States.

Although Buckhead is primarily urban, it has a surprising amount of green space and many, many parks. The Chattahoochee River flows through the western edge of the area and provides limitless opportunities for outdoor recreation (see *Natural Beauty Spots* and *Nature Preserves and Parks*).

Although it is not physically within the boundaries of Buckhead, trendy Vinings is close by. Vinings was once an important crossroads for the Western and Atlantic Railroad and one of the final places Union soldiers grouped for the assault on Atlanta. Today the fashionable area is a busy retail and entertainment mecca that strives to keep the ambience of a village center. Its hub is Vinings Jubilee, a shopping center created in the mid-1980s with multiple buildings, each featuring an architectural element from the Victorian era. Street lanterns and a large clock tower add to the turn-of-the-19th-century atmosphere.

GUIDANCE

To plan a trip specifically to Buckhead, contact the **Buckhead Coalition** (404-233-2228; www.buckhead.org/buckheadcoalition) or the **Buckhead Business Association** (404-467-7607; www.buckheadbusiness.org).

For general information about Atlanta, which includes information about Buckhead, contact the **Atlanta Convention and Visitors Bureau** (404-521-6600; www.acvb.com), 233 Peachtree Street, Suite 100, Atlanta 30303. Also consult the Web site at www.atlanta.net for up-to-date information on hotel and restaurant reservations, directions, guidebooks, maps, and help in creating an itinerary.

There are several CVB visitor centers at various locations around the city. If you are arriving by air, the **Hartsfield-Jackson Atlanta International Airport Visitor Center**, 6000 North Terminal Parkway, Suite 435, Atlanta 30320, is open 9–9 weekdays, 9–6 Saturday, and 12:30–6 Sunday. In Buckhead, the **Lenox Square Visitor Center**, 3393 Peachtree Road, Atlanta 30326, is open 11–5 Tuesday through Saturday, noon–6 Sunday. In the event that you venture out of Buckhead, there are two visitor's centers downtown at the Georgia World Congress Center and at Underground Atlanta (see the Downtown Atlanta chapter).

Also check out **AtlanTIX** at the Atlanta Convention and Visitors Bureau Underground Atlanta Visitor Center (678-318-1400). AtlanTIX is Atlanta's same-day, half-price ticket booth for tickets to a wide variety of theater, dance, and musical performances as well as Zoo Atlanta, the Atlanta History Center, High Museum of Art, the Margaret Mitchell House and Museum, and other attractions. AtlanTIX is open 11–6 Tuesday through Saturday and noon–4 Sunday. An economical way to see six of the city's major attractions and save almost 50 percent on the price of admission is to purchase the **CityPass** (see What's Where) from any of the attractions listed or online at www.atlanta.net/citypass.

Getting There

By air: See What's Where. Car rentals are available on-site at the airport.

By bus: See What's Where. A Buckhead-bound visitor arriving by bus would have to take a taxi or a MARTA bus or train (see *Getting Around*) to reach the area.

By car: Access to Buckhead is easy, with I-75 running through the western part of the area, and I-85 and GA 400, a toll road, running through the east side. There are several Buckhead exits off each of those highways. The major north/south artery through Buckhead is Peachtree Road; the primary east/west route is Piedmont Road.

By train: See What's Where. The Amtrak station is at the demarcation between Midtown and Buckhead, so access to either area is easy. Taxis are waiting at the station when the train rolls in, and a MARTA bus stop is just outside (to go north into Buckhead, the bus stop is across the street).

Getting Around

For car rental companies, see What's Where. Sometimes getting around Atlanta is best via taxi (see What's Where). Reliable taxi service is available from **Buckhead Safety Cab** (404-233-1152), which has been serving the district for 40 years. Check the Yellow Pages for many other taxi options. The **Metropolitan Atlanta Rapid Transit Authority,** known locally as **MARTA** (see What's Where), is the most cost-effective and convenient way to get around Atlanta. While in Buckhead, take advantage of the free **BUC (Buckhead's Uptown Connection)** shuttle (see What's Where). Numerous companies also offer limousine services. Check the Yellow Pages or your concierge for limousine companies.

Parking

There is little on-street parking on major thoroughfares in the commercial areas. There are free parking lots and/or decks at large shopping malls, smaller shopping centers, many restaurants, and some attractions. In addition, there are numerous paid parking decks everywhere. In the Buckhead entertainment district, some streets such as Bolling Way are closed off in the evening (especially on the weekends) to alleviate traffic congestion, which means visitors have to park farther away and walk to the restaurants and nightclubs.

Public Restrooms

Facilities are available at Lenox Square and Phipps Plaza shopping malls as well as the Amtrak Station, the Atlanta History Center, restaurants and nightspots, and in office buildings.

Medical Emergency

For life-threatening situations, call 911. In fact, if you are out and about in Buckhead and need immediate assistance, there are 20 bright-yellow emergency 911 telephone boxes with fluorescent blue signs placed throughout the business district. These give direct links to police, fire, and medical assistance 24/7 and automatically register the caller's location. Immediate care is available at Atlanta's **Piedmont Hospital** (404-605-5000), 1968 Peachtree Road.

Villages/Neighborhoods

Buckhead is made up of many areas and neighborhoods—some strictly commercial, some entirely residential, and some mixed. Just a few are described here. Any of these neighborhoods make an interesting driving tour and include examples of many kinds of architecture.

Brookhaven, on the northern edge of Buckhead, was developed as Atlanta's first country club neighborhood. In 1910, 150 acres were purchased for a golf club to be called Brookhaven, which is now the private and very exclusive Capital City Country Club. In the 1980s, the area was placed on the National Register of Historic Places as the first planned golf club community in Georgia. Enclosed by Peachtree-Dunwoody Road on the west and south, Peachtree Road on the east, and Windsor Parkway on the north, Brookhaven is an enclave of large Tudor, Colonial, and Georgian homes and English cottages. The area is characterized by broad, winding streets, rolling terrain, and densely wooded hollows.

Brookwood Hills is Buckhead's only completely enclosed neighborhood. Fighting was heavy here during the Civil War. In the 1880s, a prominent hotel tycoon built an estate here called Brookwood, and the name has survived, not only as the name of the neighborhood but also of the AMTRAK station. On the east side of Peachtree Road from I-85 to Brighton Road at Piedmont Hospital, the neighborhood features large Mediterranean, Georgian, Colonial, and Tudor homes designed by some of Atlanta's most famous architects. The oldest section of the neighborhood is on the National Register of Historic Places and is also designated an Atlanta Conservation District.

Buckhead Forest is an enclave in the V formed where Roswell and Peachtree roads split. Although it is surrounded by some of Atlanta's priciest commercial real estate, it is a quiet, eclectic area of 1920s to 1930s cottages mixed with a few brick ranches built in the 1950s and 1960s and some European-style stuccos built within the past 10 years.

Collier Hills-Ardmore Park is rich in Atlanta history. A monument at Peachtree and Palisades roads in the neighborhood marks the spot where the Echota and Peachtree Creek Indian trails crossed, where some of the most bitter fighting of the Battle of Atlanta took place along Tanyard Creek. The Collier Hills neighborhood, which runs from Tanyard Creek and the railroad line to Northside Drive, features homes primarily built right after World War II. In the Ardmore Park neighborhood, near Peachtree along 26th and 28th streets and Collier Road, brick apartments and duplexes mix with older homes. The area has three parks: Tanyard Creek, Ardmore, and Atlanta Memorial, which contains a golf course and tennis center (see *Golf, Tennis,* and *Nature Preserves and Parks*).

Colonial Homes is an area of garden apartments and town houses between Peachtree Road and Atlanta Memorial Park. Built in the 1940s, Colonial Homes was considered a party mecca in the 1960s. A broad vista of Bobby Jones Golf Course (see *Golf*) makes the area particularly desirable.

Garden Hills is a large urban forest neighborhood between Peachtree and Piedmont Roads, bordered on the north by Pharr Road and on the south by East Wesley Road. Winding streets are lined with old trees, and there's a pleasant mixture of early 20th-century homes, pocket parks, and landscaped traffic islands. Most of the homes are Georgian, Tudor, or Spanish Revival, with a few other styles mixed in. In fact, as you're riding north on Peachtree Road from Midtown, you'll pass the historic Moorish-style Alhambra Apartments, which were built in 1927 and are listed on the National Register. Garden Hills contains Sunnybrook Park, Alexander Park, Frankie Allen Park, and the Garden Hills Pool (see *Nature Preserves and Parks*).

Haynes Manor was developed in the late 1920s and takes its name from the developer. The spectacular entrance from Peachtree Road along Peachtree Battle Parkway gives the area a European flavor. The parkway, once known as Battle Avenue to commemorate the Battle of Peachtree Creek, contains a chain of parks running down the center. These parks attract joggers, bird-watchers, and strollers. The impressive homes resemble manor houses in English and French styles. The neighborhood contains three parks: Atlanta Memorial Park, which borders Peachtree Creek on the south side of Haynes Manor; Woodward Habersham Park, a densely forested conservation area; and the Haynes Manor Park and Memorial Park Trail (see *Nature Preserves and Parks*).

Peachtree Heights (also known as Peachtree Heights West) contains some of the most magnificent homes in Atlanta. This is the area that has earned Buckhead the "Beverly Hills of Atlanta" appellation. Carrere and Hastings, a well-known New York architectural firm, designed the street layout with Peachtree Battle Avenue and Habersham Road as the main streets, while spectacular mansions on sprawling grounds showcase the work of Atlanta's greatest architects. About 400 of these manor houses exist, ranging in style from classical and traditional to newer construction on subdivided lots. One of the neighborhood's most famous homes is the Swan House, which is open to the public (see *Historic Homes and Sites*). Sibley Park at Habersham Way and West Wesley Road is a densely wooded conservation park.

Peachtree Heights East isn't quite as fancy as Peachtree Heights, but still contains large homes ranging from American foursquare to bungalow, Cape Cod to Tudor. The neighborhood actually has two sections: Peachtree Heights East from Peachtree Road to Brookwood Drive, which was developed in 1908, and East Rivers between Brookwood on the west and the creek east of Acorn Avenue, which was developed in 1920. A serene lake, known locally as the Duck Pond, lies off Peachtree Road between Lindbergh Drive and East Wesley Road. The park around the lake features lush landscaping, stacked rock retaining walls, and stone bridges over streams.

Peachtree Highlands National Historic District is part of the **Peachtree Park** neighborhood. Peachtree Highlands is important because it is a living architectural museum. Despite its small size, it has good examples of three periods: Craftsman, Tudor Revival, and Minimal Traditional. There are also Dutch Colonial, Cape Cod, foursquare, and more recent ranch and split-level styles. Landscaping was part of the community plan from the beginning, which results in a parklike effect. Peachtree Highlands is also the last intact working-class neighborhood in Buckhead. A landscaped pedestrian bridge across GA 400 at the end of East Paces Ferry Road connects Peachtree Park to Lenox Square mall.

Peachtree Hills, which lies east of Peachtree Road between Peachtree Creek and Lindbergh Drive, was developed in 1910. Its eclectic, mostly Craftsman homes are painted vibrant colors and feature intimate gardens and unusual fences and walls. The neighborhood is bisected by Peachtree Hills Avenue and features antiques shops and restaurants at Kings Circle. Peachtree Battle Shopping Center is nearby.

Ridgedale Park, on the east side of Peachtree Road just north of Lenox Square and Phipps Plaza malls, was begun in the 1920s. The homes are a charming blend of early 20th-century vernacular architecture, including Tudor Revival, Georgian, and English and French cottage styles.

South Buckhead, also known as Sobu, is a destination for eclectic shopping, art enthusiasts, and diners. With a bit of the flavor of Miami's South Beach, Sobu is filled with art galleries and new restaurants. The area begins where Peachtree Road crosses I-85 at the Brookwood interchange and runs north along Peachtree to Peachtree Creek.

Tuxedo Park, a magnet for tour buses, is bounded by Valley Road on the east, Blackland Road on the north, Northside Drive on the west, and West Paces Ferry Road on the south. The neighborhood, which was begun in 1904, contains opulent mansions designed by famed architects Philip Trammell Schutze and Neil Reed in the Georgian, Greek Revival, Italianate, and Tudor styles. Most of the homes are private residences, but one of these famous houses is the **Peacock Mansion** (302 West Paces Ferry Road), which now serves as the Southern Center for International Studies. Another famous house is the Governor's Mansion. Although it was built in 1963, it was created in the traditional Southern style and blends in perfectly with the neighborhood. The heavily wooded neighborhood is particularly gorgeous in the springtime, when it turns into a fairyland of white dogwood, pink cherry, and brilliant azalea blossoms.

West Village is located in the heart of Buckhead, west of Peachtree and Roswell roads and between West Paces Ferry Road and East Andrews Drive. The village offers an array of quaint and eclectic shops, galleries, and restaurants.

To See

Cultural Sites

✐ ❦ ♿ **Chastain Arts and Crafts Center** (404-252-2927; www.bcaatlanta.com, click on "Programs & Services"), 135 West Wieuca Road Northwest. Open 9–5 June weekdays, the remainder of the year 9:30–9:30 Monday through Thursday, 9:30–4:30 Friday and Saturday. The center offers classes in all types of art media, and the gallery sponsors three artists' exhibits and two holiday shows (spring and winter) annually. Free.

✐ ❦ ♿ **Oglethorpe University Museum of Art** (404-364-8555; www.museum.ogle thorpe.edu), 4484 Peachtree Road Northeast. Open noon–5 Tuesday through Sunday; docent-led tours at 2 PM Sunday. Located on the third floor of the Philip Weltner Library on the university campus, the intimate 7,000-square-foot museum owns a permanent collection of works it describes as representational, often figurative and spiritual in nature. Paintings, sculptures, prints, and photographs range from Russian to American masters. During the year, the museum sponsors three curated exhibitions of international art as well as lectures and concerts. $5 for those 12 and older.

Public Art

Buckhead is filled with interesting architecture and public art, including wallscapes, fountains, and outdoor sculptures. A ride or stroll around the area makes a pleasant excursion.

Architecture

Some of the most famous architects in the country created magnificent homes in Buckhead, among them Neel Reid, Philip Trammel Shutze, Rudolph Satorius Adler, and Lewis Edmund "Buck" Crook Jr. Just drive up and down any of the residential streets— especially West Paces Ferry Road, Andrews and East Andrews drives, and Peachtree Battle Avenue—to admire their work (see *Neighborhoods*).

Fountains

The soothing power of moving water is well documented. A variety of handsome and whimsical fountains create relaxing oases in Buckhead, including ones at **NAVA**, 3060 Peachtree Road; **Westin Buckhead Atlanta**, 3391 Peachtree Road; **Lenox Towers**, 3390-34000 Peachtree Road; **JW Marriott Hotel**, 3300 Lenox Road Northeast; **Peachtree Palisades East**, 1819 Peachtree Road; **Monarch Tower**, Lenox Road at Buckhead Loop; **Tower Place 200**, 3348 Peachtree Road; **Swan House**, 3101 Andrews Drive; and **Pinnacle Park**, Peachtree and Lenox roads.

Outdoor Sculpture

Buckhead is dotted with important outdoor sculptures. First among them is *The Storyteller* (also known as "The Buck Man") at Buckhead Triangle Park, Peachtree Road at Roswell Road, which was described in the introduction. Some of the area's other significant sculptures include *Urban Quartet* at Monarch Tower, Lenox Road at Buckhead Loop; *Bremen Town Musicians* at Lenox Square, 3393 Peachtree Road; *Boy Holding Boy* and *Giggles* at Tower Place 200, 3348 Peachtree Road; *They Will Soar on Wings* at Lenox Towers, 3390-3400 Peachtree Road; *Great Fish* at the Atlanta Fish Market, 265 Pharr Road; *Kite Children* at Tower Place, 3340 Peachtree Road; *Temptation of Eve* at Peachtree Palisades East, 1819 Peachtree Road;

Hippocrates at Piedmont Hospital, 1968 Peachtree Road; *Untitled* at Frankie Allen Park, Bagley Street and Pharr Road; and a giant wheel-like structure at the Pinnacle Building Park, Peachtree Road at Lenox Road. For a complete list of the other sculptures, consult the Web site at www.buckhead.net/sculpture.

Wallscapes

Over many years, artists have turned blank brick walls on the sides of many buildings into an outdoor gallery of fanciful art. Some of these murals were commissioned and signed; others were graffiti. Some of the graffiti artists have actually gained acclaim and rated an exhibition at the **City Gallery at Chastain Park**. Some of the wallscapes you shouldn't miss include those at **Fellini's Pizza**, 2809 Peachtree Road; **Bolling Way** behind the World Bar, 3071 Peachtree Road; behind **Tongue and Groove**, 3055 Peachtree Road; several walls at **700 Miami Circle; Rib Ranch**, 25 Irby Avenue; and **Fadó Irish Pub**, 3035 Peachtree Road.

Guided Tours

✎ **American Sightseeing Atlanta** (404-233-9140; 1-800-572-3050; www.americansight seeing.org/atlanta.htm), 550 Pharr Road, Suite 305. The company offers two half-day tours of the Atlanta area, which include a few Buckhead sites, or an all-day combo tour, which includes both the morning and afternoon tours. The company picks up at all the major hotels. Adults $42–45, children $37–40; combo tour: adults $75–77, children $65–67. Note: A minimum of six people is required, so these tours are best for a family or a group traveling together.

✎ 🏛 **Atlanta Preservation Center** (404-688-3353; www.preserveatlanta.com), 327 St. Paul Avenue. The center offers numerous tours within the Atlanta metro area; call or con-sult the Web site for schedules. The guided walking tours showcasing the Fox Theatre, his-toric Downtown, Sweet Auburn/MLK Jr. Historic District, Inman Park, and Grant Park are described in the Downtown chapter; the tour of Ansley Park is described in the Midtown chapter; and the Druid Hills tour is described in the Decatur chapter. It's always best to check ahead because tours may be canceled due to inclement weather. Adults $10, seniors and students $5.

✎ **Gray Line** (404-767-0594; 1-800-965-6665; www.grayline.com), 705 Lively Avenue, Norcross. Gray Line offers several half-day tours or a combination all-day tour, each of which touches on Buckhead in addition to Downtown and Midtown locations. (See the Downtown chapter for a complete description of the two tours.)

Historic Homes and Sites

See **Atlanta History Center** under *Museums*.

✎ 🏛 **Fort Peachtree** (www.buckhead.net/history/fort-peachtree/index.html), 2630 Ridgewood Road. Open 9–5 weekdays. This replica of part of the first non-Native American settlement in Atlanta was constructed as part of the city's bicentennial celebra-tion. Located on a low bluff overlooking the Chattahoochee River where it meets Peachtree Creek, the fort was a major contact point for Native Americans and white traders. The vil-lage was the terminus of the Creek Indian Peachtree Trail, which ran from what is now Toccoa, Georgia, to what is now Buckhead. A historical marker at Peachtree and Palisades roads marks where the trails branched. During the War of 1812, the fort was used to control the Creek Indians. A road running from here to Fort Daniel at Hog Mountain was called Peachtree Road even that long ago. Free, but reservations are required.

 🖉 🦅 **Goodwin Home,** 3931 Peachtree Road. Open 1–4 on the third Sunday of the month. This historic home is the oldest house in the Brookhaven section of Buckhead and in all of DeKalb County. Built as a log cabin in the early 1830s on the Echota Indian Trail and expanded in the 1840s, the house was a landmark for federal troops during the Civil War. A Goodwin family member is usually on-site when the house is open to serve as a guide. A small graveyard is also on the property. Free.

 🖉 🦅 **Governor's Mansion** (404-261-1776; www.gov.state.ga.us/about_mansion.shtml), 391 West Paces Ferry Road Northwest. Open 10–11:30 Tuesday through Thursday; additional hours at Christmastime. Tour the traditionally Southern, 30-columned Greek Revival mansion, built in 1967, and learn about its history. The three-story, 24,000-square-foot home boasts 30 rooms; the ceremonial rooms on the first floor are those open for tours. Set among 18 acres of sweeping wooded lawns, the mansion contains what is considered to be one of the country's finest collections of 19th-century neoclassical furnishings from the Federal period as well as fine paintings and porcelain. The mansion is particularly beautiful at Christmastime, when it is dressed to the nines with several Christmas trees and other decorations. Free.

Museums

 🖉 🦅 **Atlanta History Center** (404-814-4000; www.atlantahistorycenter.com), 130 West Paces Ferry Road Northwest. Open 10–5:30 Monday through Saturday, noon–5:30 Sunday; last ticket sold at 4:30. Four permanent and two changing exhibits in the architecturally striking main museum give historical perspectives about Atlanta and regional history, black history, the Civil War, and folk art, among other subjects. The DuBose Civil War Collection is the largest collection of Civil War artifacts in America, with 5,000 Confederate and Union pieces including cooking gear, games, love letters, medical instruments, uniforms, weapons, and memorabilia from old soldiers' homes and battle reunions. In addition to the main museum, the complex includes two historic homes.

The newest addition to the complex is the 27,500-square-foot Fentener van Vissingen Family Wing, which has been constructed to house the Centennial Olympic Games Museum to honor the 1996 Olympic Games held in Atlanta. The spectacular collection of multimedia presentations, artifacts, images, and interactive displays is one of the most significant exhibitions on Olympic sports and history in the entire world. Visitors enter the museum over actual maple flooring from the 1996 Olympic basketball court where both the U.S. men's and women's teams won gold. The full story of the Centennial Olympic Games is explored, including how the city won the games, how the games changed Atlanta, day-to-day chronology, heroes and special moments, event results and records, the global impact of the games, and their legacy. Eight sections, 13 interactive computer kiosks, and the Olympic Mania trivia game create a different experience for each visitor. Exhibits include participation medals, posters, the only complete collection of Olympic torches from 1936 to 1996, examples of licensed merchandise, gifts from among the 197 delegations that participated in the games, puppets, costumes, country signs, sports artifacts, and uniforms, among other memorabilia. The second floor houses the interactive Sports Lab—a high-energy area where visitors test their strength and skill compared to the world's greatest athletes. An assisted long jump, two side-by-side sculls, and two bikes engage participants.

Also on the grounds of the history center is the elegant **Swan House.** Built for the wealthy Inman family in 1928, the opulent villa was designed by famed architect Philip Trammel Schutze to resemble the Palazzo Corsini in Rome. The long terraced lawn from

Among the holdings of the Atlanta History Museum is the largest collection of Civil War artifacts in America

the house to the street features a multilevel cascading fountain and stairs embellished by urns. The mansion takes its name from the swan motif found discreetly throughout the house. Among its outstanding architectural features is a striking spiral staircase. The manor is sumptuously furnished with Inman pieces—in fact, it looks as though the family just stepped out. In complete contrast to the Swan House, the house and outbuildings of the 1840s **Tullie Smith Farm,** which was moved to the site, show life on a simple farm. The modest Plantation Plain–style house is furnished with simple antiques.

The grounds surrounding all three of the main buildings comprise 33 acres of formal and natural gardens with nature trails (see *Green Space—Gardens*). The **Coca-Cola Café** serves lunch and snacks daily, while the elegant **Swan Coach House,** located in the estate's former carriage house/garage, serves lunch Monday through Saturday (see *Dining Out*). Adults $15, seniors and students older than 13 $13, children 4–12 $10. Included as an attraction in the Atlanta CityPass (see What's Where). The main building is wheelchair accessible, but there might be some difficulty managing in the grounds, the Swan House, and the Tullie Smith Farm. Free parking.

Natural Beauty Spots

The **Chattahoochee River** skirts the western side of Buckhead in the metro region as it stretches from Lake Lanier north of Atlanta for 48 miles through the city and its suburbs on its 542-mile course to Apalachicola Bay, Florida. The river corridor is one of America's premier urban greenways—a wild oasis within the metropolis. Because the river is not navigable and doesn't flow through downtown, the waterway and the land surrounding it create one of metro Atlanta's best-kept secrets. It was due to former President Jimmy Carter, a Democrat, and former Speaker of the House Newt Gingrich, a Republican—two Georgians whose outlook about many issues could hardly be more dissimilar—that this section of the river was designated the Chattahoochee River National Recreation Area (CRNRA).

Now celebrating its 35th anniversary, the 6,500-acre, 14-park recreation area is owned and maintained by the National Park Service. The CRNRA is the most popular of Georgia's 10 National Park Service units, welcoming more than 3 million visitors annually. Its parks contain more than 900 species of plants, old- and new-growth hardwood forests, 20 species of fish, and numerous other animal species. Human presence in the river corridor began as early as 10,000 B.C. and was well established by 5,000 B.C. Evidence of human habitation ranges from remnants of Native American settlements to ruins of cotton mills to significant Civil War sites. For those who know about the CRNRA, the park is a popular escape from the city for hiking, fishing, boating, and other outdoor pursuits. One of the most popular activities is "shooting the 'Hooch"—floating down the river on a raft on a hot summer day (see the Marietta and Roswell chapters for outfitters). The Palisades unit of the recreation area is described in this chapter.

To Do

Bicycling

You need to have your own bike if you're going to ride in Buckhead, because there are no rentals. You can, however, rent bikes from Skate Escape in nearby Midtown (see *Bicycling* in the Midtown chapter). **MARTA** (see *Getting Around*) allows bicycles on all its trains and there are bike racks on the front of some buses (the racks handle only two bikes at a time). Many MARTA stations have bike racks for commuters who wish to bike to the train. The **PATH Foundation** (see What's Where) has been instrumental in developing bike paths. The Atlanta/DeKalb portion of the trail system includes the 3.3-mile **Chastain Park Trail**, one of PATH's most popular. A second loop adjacent to the northern end of the park above the Galloway School is being developed.

Bird-Watching

See the Chattahoochee River National Recreation Area under *Recreation Areas*.

Boating

The **Chattahoochee River** provides numerous opportunities year-round for canoeing and kayaking, as well as motorboating and other small boat use (see What's Where).

Canoeing/Tubing

An approximate float time chart for seven possible canoe trips can be found in the Chattahoochee River National Recreation Area park brochure (see the Marietta and Roswell chapters for outfitters).

Day Camp

✧ **Horsin' Around Summer Horse Camps** at Chris and Merry Carlos Horse Park (404-252-4244, Ext. 27; www.chastainhorsepark.org), Chastain Park, 4371 Powers Ferry Road. Weekday camps offered in June and July for girls and boys age 8–11. Activities include morning riding, grooming, and horse-care lessons; afternoon crafts and games; optional Tuesday overnight with cookout ($75 extra); pizza lunch on Wednesday; and a horse show on Friday. Camp runs 8–2. $575.

Fishing

The Chattahoochee River is the southernmost habitat in the United States for trout. The state stocks the river with rainbow, brook, and brown trout, so fishing along the river's banks or from small boats is a popular activity. Several fishing outfitters, instructors, and guides are available for hire. A Georgia fishing license and trout stamp are required. There are special regulations along three sections of the river, so it's best to check ahead before planning to fish (see What's Where, call the main office at 678-538-1200, or consult the Web site at www.nps.gov/chat for details).

Golf

Bobby Jones Golf Course at Atlanta Memorial Park (404-355-1009; www.bobbyjones. americangolf.com), 384 Woodward Way. Open sunrise to sunset daily. The 18-hole, par 71 course is well suited to any level of play. The course meanders through beautiful neighborhoods and along Peachtree Creek and boasts two clubhouses. $36 Monday through Thursday, $44 Friday through Sunday; seniors $20 Monday through Thursday, $25 Friday through Sunday; Fulton County residents play for reduced rates. Check the Web site for packages and to sign up for tee times.

North Fulton Golf Course at Chastain Memorial Park (404-255-0723; www.north fulton.americangolf.com), 216 West Wieuca Road. Open sunrise to sunset daily. Opened in 1939, the 18-hole, par 71 course features 6,570 yards of challenging play. The facility features a putting green, chipping area, pro shop, snack bar, club and cart rentals, and pro instruction. $36 Monday through Thursday, $39.25 Friday through Sunday, including a $12 cart fee. Discounts for seniors and Fulton County residents.

Horseback Riding

🐎 🐴 **Chris and Merry Carlos Horse Park and Stables at Chastain** (404-257-1470; www.chastainhorsepark.org), 4371 Powers Ferry Road. The 13-acre equestrian center within Troy Chastain Memorial Park offers riding lessons, boarding, a therapeutic riding program, and summer camps for boys and girls, but not recreational riding. The facilities include four barns housing 86 stalls, three arenas, and a therapeutic area.

Rock Climbing

Dick's Sporting Goods (404-267-0200; www.dickssportinggoods.com), Lenox Marketplace, 3535 Peachtree Road. The climbing wall is available 5–8:30 Tuesday through Friday, noon–4:30 weekends. Beginning rock climbers don't have to travel to the north Georgia mountains to try out the sport. This emporium boasts a two-story rock climbing wall. Without a scorecard: adults $3, children $2; with a scorecard: adults $5, children $3.

Spa

Spa Sydell (404-255-SPAS; www.spasydell.com), Buckhead Plaza, 3060 Peachtree Road Northwest. Open 8:45–9 Monday through Saturday, 11–7 Sunday. This day spa offers many services, including various types of massage, body treatments such as exfoliating polishes and wraps, facials, manicures, and hydrotherapy. Prices vary by treatment.

Spectator Sports

There are no sports venues for professional sports in Buckhead. See the Downtown chapter for baseball, football, basketball, hockey, and arena football information.

Swimming

Most hotels in Buckhead feature outdoor pools that are open seasonally; some of them are heated.

Tennis

In addition to these major tennis centers, several Atlanta city parks offer tennis courts (see *Nature Preserves and Parks*).

✍ 🐚 **Bitsy Grant Tennis Center at Atlanta Memorial Park** (404-609-7193), 2125 Northside Drive. Open 9–9 weekdays, 9–6 Friday through Sunday. Named for tennis star Bryan M. "Bitsy" Grant, who was a dynamo on the court despite his 5-foot-4-inch frame, the complex offers 13 clay courts (open 9–8 daily) and 10 hard courts (open 9–9 daily). The center is also home to the **Georgia Tennis Hall of Fame.** $2.50–3.25 per hour for hard courts; $4–5 per hour for clay courts; seniors $3.25 for either; 50¢ extra for lighted night play.

✍ 🐚 **Chastain Memorial Park Tennis Center** (404-255-1993), 110 West Wieuca Road. Open 9–9 weekdays, 9–6 Saturday, 10–6 Sunday. The park features nine tennis courts. $2.50 before 5, $3 after 5 and on weekends, free for those younger than 18. (For more information about the park, see *Nature Preserves and Parks*.)

GREEN SPACE

Gardens

✍ 🐚 **Atlanta History Center** (404-814-4000; www.atlantahistorycenter.com), 130 West Paces Ferry Road Northwest. Open 10–5:30 Monday through Saturday, noon–5:30 Sunday; last ticket sold at 4:30. Although the complex is most noted for the museum and two historic houses (see *Museums*), the grounds are significant and contain several gardens. See the Japanese maples and U.S. and Asian species in the Cherry-Sims Asian-American Garden; azaleas and rhododendrons in the Frank A. Smith Rhododendron Garden; native plants and wildflowers in the Mary Howard Gilbert Memorial Quarry Garden; formal boxwoods, fountains, and statuary in the Swan House Gardens; the sculpture *The Peach Tree,* a gift from the Republic of Georgia, in the Garden of Peace on the Swan Woods Trail; and the house, roadside, and vegetable gardens and cotton patch at the Tullie Smith Farm. For the serious gardener, the center's Cherokee Garden Library houses more than 3,000 books and periodicals about gardening. Admission to the entire museum complex: adults $15, seniors and students older than 13 $13, children 4–12 $10. Free parking.

Nature Preserves and Parks

✍ 🐚 **Atlanta Memorial Park** (404-355-2258; www.buckhead.org/parks/atlanta-memorial), 384 Woodward Way. Open daily. The 199-acre park features the 18-hole Bobby Jones Golf Course (see *Golf*) and the 23-court Bitsy Grant Tennis Center (see *Tennis*). The site was the

The Tullie Smith Farm gives visitors a glimpse of life on a simple farm during the 1800s.

scene of part of the bloody Battle of Peachtree Creek. The land was a gift to Atlanta in 1929, and although the golf course was built in 1931 and the clubhouse in 1932, the real development of the park began in 1933 to mark Georgia's bicentennial. Access to the park is free; there are fees for golf and tennis.

Blue Heron Nature Preserve (404-814-8228; www.nbca.org/BlueHeron/index.htm), 4244 Rickenbacker Way. Open daily. This wooded area in northern Buckhead along Nancy Creek is a natural oasis in the middle of the urban area. At the 30-acre community wildlife habitat, visitors may glimpse not only blue herons, but deer, beavers, otters, minks, Canada geese, mallards, wood ducks, foxes, turtles, and raccoons. Free.

Chastain Memorial Park (404-255-0863), 135 West Wieuca Road. Open daily. The park boasts nine tennis courts (see *Tennis*), seven ball fields, a swimming pool, 18-hole golf course (see *Golf*), gymnasium with basketball court, weight facility, the Chastain Arts and Crafts Center (see *Cultural Sites*), stables (see *Horseback Riding*), a new state-of-the-art children's playground, an amphitheater (see *Entertainment*), and a 3.3-mile circuit for jogging, bicycling, and walking (see *Bicycling*). Surveys indicate that 250 cyclists, joggers, dog walkers, and in-line skaters use the trail each hour. The park was named Atlanta's Best Place for a Romantic Picnic by *Atlanta Magazine*. Access to the 158-acre city park is free; some activities have a fee.

Haynes Manor Park and Memorial Park Trail, between Sagamore Drive and Peachtree Battle Avenue. Open daily. Five acres are being developed by PATH as a park and multiuse trail from the Haynes Manor neighborhood, past the Bobby Jones Golf Course, through Tanyard Creek Park to Georgia Tech (see the Midtown chapter). Free.

Parks, Recreation and Cultural Affairs of Atlanta (404-817-6788; www.atlantaga.gov, then click on "Departments") maintains numerous parks in the Buckhead area. Call the office for information about specific parks.

Pinnacle Park, Peachtree Road at Lenox Road. Open daily. The pocket park, located by the stunning 21-story Pinnacle building, features a half-moon fountain, a curving path, benches, and a massive wheel-like sculpture. The building itself features a dramatic roofline that is one of Buckhead's landmarks. Free.

Tanyard Creek Park (404-817-6752), Collier Road at Walthall Drive in the Collier Hills neighborhood. Open daily. The 14-acre city park has been rated the Best Place to Take Your Pet by *Atlanta Magazine*. The park, once a mill site, features tree-shaded acres, historic markers, an overlook, a creek, and a playscape. Just across Collier Road, old mill stones indicate where Andrew Jackson Collier had his gristmill, which was a landmark during the 1864 Civil War Battle of Peachtree Creek. Bitter fighting took place there. Free.

Recreation Areas

Chattahoochee River National Recreation Area/East and West Palisades Unit. The headquarters for the park is in Dunwoody at the Island Ford Unit (678-538-1200; www.nps.gov/chat), 1978 Island Ford Parkway. The Palisades Unit, accessible from Northside Parkway at the Chattahoochee River, is the only unit physically within Buckhead. Open daily. The 50-acre unit features hiking, fishing, boating, tubing, picnicking, bird-watching, wildlife observation, and swimming. $3 parking fee.

Rivers

Chattahoochee River: See What's Where.

Walks

The primary shopping/entertainment area of Buckhead along Peachtree Road is not particularly pedestrian-friendly—especially if you want to cross the road, although the Buckhead Coalition is working hard to make the area safer for pedestrians. Once you leave the primary thoroughfares, however, you can stroll around Buckhead to admire the public art described in *Cultural Sites,* meander through any of the neighborhoods described in *Villages/Neighborhoods,* or take a walk through any of the parks listed in *Nature Preserves and Parks.*

LODGING

Bed and Breakfasts

& **Beverly Hills Inn** (404-233-8520; 1-800-331-8520; www.beverlyhillsinn.com), 65 Sheridan Drive. This simple, unassuming but cozy, European-style, 18-room inn attracts a clientele that's 35 percent international. Each guest chamber features antique furnishings, a balcony, hardwood floors, and a kitchen, which makes the inn particularly appealing for a long-term stay. No smoking. Wheelchair accessible on the first floor only. Continental breakfast is served in the terrace-level dining room daily. $129–199.

Inns and Hotels

Although Buckhead has some of the most luxurious hostelries in Atlanta, there are less-expensive options. Readers know what to expect from these accommodations, so consult your favorite hotel or travel site on the Internet for details about these upper-end, moderate, and economy chain hotels.

✧ & **Grand Hyatt Atlanta** (404-237-1234; www.grandatlanta.hyatt.com), 3300 Peachtree Road Northeast. Recognized by AAA as a four-star hostelry, the Grand Hyatt is known for sumptuous accommodations, superior restaurants, exciting nightlife, and a solicitous staff. It was originally opened as a Nikko hotel, and the Pan-Asian influence is still evident. The hotel's Japanese garden features a cascading waterfall dropping into a pool. Other amenities include a heated outdoor pool,

Cassis restaurant, and the Onyx lobby lounge. Smoking and nonsmoking rooms available. Wheelchair accessible. $200–400.

✧ 🐾 & **InterContinental Buckhead** (404-946-9000; www.intercontinental.com/buckhead), 3315 Peachtree Road Northeast. This newly opened, swanky, 21-floor, 421-room, four-star/four-diamond hotel features such amenities as in-room libraries, BOSE wave sound systems, marble baths, a heated outdoor pool, a whirlpool, and the Wellness Spa and Fitness Club by Jurlique. Its restaurant, **Au Pied de Cochon** (see *Dining Out*) is the Les Freres Blanc food group's first U.S. venture. The XO bar offers more than 60 different cognacs and live jazz from 6:30–10:30 Tuesday through Friday. The hotel is adjacent to the Atlanta Financial Center and within easy walking distance to two upscale shopping malls, numerous restaurants, and the Buckhead MARTA station. Pets allowed. Most rooms nonsmoking; there is one smoking floor. Wheelchair accessible. $179–479.

✧ & **JW Marriott Buckhead Atlanta** (404-262-3344; 1-800-228-9290; www.marriott hotels.com/atljw), 3300 Lenox Road. This AAA four-diamond hotel is physically connected to Lenox Square mall, which certainly makes it a favorite with shoppers. It's also within easy walking distance of the Lenox MARTA station and has easy access to Midtown, Downtown, and the suburbs. The sophisticated hotel features 377 elegantly appointed rooms and four luxury suites—all with marble and stone baths, luxury bedding, a mini bar, a CD player, plush robes, and high-speed Internet access. Service is exemplary, with minute attention to detail. Smoking is permitted on the seventh floor, otherwise nonsmoking. Wheelchair accessible. $169–189 weekends, $299 weekdays; ask about special packages.

The Ritz-Carlton, Buckhead (404-237-2700; 1-800-241-3333; www.ritzcarlton.com), 3434 Peachtree Road. Ritz-Carlton is synonymous with unparalleled luxury and service, and this AAA four-diamond hotel, one of only two in Georgia, is always voted Atlanta's best. The pampering begins the moment guests pull up outside. First they're greeted by a regally uniformed doorman, and then their car is whisked away, as is their luggage. Inside, discreetly dressed personnel ease guests through check-in. Accommodations are enhanced with ultraluxurious linens, rich upholstery, and marble baths. Guests who really want to indulge themselves choose the Club Level where, in addition to upgraded room amenities, they have access to a sumptuous private lounge where five superb complimentary food services are provided each day: a bounteous continental breakfast, midday snack, afternoon tea, cocktails and hors d'oeuvres, and evening cordials and chocolates. The swanky hotel features a swim and fitness center with an indoor heated lap pool, whirlpool, sauna, steam room, and weight machines. The hotel's five-star **Dining Room** (see *Dining Out*) is the uncontested finest dining experience in Atlanta, and The Lobby Lounge is the "in" place in Atlanta to spy visiting celebrities. The Ritz's afternoon tea, light tea, and royal tea are high-class affairs often attended by locals or those who are guests of other hotels. The Ritz, which is strategically located near Atlanta's most upscale shopping centers, restaurants, and nightspots, is known for imaginative room packages and fabulous holiday feasts. A jazz band plays in The Lobby Lounge Friday and Saturday night. Smoking and nonsmoking rooms. Wheelchair accessible. Rates from $249.

The Westin Buckhead Atlanta (404-365-0065; 1-800-253-1397; www.westin.com; www.starwood hotels.com/westin), 3391 Peachtree Road Northeast. Those who have been to Atlanta before will recognize this outstanding hotel as the former Swissotel. The AAA four-diamond property features breathtaking architecture and an outstanding expressionist art collection that includes an original by Andy Warhol. The hotel is also the home of the famed **The Palm Restaurant** (see *Dining Out*). The Westin is adjacent to Lenox Square mall and within easy walking distance of Phipps Plaza mall, two MARTA stations, and many highly rated restaurants. No smoking. Wheelchair accessible; reserve in advance one of 17 rooms with adapted bathrooms. $225–395.

WHERE TO EAT

Dining Out

In Buckhead

Anis Cafe and Bistro (404-233-9889; www.anisbistro.com), 2974 Grandview Avenue. Open 11:30–2:30 Monday through Saturday; 6–10 Sunday through Thursday, 6–10:30 Friday and Saturday. Located in a charming bungalow, the restaurant serves Provencal cuisine. Lunch choices range from quiche and pasta to beef and seafood. Adventurous dinner entrées include chicken, seafood, pork, and lamb. Smoking at the bar only. Wheelchair accessible. Lunch $8.95–16.95, dinner $13–29.

Anthony's Plantation Restaurant (404-262-7379; www.anthonysfinedining.com),

3109 Piedmont Road. Open from 6 PM Monday through Saturday. Located in an authentic 1797 Pope-Walton plantation house that was moved from Washington, Georgia, to this wooded setting in the heart of Buckhead, Anthony's exudes Old South elegance. Twelve dining rooms, many with working fireplaces, are sumptuously furnished with 18th-century pieces. Anthony's serves a variety of beef, buffalo, duck, game, pork, and seafood accompanied by excellent wines and to-die-for desserts. To top everything off, the house is said to be haunted. No smoking. Wheelchair accessible on the ground level. $18.95–35.95.

& **Antica Posta** (404-262-7112; www.antica posta.com), 519 East Paces Ferry Road. Open 5:30–10:30 daily. Operated by an Italian family with a restaurant in Tuscany, Antica Posta serves inspired Italian cuisine featuring, among other specialties, beans, chicken livers, and rustic pastas characteristic of the countryside. Decorated in the style of a rural trattoria, the restaurant is a current hot spot. No smoking. Wheelchair accessible. $15–26.

& **Aria** (404-233-7673; www.aria-atl.com), 490 East Paces Ferry Road. Open 6–10 Monday through Saturday. This upscale gourmet bistro, located in a historic house, specializes in slow-cooked food and organic produce. The sophisticated decor features unusual lighting and other flashy details. The lounge is sexy and the wine cellar table is one of the most romantic in town. No smoking. Wheelchair accessible. $19–32.

& **Atlanta Fish Market** (404-262-3165; www.buckheadrestaurants.com), 265 Pharr Road Northeast. Open 11:30–11 Monday through Thursday, 11:30–midnight Friday and Saturday, 4–10 Sunday. Look for the gigantic 65-foot steel and copper-clad spawning salmon (reportedly the largest fish sculpture in the world) outside this seafood restaurant. So fresh are the fish and seafood here that the menu is updated twice a day when the deliveries arrive. In terms of sheer variety of seafood, including everything from oysters to stone crab to halibut, no other Atlanta restaurant can compare. No smoking. Wheelchair accessible. $20–40.

& **Au Pied de Cochon** (404-946-9070; www.aupieddecochonatlanta.com), 3315 Peachtree Road. Open 24/7. Located in the new InterContinental Hotel, the fancifully decorated restaurant is based on a Parisian brasserie open since 1946. Operated by the Les Freres Blanc food group, the restaurant's menu ranges from signature pig's feet to foie gras to raw seafood trays to steaks. The signature dessert, Ile Flottante, is a floating island of poached meringue on a sea of custard. For a perfectly romantic tête-à-tête, try one of the private rooms curtained in red velvet. If you'd like to watch your meal being prepared and interact with the chef, schedule the Chef's Table in the kitchen. The restaurant's XO bar has an extensive selection of cognacs. No smoking. Wheelchair accessible. $9–26.

& **Bluepointe** (404-237-9070; www.buck headrestaurants.com), 3455 Peachtree Road Northeast. Open 11 AM–1:30 PM weekdays; 5:30–11 Monday, Wednesday, and Thursday, 5:30–midnight Tuesday, Friday, and Saturday, 5:30–10 Sunday. This restaurant, part of the Buckhead Life restaurant empire, features Pacific Rim cuisine. The scene is dramatic and glamorous, and there is an oyster and seafood bar as well as a sushi table. The bar is the place where Buckhead's gorgeous and wealthy meet. No smoking. Wheelchair accessible. Lunch $9–14, dinner $17–39.

& **Bone's** (404-237-2663; www.bones restaurant.com), 3130 Piedmont Road Northeast. Open 11:30–2:30 weekdays; 5:30–10:30 Sunday through Thursday, 5:30–11:30 Friday and Saturday. This private-club-like steak house has been a meeting place for the powerful for many years. The old-boys-network ambience is characterized by huge steaks and stiff drinks. The wine list is extensive. No smoking. Wheelchair accessible. Lunch $9.95–16.95, dinner $24.95–39.95.

& **Buckhead Diner** (404-262-3336; www.buckheadrestaurants.com), 3073 Piedmont Road Northeast. Open 11–midnight Monday through Saturday, 10–10 Sunday. Pairing nostalgia and retro style, the glitzy, chrome, 1950s-style diner is no fast food joint. Rather, it is a high-energy, upscale eatery where celebrities and other notables go to see and be seen. The American menu features chic comfort food such as sweet and sour calamari or veal meat loaf with wild mushrooms. Begin with the homemade potato chips dipped in warm Maytag bleu cheese, and finish with white chocolate banana crème pie. No smoking. Wheelchair accessible. Lunch $8–15, dinner $12–27; the blue plate special and the catch of the day can go to $40.

& **The Café at the Ritz-Carlton Buckhead** (404-237-2700; www.ritzcarlton.com), 3434 Peachtree Road. Open 6:30–11:30 for breakfast, 11:30–3 for lunch, and 6–11 for dinner Monday through Saturday; 11–2:30 Sunday for brunch; afternoon tea at 2:30 and 3:30 Monday through Saturday. Of course, the fine dining outlet at the hotel is **The Dining Room** (see below), but The Café is almost as fine, earning four stars. No smoking. Wheelchair accessible. Fixed price $36 for breakfast and lunch; $25–$100-plus for dinner; $30–40 for afternoon tea; Sunday brunch $58 for adults, $32 for children 6–12, free for children younger than 6; $69 for holiday brunch.

& **Canoe** (770-432-2663; www.canoeatl.com), 4199 Paces Ferry Road Northwest. Open 11:30–2:30 Monday through Saturday for lunch; 10:30–2:30 Sunday for brunch; 5:30–10 Monday through Thursday, 5:30–11 Friday and Saturday, 5:30–9:30 Sunday for dinner. Reservations required for dinner. This is one of the prettiest places in the metro area to dine. The Chattahoochee River just barely skirts the metro area, and this is one of the only restaurants located along its banks. In good weather the posh patio is the place to be—it's where diners are serenaded by rushing water, bird calls, and whispering leaves.

Comfort food finds a glitzy home at the upscale Buckhead Diner.

Large windows overlooking the river and lush gardens are an acceptable substitute when the weather's less than ideal. The eclectic American menu features regional cuisine such as Vidalia spring onion soup, slow-roasted Carolina rabbit, and other delicacies. Try to visit Canoe for Sunday brunch, too. A contemporary architectural masterpiece, this trendy eatery is favored by the Range Rover crowd. No smoking. Wheelchair accessible. Lunch $12.50–19.50, dinner $13–35.

& **Chops** (404-262-2675; www.buckhead restaurants.com), 70 West Paces Ferry Road. Open 11:30–2:30 weekdays; 5:30–11 Monday through Thursday, 5:30–midnight Friday and Saturday, 5:30–10 Sunday. Part of the Buckhead Life restaurant realm, this opulent surf-and-turf steak house is a longtime favorite with both locals and visitors. Not surprisingly, beef is heavily featured on the menu, but seafood is flown in fresh daily. At the Lobster Bar, which is patterned after Grand Central Station's Oyster Bar, you can feast on Savannah lump-crab cocktail or the famous batter-fried lobster tail. Smoking in the bar only. Wheelchair accessible. $15–40.

& **The Dining Room at the Ritz-Carlton Buckhead** (404-240-7040, Ext. 6109; www.ritzcarlton.com), 3434 Peachtree Road. Open 6–9 Tuesday through Thursday, 6–9:30 Friday and Saturday. Reservations required. Dine like royalty at one of Atlanta's finest restaurants—one of the very few in the city to earn five stars and diamonds. Located in the poshest hotel in the city, the restaurant's traditional decor sets an elegant backdrop for innovative gourmet cuisine. For a special occasion, splurge on the five-course menu with pairing wines. In this rarefied atmosphere, coats and ties for gentlemen and appropriate attire for ladies are required. No smoking. Wheelchair accessible. $79–138.

& **Fogo de Chao** (404-266-9988; www.fogodechao.com), 3101 Piedmont Road. Open 11–2 and 5–10 Monday through Thursday, 4:30–10:30 Friday and Saturday, 4:30–9:30 Sunday. At this Brazilian churrascaria, the first in Atlanta, diners feast on a dozen rodizio specialties cooked on live embers and brought to the table by gaucho-clad waiters who carve off whatever portion you'd like. The salad bar is a regal buffet. Smoking in the bar only. Wheelchair accessible. Fixed price is $19.50 for salad bar, $29.50 for lunch, $46.50 for dinner.

& **French/American Brasserie** (404-266-1440; www.brasserieatlanta.com), Lenox Square, 3393 Peachtree Road. Open 11:30–10 Monday through Thursday, 11:30–11 Friday and Saturday. Located inside Lenox Square mall, the French bistro combines excellent continental cuisine with attentive service and comfortable seating at cushy banquettes. No smoking. Wheelchair accessible. Lunch $7–20, dinner $15–30.

& **Haven Restaurant and Bar** (404-969-0700; www.havenrestaurant.com), 1441 Dresden Drive, Suite 160. Open 5–10 Tuesday through Thursday and Sunday, 5–11 Friday and Saturday. Although the eatery is upscale, it's not fancy. The team in the kitchen came from the Buckhead Diner, so the menu is innovative. Portions are more than ample and selections include such dishes as potato "hay" with truffle oil, clam strips with lemon aioli, fried Dover sole with saffron butter, steaks, and strawberry shortcake. The wine list primarily features choices from California. No smoking. Wheelchair accessible. $17–25.

& **Horseradish Grill** (404-255-7277; www.horseradishgrill.com), 4320 Powers Ferry Road. Open 11:30–2 weekdays; 5:30–9 Monday through Thursday, 5–10 Friday and Saturday; 11–2 Sunday for brunch and 5–9 for dinner. This serene upscale restaurant under the direction of Chef Thomas McEachern gives an elegant twist to every dish, from oysters to fried chicken. Brunch is a popular event. Any visit to the restaurant should include a stroll around the organic garden. No smoking. Wheelchair accessible. Lunch $8–14, dinner $18–33.

♿ **Imperial Fez** (404-351-0870; www.imperialfez.com), 2285 Peachtree Road. Open 6–10:30 daily; seatings on the half-hour. A visit to this Moroccan restaurant, which showcases the exotic, sensual, and indulgent, is part entertainment, part culinary experience. Remove your shoes when you enter and let your hands be washed with rosewater; then envision hand-feeding delicate morsels to your partner while reclining on posh pillows. The five-course dinner includes soup, salad, Cornish hen pastry, an entrée, and dessert with tea. Lamb, kabobs, and couscous are prominently featured. Belly dancing is part of the experience, too. Smoking in the front or outside only. Wheelchair accessible. Fixed price $45, chef's special $65.

♿ **Joël** (404-233-3500; www.joelrestaurant.com), 3290 Northside Parkway. Open 11:30–2 Tuesday through Friday; 5:30–10 Tuesday through Thursday, 5:30–10:30 Friday and Saturday. Located in the Forum Building at the Piazza de Paces, this upscale brasserie is the brainchild of Joël Antunes, who once presided over The Dining Room at the Ritz-Carlton Buckhead. The cuisine blends rustic French flavors and highly sophisticated contemporary flavors. Desserts are to die for. No smoking. Wheelchair accessible. Lunch $6–8, dinner $19–38; fixed-price three-course dinner $49 (available weekdays only).

♿ **KYMA** (404-262-0702; www.buckheadrestaurants.com), 3085 Piedmont Road. Open 5–11 Monday through Saturday. Pronounced "kee-ma," the word means "the wave." The brainchild of famed restaurateurs I. Pano Kararassos and his son, Pano I. Kararassos, Atlanta's first fine-dining Greek estiatorio features fresh seafood prepared in old family recipes and served with Greek wines. The over-the-top decor and excellent service complete the experience. Smoking in the bar only. Wheelchair accessible. $19–30.

♿ **La Grotta** (404-231-1368; www.lagrottastlanta.com), 2637 Peachtree Road. Open 6–10 Monday through Saturday. Although it has occupied a very unassuming location in a dated office building for more than 20 years, this Northern Italian restaurant remains popular because of the inspired cuisine, which features everything from linguine with calamari to quail. No smoking. Wheelchair accessible. $15.95–32.95.

♿ **NAVA** (404-240-1984; www.buckheadrestaurants.com), 3060 Peachtree Road. Open 11:30–2:30 and 5:30–11 weekdays; 5–11 Saturday, 5:30–10 Sunday. The cuisine is Southwestern with Native American and Latin influences. In addition to such dishes as enchiladas and tacos, the restaurant specializes in entrées such as suncorn-crusted snapper and cowboy-cut beef tenderloin. Unusual desserts include banana enchilada, Southwest tres leches slice, or apple-pinon empanada. Smoking in the bar only. Wheelchair accessible. $14.95–24.95.

♿ **New York Prime** (404-846-0644; www.newyorkprime.com), Monarch Tower, 3424 Peachtree Road Northeast, Suite 100. Open 5–11 Monday through Saturday, 5–10 Sunday. Jerry Greenbaum and his crew serve classic New York strip, bone-in rib steak, barrel-cut filet and other favorites such as lamb, veal, and lobster with delicious sides and salads. Diners also enjoy the martini bar and live entertainment. Smoking and nonsmoking areas in both the bar and restaurant (the entire establishment is for those 18 years and older). Wheelchair accessible. $19.50–58.50.

♿ **Nino's Cucina Italiana** (404-874-6505; www.ninosatlanta.com), 1931 Cheshire Bridge Road. Open 5:30–11 daily. Reservations required Friday and Saturday. An eatery with longtime staying power, especially in Atlanta, where restaurant turnover is notorious, this busy, noisy ristorante has been around since 1968. Signature dishes include baked stuffed mushrooms, minestrone, lasagna al forno, giant scampi, and veal marsala, but other specialties such as bresaola or escargot may appear on the menu. No smoking. Wheelchair accessible. $15–22.

& **The Palm Restaurant** (404-814-1955; www.thepalm.com), Westin Hotel, 3391 Peachtree Road Northeast. Open 6:30–11 Monday through Saturday, 7–11 Sunday. The famous full-service restaurant specializes in beef, lobster, and surf-and-turf combinations as well as chops, veal, and other seafood. No smoking. Wheelchair accessible. $35–50.

& **Pano's & Paul's** (404-261-3662; www.buckheadrestaurants.com), 1232 West Paces Ferry Road. Open 6–11 weekdays, 5–10 Saturday. For more than 25 years, this opulent restaurant has been attracting diners with an ever-evolving menu that earlier tended more toward the Continental, but now is more American contemporary. Despite the changes, favorites such as Dover sole and fried lobster tails are always on the menu. Smoking after 9 PM in lounge only. Wheelchair accessible. $24–44.

& **Pricci** (404-237-2941; www.buckhead restaurants.com), 500 Pharr Road. Open 11:30–2:30 weekdays; 5–11 Monday through Saturday, 5–10 Sunday. A creative menu of classic Italian cuisine with a modern flair combined with a dramatic interior guarantees an unforgettable dining experience. Selections include sliced Italian meats and cheeses, antipasti, salads, pizza, pasta, risotto, fish, and meat. No smoking. Wheelchair accessible. $18–30.

& **Prime** (404-812-0555; www.hereto serverestaurants.com), 3393 Peachtree Road/Lenox Square. Open 11–10 Monday through Thursday, 11–11 Friday, noon–11 Saturday, 4–9 Sunday. Many celebrities frequent this upscale surf-and-turf steak house, which offers steaks, seafood

(including sushi), and even vegetarian options. Many folks come to the bar just to enjoy the happy hour specials. The wine list is impressive, too. No smoking. Wheelchair accessible. $17–50.

& **Restaurant Eugene** (404-355-0321; www.restauranteugene.com), Aramore Building, 2277 Peachtree Road. Open 11:30–2 weekdays for lunch; 5:30–10 Sunday through Thursday, 5:30–11 Friday and Saturday. This quietly elegant restaurant serves fine cuisine with a Southern influence. The menu rotates monthly so that seasonal ingredients can be featured. Choices might include squash blossom, pork belly, lamb sweetbreads, duck foie gras, salad with chicken livers and baby artichokes, seafood, and quail. No smoking. Wheelchair accessible. $24–44.

& **Twist** (404-869-1191; www.hereto serverestaurants.com), Phipps Plaza, 3500 Peachtree Road. Open 4–10 Sunday and Monday, 4–11 Tuesday through Thursday, 4–midnight Friday and Saturday. Tom Catherall is a legendary chef in Atlanta. His handpicked team of professionals creates innovative tapas, wraps, snacks, sushi, and other finger food, as well as a few entrées and delicious desserts. Some folks come for the $5 martinis and stay for the food. Smoking allowed. Wheelchair accessible. $5–29.

In Vinings
The Vinings Inn (770-438-2282; www. viningsinn.com), 3011 Paces Mill Road. Open 11:30–2:30 Monday through Saturday; 5:30–10 Monday through Thursday, 5:30–10:30 Friday and Saturday. Located in a historic 1800s building with numerous intimate dining rooms and outdoor seating, the restaurant features innovative American cuisine. In addition to à la carte selections, there are also monthly prix fixe wine-tasting dinners. Live music is featured every evening in the Attic Bar. Smoking permitted in the bar. Downstairs

dining rooms are wheelchair accessible, but the Attic Bar is not. Lunch $7–14, dinner $18.50–31.

Eating Out

✂️🍷♿ **Corner Café** (404-240-1978; www.buckheadrestaurants.com), 3070 Piedmont Road. Open 6:30–5 weekdays, 8–5 Saturday and Sunday. Those who enjoy being able to get breakfast, brunch, or light lunch items will enjoy the café. No smoking. Wheelchair accessible. Breakfast $4–11, lunch $4–14, brunch $15–19.

✂️🍷♿ **Eclipse di Luna** (404-846-0449; www.eclipsediluna.com), 764 Miami Circle. Open 5–10 Sunday and Monday, 11:30–10 Tuesday, 11:30–11 Wednesday and Thursday, 11:30–midnight Friday and Saturday. Latin American-, Spanish-, and Brazilian-influenced cuisine is presented in small, tapas-sized portions. The artsy setting in an old warehouse creates a high-energy experience, as does the Sunday bottomless glass of sangria for $10. Live entertainment and a wine tasting on the first Tuesday of each month add to the ambience. No smoking. Wheelchair accessible. $4–7.

🍷♿ **Swan Coach House Restaurant, Gift Shop and Gallery** (404-261-0636; 404-261-4735; www.webguide.com/swan coach.html), 3130 Sloan Drive. Open 11–2:30 daily. Just to the rear of the Atlanta History Center and reached by a separate entrance is the grand coach house/garage of the sumptuous Swan House mansion (see Atlanta History Center under *Museums*). Magnificently restored and exquisitely decorated, the carriage house is a favorite place for the ladies who lunch as well as for couples and families. Dine on brunch items, soups, salads, sandwiches, and desserts. The carriage house also has an upscale gift shop. No smoking. Wheelchair accessible. $10–12.

✂️🍷♿ **White House** (404-237-7601), 3172 Peachtree Road. Open 6:30 AM–3 PM Monday through Saturday. This Peachtree Road landmark is a local favorite that serves breakfast anytime and is always packed. No smoking. Wheelchair accessible. $12–15.

Snacks

✂️🍷♿ **The Cheesecake Factory** (404-816-2555; www.cheesecakefactory.com), 3024 Peachtree Road. Open 11–11:30 weekdays, 11–12:30 AM Saturday, 11–11 Sunday. Although this restaurant features a full menu, it is especially popular as a place to drop in for dessert after dinner somewhere else or after an event. No smoking. Wheelchair accessible. Lunch $8–15, dinner $11.95–40, brunch $6.95–11.

✂️🍷♿ **Huey's** (404-873-2037; www.hueysrestaurant.com), 1816 Peachtree Road. Open 7 AM–3 PM weekdays for breakfast and lunch, 9 AM–3 PM Saturday and Sunday for brunch. Named for Louisiana politician Huey Long, the eatery has a full menu of Cajun and Creole favorites. Beignets and café au lait are available anytime. Smoking and nonsmoking areas. Wheelchair accessible. $8–12.

Coffeehouses

✂️🍷♿ **Café Intermezzo** (404-355-0411; www.cafeintermezzo.com), 1845 Peachtree Road Northeast. Open 10:30 AM–2 AM daily. The Viennese-style café, which claims to have the largest espresso/cappuccino machine in the world, has a full menu of small plates, large plates, soups, salads, and sandwiches. But after a night out on the town attending the symphony or a play, it's a great place to stop in for a nightcap or coffee and dessert accompanied by live entertainment. Choose from 100 pastries, tarts, cakes, pies, and cheesecakes, as well as scores of coffee drinks, teas, beers, wines, and other alcoholic beverages. Lunch and dinner items are available until late night. No smoking. Wheelchair accessible. Breakfast $6–12, lunch $4–13, dinner and weekend brunch $6–15.

The Swan Coach House, once a mansion's garage, is now a delightful place to eat.

Open All Night

Buckhead never sleeps, so visitors can find a quick bite, an alcoholic libation, coffee, or dessert at any time. These restaurants are always open: **Au Pied de Cochon** at the InterContinental Buckhead (404-946-9070), 3315 Peachtree Road (see *Dining Out*); **International House of Pancakes** (404-264-0647), 3122 Peachtree Road Northeast; **Landmark Diner** (404-816-9090), 3652 Roswell Road Northwest, a 1950s-style diner; **R. Thomas Deluxe Grill** (404-872-2942; www.rthomas deluxegrill.com), 1812 Peachtree Road Northwest, which serves breakfast, burgers, macrobiotic delights, vegan and vegetarian cuisine prepared with the most natural and healthful ingredients; **Starbucks** (404-261-8447), 2333 Peachtree Road Northeast, and (404-240-5596), 3330 Piedmont Road Northeast; **Steak N Shake** (404-262-7051), 3380 Northside Parkway; and three **Waffle House** restaurants: (404-261-4475), 2581 Piedmont Road; (404-231-0023), 3016 Piedmont Road; and (404-816-2378), 3735 Roswell Road.

ENTERTAINMENT

Buckhead is the entertainment mecca of the metro Atlanta area. There are 100 bars and restaurants within two blocks of the intersection of Peachtree and East Paces Ferry roads, which makes for easy walking among them. Atlanta law forbids anyone younger than 21 from entering a bar.

Music

Capitol City Opera (voice mail 678-301-8013; reservations call Petite Auberge, 404-634-6268; www.ccityopera.com), office: 1266 West Paces Ferry Road, Suite 451. The opera

The Chastain Park Amphitheatre provides a perfect setting for entertainment during the warm-weather months.

company produces two or three main operas each year, as well as children's programs and weekly "Dinner and Diva" shows at local restaurants. Call for a schedule of performances and ticket prices.

Chastain Park Amphitheatre (information 404-733-4900; single tickets 404-733-5000), 4469 Stella Drive Northwest. Atlanta's favorite outdoor venue is the site of summer concerts with big-name entertainers almost every night of the week. In fact, the amphitheater is consistently named one of the nation's top 10 outdoor venues. The concerts are just part of the appeal—the major allure is the seductive setting and the romantic accoutrements. The horseshoe-shaped amphitheater was created in 1939 as a New Deal Public Works project. The section right in front of the stage has tables for six; in the rest of the facility folks bring their own TV tables. In either case, concertgoers bring colorful table linens, dinnerware, wine goblets, floral arrangements, candles, and, of course, an elegant picnic dinner. Part of the attraction is people-watching and seeing what other concertgoers have brought. Instead of bringing their own picnic, out-of-town visitors can reserve an elegant repast from **Affairs to Remember** (404-872-7859; www.affairs.com), **Proof of the Pudding** (404-892-2359; 770-804-9880; www.proofatlanta.com), or **Glorious Events** (770-455-6600; www.gloriousevents.net) and their order will be delivered to the park. In addition, snacks, sandwiches, pizza, ice cream, soft drinks, alcoholic drinks, and even flowers and candles can be purchased at the park. Performances alternate between the **Classic Chastain** series associated with the **Atlanta Symphony Orchestra** (404-733-5000; concert hotline 404-733-4949; www.atlantasymphony.com) and the **Delta Airlines Summer Chastain Series** (404-233-2227; for single tickets call TicketMaster, 404-249-6400; www.chastainseries.com). Limited smoking. Wheelchair accessible. Call for a schedule of events and ticket prices.

Nightlife

 Andrews Upstairs (404-467-1600; www.andrewsupstairs.com), 56 East Andrews Drive Northwest, Suite 13. Open 8 PM–2:30 AM Thursday through Saturday, Sunday through Wednesday only if there are special events. The upscale music and entertainment venue (formerly the Celebrity Rock Café) features live regional and national music acts, late-night dancing with Atlanta's hottest DJs, and comedy acts. Smoking in designated areas. Wheelchair accessible. Tickets vary with the act, but normally are about $6 purchased in advance, $8 at the door.

 Beluga (404-869-1090; www.belugamartinibar.com), 3115 Piedmont Road Northeast. Open 5 PM–3 AM weekdays, 8 PM–3 AM Saturday. Beluga has been rated the Best Piano Bar by *Atlanta Magazine*. Smoking permitted (21+ facility); cigar friendly. Wheelchair accessible. Occasionally there is a cover charge; 15 types of martinis $9.50, other drinks $10, beers $3.75–4.75.

 Dante's Down the Hatch (404-266-1600; www.dantesdownthehatch.com), 3380 Peachtree Road Northeast. Open at 4 daily, except 5 Sunday; live music 6–11 Monday, 7–11 Tuesday through Thursday, 6–midnight Friday and Saturday, 7–11 Sunday. Ahoy, mateys! For a truly unique experience, descend into an 18th-century sailing ship anchored in a mythical Mediterranean village surrounded by a moat where live crocodiles lurk. Feast on fondue while listening to some of Atlanta's best live jazz, acoustic guitar, or vocalists. *Atlanta Magazine* has rated Dante's the place for the best live jazz in town. For a special treat, make reservations two nights in advance for the chocolate fondue. No smoking. Wheelchair accessible on the wharf; not wheelchair accessible on the ship. Cover charge $7 weeknights, $10 weekends to sit on the ship; no cover on the wharf.

 ESPN Zone (404-682-3776; www.espnzone.com), 3030 Peachtree Road. Open 11:30 AM–12:30 AM Monday through Thursday, 11:30 AM–1 AM Friday and Saturday, 11:30 AM–midnight Sunday. The Disney Regional Entertainment restaurant/games center features 200 televisions, a screening room, sports simulation arena, and games arcade. No smoking. Wheelchair accessible. No cover charge except for special events.

 Fadó Irish Pub (404-841-0066; www.fadoirishpub.com), 3035 Peachtree Road. Open 11:30 AM–2 AM Monday through Thursday, 10 AM–3 AM Friday and Saturday, 10:30 AM–midnight Sunday. Fadó is the No. 2 seller of Guinness in America, and the eatery's warm, welcoming ambience is a rarity in frenetic Buckhead. Irish pub grub such as corned beef and cabbage, traditional Irish music, international soccer on television, and other fun complete the package. On Tuesday there's Texas Hold 'Em Poker; on Wednesday there's a Pub Quiz. Smoking allowed (all patrons must be 18+). Wheelchair accessible. Cover charge on weekends.

 Johnny's Hideaway (404-233-8026; www.johnnyshideaway.com), 3771 Roswell Road. Open 11 AM–3 AM Monday through Saturday, noon–2 AM Sunday. The club, which has been rated the Best Matures Hangout by *Creative Loafing* and Atlanta's Best Place to Dance to '50s and '60s Songs by *Atlanta Magazine,* is definitely popular with the older crowd. The Sinatra Room displays more than 100 pieces of memorabilia and King's Corner pays tribute to Elvis. Monday night is all-request night and Wednesday evenings is devoted to rock and roll. Smoking allowed (no one under 21 admitted). Wheelchair accessible. No cover charge Sunday through Thursday; $5 after 9 PM Friday and Saturday.

 Sanctuary Latin Nightclub (404-262-1377; www.sanctuarynightclub.com), 3209 Paces Ferry Road. Open 10 PM–3 AM Friday and Saturday; dance class 9–10 Friday. The Latin nightclub features salsa, merengue, bachata, and cumbia music, as well as house music. Cover charge $10. Smoking in the bar only. Limited wheelchair access.

&. **Sambuca Jazz Cafe** (404-237-5299; www.sambucarestaurant.com), 3102 Piedmont Road Northeast. Open 6–10:30 Sunday through Thursday, 6–midnight Friday and Saturday. This upscale supper club is a full-service restaurant, but many folks go later in the evening for drinks or desserts and live jazz beginning at 7 every night. No smoking. Wheelchair accessible. No cover charge, $15 minimum for food and drink; dinner $18–30; desserts $6–8.

&. **Tongue and Groove** (404-261-2325; www.tongueandgrooveonline.com), 3089 Peachtree Road. Open 9 PM–3 AM Wednesday and Thursday; 10 PM–3 AM Friday and Saturday. Weekend nights feature a DJ playing top 40 hits; Latin music is played on Wednesday nights with free salsa lessons. The high-energy crowd is 21 to 40+. Smoking permitted. Wheelchair accessible. Cover charge $10 and up.

Summer Theater

Georgia Shakespeare Festival (404-264-0020; www.gashakespeare.org), 4484 Peachtree Road. When driving up Peachtree Road, castle- and battlement-like structures, fluttering flags, and a cheery, circular, yellow and white tentlike building come as a complete surprise. These out-of-place-and-time buildings make up Oglethorpe University. Located on the grounds of the university, the flags and tentlike building announce the **Conant Performing Arts Center**, home of the Georgia Shakespeare Festival. In midsummer and October, the Bard's classics, comedies, and opuses come to life along with works by other playwrights from Tennessee Williams to Chekhov. In the early years of the organization, performances actually took place in a tent, but Atlanta's sultry summer temperatures and tempestuous storms led to the creation of an air-conditioned building, constructed to resemble the tent of old. In fact, the sides can be raised if weather conditions are propitious. Eat, drink, and be merry by picnicking before the show with catered meals or your own from home. A small piece of trivia: TV star Jennifer Garner of Alias was an acting intern with the company in 1994. Call for a schedule of performances and ticket prices.

Theater

The Coca-Cola Roxy Theater (404-233-1062; www.livenation.com), 3100 Roswell Road. This fine old restored building was built as a movie theater in 1927 in the Spanish Baroque style. Today it serves as an intimate venue for national touring musical acts and comedians, as well as regional and local bands and even once-a-month boxing. The Roxy features an open dance floor, a balcony with reclining seats, two bars, and a lobby display of music and entertainment memorabilia. Call for a schedule of performances and ticket prices.

SELECTIVE SHOPPING

A shopper's mecca, Buckhead boasts 1,400 upscale retail shops. In addition, two of Atlanta's premier shopping malls are located in the heart of Buckhead, each within walking distance of the Ritz-Carlton Buckhead, the JW Marriott Buckhead Atlanta, the InterContinental Buckhead, the Westin Buckhead Atlanta, Embassy Suites Buckhead, the Grand Hyatt Atlanta, and several other hostelries. Between the two malls, shoppers can visit 350 trendy stores and numerous restaurants. A shuttle service whisks shoppers from one to another.

First there's upscale **Lenox Square** (404-233-6767; www.lenoxsquare.com), 3393

Peachtree Road Northeast. Open 10–9 Monday through Saturday, noon–6 Sunday. The largest mall in the Southeast features a Neiman Marcus, Bloomingdale's, Louis Vuitton, Brooks Brothers, and Hermes, among many others. The mall is adding another level, which, when complete, will give the mall 1.6 million square feet—double the size of its 1959 floor plan—and nearly 200 stores (there were 60 in 1959). Neiman Marcus is currently growing by 51,117 square feet to provide room for a new restaurant and expanded departments such as cosmetics, handbags, designer jewelry, ladies shoes, and ready-to-wear. The Atlanta Convention and Visitors Bureau offers shopping packages with terrific rates at one of eight Buckhead hotels, complimentary breakfast, parking, and a $25 gift card to use at Lenox Square. Contact the bureau at (404) 222-6688 or consult the Web site at www.atlanta.net/shopping.

Then there's posh **Phipps Plaza** (404-261-7910; 1-800-810-7700; www.phipps plaza.com), 3500 Peachtree Road Northeast. Open 10–9 Monday through Saturday, noon–5:30 Sunday. This swanky mall features a Sak's Fifth Avenue, Gianni Versace, Gucci, Giorgio Armani, and Tiffany & Co., among others. The two newest additions to Phipps Plaza are Barneys New York CO-OP and Nordstrom.

Visitors looking for the perfect antiques, works of art, or home accessories need look no further than Buckhead, which has five major interior decorator districts, each with a treasure trove of shops. It is not an exaggeration to say that Atlanta offers hundreds of antiques dealers and art galleries. **Atlanta Decorative Arts Center** (404-231-3862; www.adacdesigncenter.com), 349 and 351 Peachtree Hills Avenue, is primarily wholesale (a business license and a tax I.D. number are required for entrance), but the facility is open to members of the public who are accompanied by a designer and for occasional sales and seminars. **Miami Circle Market Center** (404-846-0449), 709 Miami Circle, is a collection of 75 antiques shops and galleries. **Buckhead Design Center** (404-876-2543; www.buckheaddesigncenter.com), 2133 Piedmont Road Northeast, is a one-stop shopping source for furniture, accessories, and lighting; and **Bennett Street** (www.buckhead.org/ bennettstreet), 22 Bennett Street Northwest, boasts more than 50 antiques and arts shops.

With all these emporia located so close together, we've listed only a few exceptional individual shops below.

Antiques

Nottingham Antiques and Reproductions (404-352-1890; 1-888-404-7463; www.notting hamantiques.com), 45 Bennett Street, Suite A. Open 10–5 Monday through Saturday. Within the 7,000-square-foot showroom, shoppers can find English antiques and other traditional designs as well as accessories for every room in the house.

Art Galleries

Buckhead's art scene stretches from Miami Circle and the Village to Bennett Street and trendy South Buckhead. New galleries are opening every month.

Fay Gold Gallery (494-233-3842; www.faygoldgallery.com), 764 Miami Circle. Open 9:30–5:30 Tuesday through Saturday. The gallery has been exhibiting the works of A-list Southern contemporary painters, sculptors, video artists, photographers, and creators of other 3-D art since 1980. Works of nationally known artists also are displayed. The gallery sponsors four major art fairs annually.

Frabel Gallery (404-467-9464; www.frabel.com), 309 East Paces Ferry Road, Suite 101.

Open 11–5 Tuesday through Saturday. Hans Godo Frabel and the artists in his studio create magnificent works of crystal and art glass, including abstracts, color abstracts, animals, flowers, fruit, hearts, and much more. His work has been presented to Gerald Ford, Jimmy Carter, and Queen Elizabeth II. Many of his pieces are used as awards. A large collection of pieces was recently displayed at the Atlanta Botanical Garden.

Thomas Deans Fine Art (404-352-3778; www.thomasdeans.com), 75 Bennett Street, Gallery K-2. Open 11–5 Tuesday through Saturday or by appointment. The gallery shows art from 1750 to the present.

Books

Cathedral Book Store (404-237-7582; www. cathedralbookstore.org), Cathedral of St. Philip, 2744 Peachtree Road. Open 10–5 weekdays, 10–1 Saturday and Sunday. The bookstore carries a large selection of religious, inspirational, and other books.

C. Dickens (404-231-3825; www.cdickens.com), 56 East Andrews Drive. Open 9–6 Monday through Saturday. Shop here for fine, rare, and collectible books, as well as for maps, historical documents, autographs, and manuscripts.

Clothing

Backstreet Boutique (404-262-7783), 3140 East Shadowlawn Avenue. Open noon–5 Wednesday through Saturday. In business for 15 years, Backstreet Boutique offers upscale resale items, including Chanel, Armani, St. John, Jimmy Choo, Manolo Blahnik, and more. The designer-only inventory of previously owned items, some of which were never worn, is priced at 90 percent off original retail.

Crash and Burn (404-365-8502; www.crashandburnatlanta.com), 3184 Roswell Road. Open noon–7 Tuesday through Saturday. The store carries shoes, boots, T-shirts, jackets, and accessories, as well as ska, punk, and rockabilly music.

Food

Piece of Cake (404-351-2253; www.pieceofcakeinc.com), 3215 Roswell Road. Open 8:30–5 weekdays, 10–1 Saturday. This bakery creates gourmet cakes, homemade cookies, and Southern specialties such as sumptuous cheese straws.

Jewelry

Brina Beads (404-816-8230; www.brinabeads.com), 3231-A Cains Hill Place. Open 10–6 Monday through Saturday with hours extended to 9 on Thursday. The shop offers beads, designer jewelry, custom-crafted jewelry, beaded gifts from around the world, jewelry-making classes, and bead parties.

Other Goods

Boxwoods Gardens and Gifts (404-233-3400), 100 East Andrews Drive. Open 10–6 Monday through Saturday. This is the place to go for antiques, plants, planters, and art.

Dog Days (404-266-8668; www.dogdaysatlanta.com), 3225 Cains Hill Place. Open 7:30–7 Monday through Thursday, 7:30–6:30 Friday, 10–3:30 Saturday, 4–6 Sunday. In addition to doggie gifts your pooch can't live without—beds, collars, garden stakes, pet-food mats, toys, accessories, premium gourmet food, and Old Mother Hubbard treats, to name just a few—the shop offers grooming and day and overnight care.

Hancock and Hartwell (404-261-6566), 3155 Roswell Road, Suite 310. Open by appointment only, 10–4 weekdays. The shop features rare U.S. coins, gold, silver, platinum bullion, and foreign delivery certificates.

Outlet Stores

Filene's Basement (404-869-4466; www.filenesbasement.com), 3535 Peachtree Road Northeast. Open 9:30–9 Monday through Saturday, 11–6 Sunday. Since 1908, Filene's Basement, the oldest and most famous off-price store, has been selling high-end, designer, and couture goods. The annual bridal gown sale is world renowned.

SPECIAL EVENTS

February: **St. Patrick's Day Family Festival** (404-523-2311; www.stpatsatlanta.com). The parade begins in Buckhead and wends its way all the way downtown to Underground Atlanta. Most events free. For more information about the festivities there, see the Downtown chapter.

April: **Fashionista Week** (404-261-7799; www.jlatlanta.org/fashionistaweek). Sponsored by the Junior League of Atlanta, this gigantic fashion sale benefits the league's many community charities. Dozens of upscale stores featuring women's, men's, children's, home, and pet items participate. The pink Fashionista Week card saves shoppers 20 percent on all purchases. The VIP card includes attendance at the Fashion Fever kickoff party and an invitation to a fashion show, as well as a tote bag full of goodies and a Fashionista T-shirt. $40 for the shopping card, $75 for a VIP Trendsetter card.

Sheep to Shawl Day (404-814-4000; www.atlantahistorycenter.com), 130 West Paces Ferry Road Northwest. A perennial favorite at the Atlanta History Center's Tullie Smith Farm, the event shows how sheep are sheared and how wool is washed, carded, spun, dyed, and woven into a shawl. In addition, old-fashioned skills such as blacksmithing, woodworking, candle-dipping, and open-hearth cooking are demonstrated. There are special games and toys for the kids, and they can meet the farm animals, too. Included in admission (see **Atlanta History Center** under *Museums*).

July: **Peachtree Road Race** (404-231-9064; www.atlantatrackclub.com). The world-class 10K Fourth of July event, which attracts 55,000 runners from all over the world and thousands of spectators, begins in Buckhead and ends at Piedmont Park in Midtown (see the Midtown chapter). The event also includes a wheelchair race and the Peachtree Junior for ages 7–12. If you want to run, you must be registered far in advance, so consult the Web site for requirements and instructions. Spectators need to be in place early because roads and streets on the route close at 5 AM. It is strongly recommended to take MARTA, because parking can be a nightmare. Fee to participate; spectators free.

July 4th fireworks at Lenox Square (404-233-6767; www.lenoxsquare.com). The oldest and largest pyrotechnic display in the Southeast takes place from the mall parking lot. Festivities begin at noon and include live entertainment on the outdoor main stage and a Kid Zone with a gigantic slide and an obstacle course. The fireworks begin at about 9:40 PM. Get there very, very early if you want a parking place. It's also highly recommended to take MARTA. Another option is to stay at a nearby hotel with a view of the fireworks. Free.

September: **Black World Music Series** at the Atlanta History Center (404-814-4000; www.atlantahistorycenter.com), 130 West Paces Ferry Road Northwest. The multisensory series seeks to create an understanding of the evolution, global influence, and legacy of black music. Events include workshops, panel discussions, live performances by local and international artists, children's activities, a film, and international food and art.

October: **Taste of Atlanta** (404-875-4434; www.tasteofatlanta.org). The two-day food festival on the streets of Atlantic Station features samplings from more than 75 restaurants, as well as live cooking demonstrations, classes, and children's activities. Tickets available at Lenox Square mall and through TicketMaster.

November: **Macy's Great Tree Lighting** (404-233-6767; www.lenoxsquare.com). A tradition for more than a half-century, the ceremony kicks off with preshow festivities, nationally known entertainers, and an appearance by Santa Claus. It culminates with the official lighting of the tree and the beginning of the Christmas season. Free.

4

DECATUR

Located just 6 miles from downtown Atlanta, DeKalb County includes Decatur, several other municipalities, and part of Atlanta itself. DeKalb County was named for Baron Johann DeKalb, a Revolutionary War hero. Decatur, named after naval hero Stephen Decatur, was formed on a rise where two Indian trails intersected. Chartered in 1823, the town predates Atlanta and, if Decatur hadn't turned down a railroad's proposal to build a major station there, Atlanta might never have existed at all.

Agriculture, including grain milling, cotton ginning, and dairy farming, was the primary industry here until the mid-20th century. Rock quarries were also an important part of the economy. Several still-existing pioneer cabins recall the hard life of early settlers, while monuments and battlegrounds bear witness to the county's role in the Civil War.

The city of Decatur is located inside the I-285 perimeter highway between Atlanta and Stone Mountain Park. Although the city limits of Decatur are practically imperceptible from neighboring Atlanta, today's Decatur is still imbued with small-town charm characterized by tree-lined streets, historic attractions and neighborhoods, and international culture and cuisine. In fact, Decatur has been described in the media as "a cross between Mayberry and Berkeley" and "Mayberry with an attitude." Delightfully walkable downtown Decatur boasts numerous restaurants, many with outdoor seating, and more than 120 retail shops including galleries, boutiques, and antiques stores. The vibrant courthouse square abuts MARTA Plaza, which features the sculpture *Celebration* by Gary Price, a fog fountain, trees, benches, art, and open areas for events. There are three MARTA stations on the east rail line within the city limits. On the serious side, the city is the home of the Centers for Disease Control, Emory University, Agnes Scott College, and several significant museums.

Beyond Decatur, some other municipalities in DeKalb County include Chamblee, Clarkston, Doraville, Dunwoody, and some sections of Atlanta.

GUIDANCE

Those planning a trip to the Decatur/DeKalb County area should contact the **DeKalb Convention and Visitors Bureau** (770-492-5000; 1-800-999-6055; www.dcvb.org), 1957 Lakeside Parkway, Suite 510, Tucker 30084. Open 8:30—5 weekdays.

For information about Norcross, consult the **Gwinnett Convention and Visitors Bureau** (770-623-3600; 1-888-GWINNETT; www.gcvb.org), 6500 Sugarloaf Parkway, Suite 200, Duluth, GA 30097.

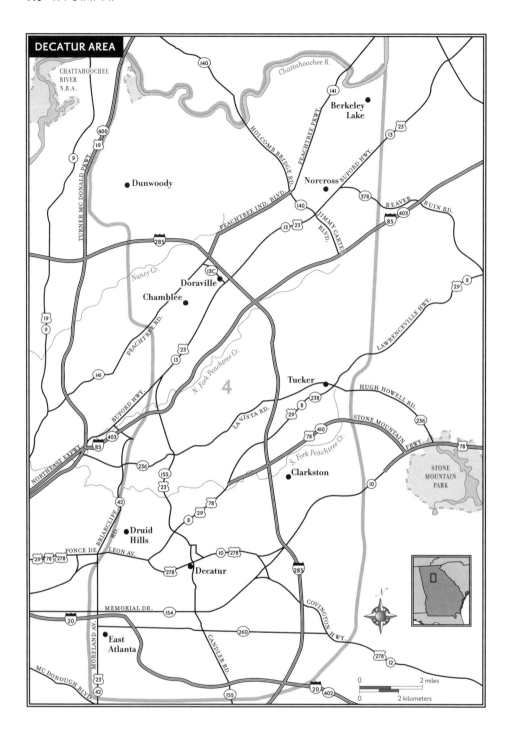

DECATUR AREA

Getting There

By air: See What's Where. Several opera-
tors offer shuttle service to destinations
throughout the metropolitan area and
beyond. These are just a few among those
that provide service to DeKalb and/or
Gwinnett counties: **Airport Metro
Shuttle** (404-766-6666), **Airport
Perimeter Connection** (404-761-0260),
and **Gwinnett Shuttle** (770-638-0666).
Some large hotels offer free shuttle service to and from the airport. Check with
your hotel when you make your reservation or contact **Atlanta Hotel
Connections** (404-312-2479) to see if
the company serves your hotel.
By bus: In addition to the Greyhound Bus
Lines station in downtown Atlanta (see
What's Where), there is also a Greyhound
bus station in Norcross (770-729-8544),
2125 Beaver Ruin Road.
By car: Decatur is most easily reached

Public art surrounds Decatur's historic courthouse

from I-20 east of Atlanta by the US 278 or
GA 155 exits. Clarkston can be reached from Decatur by US 78 and/or Ponce de Leon
Avenue. Chamblee and Doraville are just inside I-285 and can be reached by the Buford
Highway and Peachtree-Industrial Highway exits. Dunwoody can be reached off I-285 by
the Chamblee-Dunwoody Road or Ashford-Dunwoody Road exits.
By train: See What's Where.

Getting Around

Decatur offers an outlet for almost every major car rental company: **Avis** (404-296-6595),
Budget (404-284-7625), several **Enterprise** outlets (404-299-3385, 404-323-8833,
404-292-1774, 404-294-1706, and 404-286-1290), and **Hertz** (404-270-9812). Car
rentals are available in Norcross from **Avis** (770-497-1662), **Budget** (770-447-9897), and
Hertz (770-246-7955).

Mass Transit

See What's Where for information about MARTA and Gwinnett County Transit.

Taxis

Taxi service is available from **AAA Yellow Cab** (404-373-0034), **Atlanta Yellow Cab** (404-
521-0200), **Checker Cab** (404-351-1111), **Decatur Best Taxi Service** (404-377-0340),
Emory Yellow Cab (404-371-0883), as well as many others.

Parking

There's plenty of parking available in Decatur. Look for PARK HERE signs or call (404) 371-
8386 for a free parking brochure and map.

Medical Emergency

For life-threatening situations, call 911. Other immediate care is available at **DeKalb Medical Center at Decatur** (404-501-6700; www.dkmc.org), 450 North Candler Street, Decatur; **DeKalb Medical Center** (404-501-5350; www.dkmc.org), 2701 North Decatur Road, Decatur; **Children's at Egleston** (404-785-6000; www.choa.org), 1405 Clifton Road Northeast, Atlanta; and **Emory University Hospital** (404-712-2000), 1364 Clifton Road Northeast, Atlanta.

Villages/Neighborhoods

In Atlanta

Druid Hills was designed in 1893 by Frederick Law Olmstead, America's pre-eminent landscape designer, with a lush, parklike setting, curving streets, and massive plantings that are now more than 100 years old. Olmstead also designed Atlanta's Piedmont Park for the 1895 Cotton States Exposition (see the Midtown chapter), as well as New York's Central Park and the grounds of the Biltmore estate in Asheville, N.C. Although Olmstead died while the Druid Hills design was in its preliminary stages, his associates and successors implemented and refined his plans. Elegant homes of diverse architectural styles were created by renowned architects such as Neel Reid, Philip Trammel Schutze, and W. T. Downing. Visitors may recognize many locales from the movie *Driving Miss Daisy*, based on Alfred Uhry's play. Bounded by Briarcliff Road, Fairview Road, LaVista Road, and Scott Boulevard, the neighborhood is a treasure trove of architectural styles: Georgian, Gothic, Mediterranean, Neoclassical, and Tudor among them.

    East Atlanta Village, an area a mile south of Atlanta's Little Five Points neighborhood and 3 miles east of downtown Atlanta, is known for being eclectic, funky, and fun. Historically, the neighborhood sits on the site of the Sandtown Trail, a major trade route for Native Americans that connected coastal Georgia with the Chattahoochee River and crossed the Peachtree Trail. Much of the Battle of Atlanta occurred in and around what is now East Atlanta, and more than 12,000 died here, including Confederate General W. H. T. Walker and Union General James McPherson. Historic markers describing the events dot the area. East Atlanta came into its own around the turn of the 20th century and prospered until the 1960s. Because a grand dragon of the Ku Klux Klan lived in an adjacent neighborhood, East Atlanta was targeted for housing integration. Middle-class African American families were able to purchase Victorian-era and Craftsman homes, but unfortunately many whites fled the area. The construction of I-20 further disrupted the neighborhood by bisecting it, and East Atlanta began a long slide into neglect. By the 1980s, the name East Atlanta had almost disappeared and more than 60 percent of its stores were boarded up. But in 1981 the East Atlanta Community Association was founded and the neighborhood, now known as East Atlanta Village (EAV), has been on an upward track ever since. Young artists, musicians, and professionals have moved in and started rehabilitating historic houses, and the population is nearing equal proportions of blacks and whites, as was originally envisioned in the '60s. Real estate prices have doubled in recent years, and the number of quality shops and restaurants within walking distance is now rivaled only by Midtown and Virginia-Highland (see separate Midtown and Downtown chapters). Three venues bring live music to the village almost every night of the week, and EAV has become a magnet for DJs, pool, foosball, and underground and foreign films. This is also the place to go for great clothing, art, and accessories. Eateries run the gamut: Thai, vegan, burritos, burgers, pizza, continental, brunch, and even ice cream.

So many of Atlanta's Asian and Hispanic immigrants have congregated along Buford Highway that it has earned the sobriquet **International Corridor.** This is the place to go for diverse ethnic foods and items such as Asian pop music and videos, Chinese herbs, Thai iced tea, Vietnamese decor, and Hong Kong barbecued steak or dim sum, as well as Hispanic jewelry, cowboy boots, clothing, and food (see *Shopping*).

In Decatur
Historic Decatur has several historic districts. The tree-lined **Clairmont Historic District** is the northern entryway to Decatur and features architecturally interesting 1920s homes. **Historic Sycamore Street,** originally known as Covington Road, was part of a stagecoach route to Augusta. It is the location of some of the grandest houses in town, including the High House, where General William Tecumseh Sherman stopped during the Civil War. The **M.A.K. Local Historic District** (named for McDonough Street, Adams Street, and Kings Highway) was Decatur's first residential subdivision. It features many houses designed by Leila Ross Wilburn, one of only two registered female architects in 1920. The neighborhood offers excellent examples of Craftsman-style homes that were popular during the first three decades of the 20th century. **Oakhurst,** one of the oldest sections in Decatur, was actually an independent town at one time. Annexed by Decatur in the 1920s, it features many examples of bungalow-style residences. **South Candler Street**—called "the road to the depot" in Caroline McKinney Clarke's *The Story of Decatur, 1823–1899*—is home to Agnes Scott College and some of the loveliest Victorian-era homes in the city. Agnes Scott College was established in 1889 as the Decatur Female Academy and in 1907 was the first fully accredited school in Georgia. The campus covers eight blocks and includes many historic residential properties as well as the Bradley Observatory, which is open to the public on the second Friday of each month.

Norcross
Norcross, named for former Atlanta mayor Jonathan Norcross, is in adjacent Gwinnett County. The Richmond-Danville Railroad Line was the impetus for the town's development. Known in its early days as "Atlanta's favorite summer resort," Norcross attracted tourists who used to journey from Atlanta by rail to stay in the city's Brunswick Hotel. Today the city's entire 112-acre downtown is listed on the National Register of Historic Places and is marked by old-fashioned street lamps, renovated Victorian-era homes, galleries, antiques shops, gift shops, and restaurants, including one in the historic railroad depot.

To See

Cultural Sites
✐ 🐾 ♿ **Callanwolde Fine Arts Center** (404-872-5338; www.callanwolde.org), 980 Briarcliff Road Northeast, Atlanta. Office open 9–5 weekdays; gallery open 10–8 weekdays, 10–3 Saturday; conservatory open 10–4 weekdays. Although this is primarily a center for art, literary, music, and dance classes, the home itself is worthy of a visit. The sprawling 27,000-square-foot Gothic-Tudor mansion in the historic Druid Hills neighborhood was

The Callanwolde Fine Arts Center started life as a home for the oldest son of Coca-Cola founder Asa Candler.

built in 1920 for Charles Howard Candler, the oldest son of Coca-Cola Company founder Asa Candler. The designer was Henry Hornbostle, the architect who designed Emory University. One of the most outstanding features is a magnificent 3,742-pipe Aeolian organ, the largest in existence in playable condition in a residence. It's astounding that anyone would ever consider destroying this magnificent house, but it was slated for demolition in 1971 when concerned citizens organized to save it. Now listed on the National Register of Historic Places, the mansion is surrounded by 12 lush acres and several outbuildings. An on-site conservatory is the headquarters of the DeKalb County Federation of Garden Clubs. Many exhibits and performances occur during the year, the most widely anticipated of which is **Christmas at Callanwolde**, when the home is dressed up in holiday finery by local decorators and opened for tours. There are also monthly poetry readings, family storytelling evenings, Friday night jazz concerts, and Sunday afternoon classical piano concerts. Free concerts by the Callanwolde Concert Band and performances by the Atlanta Young Singers of Callanwolde are also on the schedule. Free except for events.

Schatten Gallery of the Woodruff Library (404-727-2997) on the campus of Emory University, Atlanta. The gallery provides a venue for creative exhibitions drawn from the Woodruff Library Special Collection as well as for traveling exhibitions. Shows are often mounted in conjunction with lectures, symposia, conferences, or cultural festivals. Free.

🌿 ♿ **Spruill Center for the Arts** (770-394-3447; www.spruillarts.org), 5339 Chamblee-Dunwoody Road, Atlanta. Call for a schedule of events and prices. The center provides many adult and youth art classes in numerous media and performance arts, workshops, summer camps, art exhibitions, music, dance, and theatrical performances.

🌺 **Spruill Center Gallery** (770-394-4019; www.spruillarts.org), 4681 Ashford-Dunwoody Road, Atlanta. Open 11–5 Wednesday through Saturday. Housed in a historic home built and enhanced between 1860 and 1905 but now located in the midst of modern shopping centers and high-rise office buildings, the center offers a gift shop filled with the works of local and regional artists, and also sponsors numerous exhibitions and readings by writers and poets. Special projects include the **Spruill Organic Farmers Market**, held from 8 AM to noon Wednesday, late May or June through October or until they run out of tomatoes. The market provides the opportunity for city dwellers to purchase organically grown vegetables and flowers. For more information about the market, call (706) 334-2926. Also on the grounds is the **Spruill Gallery Community Garden**, operated by the County Extension Service Master Gardener Program. The garden consists of herbs, perennials, an agronomic crop demonstration, and vegetables in the Plant a Row for the Hungry program. For more information about the garden, call (404) 298-4084 or consult the Web site at www.atlantacommunitygardens.org. Free.

Historic Homes and Sites

🍃 **Decatur Cemetery,** 299 Bell Street, Decatur. This woodsy, parklike retreat was the site of a rare Confederate victory on July 22, 1864, during a Civil War skirmish that was part of the doomed Battle of Atlanta. Visitors can trace the history of the area by examining the headstones, which range in age and style from the crude, moss-covered stones of early pioneers to ornate Victorian monuments. The oldest section of the cemetery is listed on the National Register of Historic Places. Free.

🍃 ♿ **Historic Complex of the DeKalb Historical Society** (404-373-1088; www.dekalbhistory.org), Adiar Park on West Trinity Place, Decatur. Office hours 10–4 Tuesday through Friday; call for hours the buildings are open and for guided tour reservations. The complex, which backs to a pleasant, shady park, features three antebellum structures. The oldest is the **Biffle Cabin,** which was built by a Revolutionary War veteran between 1825 and 1840. The log cabin was relocated here from a knoll overlooking Barbashela Creek. The **Thomas-Barber Cabin,** once a stagecoach stop on the Old McDonough Road, was built by Hayden Thomas. The **Benjamin Franklin Swanton House,** a one-story frame home built between 1830 and 1840, is considered Decatur's oldest house (as opposed to a cabin). Legend has it that a Yankee soldier was held captive in an upstairs closet during the Battle of Atlanta. The house serves as a small museum. Also on the property is the **Mary Gay House,** which is named for the author of *Life in Dixie During the War* and used for special events. Even when the houses aren't open, visitors can walk around them and peek in the windows. Call about **Log Cabin Hour** programs and **History Camps** held at the complex. Free.

The Mary Gay House, named for Confederate author Mary Ann Harris Gay, can be found on the grounds of the Historic Complex of the DeKalb Historical Society.

Museums

🐠 ♿ **Fernbank Museum of Natural History** (404-929-6300; tickets 404-929-6400;

Who Was Mary Ann Harris Gay?

Mary Gay (1828–1918) was a spunky Confederate author and heroine best remembered for her eye-witness history of the Civil War. She participated in a series of daring escapades, including forays across enemy lines to get food and clothing for the women and children of Decatur and hiding winter clothing in her dining room until she could smuggle it to Confederate soldiers. She refused to leave her home when it was invaded by Yankees, and when her brother was killed in the war, she supported his survivors by peddling her books door-to-door. According to Mary, her only regret was that she could not fight herself. Some of Mary's exploits are said to have inspired scenes in Margaret Mitchell's *Gone with the Wind*. Mark Twain referred to Mary Gay and included some of her poetry in *The Adventures of Tom Sawyer.*

www.fernbank.edu/museum), 767 Clifton Road Northeast, Atlanta. Open 10–5 Monday through Saturday, noon–5 Sunday. "Martinis and IMAX" 5:30–10:30 Friday evenings except December. Visitors can introduce themselves to some of Earth's earliest inhabitants at the largest museum of its type in the Southeast. The Giants of the Mesozoic gallery features the largest dinosaurs ever discovered, including Argentinosaurus; at 123 feet long and weighing 100 tons, it was not only the most massive plant eater, but also the largest known dinosaur ever to walk the earth. The much smaller, 47-foot long, 8-ton Giganotosaurus was the largest meat eater. Visitors also will see a flock of 21 Pterodaustro, small pterosaurs, and three Anhanguera, larger pterosaurs. In complete contrast, when looking down at the limestone floors, visitors see fossil remains of tiny sea creatures that lived during the Jurassic Period more than 150 million years ago. There's so much to see at this exemplary museum, it's almost impossible to describe here. Other galleries include the Star Gallery; The World of Shells, with its 900-gallon, living-reef aquarium; A Walk Through Time in Georgia; The Martha Hodgson Ellis Discovery Rooms for ages 3–5 and 6–10; First Georgians; Sensing Nature; Cultures of the World; and Wings Over Water. The **Rankin M. Smith Sr. IMAX Theatre** offers spectacular movies on its five-story-high, 72-foot-wide screen with surround sound. Fernbank also offers special programs such as "Super Saturday," "In My World," and family days. Children's crafts are offered on weekends outside the Discovery Rooms. Plan to make a day out of a visit here; there is even a café for meals or snacks (see *Eating Out*). Adults can enjoy a touch of class on Friday nights at "Martinis and IMAX," which includes a movie on the giant screen, live music, specialty martinis, a wine bar, and dinner. Hunger pangs can be staved off at the Fernbank Café (see *Eating Out*). Also on the grounds is the **Robert L. Stanton Rose Garden** (see *Gardens*). Museum only adults $13, seniors and students $12, children 3–12 $11; IMAX only, $9–11; museum and movie $13–17.

✒ ❦ ও **Fernbank Science Center** (678-874-7102; fsc.fernbank.edu), 156 Heaton Park Drive Northeast, Atlanta. Open 8:30–5 Monday and Wednesday, 8:30–10 Thursday and Friday, 10–5 Saturday, 1–5 Sunday. At this, one of the country's largest planetariums, visitors can explore the vastness of the universe with one of the center's specially choreographed shows. The center boasts an observatory, two electron microscopes, a NASA aeronautics education lab, a greenhouse, a botanical garden, and a 65-acre old-growth forest with paved walking trails, some adapted for heart patients and the visually impaired.

The forest is the largest urban woodland forest in the Piedmont region. Seasonal guide sheets identify the flora and fauna. Free except for planetarium; admission to planetarium is $4 for adults, $3 for seniors and students. Included as an attraction in the Atlanta CityPass (see What's Where).

✒ ও **Michael C. Carlos Museum of Emory University** (404-727-4282; www.carlos.emory.edu), 571 South Kilgo Street Northeast, Atlanta. Open 10–5 Tuesday through Saturday, noon–5 Sunday; docent-led tours at 2:30 Thursday and Sunday. Visitors can get

The Michael C. Carlos Museum of Emory University is the South's largest archaeological museum.

wrapped up in the art and architecture of ancient civilizations as they view the impressive collections at the South's largest archaeological museum. The museum's 16,000 objects offer a glimpse of 9,000 years of art history and include extremely rare ancient Egyptian, Greek, and Roman pieces, as well as works on paper from the Middle Ages through today. Other present-day works come from the Middle East, Near East, Asia, sub-Saharan Africa, and Oceana. From the Western Hemisphere, the collection includes ceramics from Nicaragua and Costa Rica, and burial urns from Columbia. The stunning building was designed by internationally renowned architect Michael Graves. $7; audio tours (recommended) can be rented for $3.

🖊 🐾 ♿ **Old Courthouse on the Square/Jim Cherry Museum** (404-373-1088; www.dekalbhistory.org), 101 East Court Square, Decatur. Open 9–4 Tuesday through Friday. In 1823, this site, at a point where two Indian trails met, was chosen as the location of Decatur's public square. The current courthouse, the fifth on the site, was built in 1898. Within the courthouse, which is also the headquarters of the DeKalb History Center, is the Jim Cherry Museum. The museum, named for Dr. Jim Cherry (1911–1980), a

Decatur's Old Courthouse on the Square is home to the Jim Cherry Museum and the headquarters of the DeKalb History Center

former DeKalb Historical Society president and superintendent of the DeKalb County School System for 25 years, documents county history through changing displays and four permanent exhibits: "DeKalb: The First Hundred Years," "Johnny Reb and Billy Yank: The Life of the Common Soldier," "DeKalb at War," and "DeKalb Then and Now." Free; guided tours can be arranged in advance for $2 per person.

Special Drives
Buford Highway. Begin at Lenox/Cheshire Bridge roads in Buckhead and drive north at least as far as I-285, but you can go much farther. What's interesting about this purely commercial corridor is the wide variety of Hispanic and Asian businesses readily identified by their signage.

Ponce de Leon Avenue. Starting at the Fox Theatre in Midtown Atlanta, drive east on Ponce de Leon. After some forgettable depressed areas, you'll start passing the fine old homes in Druid Hills as well as the series of six Fredrick Law Olmstead parks (see *Nature Preserves and Parks*), and will finally end at the historic courthouse on the square in Decatur.

Walking Tours
🐾 **City of Decatur Walking Tour** (404-371-8386). The Decatur Development Authority has produced a series of brochures for walking tours past points of interest. The brochures are available at city hall on the second floor.

🐾 **Ten Sites for Reflection: A Walking Tour of the Emory University Campus** (404-727-6123, ask for the Undergraduate Admissions Office receptionist; www.environment.emory.edu/who/tour/index.shtml). This 10-site, self-guided tour (print out the map and description from the Web site) focuses on how the natural world and the university have coexisted or, in some cases, not coexisted over the years. The entire tour, which is divided into two loops, takes about two hours. You can see the first four sites and stop for lunch at any of several restaurants and campus eateries clustered at this point, and then continue with the remaining six sites. Among the landmarks are the Baker Woodlands, Peavine Creek, Callaway Bridge Ravine, the gardens at the Emory Conference Center, Wesley Woods Forest and Hahn Woods, Lullwater, and several environmentally friendly buildings designed and built to comply with the Green Building Council's Leadership in Energy and Environmental Design standards. (For more information about the natural areas of the campus, see *Nature Preserves and Parks*.) Guided tours are available weekdays through the admission office. Free.

To Do

Biplane Sight-Seeing Rides

Biplane Rides Over Atlanta (770-393-3937; www.biplaneridesoveratlanta.com), 3829 Clairmont Road, Chamblee. Taking off from DeKalb–Peachtree Airport, the company offers rides, sight-seeing tours, and aerobatic flights in the Boeing PT-17 Stearman (a pilot and a single-passenger open cockpit biplane), the Waco (a pilot and a two-passenger open cockpit biplane), and the North American AT-6 Texan (a World War II advanced combat trainer). Tours include the Atlanta Skyline ($135 for one person, $195 for two), Explore Stone Mountain ($125 for one person, $195 for two), a combination of those two flights ($195 for one person, $295 for two), Lake Lanier ($275 for one person, $395 for two), Romantic Sunset Flights ($195–395 depending on length of flight), and Aerobatic Thrill Flights ($245–545 depending on length of flight).

Bicycling

✍ 🐾 **PATH Foundation** (see What's Where). The Atlanta/DeKalb portion of the trail system includes those sections described in this chapter as well as others. (See the Buckhead chapter for details about the Chastain Park Trail and the Stone Mountain chapter for information about the Stone Mountain Trail.) The most recent addition is the Arabia Mountain Greenway Trail, which uses an abandoned railroad bed to connect historic downtown Lithonia to The Mall at Stonecrest, the Arabia Mountain Nature Center (see the Stone Mountain chapter), and more than 1,000 acres of forest and rock outcroppings. The DeKalb County Trail Master Plan includes a proposed 124 miles of trails. To learn more about the trail system, including places to park and the location of nearby hospitals, restrooms, water, MARTA access, and other points of interest, purchase the Atlanta-DeKalb Greenway Trail Guide from the PATH Foundation for $5.50 plus applicable Georgia tax. The guide can be purchased online at www.pathfoundation.org.

Bird-Watching

The most natural wilderness area in the metro Atlanta region is the **Chattahoochee River Natural Recreation Area** (see *Recreation Areas*). The area's headquarters, which is at Island Ford in Dunwoody, is an ideal spot for bird-watchers. Contact the recreation area to find out about ranger-led programs.

Boating/Tubing

The Chattahoochee River, which flows through the **Chattahoochee River National Recreation Area** (see *Recreation Areas*), is popular for canoeing, kayaking, and tubing. Just keep in mind that the river has a year-round temperature of about 55 degrees, so the possibility of hypothermia is an important consideration. In addition, U.S. Coast Guard-approved personal flotation devices are required to be worn if boating, tubing, or wading on river areas between Buford Dam in Forsyth County and Morgan Falls Dam in Fulton County, which includes the portion of the river included in this chapter. All children younger than age 10 MUST wear a U.S. Coast Guard-approved personal flotation device in any vessel that is underway.

Fishing

Fishing in the Chattahoochee River is a year-round activity. Fish most likely to be caught include trout, bass, and catfish. The Chattahoochee River in this area is part of the **Chattahoochee River National Recreation Area** (see *Recreation Areas*) and is open for fishing from 30 minutes before sunrise to 30 minutes after sunset. Night fishing is not allowed. Fishermen must follow Georgia fishing regulations, which include a valid Georgia fishing license for anglers age 16 and older. Additionally, anglers must have a current trout license. Visit the Georgia Department of Natural Resources Web site at www.gofishgeorgia.com for regulations. **Fishing for Kids!**, a program for those younger than 16, is held at the Island Ford unit and includes lessons and fishing in a pond. Bait, tackle, and poles are provided.

For Families

⚓ 🍴 ♿ **Malibu Grand Prix Family Entertainment Center** (770-416-7630; www.malibu grandprix.com), 5400 Brook Hollow Parkway, Norcross. Open noon–10 Monday through Thursday, noon–midnight Friday, 11–midnight Saturday, 11–10 Sunday. The center offers something for everyone: an arcade, batting cages, bumper boats, Go-Karts, an Indy-style formula racing track, two 18-hole miniature golf courses, and a food court. Prices are charged individually for the various activities, but generally range from $1–5 per activity.

Golf

Sugar Creek Golf and Tennis Center (404-241-7671), 2706 Bouldercrest Road, Atlanta. Open daylight hours daily. The 18-hole, 6,318-yard course has a par of 71. $21 weekdays, $24 weekends—both plus $11 cart fee.

Swimming

⚓ 🍴 **DeKalb County Parks and Recreation** (404-371-2631). The county operates 12 public swimming pools from Memorial Day weekend through the first weekend in August. Call the department to find the pool nearest to where you are staying. Pools are open noon–5:30 daily, plus 7:30–8:30 Tuesday and Thursday for evening swims. Daytime swims are $3 for ages 18 and older, $2 for ages 4–17; evening swims are $2 for ages 18 and older, $1 for ages 4–17.

Tennis

⚓ 🍴 **Blackburn Tennis Center and Park** (770-451-1061), 3493 Ashford-Dunwoody Road, Atlanta. Open 9–10 weekdays, 10–6 Saturday, 10–5:30 Sunday. This popular tennis center in Dunwoody boasts 18 lighted hard-surface courts. The 49-acre park also features softball and soccer fields and trails. $2.50 per hour per person before 6 PM; $3 per hour after 6 PM.

⚓ 🍴 **DeKalb County Parks and Recreation** (404-371-2631). Twenty county parks have tennis courts. At most of them play is free and available on a first-come, first-served basis. Call the office to find the courts nearest to where you are staying.

✒️ ❧ **Sugar Creek Golf and Tennis Center** (404-243-7149), 2706 Bouldercrest Road, Atlanta. Open 8–10 weekdays, 9–8 weekends. The tennis center boasts 12 hard courts and four clay courts—all lighted. $3 per hour for hard courts, $3.50 per hour for clay courts until dusk, and then add 50 cents per hour for night play.

GREEN SPACE

Gardens

✒️ ❧ **Georgia Perimeter Native Plant Garden and Wildflower Center of Georgia** (678-891-2668; www.gpc.edu/~ddonald/botgard/george3.htm), 3251 Panthersville Road, Decatur. Open daylight hours daily; staffed 10–3 weekdays. Located on the Decatur campus of Georgia Perimeter College, the garden features examples of all of Georgia's native trees and plants. In fact, the garden's collection of 4,000 species is the largest collection of native plants in Georgia. In addition, the garden's fern collection is the 13th largest in the United States and in the Top 40 in the world. The shade garden is particularly diverse, and a trail from the garden leads to the South River. Gardening enthusiasts look forward to the spring and fall plant sales during which there are walks and talks conducted by experts. Free.

✒️ ❧ **Robert L. Stanton Rose Garden** (Fernbank Science Center 404-634-4879; www.fern bank.edu), 767 Clifton Road Northeast, Atlanta. Open daylight hours Tuesday through Sunday. This beautiful garden is located on the grounds of the Fernbank Museum of Natural History, but maintained by the Fernbank Science Center (see *Museums* for both). The garden is named in honor of Robert L. Stanton, who first established a rose garden at the museum in 1983. A trained horticulturist and employee of the science center, Stanton had a lifelong interest in roses and was a consulting Rosarian. His interest in educating the public about roses and his realization that there was no test site in Atlanta led to the establishment of this garden. Today the garden contains more than 1,000 rosebushes (the rose garden in Thomasville, "The Rose City," has only 500), with 25 to 50 different new varieties planted in test beds awaiting addition

One of the stars of the Robert L. Stanton Rose Garden

to the listing of American roses. There are 100 other varieties displayed in the garden. Another garden is devoted to test miniature roses. Free. (See Spruill Center Gallery under *Cultural Sites* for a description of the demonstration garden there.)

Nature Preserves and Parks

✒️ ❧ **Baker Woodlands/Hahn Woods/Lullwater/Wesley Woods Forest** (www.environment. emory.edu/who/tour/tour8.shtml), at Emory University in Atlanta. Emory University is known nationally for its preconstruction consultation process, including its efforts to preserve natural areas for recreation, improve air and water quality, and maintain the intrinsic value of the campus's natural environment. Baker Woodlands, an excellent example of a Piedmont hardwood forest, contains more than 100 plant species, including 60 native trees. Hahn Woods is an oasis of tranquility in the busy university area. Nature trails lead visitors through a glade of trees to South Peachtree Creek, where there is a viewing platform from which you can see the remnants of the sluiceway from the old Houston Mill. Lullwater, the spiritual heart of the Emory campus, is a 130-acre park that contains woods and meadows. Wesley Woods Forest is one of the best-preserved hardwood forests in the Piedmont region of the Southeast. In near-pristine condition, it contains a variety of plants and rare species.

🐾 **Clyde Shepherd Nature Preserve** (404-728-1411; www.cshepherdpreserve.org), 2580 Pine Bluff Drive, Decatur. Open daylight hours daily. The 28-acre park contains a healthy ecosystem of diverse wildlife and plants, including an impressive stand of huge East Coast poplar trees. The prime bird-watching area features boardwalks and observation platforms located adjacent to a beaver pond. Walking trails meander through the park. Throughout the year, the preserve is the site of neighborhood gatherings, nature tours, volunteer workdays, and special events such as an art show and a harvest celebration. Special nature tours are devoted to birds, insects, and wild edibles. Free.

🐾 **DeKalb Greenway Trails** (404-371-2540). In a public-private partnership with the PATH Foundation (see *Bicycling* and *Hiking*), the county is creating a 127-mile network of interlinking bicycle and pedestrian trails and forested greenways.

🐾 **Dunwoody Nature Center and Nature Preserve** (770-394-3322; www.dunwoody nature.org), 5343 Roberts Drive, Dunwoody. Park open sunrise to sunset daily; nature center open 9–5 weekdays. Twenty-two acres of DeKalb County's Dunwoody Park are preserved as a natural classroom for environmental education. The park features wetland, woodland, and streamside trails; display gardens; a picnic meadow; and a playground. Numerous classes, camps, and festivals occur throughout the year (see *Special Events*). Access to the park is free; some activities have a fee.

🐾 **Forty Oaks Nature Preserve** (404-508-7602), 3790 Market Street, Clarkston. Open daylight hours daily. Trails lead visitors to the 10-acre park along a stream and through forests of hardwoods and pine. A historic home within the park serves as the home of the Outbound School and the headquarters for DeKalb County's adopt-a-stream program. The preserve serves as a model site for the stream bank reclamation program designed to remove invasive, nonnative plants and restore the banks to their natural state. One of the attractions of this park is its convenient location only three blocks from the historic Clarkston square. Free.

🐾 **Olmstead Linear Park** (404-817-6760). The set of six parks follows Ponce de Leon Avenue between Moreland and Briarcliff avenues in Atlanta to the city of Decatur. The park system was designed in 1890 by Fredrick Law Olmstead, the father of American landscape architecture, and developed by Joel Hurt as part of the Druid Hills community. Over the years the parks began to deteriorate, but in 1997 a public-private partnership was established to restore and maintain them. The Oak Grove segment has been fully rehabilitated and the Dellwood, Shadyside, and Virgilee segments are being renewed.

Recreation Areas

🐾 **Island Ford Unit of the Chattahoochee River National Recreation Area** (678-538-1200; www.nps.gov/chat), 1978 Island Ford Parkway, Dunwoody. Open dawn to dusk daily.

Part of the 48-mile recreation area that runs through metro Atlanta, the Island Ford section provides hiking trails and picnicking. For more information about the recreation area, see the Buckhead and Roswell chapters. Parking $3 daily; $25 annual park pass available.

Rivers

✤ ✤ **Chattahoochee River.** See What's Where. Island Ford, the headquarters unit of the Chattahoochee River National Recreation Area, is in Dunwoody.

LODGING

Bed and Breakfasts

In Decatur

✤ **Garden House Bed and Breakfast** (404-377-3057; www.gardenhousebedand breakfastdecatur.com), 135 Garden Lane. Located just four blocks from downtown, this B&B offers a second-floor suite in a 1940s home. Guests can choose any type breakfast: continental, full, low-carb, or whatever they'd like. Relax on the screened porch overlooking the garden, pond, and waterfall. No smoking. Not wheelchair accessible. $90, discount available for multinight stay.

✤ **Sycamore House** (404-378-0685; www.city-directory.com/sycamorehouse), 624 Sycamore Street. Located in an almost 100-year-old Prairie-style mansion on a tree-lined residential street, this B&B has been lovingly restored and handsomely furnished with an eclectic mixture of antiques and contemporary pieces accented by contemporary artwork. Two upstairs rooms share a bath, while the downstairs suite has a private bath. Guests enjoy a heated pool, hot tub, and waterfall in the garden—an unexpected oasis. Full breakfast

Sycamore House is within walking distance of many Decatur attractions.

is included. The B&B is located within a five-minute walk of downtown Decatur, Agnes Scott College, and either the Avondale or Decatur rail stations. Pets accepted with advance notice. No smoking. Limited wheelchair accessibility—two steps to get into the first floor; bathrooms are not adapted. $120–145.

Inns and Hotels

All the towns in this chapter have a wide array of economical, moderate, and upscale chain hotels from A (Admiral Benbow Inn) to W (Wingate Inn). Readers know what to expect from these hostelries, so we have described only a few one-of-a-kind lodgings here.

In Atlanta

✦ **Emory Conference Center Hotel** (404-712-6000; 1-800-933-6629; www.emory conferencecenter.com), 1641 Clifton Road Northeast. The hotel, inspired by the architectural designs of Frank Lloyd Wright, provides a tranquil setting, contemporary elegance, spectacular landscapes, and exceptional service. Nestled on 28 acres of forest preserve on the Emory University campus, it offers 197 beautifully appointed rooms, a full-service restaurant serving three meals daily, a lounge, an indoor pool, whirlpool, fitness center, putting green, and spa. No smoking. Many rooms wheelchair accessible. $169–189; ask about special packages.

♂ & **Emory Inn Atlanta Bed and Breakfast** (404-712-6000; 1-800-933-6629), 1641 Clifton Road. Located adjacent to the Emory Conference Center Hotel and connected to it by a covered walkway, this more intimate inn offers 107 guest rooms, complimentary continental breakfast, a restaurant open for lunch and dinner, and an outdoor pool and hydrotherapy pool available seasonally. Some smoking rooms. Many rooms wheelchair accessible. $110.

🐾 & **University Inn at Emory** (1-800-654-8591; www.univinn.com), 1767 North Decatur Road. Guest accommodations are located in several buildings. Most rooms are large and have a microwave/refrigerator combination. The Guest House features the most economical accommodations and many of its rooms have a kitchen. Oxford Hall offers long-term housing for those who do not require daily services. For all guests, the inn offers a complimentary continental breakfast and afternoon refreshments daily. Beer and wine are available weekdays. Rooms are equipped with high-speed Internet access or modem connections and voice mail; the inn's business center offers fax, printing, and Internet access. Pet friendly. No smoking. Some rooms are wheelchair accessible. $74–159 in the Guest House, $144–154 in the inn; $280–420 weekly for efficiencies in Oxford Hall (seven-day minimum).

♂ 🐾 & **W Atlanta at Perimeter Center** (770-396-6800; www.starwood hotels.com), 111 Perimeter Center West, Atlanta. This AAA four-diamond hostelry is a boutique hotel with all the luxurious amenities a leisure or business traveler could want. Among them: guest accommodations with signature pillow-top beds, 250–thread count linens, goose-down comforters and pillows, and high-speed Internet access. The hotel also offers a fitness center with dry saunas, an outdoor pool open seasonally, an upscale restaurant, and a café. W Hotels have an exemplary pet policy—dogs and cats are not only welcomed, they are pampered. Upon check-in, pets receive a package with a toy, treat, and tag. The guest room is equipped with a custom pet bed, food and water bowls, a pet-in-room sign for the door, and a turndown treat. Pet-sitting and pet-walking services are available for additional fees. Nonsmoking rooms available. Wheelchair accessible. $129–359; extra fees apply to those traveling with pet. Ask about special packages.

WHERE TO EAT

Dining Out

In Decatur

& **Eurasia** (404-687-8822; www.eurasia bistro.net), 129 East Ponce de Leon Avenue. Open 11:30–3 and 5–10 Monday through Saturday. Low lighting and Eurasian decor set an intimate scene at this upscale restaurant. Asian, French, and Pacific Rim cuisine features such dishes as quail with Thai spices, filet mignon with a noodle cake and Indonesian curry, herb-crusted rack of lamb with Thai basil sauce, and chicken coconut soup with shiitake mushrooms. No smoking. Wheelchair accessible. $21–35.

& **Floataway Café** (404-892-1414; www.starprovisions.com, then click on Floataway), 1123 Zonolite Road. Open 6–10 Tuesday through Saturday. Reservations recommended. Operated by the same team as Midtown's Bacchanalia (see the Midtown chapter), the restaurant serves fresh California cuisine reminiscent of Napa Valley and Italian countryside cuisine embellished with local produce. Many dishes are cooked in a wood-fired oven or grill. Selections might include piccolo fritto (crispy baby squid, red onions, and lemon slices with aioli) or chilled melon soup with Parma prosciutto. The restaurant, located in a former warehouse along a purely industrial street, is named for the former tenant, the Floataway Door Company. The last time these authors were there, it was raining so hard we thought we would float away. No smoking. Wheelchair accessible. $15–26.

& **Sage** (404-373-5574; www.the bistros.com), 121 Sycamore Street. Open 5–9 Tuesday through Thursday and Sunday, 5–10 Friday and Saturday, 5–9 Sunday. Located behind the historic courthouse on the square, the restaurant serves eclectic American and international cuisine. Many restaurants claim to have an extensive wine list, but Sage delivers with 150 wines, 50 of which are available by the glass. No smoking. Wheelchair accessible. $21–30 for dinner.

✿ ❦ & **Wahoo! Grill** (404-373-3331; www.wahoogrilldecatur.com), 1042 West College Avenue. Open 5–10 Monday through Thursday, 11–11 Friday and Saturday, 10–10 Sunday (brunch served 11–3 Saturday and 10–3 Sunday). When the restaurant opened in 2005, it was named one of the Top Ten New Restaurants in Atlanta by *Atlanta Magazine*. Accolades continue to come, with kudos such as Best Patio Dining from *Creative Loafing*, Best Seafood from *Best of Citysearch*, and Best Fisherman Stew by *Atlanta Magazine*. The signature dish is naturally wahoo, but other choices might include trout, ahi tuna, and salmon as well as filet and prawns, pork chops, New York strip, pasta, and chicken. No smoking. Wheelchair accessible. $10–26.

❦ & **Watershed** (404-378-4900; www.watershedrestaurant.com), 406 West Ponce de Leon Avenue. Open 11–10 Monday through Saturday, 10–3 Sunday. The fun-loving eatery is owned by Indigo Girl Emily Saliers and three female partners. Chef Scott Peacock creates seasonal New

American cuisine with a Southern twist in a former gas station. Among the menu selections are fried chicken, light biscuits, gourmet sandwiches, fresh pasta, roasted fish, and old-timey chocolate cake. No smoking. Wheelchair accessible. $8–20 for lunch, $16–34 for dinner.

In Norcross
& **J. Alexander's** (770-263-9755; www.jalexanders.com), 5245 Peachtree Parkway. Open 11–10 Sunday through Thursday, 11–11 Friday and Saturday. The American menu features all your favorite soups, salads, burgers, and sandwiches for light eating, or steaks, prime rib, chicken, pork, ribs, and seafood for finer dining. No smoking. Wheelchair accessible. $8–23.

Eating Out

In Atlanta
& **Houston Mill House** (404-727-7878; www.houstonmillhouse.com), 849 Houston Mill Road. Open 11:30–2 weekdays. The historic fieldstone house, located in a wooded setting near the Emory University campus, offers fine dining in the main dining room and on the veranda is good weather. Entrées might include beef, pork, chicken, and seafood such as salmon and crab cakes. No smoking. Wheelchair accessible. $13–17.

❦ **Queen of Sheba** (404-321-1493), 1594 Woodcliff Drive. Open 11–midnight daily. Exotic Ethiopian cuisine is eaten with your hands, using soft injera bread to scoop up wonderful piles of vegetables, legumes, and meat stews. The coffee and chai are outstanding as well. No smoking. Wheelchair accessible. $9–11.

In Decatur
✿ ❦ & **The Angel** (404-687-5299), 426 West Ponce de Leon Avenue. Open 11:30 AM–1 AM Monday through Thursday, 11:30 AM–2 AM Friday and Saturday, 11:30

AM—midnight Sunday. The atmosphere is old English pub; the cuisine features traditional British favorites such as bangers and mash, fish and chips, and braised cabbage. Beverages include a variety of beers on tap and wine. The child-friendly pub also features outdoor seating. Smoking outside only. Wheelchair accessible. $10–20.

Café Alsace (404-373-5622), 121 East Ponce de Leon Avenue. Open 11:30 AM–2:30 PM Tuesday through Friday; 6 PM–10 PM Tuesday through Saturday; 10 AM–2 PM Sunday for brunch. This small, cozy, traditional French bistro has only 12 tables, but it's big on flavor. The French cuisine has a German twist with specialties such as spatzle with Alsatian noodles as well as a wide array of quiches, seafood, soups, salads, and sandwiches. Outdoor seating. No smoking. Wheelchair accessible. $12–20.

Café Lily (404-371-9119; www.cafelily.com), 308 West Ponce de Leon Avenue. Open 11:30–2:30 weekdays, 11–3 weekends; 5:30–10 Monday through Wednesday, 5:30–11 Thursday, 5:30–midnight Friday and Saturday, 4:30–9:30 Sunday. This friendly neighborhood bistro, named for the niece of chef/owner Anthony Pitillo, offers a variety of eclectic Mediterranean cuisine. You could make an entire dinner from appetizers such as Prince Edward Island mussels posillipo or shrimp beignets. No smoking. Wheelchair accessible. $6–13 for lunch, $10–18 for dinner.

Fernbank Café (404-929-6300; www.fernbank.edu/museum/visitor dining.html), 767 Clifton Road Northeast. Open 11–4 Monday through Saturday, noon–4 Sunday. Located within the Fernbank Museum of Natural History, the eatery serves burgers, sandwiches, salads, specialty entrées, wraps, light snacks, and refreshing beverages in comfortable surroundings with a spectacular view of Fernbank Forest. No smoking. Wheelchair accessible. $2.25–7.50.

Madras Saravan Bhavan (404-636-4400), 2179 Lawrenceville Highway. Open 11:30–10 daily. The restaurant serves South Indian cuisine, featuring many meatless dishes prepared from traditional recipes. Specialties include filled pancakes and crepes as well as grain- and legume-based snacks. No smoking. Wheelchair accessible. $7–9.

Mezza a Lebanese Bistro (404-633-8833), 2751 LaVista Road. Open 11:30–2 Tuesday through Friday; 5:30–10:30 Tuesday through Saturday. "Mezza" means "little dishes," and that's what you get at this eatery—more than 70 appetizer-size, ultra-healthy Lebanese selections, many of which are vegetarian. No smoking. Wheelchair accessible. $5–7.

Noodle (404-378-8622; www.noodle house.net), 205 East Ponce de Leon Avenue. Open 11:30–10 weekdays, 11:30–11 Friday, noon–10 Sunday. The eclectic Asian/Pacific Rim cuisine is served in an artful atmosphere and features such dishes as basil rolls, curry noodle broth with shrimp, lettuce wraps, and Vietnamese cold noodle salad with tofu. Patio dining is also available. No smoking. Wheelchair accessible. $8–15.

Udipi Café (404-325-1933; www.udipi.com), 1850 Lawrenceville Highway, Suite 700. Open 11:30–9:30 Sunday through Thursday, 11:30–10 Friday and Saturday. The South Indian restaurant serves vegetarian dishes from the buffet or from the menu. No smoking. Wheelchair accessible. $7–15.

Zyka (404-728-4444), 1677 Scott Boulevard. Open noon–10:15 Tuesday through Thursday and Sunday, noon–10:45 Friday and Saturday. The casual Indian eatery, which is located in a former church, serves spicy cuisine from Hyderabad, including a wide range of curries and chicken dishes. There's even saffron-scented ice cream served in clay flower pots. No smoking. Wheelchair accessible. $5–6.

In Norcross

✎ 🐾 ♿ **Norcross Station Cafe** (770-409-9889; www.norcrossstation.com), 40 South Peachtree Street. Open 11–9:30 Monday through Thursday, 11–10 Friday and Saturday. A charming atmosphere is created in a historic 1909 railroad depot. Dining is in various old rooms filled with railroad memorabilia, or outside on the decks overlooking the historic town center and park. The American menu features soups, quiche, burgers, sandwiches, and pasta for lighter fare, or seafood, steaks, prime rib, chops, chicken, meat loaf, or stir-fry for more substantial meals. No smoking. Wheelchair accessible. $9–16.

✎ 🐾 ♿ **Paizano's Pizza and Pasta** (770-300-0250; www.paizanos.com), 7 Jones Street. Open 11–2 and 5–9:30 Monday through Thursday, 11–2 and 5–10:30 Friday, 5–10 Saturday, 11–9 Sunday. This relaxed neighborhood favorite, located in a historic commercial building in the center of the village near the park, serves an Italian menu and New York–style pizza. No smoking. Wheelchair accessible. $11–17.

✎ ♿ **Ted's Montana Grill** (678-405-0305; www.tedsmontanagrill.com), 5165 Peachtree Parkway. Open 11–10 Sunday through Thursday, 11–11 Friday and Saturday. Founded by media mogul and hometown boy Ted Turner and George McKerrow, the restaurant offers comfort food for the 21st century. The Arts and Crafts-style architecture and authentic touches re-create the ambience of a Montana bar and grill. Everything is made fresh when you order. American bison is the specialty, but beef, chicken, and seafood are also featured. Blue plate specials are offered each day. The buffalo meat loaf is becoming a local favorite. Save room for one of the eatery's fresh-baked "scratch" cookies that come in snickerdoodle, oatmeal raisin, chocolate chip, or peanut butter. No smoking. Wheelchair accessible. $8–30.

Snacks

In Decatur

✎ 🐾 ♿ **Cold Stone Creamery** (404-378-3043), 133 East Court Square. Open noon–10 Sunday through Thursday, noon–11 Friday and Saturday. Ice cream, yogurt, and sorbets are made fresh every day. Customers choose from 15 core flavors and 40 mix-ins, then watch as the concoction is blended together on a slab chilled to 15 degrees. It's not just ice cream; it's entertainment. No smoking. Wheelchair accessible. $2–5.70.

✎ 🐾 ♿ **Pastries a GoGo** (404-373-3423; www.pastriesagogo.com), 250 West Ponce de Leon Avenue, Suite E. Opens at 7:30 AM daily except Tuesday; kitchen closes at 2:30, bakery closes at 4. Breakfast and lunch served weekdays, breakfast only on weekends. The neighborhood bakery/café concocts an array of breads and pastries fresh each day, including croissants, bagels, sticky buns, muffins, scones, and Danishes. Breakfast choices include a variety of egg dishes, pancakes, French toast, and Belgian waffles; soups, salads, and sandwiches are featured for lunch. No smoking. Wheelchair accessible. $2–7.

Coffeehouses

In East Atlanta Village

🐾 ♿ **Joe's** (404-521-1122), 510 Flat Shoals Avenue. Open 6:30 AM–11 PM Sunday through Thursday, 7:30 AM–midnight Friday and Saturday. The popular hangout serves coffees and pastries. No smoking. Wheelchair accessible. $1.57–4.75.

In Decatur

🐾 ♿ **Java Monkey** (404-378-5002; www.javamonkeydecatur.com), 205 East Ponce de Leon Avenue. Open 6:30 AM–midnight daily. In addition to coffee, the eatery serves pastries for breakfast, sandwiches and salads for brunch and lunch. No smoking. Wheelchair accessible. $1.50–10.

ENTERTAINMENT

Arts at Emory (Short Center box office 404-727-5050; www.emory.edu/ARTS), 1641 North Decatur Road. Box office open 10–6 weekdays. Emory University offers a wide range of arts programs open to the public, including Theater Emory, Music at Emory, dance performances, and visual arts exhibitions (see separate entries).

Dance

Atlanta Chinese Dance Company (office 770-449-9953; box office 770-813-7600; www.atlantachinesedance.org), 5377 New Peachtree Road, Chamblee. Call for a schedule of events, performance venues, and ticket prices. The company was created to promote the development, advancement, and appreciation of Chinese dance and culture, and has performed all over the metro Atlanta area, including the Opening and Closing Ceremonies of the 1996 Centennial Olympic Summer Games. Performances, which normally occur at the Performing Arts Center at the Gwinnett Center, include classic Chinese dance styles, ethnic folk dances, and adaptations of modern dance drama performed in authentic, historically accurate costumes. Audiences delight in the colorful fabrics, platform shoes, tall headdresses, and other adornments. Adults $20, students $10.

Beacon Dance (404-337-6927; www.beacondance.org), 410 West Trinity Place, Decatur. Call for a schedule of performances and ticket prices. What began in 1952 as the Decatur Civic Ballet has metamorphosed into a contemporary organization that promotes dance in all its forms. The company presents performances, classes, and an annual dance festival.

Several Dancers Core (404-373-4154; www.severaldancerscore.org), 133 Sycamore Street, Decatur. Call for a schedule of performances and ticket prices. The professional dance organization creates and performs experimental contemporary dance and movement. Programs consist of "Nu-Dance Exchange," "Lunchtime in the Studio," and "An Evening of Salon."

Music

Decatur Civic Chorus (770-388-9536; www.decaturcivicchorus.org). Call for a schedule of performances and venues. For more than 50 years, the organization has performed free Christmas and spring concerts as well as numerous community shows and benefit concerts. The chorus has performed with the Atlanta Symphony Orchestra, at Stone Mountain Park, and on radio and television.

DeKalb Choral Guild (678-318-1362; dcguild.home.mindspring.com), 3304 Henderson Mill Road, Atlanta. The choral group has performed for more than 26 years in community festivals and events such as the DeKalb International Choral Festival and the Emory Festival of Choirs. The guild also sponsors a biennial festival of faith featuring interdenominational choirs. The group's Chamber Singers, a small ensemble, performs Renaissance madrigals in period costume, traditional and ancient holiday selections, Broadway show tunes, and opera choruses.

DeKalb Symphony Orchestra (678-891-3565; www.dekalbsymphony.com), 555 North Indian Creek Drive, Clarkston. Call for a schedule of performances and ticket prices. The orchestra, now entering its fifth decade, presents an exciting season of performances, often featuring outstanding soloists. With the exception of children's concerts, all shows are performed in the Marvin Cole Auditorium at the Georgia Perimeter College, Clarkston campus.

Gwinnett Choral Guild (404-223-9962; www.gwinnettchoralguild.org), 286 Forest Valley Road, Norcross. Call for a schedule of events, performance venues, and ticket prices. The guild has performed throughout the metropolitan Atlanta area as well as out of state and out of the country.

Gwinnett Community Symphony Orchestra (770-789-2718; www.newschoolofmusic.com/trocinaGYS.htm), mailing address: 2847 Country House Lane, Buford. Call for a schedule of performances, venues, and ticket prices. The orchestra is a community musical organization dedicated to enriching the lives of those in Gwinnett and surrounding counties. The orchestra also mentors the Gwinnett Youth Orchestra, the Gwinnett Wind Symphony, and the Gwinnett Chamber Orchestra, all of which give a variety of performances.

Music at Emory (Short Center box office 404-727-5050; www.arts.emory.edu). Call for a schedule of performances, venues, and ticket prices. Emory University's music department presents student, faculty, and visiting artist programs in voice, organ, piano, chamber music, harpsichord, and other musical forms. Performances are held in the Donna and Marvin Schwartz Center for the Performing Arts, the Glenn Memorial Auditorium, Goodrich C. White Hall, the Performing Arts Studio, and the William Cannon Chapel.

Nightlife

🍸 ♿ **The EARL** (404-522-3950; www.badearl.com), 488 Flat Shoals Avenue, Atlanta. Open 11:30 AM–midnight Monday through Saturday, noon–midnight Sunday. This venerable venue offers a wide variety of live musical acts and upscale entrées such as rib eye, salmon, and pork chops. Admission to those 18 years of age or older only. Smoking allowed. Wheelchair accessible. Tickets to musical acts $5–20; entrées $9–15.

Eddie's Attic (404-377-4976; www.eddiesattic.com), 515-B North McDonough Street, Decatur. Open 4:30 PM–12:30 AM Sunday through Thursday, 4:30 PM–2 AM Friday and Saturday. The covered patio and pool room are for those 21+; on Friday and Saturday there is an all-ages early show from 7–8:30, otherwise 21+. The center of Atlanta's singer-songwriter scene, the club features the finest acoustic players every night. The Indigo Girls, Shawn Mullins, and Sugarland are just a few of the many musicians who got their start at Eddie's Attic. The club also has billiards and a popular covered deck. Monday is open mic night, and Friday features a happy hour on the patio with free appetizers from 5–7. No smoking in the music room; patio and pool room allow smoking. Not wheelchair accessible. It is always best to check the Web site for the most current information about acts, show times, and cover charges, which can range from $3–35 for the music room (no cover for use of other facilities); dining $6–12.

🍸 ♿ **The Flatiron** (404-688-8864), 520 Flat Shoals Avenue Southeast, Atlanta. Open 11:30 AM–2 AM daily. This laid-back bar attracts a diverse older crowd, attracted by the warm colors, local art, friendly staff, and well-stocked jukebox. Smoking allowed. Wheelchair accessible. No cover charge.

🍸 ♿ **Mary's** (404-624-4411), 1287-B Glenwood Avenue, Atlanta. Open 5 PM–3 AM weekdays, 6 PM–3 AM Saturday. Attracting an older, primarily lesbian and gay crowd, upbeat, eclectic Mary's features DJs playing mainstream dance music downstairs. The bar is upstairs. Ask about drinks such as Marytinis and Something About Marys. Participate in karaoke at 10:30 Thursday and Saturday. Smoking allowed. Wheelchair accessible. No cover charge.

🦐 ♿ **Twain's Billiards and Tap** (373-0063), 211 East Trinity Place, Decatur. Open 11:30 AM–2:30 AM Monday through Saturday; 11:30 AM–12:30 AM Sunday. Not your pool room of old, Twain's features 20 Brunswick gold-crown tables as well as shuffleboard. Typical bar fare is served. No smoking. Wheelchair accessible. $6.

Professional Sports

🏊 🦐 **Atlanta Silverbacks** (770-969-4900, tickets 1-866-GOBACKS; www.atlantasilver backs.com), office: 3299 Northcrest Road, Suite 200, Norcross. Call for a schedule of games and ticket prices, which generally run $12.50–25. Named after Zoo Atlanta's beloved silverback gorilla, the late Willie B., the United Soccer League First Division soccer team plays at RE/Max Greater Atlanta Stadium (770-896-4392), 3200 Atlanta Silverbacks Way, Atlanta. The club fields both men's and women's teams for the late-April through late-September season.

🏊 **Gwinnett Gladiators** (770-497-5100; www.gwinnettgladiators.com) belong to the East Coast Hockey League and play 36 weekend home games at Gwinnett Arena. Tickets are available by calling or consulting the Web site.

Theater

Blackfriars of Agnes Scott College (404-471-6000; www.agnesscott.edu/studentlife/p_traditions.asp), 141 East College Avenue, Decatur. Call for a schedule of events and ticket prices. The dramatic group is named for an Elizabethan theater in London where many of Shakespeare's plays were performed. The group is the oldest continuously operating theater group in Atlanta (it was chartered in 1915) as well as the oldest campus organization. Men were allowed to take part in theatrical productions starting in the 1930s; prior to that, women filled all the roles.

Dorsey Studios and Theater (404-633-3256; www.dorseystudios.com), 3593 Clairmont Road Northeast, Atlanta. Call for a schedule of events and ticket prices. For more than 20 years, the theater has been a dynamic venue for dramatic art, including plays, opera, cabaret, and musical theater.

🏊 **Jewish Theater of the South/Marcus Jewish Community Center of Atlanta** (770-393-2148; www.atlantajcc.org), 5342 Tilly Mill Road, Dunwoody. Call for a schedule of events and ticket prices. The professional theater company performs a three-play series and a children's Hanukkah play each season in the intimate Morris and Rae Frank Theatre at the center. The plays, which are meant to challenge, enlighten, and entertain, feature Jewish content with universal appeal that connects Jews to their cultural community and builds bridges to others. Among the productions are regional premieres and seldom-produced plays. The center also often hosts concerts and exhibitions. Plays run four weeks each; the Hanukkah production runs two weeks.

🏊 **Neighborhood Playhouse** (404-373-5311; www.nplayhouse.org), 430 West Trinity Place, Decatur. Call for a schedule of events and ticket prices, which range from $14 to $24. For 26 years, the professional, nonequity, nonprofit theater has been producing mysteries, comedies, musicals, and children's programs.

🏊 **Onstage Atlanta and Abracadabra Children's Theatre** (404-378-9901; www.onstage atlanta.com), 2597 North Decatur Road, Decatur. Call for a schedule of events and ticket prices. The company presents dramas, musicals, and comedies, and also boasts an interactive, educational theater for children.

⚲ **PushPush Theater/SmallTall Theater** (404-377-6332; www.pushpushtheater.com), 121 New Street, Decatur. Call for a schedule of events. Not surprisingly, PushPush Theater, which produces films, theatrical productions, and musical performances, pushes the envelope when it comes to exploring new ideas and encouraging artists to take risks more traditional organizations would not. Twelve major professional productions are presented each year as well as youth programs by the SmallTall Theater. Adults $20, children $15.

⚲ **Stage Door Players** (770-396-1726; www.stagedoorplayers.net), North DeKalb Cultural Center, 5339 Chamblee-Dunwoody Road, Dunwoody. Call for a schedule of events and ticket prices. The theatrical organization showcases the talents of up-and-coming local actors, directors, and designers through its regular productions, Stage Door Canteen cabaret series, and Stage Door Jr. Saturday productions for children.

Theater Emory (404-727-5050; www.arts.emory.edu), 1700 North Decatur Road, Decatur. Box office open 10–6 weekdays; call for a schedule of events and ticket prices. Professional and student productions of classics and new works are presented at the Donna and Marvin Schwartz Center for the Performing Arts.

Visual Arts

Arts at Emory (box office 404-727-5050; www.arts.emory.edu). Box office open 10–6 weekdays. Emory University's art history department brings well-known scholars and artists to campus through the Robert Lehman Art Lectures, the Lovis Corinth Lectureship, and the Art History Endowed Lecture. The department of film studies explores all aspects of film through the Emory Cinematheque series. The Visual Arts Program presents exhibitions, programs, and lectures in various media, which are held in the Visual Arts Building and Gallery and elsewhere on campus. (Also see the entries for the Michael C. Carlos Museum under *Museums* and the Schatten Gallery of the Woodruff Library under *Cultural Sites*.)

SELECTIVE SHOPPING

Shopping Centers or Districts

This region of metro Atlanta has some of the city's most diverse shopping. Downtown Decatur offers 1 square mile packed with 80 shops, restaurants, clubs, and galleries, while East Atlanta Village is one of the city's coolest new shopping districts. Along the International Corridor, Buford Highway's shops cater to South and Central American and Asian immigrants.

In Atlanta

East Atlanta Village, centering on the intersection of Flat Shoals and Glenwood Avenues, features funky and fine shops, restaurants, and nightclubs. You'll find rag-tag vintage clothing stores coexisting with fine art outlets and funky fashion boutiques.

Plaza Fiesta (404-982-9138), 4166 Buford Highway Northeast, Atlanta. A traditional Latin market.

In Chamblee

Atlanta's Chinatown Shopping Square (770-458-6660; www.atlantachinatown.com), 5383-C New Peachtree Road, Chamblee. Serving the estimated 50,000 Chinese Americans in metro Atlanta as well as others searching for Chinese goods and culture, the shopping center features a Chinese food court, the Oriental Pearl restaurant, Dinho Supermarket, Dinho Bakery, an herb store, World Journal Book Store, jewelry stores, and other retail shops. The center's location next to the Chinese Community Center and across from the Chamblee MARTA station makes it a busy place. Its inner courtyard boasts two murals—one of the Great Wall of China, the other of the Bright Light Festival on the River. The *World Journal* newspaper is the largest ethnic newspaper in America and the World Journal Book Store is the largest Chinese bookstore in the Southeast. A 30-minute tour of the center is available. Special events throughout the year include the Chinese New Year celebration in January, spring and fall chess tournaments, a karaoke contest in July, and the Miss Chinatown contest in October.

In Doraville

Asian Square (770-458-8955), 5150 Buford Highway, Doraville. Open 9–9 daily. Asian Square features Chinese, Japanese, Korean, and Vietnamese groceries and products such as gifts, apparel, and videos. The center's Ranch 99 Market features Asian and Hispanic foods.

Las Americas (770-458-7962), 3652 Shallowford Road, Doraville. Purveys all things Central or South American.

Antiques

Chamblee's Antique Row/Broad Street Antique Mall (770-458-6316; 1-877-645-4728; www.antiquerow.com), 3550 Broad Street, Chamblee. Open 10–5 Monday through Saturday, 1–5:30 Sunday. Find the perfect piece of furniture or decorative accessory at this site, reputed to be the largest antiques shopping area not only in the state, but in the Southeast. More than 200 dealers sell antiques and collectibles in 20 buildings—including old homes, churches, and stores—that range in size from cozy to gargantuan.

Georgia Antiques and Design Center (770-446-9292), 6624 Dawson Boulevard, Norcross. Open 10–7 Monday through Saturday, noon–7 Sunday. More than 20 merchants offer antiques, collectibles, furniture, jewelry, pottery, rare coins, and crafts from all over the world.

Great Gatsby's Auction Gallery (770-457-1903; www.gatsbys.com), 5070 Peachtree-Industrial Boulevard, Chamblee. Open 9–5 Monday through Saturday. One of the biggest antiques dealers in the metro Atlanta area, the 100,000-square-foot warehouse/showroom purveys museum-quality antique furnishings and artwork as well as offbeat items. The emporium specializes in 19th-century American and European furnishings. Garden ornaments, fountains, and statuary are displayed in a 3-acre garden.

Clothing

Rare Footage (404-215-2188; www.rarefootageatlanta.com), 493-C Flat Shoals Avenue, Atlanta. Open noon–8 Monday through Saturday, noon–6 Sunday. The emporium offers all kinds of sneakers, from stylish to utilitarian, in all sizes. This is where to find the trendiest models as well as grand old vintage shoes.

Sugar Britches (404-522-9098), 491 Flat Shoals Avenue, Atlanta. Open noon–7 Monday and Tuesday, noon–8 Wednesday through Friday, 11–8 Saturday, noon–6 Sunday. This shop sells youthful dresses and bikinis along the lines of Frederick's of Hollywood, as well as shirts and T-shirts, hats, purses, skirts, and men's clothing. It is also known for its extensive collection of all brands of jeans for both men and women.

Flea Markets

☙ **Kudzu Flea Market** (404-373-6498), 2928 East Ponce de Leon Avenue, Decatur. Open 10:30–6 Tuesday through Saturday, 12:30–6 Sunday. For shoppers who've been to this flea market when it was located in an old barn, there are new and larger facilities where dealers ply their wares. Amid the mountains of junk, shoppers can find antiques, collectibles, primitives, vintage advertising items, and furniture. Dog friendly. In fact, Kudzu's mascot is a standard poodle who greets all the shoppers and visiting canines.

Food

Buford Highway Farmers Market (770-455-0770), 5600 Buford Highway, Doraville. Open 9–10 daily. Shop here for the freshest produce, meat, and fish. You can even pick up hardware here.

International Farmers Market (770-817-9950; internationalfarmersmarket.com), 4975 Jimmy Carter Boulevard, Suite 100, Norcross. Open 9–10 daily. This market offers fresh produce, meat, fish, and bakery items from all over the world.

Your DeKalb Farmers Market (404-377-6400; www.dekalbfarmersmarket.com), 3000 East Ponce de Leon Avenue, Decatur. Open 9–9 daily. Just about every fresh-grown ingredient you can think of is available at the world's largest indoor farmer's market. Without ever leaving the metro area, you have a passport to exotic places and delicious corners of the world. The market's 140,000 square feet boast a dizzying array of selections from more than 50 countries: cheese, coffee, deli items, fish, fruit, meat, produce, regional snacks, seafood, spices, vegetables, wine, and other foodstuffs. A restaurant and bakery are on-site and tours are available.

Special Stores

Taste of Britain (770-242-8585; www.tasteofbritain.com), 73 South Peachtree Street Northwest, Norcross. Open 10–6 Monday through Saturday. Located in historic downtown Norcross across from the Norcross Station Café, the shop sells British and Scottish items such as imported teas, china, collectibles, food, hand-sculpted castles, music, and gifts.

SPECIAL EVENTS

Monthly: **Pride of Dixie Antique Market** (770-279-9853), North Atlanta Trade Center, 1700 Juergens Street, Norcross. Open the fourth weekend of the month, noon–5 Thursday, 9–5 Friday, 9–6 Saturday, 11–5 Sunday. Recognized as one of the best shows in the country, the monthly antiques extravaganza features 600 dealers displaying everything imaginable: fine antiques, furniture, crystal, artwork, silver, linens, estate jewelry, china, home decor, collectibles, and more.

April: **Decatur Arts Festival and Garden Tour** (404-371-9583; 404-371-8262; www.decatur artsalliance.org). This annual Memorial Day weekend festival is in its 17th year and includes performances by the Decatur Civic Chorus, a literary arts festival, a fine arts exhibition, film festival, ArtWalk (all around Decatur with transportation provided by the Fun Bus), children's arts festival, dance performances, concerts on the square, an artists' market, the garden tour, and more. Most events are free; tickets for the garden tour are $15.

Dream Gardens of Dunwoody Tour (770-394-3322; www.dunwoodynature.org), 5321 Roberts Drive, Dunwoody. Call for exact dates. Gardens may be toured 10–3 Friday, 10–5 Saturday, 1–5 Sunday. This event, sponsored by the Dunwoody Nature Center, allows visitors to visit six to seven private gardens at their leisure. $15.

Notoberfest (404-308-1271; 404-691-2537; www.notoberfest.com). This East Atlanta Village beer festival is sponsored by the Sweetwater Brewing Company and the East Atlanta Community Association. Admission (21+ only) purchases a glass, koozie, and tastings of specialty, microbrew, and favorite beers.

May and September: **Blue Sky Concerts** (404-371-9583; 404-371-8262; www.decaturdba.com or www.decaturga.com/events.aspx). Free concerts in Decatur are performed at noon every Wednesday.

Concerts on the Square (404-371-9583; 404-371-8262; www.decaturdba.com or www.decaturga.com/events.aspx). Every Saturday night during these months, live bands entertain picnicking concert-goers in Decatur. Free.

June: Decatur **Beach Party** (404-371-9583; 404-371-8262; www.decaturdba.com or www.decaturga.com/events.aspx). Landlocked Decatur is transformed into a tropical paradise when the city brings in 60 tons of sand and turns the square into a beach complete with wading pools, a lighthouse, flamingos, and palm trees. Activities include live bands, a street dance, children's boardwalk games, a special beach movie on a giant inflatable screen, face painting, and more. Some activities free; some have a small charge.

July: **Battle of Atlanta Day** (www.batlevent.org). Held in East Atlanta Village, this event features a dinner gala, 5K race, and an afternoon in the park listening to gospel singers and hearing stories from Union Civil War re-enactors. Participating shops, restaurants, and bars offer discounts.

Butterfly Festival (770-394-3322; www.dunwoodynature.org), 5321 Roberts Drive, Dunwoody. This is the major fund-raising event of the Dunwoody Nature Center, and its highlight is a huge tent where participants can hand-feed 700 butterflies. Fifteen discovery centers teach about butterflies, ladybugs, honeybees, and other insects. Activities include butterfly crafts, a scavenger hunt, face painting, a monarch puppet show, and a silent auction. Nature center members: adults $8, children $4; nonmembers: adults $10, children $5.

Pied Piper Parade, Concert, and Fireworks (404-371-9583; 404-371-8262). This annual Fourth of July event in Decatur includes a parade of decorated bicycles, skateboards, and wagons followed by a concert on the square and culminating in fireworks. Free.

Labor Day Weekend: **AJC Decatur Book Festival** (Decatur Arts Alliance 1-866-633-5252, Ext. 3346; www.decaturbookfestival.com). More than 100 authors participated in the 2006 event, which drew 50,000 visitors. The festival opens with a Children's Parade led by book characters such as the Cat in the Hat. Other activities include a lecture by a keynote author, author readings, music, a cooking stage, antiquarian books, booksellers, food and beverages, and more. All activities free except food, beverage, and book purchases.

September: **East Atlanta Strut** (www.eastatlantastrut.org). The neighborhood closes off the streets for a parade, after which there is an artists' market, children's activities, 5K run, live bands, food, and fun—all for the benefit of several charities. Fee for some activities.

October: **Great Decatur Beer Tasting Festival** (404-371-9583; 404-371-8262). Hundreds of local and international beers are available on the square during the city's most popular event. The festival also includes music and food. The entry fee includes a special tasting glass; proceeds benefit community charities. Children and pets are not allowed. $30.

Oakhurst Arts and Music Festival (404-371-9583; 404-371-8262). The annual Decatur event features an artists' market with more than 75 vendors, as well as children's art activities, literary arts, and musical performances. Free.

November: **Wine Tasting Festival** (404-371-9583; 404-371-8262). More than 100 wines from around the world are available for tasting at this event on the square in Decatur. The entry fee, which benefits the Decatur Arts Alliance, includes a commemorative wine glass. $30.

December: **Decatur Holiday Candlelight Tour of Homes** (404-371-9583; 404-371-8262). Tour a variety of Decatur's beautiful homes and other important points of interest decked out in their holiday best. Tickets are $15 in advance, $20 at the door.

Holiday Bonfire and Marshmallow Roast (404-371-9583; 404-371-8262). A huge bonfire is built on the square in Decatur and community members are invited to roast marshmallows. A special musical performance is presented by the Seed & Feed Marching Abominable. Free.

5

Stone Mountain Village, Stone Mountain Park, and Beyond

About 300 million years ago, intense heat and pressure forced molten rock upward. When it cooled, the molten lava coalesced into compact, granite crystals—an unusual mixture of feldspar, mica, and quartz—but it still remained 2 miles beneath the earth's surface. Over the next 200 million years, erosion not only exposed the mass, but left 583 acres uncovered at a height of 825 feet above the surface: what we know today as Stone Mountain.

Pieces of soapstone bowls and dishes found at the base of the mountain indicate that Native Americans lived around the mountain as long as 5,000 years ago. During the Spanish explorations and early colonial times, Creek Indians lived, farmed, and traded around the mountain. The first written record of the mountain was in 1597, when it was described by the Native Americans to the explorers as "very high, shining when the sun sets like fire." Long used as a landmark and gathering place by Native Americans and early American settlers, the massive mountain is now the centerpiece of Stone Mountain Park.

It was in 1909 that C. Helen Plane had the idea of memorializing the Confederacy with a carving on the mountain. In 1916 the face of the mountain was deeded to the Stone Mountain Confederate Monumental Association by Samuel H. Venable, who it turns out was a member and Imperial Wizard of the Ku Klux Klan. The Confederate Memorial Carving, which was once envisioned by Gutzon Borghum (who later created Mount Rushmore) to have included seven principal figures surrounded by thousands, was begun in 1923, but was blasted off the mountain in 1928. The state of Georgia bought the mountain in 1958; work on the carving resumed in 1964 and was finally completed in 1970. The current much-scaled-back carving depicts Confederate President Jefferson Davis and Generals Robert E. Lee and Thomas "Stonewall" Jackson astride their steeds. The area of the figures measures 90 by 190 feet and is surrounded by a 3-acre carved surface that is 400 feet above the ground and recessed 42 feet into the mountain. With the carving as a centerpiece, the ever-evolving park has developed.

Nearby Stone Mountain Village is the gateway to Stone Mountain Park, located just outside its West Gate. Established in 1845 and first named New Gibraltar, the village that is now Stone Mountain was a railroad community, center for Georgia's granite industry and a popular tourist spot from the earliest days.

Stone Mountain Depot was a strategic point for Union General William Tecumseh Sherman's troops in their campaign to destroy Atlanta during the Civil War. The Union

STONE MOUNTAIN VILLAGE, STONE MOUNTAIN & BEYOND

army destroyed much of the village and 5 miles of rail line, although buildings used as hospitals were spared. The village's historic commercial buildings once housed hotels, banks, and general stores that served the granite workers. Today, these same structures house 50 specialty stores, antiques shops, galleries, and restaurants—many with outdoor seating. Streets surrounding the commercial area are filled with antebellum mansions, Victorian-era cottages, and bungalows. Two of these operate as bed and breakfasts. In all, the National Register of Historic Places Historic District (1830–1940) contains 275 properties and two historic cemeteries.

In addition to Stone Mountain Park and Stone Mountain Village, there are several small surrounding towns that have one or more attractions that make them worthwhile to visit when you're in the area (see *Villages/Neighborhoods*).

GUIDANCE

Many of the individual entries in this chapter are located within Stone Mountain Park. In order to reduce repetitive information, we list the park's contact information only here and refer to *Guidance* when describing individual attractions. To learn more about the park, contact **Stone Mountain Park** (770-498-5690; 1-800-317-2006; www.stonemountain park.com), US 78, Stone Mountain. Park open 6 AM–midnight daily, most attractions 10–8 in summer (shorter hours in winter). It's a good idea to check the Web site for hours pertinent to your visit. The entrance fee to the park is an $8 parking fee (bicyclists and pedestrians may enter free). There are several pass options; otherwise, other attractions are priced separately, so you may pay for only what you use. It is economical, however, to purchase the One-Day All Attractions Pass: ages 12 and older $24, seniors and military $20, ages 3–11 $19; $15 after 4 PM. Ride the Ducks is an additional $12 or $8.55 as an add-on to the All Attractions Pass. Because some attractions are open seasonally, a Limited Attractions Pass, which costs $20 for those age 12 and older, $17 for ages 3–11, is sometimes available. If there's a possibility that you'll visit the park more than once in a year, you can purchase an all-year parking pass for $35 and an all-year attractions pass for $45. For information about Stone Mountain Village, contact the **Stone Mountain Village Visitors Center** (770-879-4971; www.stonemountainvillage.com), 891 Main Street, Stone Mountain 30083. Open 10–4 Monday through Saturday. Main Street Stone Mountain Self-Guided Walking Tours leave from here (see *Guided Tours*).

To learn more about Conyers, contact the **Conyers Convention and Visitors Bureau/Conyers Welcome Center** (770-929-4270; 770-602-2606; 1-800-CONYERS; www.conyersga.com), 901 Railroad Street, Conyers 30012. Open 8–5 weekdays.

When planning a trip to the Lawrenceville area, contact the **Lawrenceville Tourism and Trade Association** (678-226-2639; www.visitlawrenceville.com), 162 East Crogan Street, Suite K, Lawrenceville 30046. Open 8–5 weekdays.

Getting There

By air: See What's Where. Taking a taxi from the airport to many destinations in this chapter would be expensive. The following shuttle companies serve the cities and counties described in this chapter from the airport: **Airport Metro Shuttle** (404-766-6666), **Airport Perimeter Connection** (404-761-0260), **Daytime Transportation** (770-939-2337), and **Gwinnett Airport Shuttle** (770-638-0666).

By bus: **Greyhound Bus Lines** serves downtown Atlanta, which means there is no convenient way to get to any of the towns described in this chapter with the exception of Conyers. There is a Greyhound station there at Crusade Dominion Church (770-785-9520), 1605 GA 138 Southeast. The station is open 8–10 AM and 12:45–3 PM weekdays.

By car: See What's Where. Stone Mountain is easily accessed via US 78 from I-285, the bypass ringing the city. Lawrenceville is easily accessed via US 29 from I-285. Conyers is accessed from I-20.

By train: See What's Where.

Getting Around

If you have not rented a car at the airport, all the major rental companies are available in the area described in this chapter (consult car company Web sites before you leave on your trip or consult the Yellow Pages or your concierge once you arrive). Numerous taxi companies are available as well. Again, consult the Yellow Pages or your concierge when you arrive.

For mass transit in DeKalb County, use **MARTA** (see What's Where). The transit authority operates trains from the Atlanta airport's South Terminal near baggage claim with service to the downtown Atlanta Five Points station, where passengers can transfer to the East/West line. A rider destined for one of the towns described in this chapter would need to ride to the end of the line at Avondale and then transfer to connecting bus service. Rail stations within DeKalb County are at Avondale, Candler Park, Decatur, Dunwoody, and Indian Creek. Your own car or a rental is a much better option.

For mass transit transportation in Gwinnett County, use **Gwinnett County Transit** (see What's Where). The other counties described in this chapter do not have mass transit. A car is the only viable means of transportation in these areas.

Parking

In Stone Mountain Village there is free parking on the street as well as in lots in the center of town and at the visitor's center. Stone Mountain Park has numerous parking lots, which you have paid for in your entrance fee. Conyers offers free on-street parking, as does Lawrenceville.

Public Restrooms

In addition to the normal places that public restrooms are found, facilities are available in the pavilion adjacent to the Lewis-Vaughn Botanical Gardens (see *Nature Preserves and Parks—Gardens*) in downtown Conyers. There are also restroom facilities along the Stone Mountain Trail (see *Hiking*).

Medical Emergency

In a life-threatening situation, call 911. For immediate care in Stone Mountain, Lawrenceville, and the surrounding area, help is available at **DeKalb Medical Center at Hillandale** (404-501-8000), 2801 DeKalb Medical Parkway, Lithonia. For immediate care in Conyers and nearby towns, help is available at the **Rockdale Medical Center** (770-918-3000), 1412 Milstead Avenue Northeast, Conyers.

Villages/Neighborhoods

Conyers is the little railroad village that grew and grew. The town was founded in 1854 along the railroad line between Atlanta and Augusta. Originally called Conyers Station, the town was named for W. D. Conyers, a banker and director of the railroad who was responsible for acquiring the land that made the railroad possible. In more recent times, the community has produced country singer Brenda Lee, Academy Award–winning actress Holly Hunter, former Federal Budget Director James Miller, and three Pulitzer Prize winners. Recently revitalized, Conyers's Olde Towne district features numerous historic sites as well as a botanical garden, pavilion, streetscapes, shops, and restaurants. In addition, Conyers is home to the Georgia International Horse Park and the Haralson Mill Covered Bridge (see separate entries), as well as the annual **Conyers Cherry Blossom Festival** (see *Special Events*).

Lawrenceville, the county seat of Gwinnett County, was incorporated in 1821, making it the second-oldest city in the metropolitan Atlanta area. It was named for Captain James Lawrence, commander of the frigate *Chesapeake* during the War of 1812. Although mortally wounded, Captain Lawrence uttered the now-famous battle cry, "Don't give up the ship!" Historic downtown Lawrenceville is a mix of restaurants and antiques, craft, and retail shops. Holiday events add to its charm, and various seasonal events take place on the lawns of the Gwinnett Historical Courthouse.

Lilburn was founded in 1890 by the Seaboard Airline Railway. Previously it had been known as McDaniel, but it was renamed for the general superintendent of the railroad,

Lilburn Trigg Myers. A devastating fire and economic hard times in the 1920s almost spelled the end for Lilburn, but the Old Town district was revitalized, and shops and restaurants now occupy the historic buildings. **Lilburn Daze Arts and Crafts Festival,** held the second Saturday in October, features more than 400 artisans and vendors (see *Special Events*).

To See

Covered Bridges

✧ ❦ **Haralson Mill Covered Bridge** (770-929-4001; 770-785-5919), Haralson Mill Road off Bethel Road, Conyers. Open daily. Visitors can actually drive through this covered bridge, the first of its kind built in Georgia since the late 1890s. The bridge, which is located at the northeast corner of Randy Poynter Lake at Black Shoals Park, replicates covered bridge design similar to the 1820s Town Lattice Truss design patented by Connecticut architect Ithiel Town. The bridge consists of three 50-foot spans with solid concrete piers and spill-through abutments with granite veneer. The superstructure was built with Georgia wood products and labor. Surrounding the bridge is the Haralson Mill Historic District, which includes the Haralson Mill House, a general store, the old mill site, and a blacksmith shop. Free.

For Families

✧ ❦ **Georgia International Horse Park** (770-860-4190; 1-800-860-4224; www.georgia horsepark.com), 1996 Centennial Olympic Parkway, Conyers. Office open 8–5 weekdays. Call or consult the Web site for a schedule of events and ticket prices. Best known as the scene of the equestrian and mountain biking competitions and the final two events of the modern pentathlon at the 1996 Centennial Olympic Summer Games, the sprawling 1,400-acre multiuse park today hosts events such as rodeos, barrel-racing competitions, dressage shows, fairs, concerts, and festivals almost every day of the year. The park also boasts RV camping, the Hawthorn Suites Golf Resort Hotel, Cherokee Run Golf Club, Big Haynes Creek Nature Center, shopping for equestrian merchandise, and trails for mountain biking and horseback riding (see separate entries).

✧ ❦ ♿ **Stone Mountain Park.** See *Guidance*. Call for event schedules and fees, as they vary seasonally. The 3,300-acre park, Georgia's most-visited attraction, has something for everyone in the way of outdoor entertainment and recreation. Central to the park is the world's largest exposed mass of granite as well as the world's largest bas-relief sculpture, which depicts Civil War Confederate heroes Davis, Lee, and Jackson. Surrounding the 825-foot mountain are 3,300 acres of forests, lakes, and parkland. Attractions include an antebellum plantation, Confederate Hall Historical and Environmental Center, the 1870s town of Crossroads, a 4-D theater, The Great Barn, Ride the Ducks sight-seeing tour, a riverboat cruise, mountaintop skyride, scenic train ride, and the Lasershow Spectacular—a 40-minute extravaganza of colorful lasers, surround sound, and fantastic fireworks (see separate entries). Recreation includes canoeing, fishing, golf, hiking, miniature golf, nature trails, a water slide complex, and tennis (see separate entries). Festivals and other special events occur year-round (see *Special Events*). Accommodations are offered at two hotels and a campground (see *Lodging*), and numerous restaurants please any palate (see *Where to Eat*).

The Texas II *makes an appearance at Stone Mountain.*

🐾 🍃 **Yellow River Game Ranch** (770-972-6643; 1-877-972-6643; www.yellowrivergame ranch.com), 4525 US 78, Lilburn. Open 9:30–6 daily (last tickets sold at 5). The most acclaimed resident of this 25-acre game preserve is General Beauregard Lee, Georgia's weather prognosticator. The famous groundhog comes out of his Tara-like abode on February 2 and foretells the weather in the South just as Punxsutawney Phil does in the North, though General Lee correctly predicts an early spring much more often than his Northern cousin does. Visitors to the ranch can see 600 animals, including black bears, bobcats, one of the largest herds of buffalo east of the Mississippi, cougars, coyotes, foxes, goats, mountain lions, pigs, raccoons, sheep and lambs, white-tailed deer, and other animals indigenous to Georgia. The small-fry (and even jaded adults) are won over by feeding the deer with specially purchased feed. Spring and summer, when there are babies, are favorite months to visit. Adults $8, children $7.

Guided Tours

🍃 **Main Street Stone Mountain Village Self-Guided Walking Tours** (770-465-6776 weekdays; 770-879-4971 weekends; www.mainstreetstonemountain.com), 891 Main Street, Stone Mountain Village. Tours of the historic downtown start at the Stone Mountain Village Visitors Center (the Red Caboose). The one-hour self-guided tour highlights the development of the village between the 1830s and the 1940s. Free.

Historic Homes and Sites

🐾 🍃 **Gwinnett Historic Courthouse/Georgia Veterans Council War Museum** (770-882-5450), 185 West Crogan Street, Lawrenceville. Open 10–4 weekdays, 10–2 Saturday. One of the county's oldest buildings, this 1885 National Register of Historic Places courthouse is an architectural treasure. A room on the first floor has been set aside for the museum, which covers America's wars from the Civil War to the present with wartime artifacts, memorabilia, and uniforms from all branches of the service.

✍ ☙ **Milstead 104 *Dinky* Steam Locomotive,** Green Street, Conyers. A reminder of the days when cotton was king, the *Dinky,* a 1905 Rogers steam locomotive, hauled cotton bales from the main line to the textile mill in the nearby town of Milstead until 1961. One of only three of this design in the world, the *Dinky* is honored with a spot in downtown's Center Point Park on the side rails across from the depot.

✍ ☙ **Monastery of the Holy Spirit** (770-483-8705; www.trappist.net), 2625 US 212 Southwest, Conyers. Open 4 AM–9 PM daily. The Abbey Church is open daily at 7 AM for morning prayer and Mass, 5:30 PM for evening prayer, and 8:15 PM for night prayer. The monastery was begun in 1944 by a group of Cistercian monks. Sitting amid 2,000 acres of woodlands and lakes, the retreat offers peaceful walking paths and picnic areas. Sights to see at the monastery include the beautiful **Abbey Church, Welcome Center, Retreat House, Bonsai Greenhouse,** and **Gift Shop.** In the gift shop you'll find Monk's Fruitcake, Monk's Fudge, Monk's Coffee from a sister monastery in Venezuela, and religious items that include fine art reproductions, statuary, 14-karat and sterling silver jewelry, CDs, cassettes, software, videos, and a wide variety of books. In the greenhouse, bonsai novices and enthusiasts can purchase pottery from among the largest selection of Tokoname pots in the United States. Korean mica pots, books, videos, accessories, tools, wire, and fertilizer are also available. Free.

✍ ☙ **Stone Mountain Park Antebellum Plantation.** The plantation, created by moving 19 buildings constructed between 1790 and 1845 to this site, portrays the lifestyle of 19th-century Georgians. In addition to the graceful manor house, other typical plantation outbuildings include a cook house, slave cabins, overseer's house, and a blacksmith shop. Period gardens and a farmyard with live animals lend an air of authenticity. Several special events occur on the grounds throughout the year. Adults $9, children $3 in addition to the $8 parking fee, or included in the One-Day All Attractions Pass (see *Guidance—Stone Mountain Park*).

Museums

✍ ☙ **Antique Car and Treasure Museum at Stone Mountain Park.** This nostalgic exhibit showcases 40 vintage cars, including some that are one-of-a-kind, like Buck Rogers's Rocket Car. The short-lived Tucker displayed here was briefly built in Georgia. Other modes of transportation aren't neglected—there are 60 vintage bikes and 15 pedal cars. Music is represented by five band organs, 22 player pianos, and 30 jukeboxes. There are also carousel animals, period clothing, and thousands of other 20th-century artifacts. Adults $9, children $3 in addition to the $8 parking fee, or included in the One-Day All Attractions Pass (see *Guidance—Stone Mountain Park*).

✍ ☙ ⅙ **Confederate Hall Historical and Environmental Education Center at Stone Mountain Park.** At Confederate Hall, which is located at the base of the park's walk-up trail, visitors can learn about the geological and ecological history of Stone Mountain, explore interactive exhibits, and view "The Battle for Georgia—A History of the Civil War in Georgia," a 25-minute documentary narrated by Hal Holbrook. Exhibits include a life-size cave with a video about the origin of the mountain. A huge 3-D map enhanced by lights and sound effects depicts the Battle of Atlanta and the March to the Sea. Other exhibits include Civil War uniforms and artifacts. Free after paying the park's $8 parking fee.

✐ ✿ ♿ **Discovering Stone Mountain Museum at Memorial Hall in Stone Mountain Park.** This museum tells the story behind Stone Mountain and displays true-to-scale elements from the world's largest relief carving. In addition, exhibits tell about local history and the Civil War. The museum also hosts various traveling exhibits. Adults $9, children $3 in addition to $8 parking fee, or included in the One-Day All Attractions Pass (see *Guidance—Stone Mountain Park*).

✐ ✿ ♿ **Georgia Music Hall of Fame at Discover Mills** (866-GA-MILLS; www.discover mills.com), 5900 Sugarloaf Parkway, Lawrenceville. Open 10–9 Monday through Saturday, noon–5 Sunday. The state's official music museum, Macon's Georgia Music Hall of Fame, has a museum annex at the Discover Mills shopping mall. Situated in the Georgia Walk of Fame section of the mall, the annex features rotating exhibits, photographs, and videos. Free.

✐ ✿ **Gwinnett History Museum** (770-822-5178; www.co.gwinnett.ga.us), 455 South Perry Street Northwest, Lawrenceville. Open 10–4 Monday through Thursday, noon–5 Saturday; closed Friday and Sunday. The museum is located in the historic 1838 Lawrenceville Female Seminary, which is listed on the National Register of Historic Places. The permanent collection of Gwinnett County–related memorabilia includes historic and folk artifacts, furniture, farm tools and equipment, clothing, textiles, looming equipment, turn-of-the-20th-century kitchen items, artifacts from a one-room school, and objects related to Georgia bluegrass music. A special exhibit is devoted to Civil War satirist Bill Arp. $1 donation.

Natural Beauty Spots

See **Stone Mountain Park** under *For Families*.

To Do

Ballooning

Adventures Aloft Hot-Air Ballooning (770-356-0764; www.ballooningamerica.com), 2029 Crystal Lake Drive, Lawrenceville. Call for flight schedules and prices. Flights are conducted at dawn and about two hours after sunset, weather permitting. Each trip is custom-designed and includes refreshments and a traditional toast. Call for rates.

Bicycling

✐ ✿ **PATH Foundation**, (404-875-PATH; www.pathfoundation.org). See *Guidance*. The **Stone Mountain Trail**, a portion of the Atlanta-DeKalb Trail System, will extend 18 miles from Georgia Tech (see the Midtown chapter) to Stone Mountain Park. At this time, 12 miles have been completed from Clarkston (see the Decatur chapter) to the park. To learn more about the trail system, including the location of nearby places to park, hospitals, restrooms, water, MARTA access, and other points of interest, purchase the "Atlanta-DeKalb Greenway Trail Guide" from the PATH Foundation for $5.50 plus Georgia tax.

Bird-Watching

See **Stone Mountain Park** under *For Families* and **Davidson-Arabia Mountain Nature Preserve and Heritage Area** under *Nature Preserves and Parks*.

Boat Excursions
✧ ❦ **Ride the Ducks Adventure at Stone Mountain Park.** The amphibious sight-seeing experience makes a 40-minute tour of the park by road and then plunges into Stone Mountain Lake. These unusual vehicles are modeled after the World War II amphibious DUKWS. $12 per person in addition to $8 parking fee, or $8.55 if added to the One-Day All Attractions Pass (see *Guidance—Stone Mountain Park*).

✧ ❦ **Riverboat Cruise at Stone Mountain Park.** Relax on the first or second decks of the *Scarlett O'Hara* as the replica paddle wheeler plies the waters of 363-acre Stone Mountain Lake, cruising by natural areas, the beach and water park, the golf course, the campground, the gristmill, the Evergreen Hotel and Conference Center, and the carillon. If the time is right, passengers will hear a concert ringing out from the carillon bell tower, which was donated to the park after being exhibited at the 1964 World's Fair. Adults $9, children $7 in addition to $8 parking fee, or included in the One-Day All Attractions Pass (see *Guidance—Stone Mountain Park*).

Boating
✧ ❦ **Rental Boats at Stone Mountain Park.** See *Guidance.* The country store at the campground offers rowboats for use on Stone Mountain Lake. Pedal boats can be borrowed at the steamboat landing where the *Scarlett O'Hara* docks; their use is included in the One-Day All Attractions Pass. Note: In addition to rental boats and pedal boats, private boats are allowed on the lake, although no private boats are permitted after 11 AM on weekends and on holidays between May 1 and September 30. Private boats are limited to 10-hp motors. $8 parking fee; boat rental $20 per day.

Disc Golf
✧ ❦ **Redan Park** (404-371-2631), 1745 Phillips Road, Lithonia. Open daylight hours daily. The disc golf course has 18 stations, and the park has ball fields, trails, a tennis court, playground, and picnic area. Free.

Fishing
The Yellow, Alcovy, and South rivers as well as Lake Varner and Turner Lake offer endless opportunities for fishing year-round. Factory Shoals Park and Charlie Elliot Wildlife Center (see separate entries under *Nature Preserves and Parks*) are also open to the public for fishing. A Georgia fishing license is mandatory (ID required). If accessed through a Georgia State Park, there is a $3 parking fee; otherwise free.

For Families

In Lawrenceville
✧ ♿ **Medieval Times Dinner and Tournament** (770-225-0230; 1-888-WE-JOUST; www.medievaltimes.com), 5900 Sugarloaf Parkway Northwest, Discover Mills, Lawrenceville. Shows at 7:30 Wednesday through Friday, 5 and 7:30 Saturday, 5 Sunday (doors open one hour prior to the show). Reservations suggested. Step back in time for the splendor, pageantry, and romance of the 11th century. Thrill to the sounds of thundering hooves and the shattering of lances in the trials of mythic warriors and ancient kings. Guests are greeted by King Alfonzo and Princess Esperanza and presented with a colored crown that indicates the knight for whom they should cheer. A four-course feast includes

garlic bread, hot vegetable soup, roasted chicken, spare rib, baked potato, pastry of the castle, and two rounds of beverages—all served medieval-style with no silverware. The exciting tournament features an authentic display of classic equestrian skills astride 22 Andalusian stallions as well as the flag toss, ring pierce, javelin throw, joust, and a battle with swords, axes, maces, and bolas. After the championship has been awarded, guests gather in the Knight Club for music and dancing as well as to meet the knights and royalty, get autographs, and take pictures. No smoking. Wheelchair accessible on the top level. General admission with seating first-come, first served: adults $48, children 12 and younger $36; Royalty Package $10 additional per person for preferred seating, knights cheering banner, commemorative program, and souvenir DVD; Noble Guest and Loyalty programs also available with additional benefits.

At Stone Mountain Park
🖋️ 🍴 ♿ **Crossroads at Stone Mountain Park.** Some stores may stay open until the laser show begins at 9:30. Visitors travel back in time to an 1870s Southern village at this park-within-a-park. Here they'll meet fascinating costumed characters and skilled craftspeople who demonstrate such old-time skills as glassblowing, candle making, candy and ice-cream making, blacksmithing, and grinding meal at the gristmill. Crossroads includes Tall Tales of the South, Georgia's only 4-D theater; the Treehouse Challenge; and the Great Barn, Atlanta's largest indoor play experience (see separate entries). Admission to the village is free after paying the general parking fee of $8. Some of the individual attractions have a fee or are included in the One-Day All Attractions Pass (see *Guidance—Stone Mountain Park*).

🖋️ 🍴 **The Great Barn at Stone Mountain Park.** The gigantic barnlike structure features a series of interactive games geared toward teaching children about harvesttime. Adults $9, children $3 in addition to $8 parking fee, or included in the One-Day All Attractions Pass (see *Guidance—Stone Mountain Park*).

🖋️ 🍴 ♿ **Skyride at Stone Mountain Park.** Cable cars whisk visitors from the base of the mountain to the summit and afford a close-up view of the carving. Many visitors choose to take the Skyride to the summit and then walk down. Adults $5 one-way or $9 round-trip, children $3 in addition to $8 parking fee, or included in the One-Day All Attractions Pass (see *Guidance—Stone Mountain Park*).

🖋️ 🍴 **Treehouse Challenge at Stone Mountain Park.** The three-story outdoor attraction is actually two dueling tree houses where teams pit the boys against the girls in more than a dozen interactive games. Participants use their hands and wits to master games and try to accumulate the most points. Adults $9, children $3 in addition to $8 parking fee, or included in the One-Day All Attractions Pass (see *Guidance—Stone Mountain Park*).

Those who take the skyride can get a close-up view of Stone Mountain's famous carving

Frights

🌀 **Tour of Southern Ghosts** (770-469-1105; www.artstation.org), 5384 Manor Drive, Stone Mountain Village. For more than 20 years this project of the ART Station (see *Theater*) has been held on the lantern-lit grounds of Stone Mountain Park's Antebellum Plantation. The annual event is held after dark on several evenings during the Halloween season (check the Web site for the exact dates). The tour consists of hair-raising tales told by costumed storytellers as they guide groups from place to place around the plantation. Stories are a little scary, often humorous, but never so frightening that they're inappropriate for young audiences. The box office at the plantation opens at 6:45 and tours begin at 7; tours depart every 10 minutes. Advance reservations and tickets are strongly recommended to avoid standing in long lines and perhaps being disappointed. Adults $12, children $5 in addition to $8 parking fee; tickets purchased in advance are $10 for adults.

Golf

Cherokee Run Golf Club (770-785-7904; www.cherokeerun.com), located at the Georgia International Horse Park, 1595 Centennial Olympic Parkway, Conyers. Open 7–7 daily year-round. Designed by Arnold Palmer and Ed Seay, the semiprivate 18-hole, 7,000-yard, par 72 course features wetlands, tree-lined fairways, undulating greens, numerous water hazards, and granite outcroppings. It really plays like a mountain course. The facility also features a clubhouse with a pro shop and a full-service restaurant. $39–59; senior, PGA Passbook, replay, and twilight rates available.

Stone Mountain Golf Club at Stone Mountain Park (770-465-3278; www.stonemountain golf.com), Stonewall Jackson Drive, Stone Mountain Park. Open 7 to dusk daily. Managed by Marriott Golf, the club offers 36 championship holes on the Lakemont and Stonemont

Courses. In fact, the Stonemont Course has been named one of the Top 25 public courses in the country by *Golf Digest*. A driving range, putting green, practice facilities, pro shop, PGA instruction, clubhouse with locker rooms, and The Commons Restaurant are also available. All rates include taxes and use of a cart. Rates are dependent on day of the week and season, but range from $30–65.

Hiking

✐ ❧ **Arabia Mountain Trails** (770-484-3060; www.arabiaalliance.org), 3787 Klondike Road, Lithonia. Open daylight hours daily. The Davidson-Arabia Mountain Nature Preserve features a paved path for walking, biking, and skating, as well as several unpaved marked and unmarked paths varying in length from a half-mile to a mile. These paths can be combined for a longer hike of 3.3 miles or more. The most challenging trail is the Bradley Peak Trail, which leads to the top of the 954-foot mountain. (For more information about the site, see *Nature Preserves and Parks*.) Free.

✐ ❧ **Nature Trails of Stone Mountain Park.** See *Guidance*. The park is filled with 10 miles of easy-to-difficult trails that encourage visitors to enjoy the beauty of the seasons, the natural wonders, and the striking vistas while they get their exercise. Of the 3,200 acres encompassed by the park, more than two-thirds have been designated as a Natural District. The most difficult trail is the steep 1.3-mile **Walk-Up Trail** to the 1,683-feet-above-sea-level summit. The suggestion of these authors is that, unless you're in very good shape, you take the Skyride ($5 one-way for adults, $3 for children) to the top and walk down. If you walk up and ride down, there is no transportation back to the parking lot from which you started, so you'll have an additional walk back to your car. Along the Walk-Up Trail visitors will see the 2-inch-tall red stonecrop, golden ragweed, and the Confederate yellow daisy. Fifteen other genera of rare plants grow on the mountain outcrops and along the trails. The short loop **Nature Trail** is associated with the Nature Garden, where visitors can wander among native plants, flowering shrubs, and mountain streams. The lengthy 7-mile-plus **Cherokee Trail** with two connecting trails wraps all the way around the mountain. The site of the 1996 Centennial Olympic Summer Games archery and cycling events, the area encompasses the **Songbird Habitat and Trail,** a 1-mile trail with a variety of plant life and food for a wide array of birds. Along many of these paths, visitors can see vegetation that is native to Georgia and/or Stone Mountain Park. Parking fee $8; trail use free.

Horseback Riding

✐ ❧ **Georgia International Horse Park** (770-860-4190; 1-800-860-4224; www.georgia horsepark.com), 1996 Centennial Olympic Parkway, Conyers. Open daylight to dusk daily, but closed occasionally for special events, so check the Web site before visiting. For those who can BYOH (Bring Your Own Horse), the park features more than 15 miles of horse trails which offer scenic views of the former Olympic Endurance Course as they wind through wooded areas, across open pastureland, and past streams. Varied trail lengths and links between trails allow riders to choose their own route and tailor their own ride. A large map of the trails is posted at each check-in shelter and there are individual take-away maps as well. $5 per day trail fee collected on the honor system or $35 for an annual pass.

Miniature Golf

✐ ❧ **Stone Mountain Park Mini Golf.** The course offers 36 holes of entertainment for the whole family. Adults $9, children $3 in addition to $8 parking fee, or included in the One-Day All Attractions Pass (see *Guidance—Stone Mountain Park*).

Mountain Biking

✍ 🏕 **Georgia International Horse Park** (770-860-4190; 1-800-860-4224; www.georgia horsepark.com), 1996 Centennial Olympic Parkway, Conyers. Open daylight to dusk daily, but closed occasionally for special events, so check the Web site before visiting. The park offers 8 miles of riding and 1,032 feet of elevation change on the world's first-ever Olympic mountain biking course. A large map of the trails is posted at each check-in shelter and there are individual take-away maps as well. $5 per day trail fee collected on the honor system or $35 for an annual pass.

Swimming

Most hotels described here have swimming pools. Amazingly enough, swimming is not allowed in Stone Mountain Lake at Stone Mountain Park except in a small beach area at the water slide complex, but the two hotels in the park have pools.

Train Excursion

✍ 🏕 **Scenic Railroad and Live Show/Stone Mountain Park** (770-498-5690; www.stonemountainpark.com), US 78 East, Stone Mountain Park. Open 10–8 daily in summer, shorter hours the remainder of the year. Riding aboard vintage rail cars, passengers enjoy the 5-mile, 30-minute journey around the base of the mountain. Board the train at the Memorial Railroad Depot or the Whistle Stop Depot. The train is pulled by a 1940's diesel engine. In the summer, costumed actors perform a short show when the

A summer train ride around the base of Stone Mountain includes a short show by costumed actors.

train passes the replica of a pioneer town. Adults $9, children $3 in addition to $8 parking fee, or included in the One-Day All Attractions Pass (see *To See—For Families—Stone Mountain Park*).

GREEN SPACE

Gardens

🌿 🍂 ♿ **Lewis-Vaughn Botanical Gardens** (contact the Conyers Welcome Center, 770-602-2606; www.conyersga.com), bounded by Main, Center, Commercial, and Railroad streets. The garden features plants native to the Georgia Piedmont region. Within the garden is the old water tower, an unusual stone structure built in the early 1900s to supply water to downtown businesses. Today the tower feeds the stream and goldfish pond in the gardens. Adjacent to the site is a pavilion where many special events are held, including the Olde Town Summer Series. Through the marvels of modern technology, the pavilion is transformed into an ice-skating rink during the winter months. Free.

🌿 🍂 ♿ **Vines Botanical Gardens and Manor House** (770-466-7532; www.vinesbotanical gardens.com), 3500 Oak Grove Road, Loganville. Open 10–5 Monday through Saturday. Originally the private estate of Charles "Boe" and Myrna Adams, the 25-acre estate (valued at $6 million) was donated to Gwinnett County for use as a public park. The gardens are named in honor of Myrna's father, Odie O. Vines, an avid gardener. The property is now under the operation of the Vines Botanical Gardens Foundation. Beautifully landscaped gardens embrace curving pathways, a picturesque lake, fountains, and imported sculptures. Several niche gardens include the Whimsical Garden, Asian Garden, Southscape Garden, Pappy's Garden, White Garden, and Rose Garden. A light lunch of burgers, quiche, and sandwiches is served 11–2 weekdays. The Grand Manor House is available for weddings and special events. Adults $6, children and seniors $4.

Nature Preserves and Parks

🌿 🍂 **Big Haynes Creek Nature Center** (770-860-4190; 1-800-860-4224; www.georgia horsepark.com), 1996 Centennial Olympic Parkway, Conyers. Within the Georgia International Horse Park, 173 acres are designated as a preserve dedicated to the preservation and the study of native plants and wildlife. The preserve features 1.4 miles of riding trails and 2.6 miles of walking trails. A learning center, native plant garden, wildflower meadow, endangered species protection area, outdoor teaching theaters, elevated boardwalk, canoe trails, picnic areas, and primitive camping areas are planned, so stay tuned. Free, except for $5 trail use fee for horseback riding.

🌿 🍂 **Black Shoals Park** (770-761-1611; www.rockdalecounty.org), 3001 Black Shoals Road, Conyers. Open daily, 7–9 summer, 7–6 winter; boats must be off the water a half-hour before closing. No gasoline motors of any kind are permitted. Fishing, boating, and canoeing are the primary activities in this park surrounding Randy Poynter Lake, a 650-acre reservoir, but hiking and picnicking are popular as well. The Georgia Department of Natural Resources stocks the lake with largemouth bass, assorted bream, and catfish. The park features a boat ramp, fishing pier, and a picnic pavilion. $5 per person, $5 per boat or canoe.

✒ 🐾 **Davidson-Arabia Mountain Nature Preserve and Heritage Area** (770-484-3060; www.arabiaalliance.org), 3787 Klondike Road, Lithonia. Open daylight hours daily. The 2,000🐾-acre park, which is anchored by a 450 million-year-old mountain (100 million years older than Stone Mountain), is DeKalb County's most significant green space area and provides opportunities for wildlife recreation and environmental education. In addition to Stone Mountain, this mountain is one of three major granite outcrops in the Piedmont region. The park contains streams, waterfalls, a nature center, 3.3 miles of trails, unlimited self-guided hiking areas, a fishing lake, and historic quarry ruins. It is home to deer, tadpoles and frogs, bobcats, coyotes, chuck-will's-widows, lichen grasshoppers, and birds such as the pileated woodpecker and hawks. Plants, with two federally protected species among them, include mosses, lichens, sunnybells, sparkleberry, yellow daisies, fringe trees, and the Georgia oak. The Diamorpha is an unusual red plant found here. Programs are offered on topics such as endangered and specialized species, biodiversity, and rock outcrop ecosystems. Special events include Little Explorers of Arabia, a program for children 5 and younger, weekend group walks, and the Atlanta Audubon bird walk. Free.

✒ 🐾 **Hidden Acres Nature Preserve** (770-484-2642, www.arabiaalliance.com), 1032 Stephenson Road, Stone Mountain. Open daylight hours daily. The 66-acre park, which is under the management of the Davidson-Arabia Mountain Nature Preserve and Heritage Area, contains beautiful woodlands, wetland and stream areas, a historic barn, an open field, and a lake. Free.

✒ 🐾 **Yellow River Park** (770-932-4460), 3232 Juhan Road, Stone Mountain. The Yellow River flows through the park's 565 acres of forest and woodland. Trails are maintained for hiking, mountain biking, and horseback riding. Free.

LODGING

Bed and Breakfasts

In Stone Mountain Village
♿ **Silver Hill Manor** (770-879-6800; 1-888-381-5808; www.silverhillmanor.com), 1037 Main Street, Stone Mountain. This stately, white-columned property, constructed in 1996, does an excellent job replicating an antebellum mansion. Of the six beautifully decorated guest accommodations, several have Jacuzzis. The adjacent cottage features two bedrooms and baths as well as a kitchen and a secluded deck, making it ideal for a family or two couples traveling together. Other amenities include a Jacuzzi overlooking the B&B's swimming pool. A full breakfast is included in the nightly rate. No pets; no smoking. Wheelchair accessible. $120–140 for guest rooms, $200 for the cottage.

Village Inn Bed and Breakfast (770-469-3459; 1-800-214-8385; www.village innbb.com), 992 Ridge Avenue, Stone Mountain. Located in a stately home built in the 1820s as a roadside inn, the structure is the oldest building in Stone Mountain Village. It served as a Confederate hospital during the Civil War and was therefore spared during Sherman's March to the Sea. The inn has six guest rooms, including Scarlett's Room and Rhett's Room, each with two-person whirlpool tubs. Some also boast a gas fireplace and/or a veranda. The Ballroom Suite has a sitting area with a daybed and trundle bed, a refrigerator, microwave, shower, and whirlpool therapy tub. Full breakfast, which might consist of specialties such as raspberry-stuffed French toast with country sausage or egg casserole with cheese grits, bacon, fruit, and biscuits, is included in the nightly rate.

Complimentary snacks and beverages are also provided. Smoking outdoors only. Limited wheelchair accessibility. $139–179.

Campgrounds

In Conyers
◊ **Georgia International Horse Park** (770-860-4190; 1-800-860-4224; www.georgia horsepark.com), 1996 Centennial Olympic Parkway, Conyers. Office open 8–5 weekdays. Reservations required. The full-service park near the stable and Walker Arena complexes offers 50 sites with full water, electric, and sewer hookups. The park also offers shower facilities. The campsite price is set by the promoter of each show; check the Web site for promoter contact information.

At Stone Mountain Park
◊ ❀ **Stone Mountain Park Campground** (770-498-5710; 1-800-385-9807; www.stonemountainpark.com), US 78 East, Stone Mountain Park. Situated on 363-acre Stone Mountain Lake, the campground features 441 full- and partial-hookup sites as well as overflow and primitive sites. Amenities include a campground store from which you can rent rowboats (see *Boating*), laundry facilities, a playground, snack bar, swimming pool, and volleyball court. A 72-hour cancellation policy is strictly observed. Prices are based on up to two adults and four children as well as whether you want a full or partial hookup or a primitive site, location, and time of year. $23–50 in addition to one-time $8 parking fee to enter the park; $2 per additional person.

Inns and Hotels
Almost all familiar hotel chains are located near any of these towns and attractions, so consult the Internet for suggestions. Visitors also can consult the other metropolitan Atlanta chapters for suggestions of nearby one-of-a-kind lodgings.

Resorts

In Conyers
◊ ❀ ♿ **Hawthorn Suites Golf Resort** (770-761-9155; 1-800-527-1133; www.georgia horsepark.com; www.hawthorn.com), 1659 Centennial Olympic Parkway. Overlooking the seventh hole of the Cherokee Run Golf Club, the hotel boasts 77 one-, two-, and three-bedroom suites as well as an outdoor heated pool and whirlpool, bar, guest laundry facilities, fitness center, convenience and gift shop, business center, and valet laundry services. A hot breakfast is served daily and there's a manager's reception Monday through Thursday evening. Pets allowed. Smoking and nonsmoking rooms available. Some rooms are wheelchair accessible. $99–$139.

At Stone Mountain Park
◊ ♿ **Marriott Evergreen Conference Resort and Spa** (770-879-9900; 1-888-670-2250; www.evergreenresort.com), 4021 Lakeview Drive. In addition to 336 upscale guest rooms and 21 luxurious suites, most with lake or pool views, this AAA four-diamond resort features the Waterside Restaurant, The Commons Restaurant, Stonewall's Lounge sports bar, Starbucks Coffee, a health club, tennis courts, indoor and outdoor pools, and a spa. Stonewall's features 17 televisions, darts, pool, and shuffleboard. For information about spa services between 9 and 6, call (770) 465-3297. Nonsmoking and wheelchair-accessible rooms available. $169–199.
◊ ♿ **Marriott Stone Mountain Inn** (770-469-3311; www.stonemountainpark.com), 1058 Robert E. Lee Drive. This classic Southern inn provided the first accommodations in the park. It features the Mountainview Restaurant and 92 guest rooms, each with a refrigerator and sleeper sofa. Smoking and nonsmoking rooms available. Wheelchair accessible. $165–195.

WHERE TO EAT

Dining Out

At Stone Mountain Park

🍷 ♿ **Waterside Restaurant** (770-465-3240) at the Marriott Evergreen Conference Resort (770-498-5690; www.stonemountainpark.com), 4021 Lakeview Drive. Open 6:30–10:30 for breakfast, 11:30–2:30 for lunch and Sunday brunch, 5–10 for dinner. Elegant dining at one of DeKalb County's only white-linen restaurants features continental cuisine. Diners enjoy daily buffets and a great view of Stone Mountain Lake. One of the most popular offerings is the seafood buffet on Friday evening. No smoking. Wheelchair accessible. $12.95 for breakfast, $16.95 for lunch, $22.95 for Friday seafood buffet, $23.95 for dinner, $25.95 for Sunday brunch.

In Stone Mountain Village

♿ **The Sycamore Grill** (770-465-6789; www.thesycamoregrill.com), 5329 Mimosa Drive. Open 11:30–2:30 Tuesday through Saturday; 5:30–9 Tuesday through Thursday, 5:30–9:30 Friday and Saturday, 11–3 Sunday for champagne brunch. Named for the 150-year-old sycamore tree that shades its verandas, the restaurant is located in a circa 1836 hotel, one of the oldest structures in Stone Mountain Village. A stone stake in the front yard marks the spot from which Andrew Johnson, the first mayor of New Gibraltar (as the town was then called), laid out the town 33 yards to each side of the building. Later it was enlarged to 1,000 yards in all directions. The two-story, white clapboard house was built in the style of the basic Charleston town house. It served as the first post office of Stone Mountain and as a hospital during the Civil War, the reason it was spared during General Sherman's March to the Sea.

Exquisite dinner entrées might include fresh lump blue crab cakes, Georgia mountain trout, Angus filet mignon, pork chops, New Zealand rack of lamb, duck breast, and other delicacies. Luncheon items include soups and salads as well as entrées such as trout, salmon, steak, chicken, and pork chops. Smoking on the patio only. Wheelchair accessible downstairs and on the patio. $8–15 for lunch, $18–38 for dinner.

Worth Driving For

🍷 🐾 ♿ **Blue Willow Inn** (770-464-2131; 1-800-552-8813, www.bluewillowinn.com), 294 North Cherokee Road/GA 11, Social Circle. Open Tuesday through Sunday for lunch and dinner. Reservations recommended. Located in an imposing turn-of-the-20th-century Greek Revival mansion, the elegantly furnished restaurant earned the *Southern Living* Readers' Choice Award as Best Small Town Restaurant from 1996 until the award was retired in 2000. In 2001 and 2002, the restaurant earned the magazine's Best Country Cooking award, and it's also been recognized by *USA Today*, *Gourmet* magazine, and the Food Network. The restaurant serves a traditional, upscale Southern buffet that includes four to five meats, nine to 10 vegetables, soups, salads, biscuits, muffins, corn bread, and desserts, all served with "The Champagne of the South"—sweet tea. No smoking. Wheelchair accessible downstairs only. $10.95–13.95 for lunch, $13.95–21.95 for dinner, $15.95 for Sunday brunch.

Eating Out

In Conyers

🍷 🐾 ♿ **Seven Gables Restaurant** (770-922-8824; www.sevengables restaurant.com), 1897 GA 20 Southeast. Open 5:30–10 daily. This fine-dining restaurant, a longtime favorite, is famous for its Dover sole, filet mignon béarnaise, rack of lamb, New York strip Madagascar, scrumptious desserts, homemade breads and pasta, and fresh dressings, soups, sauces, and Italian sausage. The restaurant features a full bar and an extensive wine list. Live entertainment is offered weekends in the bar beginning at 9. Smoking in the bar only; no one younger than 18 is allowed in the bar. Wheelchair accessible. $12.95–18.95.

At Stone Mountain Park
🗡🦽♿ **Mountain View Restaurant at the Stone Mountain Inn** (770-469-3311; www.stonemountainpark.com), 1058 Robert E. Lee Drive, Stone Mountain Park. Open 7–10:30, 11:30–2, and 5–8 daily. The restaurant serves Southern-style buffets for breakfast, lunch, and dinner. Prominent on the menu are Southern favorites such as barbecue, fried chicken, Brunswick stew, okra, greens, and sweet

tea. No smoking. Wheelchair accessible. $8–15.95.

Snacks
🗡🦽♿ **Starbucks Café** at Marriott Evergreen Conference Resort (770-879-9900), 40121 Lakeview Drive, Stone Mountain. Open 6 AM–9 PM daily. Espresso, cappuccino, frozen beverages, fresh pastries, and sandwiches are among the offerings.

Coffeehouses
🗡🦽♿ **Continental Coffee and Sweets** (770-413-2045), 941-A Main Street, Stone Mountain. Open 6:30–6:30 weekdays, 9–6:30 Saturday, 11:30–5:30 Sunday. In addition to 50 whole-bean gourmet coffees, diners can enjoy specialty drinks, smoothies, fraps, shakes, gelato, fresh-baked pastries and baklava, and then shop for chocolates, wine, Georgia products, accessorized picnic baskets, or holiday gift baskets. No smoking. Wheelchair accessible. $1.45–4.

ENTERTAINMENT

Dance
Gwinnett Ballet Theatre (770-978-0188; www.gwinnettballet.org), office: 2204 Fountain Square, Snellville. Call for a schedule of performances and ticket prices, which generally range from $14–27. Gwinnett Ballet Theatre, which has been performing for more than 23 years, is one of only two nonprofit ballet schools in metro Atlanta. The company presents several annual productions at the Gwinnett Performing Arts Center, including a spring production and the ever-popular "Nutcracker" in December.

Music
Gwinnett Philharmonic (770-418-1115; gwinnettphilharmonic.org), mailing address: P.O. Box 30010, Norcross 30010. Call for a schedule of events and ticket prices, which range from $21–28. The orchestra, which recently celebrated its 10th season, performs at the Gwinnett Performing Arts Center.

Oudoor Drama
🗡🦽♿ **Lasershow Spectacular at Stone Mountain Park.** See *Guidance*. The seasonal laser show begins at 9:30 nightly in the summer, earlier on Saturdays in September and October. The world's largest laser show features a flame cannon and laser canopy, as well as surround sound and special effects choreographed to popular and patriotic music. The event culminates with a spectacular fireworks display. Free with the park's $8 parking fee.

Theater

✍ ✿ ♿ **ART Station** (770-469-1105; www.artstation.org), 5384 Manor Drive, Stone Mountain Village. Gallery open 10–5 Tuesday through Friday, 10–3 Saturday; also open Mondays during the summer. Call for schedule of theatrical performances. The contemporary, multidisciplinary arts center, which is housed in a historic trolley barn and power station that was active until 1948, stages six or seven productions each year. Galleries feature the works of prominent artists and the center sponsors numerous other events for adults and children. Gallery free, but donations are appreciated; prices for theatrical events vary.

✍ ♿ **Tall Tales of the South 4-D Theater.** See *Guidance*. Shows every 20 to 30 minutes. All your senses are engaged during the 3-D movie and 4-D special effects. Note: If you and/or someone in your party don't want to get slightly wet or are afraid of snakes, critters, or things that go bump in the night, this attraction may not be for you. You can't buy individual tickets to the shows; they are included in the One-Day All Attractions Pass (see *Guidance—Stone Mountain Park*).

SELECTIVE SHOPPING

Crafts

Southern Artistry (770-469-9456; www.southernartistrygallery.com), 965 Main Street, Stone Mountain Village. Open 10–5 Monday through Saturday, 1–5 Sunday. The shop sells quality stoneware pottery, glass, wood, jewelry, kaleidoscopes, weaving, and other traditional crafts created by artisans from Georgia and the Southeast. Dogwood motifs adorn many items.

Gifts

Stone Mountain General Store (770-469-9331), 935 Main Street, Stone Mountain Village. Open 10–6 Monday through Saturday, noon–5 Sunday. Advertising that it carries everything from "wind chimes to washboards," the emporium stocks household and kitchen gadgets, accessories, bird-feeding supplies, sun catchers, garden accessories, pottery, candles, and souvenirs.

Outlet Malls

Discover Mills (678-847-5000; 1-866-GAMILLS; www.discovermills.com), 5900 Sugarloaf Parkway, Lawrenceville. Open 10–9 Monday through Saturday, noon–6 Sunday. Among the 200 retailers are Last Call from Neiman Marcus, Off-Fifth (Saks Fifth Avenue), Kenneth Cole New York Outlet, and Pro Shops Outdoor World. The mall also has several restaurants and offers periodic entertainment such as talent shows, concerts, and other family-oriented events.

Special Stores

Bass Pro Shops Outdoor World (770-847-5500; www.bassproshops.com), 5900 Sugarloaf Parkway, Suite 129, Lawrenceville. Open 9–10 Monday through Saturday, 11–7 Sunday. The outdoor enthusiast will find everything here, from fly-fishing and saltwater fishing equipment to hunting needs, camping accessories, apparel, and footwear.

SPECIAL EVENTS

March: **Conyers Cherry Blossom Festival** (770-602-2606; www.conyerscherry
blossom.org). The festival, which is held at the Georgia International Horse Park in
Conyers, features 400 food and arts and crafts booths. Other activities include music,
dance, games, croquet and golf tournaments, a queen's pageant, hot dog– and cherry
pie–eating contests, and an Easter egg hunt. Free; $5 one-day parking pass or $8 for
both days.

March through October: **Moonlight and Music Concert Series** (678-226-2639). Concerts
are held at 8 PM on the fourth Friday of each month on the lawn of the Gwinnett Historic
Courthouse in Lawrenceville. Different styles of music are featured each time: blues, jazz,
rock, folk, country, bluegrass, Motown, swing, and others. Tables for six can be rented and
concert-goers are invited to bring a picnic to enjoy. Prizes are awarded for outstanding
table decorations. Free.

Easter: **Annual Easter Sunrise Service at Stone Mountain Park** (770-498-5690;
www.stonemountainpark.com). The park gates and the Skyride open at 4 AM, and the services begin at approximately 6:15 AM. The park sponsors two simultaneous, nondenominational Easter sunrise services—one on top of the mountain and one on the Memorial Lawn
at the base of the mountain. Parking is available at the Skyride or Crossroads lots (and
Confederate Hall lot for those walking to the top). Skyride costs $5 for adults, $3 for children who wish to ride to the top of the mountain or back one-way, $9 round-trip.
Otherwise, visitors can attend the Memorial Lawn service at no additional charge, and visitors who hike to the mountaintop service can do so for free in addition to the $8 parking
fee.

April: **Art on the Historic Courthouse Square** (678-226-2639). Jazz plays as festival-goers
stroll among artists demonstrating and selling paintings, prints, pottery, jewelry, and photography on the square in Lawrenceville. Food vendors serve throughout the day. Free.

May: **Memorial Weekend "Task Force Patriot Salute to the Troops"** (770-498-5690;
www.stonemountainpark.com). Activities at Stone Mountain Park include Air Force air-
craft flyovers, Silver Wings parachute team jumps, military exhibits and vendor booths,
band performances, a worship service, a special laser show, fireworks, and more. Free
with park's $8 parking fee; discounts for One-Day All Attractions Passes available to
active-duty, retired, and reserve military and their families with military ID; discounts for
One-Day All Attractions Passes for the general public available at specific stores (check the
park Web site).

July: **Old Town Beach Party** (770-602-2606). An end-of-summer blast (school starts in
early August in Georgia) on sand-covered Railroad Street in Conyers features food, drinks,
and entertainment. Free.

September: **Yellow Daisy Festival** (770-498-5690; www.stonemountainpark.com). The festival runs Thursday through Sunday at Stone Mountain Park; call for exact dates. In its 38th
year in 2007, the festival is considered to be America's top arts and crafts show. More than

450 artists and crafters from 38 states and two foreign countries display and sell their works. The festival also includes daily live entertainment, children's corner activities, clogging and craft demonstrations, and fabulous food. Festival admission is free with park's $8 parking fee.

October: **Autumn Artfest on the Courthouse Square** (678-226-2639). Quality handmade arts and crafts are sold at this two-day festival on the square in Lawrenceville. Free.

Highland Games (770-498-5690; www.stonemountainpark.com). In its 35th year in 2007, this event provides two days of Scottish fun at Stone Mountain Park, including Highland athletic events; Highland dancing; competitions in piping, drumming, and harping; kirking of the tartans; clan challenge events; parade of the tartans; Border collie herding demonstrations; clan and tartan information tents; many colorful Scottish shops; and traditional Scottish food. All events occur rain or shine. Admission charged in addition to the park's $8 parking fee.

Lilburn Daze Arts Festival (770-921-2210; www.lilburnbusinessassociation.com). The popular festival in Lilburn City Park features 200 food and arts and crafts vendors; children's activities such as rock climbing, pony rides, and a moonwalk; entertainment; community organizations and services exhibits; and a health fair. Free shuttle service is provided from outlying parking areas. Free admission and parking.

Pumpkin Festival (770-498-5690; www.stonemountainpark.com/pumpkin). This annual fall family festival at Stone Mountain Park actually runs Friday through Sunday throughout October. It features the *Pumpkin Express* train ride and scarecrow show, Camp Highland Outpost with a ropes course and rock wall, Stone Mountain hayrides and sing-alongs, Pumpkinpalooza competitions, pie-eating contests, arts and crafts, pumpkin bowling, the South's largest talking pumpkin tree, Kroger Pumpkin Patch, and more. Festival admission is free with park's $8 parking fee.

November: **Indian Festival** (770-498-5690; www.stonemountainpark.com). Visitors to Stone Mountain Park explore a living history tepee village with tepee styles dating back to the late 1800s. Native American demonstrations include fire starting, brain tanning, hide scraping, flint napping, pottery making, and primitive tool technology. The festival also draws Native American dancers from across the country. Visitors watch high-energy dance and drum competitions while warriors on horseback do battle in the Shield Dance. Also enjoy the Okefenokee Joe Music and Reptile Show. $9 for all ages in addition to the park's $8 parking fee.

November/December: **Stone Mountain Christmas** (770-498-5690; www.stonemountain park.com). Yes, you can have a white Christmas in Atlanta. The festival at Stone Mountain Park features a nightly "snowfall" and fireworks, the Christmas story told aboard the train, lively holiday shows, millions of lights in the Crossroads village, appearances by the Snow Angel and Santa Claus, and more. Adults $16, children 3–11 and seniors $13 in addition to park's $8 parking fee. A combo ticket is available which permits admission to the Christmas activities as well as to Coca-Cola Snow Mountain (see *To Do—For Families*).

The Chattahoochee River is responsible for much of the area's water-based fun.

6

ATLANTA'S PLAYGROUND: LAKE LANIER

Known as Atlanta's Playground, Lake Sidney Lanier, named after the beloved Georgia poet, provides innumerable opportunities for water sports and other outdoor activities. The 38,000-acre U.S. Army Corps of Engineers lake with 540 miles of shoreline, 60 recreational areas, and seven commercial marinas was formed by the damming of the Chattahoochee River in 1957. Today the lake is a major source of power and drinking water in Georgia as well as a recreational playground. One of the lake's most popular attractions is Lake Lanier Islands—a resort area with a hotel, a water park, golf, horseback riding, tennis, and other recreational activities.

Not all recreational activities are centered on the lake, however. Nearby are such attractions as the Atlanta Falcons Headquarters and Training Camp, two auto raceways, and a major winery/resort. Land-based recreational pursuits such as hiking and bird-watching can be pursued at Fort Yargo State Park and Thompson Mills Forest.

In small nearby towns such as Braselton, Buford, Duluth, Flowery Branch, and Winder, you'll find an arts colony, a major railroad museum with a large quantity of antique rolling stock, Mayfield Dairy Farms, several small museums, as well as interesting shops and restaurants. Among many appealing annual events are the Chateau Elan Summer Concert Series, Chateau Elan Vineyard Fest, and the Magical Nights of Lights at Lake Lanier Islands.

A sophisticated city such as Atlanta is blessed to have a playground so nearby where residents and visitors can get away from the hustle and bustle of the city.

GUIDANCE

For general information about all the areas covered in this chapter, stop by the **Northeast Georgia Welcome Center** (770-965-9272; www.greaterhallchamber.com), 4700 Lanier Parkway, Flowery Branch 30542. Open 9–5 daily. For other information about the entire area, contact the **Northeast Georgia Mountains Travel Association** (404-231-1820; www.georgiamountains.org).

To find out more about Braselton, Buford, or Duluth, contact the **Gwinnett Convention and Visitors Bureau** (770-623-3600; 1-888-GWINNETT; www.gcvb.org), 6500 Sugarloaf Parkway, Suite 200, Duluth 30097.

For information about Flowery Branch, contact the **City of Flowery Branch** (770-967-6371; www.flowerybranchga.org), 5517 Main Street, Flowery Branch 30542.

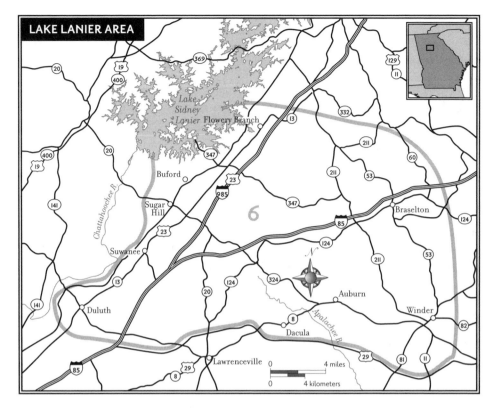

For information about Winder, contact the **Barrow County Chamber of Commerce** (770-867-9444; www.barrowchamber.com), 6 Porter Street, Winder 30680. Open 8:30–5 weekdays.

Getting There

By air: See What's Where. Car rentals are available at the airport and off-site. Several shuttle companies offer service to outlying locations. **Airport Metro Limousine** (404-766-6666), **Gwinnett Classic Limousine** (770-931-7777), and **Silver Leaf Limousine** (404-767-6657) offer shuttle service to Duluth. **Airport Metro Limousine** (404-766-6666) offers shuttle service to Flowery Branch. **Airport Metro Limousine** (404-766-6666) and **Embassy Limousine** (770-868-1448) offer service to Winder.

By bus: See What's Where.

By car: The cities and towns described in this chapter are easily accessible from either I-85 or I-985.

By train: The nearest **Amtrak** station is in Gainesville, which is outside the scope of this chapter. Contact Amtrak at (1-800-USA-RAIL; www.amtrak.com), 116 Industrial Boulevard, Gainesville. Amtrak's daily *Crescent* makes one of its three stops in Georgia in Gainesville.

Getting Around

In Buford and Duluth, taxi and limousine service is available from **A Best Gwinnett Taxi and Limo** (770-931-3313) and many others. **Gwinnett Transit** (see What's Where) operates a bus route to the Mall of Georgia in Buford. Otherwise there is no mass transit in the area described in this chapter.

Parking
There is a $7 day-use fee to get onto Lake Lanier Islands, and state parks also have a $3 parking/day-use fee.

Medical Emergency
In life-threatening situations, call 911. In Duluth, care is available at **Joan Glancey Memorial Hospital** (770-497-4800), 3215 McClure Bridge Road. Around Lake Lanier, help is available at **Northeast Georgia Medical Center** (770-535-3553), 743 Spring Street Northeast, Gainesville, or **Northside Hospital Forsyth** (770-844-3200; www.northside.com), 1200 Northside-Forsyth Drive, Cumming. In Winder, help is available at **Columbia Barrow Medical Center** (770-867-3400), 316 North Broad Street.

Villages/Neighborhoods
Barrow County has one of the most interesting histories among Georgia's 159 counties. It was formed from parts of Gwinnett, Walton, and Jackson counties, which came together in the center of a town called Jug Tavern (now Winder), a site marked today across Athens Street from the courthouse. This situation created a great deal of legal and governmental confusion.

> **The Legend of Barrow County**
> Two local men became involved in a fight. One man, standing in Gwinnett County, shot the other, who was standing in Jackson County. When the victim fell, he landed in Walton County, creating a nightmare of jurisdictional questions.

Unsuccessful attempts to create a county to alleviate this situation began as early as 1835, but it wasn't until 1914 that the governor finally signed a constitutional amendment creating Barrow County. The county was the home of Richard Russell, who was Georgia's youngest governor and also served 38 years in the U.S. Senate. Up until the 1940s, Barrow County was known as "The Work Clothing Capital of the World." Today the county is the home of the corporate headquarters of Duckhead Apparel.

Gwinnett County was founded in 1818 and opened to settlers. There was only one road at that time: Peachtree Road, an offshoot of an old Indian trail along the Chattahoochee River. It was surveyed and constructed during the War of 1812 to connect Fort Daniel with the fort at Standing Peachtree, and is still the most famous road in Georgia.

Braselton, which lies in Barrow, Gwinnett, Hall, and Jackson counties, was first settled by the Braselton family in 1876. An early Braselton family home now serves as the town hall. Braselton got national attention some years ago when native daughter Kim Basinger bought the entire town with plans to transform it into a major tourist attraction. Although those plans fizzled and Basinger later sold the town, it still has some major attractions, Mayfield Dairy and the Chateau Elan Winery and Resort being the primary ones.

Buford, named for Algernon Sidney Buford, president of the Atlanta and Richmond Air-Line Railroad, was a stop on the railroad line from Atlanta to Charlotte, North Carolina. From the very beginning, Buford was a bustling business and education center. For many years it was the largest city in Gwinnett County. In fact, a news article in 1902 referred to Buford as the New York of Gwinnett. Leather tanning and the production of

First Female Mayor in Georgia

Alice H. Strickland (1861–1947) promised to clean up the city and rid it of "demon rum." She allowed her home to be used as a hospital where children could have their tonsils removed, and she led conservation movements to protect forest lands. Her donation of an acre of land for a community forest was the first in the area.

shoes, saddles, harnesses, horse collars, and other leather products earned Buford the title "The Leather City." Today the downtown area features antique and collectible shops, restaurants, and the Tannery Row Artist Colony (see *Cultural Site*).

Duluth, in Gwinnett County, was originally called Howell Crossing or Howell's Cross Roads. The settlement evolved into a major railroad artery when a railway was built from Howell Crossing to Duluth, Minnesota. At that time, it was decided to rename the Georgia town Duluth as well. It was incorporated in 1876, and Duluth is now the second-largest city in the county. Duluth is the home of an outstanding railroad museum.

Flowery Branch was established in 1874 along the Georgia Air-Line Railroad route from Atlanta to Charlotte, North Carolina. The railroad was the primary artery for people, mail, and goods. Farmers from all over northeast Georgia brought their cotton to Flowery Branch to be ginned, sold, and shipped. Later businesses included furniture, leather goods, and buggies. Sadly, the last scheduled train stop in Flowery Branch was in 1957. From then until the late 1960s, a passenger could flag the train to stop, but now no trains stop in Flowery Branch. The town boasts lake activities, a museum, and the Falcons football team's training facility.

Winder, the county seat of Barrow County, was originally called The Jug, so named because a piece of land had been cleared in the shape of a jug. Later it was called Jug Tavern. When it was incorporated in 1893, the name was changed again to Winder in honor of notable railroad builder and manager John H. Winder. Today Winder boasts a history museum, a racing facility, and a state park.

TO SEE

Cultural Site
🌶 ⚘ **Historic Buford/Tannery Row Artist Colony** (770-904-0572; www.tanneryrowartist colony.com), 554 West Main Street, Building C, Buford. Historic Buford stretches along Main Street from South Lee Street to Hill Street. The revitalized area boasts antiques shops, art galleries, and monthly arts events. The Tannery Row Artist Colony/Tannery Row Cultural Arts Center has a 13-acre facility in the former Bona Allen Shoe and Horse Collar Factory. Today, 17 artists—including glassblowers, jewelers, painters, photographers, sculptors, and woodcarvers—open their studios from 11–9 Saturday to allow the public to view works in progress. From 6–9 on the third Saturday of each month there is a festive opening reception for a show of an outstanding artist's work. Studios are open that evening as well. Each month's show can be viewed from 1–5 Tuesday through Sunday in the Tannery Row Gallery.

For Families

✈ 🐾 ♿ **Mayfield Dairy Farms** (706-654-9180; 1-888-298-0396; www.mayfielddairy.com), 1160 Broadway Avenue, Braselton. Visitor's center open 9–5 weekdays, 9–2 Saturday; call for plant tour times. Begin at the visitor's center to see a short film, and then tour the milk-processing facility and finish up with an ice-cream treat. Free.

Museums

✈ 🐾 ♿ **Barrow County Museum** (770-307-1183; www.cityofwinder.com/museum.asp), 94 East Athens Street, Winder. Open 1–4 weekdays, Saturday only for special events. The museum is housed in the old Barrow County Jail, which was built in 1915. Listed on the National Register of Historic Places, the building features the original "hanging tower" and three original jail cells. Hundreds of artifacts have been donated by local citizens and placed into exhibits relating to native son Senator Richard B. Russell, county history, and nearby Fort Yargo, which was created as a defense against hostile Indians. Exhibits include two bales of cotton grown and ginned in Barrow County, uniforms from World Wars I and II, an old barber chair, a corn sheller, and an extensive collection of early tools. Free.

✈ 🐾 **Flowery Branch Historic Train Depot Museum and Historic Caboose** (call city hall 770-967-6371; www.flowerybranchga.org/historic_train_depot.html), Railroad Avenue and Main Street, Flowery Branch. Open 10–2 Saturday. The depot, which is more than 100 years old, is typical of the Craftsman style. The museum houses exhibits, pictures, and documents relating to the city's history. The 1914 caboose is open to visitors as well, and a simulated railroad track walkway lies along the Railroad Avenue side of the building. Free.

✈ 🐾 **Southeastern Railway Museum** (770-476-2013; www.southeasternrailwaymuseum.org), 3595 Peachtree Road, Duluth. Open April through December, 10–5 Thursday through Saturday, noon–5 Sunday of the last full weekend of the month, except Christmas and New Year's Days; January through March, 10–4 Saturday only. The 30-acre museum site, which is operated by volunteers of the Atlanta Chapter of the National Railway Historical Society and designated as Georgia's Official Transportation History Museum, is dedicated to preserving, restoring, and operating historically significant railway equipment. The chapter owns and displays 90 pieces of rolling stock, including wooden freight cars, vintage steam locomotives, Pullman cars, and maintenance-of-way equipment. Among the vintage cars are a 1910 steam locomotive; the 1911 private car *Superb,* which was used by President Warren G. Harding in 1923; and the *Washington Club,* a 1930 first-class lounge car. Also on display are a 1940s railway post office, a rare World War II troop kitchen, and a 1922 Pullman coach. The restored locomotive #97 pulls the caboose train on the third Saturday of each month. At other times vintage diesels do the work. The museum sponsors several special events throughout the year, including Romance on the Rails, a Valentine's Day dinner; Caboose Day in March; and Railfair in September. Adults $8, seniors $6, children 2–12 $4.

Spectator Sports

✈ ♿ **The Equestrian Center at Chateau Elan** (770-307-3786; www.chateauelan atlanta.com/amenities/equestrian.html), 100 Rue Charlemagne, Braselton. With a covered and lighted arena, four large and lighted all-weather rings, two smaller warm-up areas, 196 permanent stalls, and room for 200 temporary stalls, the center is the site of many equestrian and canine shows throughout the year. Concerts, arts and crafts shows, and car shows also are held here. Call for a schedule of events and prices.

Winery Tour

Chateau Elan Winery and Resort (678-425-0900, Ext. 6354; 1-800-233-WINE; www.chateauelanatlanta.com), 100 Rue Charlemagne, Braselton. Open 10–9 daily; self-guided winery tours 10–6 weekdays, guided tours 10–6 weekends. Housed in a replica of a 16th-century-style French chateau that rises out of a northeast Georgia field filled with grapevines, this full-production winery is the largest producer of premium wines in Georgia. Approximately 75 acres are planted with Vinifera French and French-American hybrid grapes from which 22 wines are produced. Tours of the operation are offered and culminate with a tasting of several varieties. The winery building also houses two restaurants, an art gallery, and a French-style wine market. Self-guided tours free; $5 for tasting four wines. Guided tours $5 including tasting four wines.

Naturally, after touring the winery and tasting some of its vintages, visitors may wish to take some home. **The Wine Market** (Ext. 6354), located just adjacent to the tasting room, sells Chateau Elan wines and a wide variety of wine-related gifts as well as Irish crystal, quality golf shirts with the Chateau logo, custom-made gift baskets, and other unique gift items. The **Art Gallery** showcases artists working in a wide variety of media. Located in the Chateau Elan Winery, it is open 10–9 daily. **Le Clos** (see *Dining Out*), the winery's fine dining restaurant, is open 6–9 Thursday through Sunday. The informal, bistro-style **Café Elan** (Ext. 6317) has the cozy ambience of a provincial European restaurant where chefs create Mediterranean dishes. It's open 11–4 and 5–10 daily; reservations recommended.

To Do

Auto Racing

✦ ♿ **Lanier National Speedway** (770-967-8600; www.lanierspeedway.com), One Raceway Drive, Braselton. Georgia's only NASCAR asphalt short track, the facility features stock-car races every Saturday evening, March through October. The speedway hosts 2,500 spectators and 100 competitors every week, with racers coming from all over the Southeast to compete for NASCAR points. Major events include the Southern All Star Stock Car Racing Series, USCS Outlaw Thunder Sprint Cars, ASA Racing Series, and NASCAR All Pro 200. The track offers spectators grandstand seating, track-side parking, and VIP suites. Call for a schedule of events and ticket prices.

✦ ♿ **Road Atlanta and Panoz Racing School** (770-967-6143; 1-800-849-RACE; www.roadatlanta.com), 5300 Winder Highway, Braselton. Office open 8–5 weekdays. The area's premier road-racing facility, Road Atlanta features one of the most challenging and exciting racetracks in the country. The 2.54-mile, 12-turn Grand Prix road course, which is home to the American LeMans Series and Panoz Motorsports, hosts internationally acclaimed events such as the Suzuki AMA Superbikes Showdown, SCCA Trans Am Southern Dash, and Petit LeMans. Other attractions include professional and amateur auto and motorcycle races, Panoz Racing School, Audi Driving Experience, Audi Teen Driving Experience, Kevin Schwartz Suzuki School, and testing for professional and amateur racing teams. Limited camping is available in the infield for all races; reservations are required. Prebooked hot laps are available to the public. Call for a schedule of events and ticket prices. Parking is free for most events; there is a fee for infield parking.

Bicycling

✈ **Chateau Elan Winery and Resort**
(678-425-6095; www.chateauelan
atlanta.com), 100 Rue Charlemagne,
Braselton. Open spring through fall 9–5
Sunday and Tuesday through Thursday,
9–6 Friday and Saturday; call for winter
hours. Seven miles of trails meander
through the 3,500-acre property through
wooded areas, quiet nature paths, around
the equestrian center, past the vineyards,
along the championship golf courses, and
through the exclusive residential area.

Local trails are a bicyclist's paradise.

Bikes, many of them Mountain Comfort models, can be rented at the Stan Smith Tennis
Center. Some spa packages include complimentary use of bicycles. Bike rental $20 for two
hours for inn guests; nonresidents with their own bikes pay a $10 trail maintenance fee.

Bird-Watching

See Fort Yargo State Park under *Nature Preserves and Parks.*

Boating

✈ 🚤 ♿ **Aqualand Marina** (770-967-6811; www.flagshipmarinas.com and navigate to the
Aqualand pages), 6800 Lights Ferry Road, Flowery Branch. Open 8:30–5:30 daily. The
full-service marina, which claims to be the largest marina in the United States, offers a
fuel dock, pump-out facilities, boat docks, shower and bath facilities, and a fully stocked

Marinas around Lake Lanier are available to assist boat owners and renters alike.

store. Jet Ski and boat rentals are available. The Windsong Sailing Academy is based here, and visitors can enjoy a meal at the Dockside Grill.

Harbor Landing (770-932-7255; www.lakelanierislands.com/harbor.asp), 7000 Holiday Road, Lake Lanier Islands. Open 9–5 Sunday through Thursday, 9–6 Friday and Saturday. With more than 90 boats, Harbor Landing marina offers the largest fleet on the lake. Choose from ski or pontoon boats or a houseboat (see *Other Lodgings*). Call for rates, as they vary widely by type of boat and length of rental; the cheapest two-hour rental is $109.

✔ ⅖ **Holiday Marina on Lake Lanier** (770-945-7201; www.westrec.com/ga-holiday.html), 6900 Holiday Road, Buford. Open 8–5 daily. The full-service marina offers boat and Jet Ski rentals, and also offers bathhouses and laundry facilities. The surrounding property features rental cabins and restaurants.

✔ **Lake Lanier Lodges, Boat Rentals** (770-967-1804; 1-866-967-1804; www.lakelanier lodges.com), 6598 Lights Ferry Road, Flowery Branch. Open 9–6 daily. The facility rents pontoon boats, ski boats, and personal watercraft. The cheapest one-hour rental is $75.

Fishing
Lake Lanier is noted for its black bass, spotted, and largemouth bass. The striped bass, which is normally found in saltwater, is stocked by the Georgia Department of Natural Resources and has adapted well.

✔ **Fishing at Lake Lanier with Bill Vanderford** (770-289-1543; www.fishinglanier.com), mailing address P.O. Box 1222, Lawrenceville. With more than 35 years of fishing and guiding, Bill is known as Lanier's most knowledgeable expert. In fact, in 1993 he was inducted into the National Freshwater Fishing Hall of Fame as a Legendary Guide. He offers a variety of half- and whole-day trips on Lake Lanier and the Chattahoochee River for fishing or to observe waterfowl, wading birds. deer, and other animals. Check Bill's Web site to purchase his books on fishing as well as lures, jewelry, and cards he creates. Call for schedules, fees, and meeting places.

The fish are always biting along the Chattahoochee

✔ **Harold Nash Lake Lanier Striper and Bass Fishing Guide Service** (770-967-6582; www.lanierfishingguide.com). The guide service specializes in trophy angling for giant stripers and bass. Call for schedules, fees, and meeting places.

Larry's Lanier Guide Services (770-842-0976; 770-844-0976; www.lanier guide.com), 8850 Bay Drive, Gainesville. Services are offered to novice anglers and pros. Call for a schedule, fees, and meeting places.

Tight Line Charters (678-898-2174; www.lanierguidefishing.com). The fishing guide service specializes in striper and bass. Call for information and fees.

Flying

Lanier Flight Center (678-898-2174; www.lanierflightcenter.com), Lee Gilmer Memorial Airport, 1660 Palmour Drive, Gainesville. Sight-seeing tours by air over Lake Lanier and the north Georgia mountains are available, as are flying lessons. Call for hours and fees.

For Families

✍ 🐾 ♿ **Atlanta Falcons Headquarters and Training Facility** (770-965-3115; 1-800-241-3489; www.atlantafalcons.com), 4400 Falcons Parkway, Flowery Branch. The team practices here from late July through late August; call or check the Web site for hours. Fans can watch practices, participate in interactive games, get autographs from players, and tour the Mobile Museum. Housed in two trailer rigs, the interactive museum chronicles the team's history with videos, photos, replica lockers, and more. Special activities for children include Junior Falcons Training Camp; punt, pass, and kick competitions; and appearances by the team's mascot, Freddie Falcon. Free; off-site parking $5.

✍ 🐾 ♿ **Lake Lanier Islands** (770-945-8787; 1-800-840-5253; www.lakelanierislands.com), 7000 Holiday Road, Lake Lanier Islands. This 1,100-acre area on the southernmost shores of Lake Sidney Lanier is a not only a year-round vacation destination, but also the most heavily visited water recreation area in the country. Facilities include a luxury hotel, lake house rentals, and lakeside camping as well as two par 72 golf courses, tennis, horseback riding, boat rentals, and a beach and water park (see next entry). Entrance fee $8 per car; annual pass $38.

The beaches of Lake Lanier attract those looking for both recreation and relaxation.

✍ ♿ **Lake Lanier Islands Beach and Water Park** (770-932-7200; 1-800-840-LAKE; www.lakelanierislands.com/bwp.asp), 6950 Holiday Road, Buford. Open weekends in May, daily late May through early August, and weekends only through late September. When open daily, hours are 10–6 Sunday through Friday, 10–7 Saturday. Located right on the lake, this exciting water park has 12 thrilling water attractions, including Wild Waves, the state's largest wave pool. The small-fry enjoy Kiddie Lagoon and Wiggle Waves. The park also boasts a mile-long sandy white beach, beach volleyball, and concessions. Sometimes there are concerts by popular groups. Adults $27.99–29.99, children $17.99; discounts for online ticket purchases.

Golf

Chateau Elan Golf Courses (678-425-6050; 1-800-233-9463; www.chateauelanatlanta.com/golf), 6060 Golf Club Drive, Braselton. Open 7:30–dusk. So passionate about golf is Chateau Elan Resort that it has four courses: two public 18-hole courses, both of which are rated as among the top four courses in Georgia by the ESPN Zagat Survey; a nine-hole, par 3 executive walking course; and a private course. The **Chateau Course** is 7,030 yards, par 71, with contoured fairways, three lakes, and two streams. Water comes into play on 10 holes. The **Woodlands Course** is considered to be the most picturesque of the resort's courses. The 6,735-yard, par 72 course has numerous elevations, lakes, and tree-lined holes. The executive walking course behind the inn is the perfect venue for the golfer without a lot of time, for beginners, or for children. Holes vary in length from less than 100 yards to more than 200 yards. Amenities within the golf complex include clubhouses with restaurants and pro shops at the Chateau and Woodlands Courses. Accommodations are available in two- or three-bedroom golf villas in addition to the inn or the spa. The practice facility, which has one of the highest ratings in the state, is home to the **Golf Academy at Chateau Elan.** The program includes comprehensive practice facilities, highly skilled instructors, and video and computer analysis. There is a driving range, short game area, and putting green. $55–85.

Emerald Pointe Golf Club (770-945-8789; 1-800-840-5253; www.lakelanierislands.com/golf.asp), 7000 Holiday Road, Lake Lanier Islands. Open 7:10–5:30 daily. This award-winning, 18-hole, par 72 course boasts 13 holes with dazzling water views of Lake Lanier. The course features instruction, a pro shop, and the Golf Club Grille. $67 Monday through Thursday, $78 Friday through Sunday.

PineIsle Golf Course (770-945-8789; 1-800-840-5253; www.lakelanierislands.com/golf.asp), 9000 Holiday Road, Lake Lanier Islands. Open 7–dusk daily. The 18-hole, 6,596-yard, par 72 resort course was designed by Gary Player and has numerous holes with lake views. The facility features rentals, lessons, a driving range, putting green, pro shop, and a clubhouse with a restaurant. $42–70 weekdays, $49–84 weekends; tee times and lessons should be booked in advance.

Horseback Riding

Lake Lanier Islands Equestrian Center (770-932-7200; 1-800-840-5253; www.lakelanierislands.com, click on "Equestrian Center"), 7000 Holiday Road, Lake Lanier Islands. Open 10–6 daily; reservations recommended. Saddle up on one of the island's gentle horses for a scenic guided trail ride through the woods and along the lakeshore. Pony rides are available for children 6 and younger. Individual and group Western or English lessons are also available. $35 for a 45-minute scenic trail ride, $15 for a 30-minute pony ride, $25 for a private half-hour lesson, $40 for a private hour lesson, $30 an hour for a semiprivate lesson.

Miniature Golf

✐ ❀ 占 **Fort Yargo State Park and Will-A-Way Recreation Area** (770-867-3489; 1-800-864-7275; www.gastateparks.org/info/ftyargo), GA 81, Winder. Open 7 AM–10 PM daily.

Sailing

✐ **Lanier Sailing Academy** (770-614-5724; 1-800-684-9463; www.laniersail.com), 6920 Holiday Road, Buford. Open 9–6 daily. One of the top American Sailing Association schools, the academy offers sailing classes from practical sailing to offshore passage, and also provides the largest sailboat rental fleet on Lake Lanier. Call for prices.

Spas

Great Restorations Day Spa (770-945-8787, Ext. 6902; www.lakelanierislands.com), 7000 Holiday Road, Lake Lanier Islands. Open 10–7 daily. Located at the Emerald Pointe Resort, the spa offers numerous ways to relax and fortify the mind, body, and spirit, including six types of massage and a wide array of body treatments, facials, manicures, pedicures, and hair services. $45–265.

The Spa at Chateau Elan Winery and Resort (678-425-6064; 1-800-233-WINE; www.chateauelanatlanta.com/spa), Haven Harbour Drive, Braselton. Open 9–5 weekdays; on weekends appointments can be made as early as 7 AM. Indulgences at the serene and romantic spa are guaranteed to make you feel renewed. Located beside a sparkling lake surrounded by trees, manicured green lawns, and flowering shrubs, the spa is contained within a French country-style spa inn, which also offers unique accommodations (see *Lodging*) and healthful gourmet dining for breakfast, lunch, and dinner at the sunny **Fleur-de-lis** restaurant. Spa treatments are available à la carte or may be purchased as an overnight package with accommodations at the inn. All-day or overnight spa packages include use of the steam room, sauna, whirlpool, indoor resistance pool, and fitness area, classes, a spa lunch, afternoon tea, and a tour of the winery; some overnight packages include other meals as well. Everyone getting a spa treatment is entitled to the whirlpool, sauna, fitness center, and afternoon tea. Guests at the resort who are not receiving a spa treatment can use the facilities for $25–35. The fitness room features a variety of health and fitness equipment. The spa also offers a wellness program with choices including a comprehensive fitness assessment, submaximal stress test, body composition, personal exercise prescription, personal training, and nutritional assessment. Spa services $42–$235; wellness program $25–90.

Tennis

🦢 **Stan Smith Tennis Center at Chateau Elan Winery and Resort** (678-425-6095; www.chateauelanatlanta.com/amenities/tennis.html), 100 Rue Charlemagne, Braselton. Open spring through fall, 9–6 Friday and Saturday, 9–5 Sunday and Tuesday through Thursday; call for winter hours. The center, designed by tennis legend Stan Smith, boasts three clay courts and four hard courts, all lighted for night play. Tennis packages ranging from $254 to $349 include accommodations at the inn, breakfast in the Versailles Room, a one-hour tennis lesson, two hours of court time, a half-hour use of the ball machine, and use of the spa facilities (fitness room, whirlpool, and resistance pool; spa services are extra). Court use for guests $14; a half-hour private lesson is $27.

GREEN SPACE

Beaches
See Lake Lanier Islands Beach and Water Park under *To Do—For Families.*

Lakes
Lake Lanier is a water-lover's paradise. The huge lake is 26 miles long, covers 38,000 acres, has 540 miles of shoreline, and touches five counties. It offers many water sports and other outdoor recreation. (See *Boating, Fishing, To Do—For Families, Golf, Horseback Riding, Campgrounds, Cottages and Villas,* and *Inns and Resorts.*)

Nature Preserves and Parks
✒ 🦢 ♿ **Fort Yargo State Park and Will-A-Way Recreation Area** (park 770-867-3489; 1-800-864-7275; Will-A-Way Recreation Area 770-867-6123;

Water lovers find plenty to do on the Chattahoochee River and Lake Lanier.

www.gastateparks.org/info/ftyargo), GA 81, Winder. Open 7–10 daily. Named for a 1792 log fort built by early settlers as protection against Creek and Cherokee Indians, the 1,814-acre park offers camping and cottages (see *Lodging*), the 260-acre Marbury Creek Reservoir with a swimming beach and boat rentals, 15 miles of hiking and biking trails along the lakeshore, picnicking, and mini golf (see *To Do*). Other recreational amenities include two boat ramps; seasonal canoe, fishing, and pedal boat rentals; and two tennis courts. The Will-A-Way Recreation Area was specifically designed for challenged populations, so most facilities in the park are wheelchair accessible. Parking $3.

Thompson Mills Forest (706-654-2666), New Liberty Church Road, Braselton. Open 8–4:30 weekdays; by appointment weekends. The 330-acre forest is the state arboretum of Georgia and features a granite outcropping, the Lee Creek Native Tree Trail, Pineturn Trail, and the 7-acre Evan Thompson Thornton Memorial Garden with a 30-minute self-guided walk. Free.

LODGING

Bed and Breakfasts

In Flowery Branch

Whitworth Inn (770-967-2386; www.whitworthinn.com), 6593 McEver Road. With its columns and verandas on both floors, the inn looks like a gracious Southern mansion of old, but it was actually built to serve as a bed and breakfast. Ten rooms with private baths are unpretentiously decorated. Some feature four-poster beds; one has two double beds. A full breakfast is included. No smoking. One room is wheelchair accessible. $65 single, $75 double.

Campgrounds

In Buford
🏊 🦽 **Shoal Creek Campground** (770-945-9541; 1-877-444-6777; www.recreation.gov), 6300 Shadburn Ferry Road. Open April through September. The U.S. Army Corps of Engineers campground features more than 100 sites with water and electric hookups on Lake Lanier. Amenities include hot showers, laundry facilities, a boat ramp, playground, dump station, and swimming area. $17–23; reservations must be made two days in advance; two-night minimum on weekends, three-night minimum on holidays.

At Lake Lanier Islands
🏊 🦽 **Lake Lanier Islands Campground** (770-932-7200; 1-800-840-LAKE; www.lakelanierislands.com, click on "Accommodations," then "Campgrounds"), 7000 Holiday Road. The campground offers 300 year-round sites, a fishing pier, pavilion, and camp store. Options include primitive campsites, primitive lakefront sites, RV or tent sites with water and electricity, RV sites with water, electricity, and sewer, and premier lakefront RV or tent sites with all hookups. $32.99–44.99.

In Winder
🏊 🦽 ♿ **Fort Yargo State Park and Will-A-Way Recreation Area** (770-867-3489; 1-800-864-7275; www.gastateparks.org/info/ftyargo), GA 81. The park offers 40 tent, trailer, and RV sites, seven walk-in sites, a pioneer campground ($50), and a group camp that sleeps 250. $15–24.

Cottages and Villas

In Braselton
🏊 ♿ **The Golf Villas at Chateau Elan Winery and Resort** (1-800-233-9463, Ext. 41; www.chateauelanatlanta.com/golf/villas.html), 100 Rue Charlemagne. The villas are located on the 15th fairway of the Chateau Course and within walking distance of the pro shop and Clubhouse Grille. Each villa has two or three bedrooms and baths, a large open plan, a fully equipped kitchen, and a living room with a fireplace. Golf packages include accommodations, breakfast, and two rounds of golf on the Chateau or Woodlands Courses. $312–407.

At Lake Lanier Islands
🏊 **The Lake Houses on Lanier** (770-945-8787; 1-800-768-LAKE; www.lakelanierislands.com), 7000 Holiday Road. The waterfront New England-style cottages are nestled among towering pines. Each cottage offers two bedrooms and baths, a great room with a fireplace, high-speed Internet access, a washer and dryer, and modern kitchen. Outside on the deck guests will find a gas grill and a heated spa. $349 off-season to $429 in-season.

In Winder
🏊 🦽 ♿ **Fort Yargo State Park and Will-A-Way Recreation Area** (770-867-3489; 1-800-864-7275; www.gastateparks.org/info/ftyargo), GA 81. The park features three fully equipped cottages. $90.

Inns and Resorts

In Braselton
🏊 ♿ **The Inn at Chateau Elan Winery and Resort** (678-425-0900, Ext. 41; 1-800-233-WINE; www.chateauelanatlanta.com), 100 Rue Charlemagne. The four-star, four-diamond property is truly a resort in every sense of the word, with multitudinous offerings in addition to exquisite guest accommodations. The property, located on the site of a winery (see *To See—Winery Tour*), is the flagship of Chateau Elan Hotels and Resorts, a group of luxury properties in the United States and overseas. The French

country chateau-style inn features 277 deluxe guest rooms, including 20 suites, a presidential suite, and 17 wheelchair-accessible rooms. Each guest accommodation boasts all the modern amenities along with a luxurious bath with an oversized tub and separate shower. The inn also features the **Versailles** restaurant, which serves breakfast and lunch buffets and à la carte dinners daily; **L'Auberge** lounge with large-screen televisions, championship-size pool tables, light foods, and live entertainment on Friday and Saturday evenings; a swimming pool; and a conference center. The centerpiece of the resort is the winery (see *Too See—Winery Tour*). The resort also boasts accommodations at the spa (see next entry) and in golf villas (see *Cottages and Villas*); several golf courses and a golf academy (see *Golf*); a spa (see *Spas*); several other restaurants and an Irish pub (see *Eating Out*); a beauty salon; a fitness room; walking/biking trails and bike rentals (see *Bicycling*); a tennis center (see *Tennis*); and an equestrian center (see *Spectator Sports*). No smoking. Wheelchair accessible. $15 nonrefundable deposit at time of booking; 72-hour cancellation policy. $189–259.

✦ **Spa Suites at Chateau Elan Winery and Resort** (678-425-0900, Ext. 41; 1-800-233-WINE; www.chateauelanatlanta.com/spa/spa-suites.html), 100 Rue Charlemagne. Located in a separate building from the main inn, the 14 luxurious spa suites exude style and comfort. Each is unique and has a separate mood, among them Country French, Victorian Wicker, High-Tech, Zimbabwe, Oriental, Vintage, Greek, Gatsby, Art Deco, Fox Hunt, Bacchus, the Camelot-inspired Excalibur, Western, and Celebration, which has a bright-red pedestal bathtub. No smoking. No children younger than 18. Wheelchair accessible. $199–274 without a Jacuzzi; $224–299 with a Jacuzzi.

At Lake Lanier Islands

✦ ✦ **Emerald Pointe Resort** (770-945-8787; 1-800-840-5253; www.lakelanier islands.com), 7000 Holiday Road. The centerpiece of Lake Lanier Islands is the resort hotel, which features 216 guest rooms and suites—many with lake views, high-speed Internet access, and spa services (see *Spas*). The resort has two restaurants: **Windows Restaurant**, open for a breakfast buffet daily as well as for special events such as monthly wine-tasting dinners and a summertime seafood buffet; and **Bullfrog's Bar and Grille**, a publike eatery serving lunch and dinner daily. Diners can eat inside or poolside. The resort also offers two championship 18-hole golf courses (see *Golf*), horseback riding (see *Horseback Riding*), a summertime beach and water park (see *To Do—For Families*), a fleet of rental boats (see *Boating*), tennis courts, a swimming pool, fitness center, gift shop, business center, and jogging trails. Girlfriends who travel together will enjoy the Girls' Getaway Package, which includes accommodations, massage, and breakfast. $139 in-season, $119 off-season.

Other Lodgings

At Lake Lanier Islands

✦ ✦ **Harbor Landings Houseboats** (770-932-7200; 1-800-840-LAKE; www.lake lanierislands.com, click on "Accommodations," then "Houseboats"), 7000 Holiday Road. Get away from it all with one of these luxurious, climate-controlled houseboats, which sleep 10 and include a full kitchen, bathrooms, a gas grill, waterslide from the upper deck, and a heated spa. Boats can be rented for 24 hours (subject to availability), three, four, or seven days. $649–699 for a 24-hour rental; $1,499–1,999 for a three-day weekend rental; $1,299–1,899 for a four-day weekday rental; $1,899–2,599 for a week rental. The marina also offers two luxury houseboats with all the above amenities plus home theaters, deluxe kitchens, a washer and dryer, and a rooftop bar with a refrigerator. $2,999–9,999.

WHERE TO EAT

Dining Out

In Braselton

& **Le Clos at Chateau Elan Winery and Resort** (678-425-0900, Ext. 6317; 1-800-233-WINE; www.chateauelanatlanta. com/dining/leclos-.html), 100 Rue Charlemagne. Open 6–9 Thursday through Sunday; reservations and "upscale casual" attire required. The intimate fine dining room resembles a Mediterranean courtyard. In this setting, seasonal French classic cuisine with American influence is served. Plan to make an evening of it, because the five-course prix fixe dinner typically takes up to two hours to complete. The staff will recommend two, three, or five wine pairings to accompany the meal for an additional $14.50 to $35 per person, or diners may purchase wine by the bottle. The wine tastings feature Chateau Elan's Georgia Founders Reserve wines. No smoking. No children younger than 12. Wheelchair accessible. Prix fixe $68 plus wines.

In Buford

Bona Allen Mansion (770-271-7637; www.turner-events.com), 395 East Main Street. Sunday brunch is served nine times yearly; call for a schedule. The lavish buffet features a delicious array of regional dishes. Ham, chicken, eggs, and crab are often accompanied by sides such as three-cheese grits, French toast soufflé, salads, fruits, breads, and desserts. The menu changes to take advantage of seasonal delicacies. The grand Italianate-style mansion was built in 1911 by a local magnate who

employed two-thirds of the town's population. Enjoy the 12-foot ceilings, original carved wood paneling, intricate moldings, stained glass windows, seven fireplaces, and original Italian mural. After dining, stroll through the 6 acres of gardens and manicured lawns punctuated by ancient magnolias, dogwoods, and mighty oaks. The terraced garden provides a flamboyant array of color from spring through fall. Daylilies, gladiolas, roses, spirea, verbena, butterfly bushes, and azaleas are just a few of the blooming plants. Adults $21.50, children 3–10 $11. Reservations required.

Eating Out

In Braselton

& **Paddy's Irish Pub at Chateau Elan Winery and Resort** (678-425-0900, Ext. 6074; www.chateauelanatlanta.com/dining/paddys-.html), 100 Rue Charlemagne. Open 4 PM–1 AM Monday through Thursday, noon–1 AM Friday and Saturday, noon–midnight Sunday. All the fixtures and furnishings at Paddy's are completely authentic: created in Ireland, shipped to the resort, and then reassembled. The pub serves traditional Irish food and beverages, and provides Irish music and song on Friday and Saturday evenings beginning at 8:30. Tuesday's open mic night begins at 8:30. No smoking. Wheelchair accessible. $9.95–22.95.

In Duluth

& **Park Café** (678-473-0071; www.parkcafeduluth.com), 3579 West Lawrenceville Street. Open 11–3 Monday through Saturday; 5–9 Tuesday through Thursday, 5–10 Friday and Saturday; 9–11 Saturday, 10–3 Sunday for brunch. Reservations suggested but not required. In this quaint, relaxing restaurant, diners can enjoy casual American dining with a Southern flair. Located in a 110-year-old house overlooking the town green, the eatery serves breakfast on Saturday, lunch, dinner, and brunch. There are chef specials almost every evening and wine tastings from 6:30–8:30 every Wednesday. Dinner entrées include seafood, steaks, salads, and Southern favorites. Some diners prefer the patio, which is enclosed and heated in winter. The café's market sells wine, cheese, gourmet food items, and gift baskets. No smoking. Wheelchair accessible. $2.95–8.95 for breakfast, $6.95–16.95 for brunch, $6.95–11.95 for lunch, $14.95–25.95 for dinner.

At Lake Lanier Islands
See **Windows** and **Bullfrog's Bar and Grille** at Emerald Pointe Resort under *Inns and Resorts*.

Snacks

In Duluth
✏ ✿ ♿ **The Soda Shop** (678-417-6600; www.TheSodaShopDeli.com), 3122 Hill Street. Open 10:30–6 Monday through Thursday, 10:30–9 Friday and Saturday, noon–9 Sunday. This old-fashioned deli on the town green serves hot and cold sandwiches, soups, and salads, as well as hand-dipped ice cream, milkshakes, sundaes, and sodas. Pizza is available after 4 PM. No smoking. Wheelchair accessible. $4.99–6.99.

ENTERTAINMENT

Professional Sports
See Atlanta Falcons Headquarters and Training Facility under *To Do—For Families*.

SELECTIVE SHOPPING

Several areas are particularly noted for shopping. The Flowery Branch Main Street Square features unique shops and restaurants.

Crafts
Raven's Nest Artisans Marketplace (678-642-6691; www.ravensnestherbals.com), 3109 South Main Street, Duluth. Open 10–6 Tuesday through Friday, 10–5 Saturday. Shop here for handcrafted potpourri, teas, herbs, spices, fragrance oils, herbal bath products, stained glass, jewelry, photography, antiques, folk art, crocheted and knitted items, woodwork, and more. Classes and live musical entertainment are often scheduled.

Other Goods

Grassroots Girls (678-475-9444; www.grassrootsgirls.com), 3579 West Lawrenceville Street, Duluth. Open 10–5 Tuesday through Saturday; Mondays by appointment. Located in the historic Knox House across from City Hall on the town green, this specialty garden shop offers garden and home accents and furnishings, live plants, and landscape design services.

SPECIAL EVENTS

July and August: **Groove with the Grapes/Chateau Elan Summer Concert Series** (678-425-0900, Ext. 41; www.chateauelanatlanta.com/winery/event-calendar.html). Popular local, regional, and national entertainers and bands perform at these outdoor concerts on Saturday nights in Braselton. Tickets ($30) include free dance lessons before each show.
August: **Chateau Elan Vineyard Fest** (678-425-0900, Ext. 41; www.chateauelan atlanta.com/winery/event-calendar.html). Activities included in the all-inclusive price: the tasting of 100 wines, wine seminars, a food pavilion, a tour of the winery in Braselton, and live entertainment. Ages 21 and older only. Even at $42 per ticket, this event is often sold out far in advance.
September: **Duluth Fall Festival** (770-476-0240; www.duluthfallfestival.com). The weekend festival in Duluth kicks off with a parade and then the action moves to the Festival Center and Amphitheater, where there are 250 arts and crafts and food vendors, continuous entertainment, a children's area, an auction, and more. Free.
November: **It's a Wonderful House** (www.itsawonderfulhouse.org). This much-anticipated event permits viewing of some of Chateau Elan's private homes bedecked in holiday splendor. Parking is at the winery in Braselton and admittance is from 10–4 (the houses are open until 6). In addition, there is a gift shop and café. Proceeds benefit the Gwinnett Children's Shelter. $25.
Mid-November through December 30: **Magical Nights of Lights** (770-932-7200; www.lake lanierislands.com). The annual extravaganza at Lake Lanier Islands claims to be the largest animated light display in the world. More than 1 million lights create gigantic animated characters and scenes along a six-mile drive. Visitors can tune their car radios to a special station to listen to holiday favorites while making the drive. At the end there is a holiday village with ice skating, shopping, refreshments, an opportunity to visit with Santa, and a bonfire for roasting marshmallows. Open 5–10 nightly; $25 per car, $35 per van.

Bulloch Hall is the most significant historic site in Roswell.

7

Hospitality Highway: Sandy Springs, Roswell, Alpharetta, Cumming, and Points North

From Metro to the Mountains: Magnolias, Moonshine, and Merlot—this is the description of Georgia's Hospitality Highway, which follows GA 400, a major north/south corridor linking the northern part of Atlanta with numerous small cities and towns, ending in the foothills of the north Georgia mountains. Recently the state legislature officially recognized GA 400 as the Hospitality Highway, and the cities and towns of Sandy Springs, Roswell, Alpharetta, Cumming, Dawsonville, and Dahlonega banded together to promote their attractions. Visitors to these towns will find everything from antebellum homes to reminders of moonshiners and revenuers to a collection of boutique wineries.

Because the Hospitality Highway stretches beyond the area defined by the Georgia Department of Economic Development's Tourism Division as Atlanta Metro, we will describe the part of the Hospitality Highway that stretches from Sandy Springs at I-285 to Cumming in Forsyth County. Dawsonville and Dahlonega, which are farther north, will be mentioned only briefly under *Worth Driving For*.

The city along the Hospitality Highway with the most interesting history is Roswell. Although the Cherokee had owned what they called the "Enchanted Land" in north Georgia, when gold was discovered there in 1828, the state of Georgia declared the Cherokee Nation illegal and took possession of the land, sending the Native Americans on the infamous Trail of Tears to reservations in the West. The land was then available to white settlers through a lottery system.

During this period, the lure of gold attracted the interest of Roswell King from coastal Darien, Georgia. But when King came to the Chattahoochee River and the rapids on Vickery Creek, he forgot about the gold and decided the location was a perfect place for a water-powered textile mill. He acquired a substantial amount of land and founded a cotton mill he called the Roswell Manufacturing Company, which produced cloth, tenting, rope, flannels, and yarn. Later he also established a woolen mill. King offered home sites and investment opportunities, and his relatives, friends, and associates migrated here from the coast. They built magnificent homes, while cottages and apartments were provided for mill workers—primarily women who ranged in age from 15 to 25. A church and an academy

SANDY SPRINGS, ROSWELL, ALPHARETTA, CUMMING & POINTS NORTH

for boys were built and the town prospered until the Civil War.

While most of the men were off fighting, the worker-class women and children kept the mills operating, making cloth for Confederate uniforms. On July 5, 1864, as Union troops advanced, retreating Confederate troops burned the covered bridge at the Chattahoochee River south of Roswell to slow their progress. Not so easily deterred, Union troops found a place to ford the river and entered Roswell anyway. Although Theophile Roche, the French foreman of the mill, tried to claim neutrality by flying the French flag, he fooled no one, and on July 7 the mills were burned. Fortunately, the town and homes were spared.

After the war, the mills were rebuilt and Roswell remained a small but successful textile town until the mid-1970s, when the mills closed for good. The town's proximity to Atlanta, however, guaranteed that rather than dying, as most Southern textile towns had done, Roswell prospered. Now, although Roswell has grown to be the sixth most populous city in Georgia and home to the offices of many national companies, it is primarily a very affluent bedroom community for Atlanta.

Because the town was spared during the Civil War, Roswell's 640-acre Historic District, of which 122 acres are listed on the National Register of Historic Places, is filled with period homes, churches, and businesses—many of which serve as museum houses, muse-

The Missing Roswell Women and Children

The most shocking part of the invasion of Roswell is that all the mill workers (remember, they were primarily young women and children) were charged with treason by orders from Union General William Tecumseh Sherman. Apparently he feared that these plucky women would somehow find a way to make the things the Confederacy needed, so by his orders they were marched west to Marietta (a railhead the Union had already captured) and put on trains for the North. Many were imprisoned for the duration of the war, while others were forced into servitude to Northern families and businesses until they could escape or the war ended. Although many returned to Roswell after the war, or at least let their families know where they were, others were never seen or heard from again, giving rise to the legend of the missing Roswell women and children. Several factual and fictional accounts of this story have been written for adults and children, including the factual account *Charged with Treason* by local historian Michael Hitt and the fictional stories *The Roswell Women* by Frances Patton Statham and *Turn Homeward, Hannalee* by Patricia Beatty.

ums, restaurants, and shops. Among these are Barrington Hall, Bulloch Hall, and the Archibald Smith Plantation Home (see *Historic Homes and Sites*). Within the city limits, nearly 20 parks encompass 880 acres and provide nature trails and numerous opportunities for outdoor activities.

GUIDANCE

For information on the **Hospitality Highway**, consult the Web site www.hospitality highway.com. The Web site describes attractions, lodgings, and events in the towns along the highway, provides links to other pertinent Web sites, and offers you the opportunity to download a brochure.

For more information about Sandy Springs, contact the **Sandy Springs Hospitality Board** (770-391-1111; www.visitsandysprings.org), Sandy Springs City Hall, 7840 Roswell Road, Building 500, Sandy Springs 30350. Open 8:30–5 weekdays. Another important source of information about Sandy Springs is **Heritage Sandy Springs** (404-851-9111; www.heritagesandysprings.org), 135 Hildebrand Drive, Sandy Springs 30328. Open 9–5 weekdays.

When planning a trip to the Roswell area, contact the **Historic Roswell Convention and Visitors Bureau/Visitor Center** (770-640-3253; 1-800-776-7935; www.cvb.roswell. ga.us), 617 Atlanta Street, Roswell 30075. Open 9–5 weekdays, 10–4 Saturday, noon–3 Sunday. Stop here to watch a film, examine historic exhibits, and get pamphlets and advice. A brochure is available for a self-guided walking/driving tour. Guided tours offered by the Roswell Historical Society (770-992-1665; www.roswellhs.org) depart from the visitor's center at 10 AM Wednesday and 1 PM Saturday. These tours and audio cassette tours cost $5.

For more information about Alpharetta, contact the **Alpharetta Convention and Visitors Bureau** (678-297-2811; 1-800-294-0923; www.awesomealpharetta.com), 3060 Royal Boulevard South, Suite 145, Alpharetta 30022. Open 8:30–5 Monday through Thursday, 8:30–4:30 Friday. Also consult or stop by the friendly **Alpharetta Welcome Center** (678-297-0102; 1-800-294-0923; www.awesomealpharetta.com), 20 North Main

Street, Alpharetta 30004. Open 9–5 weekdays, 10–4 Saturday.

For information about Cumming, contact the **Cumming-Forsyth County Chamber of Commerce** (770-887-6461; www.forsythchamber.org), 212 Kelly Mill Road, Cumming 30040. Open 8:30–5 Monday through Thursday, 8:30–4 Friday.

Getting There

Because Sandy Springs, Roswell, Alpharetta, and Cumming are located more than 30 to 40 miles north of downtown Atlanta and the airport, service into metro Atlanta by air, interstate bus, and train are some miles away from these cities. It would be prohibitively expensive to take a taxi from the airport to any of them. There is, however, shuttle service to these destinations from the airport, and the metropolitan transit service makes access to outlying areas fairly easy. The best solution, however, is to rent a car after arriving in the metro area by air, rail, or bus.

By air: See What's Where.

By bus: See What's Where.

By car: From the I-285 bypass, take Exit 25/Roswell Road to visit Sandy Springs. From downtown or I-285, take GA 400 north to Roswell, Alpharetta, and Cumming. There is a 50¢ toll collected between the Lenox and Glenridge exits.

By train: See What's Where.

Getting Around

Visitors to the northern suburbs who arrive by air can rent a car at the Atlanta airport (see What's Where). Rentals are also available in the four cities after you get there: in Sandy Springs, **Enterprise** (404-255-3873), 6189 Roswell Road Northeast; in Alpharetta, **Enterprise** (770-664-3065; www.enterprise.com), 11235 Alpharetta Highway, Suite 138; in Roswell, **Atlanta Car Rental** (770-518-5500), 1579 Holcomb Bridge Road; and in Cumming, **Econo-Ride** (770-889-8954), 818 Atlanta Highway and **Enterprise** (770-886-9604), 5925 Parkway North Boulevard or (770-888-9860), Lake Center Parkway, Suite E. For other options, check the Yellow Pages.

For limousine transportation in Sandy Springs and Roswell, contact **Southern Hospitality Limo Service** (404-863-3116); in Alpharetta, contact **Alpharetta Limousine Service** (770-772-5166); in Cumming, contact **2 Party Limousine Service** (770-652-2265). For other alternatives, check the Yellow Pages.

For cab service within the northern suburbs (not from the airport), contact **Alterna Taxi Services** (678-393-8558) or **Paddy's Taxi** (404-606-5499; www.paddystaxi.com) for service in Roswell, Alpharetta, and Cumming. For many other alternatives, check the Yellow Pages.

Bus and rail service throughout the majority of the Atlanta metropolitan area as far north as Alpharetta and North Fulton County is provided by **MARTA**—Metropolitan Atlanta Rapid Transit Authority (404-848-4711; www.itsmarta.com; see What's Where). The nearest mass transit rail station to the northern cities in this chapter is at North Springs, near Sandy Springs but about 7 miles south of Roswell off GA 400 and about 20 miles south of Cumming.

Express bus service to and from the train station is offered from the Windward Park & Ride lot in Alpharetta and from the Mansell Park & Ride lot in Roswell. Numerous bus routes serve Sandy Springs, Roswell, and Alpharetta and connect them to many destinations in the metro Atlanta area.

MARTA does not go to nor operate in Forsyth County, where Cumming is located. **Xpress Bus** (404-463-3000) provides service to and from the North Springs MARTA rail station from the Park & Ride lot at Exit 14 off GA 400. For more information about Xpress, see What's Where.

Several companies offer shuttle service to the northern suburbs. These three offer service to all of the cities in this chapter: **Greater Atlanta Shuttle** (678-851-7063), **Airport Perimeter Connection** (404-761-0260), and **Airport Metro Shuttle** (404-766-6666). Several other companies offer shuttle service to one or more of these cities, but not to all of them. For these other options, consult the Yellow Pages.

Parking

In Roswell, adequate free parking is available at the city complex, which includes City Hall, the Roswell Cultural Arts Center, and the public library. A small amount of free parking is available in a lot behind the visitor's center on South Atlanta Street. There is some free on-street parking in the Canton Street Historic District and around historic Roswell Square. Alpharetta and Cumming also have free parking downtown. There is plentiful free parking at shopping centers and malls in Sandy Springs, Roswell, Alpharetta, and Cumming.

Public Restrooms

Public restrooms in Roswell can be found at the visitor's center, Bulloch Hall, the Teaching Museum North, and the riverside parks along the Chattahoochee River. In Alpharetta, there are public restrooms at the visitor's center. Around Cumming's town square, restrooms can be found at the courthouse, county annex, and City Hall. All the towns, including Sandy Springs, have access to restrooms at attractions, shopping centers, malls, and restaurants.

Medical Emergency

For life-threatening situations, call 911. For other immediate medical care in Sandy Springs, the nearest hospitals are **Northside Hospital** (404-851-8000; wwwnorthside.com.), 1000 Johnson Ferry Road Northeast, Atlanta; **St. Joseph's Hospital** (404-851-7001; www.stjosephsatlanta.org), 5665 Peachtree-Dunwoody Road Northeast, Atlanta; and **Children's Healthcare of Atlanta at Scottish Rite** (404-785-5252, www.choa.org), 1001 Johnson Ferry Road Northeast, Atlanta. In Roswell or Alpharetta, go to the **North Fulton Regional Medical Center** (770-751-2500; www.northfultonregional.com), 300 Hospital Boulevard, Roswell. Immediate care is available in Cumming at **Northside Hospital Forsyth** (770-844-3200; www.northside.com), 1200 Northside-Forsyth Drive.

Villages/Neighborhoods

In addition to Roswell, which was described in the introduction, these cities and towns are important members of the Hospitality Highway.

Alpharetta. Just a few miles to the north of Roswell, Alpharetta is another fashionable bedroom community, although it is the home of many international companies. With nearly 200 restaurants featuring practically every cuisine imaginable, Alpharetta has become a premier dining destination in metro Atlanta. Evening entertainment includes live music ranging from rock to jazz, as well as coffeehouses with poetry readings and their own music.

Crabapple. Located between Roswell and Alpharetta, Crabapple was once a separate town, but is now part of Alpharetta, although it retains its name and identity. For more than three decades, it has been known as an antique-lover's paradise. Located at the five-way intersection of Crabapple Road, Broadwell Road, Mid Broadwell Road, Mayfield Road, and Birmingham Highway, all of which were once Indian trails, are the **Historic Shops of Crabapple** (see *Shopping*) as well as the restaurant **Milton's** (see *Dining Out*).

Cumming. Farther north and in another county, Cumming—Forsyth County's seat of government—is the gateway to Lake Lanier and the northeast Georgia mountains. Until just recently, Forsyth County was primarily rural, but over the past several years there has been a tremendous influx of new residents and the character of the county is becoming much more suburban and exurban. Cumming boasts a historic covered bridge (see *To See—Covered Bridges*) and the Sawnee Mountain Preserve (see *Green Space—Nature Preserves and Parks*). Although Lake Lanier is shared by five counties, Forsyth County boasts 260 miles of its shoreline. The lake provides innumerable opportunities for boating, fishing, and other water sports. Land-based activities include golf, tennis, camping, and hiking.

The **Chattahoochee River** is an integral part of this region, stretching from Lake Lanier for 48 miles through metro Atlanta as it makes its 542-mile way to Apalachicola Bay, Florida. The river corridor is one of America's foremost urban greenways—an untamed area within the metropolis. It is also one of metropolitan Atlanta's best-kept secrets.

Sandy Springs. Furthest south of the cities and towns along the Hospitality Highway, Sandy Springs was once part of Atlanta, but recently has become a real city with its own government and services. In fact, it is now the seventh-largest city in Georgia. It began much more humbly, of course. When the Native Americans were removed, Stephen Spruill acquired the land around the spring-fed source of water known as Sandy Springs. Because the springs were located at the intersection of two major routes, which have now become Roswell Road and Mount Vernon Highway, the site was often a stopping place for farmers and other travelers. In the 1980s the springs were threatened with development that would have buried them under storm sewers and fill dirt, so the property surrounding the springs was purchased by Fulton County in 1984 to create the Sandy Springs Historic Site. In 1986, the historic Williams-Payne House (see *Historic Homes and Sites*), which was also threatened by development, was moved to the property. Today Sandy Springs also boasts 16 miles of shoreline along the Chattahoochee River, eight parks, and the City Walk shopping area—a pedestrian-friendly shopping development at 227 Sandy Springs Place. Special events include **Concerts by the Springs** and the **Sandy Springs Festival** (see *Special Events*). When visiting Sandy Springs, be on the lookout for the large, whimsical, painted and decorated fiberglass Eastern box turtles, which are scattered throughout the city. This turtle was chosen to symbolize the city because it is indigenous to the area.

TO SEE

Covered Bridge
🦅 🐢 **Poole's Mill Park and Historic Covered Bridge** (770-781-2215; www.forsythco.com), 7725 Poole's Mill Road, Cumming. Open daily. The 1901 bridge, which spans Settendown Creek, is 90 feet long and one span wide. The surrounding 10-acre park features a walking path, picnic area, and a playground. Free.

Cultural Sites

🖉 🍴 **Abernathy Arts Center** (404-303-6172; www.fultonarts.org), 254 Johnson Ferry
Road, Sandy Springs. Open 9–10 Monday through Thursday, 9–5 Friday. Fulton County's
oldest neighborhood arts center, the facility offers art classes as well as a gallery with
monthly exhibitions. The campus includes a renovated farmhouse and a modern annex.
Gallery free.

🖉 🍴 **Roswell Art Center West** (770-641-3990), 1355 Woodstock Road, Roswell. Open
9–6:30 weekdays, noon–5 Saturday. Call for a schedule of art shows. This satellite center to
the Roswell Visual Arts Center (see next entry) focuses on works in clay. In addition to art
classes, the center sponsors many exhibitions throughout the year. The center also houses
Clay West, a local artists' cooperative that features functional and sculptural works. Free.

🖉 🍴 ♿ **Roswell Visual Arts Center** (770-594-6122), 10495 Woodstock Road, Roswell.
Open 10–6 weekdays, 10–4 Saturday. In addition to art classes, the center, which is located
within Roswell Area Park, displays the works of local, regional, national, and international
artists. Exhibits of drawings, paintings, prints, sculpture, ceramics, fiber, photography,
and mixed media are changed every six to eight weeks. Outside the center, two decks and a
sculpture garden invite visitors to enjoy
the beauty of the park. Wheelchair accessible. Free admission and opening night
receptions.

Equestrian Events

🖉 🍴 **Wills Park Equestrian Center**
(678-297-6120; www.alpharetta.ga.us/
index.php?p=221), 11915 Wills Road,
Alpharetta. Outdoor and covered show
rings provide the backdrop for an
astounding array of English and Western
horse shows, dressage events, rodeos,
bull riding, arena polo, dog shows, dog
agility trials, concerts, and fireworks.

*The Wills Park Equestrian Center hosts many horse
shows and rodeos throughout the year.*

More than 300 stalls provide accommo-
dations for the horses and an opportunity for visitors to wander among them. In addition
to plentiful paved parking, there are 30 camper hookups. Call for a schedule of events
and prices.

For Families

🖉 🍴 **Buford Trout Hatchery** (770-781-6888), 3204 Trout Place Road, Cumming. Open
7:30–4:30 daily; guided tour at 1 PM Saturday. The trout hatchery is located east of Cumming
on the banks of the Chattahoochee River just downstream from Lake Lanier and Buford
Dam. Visitors can view up to a million brown and rainbow trout ranging from a few inches
long up to ones that weigh 10 pounds, walk along the Hatchery Nature/Bird Trail, and fish
in the Family Fishing Pond. The hatchery produces trout for the traditional Georgia stock-
ing season as well as the Delayed Harvest and Big Fish programs. The bird trail, which
offers visitors an opportunity to see transient and breeding songbirds, waterfowl, and
occasional upland birds, ends in a boardwalk and viewing platform overlooking a beaver
swamp. The Family Fishing Pond offers catch-and-release programs for small bluegill and

catfish. Bream and catfish also can be caught. Anglers are welcome to bring their own equipment, or the hatchery has a limited number of loaner fishing poles. Visitors are asked to register. Children younger than 16 may fish free, but adults and teens must have a valid Georgia fishing license. The guided tours explain how trout are reared and how the hatchery works. Tour participants will be able to feed the fish. Free.

Guided Tours

🐾 🐟 **Ghost Talk-Ghost Walk** (770-753-0037; 1-800-273-0371), 617 Atlanta Street, Roswell. Tours 6:30–8 Friday; reservations requested. The one-hour, easy-walking tour of Roswell's Historic District includes plenty of chills and thrills concerning the spirits that are said to live behind the walls of the mansions and workers' dwellings in the mill village. $10.

🐟 **Historic Tours** (770-640-3253; 1-800-776-7935), 617 Atlanta Street, Roswell. Tours are given at 1 PM Saturday and 10 AM Wednesday. Stroll the historic streets with a guide and hear about Roswell's early settlers and the turbulent Civil War era. $2.

🐟 ♿ **Roswell Ghost Tour** (770-649-9922; 404-644-8051; www.roswellghosttour.com), meet at the bandstand in the square across from the visitor's center at 617 Atlanta Street. Most Friday and Saturday evenings; some tours are at 7 PM and some at 8 PM, so be sure to clarify the time. Tours depart rain or shine. During the two-hour tour, experienced guides lead you on an exploration of the Historic District and tell the stories of spirits in the city's antebellum mansions, workers' apartments, deep ravines, and ruined mills. Once a month, there is a pet-friendly tour on which your leashed pet is welcome to accompany the group. Wear comfortable walking shoes and bring a flashlight, a camera, and an umbrella and/or insect repellent if appropriate. Note: A minimum of six people is required for the tour to depart, although they do not all have to be in the same party. Adults $15, children 12 and younger $10; wheelchair rental $10.

🐾 **Storytelling Tours** (770-640-3253; 1-800-776-7935), 617 Atlanta Street, Roswell. Tours, led by storytellers who weave tales of Roswell's mills and settlers, are given on the third Sunday of each month. Call for exact times. $8.

Historic Homes and Sites

🐾 🐟 **Archibald Smith Plantation Home** (770-641-3978; www.archibaldsmith

The Archibald Smith Plantation Home is filled with original furnishing and surrounded by 10 outbuildings.

plantation.org), 935 Alpharetta Street, Roswell. Open 10–3 Monday through Saturday, 1–3 Sunday. The original 300-acre farm was created by Archibald Smith, one of those who had migrated from coastal Georgia. His home and farm were on the outskirts of town about a mile north of the Roswell town square. Built in 1845, the house was lived in for 150 years by three successive generations of the Smith family until they donated the property to the city. All the furnishings, therefore, are original, which is very unusual in a period museum home. What is even more interesting, considering that the remaining 3-acre property is now completely surrounded by the bustling city of Roswell, is that 10 original outbuildings survive, including barns, the carriage house, corn crib, greenhouse, kitchen building, slave cabin, springhouse, and well. Adults $8, children 6–12 $6. An $18 combination ticket includes admission to Barrington Hall and Bulloch Hall.

♂ ☙ Barrington Hall (770-640-3855; www.barringtonhall-roswell.com), 535 Barrington Drive, Roswell. Open 10–3 Wednesday through Saturday. City of Roswell cofounder Barrington King chose the highest point in town to build his Greek Revival home in 1842. When Roswell was invaded by Union troops during the Civil War, Union General Theophilus T. Garrard briefly occupied the house as his headquarters. The home

Beautiful Barrington Hall was built in 1842

was lived in by descendants of Barrington King until Katherine Simpson died in 1995 at age 99. Her adopted daughter, Lois, continued to live in the house until her death in 2003. The National Register of Historic Places home, now owned by the City of Roswell, has been named one of the 50 Most Beautiful Homes in Metro Atlanta by *Atlanta* magazine. In 2005, the home received an Outstanding Restoration award from the Georgia Trust for Historic Preservation. Adults $8, children 6–12 $6. An $18 combination ticket includes admission to the Archibald Smith Plantation Home and Bulloch Hall.

♂ ☙ Bulloch Hall (706-992-1731; www.bullochhall.org), 180 Bulloch Avenue, Roswell. Open 10–4 Monday through Saturday, 1–4 Sunday, with tours on the hour until 3. The most significant historic site in Roswell, Bulloch Hall, which was built in 1840, was the home of Major James Stephens Bulloch, one of the town's first settlers and the grandson of an early Georgia governor, Archibald Bulloch. Constructed of heart pine, it was built in the Greek temple style with a full pedimented portico and is considered one of the best examples of the style in Georgia. The interior style, typical of the period, was called "four-square"— four principal rooms and a central hall on each floor. The kitchen is in the basement rather than in a separate building (as was more common at the time), and it features a beehive oven. Because of their ability to discourage flies and rodents, Osage orange trees were planted near the house, and many of them still survive along with shade and fruit trees. In fact, 142 trees on the property are listed on the Historic Tree Register. Major Bulloch's daughter, Martha "Mittie" Bulloch, married Theodore Roosevelt Sr. in the dining room of Bulloch Hall on December 22, 1853. They went on to become the parents of President Theodore Roosevelt Jr. and, through their other son Elliott, the grandparents of first lady Eleanor Roosevelt. In 1905 President Teddy Roosevelt visited his mother's former home and spoke to Roswell residents from the bandstand in the town square. Today the lovingly restored home is filled with gracious period pieces, including some original china used by the Bullochs. Guided tours are offered of the house; self-guided tours include the reconstructed slave quarters and colonial garden. The dog-trot-style slave quarters, which were reconstructed on the original site, include a period room and an exhibit, "Slave Life in the Piedmont." Bulloch Hall is home to many active guilds which demonstrate old-time skills at special events. These guilds include quilting, open-hearth cooking, sampler (needlework), gardening, and archaeology. Several special events—the monthlong Christmas at Bulloch Hall, Civil War encampments, Osage Orange Festival, storytelling programs, and summer camps for children—occur throughout the year. Adults $8, children 6–12 $6. An $18 combination ticket includes admission to Barrington Hall and the Archibald Smith Plantation Home.

🕭 **Founders Cemetery**, Sloan Street, Roswell. Open daily. The oldest cemetery in the city contains the graves of members of some of Roswell's founding families, including Roswell King, James Bulloch, and John Dunwoody. Unmarked graves contain the remains of family servants. Free.

🕭 **Historic Mansell House and Gardens** (770-475-HOME; www.ahsga.org), 1835 Old Milton Parkway, Alpharetta. Open 10–4 weekdays. The 1910 Queen Anne Victorian home is owned by the City of Alpharetta and managed by the Alpharetta Historical Society. Inside, six rooms feature heart pine floors, 12-foot ceilings, antique mantels above decorative fireplaces, and period antiques. The house is surrounded by Southeast Historic Gardens Award-winning floral displays created and maintained by the Alpharetta Garden Club. The romantic gardens feature a gazebo, an arbor, and statuary. Free.

🕭 **Lost Mill Workers of Roswell Monument**, Old Mill Park on Sloan Street, Roswell. Open daily. The simple monument is dedicated to the 400 women and children who were sent north when the Union Army occupied Roswell. Free.

✍🕭 **Milton Log Cabin** (770-475-HOME; www.ahsga.org), 86 School Drive, Alpharetta. Call the Alpharetta Historical Society between noon and 4 Friday to have someone open the cabin for you. It will only take a few minutes to examine the late 1800s and early 1900s period furnishings and tools in this tiny log cabin, which was built in 1935 by the Future Farmers of America at Milton High School (now Independence High School). The one-room cabin has a customary loft, and split log benches line the walls from when the cabin was used in the 1930s and 1940s for dances, meetings, weddings, and suppers. Today it holds donated tools, farm equipment, a spinning wheel, rope bed, straw mattress, and a model of an old Alpharetta farm. In 1985 the cabin was to be torn down so the land could be used for a parking lot at the school, but the Alpharetta Historical Society offered to lease the cabin and restore it. Free.

✍🕭 **Sandy Springs Historic Site/Williams-Payne House** (404-851-9111; www.heritage sandysprings.org/museum), 6075 Sandy Springs Circle, Sandy Springs. Site and gardens open dawn–8 daily; museum open 9–5 Friday; tours of the house by appointment. The original double-pen farmhouse with detached kitchen was built in 1869. As the family that lived there grew to 12 children, an additional bedroom and kitchen were added. To save the house from destruction in the face of encroaching development, the structure was moved to this location in 1986. Fully restored, the house is furnished to depict a typical Sandy Springs farmhouse between 1870 and 1910. On the grounds are the original well shelter surrounded by antique roses and other heritage plants, the milk house and its kitchen garden, a gazebo band shell surrounded by flower beds planted in designs to resemble carpets as was the style in Victorian times, and a 19th-century two-hole privy with a large hole for adults and a small one for children. Concerts are held on the lawns June through September (see *Special Events*). Free.

Museums

✍🕭 **Roswell Fire and Rescue Museum** (770-641-3730), 1002 Alpharetta Street, Roswell. Open 9–6 daily unless personnel are responding to a fire or EMS call. This small museum, located in a working fire station, uses antique alarms, bells, and fire-fighting equipment to trace the history of the Roswell Volunteer Fire Department. Free.

🐾🐾 **Teaching Museum North** (770-552-6339; www.fultonschools.org/dept/teaching museumnorth), 791 Mimosa Boulevard, Roswell. Open 8–3 weekdays. The museum uses exhibits of historical, political, and social interest to document the history of the United States, Georgia, and Roswell. Exhibits include how a bill becomes a law, U.S. presidents, Georgia authors, the changing roles of women in the White House, the history of transportation, the Great Depression, World War II, and more. The museum occupies one wing of Crossroads High School, which sits on the site of the first academy in Roswell. Free.

Natural Beauty Spots

See the **Chattahoochee River** under *Rivers* and the **Vickery Creek Unit of the Chattahoochee River National Recreation Area** under *Nature Preserves and Parks*.

Special Places

🐾🐾 ♿ **Vietnam War Memorial: "The Faces of War,"** 38 Hill Street, Roswell. Open 24/7. Located in the Memorial Garden at City Hall, the life-size bronze sculpture depicts a child leading a soldier out of a sea of 50 faces, each touched by war and showing a variety of emotions. As water courses over the monument, it seems to weep. The sculpture was designed by two Roswell artists, Don Haugen and Tina Stern. Free.

The Faces of War, *the Vietnam War Memorial in Roswell, was designed by two local artists.*

Worth Driving For

Just a few miles beyond our parameters for metro Atlanta are **Dawsonville** and **Dahlonega.** Dawson County bills itself as "Where the Mountains Meet the Lakes." It was once an area notorious for moonshiners and revenuers. Their wild chases through the mountains led to auto racing's rise in popularity. NASCAR legend Bill Elliott, "Awesome Bill from Dawsonville," hails from these parts. Today the area's greatest coup is that it is the home of the Kangaroo Conservation Center, which contains the largest concentration of kangaroos outside Australia. A few other attractions in and around Dawsonville are the North Georgia Premium Outlets, Amicalola Falls State Park, the Len Foote Hike Inn, the southernmost terminus of the Appalachian Trail, the Bowen Center for the Arts, the Dawsonville Pool Room (filled with Bill Elliott memorabilia), Burt's Pumpkin Farm, and Uncle Shuck's Corn Maze and Pumpkin Patch. (The last two attractions operate seasonally.)

Gold was discovered in the area around Dahlonega before it was discovered in California, leading to the saying "Thar's gold in them thar hills." Before the Civil War there was a U.S. Mint in Dahlonega. Today reminders of the first gold rush include Consolidated Gold Mines, Crisson Gold Mine, and the Dahlonega Gold Museum Historic Site. Among other attractions in Dahlonega are the Historic Holly Theater and the Chestatee Wildlife Preserve as well as several wineries: Blackstock Vineyards and Winery, Frogtown Cellars, Three Sisters Vineyard and Winery, and Wolf Mountain Vineyard and Winery.

To find out more about Dawsonville and Dawson County, call 706-265-6278 or 1-877-396-6288 or consult the Web site www.dawson.org. To learn more about Dahlonega, call 706-864-3711 or 1-800-231-5543 or consult the Web site www.dahlonega.org.

To Do

Bicycling

🚲 Roswell Bicycles (770-642-4057: www.rowsellbicycles.com), 670 Houze Way, Roswell. The store, which carries everything you could need for cycling but which rarely has bikes to rent, sponsors organized rides. There are three different rides, but at 30, 50, and 75 miles long, they're not for the inexperienced or fainthearted. The length of the ride is dependent on the number of participants and the weather.

Boating

The **Chattahoochee River** provides numerous opportunities for canoeing and kayaking (see below), as well as motorboating and other small boat use year-round (see What's Where).

Canoeing, Kayaking, Tubing

On a hot summer day, there's nothing more refreshing than floating down the Chattahoochee River in a raft. This popular activity is known as "Shootin' the Hooch." The water stays about 55 degrees, so if you get too hot all you have to do is splash yourself with water. Bring your own picnic, because the leisurely trip takes between two and six hours, depending on the outpost location and the speed of the river flow. U.S. Coast Guard–approved life jackets are required, and anyone younger than 18 must be accompanied by an adult. An approximate float-time chart for seven possible canoe trips can be found in the Chattahoochee River National Recreation Area brochure (see www.nps.gov/chat).

🚣 **Chattahoochee Outfitters** (770-650-1008; 404-274-6912; www.shootthehooch.com), Azalea Landing at Chattahoochee River Park, 203 Azalea Drive, Roswell. Open 9–sunset daily, Memorial Day through Labor Day; the remainder of the year 10–6 weekends. Canoe, kayak, tube, or raft the Chattahoochee River as it flows through Roswell, or just paddle around the park on a water bicycle or paddle boat. For rafters who want to float down the river, the company provides shuttle service—$5 for Island Ford or $10 for Gerald's Landing. Canoe rentals are $50 per day or $20 per hour; one-man kayak rentals are $60 per day or $35 per hour; two-man kayak rentals are $90 per day or $40 per hour; raft rentals are $100 for a four-man raft, $120 for a six-man raft, $160 for an eight-man raft, $200 for a 10-man raft; water bicycles $10 per hour; two-man paddleboats $15 per hour, four-man paddleboats $20 per hour; tube rentals $25–30 per hour. A deposit is required. The company also operates a riverboat that runs from Azalea Landing to Morgan Falls Dam and back—a two- to three-hour trip. Call for a schedule of cruises and prices.

Day Camps
See *Summer Youth Programs.*

Disc Golf
Central Park (Recreation Center 678-455-8540), 2300 Keith Bridge Road, Cumming. Office open 8:30–5 weekdays. Park facilities available during daylight hours daily year-round. The park offers a 27-station course. Free.

✐ 🌹 **East Roswell Park** (770-594-6134), 9000 Fouts Road, Roswell. Office open 9–6 Monday through Saturday. Park facilities available year-round during daylight hours. The 18-station course winds through the park. Free.

✐ 🌹 **Wills Park** (678-297-6150), 11915 Wills Road, Alpharetta. Available year-round during daylight hours. The 18-station course winds around the park's ball fields and other facilities. Free.

Fishing
Part of the **Chattahoochee River** and the **Chattahoochee River National Recreation Area** meander along the southern edge of Roswell. Fishing along the riverbanks is a popular activity (see What's Where).

✐ 🌹 **Rainbow Ranch** (770-887-4797; www.rainbowranchtrout.com), 41 Ruth Lane, Cumming. Open 10–5 Tuesday through Sunday. Heavily stocked ponds continuously refreshed from the Chattahoochee River provide opportunities for anglers to hook a rainbow trout. $4.29 a pound for fish caught, $1 to ice your catch, 10 percent to clean. No limit.

For Families
✐ **StarTime Entertainment Complex** (770-993-5411; www.startimeentertainment.com), 608 Holcomb Bridge Road, Roswell. Open 11 AM–2 AM Monday through Saturday, 11 AM–midnight Sunday. The complex features two miniature golf courses, two Go-Kart tracks, bumper cars, batting cages, a 14-seat motion simulator, an arcade with 200 video/skill games, billiards, the Funny Farm comedy club, and a 10-screen movie theater. The Studio Café and the StarTime Sports Bar offer refreshments. Prices vary depending on the activity.

Hiking
✐ 🌹 **Roswell Trail System and River Walk** (770-640-3253; 770-641-3705; 1-800-776-7935). Open dawn to dusk. Sixteen miles of trails wind through the city and along the Chattahoochee River. Maps are available at the visitor's center. One of these trails, the 1.8-mile **Oxbo Trail**, combines an easy, level walk along the banks of Vickery Creek and an energetic climb to Roswell's first city park, passing Hog Waller Creek along the way. The trail also provides access to the Chattahoochee River National Recreation Area. The 7-mile linear city park along the Chattahoochee River is dotted with parks and recreational facilities such as playgrounds, picnic areas, boat ramps, places to fish, and restrooms. Free.

Vickery Creek Unit of the Chattahoochee River National Recreation Area (see *Nature Preserves and Parks*), at South Atlanta Street and Riverside Drive, Roswell. The unit contains 6 miles of trails for all abilities along the creek or rigorous climbs over ridges. Steep bluffs create a rugged terrain that is quite unique in the metro Atlanta area.

Horseback Riding
Bowman's Island Unit of the Chattahoochee River National Recreation Area, Island Ford Road near Buford Dam, Cumming. Horseback riding (BYOH—Bring Your Own Horse) is allowed along the trails of the Forsyth County section of Bowman's Island. There are no facilities from which to rent horses. For more information about riding your own horse at this unit, call the National Park Service's visitor center at Island Ford in Dunwoody (678-538-1200).

Hot Air Ballooning
Balloons Over Georgia (678-947-9866; www.balloonsovergeorgia.com). Flights Saturday and Sunday morning and evening, March through October or November, weather permitting. Soar over beautiful north Georgia on a romantic balloon flight. $200 per person for a nonexclusive flight of four people; $600 for a private flight for a couple.

Skating
🕊🦐 **Alpharetta Family Skate Center/The Cooler** (770-649-6600; www.cooler.com), 10800 Davis Drive, Alpharetta. Hours for public use vary widely depending on school schedules and team requirements. Call the special events hotline to get the most current hours. Two ice arenas and one inline skating arena provide opportunities for figure skating, ice hockey, roller hockey, public skating, inline skating, birthday parties, and special events. In addition, the complex has stadium seating for watching the action, and areas for adults and toddlers to wait. There's also a video arcade and skate rentals. Call for admission and skate rental fees.

🕊🦐 **Grimes Bridge Skate Park** (770-594-6430), 830 Grimes Bridge Road. Open daylight hours daily unless conditions are wet. The Roswell Recreation and Parks Department maintains the skating facility, which features half-pipes, quarter-pipes, ramps, rails, ledges, and a four-level pyramid with stairs. Participants are required to wear a helmet and knee pads or long pants; shoes are required for skateboarders. Elbow and wrist pads are encouraged. Parents must accompany first-time participants under age 18 to sign a liability waver. Free.

Sports Experiences
Andretti Speed Lab (770-992-5688; www.andrettispeedlab.com), 11000 Alpharetta Highway, Roswell. Open 11 AM–10 PM Sunday through Thursday, 3 PM–1 AM Friday, 11 AM–1 AM Friday and Saturday. This indoor complex boasts racing-related entertainment for the on-the-edge adventure seeker. Visitors can suit up in authentic racing gear and get behind the wheel of a high-performance, Italian-designed SuperCart. Two indoor courses were patterned after famous European courses. The Game Lab is an interactive arcade with the latest in video and virtual reality games, including football, basketball, soccer, and racing simulators. The high-energy facility also offers a three-story rock-climbing wall, a ropes course, and 100 satellite-linked televisions as well as SkyBox Sports Bar and a Fuddrucker's restaurant. Racing is not suitable for preteen children. Prices: $7 for a license good for one year; $18 per race or $48 for three races; $9 for three climbs on the rock wall; 50¢–$1.50 for arcade games.

Summer Youth Programs
🕊 **Camp Bulloch** (770-992-1731; www.bullochhall.org), 180 Bulloch Avenue, Roswell. Held on the grounds of historic Bulloch Hall (see *Historic Homes and Sites*) for a week in June or July, the 1800s heritage day camp for children 6–11 makes history fun. Activities

include archaeology, open-hearth cooking, candle dipping, walking tours of the Historic District, and much more. $170, $150 for members of Friends of Bulloch Hall.

♂ **Camp Yesteryear** (770-641-3978; www.roswellgov.com), 935 Alpharetta Street, Roswell. Held 10–1:30 weekdays one week in June on the grounds of the historic Smith Plantation. This summer camp for ages 7–12 includes games, crafts, and activities involving old-time skills. $150.

Swimming
♂ ❧ **Roswell Area Park** (770-641-3768), 10495 Woodstock Road, Roswell. Open Memorial Day weekend through Labor Day: 1–5:15 and 7:30–9:30 Tuesday through Friday, 1–7 Saturday and Sunday. The 50-meter, Olympic-size pool has eight lap lanes, a diving well with two springboards, and a children's wading pool with a waterfall mushroom. Programs include aquatic exercise, swim lessons, lap swimming, and open swim times. Friday nights are "Noodle Nights" from 7:30–9:30. $4; season swim passes available for individuals and families.

♂ ❧ **Wills Park** (678-297-6107), 11925 Wills Road, Alpharetta. Open seasonally, noon–5 weekdays, 8–10 Saturday, noon–8 Sunday. The park features an Olympic-size pool. $3.

Tennis
Four of the parks operated by the Alpharetta Parks and Recreation Department offer tennis courts: **Wills Park** (678-297-6130), 11925 Wills Road; the **Senior Activity Center** (678-297-6140), 13453 Cogburn Road; **Webb Bridge Park** (678-297-6100), 4780 Webb Bridge Road; and **Alpharetta North Park** (678-297-6100), 13450 Cogburn Road.

Six of the parks operated by the Forsyth County Parks and Recreation Department offer tennis courts in and around Cumming: **Bennett Park** (770-886-2851), 5930 Burruss Mill Road; **Central Park** (770-781-2215), 2300 Keith Bridge Road; **Coal Mountain Park** (770-781-2151), 3560 Settingdown Road; **Midway Park** (770-781-2152), 5100 Post Road; **Sawnee Mountain Park** (770-886-4085); and **Sharon Springs Park** (770-205-4646), 1950 Sharon Road.

North Fulton Tennis Center (404-303-6182; www.northfultontennis.com), 500 Abernathy Road, Sandy Springs. Open 9–10 Monday through Thursday, 9–9 Friday, 9–7 Saturday, 9–6 Sunday (closed Christmas and New Year's Days; closes early New Year's Eve). The center maintains 20 hard-surface courts and four clay courts—all lighted for night play, as well as a pro shop and a clubhouse. Lessons are available. Hourly rates $2.60 days or $3 nights and weekends for hard courts; $3 days or $3.50 nights and weekends for soft courts.

Four of the parks operated by the Roswell Recreation and Parks Department have tennis courts: **East Roswell Park** (770-594-6505), 9000 Fouts Road; **Hembree Park** (770-569-9746), 850 Hembree Road; **Roswell Area Park** (770-641-3775), 10495 Woodstock Road; and **Waller Park Extension** (770-594-6147), 160 Dobbs Drive.

Tubing
See *Canoeing, Kayaking, Tubing.*

Waterfalls
The natural shoals on Vickery Creek inspired Roswell King to locate his textile mills in Roswell. These shoals were harnessed by a mill dam, which still exists and creates a

striking waterfall. Access to the falls is from two different sides, but the easiest path is from the mill parking area off Sloan Street. Walk upstream and the path will lead you to the dam and falls, which are very photogenic.

GREEN SPACE

Nature Preserves and Parks

✒ 🐾 **Alpharetta Parks and Recreation** (678-297-6100). The city parks department operates 10 parks. Although every park does not offer every amenity, among them you'll find baseball, soccer, football, and softball fields, tennis courts, playgrounds, a disc golf course, hockey arena, gymnasium, equestrian facilities, arts and crafts center, swimming pool, walking trails, and gymnastics and dance facilities. Most facilities are free.

✒ 🐾 **Autrey Mill Nature Preserve and Heritage Center** (678-366-3511; www.autreymill.org), 9770 Autrey Mill Road, Alpharetta. Preserve open daily daylight hours; heritage center open 10–4 weekdays, 10–2 Saturday. Located on 46 acres of forest and the site of an old cotton plantation, Autrey Mill offers scenic creeks, rocky shoals, spring seeps, picturesque cliffs, mature trees, wildflowers, native plants, wildlife, and one mile of hiking trails. Circa late 1800s farmhouses from the plantation days remain: The Tenant Farmhouse is filled with tools and furnishings from bygone days; the 1880s Summerour House is being restored; and the rustic visitor's center houses exhibits. The park offers special programs and events, including an Easter egg hunt, environmental activities, music programs, summer camp, trail walks, and Young Artist Days. Free.

✒ 🐾 **Big Creek Greenway** (678-297-6100), contact the Alpharetta Recreation and Parks Department, 1825 Old Milton Parkway, Alpharetta. Open 8–6 daily. The 6-mile paved path meanders through forests alongside Big Creek parallel to North Point Parkway from Webb Bridge Road on the north end to Mansell Road on the south end. It is widely used by locals for walking, jogging, skating, and cycling. Its location near several hotels makes it a popular diversion for visitors as well. A soft mulch trail that leads around a large wetland between Haynes Bridge and Mansell roads provides opportunities to view blue herons, deer, ducks, and Canada geese. The greenway can be accessed from three points: the Alpharetta YMCA on Preston Ridge Road, Haynes Bridge Road, and North Point Parkway. The last two access points offer parking and the North Point Parkway access also has restrooms. A special 1.2-mile section at the Webb Bridge Road end is set aside for mountain bikers. The greenway is patrolled by park rangers and police, and several call boxes with emergency-only phones are located along the path. Free.

✒ 🐾 **Bowman's Island Unit of the Chattahoochee River National Recreation Area** (call Island Ford visitors center in Dunwoody at 678-538-1200; www.nps.gov/chat), Island Ford Road, Cumming. Open 9–5 daily. In addition to an opportunity to ride your own horse (see *Horseback Riding*), this unit offers hiking, boating, and trout fishing. $3 parking fee.

✒ 🐾 **Chattahoochee Nature Center** (770-992-2055; www.chattnaturecenter.com), 9135 Willeo Road, Roswell. Open 9–5 Monday through Saturday, noon–5 Sunday. Visitors can get in touch with nature at this facility, where boardwalks and nature trails allow access to the 127-acre site and miles of freshwater ponds, river marshes, and wooded uplands that hug the Chattahoochee River. More than 30 species of wildlife call the nature center home. Among the popular exhibits is a beaver dam complete with beavers. Raptor aviaries display

Trails at the Chattahoochee Nature Center in Roswell allow guests to explore flora and fauna that surround the Chattahoochee.

birds of prey that have been rehabilitated here but can't be returned to the wild. The nature center offers tours and hosts educational programs and special events throughout the year, including seasonal canoe trips on the river. Adults $5, children 3–12 and seniors $2.

✈ 👣 🐾 **Forsyth County Parks and Recreation** (770-781-2215), administrative offices in Central Park, 2300 Keith Bridge Road/GA 306, Cumming. The county operates 11 parks. Although each park does not have every facility, together they offer baseball, softball, football, and soccer fields, outdoor basketball courts, tennis courts, playgrounds, and walking trails. **Central Park** features a recreation center with two gymnasiums, a game room, fitness area, arts and crafts room, walking area, aerobics room, and dance room. In addition, Central Park has a 27-hole disc golf course (see *To Do—Disc Golf*), a new 3.7-mile cross-country mountain biking trail, and a bike park with an obstacle course. The parks department is adding boating, camping, fishing, nature trails, and passive outdoor recreation to its offerings with the acquisition of two U.S. Army Corps of Engineers parks on Lake Lanier: 7-acre **Young Deer Creek Park** and 157-acre **Charleston Park**. One of the department's units is the **Sawnee Mountain Preserve** (see separate entry).

✈ 👣 🐾 **John Ripley Forbes Big Trees Forest Preserve** (770-673-0111; www.bigtreesforest .com), 7645 Roswell Road, Sandy Springs. Open sunrise to sunset daily. The hilly 30-acre site comes as a surprise along busy Roswell Road in the heart of Sandy Springs. Step into the forest and leave the chaotic world behind. The preserve offers one mile of hiking trails through middle-growth forests with 100- to 200-year-old white oak trees. No smoking; leashed pets welcome. Free parking and trail use; donations appreciated.

✈ 👣 🐾 **Roswell Recreation and Parks Department** (administrative offices 770-641-3705), 38 Hill Street, Suite 100, Roswell. Open daylight hours daily. The department maintains nearly 20 parks around the city. Although every park does not offer every amenity, together they feature several types of athletic fields, picnic areas, playgrounds, gymnasiums, a swimming pool, tennis courts, nature and hiking trails, an inline skating and skateboard park, fishing, and a formal garden. Some of the most popular parks are the three along the Chattahoochee River. Free.

✈ 🐾 **Sawnee Mountain Preserve** (parks and recreation office 770-781-2215; Sawnee Mountain Foundation 678-936-0308; www.sawneemountain.org), 2500 Bettis–Tribble Gap Road, Cumming. Open 8 to dusk daily except Thanksgiving, Christmas Eve, Christmas Day, and New Year's Day. A unit of the Forsyth County Parks and Recreation, the preserve occupies 720 acres on the southernmost mountain in the Blue Ridge Mountains range. The summit of the mountain, which was named for a friendly Cherokee chief, rises to 2,000 feet. At the summit are the Indian Seats, a natural rock formation where visitors can sit and admire the views of the north Georgia mountains, Lake Lanier, and even the Atlanta skyline. Winner of the Georgia Urban Forestry Council's Most Outstanding Green Space Plan in 2005, the park has completed Phase I of a three-phase development project

Cooling off at the Vickery Creek Unit of the Chattahoochee River National Recreation Area

designed to keep the mountain in its most pristine condition while providing facilities for it to be enjoyed by the public. Completed so far are three miles of easy to strenuous trails for foot traffic only, an amphitheater, restrooms, and picnic pavilions. An area is set aside for rock climbing and rappelling (a $3 permit is required). Pets are not allowed. Free.

✐ ✤ **Vickery Creek Unit of the Chattahoochee River National Recreation Area** (call the Island Ford Headquarters at 678-538-1200; www.nps.gov/chat), Riverside Drive, Roswell. Open 9–5 daily. The topography of the heavily wooded park includes steep cliffs and rocky outcroppings as well as level terrain. A total of 11 miles of trails crisscross the park. Within the park are the ruins of several mill buildings and a man-made mill dam from the 1860s that creates a cascading waterfall. $3 parking fee.

✐ ✤ **Webb Bridge Park** (678-297-6100), 4780 Webb Bridge Road, Alpharetta. Open daily. This 70-acre park has wooded walking trails, soccer fields, tennis courts, and the Webb Zone playground, which includes a wading stream, sand play area, and butterfly garden. Free.

✐ ✤ **Wills Park** (678-297-6120), 11915 Wills Road at Old Milton Parkway, Alpharetta. Open daily. The 110-acre park features an Olympic-size swimming pool (open summer only); football, baseball, and soccer fields; a disc golf course; lighted tennis courts; walking trails, and Wacky World Playground. The **Wills Park Equestrian Center** (see *Equestrian Events*) is attached to the park. Free.

Rivers

Chattahoochee River. The river and its banks offer opportunities for fishing, hiking, picnicking, canoeing, and rafting. Visitors may see wildflowers, wildlife, and waterfowl. The City of Roswell created a River Parkway, an important link in the Roswell Trail System, along several miles of the river (see *Hiking*). Dotted along the River Parkway are the **Chattahoochee River Park** on Azalea Drive, **Riverside Park** on Riverside Road, and the **Don White Memorial Park** on Riverside Drive. (Also see What's Where).

Walks

From the **Roswell Visitors Center** (see *Guidance*), pick up a brochure for a walking/driving tour of Roswell's Historic District. Around the town square and down Bulloch Avenue and Mimosa Boulevard, visitors can walk or drive by **Barrington Hall**, which was in the family of Roswell King's son and his descendants until after the turn of the 21st century and is now open for tours; **Bulloch Hall**, the home of James Stephens Bulloch; **Mimosa Hall** and Holly Hill, private homes; **Primrose Cottage**, now a special events facility; the **Roswell Presbyterian Church**; **Great Oaks**, once the home of Roswell's first schoolmaster and now a special events facility; and **Kimball Hall**, also a special events facility. Down Sloan Street is the **Roswell Historic Mill Village District**, which includes **The Bricks**, the first row houses in the area, built for mill workers to live in dormitory-style and now converted to condominiums; the ruins of one of the old mills; a later mill now used as offices; numerous cottages built for supervisory mill workers and now in use as private homes; the **Lost Mill Workers of Roswell Monument**; and **Founders Cemetery**. In the **Heart of Roswell/Canton Street Historic District** are **Founders Hall** and **Naylor Hall**, both once residences and now special events facilities. **Roswell Area Park** on Woodstock Road (see *Swimming* and *Tennis*) has an interlocking series of paved walking paths. These are color-coded by distance so you can take long or short walks.

Lodging

Bed and Breakfasts

In Sandy Springs
Bentley's Bed & Breakfast (770-396-1742; www.bentleysbandb.com), 6860 Peachtree-Dunwoody Road. Nestled in a serene setting of magnolias, oaks, dogwoods, and pines, the bed and breakfast is located in a 1930s mansion. Six guest rooms feature antiques, hardwood floors, private baths, and Ralph Lauren linens. The Malcomb and Hannah Rooms can be combined to create a suite with a common area. A Southern breakfast is served. Because the B&B also serves as a special events facility, weddings or other events might occur, primarily on weekends. No pets. Limited smoking. Limited wheelchair accessibility (two steps to get into house). $150–175.

Campgrounds

In Cumming
There are eight U.S. Army Corps of Engineers campgrounds on Lake Lanier. Only one—Bald Ridge—falls within the parameters of this chapter, although the others are very close. For all COE campgrounds, reservations must be made at least two days in advance. There is a minimum two-day stay on weekends and a three-day stay on holiday weekends. Attendants are on duty 7 AM–10:30 PM, then the gates are locked overnight. There are limits on the number of vehicles and campers allowed on each site. Alcoholic beverages are prohibited. To get more details about this and the other seven campgrounds or to make reservations, consult the Web site at www.recreation.gov.

🚲 🐾 **Bald Ridge Creek Campground** (770-889-1591), 4100 Bald Ridge Road. Open daily from March through October, the campground is located on a peninsula jutting out into the lake, guaranteeing lake views from almost every site. In addition to 82 sites with water and electric hookups, the campground features a dump station, laundry facilities, restrooms with hot showers, a boat ramp, and a swimming pool. $23–25 per night.

🚲 🐾 **Twin Lakes RV Park** (770-887-4400; www.campgroundinfo.com), 3300 Shore Drive. The campground offers 132 sites with full hookups and a dump station, but no tent sites. There is a stocked pond for campers. $21 per night.

Inns and Hotels
There are no historic, one-of-a-kind, or luxury hotels in any of the cities in this chapter. Sandy Springs, Alpharetta, and Roswell offer a plethora of upper-end chain hotels and motels as well as a few economy hotels; Cumming offers only a few lodgings. Readers should be familiar enough with these chains that we don't need to describe them in detail. The two most upscale hotels in the area described in this chapter are the **Atlanta Marriott Alpharetta** (770-754-9600; 1-800-228-9290), 5750 Windward Parkway, and the **DoubleTree Hotel Atlanta/Roswell** (770-992-9600; 1-800-222-TREE), 1075 Holcomb Bridge Road.

WHERE TO EAT

Dining Out

In Alpharetta

Alpharetta has become a dining mecca among the northern suburbs and is reputed to have more than 200 restaurants, but we can only give a small sampling here. When you arrive in the area, ask your concierge for additional suggestions.

& **Cabernet** (770-777-5955; www.cabernet steakhouse.com), 5575 Windward Parkway. Open 11–2 weekdays; 5–10 Sunday through Thursday, 5–11 Friday and Saturday. The menu features the highest grade of prime aged beef and fresh seafood flown in daily. Specialties include escargot baked in pastry crocks, tuna and salmon tartar, Cabernet salad, and herb-roasted veal chop. The restaurant offers an award-winning wine list from which selections can be purchased by the glass or bottle. Chef Richard Holley also has introduced prix fixe dinners on Friday and Saturday; the three-course meal includes an appetizer, entrée, dessert, and a glass of cabernet for $35. Thursdays with a Twist or an Olive features classic martinis, complimentary hors d'oeuvres, and live jazz from 5:30–7:30. Smoking in the cigar bar only. Wheelchair accessible. Lunch from $9.95, dinner $19.95–38.95.

& **Milton's Restaurant and Bar** (770-817-0161; www.miltons-atl.com), 780 Mayfield Road. Open 5–10 Monday through Thursday, 5–11 Friday and Saturday, 5–9 Sunday; 10–3 Sunday for brunch. Located in a 150-year-old farmhouse and attached 1930s cottage in the Crabapple historic district, Milton's is a comfortable and quaint alternative for dining in style. Chef Jay Pollock, formerly of the Vinings Inn, the River Room, and Killer Creek, presents continental/American comfort food. Appetizers, soups, salads, pastas, and entrées feature chicken, veal, catfish, trout, shrimp and grits, scallops, steaks, and pork chops. Sunday brunch might include waffles, eggs Benedict, salmon, a variety of omelettes, crepes, biscuits and gravy, and huevos rancheros. Sundown Suppers feature smaller portions of a select group of entrées from 5 to 6. No smoking. Wheelchair accessible. $15–32; Sundown Suppers $11–15; brunch $10–15.

& **Rainwater** (770-777-0033; www.rainwater restaurant.com), 11655 Haynes Bridge Road. Open 11:30–2:30 weekdays; 5:30–9 Monday through Thursday, 5:30–10 Friday and Saturday. Rainwater's new American cuisine is heavily influenced by that of northern California and the Pacific Northwest. Dinner, a somewhat formal affair, features such highlights as certified Angus filet, roasted halibut, and Rainwater's signature crab cake. Lunch, which is more casual, might offer a fried shrimp, warm Brie, and spinach salad; spring vegetable pasta; or Italian Otto ham and smoked mozzarella panini. Be sure to save room for the signature dessert: Raspberry Staircase, an elegant presentation of white and dark chocolate mousse with raspberry coulis. Smoking allowed in one room. Wheelchair accessible. Lunch $10–16, dinner $19–38.

& **Ray's Killer Creek** (770-649-0064; www.raysrestaurants.com), 1700 Mansell Road. Open 11–2 weekdays; 5–10 Monday through Thursday, 5–11 Friday and Saturday, 5–9 Sunday; Sunday brunch 10:30–2:30. Voted one of the best steak houses in Atlanta by *Creative Loafing* and a Taste of Alpharetta winner, this upscale restaurant offers premium steaks and fresh seafood. In addition, Killer Creek has been recognized with a *Wine Spectator* Award of Excellence. Signature cocktails and live entertainment are featured on Wednesday, Friday, and Saturday night. Smoking in the bar only. Wheelchair accessible. Lunch under $10; dinner $19.95–39.95; brunch: adults $23.95, children $12.95.

& **Sage** (770-569-9199; www.sagewood

firetavern.com), 11405 Haynes Bridge
Road. Open 11–10 Monday through
Thursday, 11–11 Friday, 5–11 Saturday and
Sunday; lounge and bar open until 1 AM.
Casual ambience paired with city chic
serves as a pleasant backdrop for contemporary American cuisine with global influences. Fresh fish, hand-cut steaks, chops,
and chicken are prepared over a hickory-
oak wood-fire grill. Live music is offered
6–10 Monday through Saturday; DJs take
over after 10. Thursdays they spin '60s and
'70s tunes; Friday the DJ plays hot dance
music. No smoking. Wheelchair accessible.
Lunch $7.97–11.95, dinner $10.95–34.95.

&Village Tavern (770-777-6490; www.
villagetavern.com), 11555 Rainwater Drive.
Open 11–10 Monday through Thursday,
11–11 Friday, 4–11 Saturday, 10–10 Sunday
with brunch served 10–3. In this upscale yet
casual restaurant, exposed timber beams,
warm colors, and a stone fireplace set the
stage for traditional and modern fare and
an award-winning wine list. No smoking.
Wheelchair accessible. $13–27.

& Vinny's (770-772-4644; www.know
wheretogogh.com), 5355 Windward
Parkway. Open 11–3 weekdays; 5–10:30
Monday through Thursday, 5–11:30 Friday
and Saturday, 5–10 Sunday. A sibling to the
original Bistro VG in Roswell (see separate
entry), Vinny's is also a salute to Vincent
Van Gogh. The Italian-inspired menu
depends on the freshest ingredients such
as imported Parmesan-reggiano cheese,
real Parma ham, delicate truffles, organic
greens and vegetables, and imported
chocolates. Lunch starters include gazpa-
cho, tomato-ciabatta bread soup, pear and
arugula salad, fresh buffalo milk mozzarella
and tomatoes, and prosciutto and spinach
pizza followed by entrées such as leg of
lamb sandwich, shaved pork tenderloin,
lasagna, or veal meatballs. Dinner entrées
range from sea bass to lamb to cowboy rib
eye, with many other meat and seafood
choices filling out the menu. Diners also

can sample from an eclectic selection of
beers on tap as well as fine Italian wines,
California reserve labels, and even grappa.
The artistry here extends beyond the menu
and beverage selections: Vinny's has
invited several well-known galleries to
share their classical and contemporary artwork with patrons. No smoking.
Wheelchair accessible. Lunch entrées average $12, dinner entrées $16–30.

In Cumming

&Atkins Park Tavern (678-513-2333;
www.atkinspark.com), 5820 South Vickery
Street. Open 11 AM–1 AM Monday through
Thursday, 11 AM–2 AM Saturday, 11 AM–
midnight Sunday. The third and newest
location of the oldest continuously licensed
tavern in the metro Atlanta area is located
in the newly created live/work/play community of Vickery. In addition to an array of
appetizers, soups, salads, sandwiches, and
burgers, the eatery serves entrées such as
lamb, rib eye, chicken, pork, bass, trout,
scallops, and salmon. Brunch, which is
served from 11–4 on weekends, features
biscuits and gravy, omelettes, shrimp and
grits, French toast, steak and eggs, and crab
cake Benedict. No smoking. Wheelchair
accessible. $12–21.

& The Foster House (770-887-9905), 305
West Main Street. Open 7:30–10 and
11–2:30 weekdays; 5–8:30 Thursday, until
9:30 Friday and Saturday. Mother-daughter
team Patricia and Amanda Hamby restored
this 1800s house complete with wraparound
porch, and now operate a popular dining
establishment from it. This charming
restaurant is often filled with the ladies who
lunch (as well as some businessmen and
other gentlemen), and the menu reflects
that with an array of salads, sandwiches, and
other lighter fare. Dinner is a more substantial meal with a country buffet that
includes two meats, vegetables, salads, and
beverages. You can order off the menu on
Friday and Saturday evening, when steaks

and seafood are featured. Save room for the homemade desserts. The restaurant serves wine and beer, but not liquor. The stone patio is an enticing place to eat in good weather, and the carriage house has been converted to a wedding chapel, so you could actually have a small wedding and reception or a very private romantic dinner here. No smoking. Wheelchair accessible. Breakfast $3.95–5.95, lunch $5–10, dinner $10–25.

♨ ♿ **Tam's Backstage** (678-455-8310; www.tamsbackstage.com), 125 Ingram Avenue. Open 11–9:30 Monday through Thursday, 11–10 Friday and Saturday. Located in the lower level of the historic 1927 Cumming Schoolhouse, now home of the Cumming Playhouse, the eatery serves a blend of American cuisines with a bit of Italian pizzazz. In keeping with its association with the theater, the cozy restaurant's courses are titled dramatizers, spotlights, headliners, supporting roles, and curtain calls. Entrées feature chicken, steak, pork, seafood, and pasta. No smoking. Wheelchair accessible. $4–10 for lunch, $15–20 for dinner.

In Roswell

♿ **Amalfi Ristorante** (770-645-9983), 292 South Atlanta Street. Open 5:30–10 Monday through Saturday; reservations not accepted. Salvatore Mattielo serves Neapolitan-influenced Italian cuisine. Some specialties include linguine with seafood, veal with tomato and mushrooms, pasta fagioli, calamari with marinara sauce and yellow peppers, penne all'amatriciana, and homemade cannoli. Smoking at the bar only. Wheelchair accessible. $12–25.

♿ **Bistro VG** (770-993-1156; www.know wheretogogh.com), 70 West Crossville Road. Open 11:30–2:30 daily; bar food 2:30–5 daily; dinner 5–11 Saturday, 5–9 Sunday. The Zagat Survey considers Bistro VG's to be one of the best restaurants in the entire metropolitan Atlanta area. The contemporary stone and rustic wood structure once housed a California-style restaurant. These days, the formal traditional furnishings and crisp white linens are somewhat at odds with the casual structure, but nothing takes away from the fabulous cuisine or the extensive wine list. Bistro VG's wine cellar, which features more than 500 selections representing the world's greatest wine regions, has received *Wine Spectator's* Award of Excellence several years running—one of only five such awards in the state. Lunch might include such delicacies as calamari, Thai chicken salad, shaved beef carpaccio, tuna tartar, or hot smoked trout for starters, followed by a grilled salmon BLT, grilled bison burger, or a crab cake sandwich. Dinner choices include Cabrales blue cheese and basil risotto fritters, or garnet beet and bucheron Napoleon for starters, followed by seared sea scallops, grilled chipotle marinated pork tenderloin, roast rack of lamb, or confit and crisp-seared breast of duck. To-die-for desserts include crème brûlée, pots de crème, beignets, chocolate turtle truffle tortes, and other specialties. The bar, with its comprehensive selection of top-quality liquors and liqueurs, is a favorite hangout for locals. No smoking. Wheelchair accessible. Lunch entrées average $12, dinner entrées $16–24.

♿ **dick and harry's** (770-641-8757; www.dickandharrys.com), 1570 Holcomb Bridge Road, Suite 810. Open 11:30–2:30 weekdays; 5:30–10 Monday through Thursday, 5:30–11 Friday and Saturday. Dick and Harry are brothers Richard and Harold Marmulstein. Their contemporary American cuisine at this upscale casual restaurant features fish, seafood, steaks, chops, and award-winning crab cakes. In fact, their menu is so diverse, you can get everything here from special Passover meals to ice cream. No smoking. Wheelchair accessible. $17–30.

Pastis (770-640-3870; www.roswell pastis.com), 936 Canton Street. Open

11:30–2:30 and 5:30–10 daily. This restaurant has an award-winning wine list and menu featuring French cuisine. This trendy little eatery in the heart of the Roswell art gallery district makes you feel as if you have, indeed, been whisked off the French Riviera. Popular places to dine are by the fireplace or on the balcony overlooking historic Canton Street. Among the accolades heaped on Pastis by *Jezebel* and *Creative Loafing* are Best Steaks, Best French Food, Best Live Music, Best Neighborhood Bar, Best Trendy Hangout, Best Romantic Restaurant, and Best Overall Restaurant. No smoking. Not wheelchair accessible. $17–30.

In Sandy Springs

&. 5 Seasons Brewing Company (404-255-5911; www.5seasonsbrewing.com), 5600 Roswell Road at the Prado Shopping Center. Open 11–10 Monday through Wednesday, 11–10:30 Thursday, 11–11 Friday and Saturday, noon–10 Sunday. A serious brewery, the establishment creates 60 beers, including Seven Sisters Munchner, Munich Helles, Me262 Maibock, and Sledgehammer. Gourmet meals feature local produce, all-natural meats, and artisanal cheeses. In addition to appetizers, salads, and grilled pizzas, menu items might feature entrées such as salmon trout, duck, lamb, rib eye, filets, pork, and chicken. Popular events include beer tastings, organic dinners, and barbecue demonstrations. Smoking is allowed in a separate dining room and bar. Wheelchair accessible. $13–25.

Eating Out

In Alpharetta

&. Alpha Soda (770-442-3102; www.alphasoda.com), 11760 Haynes Bridge Road. Open 7 AM–10 PM weekdays, until 11 Friday and Saturday. Alpha Drug has been a fixture in Alpharetta since the 1920s, when a local drugstore opened a soda fountain.

Although the casual eatery has moved to a new home and changed its name to Alpha Soda, its decor is reminiscent of the 1920s and 1930s. Breakfast choices include eggs any style, pancakes, waffles, and more substantial fare such as steak and eggs, pork chops, or eggs with crab. Lunch and dinner feature soups, salads, burgers, sandwiches, chops, seafood, and Southern specialties such as fried chicken or ribs. Alpha Soda also features a full bar and a covered patio for outdoor seating. No smoking section. Wheelchair accessible. $7–20; senior citizens get a 10 percent discount.

&. Champps Americana (770-642-1933), 7955 North Point Parkway. Open 11 AM–midnight Monday through Wednesday, 11 AM–1 AM Thursday through Saturday, 10 AM–midnight Sunday. The spacious restaurant serves gargantuan portions of steaks, chops, ribs, pasta, burgers, and great desserts. Most likely you'll be taking home enough for another meal. A plethora of large-screen televisions are tuned to various sports shows and events, which leads to a lively atmosphere as diners cheer on their favorites. No smoking. Wheelchair accessible. $9–20.

&. di Paolo Cucina (770-587-1051), 8560 Holcomb Bridge Road. Open 5:30–10 Tuesday through Thursday, 5:30–11 Friday and Saturday, 5:30–9 Sunday. Reservations recommended. One of metro Atlanta's finest trattorias, casual di Paolo's features Tuscan cuisine cooked in a wood-burning brick oven in an open kitchen. The menu changes seasonally so that ingredients can always be the freshest, but diners can expect antipasti (appetizers), misto (mixed platters), salads, and traditional Italian entrées such as ravioli, lasagna, and other pastas along with gourmet selections such as lamb and seafood. An extensive wine list provides perfect accompaniments to dinner. No smoking. Wheelchair accessible. $12–20.

&. Mittie's Café (770-772-0850; www.mitties.com), 62 North Main Street.

Open for breakfast, lunch, and high tea 8–3 daily. Mittie, of course, was Mittie Bulloch, who married Theodore Roosevelt Sr. (see **Bulloch Hall** under *Historic Homes and Sites*). The restaurant, located in a small brick house in the center of Alpharetta, consists of numerous intimate dining rooms decorated with antiques and teacups. Breakfast delicacies include cranberry scones; ham, egg, and cheese croissants; New Orleans toast; Monte Cristo sandwiches; oatmeal soufflé; and other specialties. Typically Southern ladies' luncheon specials include Ms. Emily's chicken salad as a plate or a croissant sandwich, quiches, crêpes, soups, salads, sandwiches, and wraps. High tea, which is by appointment, includes several specialty canapés, sandwiches, quiches, and salads. No smoking. Wheelchair accessible. There is a sister restaurant (in fact, it was the original) in Roswell on Canton Street (770-594-8822). Its recent move into a space that once housed a Southwestern restaurant and minimal redecorating has resulted in a very un-tea-room-like atmosphere. Besides that, it's very noisy. The excellent menu, however, is the same as that of the Alpharetta location. No smoking. Wheelchair accessible. Breakfast $7–9, lunch $6–10, high tea $15 adults, $10 children.

✍🦞♿ **Pure Taqueria** (678-240-0023), 103 Old Roswell Street. Open 11–11 daily. Located in a remodeled old Pure gas station, the casual eatery serves authentic Mexican food. The specialty is fish tacos. Reservations are not taken and there is often a line spilling out onto the street. No smoking. Wheelchair accessible. $9–25.

In Cumming

✍🦞♿ **Norman's Landing** (770-886-0100), 365 Peachtree Parkway. Open 11:15–10 Monday through Thursday, 11:15–11:30 Friday, 11:30–11:30 Saturday, 11:30–9:30 Sunday (brunch served on Sunday morning); bar open 11:30–2 AM Monday through Saturday. A serious seafood place, casual Norman's has a menu with cute titles such as The Lures (appetizers), The Lines (side dishes), and The Sinkers (desserts). Entrées run the range from all kinds of seafood to beef, ribs, and chicken. Brunch includes such hearty dishes as eggs Benedict, crab Benedict, filet and eggs, and pork chop and eggs. No smoking. Wheelchair accessible. Lunch $4.95–9.95, dinner $10.95–35.95 (lobster and some other items are market price), brunch $8.95–14.95.

✍🦞♿ **Pappy Red's Barbecue** (770-844-9446), 302 Tri-County Plaza. Open 11–7 daily. The small airplane that seems to have crashed into the roof might be the first clue that this popular eatery doesn't take itself too seriously. A conglomeration of interesting-to-tacky memorabilia covering the walls and ceiling inside confirms that first impression. What the restaurant does take seriously, however, is its barbecue. Sandwiches, plates, and ribs are available along with several comfort-food-type side dishes. No smoking. Wheelchair accessible. $3 for a sandwich, $8 for a dinner.

In Roswell

✍🦞♿ **Anna Lee's** (770-998-0086), 425 Market Place. Open 11:30–2:30 weekdays. A favorite place for the ladies who lunch, the intimate eatery is known for its homemade soups, desserts, and creative sandwiches at very affordable prices. The best bargain is the soup/entrée/dessert combo for $6. This includes a choice of about three soups, three to five entrées, and a half-dozen desserts. Businessmen eat here as well, and there is a communal table stacked with magazines and newspapers so a single diner can mingle with others. Wheelchair accessible. $5–10.

✍🦞♿ **Byblos** (678-352-0321; www.byblos -atlanta.com), 10864 Alpharetta Highway. Open 11–2:30 and 5:30–10 Tuesday through Sunday. This Lebanese restaurant offers traditional food and entertainment. The lunch buffet is a great bargain, especially on weekends. The mezza (appetizers) are terrific, too. In addition to the great food, diners can smoke a water pipe on the patio or watch belly dancers. No smoking. Wheelchair accessible. $11.50–18.

🛥🍴♿**Dreamland Barbecue** (678-352-7999; www.dreamlandbbq.com), 10730 Alpharetta Highway. Open 10–10 Monday through Saturday, 11–10 Sunday. The one-of-a-kind Dreamland has been an institution in Tuscaloosa, Alabama, where it was a favorite of local citizens, University of Alabama students, Crimson Tide football players and coaches, and tourists. It was a bit of a drive, however, if Roswellians got a hankering for Dreamland barbecue, so it was exciting when a sister restaurant opened here. The choices are primarily ribs and sandwiches served with side dishes such as coleslaw and baked beans and a pile of napkins. No smoking. Wheelchair accessible. $7–18.

🛥🍴♿**Edible Expressions** (770-992-7700; www.edibleexpressions.com), 555 South Atlanta Street. Open 9–4 weekdays. Located in the Founders Square shopping center, this casual European-style café features an outdoor deck overlooking the historic Roswell Mill. Menu items include gourmet salads, sandwiches, and pastas accompanied by to-die-for desserts and specialty coffees. No smoking. Wheelchair accessible. $3.75–8.25.

🛥🍴♿**Fratelli di Napoli** (770-642-9917; www.fratelli.net), 928 Canton Street. Open 5–10 Monday through Thursday and Sunday, 5–11 Friday and Saturday. Bring big appetites or several people to this casual restaurant where Southern Italian chicken, steaks, chops, veal, seafood, and pasta are served in portions for two or more. The full bar has an extensive wine list. No smoking. Wheelchair accessible. $13.

🛥🍴♿**Greenwood's on Green Street** (770-992-5383), 1087 Green Street. Open 5–9

Wednesday and Thursday, 11:30–10 Friday and Saturday, 11:30–9 Sunday. At this casual, down-home Southern eatery, owner Bill Greenwood creates signature dishes from meat loaf, pork chops, chicken pot pie, trout, vegetables, and luscious homemade desserts, but even items as fine as duck are featured. No smoking. Limited wheelchair accessibility in one area of the restaurant; restrooms are not wheelchair accessible. $10.95–25.95. Credit cards are not accepted, but checks are.

🛥🍴♿**Slopes BBQ** (770-518-7000; www.slopesbbq.com), 34 Crossville Road. Open 11–9 Monday through Thursday, 11–9:30 Friday and Saturday in the summer; closes a half-hour earlier in the winter. The menu features hickory-smoked, hand-pulled pork and chicken as well as ribs, Brunswick stew, homemade cobblers, and other comfort foods. No smoking. Wheelchair accessible. $1.99–10.99.

🛥🍴♿**The Southern Skillet** (770-993-7700; www.theskillet.com), 1037 Alpharetta Street. Open 6 AM–9 PM weekdays, 6 AM–3 PM Saturday, 8 AM–3 PM Sunday. Billed as a place "Where local folk meet and eat," this restaurant has been a local favorite for almost a quarter-century. It serves old-fashioned Southern dishes for breakfast and lunch daily and for dinner on weekdays. Get the day off to a good start with a typical Southern breakfast of biscuits and gravy, eggs, bacon, sausage, pancakes, and grits. For lunch or dinner choose from dishes such as country-fried steak, meat loaf, ham, pork chops, trout, catfish, or liver, each served with vegetables and a roll, biscuit, or corn bread. Live bluegrass music entertains diners most Friday nights. Smoking allowed. Wheelchair accessible. $5.99–10.55.

🛥🍴♿**Swallow at the Hollow** (678-352-1975; www.theswallowatthehollow.com), 1072 Green Street. Open 11–2:30 and 5–9 Wednesday through Sunday; for shows 8:30–midnight Friday and Saturday. Are the terms "gourmet" and "backyard country barbecue" an oxymoron? Find out at this simple restaurant located in an old barn. Owner Bill Greenwood (of Greenwood's on Green Street, above) offers everything from barbecue to fried green tomatoes to pit-cooked portobello sandwiches with fresh Gouda to banana pudding with chocolate chip cookies. Bill bakes all his own breads, too. Live bands play as background music Wednesday and Sunday evenings; country bluegrass shows are performed Friday and Saturday nights. No smoking. Wheelchair accessible. $10.95–21.95. Cover charge for Friday and Saturday night shows $15–30; no cover charge Wednesday and Sunday.

In Sandy Springs

✆ 🍴 ♿ **China Cooks** (404-252-6611), 215 Northwood Drive. Open 11 AM–2 AM weekdays, noon–2 AM weekends. Menu items might include Peking duck with all the trimmings, duck palms in oyster sauce, shrimp balls and bean thread noodle hot pot, or steamed minced chicken with salt fish. No smoking. Wheelchair accessible. $9–15.

✆ 🍴 ♿ **Persepolis** (404-257-9090; www.persepoliscuisine.com), 6435 Roswell Road. Open 11:30–10 Sunday through Thursday, 11:30–11 Friday and Saturday. You'd think you were in the posh dining room of a private home with ornate columns, corner fireplaces, and elegant decorating touches at this Persian restaurant where beef, chicken, lamb, seafood, and vegetarian kabobs lead the menu. Baklava, Persian ice cream, and other Persian delicacies star on the dessert menu. Several drinks feature yogurt. Belly dancing is performed Thursday through Saturday evenings. No smoking. Wheelchair accessible. $11–20.

✆ 🍴 ♿ **Rumi's Kitchen** (404-477-2100; www.rumiskitchen.com), 6152 Roswell Road. Open 11:30–10 Monday through Thursday, 11:30–11 Friday, noon–11 Saturday and Sunday. Owner and head chef Ali Mesghali was formerly the inspiration behind Persepolis and now brings his expertise to Rumi's—named for Jelauddin Rumi, a famous poet of the ancient Persian Empire. At Rumi's Kitchen, "hospitality, love, and friendship come together for the joy of the exquisite cuisine and traditions of Persia." The inviting and cozy bar opens into an intimate dining room with Middle Eastern accents. On the large covered patio, guests can sit in lavish wicker chairs and sample Turkish tobacco in an authentic hookah after 10 PM. In addition to such traditional dishes as hummus, tabbouli, and dolmeh, visitors can feast on vegetable, chicken, beef, lamb, and shrimp kabobs. Traditional Persian flatbread is baked daily in a wood stone oven resembling the old-fashioned tanoor ovens of ancient Persia. No smoking except hookahs on the patio after 10. Wheelchair accessible. $12–22.

Snacks

In Alpharetta

✆ 🍴 ♿ **Theo's Brother's Bakery** (770-740-0360), 12280 Houze Road in the Silos Corner Shopping Center. Open 8–5 Tuesday through Saturday. All Theo's breads are baked with the freshest ingredients and no preservatives. Breads include such favorites as dried cranberry pecan, focaccia, traditional French baguettes, Moroccan and kalamata olive, brioche, corn-studded sweet potato semolina, and Theo's daily specials. Every day the bakery also creates a fresh assortment of cookies, tarts, scones, biscotti, sandwiches, and homemade soups. Buy these to take home or enjoy them at the bakery. There are no tables inside, but in good weather you can sit café-style at one of the two tables on the sidewalk outside. No smoking. Wheelchair accessible.

Tea Shops

In Alpharetta
✧✿❧ **Vintage Tea** (770-752-8422; www.vintagetea.com), 3005 Old Alabama Road. Open
10–4:30 Tuesday through Friday, 10–5 Saturday. The tea parlor features vintage hats, gloves,
and furs for guests to don while experiencing a tea party menu served on English china.
Light afternoon tea includes scones, fruit, clotted cream and lemon curd, finger sandwiches, delectable sweets, and a bottomless pot of tea. Full afternoon tea also includes a
savory soup and a salad. In addition, Vintage Tea sells a fine selection of teas and gift items.
No smoking. Wheelchair accessible. $17.95–23.95.
Also see **Mittie's Café** under *Eating Out—In Alpharetta*.

ENTERTAINMENT

Music
Atlanta Wind Symphony (for tickets, call the Georgia Ensemble Theater 770-641-1260;
www.atlantawindsymphony.org). Call for a schedule of performances. In existence since
1979, this nationally and internationally respected symphony is comprised of professional
and amateur (but highly accomplished) musicians. The AWS presents a Master Concert
Series and several other concerts at parks, adult living centers, and civic celebrations.
Tickets for performances at the Roswell Cultural Arts Center are: adults $10, seniors $7,
students $5, children 12 and younger free, but a ticket is required. Admission to the
"Sounds of the Spirit" concerts at the Roswell United Methodist Church is free, but a ticket
is required. All concerts are general admission.
Georgia Philharmonic Orchestra (770-594-6232). In existence since 1984, the orches-
tra, which performs at the Roswell Cultural Arts Center and Alpharetta United Methodist
Church, contributes to the cultural life of residents in the northern metropolitan Atlanta
suburbs. The orchestra performs the highest caliber of music with noted guest artists.
Jam Sessions at the Roswell Visitors Center (770-640-3253; 1-800-776-7935). Bluegrass
held 1–4 on the first Sunday of each month; folk music 1–4 on the second and fourth
Sunday of each month. Bring your instrument and join the fun or just listen and tap your
toes. Free.

Theater
Alpharetta Christian Theater (770-663-8989; www.act1theater.com), Alpharetta
Presbyterian Church, 180 Academy Street, Alpharetta. The community theater, an outreach
of the church, presents family-oriented productions. Call for a schedule and ticket prices.
Cumming Playhouse (770-781-9178; www.playhousecumming.com), 101 School Street,
Cumming. Building open 9–noon and 2–4 weekdays. Call for a schedule of events and
ticket prices. The community theater is located in the restored 1923 Cumming Public
School, which is on the National Register of Historic Places. Numerous productions from
comedy to drama to musicals are performed each year. The facility also houses the
Historical Society of Forsyth County and the Colonel Hiram Parks Bell Center for Southern
History and Genealogical Research. Dinner theater is offered on select performance nights
at **Tam's Backstage** downstairs (see *Dining Out*).

Georgia Ensemble Theater (770-641-1260; www.get.org), 950 Forrest Street, Roswell. The season of professional dramas, comedies, and musicals lasts from February through August. Both season subscriptions and single tickets are available. Call for a schedule and ticket prices.

🎭 **Kudzu Playhouse of Roswell** (770-594-1020; 770-998-3526; www.kudzuplayhouse.com), 608 Holcomb Bridge Road, Suite 140-B, Roswell. The 125-seat community theater features seven professional and amateur performances per year as well as a popular children's theater, a drama camp, and drama lessons. Shows are held at 8 PM Thursday through Saturday; children's shows are performed at 2 PM Saturday and Sunday. Call for a schedule of performances and prices.

Roswell Cultural Arts Center (770-594-6232; 770-641-1260; www.roswellgov.com), 950 Forrest Street, Roswell. Box office open 12:30–6 Tuesday through Saturday. The center hosts theater, dance, musical, and puppet show performances as well as cultural events such as pageants, celebrations, and exhibits year-round. It is the home of the Georgia Ensemble Theater (see above). Call for a schedule of performances and prices.

SELECTIVE SHOPPING

The historic downtowns of Alpharetta, Crabapple, and Roswell offer upscale shopping. **Historic Downtown Alpharetta** is lined with shops and restaurants. The works of local artists and craftsmen are displayed during the Main Street Market events held the third weekend of each month from April through October. Antique festivals are held in May and October. The **Historic Shops of Crabapple** have constituted an antiques haven since the late 1960s. The former stop on Cherokee Indian trails is now a popular stop for shoppers in search of something a little different. Peddlers are located in small historic structures. Twice a year, in May and October, 100 roving antiques vendors converge here and set up shop outdoors all around the village. At the **Shops of Historic Roswell** (Canton Street and Elizabeth Way), period storefronts, benches, and lighting create an upscale shopping atmosphere. **City Walk** in Sandy Springs contains numerous trendy boutiques such as Fab'rik, Sandpiper, Chelsea Parkes, and Potpourri.

Antiques

The Board of Trade Fine Consignments (770-640-7615), 1078 Alpharetta Street, Roswell. Open 10–5:30 Monday through Saturday, noon–5 Sunday. Owned by accredited antiques appraisers, the shop features antiques, fine furniture, artwork, porcelain, lamps, silver, china, jewelry, and collectibles.

Historic Crabapple Antique Village (contact the Alpharetta CVB at 678-297-2811). Several antiques and specialty shops clustered around the intersection of Crabapple, Broadwell, Mid Broadwell, and Mayfield roads and Birmingham Highway occupy early homes, a former country store, and a circa 1860 cotton gin. The particular shops may come and go, but there's always a delightful array of choices, Southern-style gifts, folk art, and one-of-a-kind items.

Historic Roswell Antique Market (770-587-5259; www.roswellantiques.com), 1207-C Alpharetta Street, Roswell. Open 10–6 Monday through Saturday, 1–5 Sunday. Shoppers can find antiques, vintage furniture and accessories, collectibles, antique clocks, and Oriental rugs.

Main Street Antique Market (770-521-1555), 43 Marietta Street, Alpharetta. Open 10–6 Monday through Saturday. The shop features everything from French to country, including furniture, collectibles, porcelain, china, silver, lamps, and more.

Red Baron's Antiques (404-252-3770; www.redbaronsantiques.com), 6450 Roswell Road, Sandy Springs. Open 9–6 Monday through Saturday. A not-to-be-missed event is one of the auctions at Red Baron's, where the well-heeled gather to bid on spectacular antique cars, furniture, garden accessories fit for a royal palace, architectural elements, fine arts, and collectibles. At these auctions, which are held two or three times per year, you can purchase everything from an entire dismantled room from a European castle to a motorized life-size elephant to the contents of an entire museum. Red Baron's specializes in the etchings of Louis Icart. A reservation for the auction will run you $100 (the amount is fully credited to any purchase you make). If you can't make it to an auction, items may be purchased at the wholesale price up to one week prior to an auction.

Roswell Clock And Antique Co. (770-992-5232; www.roswellclockandantique.com), 955 Canton Street, Roswell. Open 10–5 Tuesday through Friday, 10–4 Saturday. In addition to antique clocks, the shop offers furniture, china, silver, and accessories, as well as expert clock repair and restoration.

Art Galleries

Ann Jackson Gallery (770-993-4783; www.annjacksongallery.com), 932 Canton Street, Roswell. Open 10–5:30 Monday though Saturday, noon–5 Sunday. The gallery is the exclusive dealer of Dr. Seuss, Mackenzie Thorpe, Pino, Roy Fairchild, and other international artists.

Art Galleries of Historic Roswell (706-640-3253; 1-800-776-7935; www.cvb.roswell.ga.us). Numerous art galleries and artists' studios are located primarily on historic Canton Street in Roswell.

Heaven Blue Rose Contemporary Gallery (770-642-7380; www.heavenbluerose.com), 934 Canton Street, Roswell. Open 11–5:30 Tuesday through Saturday, 1–4 Sunday. The facility, an artist-owned contemporary gallery, sponsors six exhibits each year.

Raiford Gallery (770-645-2050), 1169 Canton Street, Roswell. Open 10–6 Tuesday through Friday, 10–5 Saturday. The gallery represents 350 artists working in mediums such as ceramics, furniture, glass, jewelry, painting, and sculpture.

Books

Roswell Bookstore (770-992-8485; www.roswellbookstore.com), 11055 Alpharetta Highway, Suite 4, Roswell. Open 10–6 Monday, Tuesday, Wednesday, and Friday, 11–7 Thursday, 10–5 Saturday. Essentially a used book store/paperback exchange, the shop also sells new books, books on tape, and gifts.

Children's Things

Abbotts Kids Village, 5075 Abbotts Bridge Road. Located at Abbotts Bridge and Jones Bridge roads, the shopping center is just for kids, with bright awnings, colorful signs, and sidewalks painted with train tracks and hopscotch squares. The shopping center features the Dynamo Swim Center, Gym Zone, Kuts 4 Kids, Plaster Palace, My Storyhouse Toys, Peek a Boo kids' clothing, and Child Time Day Care.

Crafts

American Sampler (770-993-1843), 959 Canton Street, Roswell. Open 10–5 Monday through Saturday, 1–5 Sunday. The store purveys original folk art, country and primitive carvings, pottery, furniture, and folk Santas year-round.

Food

Cookies by Design (770-992-0355; www.cookiesbydesign.com), 900 Mansell Road, Suite 16, Roswell. Open 9–6 weekdays, 9–3 Saturday. The sweetest bouquet in town, these gourmet cookie arrangements are perfect for many occasions.

Farmer's Market (770-781-3491), Cumming Fairgrounds, 235 Castleberry Road, Cumming. Open every Wednesday and Saturday from 7 AM until all the produce is sold, which is usually between 11 AM and noon. This is an opportunity to buy fresh, locally grown produce.

Harry's Farmer's Market (770-664-6300), 1180 Upper Hembree Road, Roswell. Open 8–9 Monday through Saturday, 8–8 Sunday. Residents of the northern suburbs don't have to go to Decatur or south of the airport to shop at a farmer's market. Some visitors have likened Harry's to a culinary theme park or a chef's playground. You can get all kinds of exotic ingredients from around the world here.

Gifts

The Chandlery (770-993-5962; 1-800-440-4789; www.chandlerygifts.com), 950 Canton Street, Roswell. Open 9:30–6 Monday through Saturday (until 8 on Wednesday), 1–5 Sunday. The shop features gifts and accessories from the world's finest designers, as well as many lines exclusive to The Chandlery.

Olive and Fig (770-998-2505; www.oliveandfig.com), 1025 Canton Street, Roswell. Open 10–5 Tuesday through Saturday. Located in a cottage in the historic district, the shop offers unique home furnishings, custom lighting, interesting finds, stylish accessories, and unusual gifts. Enjoy a beverage from the rejuvenating coffee bar while browsing.

Parsons (770-887-9991), 525 Lakeland Plaza, Cumming. Open 10–7 weekdays, 10–6 Saturday. Parsons carries one of the biggest collections of gifts, collectibles, and home decor in the metropolitan Atlanta area. The shop holds a special sale every month and an entire Christmas store in November and December.

Other Goods

Bonsai Trees Intl. Co. (770-993-1144), 352 South Atlanta Street, Roswell. Open 10–6 Monday through Saturday. Since 1972, the nursery/shop has been selling indoor and outdoor varieties of bonsai trees as well as bonsai supplies, books, tools, and pots.

Moss Blacksmith Shop (770-993-2398), 1075 Canton Street, Roswell. Open 7:30–5 Wednesday through Friday, 7:30–4 Saturday. This artisan creates custom ironwork, railings, and iron furniture, and also performs general repairs and welding.

Special Stores

Cherokee Music Company (770-887-7580), 5515 Setting Down Road, Cumming. Huge whimsical figures of the Pink Panther, Inspector Clouseau, a Viking, and even Santa Claus call attention to this unusual store, where nostalgia enthusiasts can purchase a restored 1940s or 1950s jukebox, a soda fountain, or a pinball machine.

SPECIAL EVENTS

March: **Great American Cover-Up Annual Quilt Show** (770-992-1731), 180 Bulloch Avenue, Roswell. Open 10–4 Monday through Saturday, 1–4 Sunday. The one-week show features more than 100 antique and new quilts filling the rooms of historic Bulloch Hall. Demonstrations and other activities also are part of the show. $8.

May: **Colors Festival of Arts** (770-640-3253; www.cvb.roswell.ga.us/festivals.html). Sponsored by the Roswell Junior Woman's Club and the Roswell Visitors Center, the festival in the historic town square features fine arts and original crafts created by artists from around the Southeast. Performing arts and children's entertainment are also part of the event. Free.

Taste of Alpharetta (678-297-6078; www.awesomealpharetta.com). This festival draws more than 40,000 hungry fans to Wills Park in Alpharetta. Sample foods from Alpharetta's finest restaurants and enjoy children's activities and rides, an arts and crafts show, live entertainment on two stages, and businesses showcasing their products. Fifty cents–$3 for food samples.

May through October: **Roswell Riverside Sounds** (770-594-6187; www.roswellgov.com), Riverside Park, 575 Riverside Road, Roswell. Held at 7:30 PM on the first Saturday of each month, May through October, the outdoor concert series features a wide variety of musical genres that might include roots rock, country, rock and roll, jazz, rhythm and blues, soul, swing, or Latin American. Food concessions are available, as are free parking and restrooms. Free.

June: **Roswell Magnolia Storytelling Festival** (770-640-3253; 1-800-776-7935), 180 Bulloch Avenue, Roswell. The general public is invited to the grounds of historic Bulloch Hall to listen to storytellers, musicians, and interpreters from around the Southeast who gather to share stories passed down through generations. The event includes performances, workshops, open mic programs, and more. $10–20.

June and July: **Roswell Cultural Arts Center Summer Puppet Plays and Workshops** (770-594-6232; www.roswellgov.com, click on "Culture & Arts"). Shows at 10 AM weekdays, 11 AM Saturday. After-show workshops at 11 AM weekdays. A series of traditional fairy tales and children's stories is presented by local and national puppeteers. Shows $4, workshops $3.

June through September: **Concerts by the Springs** (404-851-9111, Ext. 203; www.heritage sandysprings.org/ConcertsByTheSprings/Concerts_index.html). In its 12th year in 2008, the concert series is held from 6:30–8 on the first Sunday evening in June, July, August, and September on the Sandy Springs Society Entertainment Lawn at the Sandy Springs Historic Site. Prior to the concert there are free tours of the gardens and museum, children's activities, and a balloon artist. Food is available from Slope's BBQ and Bruster's Ice Cream, or you can bring your own picnic. Pets and smoking are not allowed. General lawn seating free; tables for six are available with a prepaid reservation for $45–50, tented tables are $10 more.

July: **July Fourth Festivities and Steam Tractor Parade** (770-781-3491). The celebration in downtown Cumming begins on July 3 with a live band and an all-age dance contest followed by an amazing fireworks display. The morning of the Fourth features the unusual parade, which includes antique tractors and cars, steam engines, and floats decorated in the spirit of the holiday. After the parade, many of the tractors and engines are displayed at the Cumming Fairgrounds for a short time. Free.

August: **Old Soldier's Day Parade** (678-297-6078; www.awesomealpharetta.com). In its 54th year in 2008, the parade recognizes the living memory of all war veterans with floats, bands, military groups, antique vehicles, and civic organizations. Other activities include entertainment, children's activities, and prizes. Memorial services begin at 9:30 AM in front of Alpharetta's City Hall. After the parade, free hot dogs and soft drinks are served until 4 PM at the American Legion Post 201 on Wills Road. Free.

September: **Roswell Arts Festival** (770-640-3253; 1-800-776-7935). Sponsored by the Roswell Recreation Association and held at Roswell's historic town square, the event features fine arts, original crafts, and lots of fun. Free.

Sandy Springs Festival (404-851-9111, Ext. 203; www.sandyspringsfestival.com). Held the third weekend in September on the grounds of the Sandy Springs Historic Site, the festival includes live entertainment, children's rides, heritage education, an artists' market, collector car show, food court, and the Doug Kessler Lighting 10K Road Race—a qualifier for the Peachtree Road Race. Free; fee for some activities.

October: **Forsyth County Fair** (770-781-3491; www.cummingfair.com). The 10-day fair is open 4–10 Monday through Thursday, 4–midnight Friday, 10–midnight Saturday, 12:30–7 Sunday. Daily attractions at the fairgrounds in downtown Cumming include demonstrations by craftsmen, a petting zoo, pony rides, shows such as "Bear Mountain Wildlife Encounter," and midway rides and games. Nightly entertainment is offered by big-name headliners. Throughout the run of the fair, a heritage village—including a barbershop, blacksmith, cider press, cotton gin, doctor's office, general store, printing press, sawmill, syrup mill, waterwheel corn mill, gristmill, dentist's office, steam engine shed, old Baptist church, old Methodist church, one-room schoolhouse, and chicken house—is open and staffed. An extensive collection of antique steam tractors and gasoline engines are also on display. Adults $5, students 7–18 $2; discounts for advance purchases. Midway and chairlift rides are charged separately.

Halloween Hikes (770-992-2055). For four nights from 6:30–10 at the Chattahoochee Nature Center in Roswell, guests take guided hikes along the nature trail and meet costumed characters who educate hikers about wildlife in Georgia. Other activities include live musical entertainment, arts and crafts for kids, natural snacks, and a campfire. Children in costume get a special treat. $7 all ages.

November: **Annual Cumming Steam, Antique Tractor, and Gas Engine Exposition** (770-781-3491), Cumming Fairgrounds. If you missed the antique equipment during the Fourth of July parade or at the Forsyth County Fair, this is another opportunity to see both the equipment and the Heritage Village. $5 ages 13 and up.

Tellabration (770-640-3253; 1-800-776-7935). Tellabration, held at the Roswell Adult Recreation Facility on Grimes Bridge Road, is part of a worldwide storytelling event. Outstanding regional storytellers celebrate their art. $5

December: **Christmas in Roswell** (770-640-3253; 1-800-776-7935; www.cvb.roswell.ga.us), contact the Historic Roswell Convention and Visitors Bureau, 617 Atlanta Street, Roswell. Barrington Hall, Bulloch Hall, and the Archibald Smith Plantation Home are dressed up in period Christmas finery and are open for special tours all month. Among the highlights of the holiday are the re-enactment of Mittie Bulloch's 1853 wedding to Theodore Roosevelt Sr., a series of high teas at Bulloch Hall, and a candlelight tour of all three properties. (These events fill up early, so make reservations way in advance.) Wedding re-enactment, teas, and candlelight tours are priced in addition to regular home tours, at $8 for each house or $18 for all three.

8

Marietta

Founded in 1834, Marietta (pronounced May-retta by locals) became a summer resort town for south Georgia planters seeking relief from the heat and malaria of the coastal region. The town's location at the foothills of the mountains contributes to its milder, very appealing climate. Fine hotels like the Kennesaw House, which now houses the Marietta Museum of History, welcomed visitors, many of whom stayed for months. Others built large Victorian "cottages" radiating from the square.

During the Civil War, Andrew's Raiders stayed in Marietta the night before they began the famous Great Locomotive Chase by stealing a train pulled by a locomotive called *The General*. Union General William Tecumseh Sherman ordered most of the buildings around the town square burned during the war, but spared many of the residential areas. It was also from Marietta that Sherman had the captured women and children mill workers from Roswell and Lithia Springs charged with treason and shipped to the North (see the Hospitality Highway chapter for this fascinating story).

In the 20th century, the Dixie Highway, which passes through Marietta, was a major route for Northerners on their way to and from Florida. Until the construction of the interstate highways, many travelers stayed, ate, or went sight-seeing in Marietta, Kennesaw, and Smyrna during their trips.

Today, Marietta has a population of 61,000 and is the state's ninth-largest city. Five National Register Historic Districts showcase more than 150 antebellum and Victorian-era historic buildings, and many consider the charming turn-of-the-20th-century town square to be the prettiest in Georgia. More than 70 antiques and specialty shops, restaurants, theaters, and museums surround the square, and several bed and breakfasts are located nearby. Marietta is also the gateway to the state-designated Blue and Gray Civil War Trail and Georgia's Dixie Highway Trail, as well as the northwest Georgia mountains.

Kennesaw Mountain National Battlefield Park

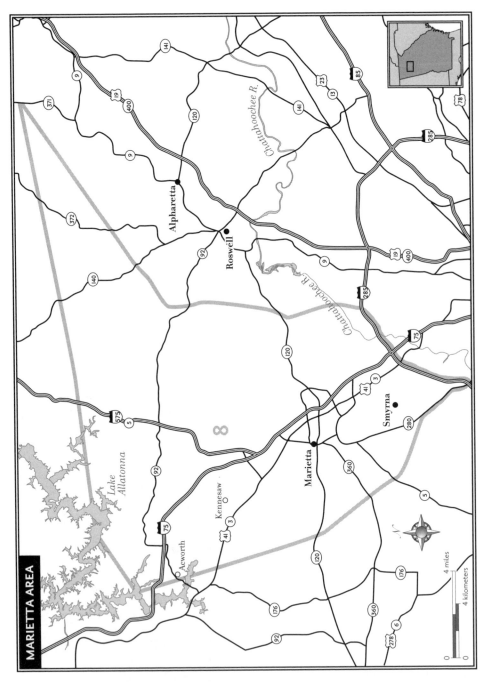

The nearby towns of Acworth, Kennesaw—famous for a Civil War battlefield—and Smyrna attract visitors as well with museums, restaurants, shops and recreation on Lakes Acworth and Allatoona. When the lakes were created in the 1950s, Acworth became known as "Lake City."

The Big Chicken

When relating Marietta's rich historical background, one can go from the sublime to the ridiculous. Around Marietta, all things point to or away from the much beloved Big Chicken, so directions anywhere in the vicinity generally include references to the giant fowl: "Turn right at the Big Chicken," "Go 4 miles past the Big Chicken"—you get the idea. The 56-foot-tall, red and white sheet-metal chicken with its opening and closing beak and rolling eyes presides over the intersection of US 41/Cobb Parkway and GA 20/Roswell Road east of Marietta proper, where it has been since it was erected as the landmark identifying a local fast food joint in 1963. In addition to metro Atlantans, scores of Northerners saw the big bird on their way to and from Florida when US 41 was the main route, though fewer people see it in these days of interstate highways.

The eatery was bought by Kentucky Fried Chicken in 1980, and as the end of the century approached, company executives began making noises about tearing the chicken down to make this KFC conform to all the others. But the citizenry grumbled. In 1993 a tornado severely damaged the big fella, and KFC decided once and for all to tear it down, but the company headquarters was soon flooded with protests from locals and folks around the world. The company even had to install a special toll-free number to handle the volume of calls that were coming from as far away as Japan. Bowing to the inevitable, executives spent $700,000 to restore the big guy to his former glory. Thank goodness the icon remains at his post. How else would we be able to find our way?

GUIDANCE

When planning a trip to the Marietta area, contact the **Marietta Welcome Center and Visitors Bureau** (770-429-1115; 1-800-835-0445; www.mariettasquare.com), 4 Depot Street, Marietta 30060. Open 9–5 weekdays, 10–4 Saturday, 1–4 Sunday. Located in the charming 1898 Nashville, Chattanooga, and St. Louis Railway Company passenger train depot, the welcome center features the video "Marietta, My Hometown," narrated by former Marietta resident Joanne Woodward. The depot was built on the site of the 1840s Western and Atlantic Railroad depot, which was destroyed by Union troops in 1864.

To find out more about Acworth, contact the **Acworth Area Convention and Visitors Bureau** (770-974-8813; www.acworth.org), 4415 Senator Russell Avenue, Acworth 30101. Open 8–5 weekdays. Pick up a brochure for a 30-site walking tour of historic Acworth here.

To find out more about Kennesaw, call the **City of Kennesaw** (770-422-9714; www.kenne saw.ga.us). Open 8–5 weekdays. For information on all of Cobb County, contact the **Cobb County Convention and Visitors Bureau** (678-303-2622; 1-800-451-3480; www.cob-bcvb.com), One Galleria Parkway, Atlanta 30339. Open 8–5 weekdays.

For information about Smyrna, contact the **Smyrna Welcome Center/Aunt Fanny's Cabin** (770-805-4277), 2875 Atlanta Road, Smyrna 30080. Open 10–4 Monday and Wednesday through Friday, 10–5 Saturday. Aunt Fanny's Cabin was a famous restaurant and many were brokenhearted when it closed, but today the landmark serves as Smyrna's Welcome Center. Inside are photos and autographs left by the many celebrities who ate there over the years. You also can get more information on Smyrna by calling 770-434-6600 or consulting the Web site at www.smyrnacity.com.

Getting There

By air: See What's Where. The following shuttle companies offer service to Cobb County and the towns described in this chapter: **Around Town Tours** (770-909-9091), **Airport Perimeter Connection** (404-761-0260), **Daytime Transportation** (770-939-2337), **Airport Metro Shuttle** (404-766-6666), **Galleria Direct** (770-955-1550), and **Interstate Airport Jitney** (770-932-6757). Limousine service to this area is offered from the airport by **A&M Limousines** (770-955-4565). In Acworth limousine service is available from **Super VIP Transportation and Limo Service** (1-866-969-4200).

By bus: **Greyhound Bus Lines** (770-427-3011; 1-800-231-2222; www.greyhound.com), 1250 South Marietta Parkway Southeast, Marietta, provides incoming and outgoing bus service.

By car: Marietta is located on I-75, 18 miles northwest of Atlanta and 8 miles from I-285, the perimeter highway that bypasses the city. The original Dixie Highway, US 41, runs north/south through Cobb County as well. GA 120 runs east/west right through downtown Marietta, but if you don't want to go downtown, bypass it by taking the GA 120 Loop. Your own car or a rental is the preferred method of transportation.

By train: See What's Where.

Getting Around

In Marietta, rental cars are available from **Rent a Wreck of Marietta** (770-926-9294) and **Thrifty Car Rental** (770-421-0729; www.thrifty.com). Every major rental car company is represented at Atlanta Hartsfield-Jackson International Airport (see *Getting There—By air*) and at various locations around the metro area. Limousine service is available from **A&M Limo Inc./Galleria Direct Shuttle** (770-955-4565; www.aandmlimo.com; www.galleria direct.net).

Mass transit is provided by **Cobb Community Transit** (see What's Where).

Taxis are available from **Victory Cab of Marietta** (770-428-2626), 1310 South Cobb Drive Southeast. Carriage rides are available on the historic Marietta Square during special events (see *Carriage Rides*). The carriage is parked at the northwest corner of the square.

Parking

There is free parking at the Mill Street lot directly behind the Marietta Welcome Center (two-hour limit). There is also free all-day parking on North Marietta Parkway by the Root House Museum. Parking spots around the square are metered (free in the evening). There is a minimal charge to park at the Cobb County Parking Deck on Cherokee Street. Acworth, Kennesaw, and Smyrna offer free on-street parking.

Public Restrooms

Facilities are available at the Marietta Welcome Center (see *Guidance*) and at four trail-heads along the Silver Comet Trail (see entry under *Hiking*).

Medical Emergency

For life-threatening situations, call 911. For other situations needing immediate attention, care is available at **WellStar Kennestone Hospital** (770-793-5000; www.wellstar.org), 677 Church Street, Marietta. In Smyrna, immediate care is available at **Emory-Adventist Hospital** (770-434-0710), 3949 South Cobb Drive Southeast.

Villages/Neighborhoods

Because Marietta's residential areas survived the Civil War, the city is blessed with five historic districts. **Northwest Marietta Historic District,** Marietta's oldest designated historic district, runs from Kennesaw Avenue to Powder Springs Road and includes numerous historic Greek Revival–style homes. **Whitlock Avenue Historic District,** which borders the Kennesaw Mountain National Battlefield Park, includes several historic homes. **Atlanta/Frazier Street Historic District,** Marietta's most

Union troops stole The General *from Kennesaw during the Civil War.*

recently designated district, borders the railroad tracks near the Confederate Cemetery and includes several more historic homes. **Washington Avenue Historic District,** on the east side of Marietta, includes the Marietta National Cemetery and "Lawyer's Row," mid- to late-19th-century houses now adapted for use as attorneys' offices. **Church/Cherokee Historic District** includes the two parallel tree-lined streets that head north from the square. This neighborhood includes Victorian-era homes and several historic churches.

Pick up a copy of the "Historic Marietta Walking/Driving Tour" brochure from the Marietta Welcome Center. It describes 57 historic structures you can walk or drive by, most of which are private homes.

During the Civil War, Union troops camped in **Acworth,** and homes and churches were used as field headquarters and hospitals. General Sherman himself was headquartered in Acworth for several days. When the Union troops left Acworth, they burned much of the town. The cotton economy brought prosperity to Acworth by the late 1870s, and new homes and businesses were built. These are the historic buildings visitors see today. The small town's **Collins Avenue Historic District** showcases 150 years of architecture. **Lake Allatoona** and **Lake Acworth** were built in the 1950s, earning Acworth the nickname "Lake City" and providing numerous recreational opportunities (see separate entries).

Kennesaw, just north of Marietta, was originally called Big Shanty because it was a construction camp for Irish railroad workers who lived in shanty houses there in the 1830s and 1840s. During the Civil War, Union raiders stole *The General* from here and attempted to flee to Chattanooga. Their intent was to tear up tracks behind them to disrupt rail service to the Atlanta area, but they failed. At nearby Kennesaw Mountain, Confederate troops held off Union troops for several weeks. After the war, the name of the town was changed to commemorate the battle, and the battlefield became a National Battlefield Park (see entry under *Historic Homes and Sites*).

Today the town has five historic districts and the Museum of Civil War and Locomotive History (see entry under *Museums*). Kennesaw's 1908 railroad depot has been restored and is often the site of fairs and festivals. The small town's position as home to Kennesaw State University ensures that there are numerous cultural activities throughout the year. Kennesaw is also a site on the Blue and Gray Civil War Trail and the Dixie Highway Trail.

The only reason you might have heard of **Smyrna** is because Julia Roberts is its most famous native daughter. The small city has a rich history, however. Smyrna grew up as a stop on the railroad, but it also was known for the nondenominational campground that was built there. In friendly Smyrna, known as "The Jonquil City," there's always something going on at the Village Green. The town has a new Market Village with unique shops and restaurants, as well as the **Concord Covered Bridge Historic District**, parks, trails, and golf courses.

TO SEE

Covered Bridge
✍ ✿ **Concord Covered Bridge** (770-431-2858), Concord Road between Hicks Road and South Cobb Drive, Smyrna. Open daily. Listed on the National Register of Historic Places, the bridge is the centerpiece of the Concord Covered Bridge Historic District, which also contains four historic homes, a railroad trestle bridge, and a gristmill. The bridge, which was built around 1840, was burned during the Civil War, but was reconstructed. The only covered bridge still in use on a public highway in metropolitan Atlanta, it is 133 feet long, 16 feet wide, and 13 feet high. Ruff's Mill, which was originally built in the 1840s, saw action during the Civil War's Battle of Atlanta and was burned. It was rebuilt in 1873 and operated until the 1930s. The Rock House, a fieldstone structure built in 1910 as a summer residence for a wealthy Atlanta family, is particularly interesting because no two windows are alike. Free.

Cultural Sites
✿ **Horace W. Sturgis Library Art Gallery/Kennesaw State University Art Gallery** (770-499-3223), 1000 Chastain Road, Kennesaw. Open during the day Monday through Thursday and in the evening Wednesday and Thursday; Sturgis Library Art Galley also open 1–4 Saturday. (Note: Galleries may be closed during university holidays.) The galleries feature a wide variety of art, including paintings, photography, pottery, and sculpture, as well as faculty and student works and regional, national, and international traveling exhibitions. Free.

Historic Homes and Sites
✿ **Antebellum Brumby Hall and Gardens** (770-427-2500; 1-888-685-2500; www.brumby hall.com), 500 Powder Springs Road, Marietta. Open 9–5 weekdays; for weekend access contact Guest Services at the Marietta Conference Center and Resort (see *Lodging*). The lovely raised Greek Revival–style house was built by Colonel Anoldus VanderHorst Brumby, the first superintendent of the Georgia Military Institute, which was located on adjacent property until it was destroyed during the Civil War. Brumby Hall served as a Union hospital during the war, and legend has it that General Sherman spared the house because he and Brumby had been friends at West Point. From the 1920s to the 1990s, Brumby Hall was a private residence, but it now belongs to the city and is part of the Marietta Conference Center and Resort. Make time to wander in the formal boxwood, topiary, rose, annual, perennial, and knot gardens, which were designed in 1930 by Hubert Bond Owens, founder of the School of Landscape Architecture at the University of Georgia. His original 1925 drawings were used to restore the gardens to their former splendor. Free.
✍ ✿ ♿ **Kennesaw Mountain National Battlefield Park** (770-427-4686; www.nps.gov/kemo), 900 Kennesaw Mountain Drive off Old US 41 and Stilesboro Road, Kennesaw. Open dawn

to dusk daily; visitor's center open 8:30–5 weekdays, 8:30–6 Saturday and Sunday. Hours extended in the summer. The site of a major Civil War battle on June 27, 1864, which temporarily thwarted the advance of Union troops from Chattanooga to Atlanta, the 2,884-acre park commemorates the Atlanta Campaign. A film at the visitor's center describes the battle and exhibits depict the life of Civil War soldiers. Living history programs and ranger talks are presented in the summer. The park features 16 miles of hiking trails, monuments, and

A cannon stands watch over the Kennesaw battlefield.

re-created military positions as well as recreation areas and picnicking facilities. On summer weekends a shuttle bus carries visitors almost to the summit of the mountain. From there they can walk the rest of the way to the top where, on a clear day, they'll be rewarded with an amazing view of downtown Atlanta. Free. The Marietta Heritage Passport (see *Museums*) offers a 20 percent discount in the park's bookstore.

🐾 **The Root House Museum** (770-426-4982), 145 Denmead Street, Marietta. Open 11–4 Tuesday through Saturday. One of the oldest surviving frame houses in Marietta, the 1845 Plantation Plain–style Root House offers a glimpse into the life of a middle-class merchant family. William Root was the city's first druggist and the first merchant to receive a shipment of goods on the Western and Atlantic Railroad. The simple frame house is furnished with period pieces typical of the 1850s. Also on the property is a re-created kitchen house with a working 1850s cook stove as well as flower beds and vegetable plots with plants that were available in Cobb County before 1860. Adults $4, seniors $3, children $2.

Museums

The **Marietta Heritage Passport** allows admission to three heritage museums at a savings of 25 percent off the single ticket price of each individual attraction. The passport, which includes the Marietta Museum of History, the Root House Museum, and the Marietta *Gone with the Wind* Movie Museum/Scarlett on the Square, is available for $10 at the Marietta Welcome Center (see *Guidance*). The card is valid for one year from purchase, but is not valid for special exhibits or with other discounts.

🐾 ♿ **Marietta/Cobb Museum of Art** (770-528-1444; www.mariettacobbartmuseum.org), 30 Atlanta Street, Marietta. Open 11–5 Tuesday through Saturday, 1–5 Sunday. The only all-American museum in the metro area, this museum features 19th- and 20th-century regional art and sponsors four special exhibits and children's activities each year. It is housed in an imposing, many-columned Classical Revival building that was originally constructed to serve as a federal post office. It was later used as a library. Adults $5, seniors and children $3.

✏️🐾♿ **Marietta Fire Museum** (770-794-5460; www.mariettasquare.com/fire_museum.html), 112 Haynes Street, Marietta. Open 8–5 weekdays. Housed at the Marietta Fire Station and featuring fire-fighting equipment from the 1800s to the present, the museum is the home of *Aurora*, a horse-drawn Silsby Steamer fire engine in service from 1879 to 1921.

🎣 🐾 ♿ **Marietta** *Gone with the Wind* **Movie Museum/Scarlett on the Square** (770-794-5576; www.gwtwmarietta.com), 18 Whitlock Avenue, Marietta. Open 10–5 Monday through Saturday. Housed in an 1880s warehouse just off the square, the museum features a privately owned collection of movie memorabilia, including original costumes, conceptual artwork, scripts, props, photographs, rare press and publicity books, premiere programs, promotional items, and more. Among the treasures are the original Bengaline silk honeymoon gown worn by Vivien Leigh, Margaret Mitchell's personal volumes of the novel, contracts, foreign versions of the novel, and foreign film posters. One display is dedicated to the African American members of the cast. Adults $7, seniors and students $6, children younger than 8 free.

🎣 🐾 ♿ **Marietta Museum of History** (770-528-0430; www.mariettasquare.com/history_museum.html), 1 Depot Street, Marietta. Open 10–4 Monday through Saturday. The second floor of the old 1855 Kennesaw House hotel provides a home for the local history museum and its collections of artifacts that tell Marietta's story from the time of the Native Americans to the present. Operating under the name Fletcher House in 1862, the hotel was the base from which Andrew's Raiders launched their bold move to steal *The General,* so naturally there is an exhibit devoted to this momentous event. Other displays include antique quilts and furnishings, mannequins in vintage clothing from various periods, and sewing arts. The Homelife Gallery houses 19th- and 20th-century clothing and accessories, inventions from the turn of the 20th century, a complete 1940s kitchen, and a vignette featuring the bachelor suite of Yankee spy Henry Green Cole. The Civil War Gallery features uniforms, weapons, a battle flag, and a military document signed by Abraham Lincoln. The General History Gallery tells the story of Native Americans, the Gold Rush, local businesses, influential Mariettans, the growth of the Bell Bomber Plant (which became Lockheed Martin), and displays from all of America's wars. Adults $3, seniors and students $2, children $1.

🐾 **Smyrna Museum** (770-431-2858; www.rootsweb.com/gashgs), 2861 Atlanta Street, Smyrna. Open 10–4 Tuesday through Saturday. The museum, which is housed in a reconstructed replica of the 1910 Smyrna train depot, contains historical materials, memorabilia, photographs, publications, and historical and genealogical research materials. Free, but donations are appreciated.

🎣 🐾 ♿ **Southern Museum of Civil War and Locomotive History** (770-427-2117; www.southernmuseum.org), 2829 Cherokee Street, Kennesaw. Open 9:30–5 Monday through Saturday, noon–5 Sunday. This Smithsonian-affiliated museum describes how the locomotive has shaped history. Visitors learn the crucial role railroads played during the Civil War and how a locomotive factory aided in rebuilding the South after the war. On display is one of the most famous loco- motives in the South: *The General,* which

The Southern Museum of Civil War and Locomotive History

was hijacked by Union raiders during the Civil War, but recaptured by Southerners after an 86-mile chase. The museum includes a multimillion-dollar collection of Civil War relics as well as the Glover Iron Works collection and traveling Smithsonian exhibits. The Glover Steam Locomotive Collection includes patterns and parts for the original small-gauge steam locomotive. Adults $7.50, seniors $6.50, children 6–12 $5.50.

Natural Beauty Spots

See **Kennesaw Mountain National Battlefield Park** under *Historic Homes and Sites* and *Scenic Drives*.

Scenic Drives

The Cannonball Trail. For a driving tour of Marietta's Civil War sites, pick up a brochure from the **Marietta Welcome Center and Visitors Bureau** (770-429-1115; 1-800-835-0445; www.mariettasquare.com), 4 Depot Street.

🚗 ⚑ ♿ **Kennesaw Mountain National Battlefield Park** (770-427-4686; www.nps.gov/kemo), 900 Kennesaw Mountain Drive off Old US 41 and Stilesboro Road, Kennesaw. The visitor's center will provide a brochure for a self-guided walking/driving tour of the park. The four sites on the trail are the overlook at the summit of Kennesaw Mountain, where visitors can get a panoramic view of North Georgia, including the Atlanta skyline; Pigeon Hill entrenchments reached by a foot trail; Cheatham Hill, known as The Dead Angle, where fierce fighting occurred during the Civil War; and Kolb's Farm, where a 1836 log house has been restored but is not open to the public.

Special Places

⚑ **Marietta Confederate Cemetery/Marietta City Cemetery** (770-794-5606; www.marietta square.com/confederate-cemetery.html), 381 Powder Springs Road, Marietta. Open dawn to dusk daily. In 1863, Jane Glover, the wife of Marietta's first mayor, donated land beside the Marietta City Cemetery to inter Confederate soldiers killed in a train wreck nearby. The hilly land on the southern edge of town became the final resting place for Confederate soldiers who died in local hospitals and at military battles such as the Battle of Chickamauga and the Battle of Kennesaw Mountain. More than 3,000 Confederate soldiers are buried here; 1,000 of them are unknown. Today the parklike setting is a quiet oasis where visitors can examine the headstones, stroll around, or simply relax. The adjacent city cemetery is even older, having been founded in the 1830s. It is the final resting place of several historical figures. Free.

⚑ **Marietta National Cemetery** (770-428-5631; www.cem.va.gov, and then follow the prompts), 1 Depot Street, Marietta. Open dawn to dusk daily. The graveyard, still an active veteran's cemetery, was created in 1866 on acreage donated by two Marietta citizens who were fervent Union supporters. In hopes of healing the wounds of each side, they first proposed donating the land for a cemetery where both Union and Confederate soldiers could rest together. When that offer was declined, they donated it for the federal cemetery. Nearly 10,000 Union soldiers who were killed in Civil War battles all over Georgia are buried here. Of those, 3,000 are unknown. Over the past 140 years, 7,000 other soldiers who died in all of America's other wars since the cemetery's creation have been interred here as well. Free.

🚗 ⚑ ♿ **Marietta Square/Glover Park.** The original 1852 layout of the centrally located square, also known as Antebellum Square, was planned to be similar to the squares in downtown Savannah. The lushly landscaped Glover Park, named for John Glover, the first mayor of Marietta who also donated the land for the park, serves as the heart of the community and is the scene of many special events. When Glover donated the land, he stipulated that if the land were ever used for anything other than a park, it would revert to his estate. There was no need to worry. The park gets better every day. Among its interesting attractions are a gazebo; a bandstand; a fountain; a statue of Alexander Stephens Clay, a prominent politician between 1880 and 1910; and a children's play area with a pint-size representation of *The General*. On the last Friday evening of the month from April through August, free concerts are performed in the park.

To Do

Agricultural Fair

✔ 🐾 ♿ **North Georgia State Fair** (770-423-1330 year-round; 770-528-8989 in September; www.northgeorgiastatefair.com), 2245 Callaway Road, Marietta. Open eight days in September: 4–11 Monday through Thursday, 4–midnight Friday, 10–midnight Saturday, 12:30–7 Sunday. Jim R. Fowler Park is the scene of competitions and exhibits of award-winning fruits, vegetables, and flowers grown by locals as well as arts and crafts created locally. The fair features the Great James H. Drew Exposition Carnival Midway with the Mega Drop—the tallest, fastest, scariest traveling drop tower in the country. Fair-goers also can see a beauty pageant, BMX bike stunt show, pig racing, the Talking Treeman, a stunt dog show, Oscar the Robot, the Human Cannonball, a petting zoo, pony rides, and entertainment on the Market Plaza Local Entertainment Stage. Adults $5, children $2; 10-ride Ride Ticket Book $10; advance discounts available.

Bicycling

The **PATH Foundation** (404-875-7284; www.pathfoundation.org), mailing address: P.O. Box 14327, Atlanta 30324, has been instrumental in developing bike paths in the metropolitan Atlanta area. The most ambitious of these trails is the **Silver Comet Trail** (see *Hiking*), which begins in Smyrna and ends 60 miles later at the Alabama line, where it connects with the 33-mile Chief Ladiga Trail. The section pertinent to this chapter begins between Smyrna and Mableton (see the Westside chapter). For information on renting regular and three-wheel recumbent bikes and skates or obtaining other related services, visit the **Silver Comet Depot** (770-819-3279; www.silvercometdepot.com), 4342 Floyd Road, Mableton. Open 10–6 Monday through Wednesday and Friday through Sunday, 9–7 Thursday; longer hours in summer. The company also sponsors group walks and rides, and provides some shuttle service. For other trail information, consult the Web site www.trailexpress.com.

Bird-Watching

Chattahoochee River National Recreation Area (visitor's center 678-538-1200; www.nps.gov/chat), office: 1978 Island Ford Road, Dunwoody. Office open 9–5; park units open dawn to dusk daily. Several units of the 48-mile-long park are within the boundaries of this chapter: **Cochran Shoals, Sope Creek, Powers Island, Johnson Ferry North,** and **Johnson Ferry South.** Hiking trails provide numerous opportunities for bird and wildlife observation. Proximity to the river means visitors will often see ducks and herons. Hawks and many other species also are frequently seen. Use of the park requires a $3 daily parking fee or a $25 annual park pass.

Boating

Chattahoochee River/Chattahoochee River National Recreation Area (see What's Where). The river, which is flat and calm in the section described in this chapter, offers endless opportunities for rafting, canoeing, kayaking, and motorboating.

Canoeing, Kayaking, Tubing

On a hot summer day, there's nothing more refreshing than floating down the Chattahoochee River in a raft. This popular activity is known as "Shootin' the Hooch." The water stays between 50 and 55 degrees year-round, so if you get too hot all you have to do is splash yourself with water. Rentals and return shuttle service are available seasonally from **Chattahoochee Outfitters** (770-650-1008; www.shootthehooch.com) at its Johnson Ferry and Powers Island outposts. Bring your own picnic, because the leisurely trip takes between two and six hours, depending on the outpost location and the speed of the river flow. Canoe rentals are $50 per day or $20 per hour; one-man kayak rentals are $60 per day or $35 per hour; two-man kayak rentals are $90 per day or $40 per hour; raft rentals are $100 for a four-man raft, $120 for a six-man raft, $160 for an eight-man raft, $200 for a 10-man raft; tube rentals are $25–30 per hour. A deposit is required. See What's Where for other information about requirements for trips on the river.

Carriage Rides

During special events, **Yellow Rose Carriage Service** (770-499-9719) offers Friday and Saturday evening carriage rides around Marietta's Glover Square in the company's vis-à-vis carriage, weather permitting. The company also offers a 1904 Studebaker freight wagon for groups. Short rides cover a half-mile; long rides cover a mile. Note: It's best to call ahead to make sure they will be there. $5 per person for the short ride; $10 per person for the long ride.

Fishing

The **Chattahoochee River** runs through Cobb County on its way from northeast Georgia to the Florida line and Lake Seminole. During its course through metro Atlanta, 48 miles of the river are designated as the **Chattahoochee River National Recreation Area** (678-538-1200). Fishing for trout, bass, catfish, and other species is a popular year-round activity and is available from 30 minutes before sunrise to 30 minutes after sunset. Night fishing is not allowed. Anglers 16 and older must have a valid Georgia fishing license and nonresidents age 16–64 must have a trout license, which is available from the Georgia Department of Natural Resources (www.gofishgeorgia.com). Sope Creek and Sibley Pond are excellent fishing spots, and the area from the Sope Creek unit off Columns Drive downstream to Cobb Parkway is a special delayed harvest area. This means that anglers must release all trout and use only artificial lures with single hooks from November 1 through May 14. Those fishing for other species also must abide by the artificial lure regulation. Keep in mind that the river is usually about 50–55 degrees year-round, which is good for fish, but not for humans. Hypothermia is a concern in cooler weather. A $3 daily parking fee or a $25 annual park pass is required.

For Families

✒ ❀ **Brunswick U.S. Play** (770-427-7679; www.bowlbrunswick.com/center_info?center Num=2910), 775 Cobb Place Boulevard, Kennesaw. Call or consult the Web site for hours, as they vary widely. The games emporium features cosmic bowling, billiards, karaoke, and video games. Prices vary widely depending on the activity, but are generally under $10. Shoe rentals $4.

✒ ❀ **Mountasia Family Fun Center** (770-422-7227; www.mountasia.com), 175 Ernest Bennett Parkway, Marietta. Golf and games open 10–10 Monday through Thursday,

10–midnight Friday and Saturday; speedway and boats open 10–10 Monday through Thursday, 10–11 Friday and Saturday, noon–9 Sunday. The family-fun park offers Go-Karts, bumper boats, 54 holes of miniature golf, an arcade with 60 video games, and a snack bar. Miniature golf: adults $7, seniors and children $6; speedway or bumper boats $5.50. Specials and ride combination packages are available.

✍ ♿ **Six Flags American Adventures** (770-948-9290; www.sixflags.com/american adventures/index.aspx) 250 Cobb Parkway, Marietta. Open weekends March through May and mid-August through October; daily June through mid-August; closed November through February. Call for exact hours or check the Web site. This nostalgic, family-oriented theme park was created to resemble a turn-of-the-20th-century town. Popular activities include the four-story, 40,000-square-foot Foam Factory and the outdoor Fun Forest, which features Go-Kart rides, bumper cars, a mini roller coaster, carousel, kiddie play area, arcade, laser tag, and miniature golf. Hungry fun-seekers can visit the on-site restaurant. $6–15; parking $10. Rates vary by season and there are numerous specials.

✍ ♿ **Six Flags White Water** (770-948-9290; www.sixflags.com/whitewater/index.aspx), 250 Cobb Parkway, Marietta. Open 10–6 weekends in May and the week before Memorial Day, then 10–8 daily Memorial Day weekend through Labor Day. This park is the place to dive into the Southern tradition of fun in the sun. Named one of the Top Ten water parks in America as well as the Most Scenic Water Park in the country by *USA Today,* the complex offers 50 "splash-tastic" water rides that are fun for the whole family. The 35-acre site contains all the necessary ingredients for cooling off on hot summer days. Millions of gallons of water create experiences that range from relaxing to high-thrill. The 90-foot-tall Cliffhanger, for example, provides one of the world's largest free falls, while the Tornado sends thrill-seekers down a 132-foot-long tunnel, throws them into a giant open-ended funnel, and drenches them under a waterfall. The park also features tree-shaded waterfalls, a lazy Little Hooch River, the Atlanta Ocean wave pool, a family raft ride, and the four-story Tree House Island. Five food concessions, a gift shop, and the after-dark "Dive-In Movie" provide even more fun. Adults $35, seniors and children shorter than 48 inches $26; parking $10.

Golf

City Club Marietta (770-528-GOLF; www.cityclubmarietta.com), 510 Powder Springs Street, Marietta. Open daylight hours daily. The original nine-hole layout was designed and constructed in 1912 on the former site of the Georgia Military Institute. An additional nine holes were added in the 1960s. The property was bought by the City of Marietta and, after extensive renovations, opened to the public in 1991. Rolling hills and tall pines make the facility play like a mountain course. Also on-site are three putting greens, a chipping and putting green, fairway bunker, greenside bunker, pro shop, and instruction. The Marietta Conference Center and Resort hotel is located adjacent to the course. $42–53; junior and senior discounts available; practice facility $3.50–6.30 per basket of balls.

Hiking

✍ 🍂 **Chattahoochee River National Recreation Area** (678-538-1200; www.nps.gov/chat). The Sope Creek unit of the 48-mile-long park is located on Paper Mill Road between Terrell Mill Road and Johnson Ferry Road in Marietta. It offers several miles of easy to difficult hiking trails, and mountain biking is allowed on designated stretches of the trails. A moderate hike takes you to the ruins of the Marietta Manufacturing Mill. The Powers Island unit has an easy 1-mile trail; the Johnson Ferry South unit has a 1.5–mile trail; and the Johnson Ferry North unit has 2.5 miles of easy trails. The Cochran Shoals unit contains easy to difficult trails, including a 3-mile fitness trail and a 3-mile bike loop. $3 daily parking fee or $25 annual parking pass.

✎ ☙ **Kennesaw Mountain National Battlefield Park** (770-427-4686; www.nps.gov/kemo), 900 Kennesaw Mountain Drive off Old US 41 and Stilesboro Road, Kennesaw. The park's trails offer short walks and long hikes. Various starting points on the trails create 2-, 5-, 10-, and 16-mile round-trip hikes. All the trails require moderately steep climbing. There is limited water and no shelter or food along the trails. Free.

✎ ❦ ☙ ⑆ **Silver Comet Trail** (770-819-3279; www.pathfoundation.org). The trail, which begins at South Cobb Drive and the East-West Connector in Smyrna, connects the Atlanta metropolitan area to the Alabama state line—a 60-mile journey. A former railroad route for the *Silver Comet* passenger train, which ran from Boston to Birmingham between 1947 and 1968, the track has been taken up and paved so that the roadbed provides opportunities for walking, jogging, hiking, cycling, and skating. The trail is also suitable for baby strollers and wheelchairs. Leashed pets are welcome and those visitors with their own horse can avail themselves of portions of the trail. No motorized vehicles are allowed. The trail, which crosses six trestles and bridges, offers scenic views and access to Heritage Park, a 105-acre nature preserve. A 1.7-mile spur trail goes to the ruins of a woolen mill. One of the highlights of the trail is crossing the Pumpkin Vine Creek Trestle, a 750-foot-long, 126-foot-high bridge. Another special place is the 800-foot Brushy Mountain Tunnel. Four trailheads offer parking, restrooms, and water fountains. The trail can also be accessed from several cross streets. It is patrolled by bicycle-mounted Cobb County police officers. For more information about the trail, contact Cobb County Parks, Recreation and Cultural Affairs (770-528-8840; www.cobbcounty.org) or the Web site at www.trail express.com, which provides directions to the trailheads. The trail connects to the Wild Horse Creek Trail in Powder Springs and to the 33-mile Chief Ladiga Trail at the Georgia/Alabama line, then continues on to Anniston, Alabama, which creates even more possibilities. See *Bicycling* for information about the shuttle service (reservations required) provided by **The Silver Comet Depot,** which is a year-round Volksmarch center.

Ice Skating

✎ ☙ **IceForum at Town Center** (770-218-1010; www.iceforum.com), 3061 George Busbee Parkway, Kennesaw. Open daily. Schedules are too complicated to include here, but in general there are three public skating sessions on Friday; two sessions on Monday, Wednesday, and Saturday; and one session on Tuesday, Thursday, and Sunday. Ice skating, a rare treat in Atlanta, is available here year-round. In addition to skating on regulation NHL-size surfaces, the facility offers a full-service snack bar, pro shop, skate rentals (figure and hockey), skate repairs and sharpening, instruction for all ages and levels, video games, and seating for spectators. $6–7; rentals $3.

Miniature Golf

See **Mountasia Family Fun Center** and **Six Flags American Adventures** under *For Families.*

Tennis

The Atlanta Lawn Tennis Association is one of the largest in the country, and Cobb County is considered a mecca for tennis players. The **Cobb County Department of Parks, Recreation and Cultural Affairs** (770-528-8800; www.cobbcounty.org), operates several tennis centers, three within the boundaries of this chapter: **Fair Oaks Park** (770-528-8480), 1460 West Booth Road; **Harrison Park** (770-591-3151), 2653 Shallowford Road; and **Terrell Mill Park** (770-644-2771), 480 Terrell Mill Road. Four to eight tennis courts also can be found at these county parks in Marietta: **Bells Ferry Park**, 2334 Bells Ferry Road; **Fullers Park**, 3050 Robinson Road; **Hurt Road Park**, 990 Hurt Road; **Larry Bell Park**, 592 Fairground Street; **Oregon Park**, 145 Old Hamilton Road; **Sewell Park**, 2055 Lower Roswell Road; **Shaw Park**, 3016 Canton Road; and **Sweat Mountain Park**, 4346 Steinhauer Road; and in Smyrna at **Rhyne Park**, 4145 King Springs Road.

GREEN SPACE

Gardens
See **Antebellum Brumby Hall and Gardens** under *Historic Homes and Sites.*

Lakes
♂ ❀ ♿ **Lake Acworth** (770-974-3112), City of Acworth Parks and Recreation Department, 4375 Russell Square, Acworth. Open daylight hours daily. The 90-acre urban lake offers fishing, boating (electric motors only), boat ramps, picnicking, swimming in the summer, a playground, and a concession stand. The lake is stocked with channel catfish, largemouth bass, bluegill, redear sunfish, crappie, carp, and bullheads.

Nature Preserves and Parks
♂ ❀ ♿ **Acworth Beach/Cauble Park** (770-917-1234; www.acworth.org), Beach Street, Acworth. Park open 7–11 daily year-round; beach open Memorial Day through Labor Day. Boating, fishing, swimming, and occasional outdoor concerts keep families busy here. Free admission; parking $5 on weekends.

Cobb County Parks, Recreation and Cultural Affairs (770-528-8800; www.cobbcounty.org), 1792 County Services Parkway, Marietta, operates 40 parks. Although each park does not have every feature, together they offer ball fields, batting cages, fitness trails, horseshoe pits, jogging tracks or trails, playgrounds, picnicking facilities, and volleyball courts. A few parks boast an aquatic center, tennis center, gymnasium, and/or community center.

Recreation Areas
Chattahoochee River National Recreation Area (678-538-1200) is a 48-mile stretch of the Chattahoochee River (see the Roswell chapter for details). Along the way are numerous day-use parks where visitors can enjoy boating, fishing, hiking, and wildlife observation (see separate headings). The units in the area described by this chapter include Cochran Shoals, Sope Creek, Powers Island, Johnson Ferry North, and Johnson Ferry South. Cochran Shoals offers several trails, including one that is wheelchair accessible, as well as a 3-mile bike loop. Sope Creek also offers hiking and mountain biking as well as stone ruins from a paper manufacturing company that produced much of the South's paper from 1855 to 1902. Powers Island, named for James Powers, who ferried travelers across the river before there were bridges, has a hiking trail. The two Johnson Ferry units also offer trails. See *Hiking.*

Rivers
See *Boating, Fishing, and Recreation Areas.*

LODGING

Bed and Breakfasts

In Marietta

The Stanley House Inn (770-426-1881;
877-426-1881; www.thestanleyhouse.com),
236 Church Street. When visitors see this
large, stately, Queen Anne Victorian, they
find it hard to imagine that the house was
built in 1895 as a summer "cottage" by Felie
Woodrow, an aunt of Woodrow Wilson. Now
an elegant bed and breakfast, the inn offers
five guest rooms. No smoking. Not wheelchair accessible. $135–175.

The Whitlock Inn Bed and Breakfast
(770-428-1495; www.whitlockinn.com), 57
Whitlock Avenue. Built around 1900, this
lovely home was the residence of one family
for 60 years. It's a perfect example of the
"wedding cake" style of architecture so
popular at the turn of the 20th century, so
it's no surprise that many weddings are
held here. The Whitlock House has operated as an inn with five luxurious, individually decorated guest rooms furnished with
period antiques since 1994. No smoking.
Limited wheelchair accessibility. $125–150.

Campgrounds

In Acworth

🐾 🐕 **Holiday Harbor Marina, Campsites,
and Resort** (770-974-2575; www.lakealla
toona.net), 5989 Groovers Landing Road.
The campground offers 28 campsites with
partial hookups as well as a camp store,
restaurant, and boat rentals. Seven waterfront cabins offer a kitchen, living room
with fireplace, dining room, two bedrooms,
one or two bathrooms, a deck, and a cour-
tesy boat dock. Smoking and nonsmoking
cabins available. Not wheelchair accessible.
$115–135 per night, $545 per week.
Campsites $20.

In Marietta

🐾 🏕 🐕 **Brookwood RV Resort Park**
(770-427-6853; 1-877-727-5787;
www.bkwdrv.com), 1031 Wylie Road
Southeast. Located on a peaceful wooded
site convenient to the cities described in
this chapter, the park provides full electric,
water, and sewer hookups. Television,
phone, and Internet services are available.
The campground also has a swimming pool,
Laundromat, and LP fuel service. Children
and pets are welcome. No tents or dry
camping are allowed. $45 nightly; dis-
counts available.

Cabins

In Acworth

See **Holiday Harbor Marina, Campsites,
and Resort** under *Campgrounds.*

Inns and Hotels

Renaissance Waverly Hotel (770-953-
4500; 1-888-391-8724; www.renaissance
hotels.com), 2450 Galleria Parkway,
Atlanta. One of the most luxurious hotels in
the immediate area, the Renaissance
Waverly is one of the only AAA four-
diamond hostelries in the northwest
quadrant of metro Atlanta. The 14-floor
hotel features 497 upscale guest rooms,
24 elegant suites, and a concierge level as
well as indoor and outdoor pools, a fitness
center, spa services, and room service until
1 AM. Restaurants include The Atrium Café
and the Waverly Coffee Bar for breakfast
and lunch, and Tosca Blu and Medici for
dinner. $100–200; many specials and
packages available.

Resorts

In Marietta

🐾 ♿ **Marietta Conference Center and
Resort** (770-427-2500; 1-888-685-2500;
www.mariettaresort.com), 500 Powder
Springs Road. This magnificent AAA

four-diamond hotel, which resembles the world-famous Greenbrier in West Virginia, sits on the site of the old Georgia Military Institute, which was destroyed by Union troops during the Civil War. The modern resort features shiny marble floors, burnished paneling, glittering chandeliers, imposing oil paintings, and a life-size diorama depicting an event at the military school. Choose from 199 elegantly furnished guest rooms or nine parlor suites. Each offers a spectacular view of the Atlanta skyline or the golf course and Kennesaw Mountain. Other amenities include a restaurant, bar, billiard room, outdoor pool, fitness club, lighted tennis courts, and a golf course. On the grounds is the historic Antebellum Brumby Hall and Gardens, the only surviving building from the school era (see *Historic Homes and Sites*). Smoking and nonsmoking rooms available; no smoking in the restaurants; smoking allowed in the pub. Wheelchair accessible. $119–199.

WHERE TO EAT

Dining Out

In Atlanta

& **Ray's on the River** (770-955-1187; raysrestaurants.com), 6700 Powers Ferry Road. Open 11–2:30 weekdays; 5–10 Monday through Thursday, 5–11 Friday and Saturday, 5–9 Sunday; 9:30–3 Sunday for brunch. Enjoy live music in the bar from 7–10 Thursday, and a cookout and music on the patio from 5–8 Friday, weather permitting. Ray's is one of a very few restaurants in metro Atlanta blessed with a location on the banks of the languid Chattahoochee River. Diners vie for window or patio seating to couple a fine dining meal with a beautiful view. At both lunch and dinner you can begin with hot and cold appetizers,

raw bar selections, and fresh Florida stone crab claws. Seafood is prominently featured for both meals. At dinner, guests also can choose among pork chops, chicken, prime rib, steak, and lobster. The award-winning Sunday brunch features 80 items from peel-and-eat shrimp to mussels marinated in vinaigrette, a carving station, made-to-order omelettes, a waffle station, and a vast assortment of desserts. No smoking (even outside). Wheelchair accessible. $5.75–16 for lunch; $16.50–37 for dinner; adults $23.95, children $12.95 for brunch.

In Marietta

♪ & **Hamilton's** (770-427-2500; www.mariettaresort.com), 500 Powder Springs Road. Open 6:30–10 AM, 11:30 AM–2 PM, and 6–10 PM daily. Located at the Marietta Conference Center and Resort, the elegant restaurant is fashioned after Southern estates of the 1800s. New South cuisine features seasonally changing menus. No smoking. Wheelchair accessible. $11 for breakfast, $13 for lunch, $17–29 for dinner, $22 for Sunday brunch.

Shillings Top of the Square (770-428-9520), 19 North Park Square. Open 5–11 Tuesday through Saturday. Located above Shillings on the Square (see *Eating Out*), the restaurant offers formal dining with crisp table linens and candlelight, while its large windows provide a romantic view of Marietta Square. Dinner choices might include seafood, steaks, chops, chicken, or lamb. Live piano music and a full bar add to the ambience. No smoking. Not wheelchair accessible. $18–23.

& **Slovakia Restaurant** (770-792-4443; www.slovakiarestaurant.com), 164 Roswell Street. Open 6–10 Tuesday through Saturday, 11:30–2 Sunday for brunch. Aged wood and traditional costumes create an Old World ambience that serves as an elegant backdrop for delicious dishes. Native Slovakians Stefan and Ivana Bencik create traditional dishes such as sauerkraut soup, tarator (cold cucumber soup), halusky (Slovakian potato spatzle with cheese and bacon), pierogies, goulash, and entrées using beef, pork, sausage, duck, veal, chicken, and seafood. Specialties include chateaubriand and beef Wellington. Save room for desserts such as strudels or palacinky Patrik, Slovakian pancakes with jam, strawberries, whipped cream, chocolate, pecans, and ice cream. $11.95–24.95. On Saturday evenings, the banquet facility portion of the restaurant becomes Murder on the Square, a dinner theater that presents a different play each month. A three-course dinner and the play cost $41.95.

Eating Out

Just about every chain restaurant imaginable has one or more outlets in the immediate area.

In Kennesaw

♿ **The Trackside Grill** (770-499-0874; www.tracksidegrill.com), 2840 South Main Street. Open 11–3 daily; 5–9 Monday through Thursday, 5–10 Friday and Saturday. Fried green tomatoes, hush puppies, and house-made potato chips are specialty appetizers. At lunchtime, choose from soups, salads, sandwiches such as the fried green tomato BLT, and entrées such as seafood, chicken, beef, and meat loaf. Dinner choices include those as well as pork chops, steaks, and pot roast. Weekend brunch choices run the gamut from a fried green tomato Benedict to all kinds of egg dishes to Charleston shrimp and grits to surf and turf. Save room for the maple-bourbon bread pudding with praline ice cream and caramel sauce or any of the other tempting desserts. Try a specialty coffee cocktail, too. Monday features wine by the glass or bottle for half price. Every Wednesday is designated for catfish and blues, so wear blue (denim's good) and enjoy barbecue ribs, fried pickles, and catfish. Every Thursday is Pasta Night, with an array of dishes for $10. The restaurant also offers a special wine dinner on the third Tuesday of each month, when four special courses are paired with four wines for $49.95 per person. $6–9 for lunch; $14–23 for dinner; $7–13 for brunch.

In Marietta

♿ **The Big Chicken KFC** (770-422-4716), 12 North Cobb Parkway. Open 10 AM–midnight. When is a Kentucky Fried Chicken not just a KFC? When it's The Big Chicken. This beloved landmark has a small gift shop as well as fast food. No smoking. Wheelchair accessible. $5–10.

♿ **Dave and Buster's** (770-951-5554; www.daveandbusters.com) 2215 Dave and Buster's Drive. Open 11:30 AM–midnight Sunday through Wednesday, 11:30 AM–1 AM Thursday, 11:30 AM–2 AM Friday and Saturday. Food, while plentiful and good, takes second place to the state-of-the-art interactive video games, virtual-reality simulators, pocket billiards, shuffleboard, entertainment, and other recreational facilities to be found here. Fine dining is offered in the Grand Dining Room; lighter and more casual fare is available at the Viewpoint Bar and the Midway Bar. Patrons younger than 21 are allowed only when accompanied by adults older than 25, but their curfew is 10. No smoking in dining areas. Wheelchair accessible. $8–20.

Hemingway's Tropical Bar and Grill (770-427-5445), 29 West Park Square. Open 11:30–11:30 Monday through Thursday, 11:30–1 AM Friday and Saturday, 11:30–7 Sunday. Casual dining is offered in a typical barlike atmosphere. There's really not much tropical about the decor, although you may hear Jimmy Buffet-like music. Typical pub grub includes everything from burgers to steaks to seafood. In nice weather, diners enjoy the umbrella tables in the cobblestone side alley. Live rock bands perform on Friday and Saturday nights. There is a nonsmoking section of about eight tables until 10 PM, after which smoking is allowed throughout. The downside is that there is no barrier between the smoking and nonsmoking sections, so some tables are adjacent to the smoking section. Not wheelchair accessible. $8–15.

&. **Shillings on the Square** (770-428-9520), 19 North Park Square. Open 10:30–11 Sunday through Thursday, 10:30–midnight Friday and Saturday. It's hard to imagine that this structure was built in 1900 as a hardware store. Of the two restaurants housed here (see Shillings Top of the Square under *Dining Out*), this is the more casual and economical. Dining options include soups, salads, sandwiches, and traditional entrées. No smoking. Wheelchair accessible. $9–23.

In Smyrna
Atkins Park Tavern (770-435-1887;

www.atkinspark.com), 2840 Atlanta Road. Open 11 AM–4 AM weekdays, 11 AM–3 AM Saturday, 11 AM–midnight Sunday. The original Atkins Park, one of Atlanta's oldest restaurants, has been around since 1922. This popular sister eatery has an award-winning chef, a Cheers-like tavern atmosphere, patio dining, and an extensive selection of beers. Smoking in the bar only. Wheelchair accessible. $16–30.

Coffeehouses

In Marietta
Cool Beans Coffee Roasters (770-422-9866), 31 Mill Street, Suite 100. Open 8–10 Monday through Thursday, 8–11:30 Friday, 9–11:30 Saturday, 10–7 Sunday. Come here for coffee, cappuccino, tea, pastries, and desserts. No smoking. Wheelchair accessible.

ENTERTAINMENT

Dance

Georgia Ballet (770-528-0881; www.georgiaballet.org), office: 1255 Field Parkway, Marietta. Box office hours 9–5 weekdays; call for a schedule of events and ticket prices, which are in the $19–26 range. The 45-year-old professional dance company and dance school offers performances of classical ballets and new works at the Jennie T. Anderson Theatre at the Cobb County Civic Center, 548 South Marietta Parkway, during its September-to-May season.

Music

Cobb Symphony Orchestra (770-426-1509; www.cobbsymphony.com), mailing address: P.O. Box 680993, Marietta 30068. Founded almost 60 years ago, the professional orchestra and a variety of well-known guest artists present a full season of classical and chamber works in an audience-friendly atmosphere. Local citizenry look forward to several outdoor performances such as those at Marietta Square/Glover Park.

Department of Music/Kennesaw State University (770-423-6650; www.kennesaw .edu/arts), mailing address: 1000 Chastain Road, Kennesaw 30144. Call for a schedule of performances and ticket prices or send an e-mail to boxoffice@kennesaw.edu. The department presents many faculty and student recitals, operas, and jazz concerts as well as performances by guest artists, world-class musical ensembles, and the Georgia Young Singers at the university's Stillwell Theater. The Legacy Gazebo Amphitheater is host to the popular Starlight Summer Concert Series of jazz and pops concerts.

Nightlife

Cowboys Atlanta (770-426-5006), 1750 North Roberts Road, Kennesaw. Open 7 PM–2 AM Thursday and Friday, 7 PM–3 AM Saturday, 4–11 Sunday. Cowboys is a mega country music venue with a huge dance floor and local and nationally known bands. You'll find everyone here, from boot-scootin' rednecks to city slickers—often decked out in rhinestones and fringe. Free line dancing lessons are given on Thursday and Sunday evenings; couples dance lessons start at 7 PM Saturday. And, oh yes, just as in *Urban Cowboy*, there's even a mechanical bull. Although it is generally an adult club, on Sunday Cowboy's sponsors family night with free dance lessons and free pizza (while it lasts). No alcohol is served, the club is smoke-free, and all ages are welcome. Smoking is allowed Thursday through Saturday only. Wheelchair accessible. $7 cover charge Thursday through Saturday (ladies free on Thursday), $10 Sunday.

Theater

Cobb Playhouse and Studio (770-565-3995; www.cobbplayhouse.com), 4857 North Main Street, Suite 240, Acworth. The theater organization is actually a collection of six theater companies, an arts education program, and an art studio. The **Barnbuster Musicals** troupe presents several full-length musicals each year; **Cobb Players** performs several plays; **Little General Players**, composed of youth age 8 to 16, presents eight or more productions; **Little General Junior Players**, composed of young people in first through eighth grade, performs four plays; **School Day Theater** is an outreach program for schoolchildren; and **Lake City Players**, the most recent addition to the theater family, is a professional company of adults who perform dinner theater at Cott'n Eyed Joe's Restaurant in historic downtown Acworth. Call for a schedule of events and ticket prices, which range from $8–16. Dinner theater tickets are $38, which includes your meal.

Department of Theatre and Performance Studies/Kennesaw State University (770-423-6650; www.kennesaw.edu/arts), mailing address: 1000 Chastain Road, Kennesaw 30144. Call for a schedule of performances and ticket prices or send an e-mail to boxoffice@kennesaw.edu. The department presents a full season of performances by students and faculty as well as guest artists and the KSU Tellers.

Jennie T. Anderson Theatre (770-528-8490), 548 South Marietta Parkway, Marietta. Located at the Cobb Civic Center, this intimate space for the performing arts is the performance venue for the Georgia Ballet, the Cobb Symphony Orchestra, and many special productions.

John A. Williams Theatre at the Cobb Energy Centre for the Performing Arts (770-989-5035; www.cobbenergycentre.com), 2800 Cobb Galleria Parkway, Atlanta. Call for a schedule of events and ticket prices. New in 2007, the Cobb Energy Centre is the first major performing arts facility built in metro Atlanta in the past 40 years. The 2,750-seat theater hosts Broadway shows, ballet, concerts, and other performances, and is the performance home of the Atlanta Opera. Wheelchair accessible.

& **Theatre in the Square and Alley Theater** (770-422-8369; www.theatreinthesquare.com), 11 Whitlock Avenue, Marietta. Call for a schedule of performances and ticket prices. This intimate theater, housed in a charming restored cotton warehouse, offers award-winning Broadway-caliber productions year-round, including holiday shows, shows for young people, and a play-reading series featuring works by regional playwrights. The theater has been called "the most charming performing space in the Southeast" by *Southern Living* magazine. A second set of plays is offered in the very intimate Alley Theater. Both theaters are wheelchair accessible, but be sure to let the box office know if the patron needs to stay in the wheelchair.

SELECTIVE SHOPPING

Antiques

Cobb County is rich in antiques stores. There are nearly 20 shops around the square in Marietta, and Kennesaw's Main Street is a gold mine of antique treasures. Smyrna's antiques district is found on Atlanta Road. You'll also be captivated by Acworth's Victorian village-style downtown, where you'll find many antiques shops.

DuPre's (770-428-2667; 1-877-894-2293; www.dupresai.com), 17 Whitlock Avenue, Marietta. Open 10–6 Monday through Saturday, 1–6 Sunday. DuPre's is located in a circa 1880 building that was once a general store and an unofficial post office where friends could leave letters and parcels for each other. Today it's is an antiques mall with 90 dealers who purvey all kinds of antiques, collectibles, and other goods. The front of the store is wheelchair accessible, but the back is not.

Food

Church Street Market (770-499-9393; www.churchstreetmarket.com), 131 Church Street, Marietta. Open 11–5 daily; farmer's market Saturday mornings, May through September. In general, the store purveys Georgia products and foods such as preserves and jellies. On Saturday mornings from spring through fall, the store operates a farmer's market where customers can get fresh produce.

Other Goods

The Brumby Chair Company (770-425-1875; www.brumbyrocker.com), 37 West Park Square, Marietta. Open 10–5 Monday through Saturday. In 1875, the Brumby family began to make generous oak rocking chairs for Southern verandas. Over time, the popularity of the jumbo rockers led the company to produce other sizes: a double-courting rocker, a smaller lady rocker, a baby rocker, a footstool, and now, in the age of laptop computers, a lap desk rocker. The solid Appalachian red oak rockers come in six stained finishes and two paint colors. No matter what size you choose, the rocker is bound to become a family heirloom. Craftspeople actually assemble the chairs and cane the seats at the store, where visitors also can examine antique Brumby rockers and photographs of famous Georgians with their Brumby rockers. When Jimmy Carter was president, he took them to the White House.

Eddie's Trick Shop (770-428-4314; 1-800-429-4314; www.eddiestrickshop.com), 70 South Park Square, Marietta. Open 10–6 Monday through Saturday. Guaranteed fun whether you buy anything or not, Eddie's carries costumes (rentals and sales), costume accessories, wigs, hats, masks, theatrical makeup, novelties, balloons, puppets, theatrical books, and clown, juggling, and magic supplies.

Kreature Komforts of Marietta (770-428-8616; www.kreaturekomfortsofmariettainc.com), 31 Mill Street, Suite 300, Marietta. Open 8:30–5:30 Tuesday through Saturday. Created for those who spoil their pets shamelessly, Kreature Komforts features exclusive lines of pet essentials and pet-related human essentials. The shop boasts a gourmet bakery with all-natural, preservative-free treats for your special pets, as well as wheat-, corn-, and soy-free treats for those on special diets. In addition, the day spa pampers pets with specialized coat-conditioning botanical treatments.

Special Stores

Galleria Specialty Mall (770-955-8000; www.galleriaspecialtymall.com), 1 Galleria Parkway, Marietta. Mall open 11–6 daily; individual store hours may vary. Located at I-285 and Cobb Parkway, the upscale mall is home to some of the most unique shops in metro Atlanta, from fine home furnishings to art shops to clothing boutiques. The mall also features several restaurants and an eight-screen cineplex.

SPECIAL EVENTS

April: **Spring Jonquil Festival** (770-805-4277). The weekend arts and crafts festival on the Village Green in Smyrna features works by more than 150 artisans and crafters from around the country, continuous entertainment, a children's area, and a wide selection of food. $1, children and seniors free.

    Taste of Marietta (770-429-1115; 1-800-835-0445; www.mariettasquare.com). This is a fun way to sample the cuisine of a variety of Cobb County restaurants and to experience Marietta's history, culture, and shopping at Marietta Square. There are children's activities and a car show, too. A variety of outdoor entertainment is scheduled from 11–7, culminating with a sunset concert featuring a well-known guest artist or artists. Concert table reservations are available. Admission free; fee for food and special seating.

April through August: **Glover Park Concert Series** (770-429-1115; 1-800-835-0445; www.mariettasquare.com). Bring a blanket and enjoy a concert under the stars at historic Marietta Square/Glover Park. Concerts are held the last Friday of the month. Free.

Summer: **Starlight Movie Series** (770-422-9714). Call for dates. The Depot in Kennesaw is the place to gather for major motion pictures shown on a four-story-tall inflatable movie screen at dusk. There are games and music beforehand. Bring a blanket or lawn chairs and a picnic. Food is also available for purchase. June through August. Free.

    Summer Concert Series (770-422-9714). Call for dates of these concerts, also held at The Depot in Kennesaw. Local, regional, and national headliners entertain. May through August. Free.

July: **Fourth in the Park** (770-429-1115; 1-800-835-0445; www.mariettasquare.com). The celebration at Marietta Square lasts from morning until evening, beginning with a parade, followed by food and festivities throughout the day, and culminating with a fireworks extravaganza. Free.

September: **Art in the Park** (770-429-1115; 1-800-835-0445; www.mariettasquare.com). Held Labor Day weekend in Marietta's Glover Park, the juried art show is one of the largest in the Southeast. The show focuses on original fine arts and crafts. Free.

    Marietta Antique Street Festival (770-429-1115; 1-800-835-0445; www.mariettasquare.com). More than 100 antique dealers display and sell their wares at this festival in Glover Park. There is also entertainment and demonstrations of caning, furniture refinishing, upholstery, spinning, and quilting. Appraisals of one item per family are held from 11–2, a classic car show is held in East Park Square, and 20 local antiques shops have sidewalk sales. There are carriage rides, too. Festival free; fee for carriage rides.

Spice of Life Food and Cultural Celebration (770-434-6600; 770-319-2526). This event, held on the Village Green in Smyrna, showcases the culture and tastes of Smyrna restaurants as well as musical entertainment. Free admission.

October: **Fall Festival** (770-805-4277). This event, the sibling to Smyrna's Spring Jonquil Festival, features arts and crafts, entertainment, games, and food on the Village Green. Free.

Folk Tales on the Rails (770-422-9714). Storytellers portraying pirates, settlers, and Georgia founder James Oglethorpe will mesmerize children and adults. The festival, held at the Southern Museum of Civil War and Locomotive History in Kennesaw, also includes hayrides and a treasure hunt. Free.

Kennesaw Fall Antique Festival (770-428-2262; www.kennesawmerchants.com). Downtown Kennesaw bustles with antiques dealers, crafts, entertainment, and food, as well as a display of antique cars, tractors, farm equipment, and other old-time items. Free.

November and December: **A Merry Olde Marietta Christmas** (770-429-1115; 1-800-835-0445; www.mariettasquare.com). Two months of special events include holiday theater performances and the much anticipated **Marietta Pilgrimage Christmas Home Tour,** which is held on the first full weekend in December. The tour visits six historic private homes and eight public buildings. Shuttle service is provided along the route for the day tour, but not the candlelight tour. Pilgrimage hours are 9–6 Saturday, 10–6 Sunday; candlelight tour runs 7–9:30 Saturday. $12–25.

9

Westside

Austell, Douglasville, Lithia Springs, Mableton, Powder Springs, Villa Rica

The small municipalities in this chapter stretch from urban towns just west of Atlanta through charming suburban hamlets farther out and finally through rural areas—all liberally sprinkled with green spaces. The region is rich in Native American history and was the site of the first gold strike in Georgia, and several springs believed to have medicinal properties led to a brief resort era. The railroads were important in the formation of many of the towns in the late 19th century, and most of the villages have preserved historical architecture from that period.

Today the Westside towns feature historic homes, museums, theater, and musical performances as well as plenty of opportunities for outdoor activities such as biking, hiking, fishing, and swimming. Several outdoor attractions of note include Sweetwater Creek State Park, the Silver Comet Trail, and the Wild Horse Creek Trail. Favorites with families include Six Flags Over Georgia and Sun Valley Beach.

Perhaps most important of all for travelers who may have just left the frenetic pace of the city is the friendly, relaxed, laid-back ambience of the Westside.

Canoes are ready to be taken out on the water at Sweetwater Creek State Park.

GUIDANCE

To learn about Douglasville, contact the **Douglasville Convention and Visitors Bureau and Welcome Center** (770-947-5920; 1-800-661-0013; www.douglasvillecvb.com), 6694 East Broad Street, Douglasville, open 8–5 weekdays; or the **Douglas County Local Welcome Center** (770-942-5022; www.douglas countygeorgia.com), 2145 Slater Mill Road, Douglasville, open 9–5 weekdays.

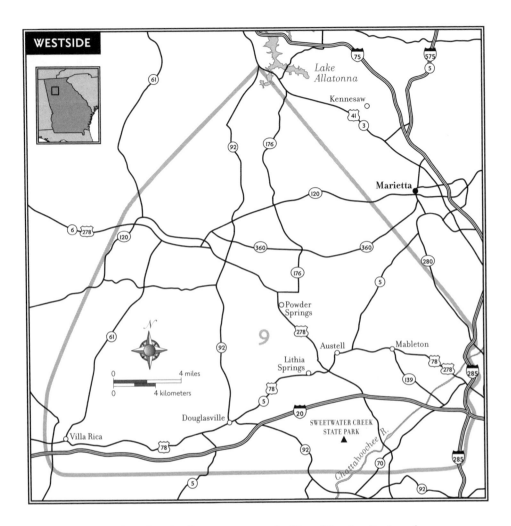

To learn more about Powder Springs, contact the **City of Powder Springs** (770-943-1666; www.cityofpowdersprings.org), 3930 Austell-Powder Springs Road Southwest, Powder Springs. For information on all of Cobb County, contact the **Cobb County Convention and Visitors Bureau** (678-303-2622; 1-800-451-3480; www.cobbcvb.com), One Galleria Parkway, Atlanta, open 8–5 weekdays.

For more information about Villa Rica, contact the **Villa Rica Tourism Board** (678-785-1014; www.villaricatourism.com), 571 West Bankhead Highway, Villa Rica.

Getting There

By air: See What's Where. The following shuttle companies offer service to Austell, Mableton, and Powder Springs: **Around Town Tours** (770-909-9091), **Airport Perimeter Connection** (404-761-0260), **Daytime Transportation** (770-939-2337), **Airport Metro Shuttle** (404-766-6666), and **Galleria Direct** (770-955-1550). Limousine service to these towns is offered from the airport by **A&M Limousines** (770-955-4565). For transportation to the remainder of towns described in this chapter, a visitor needs a car.

By bus: See What's Where.

By car: These towns are located just north or just south of I-20 west of Atlanta. Austell, Douglasville, Lithia Springs, Mableton, and Villa Rica are on US 78. Powder Springs is on US 278.

By Train: See What's Where.

Getting Around

Car rentals are not only available at the airport, but in each of the towns described, and as such they are too numerous to list here. Consult the Yellow Pages, the Internet, or the concierge at your hotel.

Within and between the Cobb County municipalities described in this chapter, mass transit is available from **Cobb Community Transit** (see What's Where). There is no mass transit available in the other towns.

When to Go

A few attractions such as Six Flags Over Georgia have severely curtailed hours in winter, so check their Web sites when planning a trip.

Medical Emergency

In life-threatening situations, call 911. For less serious situations needing immediate care, visitors to Austell, Mableton, and Powder Springs can get help at **WellStar Kennestone Hospital** (770-793-5000; www.wellstar.org), 677 Church Street, Marietta, or at **Emory-Adventist Hospital** (770-434-0710), 3949 South Cobb Drive, Smyrna.

Villages/Neighborhoods

Austell was once known as Cincinnati Junction because the railroad line from Atlanta west branched here, with one line going to Birmingham, Alabama, and the other going to Cincinnati, Ohio. The City of Austell, named for General Alfred Austell, was incorporated in 1885.

Douglasville was a turn-of-the-20th-century railroad town, but its significance was evident much earlier. The boundary between the Cherokee Nation to the north and the Creek Nation to the south was marked by a chestnut tree located at the summit of the ridge where Douglasville now stands. Today the quaint downtown is listed on the National Register of Historic Places and the historic buildings house shops, restaurants, boutiques, and professional services. The old courthouse is interesting in itself. Although it was built in 1956, it is listed on the National Register of Historic Places because it is one of only four courthouses in the United States built in the International style of the 1950s. It has since been replaced by another courthouse. Today the old courthouse houses the Douglas County Museum of History and Art, the Jocada Museum of Jazz History (see separate entries), and a *Gone with the Wind* exhibit.

Concerts are often held at O'Neal Plaza, a city park in Douglasville's quaint downtown.

Lithia Springs was a resort town in the late 1800s. Even before that, Native Americans prized the area and lived at the salt (lithium) springs. The Brevard Fault zone passes directly through the Sweetwater Creek basin and its movement has resulted in a more mountainous environment than the surrounding region.

Mableton was named for Robert Mable, a Scottish immigrant who gave land for railroad right-of-way. Mableton was incorporated in 1912, but residents decided they didn't need to be a city and petitioned to have the charter repealed. Robert Mable's home, Mable House, served as a hospital during the Civil War. Now restored and open for tours, the property is also the home to the South Cobb Arts Alliance as well as the Mable House Barnes Amphitheatre, which hosts various concerts throughout the year.

Powder Springs was originally known as Springsville because it had seven springs valued by Native Americans and white settlers for their reputed medicinal properties. The first settlers came searching for gold, but found little in the mines at Lost Mountain and off Brownsville Road. The name of the town was changed to Powder Springs in 1859 because the minerals in the springs turned the surrounding sand black like gunpowder.

Villa Rica was the site of the first gold strike in Georgia, although it didn't amount to much. The small town was the home of Asa Candler, founder of Coca-Cola, and Thomas A. Dorsey, the father of gospel music. Dorsey, who played with Ma Rainey (another Georgian) and her Wild Cat Jazz Band, had a breakdown after the death of his wife and newborn. He turned to his faith for solace and composed more than 400 blues and gospel songs, including "Take My Hand Precious Lord," which has been translated into 32 languages, and "Peace in the Valley," which was recorded by Elvis Presley. A popular annual festival honors Dorsey. The **North Villa Rica Commercial Historic District**, roughly bounded by Southern Railroad, North Avenue, East Gordon, and West Church streets, is a collection of buildings dating from 1875. The district contains the police department, antiques shops, restaurants, and other commercial businesses.

To See

Cultural Sites

♦ ♿ **Cultural Arts Center of Douglasville/Douglas County** (770-949-ARTS; www.artsdouglas.org), 8652 Campbellton Street, Douglasville. Open 9–5 weekdays, 1–5 Sunday, and for special events (call for a schedule). Housed in the gracious 1901 Neoclassical Roberts-Mozley House—former home of three mayors of Douglasville—the state-of-the-art center is headquarters for cultural activities such as artist's receptions,

Art can be found both outside and inside the Cultural Arts Center of Douglasville/Douglas County.

rotating exhibits, and special programs. One of the few historic structures remaining in Douglasville, the building is listed on the National Register of Historic Places. Among the center's permanent works is an outdoor sculpture by Georgia artist Joel Yawn, which is listed on the Smithsonian's public art inventory and part of the Save Outdoor Sculpture program. The center also maintains a downtown sales gallery at the Chamber of Commerce where works of local artists are sold. While visiting the center, be sure to admire the grand front porch, stained glass doors, heart pine floors, and fireplaces embellished with tortoise-shell tiles. Free; fees for some events.

Historic Homes and Sites

❦ ⟺ **Mable House** (770-819-3285; www.mablehouse.org), 5239 Floyd Road, Mableton. House open by appointment; arts center open 10–5 weekdays. Listed on the National Register of Historic Places, Mable House was built in 1843 and is furnished in turn-of-the-20th-century pieces. With its outbuildings and family cemetery, the historic property represents a mid-19th-century architectural complex. On the grounds are a cultural arts center and an amphitheater (see *Entertainment*). House tour free; fees for concerts.

❦ **Wick Tavern** (770) 456-0201), 212 West Wilson Street, Villa Rica. Open by appointment. Wick Tavern, which is the oldest commercial structure in West Georgia, dating from 1830, is a classic example of the Dutch-style timber-framing method. The tavern was used as a bar and hotel for travelers. It was originally located in Gold Village, also known as Old Town or Hixtown, and was moved to this site in 1998 to serve as a living history museum. Free.

Museums

❦ ❦ **Douglas County Museum of History and Art** (770-949-4090; www. douglas countymuseum.com), Old Courthouse Building, 6754 West Broad Street, Suite 205, Douglasville. Open 1–5 Tuesday and Thursday. Rotating mid-20th-century exhibits reflect the 1956 construction date of the courthouse in which the museum is situated. Private collections include a display of cocktail shakers, school lunch boxes, Coca-Cola articles, and children's phonographs. Free.

The old Douglas County Courthouse now houses the Jocada Museum of Jazz History and the Douglas County Museum of History and Art

❦ **Jocada Museum of Jazz History** (770-947-1187 answers during museum hours; www.mindspring.com/~dmerriman/Jazz/index.htm), Old Courthouse Building, 6754 West Broad Street, Suite 205, Douglasville. Open 11–5 Friday and Saturday. This multicultural establishment tells the story of those who contributed to the legacy of jazz history dating back to the early 1900s. Big Band, swing, bebop, and Dixieland styles are explored through displays of rare and antique instruments, paintings, photos, biographies, and memora-bilia. The James Patterson Collection features instruments used in the 1920s and 1930s in the music education department of Clark College (now Clark Atlanta University). $6.

❦ ❦ **Seven Springs Museum** (678-567-5611; www.cityofpowdersprings.org/history.html), 3899 Brownsville Road, Powder Springs. Open 3–4 Wednesday, 9–1 Saturday, 1–4 Sunday. Located in Powder Springs Park and operated by volunteers from the Seven Springs Historical Society, the museum houses a collection of artifacts and photographs that trace the history of the area. Among the exhibits are those relating to the Cherokee Indians, the 1828 Gold Rush, and the Civil War. Free.

To Do

Bicycling
See the **Silver Comet Trail** under *Hiking.*

Fishing
✧ ❧ ♿ **Sweetwater Creek State Park** (770-732-5871; www.gastateparks.org/info/sweetwater), Mount Vernon Road, Lithia Springs. Park open 7–dusk, visitor's center open 8–5, bait shop open 7–7; trails close at dark. The park's 215-acre George Sparks Reservoir is popular with anglers. Stream fishing is available as well. There are two fishing docks, and fishing supplies, canoes, and fishing boats are available from the park bait shop. Only electric motors are permitted. Parking $3, boat ramp fee $2.

For Families
✧ ♿ **Six Flags Over Georgia** (770-948-9290; www.sixflags.com/overGeorgia/index.aspx), 275 Riverside Parkway, Austell. Open weekends March through Memorial Day, daily in the summer, and weekends again Labor Day through the end of October. Park hours are generally morning through late evening, but they vary widely, so call ahead or consult the Web site before traveling. It's always playtime at this family-oriented theme park, which features 100 rides, including eight white-knuckle coasters and other not-for-the-faint-of-heart thrill rides as well as moderate and mild rides suitable for everyone in the family. Along with the rides, numerous food outlets and a variety of shows and other entertainment extravaganzas on 10 stages keep the fun going late into the night. Hair-raising thrill rides include Superman: Ultimate Flight; Batman: The Ride; Georgia Cyclone, the South's only twister

The twists and turns of a roller coaster at Six Flags Over Georgia

coaster; Acrophobia, a 200-foot rotating tower drop; Georgia Scorcher, one of the South's tallest and fastest stand-up coasters; Déjà Vu; Ninja; and the newest coaster, Goliath, a 200-foot-tall, 4,400-foot-long monster coaster that reaches speeds of 70 mph and covers 8.5 acres. Another popular attraction is Skull Island, the world's largest interactive water play structure. Recent additions include two dozen new characters and additional seats in the eating area. Adults $50, children $30; $15 parking. Unlimited season pass $70.

⚓ ♿ **Sun Valley Beach** (770-943-5900; 1-888-811-7390; www.sunvalleybeach.com), 5350 Holloman Road, Powder Springs. Open weekends May through Memorial Day, daily Memorial Day to Labor Day, weekends in September (hours are too variable to include here, so check the Web site). Landlocked metro Atlantans will think they're in paradise at this inland beach. Sun Valley Beach was the forerunner of modern water parks. In operation since 1964, the facility is nestled in 40 acres of pines and features the Southeast's largest swimming pool, which is surrounded by white sandy beaches. The complex boasts 10 water slides, a dolphin fountain, showering umbrella, log roll, Tarzan ropes, a zip line, diving platform, the Pirate Obstacle Course, and Cruisin' in the Valley Car Show. Beach volleyball courts, sports fields, a Go-Kart track, tennis courts, horseshoes, ball fields, and picnicking facilities add to the fun. Adults $17.95, children 2–11 $15.95.

Frights

⚓ ♿ **Six Flags Over Georgia** (770-948-9290; www.sixflags.com/overGeorgia/index.aspx), 275 Riverside Parkway, Austell. Friday through Sunday in October. The hours vary widely, so call ahead or consult the Web site. Ghouls and goblins transform the entire park into an eerie city filled with haunted houses, new shows, and other frightfully good fun. Adults $50, children $30; $15 parking.

Hiking

See Annie Clinton Farms and Nature Preserve and Sweetwater Creek State Park under *Nature Preserves and Parks*.

⚓ 🎃 🐾 ♿ **Silver Comet Trail** (PATH Foundation 770-875-7284; silvercomet.tripod.com; www.pathfoundation.org). Open daylight hours daily. The 59-mile trail, which begins in Smyrna (see the Marietta chapter), connects the Atlanta metro area to the Alabama state line. A former railroad route for the Silver Comet passenger train, the track has been taken up and paved so that the 12?-mile roadbed provides opportunities for walking, jogging, hiking, cycling, and skating. The trail is also suitable for baby strollers, wheelchairs, and leashed animals. Crossing six trestles and bridges, the trail offers scenic views and access to Heritage Park, a 105-acre nature preserve. A 1.7-mile spur trail goes to the ruins of a woolen mill. A section beginning at Florence Road in Powder Springs is open to horses (BYOH—Bring Your Own Horse). Four trailheads offer parking, restrooms, and water fountains. The trail also can be accessed from several cross streets. It is patrolled by bicycle-mounted Cobb County police officers. The trail connects to the Wild Horse Creek Trail (see next entry). For more information about the trail, visitors also can contact **Cobb County Parks, Recreation, and Cultural Affairs** at (770) 528-8840 or www.cobbcounty.org. (See *Shopping—Bicycle Shops* for information on bicycle and skate rentals.) Free.

⚓ 🐾 ♿ **Wild Horse Creek Trail** (City of Powder Springs 770-439-2500; www.cityofpowder springs.org/areatrails/areatrails.html). Open daylight hours daily; closed immediately after a rainstorm. In 1864 this area saw much action as Union troops advanced on Atlanta. Today, a 10-foot wide, 1.5-mile paved trail is used by cyclists, skaters, runners, and walkers.

The trail, which begins at Wild Horse Creek Park on Macedonia Road and ends at the Silver Comet Trail (see previous entry) at Carter Road, is the first in a proposed citywide network of trails. It is appropriate for baby strollers, wheelchairs, and pets on leashes. Motorized vehicles and horses are not permitted. Along the way users may see the largest red maple tree in the state, and there is an observation tower south of Hopkins Road from which to view the wetlands. Amenities include a rest area near Powder Springs Road, two emergency call boxes, and parking and restroom facilities at Wild Horse Creek Park. The bicycle unit of the Powder Springs Police Department provides security. Free.

Swimming

✐ **West Cobb Aquatic Center** (770-222-6700), 3675 MacLand Road, Powder Springs. Open 6 AM–9 PM weekdays, 9–5 Saturday, 2–5 Sunday, but the hours are different for open swim times, so check ahead. Operated by the Cobb County Department of Parks, Recreation and Cultural Affairs, the facility has a large pool and a diving well. Adults $3, children $2.

Tennis

Cobb County Department of Parks, Recreation and Cultural Affairs (770-528-8800; www.cobbcounty.org) operates several tennis centers: **Sweetwater Park** (770-819-3221), 2447 Clay Road, Austell, and **Lost Mountain Park** (770-528-8525), 4845 Dallas Highway, Powder Springs. There are four or more tennis courts at the following parks: **Nickajack Park**, 3630 Oakdale Road, Mableton; **Wallace Park**, 6289 Pisgah Road, Mableton; and **Wild Horse Creek Park**, 3820 Macedonia Road, Powder Springs. Call the department 8–5 weekdays for more information.

GREEN SPACE

Nature Preserves and Parks

Contact **Cobb County Department of Parks, Recreation and Cultural Affairs** (770-528-8800; www.cobbcounty.org), 1792 County Services Parkway, Marietta, for information on parks in the county. Office open 8–5 weekdays.

✐ 🌼 🐾 ♿ **Annie Clinton Farms and Nature Preserve** (Douglas County Parks and Recreation superintendent 770-920-7191; www.celebratedouglascounty.com, and then follow the prompts), Ephesus Church Road, Winston. Open daylight hours daily. Annie Clinton bequeathed the 200-acre historical preserve to the county provided that it remains in as natural a state as possible. The property features the antebellum Carnes Cabin—a log structure listed on the National Register of Historic Places—a picnic area, walking and nature trails, a walking track, fishing, open exploration areas, and an outdoor amphitheater. The trails, which are also popular with mountain bikers, have very challenging sections and lots of climbing. The Junior League donated a disabled-accessible playground/play garden. Pets are welcome. Free.

✐ 🐾 ♿ **Powder Springs Park** (770-528-8800; www.cobbcounty.org and follow the prompts), 3899 Brownsville Road, Powder Springs. Open daily; pool open 1–6 Tuesday through Sunday, Memorial Day weekend through the first weekend in August. The 17.5-acre park offers ball fields, playgrounds, picnic areas, an outdoor pool, and paved trails. Free; pool $1.75 for adults, $1.25 for seniors and youth younger than 16.

✎ 🐾 ♿ **Sweetwater Creek State Park** (770-732-5871; www.gastateparks.org/info/sweet water), Mount Vernon Road, Lithia Springs. Park open 7–dusk; visitor's center open 8–5; bait shop open 7–7; trails close at dark. This is the third-most-visited park in the state system and the most-visited park without overnight facilities. More than 2,500 acres of peaceful wilderness are located just west of Atlanta. A forest trail follows a stream to the ruins of the New Manchester Manufacturing Company, a textile mill that was burned during the Civil War. Its workers (mostly women and children) were charged with treason, marched to Marietta, and put on trains for the North, where they were either imprisoned or forced into servitude to Northern families and businesses for the duration of the war (see the Roswell chapter for more information about this fascinating Civil War story). From the mills, the trail climbs rocky bluffs and affords views of the shoals below. Within the park, there are 9 miles of trails. The streams and 215-acre George Sparks Reservoir provide recreation for anglers. Electric motors only are allowed. Fishing supplies and snacks are available in the park's bait shop, and canoes and fishing boats are rented as well. The park also features picnicking facilities, a butterfly garden, and periodic interpretive programs such as **History Walks** in February, **Wildflower Walks** in April, an **Intertribal Powwow** and a **Summer Festival**, both in June (see *Special Events*). Children love to feed the ducks in the pond. Maps and park information can be found at the new visitor's center, where there are exhibits covering the Civil War and the New Manchester Manufacturing Company as well as the park's geography and animals. The building is Leadership in Environmental and Energy Design–certified, which means that it meets environmentally friendly building standards with solar panels, waterless toilets, and even a roof that grows flowers. Parking $3, boat ramp fee $2.

✎ 🐾 ♿ **Wild Horse Creek Park** (770-528-8800; www.cobbcounty.org and follow the prompts), 3820 Macedonia Road, Powder Springs. Open daily. In addition to ball fields, lighted tennis courts, a playground, and picnicking facilities, this 70-acre park features a fitness trail, lake, horseshoe pit, BMX track, and an equestrian ring. Free.

LODGING

Bed and Breakfasts

♿ **Twin Oaks Bed and Breakfast at MelaCari Cottages** (770-459-4374; www.twinoaksmc.com), 9565 East Liberty Road, Villa Rica. Visitors get the better of two worlds at this upscale 23-acre farm. City slickers who want to get away from it all can enjoy the farm menagerie that includes Canadian geese, a peacock, and mute swans. Ponds feature goldfish and koi. But there are no bunkhouse accommodations here. Guest quarters are in swanky, sophisticated private cottages. Scarlett's Cottage is done in *Gone with the Wind* style and overlooks the goldfish and koi pond. Swan Cottage boasts a large porch overlooking the ponds and gardens. Full-day spa services are available at the Cozy Spa Cottage. A country breakfast can be served in your cottage or in the main dining room. No smoking. Wheelchair accessible. $139–189; romance,

Rhett's Cottage, one of the unique accommodation choices at the Twin Oaks Bed and Breakfast

honeymoon, and anniversary packages with additional amenities are available.

Campgrounds

✐ ✿ **Atlanta West Campground** (770-941-7185), 2420 Old Alabama Road, Austell. Shady wooded sites have water, electric, and sewer hookups. The campground also offers a bathhouse with showers. $20.50–24.50.

Inns and Hotels

The entire area along I-20 from Atlanta west is filled with just about every chain hotel imaginable. Consult your favorite hotel or travel site on the Internet.

WHERE TO EAT

Eating Out

In Douglasville

✐ ✿ ⅊ **Gumbeaux's—A Cajun Café** (770-947-8288), 6712 East Broad Street, Douglasville. Open 11–2 and 5–10 Tuesday through Saturday. This is the best place to go in west Georgia for Cajun dishes such as gumbo and jambalaya. No smoking. Wheelchair accessible. $8–12.

✐ ✿ ⅊ **Szechuan Village Restaurant** (770-949-6167), 9559 Highway 5, Douglasville. Open 11–9 Monday through Thursday, 11–10 Friday and Saturday, 11–9:30 Sunday. The restaurant specializes in spicy Szechuan Chinese cuisine. No smoking. Wheelchair accessible. $7–10.

In Villa Rica

✐ ✿ ⅊ **The Georgian Grill** (770-459-4400, Ext. 6; www.golfthefrog.com), 1900 Georgian Parkway, Villa Rica. Open 7–4 Sunday through Thursday, 7–5:30 Friday and Saturday. Overlooking the 18th hole of the Frog Golf Course at the Georgian Resort, the casual eatery is open for break-

Gumbeaux's serves up Cajun food in Douglasville

fast and lunch daily. A wide array of sandwiches, soups, and entrées are offered. Try the Frog Lager, a one-of-a-kind treat. No smoking. Wheelchair accessible. $4–22.

✐ ✿ ⅊ **Shucker's Oyster Bar** (770-459-2600), 660 West Bankhead Highway, Villa Rica. Open 11–10 weekdays, 11–midnight Friday and Saturday, 1–9 Sunday. The laidback, beachy atmosphere features beach music played on the jukebox. Fresh seafood—steamed, broiled, or grilled—is the main focus of the menu, but chicken and beef are served as well. Smoking on the deck only. Wheelchair accessible. $6–25.

ENTERTAINMENT

Music

✐ ⅊ **Mable House Barnes Amphitheatre** (770-819-7765; www.themhba.com), 5239 Floyd Road, Mableton. Box office open

10–4 Monday through Saturday. Call for a schedule of performances and ticket prices. One of the Atlanta metro area's newest performance venues, the 2,200-seat concert venue is located in a wooded setting on the property of the historic Mable House (see *Historic Homes and Sites*).The publicly owned outdoor venue provides all kinds of performing arts entertainment, including concerts, musical theater, dance, plays, and multidiscipline performances. The facility offers tables for four, fixed seats, and lawn seating.

Theater

Community Alliance of Stage and Theater/Whistlestop Players (contact the Cultural Arts Center of Douglasville/Douglas County, 770-949-2787; www.artsdouglas.org/Satellites/cast.htm). Call for a schedule of events and ticket prices. The community theater presents plays at the Old Courthouse, as well as dinner theater and a summer series of one-act plays.

♪ ♿ **Cultural Arts Center of Douglasville/Douglas County** (770-949-2787; www.arts douglas.org), 8652 Campbellton Street, Douglasville. Open 9–5 weekdays, 1–5 Sunday. Located in a 1901 Neoclassical-style home, the CAC hosts concerts, festivals, holiday events, and other cultural activities including monthly artists' receptions, exhibits, and special programs. Prices vary by activity.

Also see **Mable House Barnes Amphitheatre** under *Music*.

SELECTIVE SHOPPING

Antiques

Cobb County is dotted with little shops where treasures can be found. Historic downtown Austell features several dealers. Mableton's Bankhead Highway is a treasure trove of antiques shops. In Powder Springs, shops are concentrated on Marietta Street and Lost Mountain Road. In Douglas County, Douglasville boasts an antiques alley downtown.

Bicycle Shops

Bone Shakers Bicycle Shop (770-222-BONE; www.boneshakersbicycle.com), 3279 New MacLand Road, Powder Springs. Open 11–7 weekdays, 11–5 Saturday. Located within riding distance of the Silver Comet Trail, the Wild Horse Trail, and the BMX track at Wild Horse Creek Park, the shop offers sales, repairs, and a limited number of rentals.

Silver Comet Depot (770-819-3279; www.silvercometdepot.com), 4342 Floyd Road Southwest, Mableton. Open 10–7 Sunday through Thursday, 10–6 Friday, 9–6 Saturday during the summer; shorter hours the remainder of the year, so call ahead. The shop rents regular and three-wheel recumbent bikes and skates, and provides other related services in addition to sponsoring group walks and rides.

SPECIAL EVENTS

February: **Annual Cowboy Poets Gathering.** Sponsored by the Cultural Arts Center of Douglasville/Douglas County (770-949-2787; www.artsdouglas.org) and the Douglas County Cowboy Poets, the event features the very best in cowboy poetry and music performed by poets and musicians from all over the country. Performances are given at the Mashburn Center for the Performing Arts at Douglas County High School. $10.

May and September: **Concerts on the Plaza** at O'Neal Plaza on Church Street in downtown Douglasville. Sponsored by the Cultural Arts Center of Douglasville/Douglas County (770-949-2787; www.artsdouglas.org), these free-to-the-public outdoor concerts are held from 7–9 on Saturday in May and on Saturday after Labor Day in September. A variety of musical forms are presented. Bring your own chairs. Free.

June: **Sweetwater Creek Intertribal Powwow** (park 770-732-5871; festival 770-823-7659; www.gastateparks.org/info/sweetwater; www.friendsofsweetwatercreek.org). Held on the grounds of Sweetwater Creek State Park in Lithia Springs (see *Nature Preserves and Parks*), the festival features Native American drumming, music, dancing, arts and crafts, demonstrations, food, and an auction. $3–5 plus $3 parking fee.

Sweetwater Creek Summer Festival (park 770-732-5871; festival 770-823-7659; www.gastateparks.org/info/sweetwater; www.friendsofsweetwatercreek.org). Held on the grounds of Sweetwater Creek State Park in Lithia Springs (see *Nature Preserves and Parks*). In addition to arts and crafts demonstrations and sales, the festival features children's activities, music, and craft demonstrations. $3 parking fee.

Thomas A. Dorsey Festival (678-785-1014). The father of gospel music is honored with a festival featuring jazz, gospel singing, blues, and barbecue at various locations around town. Free.

December: **Old-Fashioned Holiday Celebration, Candlelight Tour of Historic Homes, and Kris Kringle Market** (770-947-5920; 1-800-661-0013; www.ci.douglasville.ga.us). The opportunity to see some of Douglasville's most beautiful houses resplendent in holiday finery as well as chances to shop for one-of-a-kind gifts make these among the most anticipated activities of the year. $10 for home tour; other activities free.

10

THE SOUTHERN CRESCENT

This area is called the Southern Crescent because it hugs and curves around the south side of Atlanta. To the casual observer, the municipalities of College Park, East Point, Fairburn, Fayetteville, Forest Park, Hapeville, Jonesboro, Morrow, Palmetto, Peachtree City, Riverdale, Stockbridge, and Union City seem to blend imperceptibly with each other and with the city of Atlanta, but in reality each is distinct from the others and is imbued with civic pride.

In years past, this was *Gone with the Wind* territory. Margaret Mitchell's grandparents lived here, and when young Peggy visited them, she met their neighbors and heard fascinating stories that inspired her to create the characters in her book. Don't come looking for Tara, however, or you'll be disappointed. It never actually existed. There are, however, homes from the antebellum period that are open for tours.

The Patrick Cleburne Confederate Memorial Cemetery in Jonesboro

Clayton County saw heavy fighting as part of the Atlanta Campaign. After the Battles of Rough and Ready and Jonesboro, Confederate troops had to evacuate. The Battle of Jonesboro was a decisive event in Union General William Tecumseh Sherman's capture of Atlanta and, in fact, marked the end of the Atlanta campaign. When federal troops seized control of the railroad in Jonesboro, all supplies to Atlanta were cut off. Following the battle, Sherman embarked on his March to the Sea. Jonesboro is the grand finale on the Atlanta Campaign Heritage Trail, part of the Georgia Civil War Heritage Trail. Markers along the trail feature a description of the importance of the site as well as a map and a photograph or drawing.

It's somewhat surprising, considering the area's proximity to Atlanta, that there are so many parks, nature preserves, and green spaces, but nature lovers are in seventh heaven to have the best of both worlds—urban and rural.

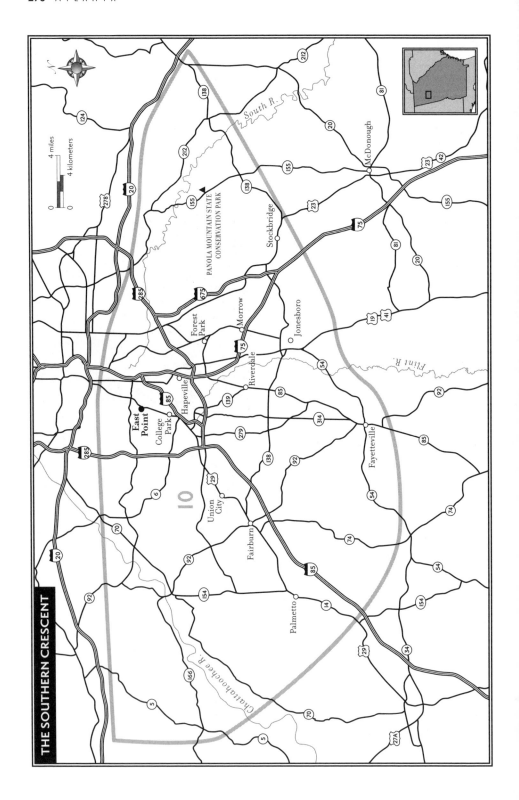

THE SOUTHERN CRESCENT

GUIDANCE

To plan a trip to College Park, East Point, Fairburn, Hapeville, Palmetto, or Union City, contact the **Atlanta Convention and Visitors Bureau** (404-521-6688; 1-800-ATLANTA; www.acvb.com), 233 Peachtree Street Northeast, Suite 100, Atlanta 30303. Open 8:30–5:30 weekdays. Also consult the Web site www.atlanta.net for up-to-date information on hotel and restaurant reservations, directions, guidebooks, maps, and help in creating an itinerary. There is an Atlanta CVB **Visitor Center at Hartsfield-Jackson Atlanta International Airport**, 6000 North Terminal Parkway, Atlanta, which is open 9–9 weekdays, 9–6 Saturday, 12:30–6 Sunday.

For specific information about Fairburn, contact **Fairburn City Hall** (770-964-2244; www.fairburn.com), 56 Malone Street, Fairburn 30213. Open 8–5 weekdays.

To learn more about Fayetteville and Peachtree City, consult the **Fayette County Chamber of Commerce** (770-461-9983; www.fayettechamber.org), 200 Courthouse Square, Fayetteville 30214. Open 8–5 weekdays.

When planning a trip to the Jonesboro or Morrow area, contact the **Clayton County Convention and Visitors Bureau/Jonesboro Depot Welcome Center** (770-478-4800; 1-800-662-7829; wwwvisitscarlett.com), 104 North Main Street, Jonesboro 30236. Open 8:30–5:30 weekdays, 10–4 Saturday. Pick up a brochure for the *Gone with the Wind* Historic District Driving Tour (see *Scenic Drives*) here.

To find out more about Morrow, contact the **Morrow Tourist Center** (770-968-1623; www.morrowtourism.com), 6475 Jonesboro Road, Morrow 30260. Open 8:30–5 Tuesday through Saturday.

Learn more about Stockbridge by contacting the **Henry County Convention and Visitors Bureau** (770-957-5786; 1-800-436-7926); www.henrycvb.com, 1709 Highway 20 West, McDonough 30253. Open 8–5 weekdays, 10–4 Saturday.

Getting There

By air: See What's Where. There are numerous shuttle companies that operate from the airport, and several hotels have free shuttles to their properties, so check ahead when you make your hotel reservation. Shuttle service to College Park, Fairburn, Fayetteville, Peachtree City, and Riverdale is provided by **Sherwood Shuttle** (770-631-0989; www.phoenixstar.us).

By bus: The **Greyhound Bus Lines** (404-762-9581) station at 438 Henry Ford II Avenue in Hapeville serves the municipalities in this chapter. The next nearest station is in downtown Atlanta (see What's Where). A passenger arriving by bus could take a taxi to his hotel, but would then still need a rental car to get around.

By car: All the municipalities in this chapter can be reached easily from I-75, I-85, and I-285.

By train: See What's Where.

Getting Around

Taxis and limousines are too plentiful to list here. Consult your concierge or the Yellow Pages. Two companies offer mass transit. The **Metropolitan Atlanta Rapid Transit Authority,** known locally as **MARTA,** and **Xpress** (404-463-4782; www.xpressga.com). For more information about fares and connections, see What's Where.

Parking
The historic downtowns generally have free on-street parking.

Medical Emergency
For life-threatening emergencies, call 911. For other urgent care, there are numerous hospitals in the Southern Crescent: **South Fulton Medical Center** (404-305-3500), 1170 Cleveland Avenue, East Point; **Piedmont Fayette Hospital** (770-719-7070), 1255 Highway 54 West, Fayetteville; **Southern Regional Medical Center** (770-991-8000), 11 Upper Riverdale Road Southwest, Riverdale; and **Henry Medical Center** (770-389-2200), 1133 Eagles Landing Parkway, Stockbridge.

Villages/Neighborhoods
College Park was established in 1896 along the tracks of the Atlanta & West Point Railroad. The historic city center is well preserved and, along with several residential neighborhoods, 606 acres are recognized as a National Historic Register District, the fourth-largest in the state. Among the 857 designated structures, 29 architectural styles are represented. The east/west streets were named for colleges and universities; the north/south streets for people. Many of the historic buildings along Main Street house specialty shops and restaurants. College Park is also the home of Woodward Academy and the new state-of-the-art Georgia International Convention Center, where large conventions, trade shows, and other events are held.

    East Point was the easternmost terminus of the Atlanta & West Point Railroad. Today it is one of the state's fastest growing cities, fueled partly by its accessibility to public transportation, major highways, and Hartsfield-Jackson Atlanta International Airport. The municipality is the home of R&B and hip-hop groups TLC, Outkast, Coolbreeze, Organic Noise, and Goodie Mob.

    Fairburn's slogan is "History Lives Here." The historic downtown is a cluster of antiques shops, boutiques, and restaurants. Visitors should see the Confederate flag monument, the Confederate soldiers' monument, the Fairburn cemetery, the grave of the first female sheriff, and the World War I monument. Also make time to visit the Old Campbell County Museum (see *Museums*) and attend a production of the Southside Theatre Guild (see *Theater*). The Georgia Renaissance Festival brings a quarter-million visitors to Fairburn each spring (see *Special Events*).

    Fayetteville was established in 1823 and later became the county seat of Fayette County, which had been formed two years earlier. Both the town and the county are named for the Marquis de Lafayette, a French nobleman who aided the colonists during the Revolutionary War. Fayetteville's courthouse, which was built in 1825, is the largest in Georgia. It is listed on the National Register of Historic Places and claims to have the world's longest courthouse bench. Margaret Mitchell did a lot of research for *Gone with the Wind* at the courthouse, and some of her great-grandfather's family members are buried in the Fayetteville City Cemetery. Today Fayetteville has several museums and historic homes open to the public and is the site of several festivals (see *Historic Site, Museums,* and *Special Events*). Drive by the historic Hollingsworth House, 200 Stonewall Avenue West, which was built in 1905 for Waymon and Irene Felker Hollingsworth as a wedding gift from her father. The beautifully restored and furnished house is a special events facility.

    Hapeville, which was chartered in 1891, is Atlanta's next-door neighbor and located immediately adjacent to Hartsfield-Jackson Atlanta International Airport. It is the home to the original Dwarf House Chick-fil-A, Delta Airlines corporate headquarters, the Federal Aviation Administration, the U.S. Army Forces Command and the Third Army Headquarters, and one of Ford Motor Company's manufacturing plants. With all this modern-day activity, Hapeville respects its past and preserves its historic downtown and neighborhoods.

Jonesboro is the legendary land of *Gone with the Wind.* More than 70 years after the burning of Atlanta, Margaret Mitchell spun a tale about her relatives and local characters in Clayton County. Her book became the best-selling novel of all time and was made into a movie in 1939, introducing Jonesboro and Clayton County to people all over the world. Thousands of visitors from around the globe come searching for Mitchell's mythical Tara. Although they are disappointed not to find it, there are plenty of other attractions connected with the author and her opus.

Morrow began as Morrow Station in 1846, a stop on the railroad line between Jonesboro and Atlanta. It was named for Radford E. Morrow, who owned a 1,000-acre plantation there. The train would stop for a few hours while workers loaded cotton, tobacco, and other agricultural products from the surrounding farms. Known as the "Whistle Stop," the area gained popularity and was transformed from a farming community to a business and retail center. Today Morrow is the home of Spivey Hall (see *Entertainment*) and Clayton College and State University.

Palmetto got its name from South Carolina's Palmetto Rifles troops, who marched through the area on the way to fight in Mexico. Palmetto is the home of an outstanding bed and breakfast, several well-known restaurants, and a nature center.

Peachtree City, the largest city in Fayette County, is a planned community developed with villages, each of which has its own shopping areas, recreational facilities, and elementary schools. The city boasts 90 miles of pedestrian and golf cart paths, three championship golf courses, two lakes, a state-of-the-art tennis center, a full-size BMX course, and an aquatic center.

The village of **Stockbridge** traces its beginnings to 1829, when a settlement sprang up around the Old Stockbridge Concord Methodist Church, but it didn't really begin to grow until the 1880s. Today the city boasts a variety of parks: Clayton County International Park, Stockbridge Municipal Park, and Panola Mountain State Conservation Park among them.

Union City was incorporated in 1908. It got its name because the Farmer's Union had its national headquarters there and because it was the location where the Atlanta & West Point Railroad and the Atlanta, Birmingham & Atlantic Railroad met.

To See

Cultural Sites
🐚 **Arts Clayton Gallery** (770-473-5457), 136 South Main Street, Jonesboro. The art gallery promotes Georgia artists with an emphasis on those from Clayton County and the south metropolitan area of Atlanta. Free.

For Families
🐚 **Margaret Mitchell Playhouse/Antique Funeral Museum** (770-478-7211), 168 North McDonough Street, Jonesboro. Open daylight hours daily. Once located on the famous

author's grandmother's Fitzgerald Plantation, the fully decorated one-room playhouse Margaret used as a child has been relocated to the grassy lawns in the rear of the Pope-Dixon Funeral Home, where visitors can peek in the windows. Also in the rear of the funeral home building itself is the **Antique Funeral Museum,** the only drive-through funeral museum we know about anywhere. Visitors can drive by a large, glass-enclosed bay in the rear of the funeral home to view a pre-Civil War casket, Civil War embalming equipment, and the antique horse-drawn hearse used for the funeral of A. H. Stephens, vice president of the Confederacy. Free.

Guided Tours
𝄢 **Landmarks Through History Tour** (800-662-7829; www.visitscarlett.com), 100 Carriage Lane, Jonesboro. The trolley tour leaves from Stately Oaks Plantation at 11, noon, and 1 Monday through Saturday.

Margaret Mitchell's playhouse can be found behind the Pope-Dixon Funeral Home in Jonesboro.

Peter Bonner of Historical and Hysterical Tours relates a story outside the gates of the Patrick Cleburne Confederate Memorial Cemetery.

More than 100 years of history is described as the trolley explores the Historic District and drives by several important landmarks. The tour includes admission to the Road to Tara Museum, Stately Oaks, and the Old Jail/Clayton County Museum. Adults $18.95, children $13.95.

𝄢 **Peter Bonner's Historical and Hysterical Tours** (770-477-8864; www.peterbonner.com), 104 North Main Street, Jonesboro. *Gone with the Wind—* **The Tour** is offered for groups (but even as an individual traveler you should call to see if you can join a scheduled group) from the 1867 train depot/welcome center in the center of Jonesboro. Peter, costumed as a common Confederate soldier, is a font of local knowledge. As he guides visitors around town, he spins tales about the Battle of Jonesboro and about the true local stories that influenced Margaret Mitchell to write *Gone With the Wind*. In fact, in a letter dated July 11, 1936, Mitchell declared "... all the incidences in the book are true." The 90-minute tours cost $15 per person.

Historic Site

🌿 ♿ **Patrick Cleburne Confederate Memorial Cemetery** (770-478-4800), Johnson and McDonough streets, Jonesboro. Open daily. This peaceful cemetery is the final resting place of 1,000 unidentified Confederate soldiers who died in the Battle of Jonesboro. The pattern of the headstones is laid out to form the shape of the Confederate battle flag. Free.

Museums

🌿 ♿ **Holliday-Dorsey-Fife House** (770-716-5332; www.hdfhouse.com), 140 West Lanier Avenue, Fayetteville. Open 10–5 Thursday through Saturday. Located in an 1855 Greek Revival house built by the uncle of infamous outlaw Doc Holliday, the museum features *Gone with the Wind* memorabilia; Civil War relics and documents, particularly from the Fayette Rifle Greys, Company I, 10th Georgia Volunteers; Fayetteville artifacts; and genealogical information about the three families who owned the house, which Doc Holliday actually visited. Margaret Mitchell's grandmother stayed in this house when it was used as a dormitory for the Fayetteville Academy. Be sure to stop at the Down South Treasures Museum Shop (see *Shopping*). Adults $5, seniors $4.

♿ **Old Campbell County Museum** (770-964-6007; 770-996-6796), East Broad Street, Fairburn. Open 11–4 Tuesday and by appointment. The museum, located in the historic Old Campbell County Courthouse, chronicles the history of Campbell County. Free.

🐾 🌿 **Old Jail/Clayton County Historical Museum** (770-473-0197), 125 King Street, Jonesboro. Open 10–4 weekdays with tours on the hour. Built in 1869, the building served as both a jail and the home of the jailer.
He and his family lived downstairs; pris-
oners were kept upstairs. The only man
ever hanged in Clayton County was a pris-
oner from 1880 to 1881. He had murdered
Judge Hilliard Moore during a robbery.
Today the building houses exhibits about
the building's jail house days as well as
displays about county history. Adults $12,
seniors $9, children $6.

🌿 ♿ **Road to Tara Museum** (770-478-
4800; 1-800-662-7829; www.visit
scarlett.com), 104 North Main Street,
Jonesboro. Open 8:30–5:30 weekdays,
10–4 Saturday; last ticket sold 45 minutes
before closing. Located in the warehouse
portion of the historic Jonesboro depot,
which also houses the town's welcome
center, the museum focuses on
Jonesboro's part in the Civil War and the
book *Gone with the Wind*. The museum
boasts the Herb Bridges collection, the
largest collection of *Gone with the Wind*

An exhibit inside the Road to Tara Museum

book and movie memorabilia in the country, including seats from the Lowe's Grand Theater in Atlanta, where the 1939 premiere was held. An original oil mural depicts scenes from the movie. Adults $7, students and seniors $6. A Premier Pass that permits entrance to five Margaret Mitchell/*Gone with the Wind*/Civil War sites in Jonesboro and Atlanta is available here for $34.95.

✒ ❧ ♿ **Stately Oaks Plantation** (770-473-0197; www.historicaljonesboro.org), 100 Carriage Lane, Jonesboro. Open 10–4 weekdays and most Saturdays (but check ahead). The grand, white-columned planter's home was built in 1839. Soldiers camped on the lawns during the Civil War. Tours of the home are conducted by costumed docents who interpret customs and lifestyles of the rural South. Also on the grounds are a log cook house, blacksmith shop, the 1894 Juddy's Country Store, and the last one-room schoolhouse used in Clayton County. Living history demonstrations are conducted periodically, and many festivals and special events (see *Special Events*) occur year-round. Adults $12, seniors $9, children $10.

Special Places

✒ ❧ ♿ **Starr's Mill Scenic Stop** (770-716-4320), GA 85 South Connector, Fayetteville. Open daylight hours daily. Visitors may recognize the red mill on Starr's Mill Lake from the film *Sweet Home Alabama*. Although the mill is not open for tours, residents and visitors alike come here for fishing, picnicking on the grounds, enjoying the waterfall created by the mill's dam, and photo ops. Free.

Scenic Drives

Gone with the Wind **Historic District Driving Tour.** Available from the Jonesboro Depot Welcome Center, the self-guided driving/walking tour features 25 sites, including the Patrick Cleburne Memorial Confederate Cemetery, Margaret Mitchell's Playhouse, the Drive-Up Antique Funeral Museum, and other sites described here separately. Free.

Walking Tour

Historic Fayetteville Walking Tour. Stop by the Fayette County Historical Society (770-716-6020; fayettehistoricalsociety.com), 195 Lee Street, to pick up a brochure for a self-guided tour of the town's historic area. Open 6–9 Tuesday, 10–1 Thursday, 9–1 Saturday. Free.

To Do

Bicycling

✒ **Dick Lane Velodrome** (the Velodrome is run by volunteers, so contact the facility via the Web site, www.dicklanevelodrome.com, for information), 1889 Lexington Avenue, East Point. Public hours and events can be found on the Web site.

What's a Velodrome?
The steeply banked tracks feature two 180-degree bends and two straightaways. When bicycle speed, inertia, and gravitational force are balanced, riders can zoom around the track even though it looks as if they would fall over.

The facility was used as a training ground for the Olympic trials leading up to the 1996 Centennial Olympic Summer Games in Atlanta. Several teams practice at the facility, including the Georgia Velo Bellas female team, the Fulton Flyers Cycling Team, and the Atlanta Velos professional team. There are several open training sessions and beginner lessons are available. If you're not up for working out yourself, there are a wide variety of programs to enjoy as a spectator, including weekly events, grand prix races, and a bike stunt show. September sees the Festival of Speed, an event with a $1,999 purse. A garden planted with native Georgian and Southeastern species is on the grounds of the facility, and three seasons of color attract birds and butterflies.

✒ **William Davis BMX Track** (770-631-2542), 191 McIntosh Trail, Peachtree City. The track offers scheduled races and events, but the unsupervised facility can be used with proper safety equipment at other times.

See also **The Beach at Clayton County International Park** under *To Do—For Families.*

Bird-Watching

See Cochran Mill Nature Preserve and W. H. Reynolds Memorial Nature Preserve under *Nature Preserves and Parks.*

Fishing

See The Beach at Clayton County International Park under *To Do—For Families.*

For Families

✒ 🐾 ♿ **The Beach at Clayton County International Park** (770-473-5425; www.thebeach ccip.com), 2300 Highway 138 Southeast, Jonesboro. Beach open Memorial Day weekend through Labor Day weekend—daily except Monday in June and July, weekends only in August. Hours 10–6 Tuesday through Friday, 10–7 weekends, 10–8:30 holidays. Park open 8–8 daily year-round. This multiuse park offers a little bit of everything to keep families busy. The **Beach Water Park** (770-477-3766) is a spring-fed lake with a sandy beach, an adventure kiddie pool, water slides, a water trampoline, and a sun deck. In the same area, the Nassau Arcade Center features an indoor playground, snack bar, beach store, and changing facilities. The **Tennis Center** (678-479-5016) offers 17 hard courts, a pro shop with showers, lessons, and league play. There are often drills and round robins, too. **Muscle Beach Fitness** (770-472-8093) is a full gym with strength machines, free weights, cardio equipment, and International Sports Science Association trainers. Classes include body sculpting, cardio, kick boxing, and yoga. A park-within-a-park, the **hiking and biking trails** (770-477-3766) offer paved and naturalized trails accessible 8–8 year-round. Eleven **volleyball courts** (770-477-3766) allow beach volleyball play where the world's greatest athletes competed during the 1996 Centennial Olympic Summer Games. Or bring your own gear and drop a line into the **fishing lakes** (770-477-3766) for bass, bream, or catfish. A proper fishing license is required. Several concession stands are available. Adults (13–54) $10, seniors and children 3–12 $8. Parking $3. Season beach admission and parking passes available.

✒ 🐾 ♿ **Dixieland Fun Park** (770-460-5862; www.dixielandfunpark.com), 1675 US 85 North, Fayetteville. Open noon–11 weekdays, 11–11 Saturday, 1–11 Sunday late May through early August; 4–11 Friday, 11–11 Saturday, 1–9 Sunday the remainder of the year. Fun-filled family activities can be found both indoors and out. Outdoors there are batting cages, bumper boats, three Go-Kart tracks, a giant swing, road course, adult slick track, antique car track, 54 holes of miniature golf, and a zip line. Indoors, visitors find an arcade, indoor playground, play maze, and laser tag. There are some age and height requirements for rides. Admission tokens for rides are $2.50 each (some rides take multiple tokens); miniature golf $6.

Frights

⚓ **Halloween Hayride and Family Festival** (770-306-0914), Cochran Mill Nature
Preserve, 6875 Cochran Mill Road, Palmetto. Call for date and price. The spooky event features a haunted hayride, haunted canoe rides, and a haunted house as well as arts and
crafts, food, and a bonfire.

Genealogy/Historical Research

🏛 ♿ **Georgia State Archives/National Archives Southeast Region** (Georgia State Archives
770-364-3700; www.sos.state.ga.us/archives; National Archives 770-968-2100;
www.archives.gov/southeast), 5780 Jonesboro Road, Morrow. Open 8:30–5 Tuesday
through Saturday. Housed under one roof, the state and national archives are the place to
go for historical research about genealogy and general history in Georgia and the
Southeast. The state archives houses 10,000 square feet of records covering the period
1732 to the present, including 6,500 reels of microfilm. Changing exhibits display important documents and photographs. Material in the microfilm and archival research rooms at
the national archives covers the period 1760 to the 1980s. Free workshops offered. Snack
bar (or you may bring your own food), gift shop, lockers. Children younger than 14 are
admitted only if under an adult's supervision at all times. Free.

Golf

College Park Golf Course (404-761-0731; www.collegeparkgolfcourse.com), 3711 Fairway
Drive, College Park. Open sunup to sundown daily. This nine-hole course is exceptionally
affordable. Play is on a first-come, first-served basis; there are no tee times. $8.29 for
nine holes walking, $14.98 with a cart; for a second nine, $6.69 walking, $11.58 with a cart.
Fayetteville Golf Club (770-460-1098; www.fayettevillegc.com), 40 Southern Golf Court,
Fayetteville. Open 7:15–dusk daily. The 18-hole championship course, a sister course to
the Lake Spivey Golf Club, is par 72, 6,810 yards. The facility features the River's Edge Grill
and, on weekends and holidays, roaming hospitality carts with snacks and beverages.
$29–35 weekdays, $27–45 weekends.
Lake Spivey Golf Club (770-477-4653; www.lakespivey.net), 8255 Clubhouse Way,
Jonesboro. Open 7:15–dusk daily. Lake Spivey Golf Club, a sister course to River's Edge
Golf Club, is actually three nine-hole courses. The Clubside Course is 3,312 yards and par
36; the Hillside Course is 3,089 yards, par 36; and the Lakeside Course is 3,503 yards, par
37. The club also has the Lake Spivey Grill and, on weekends and holidays, roaming hospitality carts with snacks and beverages. $35 weekdays, $45 weekends; discounts available.
Links Golf Club (770-461-5100), 340 Hewell Road, Jonesboro. Open 6:45 AM–dark daily.
The challenging public course—27 holes, 6,376 yards, par 70—also features a driving range,
putting green, pro shop, and grill. $29–37; discounts for seniors and after 3 PM.
Rum Creek Golf Club (770-507-3538), 107 St. Ives Court, Stockbridge. Henry County's
only fully lighted golf facility, Rum Creek is a nine-hole, 1,400-yard, par 3 public course
that also offers a driving range. $13 weekdays, $15 weekends.

Hiking

See The Beach at Clayton County International Park under *To Do—For Families* and Panola
Mountain State Conservation Park under *Nature Preserves and Parks*.

Miniature Golf

See **Dixieland Fun Park** under *To Do—For Families*.

Shooting Sports

Tom Lowe Trap and Skeet Range (404-346-8382; www.atlantaskeetshooting.com), 3070 Merk Road Southwest, Atlanta. Open 1–8 Monday through Thursday, 10–6 Saturday, 1–6 Sunday. Built as the shooting sports venue for the 1996 Centennial Olympic Summer Games, the center features 25 skeet fields, 20 trap fields, sporting clays, a five-stand course, and a clubhouse where shooters can purchase ammunition and other supplies. Protective eye and hearing devices required. $5.25 per round, not including shells.

Skateboarding

Shakerag Knoll Skateboard Park (770-631-2542), 191 McIntosh Trail, Peachtree City. Call for hours, which vary by season, school year, holidays, and daylight-saving time. The park offers facilities for skateboarding and in-line skating such as a half-pipes and other apparatus. This is a supervised and monitored area. No bicycles allowed. Free.

Swimming

Kedron Fieldhouse and Aquatic Center (770-631-2525; www.peachtree-city.org/kedron), 202 Kedron Drive, Peachtree City. Open 9–9:30 Monday through Saturday, 1–5:30 Sunday. The facility boasts a 25-yard competition pool and a heated instructional pool. Adults $3, seniors and children 3–11 $2.

See also **The Beach at Clayton County International Park** under *To Do—For Families* and **City of Stockbridge Municipal Park** under *Nature Preserves and Parks.*

Tennis

Burdett Tennis Center (770-996-3502), 5975 Old Carriage Lane Southeast, College Park. Open 11–8:30 Monday through Thursday, 9–1 Friday, 10–4 Saturday. The center features eight lighted courts. $2 per hour.

Peachtree City Tennis Center (770-486-9474; www.tenniscenter.net), 10 Planterra Way, Peachtree City. Open 8–10 weekdays, 8–6 Saturday, 12:30–6 Sunday. The tennis center has 12 hard courts and six clay courts. Six of the courts are covered for all-weather play. There is also a pro shop. $3.50 per hour for hard courts, $5 for clay.

South Fulton Tennis Center (770-306-3059), 5645 Mason Road, College Park. Open 9–7 Monday and Friday, 9–9 Tuesday through Thursday, 8:30–3:30 Saturday, 11–3 Sunday. This center boasts 20 hard courts and four clay courts, all lighted, as well as a clubhouse. $3 per hour for hard courts, $4 for clay.

GREEN SPACE

Gardens

See **City of Stockbridge Municipal Park** under *Nature Preserves and Parks* and **Dick Lane Velodrome** under *Bicycling.*

Lakes

See **The Beach at Clayton County International Park** under *To Do—For Families.*

Nature Preserves and Parks

City of Stockbridge Municipal Park (770-389-7900), 4545 North Henry Boulevard,

Stockbridge. Open daily. The park, which surrounds City Hall, features beautiful gardens, fountains, and a swimming pool with a water slide. Free; fee for swimming pool. The city also operates several other parks. **Gardner Park**, 160 East Atlanta Road, has playground areas, a walking trail, and tennis courts. **Clark Community Park**, 111 Davis Road, has a playground and walking trail. **Cochran Ball Park**, 302 East Atlanta Road, features softball and baseball fields operated by the Henry County Recreation Department. **Dabney-Hunter-Simmons Memorial Park,** 106 Cemetery Street, offers a basketball court, playgrounds, and a walking trail. Free.

🌿 🐾 ♿ **Cochran Mill Nature Center** (770-306-0914; www.cochranmillnaturecenter.org), 6300 Cochran Mill Road, Palmetto. Open 9–3 Monday through Saturday. Fifty heavily wooded acres provide opportunities for hiking, wildlife observation, and environmental education programs. The center has many reptiles, birds, and amphibians. All have been rehabilitated from injuries but can't be released back into the wild. Several special events include Snake Day in August, the Wild Trail Trot 5K Run in September, and the Halloween Hayride and Family Festival in October (see *Frights*). Adults $2, children $1. **Cochran Mill Park,** located adjacent to the nature preserve, offers hiking, jogging, horse trails (BYOH—Bring Your Own Horse), a playground, and primitive camping. Free.

🌿 🐾 ♿ **Flat Creek Nature Center** (770-486-7774), 201 McIntosh Trail, Peachtree City. Open daylight hours daily. Operated by the Southern Conservation Trust, the 513-acre center is adjacent to 3 miles of paved paths, a 1,200-foot boardwalk, and two viewing platforms extending into the wetlands. The area sustains a wide variety of trees and plants. The educational center offers classes, camps, workshops, and programs throughout the year. Free.

🌿 🐾 ♿ **Panola Mountain State Park** (770-389-7801; www.gastateparks.org/info/panolamt), 2600 GA 155 Southwest, Stockbridge. Open 7–6 daily, September 15 through April 14; 7–9 daily, April 15 through September 14. Interpretive center open 8:30–5 Tuesday through Friday, noon–5 Saturday and Sunday. The 100-acre granite mountain, designated a National Natural Landmark, is located within a 1,026-acre park that provides a home for rare plants and animals. Visitors can explore 2 miles of nature trails and a 1-mile fitness trail on their own, or join ranger-led nature programs and 3.5-mile guided hikes of the restricted-access mountain Tuesday through Saturday (reservations required). An interpretive center features animal exhibits. Pets and bicycles are not permitted on the trails. $3 parking fee.

🌿 🐾 ♿ **W. H. Reynolds Memorial Nature Preserve** (770-603-4188; web.co.clayton.ga.us/reynolds/about.htm), 5665 Reynolds Road, Morrow. Visitor's center open 8–5 weekdays, park open 8:30–dusk daily. The 146-acre woodland and wetland preserve is dedicated to conservation. The center began with the donation of 130 acres by Judge William "Bill" Huie Reynolds in 1976. To that 16 additional acres were added in 1997. Among the park's attributes are ponds, streams, hardwood forests, piers, pavilions, bridges, a demonstration heritage herb and vegetable garden featuring varieties from the late 1800s, a butterfly and hummingbird garden, and a historic barn with displays of late-19th- and early-20th-century farm implements. The Nature Center houses a collection of native reptiles and amphibians as well as an observation honeybee hive and environmental education exhibits. Visitors can enjoy 4.5 miles of well-defined trails which run in half-mile loops that bring hikers back to their starting point. The Georgia Native Plants Trail is wheelchair accessible and also features Braille trail markers. Free.

Lodging

Bed and Breakfasts

In Palmetto

✪ **Inn at Serenbe** (770-463-2610;
www.serenbe.com), 10950 Hutcheson Ferry
Road. Guests experience farm life with an
elegant twist at this superb B&B, where
accommodations and cuisine are decidedly
upscale. Guest rooms are in the main house
(16+ only); a restored 1930s horse barn; a
lake house; and two newly constructed,
environmentally friendly cottages. More
than 100 animals live at Serenbe: chickens,
bunnies, goats, pigs, horses, donkeys, lla-
mas, and cows (check the Web site to see
the latest births). Yes, you can feed the animals or gather eggs, but you can also enjoy
afternoon tea, bedtime snacks, and a full
country breakfast. Swim in the pool or soak
in the outdoor hot tub, both of which are
surrounded by glorious gardens. Play croquet or hike the trails to streams, waterfalls, or a lake, and then take some time to
laze in the pool cabana's twin-bed-size
swings. Hayrides and roasting marshmallows around a campfire are sometime highlights. The inn also operates a restaurant
Thursday through Sunday (see *Dining Out*).
No smoking. Limited wheelchair accessibility. $140–275.

*The Inn at Serenebe offers B&B accomodations and a
gourmet restaurant.*

Inns and Hotels
The Southern Crescent offers a vast array of
economy, mid-range, and luxury chain
hotels from A (Amerihost Inn) to W
(Wingate)—far too many to describe here.
Most readers will be familiar with what
these chains have to offer, so consult a specific chain's Web site or Internet travel sites
such as Orbitz, Priceline, Travelocity, or
Hotels.com.

Where to Eat

Dining Out

In College Park

✪ ♿ **The Feed Store** (404-209-7979), 3841
Main Street. Open 11–2 weekdays; 5–10
Monday through Thursday, 5–11 Friday and
Saturday. Look for the mural of a horse on
the side of the historic building, which
actually was a feed store operated well into
the 1980s by the current owner's grandmother. Many rustic architectural elements
such as exposed brick have been retained
and combined with sleek modern touches
for an eclectic look. Antique farm implements grace the walls. The cuisine is
described as artful New American. Outdoor
seating on the patio is a popular option in
good weather. No smoking. Wheelchair
accessible. $8–14 for lunch, $13–26 for
dinner.

In Palmetto
♿ **The Farmhouse at the Inn at Serenbe**
(770-463-2610;
www.serenbefarmhouse.com), 10950
Hutcheson Ferry Road. Open 6–9 Thursday
through Saturday, noon–5 Sunday. This
1905 farmhouse inn has been the brainchild of famous Atlanta restaurateurs Steve
and Marie Nygren since 1990 (it actually
opened in 1995). In 2006 the Nygrens
added a restaurant under the direction of

Chef Tony Seichrist, who was an acolyte of Hugh Acheson of Athens's renowned Five and Ten. A dining experience at the farmhouse has the simplicity and intimacy of eating in someone's home. The main dining room and the sun porch offer bucolic views of the barns, outbuildings, and fields. Seichrist's farm-to-table concept makes use of organic produce grown at Serenbe as well that of other local growers. Dinner is a prix fixe affair with a first course, an entrée accompanied by two sides, and dessert. Sunday is reminiscent of the old family-style meat-and-three dinner—always including fried chicken. A discreet chalkboard lists the daily offerings. Sometimes an optional extra course is offered at a small additional price. Because the restaurant does not yet have a liquor license, at this time you can bring your own bottle and there is no corkage fee. No smoking. Wheelchair accessible. $33 Thursday through Saturday, $22 Sunday; extra optional courses about $10.

Eating Out

In College Park

𝄞 🦐 ♿ **The Brake Pad** (404-766-1515), 3403 Main Street. Open 11 AM–2 AM daily. An old gas station has been transformed into a funky bar and eatery where you can fuel up with appetizers, burgers, quesadillas, sandwiches, salads, and other pub food. In nice weather, diners enjoy eating and drinking on the patio. The Brake Pad has an extensive selection of beers, and you can get late-night fare until closing. Smoking allowed after 8 PM. Wheelchair accessible. $7–15.

𝄞 🦐 ♿ **Fina, Your Italian Bistro** (404-767-9292), 3823 Main Street. Open 11–10:30 weekdays, 5–10 Saturday. All your favorite Italian dishes are served here in a cheerful, casual atmosphere. No smoking. Wheelchair accessible. $7.50–12.

𝄞 🦐 ♿ **Lunch on Main** (404-767-0470),

3569 Main Street. Open 6:30–10 AM and 11 AM–2 PM weekdays; 4:30–9 Thursday and Friday. The vinyl booths, shiny counter, and gingham curtains give this casual eatery, which occupies a former 1930s gas station, a small-town diner ambience. The menu focuses on pork, catfish, veggies, sandwiches, salads, and burgers as well as desserts like banana pudding and pecan pie. The sweet potato pie is to die for. No smoking. Wheelchair accessible. $2–7 for breakfast, $5–7 for lunch, $8 for dinner.

In East Point

𝄞 🦐 ♿ **Matilda Bean** (404-762-5136), 1603 White Way. Open 11–8 Monday through Saturday. This burrito joint puts a fresh twist on Tex-Mex cuisine. Gourmet tortillas are made from wheat with additions such as spinach or tomato basil. Fillings include pork, steak, chicken, shrimp, grilled veggies, peppers, rice, pinto or refried beans, and cheese. The vegetarian burrito, called the Mean Green burrito, is packed with peppers, onions, rice, spinach, salsa, cheese, and sour cream. Each is accompanied by a choice of salsas from mild to lethally hot. The decor is cheery, with brightly painted chairs and Cuban and Mexican advertisements serving as wall and table art. No smoking. Wheelchair accessible. $5–6.

In Forest Park

𝄞 🦐 ♿ **Oakwood Restaurant** (404-214-5660), 16 Forest Parkway. Open 6 AM–8 PM weekdays, 7 AM–8 PM Saturday. Located on the grounds of the Atlanta State Farmer's Market, the bustling restaurant is often packed with diners looking for down-home comfort foods such as fried chicken or fried whole catfish; steaks and seafood; vegetables; fresh rolls and corn muffins; and desserts like pies and cobblers. The restaurant smokes its own hams and turkeys, and you *must* order a plate of fried-green tomatoes. Breakfast includes traditional

Southern favorites such as grits, biscuits, and country ham. While you're dining, enjoy the eatery's murals, which depict scenes of Atlanta and Europe. No smoking. Wheelchair accessible. Under $10.

Coffeehouses

In East Point

🎵 🍴 ♿ **Mocha Delites** (404-762-7765; www.mochadelites.com), 1513 East Cleveland Avenue. Open 7–6 Monday through Saturday. In addition to signature drinks, the coffeehouse also offers espressos, cappuccinos, lattes, frozen coffee drinks, and smoothies. In addition, diners can get breakfast items, salads, paninis, wraps, and quesadillas. No smoking. Wheelchair accessible. $4–6.50.

In Hapeville

🎵 🍴 ♿ **Perk Place Coffee Shop** (404-768-5678; www.perkplacecoffee.com), 673 North Central Avenue. Open 6:30–6:30 Monday through Saturday. The focus of the coffeehouse is organic, shade-grown, fair-trade coffee in all its hot, cold, and frozen incarnations, but pastries, muffins, Danishes, bagels, scones, egg sandwiches, soups, chicken salad sandwiches, BLTs, salads, cakes, other desserts, and ice cream are also on the menu. Customers also can make use of free wireless Internet access. Special events include free outdoor movies shown out back (check the Web site for dates and titles). Prior to the movies, hot dogs, nachos, and popcorn are served. No smoking. Wheelchair accessible. $1–1.75 for coffee; $2–6 for food items.

ENTERTAINMENT

Music

🎵 ♿ **Frederick Brown Jr. Amphitheater** (770-631-0630; www.amphitheater.org), 201 McIntosh Trail, Peachtree City. Office open 8–5 weekdays; box office open on nights of performances until 9. Call for a schedule of events and ticket prices. Affectionately known as The Fred (as opposed to the Atlanta sports stadium, which is known as The Ted), the amphitheater is an intimate setting in which to enjoy a wide variety of entertainment including a summer concert series with a variety of top acts.

🎵 ♿ **HiFi Buys Amphitheatre** (404-627-9704; www.hob.com/venues/concerts/hifibuys), 2002 Lakewood Way, Atlanta. Call for a schedule of performances and ticket prices. This outdoor performance venue, built in 1989, is designed to offer a state-of-the-art musical experience for artists and patrons alike. Some seats are under a covered area and there's plenty of lawn seating. Nationally renowned acts stop by regularly.

🎵 ♿ **Spivey Hall** (770-960-4200; www.spiveyhall.org), 5900 North Lee Street, Morrow. Box office open 9–5 weekdays. Call for a schedule of performances and ticket prices. Located on the campus of Clayton College and State University, this magnificent performance hall is the scene of the finest in piano, vocal, chamber, choral, classical, jazz, organ, string, and other musical entertainment. The acoustically perfect Spivey Hall is also the home of the magnificent Albert Schweitzer Memorial Pipe Organ, a 4,413-pipe organ built in Italy. The hall's acclaimed concert series receives national attention thanks to frequent appearances on National Public Radio's *Performance Today*. There is also a summer jazz and pops series. Recent developments have included the formation of the Spivey Hall Children's Choir, the Spivey Hall Young Artists, and the Children's Concert Series.

🎵 ♿ **The Villages Amphitheater** (770-460-0686; www.villagesamphitheater.com), 301 Lafayette Avenue, Fayetteville. Call for a schedule of events and ticket prices. This state-of-the art venue in the heart of downtown Fayetteville provides a full schedule of local, regional, and national entertainment and concerts. Orchestra tables and tiered table areas are popular choices for enjoying the shows.

Nightlife

& **B-52's** (404-765-0280), 3420 Norman Berry Drive, Hapeville. Open 4 PM–2 AM weekdays, 6 PM–2 AM Saturday and Sunday. The bar/pub has more than 15 beers on tap and offers pool tables, darts, a dance floor, live music on occasion, Texas Hold 'Em poker on Tuesday and Sunday, karaoke on Monday, and a DJ on Friday and Saturday. Smoking allowed. Wheelchair accessible. No cover charge.

Theater

Clayton County Schools Performing Arts Center (770-473-2875), 2530 Mount Zion Parkway, Jonesboro. Call for a schedule of performances and ticket prices. The state-of-the-art theater hosts local, regional, and national performances from concerts to theatrical productions.

✍ ☙ **Fayette-Coweta Family Theatre** (770-251-7611; www.fcft.net), Fayetteville. Call for a schedule of performances and ticket prices, which average $8. The theater offers six productions each season, which are divided into three age-appropriate categories. The Little-One's Theatre Series, designed for children age 2–8, features plays with music, plenty of onstage action, and lots of interaction with the audience. Youth Productions are designed for children age 7–16 and include both musicals and plays. The Family Theatre Series musicals and plays are suitable for all ages. FCTC also has two professional theater ensembles that each produce a play every season. The Senior Professional Ensemble performs well-known dramas and comedies for adult audiences, while the Junior Professional Ensemble performs musicals and plays for a family-oriented audience. Dinner theater includes a catered meal, beverages, and dessert. Plays are staged at various Fayette County schools, local YMCAs, Sams Auditorium, and churches.

Southside Theatre Guild (770-969-0956; www.stgplays.com), 20 West Campbellton Street, Fairburn. Call for a performance schedule. One of metro Atlanta's oldest community theaters, the organization has been staging productions year-round for more than 30 years. The group presents five plays including a drama, a comedy, and a family show. The entire staff is made up of volunteers. Adults $15, children $12.

SELECTIVE SHOPPING

Antiques

My Favorite Things Antique Shop (770-463-3010), 503 Toombs Street, Palmetto. Open 10–5 Saturday and Sunday, by appointment, or by chance. Located in the heart of Palmetto, the shop, which is operated by the folks from Oak Grove Plantation and Gardens (see the Newnan chapter), specializes in furniture from the 1800s, porcelain, and one-of-a-kind pillows. You'll also find heirloom handmade items (old and new) like quilts, rag dolls, topsy-turvy dolls, dried flower arrangements, holiday dresses for girls, crazy quilt pictures, and more made by the owner, her daughters, and friends. There is an adjoining garden shop with items to make your garden special.

Food

♂ ☜ ♿ **Atlanta State Farmer's Market** (404-361-7577; 1-800-662-7829), 16 Forest Parkway, Forest Park. Open 24/7 except Christmas Day. The South's largest farmer's market and one of the biggest in the world, the 150-acre site offers a dizzying array of produce; fruit; plants and flowers; homemade items such as pickles, jams, and relishes; and seasonal items such as pumpkins in October and Christmas trees at holiday time. Take a tour of the farmer's market via the **Fresh Express Trolley Tour** ($3 per person). The open-sided trolley operates four days a week in good weather. **Georgia Grown Visitors Center and Gifts**, which is located on the grounds of the farmer's market, is a place to purchase a variety of Georgia foodstuffs and souvenirs. The facility also dispenses travel information for the entire state of Georgia. Events at the market include the **Peachblossom Bluegrass Festival** in April and the **Georgia Grown MarketFest**, an arts and crafts festival in October.

> **Farmer's Market Facts**
> • 90 tractor-trailer loads of goods are unloaded every day.
> • The market has a $3 billion annual impact on the area.
> • 3,500 vendors, purchasers, and others visit the market daily.

Gifts

Down South Treasures Museum Shop (770-716-5332; www.hdfhouse.com), 140 West Lanier Avenue, Fayetteville. Open 10–5 Thursday through Saturday. The shop at the Holliday-Dorsey-Fife House Museum carries antiques, artifacts, Civil War items, replicas of Confederate kepis, reproduction swords, and a series of Fayetteville Christmas ornaments.

Jonesboro Depot Welcome Center/Road to Tara Museum Gift Shop (770-478-4800; 1-800-662-7829), 104 North Main Street. Open 8:30–5:30 weekdays, 10–4 Saturday. The gift shop at the welcome center carries *Gone with the Wind* items, Southern food, and gifts.

SPECIAL EVENTS

Mid-April through early June: **Georgia Renaissance Festival** (770-964-8575; www.garenfest.com). Open 10:30–6 weekends plus Memorial Day from mid-April through the first weekend in June, rain or shine. The multiacre kingdom in Fairburn re-creates a 16th-century European country faire in a village of Tudor homes and enchanting cottages. There you can shop like a queen for handcrafted treasures, watch demonstrations of age-old arts, feast like a king on treats like steak on a stake or smoked turkey legs, enjoy dozens of games and rides for all ages in the medieval amusement park,

The fun of a 16th-century European faire is re-created at the Georgia Renaissance Festival.

and revel with a cast of costumed characters (costumes are even available for rent if you want to participate). Ten stages of music and comedy shows present such acts as the Ded Bob Sho, the Washing Well Wenches, Parrots of the Caribbean: The Birds of Prey Show, Curious Magic and Impossible Illusions, rope walking, balancing stunts, sword swallowing, and juggling. You also can cheer on your favorite in the joust or the Hack and Slash sword fight. Wheelchair accessible. Adults $16, seniors $14, children 6–12 $9.50; games and rides $1–5.

May: **Old Courthouse Art Show/Taste of Fayette** (770-461-9983). This Fayetteville festival, sponsored by the Fayette Arts Association, features the juried work of Southeastern artists and students, live musical entertainment, a 5K run, children's activities, and samplings from some of Fayetteville's best restaurants. Free; fee for some activities.

Old Stockbridge Days (770-957-5786; 1-800-436-7926). The event in Stockbridge features a 5K road race, an old-engine car show, and other activities. Free.

June: **A Taste of Main Street** (404-270-7001). From 5–10 PM, Whiteway between Main and East Point streets in East Point is shut down for the free festival, which offers an opportunity to sample culinary concoctions from a dozen or more of the town's eateries while being entertained by DJs and live jazz, pop, rock, funk, and blues bands. From 2–5, there are children's activities with storytelling, a puppet show, games, balloon artists, and stilt walkers. There are also visits from many favorite cartoon characters. Free; fees for food.

Summer: **Music in the Park** (770-957-5786; 1-800-436-7926). Concerts are held from 7–10 PM on the fourth Saturday of each month, June through September, at Memorial Park, 106 Cemetery Street in Stockbridge. Free.

July: **Fourth of July Golf Cart Parade** (770-487-7657; www.peachtree-city.org). The patriotic, family-oriented festival in Peachtree City features floats and golf carts bedecked with red, white, and blue decorations parading through streets and along golf cart paths (which can become congested). Folks then proceed to Picnic Park for an old-fashioned community picnic, musical entertainment, and fire department demonstrations before heading for the boat dock on Lake Peachtree to watch the fireworks. Several roads are blocked off during the parade and there are parking restrictions all day and evening. Free.

September: **Happy Days** (404-669-2136; www.hapeville.org). This festival, held at Jess Lucas Park in Hapeville, is actually a weekend filled with arts and crafts, children's activities, festival rides, food, entertainment, games, a parade, and other activities. Free admission and free parking.

Historic College Park Arts Festival (404-521-6688; www.hcpna.org). The annual free festival in College Park features a juried artist's market, vendors, live musical performances, a fine cuisine food court, children's area, and a raffle for something wonderful (one year it was round-trip airline tickets). Free.

Shakerag Arts and Crafts Festival (770-631-2542). Peachtree City's Shakerag Knoll got its name because it was a place to signal a train to stop by waving a handkerchief or rag. Today, as part of the city park system, it is the home of a festival with arts and crafts, musical entertainment, food, and children's activities. Admission and parking are free.

October: **Autumn Oaks Arts and Crafts Festival and Battle of Jonesboro Civil War Re-enactment** (770-473-0197; 1-800-662-7829; www.historicaljonesboro.org; www.visit scarlett.com). Held on the grounds of Stately Oaks Plantation for a weekend in October, the festival includes arts and crafts, living history demonstration of soldiers' camps and sutlers' tents, a carnival midway, food, tours of Stately Oaks, and a re-enactment at 2 PM each day. Other activities include a seminar by local historians on Friday evening and a Run with the Wind 5K race on Saturday. (Note: The exact date of the re-enactment is highly dependent on the availability of re-enactors. It is best to call ahead to find out about the exact dates, individual events, and times.) Adults $8, seniors $6, children $4.

Falling For Henry Fine Arts Festival (770-957-5786; 1-800-436-7926; www.henry cvb.com). The arts festival features a juried exhibition of gallery-quality art and fine crafts including ceramics, oil and acrylic paintings, wood, glass, jewelry, and sculpture. Activities include a children's interactive arts area. Free.

The Great Georgia Air Show (www.thegreatgeorgiaairshow.com). The annual two-day air show in Peachtree City features performances by professional civilian performers and military demonstration teams. Thirty World War II planes do a flyby and some are available for rides. There are also arts and crafts, children's activities, rock climbing, food and beverages, and World War II memorabilia for sale. For safety reasons, no coolers or backpacks are permitted; also no pets. Tickets are available at some Kroger stores and online at www.aircraftspruce.com. In advance, adults $13, children 6–12 $5; at the gate, adults $18, children $7. Free parking with shuttle service is available at Starr's Mill High School.

December: **In the Fullness of Time** (770-603-1099; www.inthefullnessoftime.com). This community musical, written and directed by Melly Meadows, tells the old story of Christmas with new perspective and is presented free to the community in Morrow. Melly, a playwright, director, and choreographer, is best known as the international spokesperson for Georgia as Scarlett O'Hara, in which capacity she has toured the world and greeted visitors in Georgia. Performances are given Friday evening, Saturday afternoon, and Sunday evening. Free. Tickets can be ordered via the Web site or e-mail, fullness@aol.com; tickets also available at the door.

11

McDonough, Hampton, Lovejoy, and Locust Grove

McDonough makes a good base of operations for exploring the surrounding small towns that are rich in attractions, historical sites, sporting venues, outdoor pursuits, and special events. Easy access to I-75 gives visitors the convenience of going into Atlanta or Macon as well. Venture onto the back roads to see rolling green pastures, quiet leafy woodlands, serene lakes, and quaint towns.

McDonough, now known as "The Geranium City," was incorporated in 1823, two years after Chief William McIntosh of the Creek Indian Nation stood on a large rock at Indian Springs and signed a treaty giving the state of Georgia all rights to the Creek territory between the Ocmulgee and Flint rivers. Henry County was created from these lands and was named for statesman and orator Patrick Henry. Eventually, five counties were carved out of Henry County, earning it the sobriquet "Mother of Counties."

Because the area was located in a highly productive area of Georgia, it was important to the Confederacy. That significance put it high on General William Tecumseh Sherman's list to be destroyed by Union troops on his March to the Sea. During Reconstruction, cotton came into importance and prosperity returned.

McDonough grew and prospered until 1843, when it was bypassed by the railroad. In recent years, Pennsylvanian Bob Oglevee was instrumental in getting Oglevee Products to set up a nursery in McDonough to test their hot-weather geraniums. The company offered to plant hundreds of geraniums in the town square and the town agreed. The City Council then had McDonough recognized as "The Geranium City" and it now hosts a Geranium Festival

Hampton's historic railroad depot was built around 1881.

on the courthouse square, one of metro Atlanta's most popular events. The landscaped square around the 1897 Romanesque-style courthouse also boasts ancient oaks and a Confederate monument. Surrounding the square are bustling specialty shops, antiques stores, and boutiques. Residents and visitors don't have to drive to Atlanta for cultural experiences, either. Henry County is home to the **Atlanta Festival Ballet**, the **Southern Crescent Symphony Orchestra**, and **The Henry Players** (see separate entries under *Entertainment*).

GUIDANCE

When planning a trip to the McDonough area, contact the **McDonough Hospitality and Tourism Bureau/McDonough Welcome Center** (770-898-3196; www.tourmcdonough.com), 5 Griffin Street, McDonough 30253. Open 8–5 weekdays and 10–4 Saturday. Stop at the 1920s prototype Standard Oil gas station for local tourism information and admire the black 1920 Model T Ford waiting for a fill-up at the hand-cranked gas pumps. Pick up the brochure, "Historic Sites of McDonough, Georgia," for a walking/driving tour.

For more information about the area, including Hampton, Lovejoy, and Locust Grove, consult the **Henry County Chamber of Commerce, Convention and Visitors Bureau and Welcome Center** (770-957-5786; 1-800-HENRYCO; www.henrycvb.com), 1709 GA 20 West, McDonough 30253. Open 8–5 weekdays, 10–4 Saturday.

Getting There

By air: See What's Where.
By bus: **Greyhound Bus Lines** does not serve any of the towns described in this chapter.
By car: Most of the towns described in this chapter are easily accessed from I-75 south of Atlanta.
By train: The nearest **Amtrak** station is in Atlanta (see What's Where).

Getting Around

Car rentals are available from **Enterprise** (678-432-0130). Taxi service is available from **Anthony's Taxi** (678-610-0035). Limousine service is available from **Ace of Hearts Limousine Service** (770-305-9434) and **First Impressions** (770-507-9090). Public transportation is available from **Xpress** (see What's Where). The service provides an easy-to-use connection from Hampton and McDonough to downtown Atlanta, where passengers can transfer to the MARTA bus/rail system.

Parking

There is free parking at Tarpley and Hampton Streets, at the First Baptist Church on Macon Street, on John Frank Ward Boulevard east of the courthouse, behind the McDonough Police headquarters, and behind the courthouse (weekends only). There is some metered parking on the square in McDonough. The other towns have plenty of free parking.

Public Restrooms

Facilities are located in the **McDonough Welcome Center** on the Square (see *Guidance*).

Medical Emergency

Call 911 for life-threatening situations. For other medical attention, go to the **Henry Medical Center** (770-389-2200; www.henrymedical.com), 1133 Eagle's Landing Parkway, Stockbridge.

Villages/Neighborhoods

When the railroad bypassed McDonough, **Hampton,** then known as Bear Creek because two surveyors had seen two bears in a tree, profited from being on the Central of Georgia Railroad route. The center of all business activity in the area, the town shipped all the cotton for the surrounding counties. It wasn't unusual to see hundreds of wagons lining the roads, waiting to be unloaded. The town changed its name in 1873 to honor Civil War hero General Wade Hampton of South Carolina. Hampton's historic railroad depot, circa 1881, was constructed with fireproof brick—both an innovation and an extravagance in the 1880s—and is graced with ornate brick detailing in several patterns. Today, Hampton is best known as the home of the Atlanta Motor Speedway. The speedway's two NASCAR Nextel Cup series races draw more visitors than any other sporting event in Georgia. Beautiful historic homes and ancient oaks line the streets. In the spring, dazzling daylilies line the streets as well.

City government offices now occupy what was once the main building of the Locust Grove Institute.

Locust Grove was named for a grove of flowering locust trees that could be seen throughout the town. It was a major rail distribution center for cotton, peaches, and other farm products, and had three cotton gins and several warehouses. Beginning in 1894, the prosperous town was the home of the Locust Grove Institute, a top-notch college preparatory school founded by the Locust Grove Baptist Church and Mercer University. It was one of the first schools in Georgia to be accredited by the Association of Schools and Colleges of the Southern States. The Great Depression and the introduction of public schools led to the demise of the school in 1930, but its beautiful main building now houses city government offices. Today, Locust Grove is the home of Noah's Ark, a facility for animal rehabilitation, and the Tanger Outlet Mall.

TO SEE

For Families
🐾 🐾 ♿ **Noah's Ark Animal Rehabilitation Center** (770-957-0888; www.noahs-ark.org), 712 LG-Griffin Road, Locust Grove. Office open 9–4 Tuesday through Saturday, facility open for self-guided tours noon–3 Tuesday through Saturday; closed on major holidays. (Note: All tours are subject to cancellation because of rain, extreme heat or cold, or lack of volunteers, so call ahead.)

A friendly, furry face at Noah's Ark, an animal rehabilitation facility in Locust Grove.

Noah's Ark Facts
- The center rehabilitates more than 1,000 animals each year.
- 800 to 900 animals are usually in residence at any one time.
- Animals come from the Department of Natural Resources, zoos, and the general public.
- It costs $600 per day to feed all the animals.
- The yearly budget at Noah's Ark is $900,000.
- There are only 27 full-time and part-time employees.
- It takes 300 volunteers to help with animal care and feeding, tours, group projects, and annual events.
- Noah's Ark had to turn away 2,450 animals last year for lack of funds.
- Funds come from donations, fund-raisers, and a few foundational grants.

Noah's Ark, which is located on 250 acres, was created to provide a home for abused, unwanted, and orphaned wild, domestic, and exotic animals and birds. Rehabilitated animals are returned to the wild or their place of origin; animals that can't be released live out their days here in as natural a habitat as possible, as do unwanted exotic animals such as lions, monkeys, and tigers that have no natural habitat in North America. Visitors can walk the nature trails through 40 acres and view the animal habitats. The facility also provides a home to abused and orphaned children. The philosophy of Noah's Ark is to bring children and animals together for the mutual rehabilitation of both. Free, but donations are welcome.

Historic Homes and Sites
✔ ✿ �& **Heritage Park** (Henry County Extension Service 770-288-8421; www.co.henry.ga.us/extensionservice/extensionservicemain.htm), 101 Lake Dow Road, McDonough. Park open daylight hours daily; museum open 9–1 Monday, Wednesday, and Friday. The 129-acre park straddles two centuries. The historic village, which represents what Henry County was like at the turn of the 20th century, was created by moving historic structures from around the county to one location. It includes a 100-year-old corncrib, an 1827 settler's log cabin, an original two-room country schoolhouse, a typical detached cook house, the first library building in the county, a 1933 steam locomotive, and Lane's Store, which was built in 1921 and served as a general store for quarry workers as well as a service station and local gathering place. The Barn Museum houses county artifacts. A unit in the county's Extension Service, the park also features a community garden, the 0.9-mile paved Brian Williams Trail, two playgrounds, a senior center, and a softball complex. Free.

✔ ✿ **Nash Farm Battlefield** (Henry County Parks and Recreation 770-288-7300; 1-800-436-7926; www.henrycountybattlefield.com), 4361 Jonesboro Road, Hampton. Open for special events at this time; call Parks and Recreation for details. The 204-acre battlefield was the site of the largest cavalry raid in Georgia's history and a massive Confederate campsite. It is one of the few Civil War battlefields that remains intact and is meticulously preserved. In fact, Henry County purchased the land only a few years ago to preserve it from development and turn it into a park. An archaeological survey revealed hundreds of artifacts. Two important events at the battlefield are Folktales and Moonlight Storytelling at Nash Farm Battlefield in October and the Battle of Atlanta Re-enactment in November.

To Do

Auto Racing
✔ �& **Atlanta Motor Speedway** (office 770-707-7904; gift shop/tours 770-707-7970; www.atlantamotorspeedway.com; www.gospeedway.com), 1500 Tara Place/US 41 North, Hampton. Office open 8:30–5 weekdays; gift shop/tours open 9–5 Monday through Saturday, 1–5 Sunday. Call for a schedule of events and ticket prices. Track tours operate daily from the gift shop. The 1.54-mile track is one of the premier motor sports facilities in America and is considered to be the fastest track on the NASCAR circuit. Its two NASCAR Nextel Cup Series races are the two largest single-day sporting events in Georgia. In fact, the track is the biggest revenue-producing sports venue in the state. Approximately 160,000 fans converge there to watch their favorite drivers "put the pedal to the metal" as

they race around the track at heart-stopping speeds. In addition, the track sponsors the NASCAR Craftsman Truck Series and Busch Series racing. Thursday Thunder Legends, Bandolero, and Roadster racing showcase the talents of up-and-coming drivers for 10 weeks during the summer. The Richard Petty Driving Experience provides visitors a year-round opportunity to travel around the track at speeds over 100 miles per hour.

In use more than 300 days a year, the track also hosts concerts, air shows, dog shows, circuses, weddings, and car shows such as the Number One Parts Incorporated compact car show (the largest in the world), which brings in more than $455 million annually. The facility also offers tours and behind-the-scenes looks at the entertainment complex. Official track tours include track history, a visit to Petty Garden, a tour of a luxury suite, a peek at the garages and Victory Lane, and two laps in the speedway van. The facility was heavily damaged in a storm in 2006, but was able to open for the season. Renovations and expansions in 2007 included a new luxury seating option called Club One, which features 1,000 premium enclosed theater-style seats. Patrons of Club One enjoy upscale dining and premium video and sound. The speedway also added 13,000 new grandstand seats in Turn One—7,000 of these are individual chair-back seats with drink holders. Camping is also available.

Bicycling
Sandy Ridge Park (770-957-8836), 1200 Keys Ferry Road, McDonough. The park features a BMX track.

Bird-Watching
See Newman Wetlands Center and Cubihatcha Outdoor Center under *Nature Preserves and Parks*.

For Families
✐ **Fun Town of Henry County** (770-898-4272), 300 GA 155, McDonough. Open 9 AM–midnight Monday through Thursday, 9 AM–3 AM Friday and Saturday, noon–midnight Sunday. The 8-acre indoor/outdoor family entertainment complex offers two video arcades, billiards, 32 lanes of bowling, a climbing wall, Go-Karts, laser tag, 18 holes of mini golf, an eight-station batting cage, and a snack bar. Limited wheelchair accessibility on some rides. $2.75–4 per activity depending on season and time of day.

Fruit/Berry Picking
✐ 🍴 ♿ **Little Billie's Strawberry Farm** (770-957-8524; www.littlebillies.com), 2501 GA 20 West, McDonough. The season typically runs from the first week in April through the first week in June. Hours are 9–7 Monday through Saturday, noon–6 Sunday. A veritable sea of strawberries, the farm has 10 acres planted—that's 140,000 plants. The owners say that if they were lined up end to end, the line would be 26 miles long. Visitors can pick their own succulent strawberries fresh from the vine or purchase those already picked. Don't leave without savoring some of the luscious homemade strawberry ice cream made with their very own strawberries. Price: you-pick $1.75 per pound, they-pick $2.50 per pound; $7.50 per gallon if you supply the bucket, $8.50 per gallon if they supply the bucket; $2 for a cup or cone of strawberry ice cream.

Hiking
See **Cubihatcha Outdoor Center** under *Nature Preserves and Parks*.

Miniature Golf
See **Fun Town of Henry County** under *To Do—For Families*.

GREEN SPACE

Nature Preserves and Parks
⚓ ✿ **Cubihatcha Outdoor Center/Towaliga River Preserve** (678-583-3930; www.hcwsa.com/community/cubihatcha.asp), 100 Collins Road, Locust Grove. Loop Trail open 8–5 daily year-round; River Trail parking lot open 8–5 weekdays, April through October, but you can park outside the gate and walk the trail anytime. The center is a wetland enhancement and protection corridor created to improve and protect existing wildlife habitats, as well as for public education and enjoyment. Almost 1,000 acres of bottomland, hardwood forest, wetlands, and uplands typical of the Piedmont region provide diverse habitats for mammals, birds, fish, reptiles, amphibians, and insects. The 8-mile River Trail runs along the Towaliga River, while the Loop Trail is 2 miles around. Visitors can take a self-guided tour or arrange in advance for a walk led by a staff naturalist. Free.

⚓ ✿ ♿ **Newman Wetlands Center** (770-603-5606; www.ccwa.us), 2755 Freeman Road, Hampton. Trail open 7–7 daily, March through October; 7–5 daily, November through February. Visitor center open 8:30–5 weekdays, September through May; 8:30–5 Tuesday through Saturday, June through August. The 32-acre facility consists of a trail and a visitor's/interpretive center. The easy half-mile trail alternates between crushed stone through forested areas and a boardwalk over the swamp. Wheelchairs and strollers can be accommodated on the trail. The visitor's center contains a central exhibit/learning lab area, an auditorium where a wetlands video is presented, and restrooms. During the summer, weekday guided walks are often scheduled. In addition to 130 species of birds, other wildlife such as beaver, river otter, fox, raccoon, muskrat, deer, wild turkey, opossum, mink, reptiles, and amphibians have been sighted. Some species stop here during their migrations; others are permanent residents. The Atlanta Audubon Society holds Saturday morning bird walks here all year. Birding classes and workshops are offered, too. Special programs on topics such as waterfowl, bats, reptiles, or gardening are scheduled annually. The **Wetlands and Watershed Festival** is held on the first Saturday after Labor Day. No jogging, bicycles, trail bikes, grills, or open fires are permitted. Free.

LODGING

Campgrounds

In McDonough
⚓ ✿ ♿ **Atlanta South RV Resort** (770-957-2610; 1-800-778-0668; www.atlanta southrvresort.com), 281 Mount Olive Road, McDonough. The campground provides 170 sites with water, sewer, and electric hookups as well as camping, cabin, and tent sites.

Other amenities include restrooms, laundry facilities, showers, a dump station, pool, and a playground. The new clubhouse features a TV viewing area and Internet access. $35.

WHERE TO EAT

Dining Out

In McDonough

♿ **Pilgreen's on Lake Dow** (770-957-4490), 1720 Lake Dow Road. Open 5–9 Monday through Thursday, 5–10 Friday and Saturday. A favorite with locals and well-known for steaks and seafood for more than a half a century, Pilgreen's offers white-table service with a view of the lake. No smoking. Wheelchair accessible. $13–30.

♿ **Truman's** (770-320-8686), 32 Jonesboro Street. Open 11–3 Tuesday through Sunday; 5–10 Tuesday through Saturday. Dine in luxury at a historic home just off the square, where the cuisine is described as "fancy French to down-home." White tablecloths and soft music enhance the romantic atmosphere. Lunch choices include a wide variety of soups, salads, and sandwiches. Dinner entrées range from pasta to filet mignon. You'll also find everything from quesadillas to shrimp po'boys. Don't forget the delicious homemade desserts. No smoking inside; smoking permitted in outdoor seating area. Wheelchair accessible. $7–19.

Eating Out

In McDonough

Gritz Family Restaurant (770-914-0448), 14 Macon Street. Open 7–3 Monday through Saturday. Down-home Southern cooking is served for breakfast and lunch in a casual atmosphere. Start the day with a hearty breakfast of pancakes, omelettes, or eggs fixed any way. Breakfast meats include bacon, sausage, ham, steak, chicken, pork, or corned beef hash. Of course, grits and biscuits make an appearance. Lunch entrées such as chicken and dumplings, salmon patties, fried chicken livers, and country-fried steak include two sides and bread. No smoking. Wheelchair accessible. $5–10.

PJ's Café (770-898-5373), 30 Macon Street. Open 11–9 Tuesday through Thursday, 11–10 Friday and Saturday, 11–3 Sunday. Steaks, seafood, and pasta are served in a casual atmosphere. The restaurant features a wine bar, international beers, and outdoor dining. Enjoy the cozy bar and the beautiful mural in the dining room. No smoking inside; smoking permitted in outdoor seating area. Wheelchair accessible. $4–10 for lunch, $11–16 for dinner. Early Bird Specials between 4 and 6:30 start at $6.95.

ENTERTAINMENT

Dance

Atlanta Festival Ballet (770-507-2775; www.atlantafestivalballet.com), mailing address: 416 Eagle's Landing Parkway, Stockbridge 30281. The only professional dance company on the south side of metro Atlanta, the organization has 18 full-time professional dancers and more than 40 student apprentices in the Festival Ballet School. The company presents two to three full-length productions each year, including "The Nutcracker" at holiday time and a spring production. Although the company is based in nearby Stockbridge (see the Southern Crescent chapter), performances are held at the Henry County Schools Performing Arts Center (770-914-7477), 37 Lemon Street, McDonough, as well as the Clayton County Schools Performing Arts Center (770-473-2875), 2530 Mount Zion Parkway, Jonesboro. Adults $15, seniors and students $12.

Music

The Henry Singers (770-957-0987; www.henrysingers.com). The 20-member vocal group performs three concerts annually, including a holiday concert in December, a spring performance, and a patriotic concert in the summer. Performances are held at the McDonough Presbyterian Church, 427 McGarity Road, McDonough, or the Henry County Schools Performing Arts Center (770-914-7477), 37 Lemon Street, McDonough.

Southern Crescent Symphony Orchestra (770-389-1625; www.scsymphony.org), mailing address: 950 Eagle's Landing Parkway, Suite 241, Stockbridge 30281. Call or check the Web site for a schedule of events and ticket prices; some concerts are free. The 75-member volunteer community orchestra composed of professional musicians, music educators, amateur musicians, and students presents four to six concerts annually ranging from Christmas sing-alongs to movie music, children's favorites to classical concertos. Although the symphony is based in Stockbridge (see the Southern Crescent chapter), it performs at the Henry County Schools Performing Arts Center (770-914-7477), 37 Lemon Street, McDonough, as well as the Clayton County Schools Performing Arts Center (770-473-2875), 2530 Mount Zion Parkway, Jonesboro, the Coweta County Centre for Performing and Visual Arts (770-252-5456), 1523 Lower Fayetteville Road, Newnan, and other venues.

Theater

The Henry Players (770-914-1474; www.henryplayers.com), mailing address: P.O. Box 3083, McDonough 30253. Call or check the Web site for a schedule of performances and ticket prices, which generally run about $12. Tickets are also available at several businesses and online. The theatrical company, which is composed entirely of volunteers, presents five productions annually and some charity performances as well. Productions are held at the Henry County Schools Performing Arts Center (770-914-7477), 37 Lemon Street, McDonough. $10–12.

SELECTIVE SHOPPING

McDonough's historic town square abounds with antiques shops and also features an old-fashioned hardware store and an art design studio. Many of the merchants in McDonough have banded together to offer a booklet of discounts at many of the town's shops, restaurants, and activities. The booklet can be obtained from the **McDonough Hospitality and Tourism Bureau** (see *Guidance*).

Flea Markets

Peachtree Peddlers Flea Market (770-914-2269; 1-888-661-3532; www.peachtreepeddlers.com), 155 Mill Road, McDonough. Open 9–6 Saturday, 10–6 Sunday. The 200,000-square-foot, all-weather flea market features antiques and craft booths as well as booths for just about every item imaginable. Find antiques, books, floral arrangements, Georgia produce, gifts, and much, much more. In addition, the facility has a restaurant and hosts craft shows and other special entertainment events. The **Peachtree Antique Market** is at the same location (open 10–6 daily). Free.

Sweetie's Flea Market (770-946-4721), 2316 US 19 and 441, Hampton. Open 8–4:30 Friday through Sunday year-round. Georgia's oldest flea market has a fun country fair atmosphere and bargains galore. More than 100 dealers sell antiques, collectibles, farm and country items, primitives, and more. There is a snack bar on the premises.

Other Goods

Atlanta Motor Speedway Gift Store (770-707-7970; www.atlantamotorspeedway.com; www.gospeedway.com), 1500 Tara Place/US 41 North, Hampton. Open 9–5 Monday through Saturday, 1–5 Sunday. Shop here for Atlanta Motor Speedway and NASCAR apparel, flags, pins, jewelry, pens, postcards, electronics, and kitchen supplies. The gift shop is in the same building as the ticket office.

Nutmeg's (770-957-6199), 16 Macon Street on the Town Square, McDonough. Open 10–5:30 Monday, Tuesday, and Thursday through Saturday. The gift shop offers gourmet cookware, tableware, cookbooks, and housewarming gifts. Cooking and tea classes also are offered.

Outlet Malls

Tanger Outlet Center (770-957-5310; 1-800-406-0833; www.tangeroutlet.com), 1000 Tanger Drive, Locust Grove. Open 9–9 Monday through Saturday, noon–6 Sunday; longer hours on Thanksgiving weekend; closed Easter, Thanksgiving, and Christmas Day. One of the largest outlet centers in the country, this one features more than 60 of the nation's leading brand-name stores with quality merchandise at discount prices. It attracts more than 3.5 million shoppers annually. A recent expansion has added 58,000 square feet of retail space and tenants such as Polo Ralph Lauren, Children's Place, Nautica, Strasburg Children, Rack Room Shoes, Stride Rite, and Kirkland's.

SPECIAL EVENTS

Spring: **Geranium Festival** (678-432-7112). A more-than-quarter-century tradition on the Square in McDonough, the festival features an arts and crafts exhibition and sale, music, other entertainment, and great food. Free.

Summer: **Music on the Square Summer Concert Series** (770-898-3196). Music on the Square concerts are held from 7–11 on specific dates in May, July, and August at the McDonough Square. Talented bands and soloists perform jazz, rock and roll, classical, and pop music. Concert-goers are invited to bring blankets or chairs, snacks, and beverages to enjoy while listening to music outdoors. Free.

October: **Fall Festival and Chili Cook-Off** (770-898-3196). The event, held on the McDonough Square, features a different kind of chili cooking contest. Instead of being judged according to certain criteria, participants are judged by the public. Participants (applications required) prepare their secret chili recipe ahead of time and bring it to the festival, where they sell it in sample-size cups. The person who sells the most cups wins. Other festival activities include entertainment, arts and crafts, and children's activities. Free admission; nominal fees for some activities.

December: **McDonough Holiday Tour of Homes** (770-957-4150). The tour allows glimpses into six to eight private homes each year to get visitors into the holiday spirit and perhaps give them decorating ideas. Note: The tour is not wheelchair-friendly because there are so many steps involved. $8 in advance, $10 on the day of the tour.

The Coweta County Courthouse sits at the center of Newnan's bustling town square.

NEWNAN

Coweta County was named for the Coweta Indians, a Creek tribe, and its name means "water falls." The county was formed in 1825, when Chief William McIntosh—who was part Scot, part Indian—signed the Treaty of Indian Springs, for which he was later killed by angry fellow tribesmen. He was married to Senoya He-ne-ha, and it is believed that the town of Senoia was named after her. As for McIntosh, a large preserve is named for him (see *Nature Preserves and Parks*).

Coweta County has produced loads of famous folks, from literary giants to entertainers. In addition to authors Erskine Caldwell and Lewis Grizzard (see *Museums*), other celebrities include David Boyd, who illustrates the *You Might be a Redneck If...* books; Margaret Anne Barnes, who wrote *Murder in Coweta County*; country music stars Alan Jackson and Doug Stone; classical music personality Charles Wadsworth, who serves as the musical director of Charleston's Spoleto festival; and football great Drew Hill. Minnie Pearl began her career as a drama coach here as well.

The area should be familiar to moviegoers who have seen *Fried Green Tomatoes, Driving Miss Daisy, Pet Sematary II,* and *The War.* Numerous television series and productions have been filmed here as well: *I'll Fly Away, Passing Glory, A Christmas Memory,* and *Andersonville,* just to name a few. Riverwood Studios, located on 105 acres in Senoia, is a complete production facility with several soundstages.

Newnan, Grantville, Moreland, and Senoia boast historic neighborhoods with designated driving or walking tours. Whitesburg is the home of the McIntosh Reserve (see *Nature Preserves and Parks*) and a lovely resort.

Two of the state's designated Scenic Trails travel through this area: the **Chattahoochee-Flint Heritage Highway** and the **Georgia Antiques Trail**.

GUIDANCE

When planning a trip to the Newnan area, contact the **Coweta County Convention and Visitors Bureau and Welcome Center** (770-254-2627; 1-800-826-9382; www.coweta.ga.us), 100 Walt Sanders Memorial Drive, Newnan 30265. Open 9–5 Monday through Saturday, 1–5 Sunday. Pick up a brochure for the Newnan Antebellum and Victorian Driving Tour as well as brochures for Moreland, Senoia, and Grantville tours.

Visitors also can consult the **Newnan-Coweta County Chamber of Commerce** (770-253-2270; www.newnancowetachamber.org), 23 Bullsboro Drive, Newnan 30264. Open 9–5 weekdays. For information about Senoia, call **Senoia City Hall** (770-599-3679). Open 8-5 weekdays.

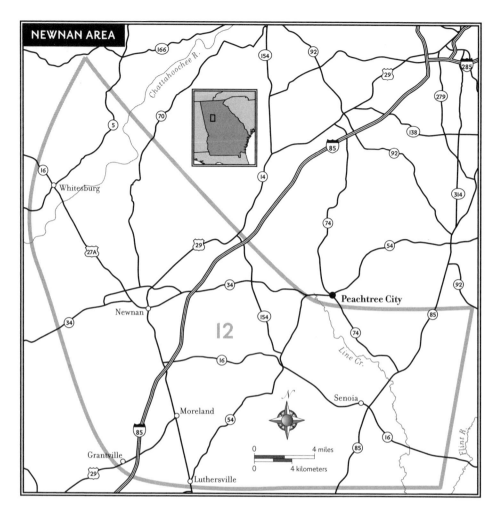

Getting There

By air: See What's Where. Car rentals are available on-site.

By bus: The nearest bus stations are in Atlanta—downtown and at the airport (see What's Where). Visitors arriving in Atlanta by bus would need to rent a car to get to the towns in this chapter and to get around between them, because taxis and mass transit are not a feasible way to travel.

By car: The towns described in this chapter are clustered around I-85 south of Atlanta. Newnan is directly off the interstate on US 27 Alt., and Whitesburg is farther northwest from Newnan. Grantville is north on US 29. Moreland is south of the interstate via either US 27Alt. or US 29. Senoia is reached by GA 16.

Getting Around

Taxi service is available in Newnan from **Atlanta South Taxi** (770-252-2828). Limousine service is available in Newnan from **Ace of Hearts Limousine Service** (770-305-9434) and **Eternity Limousine Service** (678-423-0058). The other towns do not have taxi or limousine services, so it is necessary to have a car.

Parking
All of these towns have ample free on-street parking. In Newnan, there is a two-hour limit downtown around the square and the courthouse. There is also a municipal lot behind the courthouse.

Public Restrooms
In Newnan facilities can be found at both the Coweta County Convention and Visitors Bureau Welcome Center and the Newnan-Coweta County Chamber of Commerce.

Medical Emergency
For life-threatening emergencies, call 911. Otherwise, urgent care is available at **Piedmont Newnan Hospital** (770- 253-2330), 60 Hospital Road.

Villages/Neighborhoods
Newnan, the largest town in the area, was founded in 1828 and named for General Daniel Newnan, a War of 1812 veteran and Georgia General Assemblyman, after the area was opened up for settlement in the Land Lottery of 1827. Many of those early settlers became successful farmers and businessmen. Newnan later became known as the "Hospital City of the Confederacy" because six field hospitals, which served as many as 10,000 wounded soldiers from both the South and North, were located in churches, homes, and other buildings there. A monument erected in 1885 on the east side of the courthouse square honors the Confederate soldiers lost in that war, 63 of whom were laid to rest in Oak Hill Cemetery.

Newnan is also renowned for its historic homes built before the Civil War and during the Victorian era. In fact, the motto "The City of Homes" is emblazoned in lights on the old Carnegie Library building downtown.

There are numerous historic districts in and around Newnan. The **Newnan Historic District,** a nine-square-block area, was laid out in 1828 in the Washington plan, which includes wide avenues and a public square. This district contains the Neo-Greek Revival 1904 courthouse, the first Carnegie-endowed library in Georgia, four religious structures, and the historic black commercial district along Broad Street—a reminder of the days of segregation.

The **Cole Town Historic District,** founded in 1854, is a residential neighborhood with a wide variety of architectural styles.

The **College-Temple Historic District,** laid out in 1828, is an example of a well-planned residential neighborhood where walkways, fences, formal gardens, open lawns, and hedges accent the varied architectural styles. The academy lot was the site of seven schools between 1829 and 1975. The last of those schools now houses the Male Academy (see *Museums*).

In contrast to the planned residential neighborhoods, the **Greenville Street/LaGrange Street Historic District** is a patterned development where the principal streets have the oldest and grandest homes, while the infill streets have newer, smaller houses. One of the houses, Buena Vista, served as a Confederate headquarters during the Battle of Brown's Mill in July 1864.

Although it began in 1895, a collection of homes known as the **Platinum Point Historic District** was built by wealthy Newnan citizens and developed with increased use of automobiles. Built in a parklike atmosphere, the district contains a variety of the Revival architecture popular at the turn of the 20th century.

Roscoe/Dunaway Gardens Historic District is actually in Roscoe, a small crossroads community surrounded by farmsteads. The hamlet, which is listed on the National Register of Historic Places, features antebellum homes as well as architectural styles representing the late 19th and early 20th centuries. These farmhouses, fields, and large wood-framed barns depict the prominent role agriculture played and still plays in Coweta County. The only retail establishment left in town is the Roscoe General Store. A mural depicting Roscoe's busier times, when it had eight steam gins, five sawmills, four gristmills, four stores, six churches, and five schools, is painted on the side of the building. Dunaway Gardens was recently reopened after a slumber of more than a quarter-century (see *Gardens*).

The small town of **Grantville**, which was originally named Calico Corners, was renamed in 1852 for L. P. Grant, president of the Atlanta and LaGrange Railroad. In the late 19th and early 20th centuries, the town flourished with three factories, two banks, a theater, civic auditorium, and a telephone and telegraph office—all of which earned it the name "Gem of Coweta County." Unfortunately, Grantville declined, and today it is a very small but friendly town.

The **Grantville Historic District** represents a small railroad town that grew up along the tracks. Two historic mills and mill villages remain within the district along with several churches and the passenger and freight depot. One of the most significant homes is Bonnie Castle, an elaborate Romanesque brick home built in 1896 using a variety of styles.

Moreland, originally a railroad stop called Puckett's Station, was once a booming cotton town with a hosiery mill. Today the small town boasts three museums (see *Museums*), a bike/pedestrian path that winds through the small hamlet, and a huge Fourth of July weekend celebration (see *Special Events*).

Senoia was developed from a cluster of farms in 1827. When the coming of the railroads brought about the need for an organized community, the town was founded in 1860, then incorporated in 1864. Two railroads intersected in Senoia, and cotton and peaches were shipped from there. Much of the original town remains intact as a nationally designated historic district (see *Scenic Drives*). No trip to Senoia would be complete without a visit to the **Buggy Shop Museum** (see *Museums*), a stay at the **Culpepper House Bed and Breakfast** or the **Veranda Historic Bed and Breakfast Inn** (see *Bed and Breakfasts*), and shopping at the old-time Hutchinson Hardware.

> **Pronounce It Correctly**
> Senoia looks as if it would be pronounced Seh-noy-yuh, but locals say Seh-noy. You'll show that you're a visitor if you mispronounce it.

The **Senoia Historic District** contains 150 historic structures representing architectural styles from Greek Revival to Queen Anne. It also includes several antebellum homes that predate the town's development. Most, however, are from the turn of the 20th century.

To See

Museums

🗡 🐾 ♿ **Buggy Shop Museum** (770-253-1018), Main Street, Senoia. Open 1–4 on the third Saturday and Sunday of each month, April through October, or by appointment. Relive history by viewing buggies, old-time tools and machinery, antique cars, player pianos,

The Buggy Shop Museum and other buildings in Senoia

Coca-Cola memorabilia, and collectibles from a bygone era. The rustic building that houses the museum was built in 1867. Small admission fee.

Coweta County African American Heritage Museum and Research Center (770-683-7055; www.africanamericanalliance.net), 92 Farmer Street, Newnan. Open 10–4 Monday and Wednesday. The shotgun house in which the museum is located is an example of historical African American architecture. The museum serves as a repository for artifacts concerning Newnan's African American history and is an active research center. On the grounds is a slave cemetery under centuries-old giant oak trees. An authentic slave cabin is being relocated on the property and will be restored. Free; donations accepted.

"The Little Manse"—Erskine Caldwell Museum (770-254-8657; www.coweta.ga.us), East Camp Street on the Moreland Town Square, Moreland. Open 11–3 Thursday through Saturday (call ahead to make an appointment, or if you arrive and no one is there, go across the square to the art shop and someone will let you in). "The Little Manse" was the birthplace of native son and world-famous author Erskine Caldwell. The small wooden house has been restored to its 1903 appearance and relocated to the town square to serve as a house museum documenting Caldwell's life and accomplishments, and to reflect life when the mill dominated the South. The museum features biographical exhibits, personal items, and copies of his books in different languages. Although Caldwell penned 25 novels, he is best remembered for his compelling depictions of the rural South during the Great Depression in *Tobacco Road* and *God's Little Acre*. Adults $2, children $1.

Lewis Grizzard Museum (770-251-0424; www.coweta.ga.us), 2769 US 29 South, Moreland. Open 11–2 Tuesday through Saturday (if no one is there, go next door to the monument company that shares the same building and someone will let you in). Native son Lewis Grizzard was beloved as a Southern humorist, author, and entertainer before his premature death in 1994 at age 47 from heart problems. Grizzard put Moreland on the map with his syndicated columns and books such as *Don't Sit Under the Grits Tree with Anyone Else But Me* and *Elvis is Dead and I Don't Feel So Good Myself* in which he fondly told about his childhood in the small rural town. The museum showcases old typewriters, family photos, mementos, and manuscripts. $1.

✿ ❀ ⚷ **Male Academy Museum** (770-251-0207; www.nchistoricalsociety.org/mam.htm), 30 Temple Avenue, Newnan. Open 10–noon and 1–3 Tuesday through Thursday, 2–5 Saturday and Sunday. Once a private school for boys, the museum features a replica of a classroom with the original teacher's desk as well as a student's desk, teacher's dress, stu-

dent uniform, bell, stove, and lunch pail. The museum boasts an extensive Civil War exhibit with an authentic Confederate battle flag, uniforms, soldiers' personal items, artifacts, weaponry, maps, and paintings of the Battle of Brown's Mill. The museum is also noted for its extensive collection of 19th- and early-20th-century clothing. In addition, the museum contains Native American artifacts and a collection of photos concerning the life of native son and country music star Alan Jackson. Adults $3, children $2.

❀ ⚷ **Old Mill Museum** (call the City of Moreland 770-251-3428), Main Street on the downtown square, Moreland. Open by appointment only. The massive brick Moreland Mill on the square was once a hosiery mill. Today it houses town offices, meeting space, and the town museum. Exhibits include artifacts from the build-

The Male Academy Museum was once a school for boys.

ing's days as a mill, antique farming equipment, World War II memorabilia, rural Georgia collectibles, and a Smithsonian textile display. Dr. Quigg Young's medical office, which closed years ago, is always open as an exhibit. Outside is a garden planted in memory of longtime resident Lamar Haynes. $2.

Scenic Drives
Pick up the brochures for all these tours from the Coweta County Convention and Visitors Bureau and Welcome Center (see *Guidance*).

The Chattahoochee-Flint Heritage Highway. This scenic highway and bike route runs through Coweta, Troup, Harris, and Meriwether counties from Roscoe to St. Marks. The Creek Indians originally inhabited this land. Today the route is filled with historic sites. Free.

Historic Grantville Driving Tour. Drive past lovely homes, among them the Smith-Wilson House and Bonnie Castle. The Renaissance Revival home with its round battle-ment-like tower is surrounded by an original decorative wrought iron fence. The original hitching post is still in place as well. Free.

Moreland Driving Tour. The tour takes visitors past the restored history of the town, including the Old Mill Building (1894), the Old Moreland Post Office (1876), Founders Cemetery, and historic homes. Browse for antiques in the old general store. Free.

Newnan Driving Tour. The tour includes five historic districts. Antebellum and Victorian-era houses, which are marked with black metal signs, represent Gothic, Queen Anne, Eastlake, Second Empire, and Colonial Revival styles. Particularly interesting are the "Painted Ladies," those Victorian-era houses painted in three or more colors. Free.

Senoia Driving Tour of Homes. Developed by land grant round 1830 as a cluster of farms, the town features tree-lined streets, 150 historic structures, and a commercial district. Senoia was named for the wife of Chief William McIntosh of the Lower Creek Indians, and Princess Senoia appears as the symbol of the Senoia Historical Society. The tour points out historic homes, businesses, and churches. Free.

Smokey Road Scenic Drive. Head south out of Newnan on Jackson Street, which becomes LaGrange Street, and finally Smokey Road, where you'll see one panoramic vista after another of horse country and farm estate homes. Free.

To Do

Auto Racing

New Senoia Raceway (770-599-6161; www.newsenoiaraceway.com), 171 Brown Road, Senoia. Call for a schedule of events. For night races, the gates open at 4:30 and races begin at 6:45; for day races, the gates open at 12:45 and races begin at 2:45. Events at the speedway include many classes and series: the O'Reilly United Sprint Car Series, the Georgia Asphalt Series, Pro Challenge, Bandoleros, Street Stock, Legends-Pro, Legends-Semipro, Sportsman, and Iceman classes. The demolition derby is another popular event. Adults $10, children younger than 10 $2. For special events, general admission is $15, $20 for positions at the fence, and $30 for positions at the pits.

Bicycling

McIntosh Reserve (770-830-5879; www.carrollcountyga.com), 1046 West McIntosh Circle, Whitesburg. Open 8–dusk daily. (Note: The park's gates close promptly at sundown during the week or when there are a large number of campers in the park. Be sure to be out by then if you are not camping there.) Several interconnecting mountain biking trails in the reserve provide 17 miles of riding. Good places to start are the park station and Council Bluff. The trails provide a variety of flat and hilly terrain for beginning and intermediate riders, but there are some sandy, rocky, and eroded areas. And look out: Horses also use the trails and often leave a calling card behind. There is a yearly foot race in August. $2.

Canoeing, Kayaking, Rafting

McIntosh Reserve (770-830-5879; www.carrollcountyga.com), 1046 West McIntosh Circle, Whitesburg. Open 8–dusk daily. (See the warning above about the gates closing at sundown.) The Chattahoochee River, which forms the southern boundary of the reserve, provides an excellent venue for these paddling sports. $2.

Frights

Horror Hill Haunted Trail and Vertigo Haunted Trail (770-253-4983; www.horrorhill.com), Newnan. (Note: the telephone number is active only a few weeks before the event; call to get the exact location to begin the tour.) Open evenings at Halloween time. In operation since 1984 and considered to be the largest haunted trail in the Southeast, the route features buildings, cabins, mazes, tunnels, bridges, trapdoors, fog machines, lasers, and strobe lights to create spooky effects. $12 for the Horror Hill Haunted Trail alone or $20 for both trails.

Horseback Riding/Summer Riding Camp

Blue Moon Stable (770-252-3300; www.bluemoonstables.net), 493 Boone Road, Newnan. Open 8–6 Monday through Saturday, 9–4 Sunday. Lessons are given for riders age 5–15, whether they're novices or have had some lessons. Riders are grouped according to age and skill. Classes consist of riding and horse care. With an indoor arena, riders never have to worry about a rainy day. Call for prices.

GREEN SPACE

Gardens

🎨🌿 ♿ **Dunaway Gardens** (678-423-4050; www.dunawaygardens.com), 3218 Roscoe Road, Newnan. Open March 15 through November 30, 10–5 Thursday through Saturday, 1–5 Sunday. One of the South's largest natural rock and floral gardens, 25-acre Dunaway Gardens features spring-fed pools, stone waterfalls, and extensive rock paths, walls, and staircases. Once a magnificent treasure, the gardens were allowed to fall into such disrepair that the original beauty was totally choked out by weeds and vines until rescued in 2000.

Dunaway Gardens was created on a former cotton plantation by vaudeville Chautauqua actress Hetty Jane Dunaway and her husband, Wayne Sewell, as part of a larger complex that included a theatrical training center, said to be one of the largest in the 1920s. Many of the company's ballet and theatrical productions were originally previewed at the 1,000-seat amphitheater on the grounds. Walt and Roy Disney were frequent visitors, and Sarah Ophelia Colley created her Minnie Pearl character here in the 1930s. The gardens remained popular up until the 1950s, when the tearoom was often used for parties and plays were produced in the Patchwork Barn.

Dunaway died in 1961 and the gardens were abandoned. Over the years of neglect the historic buildings disappeared, but the walls, walkways, patios, pools, ponds, and waterfalls were salvageable. Jennifer Rae Bingham bought the property in 2000 and spent three years reclaiming the gardens. Today visitors can enjoy the arrowhead pools, an amphitheater, butterfly rockery, hanging garden, sunken garden, pink patios, octagon pool, wedding tree, Japanese garden, twin pools, hillside rock garden, moss garden, the great pool, and a rose garden. Little Stone Mountain is a huge outcropping of exposed granite, the base of which underlies the entire garden. It was said to be a favorite campsite of Chief William McIntosh. Adults $10, children $8.

🌿 ♿ **Oak Grove Plantation and Gardens** (770-463-3010; www.oakgrovega.com), 4537 US 29, Newnan. Open periodically for tours. Central to the plantation is the 1830s four-over-four house, which reflects early Plantation Plain and Federal styles. The owners live in the house and it is only open on special occasions, but visitors can admire the exterior architectural details such as intricate moldings, pilasters, and chimneys. A restored carriage house offers bed and breakfast accommodations (see *Lodging*). Four acres of gardens feature old-fashioned flowers and shrubs as well as herbs and vegetables. There are also other themed areas such as the pool, meditation, secret, formal, patience, shade, rhododendron, and sin el agua (without water) gardens. The sunken garden is designed for outdoor entertainment and planted with only white blooming flowers. The Arnold family cemetery is on the property (they were former owners) and is attractively planted as well. Oak Grove Plantation Nursery specializes in old-fashioned flowers and shrubs. $5.

Nature Preserves and Parks

✏ 🐾 ♿ **Coweta County Fairgrounds** (770-254-2685), 275 Pine Road, Newnan. Office open 8–5 weekdays. Call for a schedule of events and prices. The 65-acre facility hosts the five-day Coweta County Fair in September, 4-H events, horse shows in the **W.C. Adamson Horse Arena**, the Coweta Cattleman's Association benefit rodeo, dog shows, circuses, and other events. The **Walker Horne Open Air Theater** is a popular site for concerts, stage performances, and weddings. Also within the facility is the **James E. McGuffey Nature Center**, 30 acres of green space with a small pond, wetland environment, forest, and nearly 3 miles of nature trails. The complex also has a hard-surface, wheelchair-accessible trail.

✏ 🐾 ♿ **McIntosh Reserve** (770-830-5879; www.carrollcountyga.com), 1046 West McIntosh Circle, Whitesburg. Open 8–dusk daily. (Note: The reserve is a gated facility and is closed at sundown unless camping arrangements have been made.) The reserve is named for Chief William McIntosh Jr., the son of a Scottish captain in the British Army and a full-blooded Creek Indian woman who belonged to the

Enjoying the horse trails at McIntosh Reserve

Chief William McIntosh

McIntosh, a Lower Creek chief, served America as a distinguished soldier in several battles—including Autossee, Horseshoe Bend, the Creek Indian War, and the Seminole Wars—for which he was awarded the rank of brigadier general in the U.S. Army (the only Indian to ever reach that rank). He fought with Andrew Jackson and even dined with President Thomas Jefferson at the White House. Raised as an Indian, he never knew his Tory father, but since descent was determined through the mother, that was of little importance to the Creeks. He owned a plantation and operated an inn, two taverns, a trading post, and a ferry across the Chattahoochee River. He also owned 72 slaves and had Indians and white men working for him. McIntosh and other Lower Creeks ceded all Creek lands in Georgia west of the Flint River to the U.S. government. He then planned to leave for lands he had been promised in Arkansas. Before he could do that, however, the Upper Creeks killed him, burned the plantation, and destroyed what stock they didn't take, but spared the lives of the women and children.

Wind Clan of the Creek Nation. The park contains part of his plantation, which he called "Lochau Talofau," or Acorn Bluff. McIntosh rose to the rank of chief in the Coweta tribe of the Lower Creeks, but was killed May 1, 1825, by his own people, who were angered that he had ceded land to the white settlers.

This area is called a "reserve" because McIntosh reserved some of it for himself. His simple grave is here, as well as a reproduction of his rustic dogtrot-style house. Today the property—which combines recreational activities; preservation of cultural heritage; education, fish and wildlife management; and conservation of the Chattahoochee River corridor—is used for camping, hiking, fishing, canoeing, rafting, and picnicking. More than 17 miles of trails, enjoyed by hikers, cyclists, and equestrians, wind through the reserve and along the Chattahoochee River, which forms the southern boundary. Model airplane enthusiasts enjoy the grass airstrip in the lower park near the camping area. Primitive camping can be arranged for weekends only. During the summer, the Spray and Splash Water Park is open daily ($1). Annual events include the Easter Festival, Fall Festival, Native American Powwow, Halloween Carnival, and Chattahoochee Challenge Car Show. $2.

Lodging

Bed and Breakfasts

In Newnan
Oak Grove Plantation and Gardens
(770-463-3010; 770-841-0789; www.oak grovega.com), 4537 US 29 North. Located on 20 acres, the plantation is listed on the National Register of Historic Places (see *Historic Homes and Sites*). Guest accommodations are offered in the restored tin-roofed carriage house, where two suites boast antique furnishings and private baths with Jacuzzi tubs. The cottage also features a common room with games, puzzles, television, a video and DVD player, and books. There is also a vintage kitchen, which guests are free to use. In addition to enjoying the many different gardens, guests can use the outdoor pool and the playhouse area. Homemade cookies are served in the evening, and the day begins with a hearty breakfast. No smoking. Not wheelchair accessible. $155.

In Senoia
Culpepper House (770-599-8182; www.culpepperhouse.com), 35 Broad

Oak trees shade Culpepper House, a bed and breakfast in Senoia.

Street. The house was built in 1871 by Dr. John Addy, a Confederate veteran. The oak trees he planted during that era continue to shade the house and property. The house later belonged to Dr. Wilbur Culpepper and has retained his name. Twelve-foot ceilings and other architectural elements of the period create gracious public rooms and three guest rooms. Guests particularly enjoy the wraparound porch. A generous breakfast buffet is included in the nightly rate. No smoking. Not wheelchair accessible. $95–105.

The Veranda Historic Bed and Breakfast Inn (770-599-3905; www.verandaband binn.com), 252 Seavy Street. On a recent visit to Senoia, we were overjoyed to find that The Veranda had reopened after a two-year hiatus and change of ownership. The stately Greek Revival mansion with its sweeping verandas was built in 1906 as the Hollberg Hotel and featured the first commercial use of electricity in town. Famous guests have included William Jennings Bryan and Margaret Mitchell. More recently, the Burt Reynolds film *Broken Bridges* was filmed at the inn. Many of the architectural elements are original: tin ceilings, chandeliers, claw-foot tubs, pedestal sinks, and 11 fireplaces. Nine guest rooms have been updated with modern baths and king or queen beds. The Bridal Suite boasts a whirlpool tub. Guests enjoy a full breakfast, browsing in the gift shop, rocking or swinging on the verandas, or wandering through the lush gardens. Five-course dinners can be arranged by reservation at an additional cost. No smoking or pets. Well-behaved children are welcome. Not wheelchair accessible. $125–150.

Campgrounds

In Whitesburg
McIntosh Reserve (770-830-5879; www.carrollcountyga.com), 1046 West McIntosh Circle, Whitesburg. Reservations for primitive camping are restricted to weekends only and can be arranged by calling the office between 9 and 5 weekdays. $10 for county residents, $15 for nonresidents.

Inns and Hotels

Newnan has a variety of chain hotels, including **Best Western Shenandoah Inn** (770-304-9700), **Comfort Inn** (770-502-8688), **Country Inn and Suites** (770-304-8500), **Hampton Inn** (770-253-9922), **Holiday Inn Express** (770-251-2828), **Howard Johnson** (770-683-1499), **Jameson Inn** (770-252-1236), **LaQuinta Inn** (770-502-8430), and **Spring Hill Suites** (770-254-8900).

Resorts

In Whitesburg
The Lodges at Historic Banning Mills Country Inn, Executive Retreat and Spa (770-834-9149; 1-866-447-8688; www.historicbanningmills.com), 205 Horseshoe Dam Road. The retreat is nestled on 700 wooded acres overlooking the Snake Creek Gorge. Guest accommodations take the form of rooms in the lodge, log cabin suites, and cozy cottages. Many rooms feature a Jacuzzi, gas-log fireplace, refrigerator, microwave, and a deck with a spectacular view. Dining includes a full breakfast, deli box lunch or gourmet picnic basket, and dinner. Amenities at the resort include an Olympic-size swimming pool; tennis, basketball, and sand volleyball courts; an 18-hole putting green; a baseball field; and a horseshoe pit. Hiking along old town trails, Creek Indian paths, old water raceways, and along the Snake River can range from mild to moderately strenuous. Other activities, which are charged separately and range in price from $10 to $70, include skeet shooting, pistol shooting, and kayaking. An on-site spa offers numerous packages and body treatments ranging in price from $30 to $235. No smoking. One wheelchair-accessible room. $99–159; ask about special packages.

WHERE TO EAT

Dining Out

In Newnan
& **Andre's** (770-304-3557), 11 Jefferson Street. Open 5–9:30 Tuesday through Saturday. The upscale restaurant serves creative American cuisine and features fresh seafood every night. No smoking. Wheelchair accessible. $14–26.
& **Ten East Washington** (770-502-9100; www.teneastwashington.com), 10 East Washington Street. Open 5–9 Tuesday

through Thursday, 5–9:30 Friday and Saturday. Located just off the square, Ten East Washington, one of Newnan's finest restaurants, has earned a reputation for superbly prepared seafood, steaks, and continental cuisine. Chef George Rasovsky concentrates on refinement and fresh products. Live entertainment is offered once a month. No smoking. Wheelchair accessible. $14–26.

Eating Out

In Newnan

✍ ☏ ♿ **Catfish Hollow** (770-502-1223), 2826 GA 154. Open 4:30–9 Tuesday through Saturday. Naturally, the restaurant serves a multitude of seafood choices, but diners also can choose among steaks, burgers, veggie plates, and more. No smoking. Wheelchair accessible. $8.75–19; all-you-can-eat crab legs are $30.

✍ ☏ ♿ **Golden's on the Square** (770-251-4300), 9 East Gordon Street. Open 11–9 Tuesday through Sunday. Located in a historic downtown building, Golden's has been feeding the citizenry of Newnan for 28 years. Every day, the kitchen staff prepares six to eight made-from-scratch entrées, 12 to 14 freshly steamed vegetables, six to eight salads, and a variety of desserts. All meals are the same price and include a beverage, roll, and butter. No smoking. Wheelchair accessible. $7–17.

✍ ☏ ♿ **Redneck Gourmet Corner Cafe** (770-251-0092; www.redneckgourmet.com), 11 North Court Square. Open 7:30–10:30 and 11–9 Monday through Saturday. Breakfast is cooked to order and includes anything you could want, from eggs and breakfast meats to pancakes and French toast. For lunch, diners can enjoy hot and cold sandwiches, salads, soups, daily specials, as well as homemade desserts and cookies. The café, which has been operated by the Smith family for 14 years, is noted for its wide array of hot sauces. Monday's special is barbecue and their "Nearly

Famous" Brunswick stew; Thursday features the "Red" Plate Special; and Friday and Saturday are Hot Dawg Days. A new addition is Redneck-without-the-wait take-out. Call 770-683-NECK to place your order. The menu is complemented by a diverse selection of beer and wine. No smoking. Wheelchair accessible. $5 for breakfast, $4–7 for lunch, $5–13 for dinner.

✍ ☏ ♿ **Sprayberry's Barbecue** (770-253-4421; 770-253-5080; www.sprayberrysbbq.com), 229 Jackson Street and (770-253-5080), GA 34 West (Exit 47 off I-85). Open 10:30–9 Monday through Saturday. Sprayberry's was humorist Lewis Grizzard's favorite place to eat, and there's even a dish named after him. Using a vinegar-based sauce and slow roasting meat over an oak and hickory fire, Sprayberry's offers barbecue chicken and slow-roasted pork, Brunswick stew, and baby-back ribs. Grilled fish tacos, meat loaf, and a full menu are also featured at the original 1926 location in a former gas station on Jackson Street as well as at the new location on GA 34 West. Sprayberry's is also renowned for its homemade pies—especially its fried pies. No smoking. Wheelchair accessible. $3.75–14.95.

Sprayberry's Barbecue

The now legendary eatery had its beginning as Houston Sprayberry's gas station. Sprayberry began selling barbecue sandwiches made on-site with his special sauce, and soon he was selling so many he closed the pumps and became a restaurant. Politicians from U.S. presidents to governors have campaigned here, and entertainers and athletes stop in as well. Country music star Alan Jackson waited tables here when he was in high school, so whenever he's in the area he stops in for barbecue, Brunswick stew, and lemon pie. Lewis Grizzard proclaimed Sprayberry's "merely the best barbecue joint on earth." His choice of meal was a barbecue sandwich, Brunswick stew, and onion—a combination now known as the Lewis Grizzard Special.

ENTERTAINMENT

Nightlife

Alamo and Alamo Jacks (770-683-2526), 19 West Court Square, Newnan. Open 5 PM–2 AM daily, except Saturday 5–midnight. The nightclub features live music from national acts and local bands on Friday and Saturday nights, a DJ, karaoke night, trivia night, and two Texas Hold 'Em Poker nights as well as monthly theme parties. Ribs, wings, and other pub grub are served at the adjoining restaurant. Smoking allowed in the bar, but not in the restaurant. Limited wheelchair accessibility. Cover charge varies with the act, but is generally $5.

Theater

Newnan Theatre Company (770-683-NCTC; www.newnantheatre.com), 24 First Avenue, Newnan. The troupe, which has been in existence since 1975, produces comedies, dramas, musicals, works by Shakespeare, experimental pieces, and children's productions. Although the company has performed in converted warehouses, old cotton mills, churches, and even open fields, it now has a home in the former Johnson Hardware Building. Call for a schedule of performances and ticket prices, which run about $12 for adults, $10 for seniors and students for the Main Stage Series; $2 less for the Artist Series and the Popcorn Theatre Series.

SELECTIVE SHOPPING

Antiques

Re-Use the Past (770-583-3111; www.reusethepast.com), 98 Moreland Street, Grantville. Open noon–5 Wednesday through Monday. The firm's motto is "if it's old, we probably have it." Located in an 1895 hosiery mill, the company serves as an architectural salvage and antiques store. If you're remodeling a historic house, this is the place to get antique heart-pine floorboards, ceiling tin, doors, Victorian-era stained glass, bricks, pavers, hinges, doorknobs, chair rails, and molding, just to name a few items. If you simply want to add to your furnishings and decor, the store carries mirrors, coat hangers, wall sconces, antique furniture, and regional pottery.

Books

Scott's Book Store (770-254-9862; www.newnangaonline.com/businesses/scotts/scotts.html), 28 South Court Square, Newnan. Open 9–6 weekdays, 9–4 Saturday. In addition to a wide selection of books and an extensive children's section, the store carries plush toys, American Girl dolls, and other items. You also can purchase tickets for local events here.

Gifts

Collectors' Corner (770-251-6835; www.collectors-corner.net), 8861 GA 54, Sharpsburg. Open 10–6 Monday through Saturday, 1–5 Sunday. This vast shop features antiques, collectibles, gifts, furniture, heritage lace, home and garden accessories, lamps, pictures, mirrors, custom florals, baby and toddler clothing, and much more. Take a break from shopping with a bite in the Jasmine Tea Room and Restaurant. The store has several special

Delightful shops dot Senoia's Main Street.

events throughout the year: Spring Fling in April, Customer Appreciation Days in May, Christmas in July, Antique Dealer Appreciation Day in September, and a Christmas open house every weekend in November and December.

SPECIAL EVENTS

February: **Charles Wadsworth and Friends Concert** (770-251-4156). The native son, pianist, and Spoleto musical director performs with some of his friends at Wadsworth Auditorium in Newnan. $30.

April: **Senoia Tour of Homes and Progressive Dinner** (770-599-1929). The Senoia Area Historical Society presents this much-anticipated event, which allows visitors to get a glimpse into several historic homes. $40.

Tour of Homes (770-251-0207). Sponsored by the Newnan-Coweta Historical Society, the tour includes some of Newnan's most beautiful antebellum and Victorian-era homes as well as an art show, antique car show, and trolley tour. $13.

June: **Grantville Day** (770-583-3212). A pleasant country blend of fun and entertainment, Grantville Day is celebrated with live bands and other entertainment, food, a late movie, and shopping bargains throughout town. Although the festival is called Grantville Day, it is actually held Saturday and Sunday. There is plenty of street parking and there are also remote parking lots. Free.

Fourth of July weekend: **Moreland Independence Day Barbecue** (770-251-3428) and **Puckett's Station Arts and Crafts Festival** (770-583-2200; 770-251-3428). For more than half a century, three Moreland area churches have prepared barbecue pork and stew, which is now served at the Lewis Grizzard Pavilion behind the old Moreland Mill for $6 a plate. Chefs work through the night to cook about 3,000 pounds of meat, and there's already a long line when sales begin at 11 AM. The arts and crafts fair, which is named for Moreland's original name, begins at 9 AM. Free except for dinner.

July: **Annual Watermelon Festival** (770-252-9400). Everyone gets free watermelon at this popular Sharpsburg event, and there's also a watermelon seed-spitting contest, antique dealers, craft vendors, and old-fashioned games. For more information, visitors also can call 770-254-2627 or 1-800-826-9382. Free.

Labor Day Weekend: **Powers' Crossroads Country Fair and Art Festival** (770-253-2011; www.newnan.com/cowetafestivals/powers). Open 9–5 Saturday through Monday. One of the outstanding events in the nation, the fair at historic Powers' Plantation in Newnan features 250 or more juried artists and craftsmen from all over the United States; continuous country, gospel, folk, contemporary, and clogging acts; a wide variety of food; a children's play area; and demonstrations of plantation skills such as blacksmithing. Visitors can see a sorghum sugar mill and the original Powers' Plantation gristmill. Free parking and shuttle buses are provided at remote lots. Be sure to pick up your free program at the gate for a list of performers and a map to exhibitor locations. Adults $5, seniors and military $4, children 5–12 $2.

December: **"Light Up" Senoia** (770-254-2627; www.senoia.com). Downtown Senoia is lit up with holiday decorations, and there's a Christmas tree lighting, a parade, entertainment, and an appearance by Santa Claus and his elves. Free.

Newnan Candlelight Tour of Homes (770-253-8866). Sponsored by the Newnan Hospital Auxiliary, the tour features homes, churches, and businesses with evening entertainment. $15.

Index

A

Abbotts Kids Village, 239
Abernathy Arts Center, 217
Ace of Hearts Limousine Service, 297, 308
Acworth, 247, 256, 257
Acworth Area Convention and Visitors Bureau, 245
Acworth Beach/Cauble Park, 256
Adventures Aloft Hot-Air Ballooning, 17, 178
Affairs to Remember, 138
African American Panoramic Experience (APEX), 13, 34, 61
African American sites, 13
Agatha's-A Taste of Mystery, 41, 74
Agave, 70–71
agricultural fairs, 13, 252
air tours, 14
Airport Metro Limousine, 194
Airport Metro Shuttle, 147, 173, 215, 246, 266
Airport Perimeter Connection, 147, 173, 215, 246, 266
airports/airlines, 13–14
AJC Decatur Book Festival, 169
Alamo and Alamo Jacks, 319
Alliance Theater Company, 41, 108–9
Alpha Soda, 233
Alpharetta Christian Theater, 237
Alpharetta Convention and Visitors Bureau, 213
Alpharetta Family Skate Center/The Cooler, 224
Alpharetta Limousine Service, 214
Alpharetta North Park, 225
Alpharetta Parks and Recreation, 226
Alpharetta Welcome Center, 213–14
Alterna Taxi Services, 214
A&M Limousines, 246, 266
Amalfi Ristorante, 232
Amen Carriage Tours, 22, 30, 63
American Museum of Papermaking, 86
American Sampler, 240
American Sightseeing Atlanta, 122
Amsterdam Walk, 84
Amtrak, 14, 194
amusement parks, 14
Andre's, 317
Andretti Speed Lab, 224
Andrews Upstairs, 139
Angel, The, 160–61
Anis Cafe and Bistro, 130
Ann Jackson Gallery, 239
Anna Lee's, 234
Annie Clinton Farms and Nature Preserve, 272
Annual Cowboy Poets Gathering, 275
Annual Cumming Steam, Antique Tractor, and Gas Engine Exposition, 242
Annual Easter Sunrise Service at Stone Mountain Park, 190
Annual Watermelon Festival, 321
Ansley Inn Bed and Breakfast, 96
Ansley Park, 54, 83, 96
Ansley Park Playhouse, 109
Antebellum Brumby Hall and Gardens, 28, 31, 248
Anthony's Plantation Restaurant, 130–31
Anthony's Taxi, 297
Antica Posta, 131
Antique Car and Treasure Museum at Stone Mountain Park, 177
Antique Dealers Association of Marietta, 15
antiques, 15
Aqualand Marina, 33, 199–200
aquariums, 15
Arabia Mountain Trails, 31, 182
Archibald Smith Plantation Home, 218–19
Arden's Gardens, 76
area codes, 15–16
Aria, 131
Around Town Tours, 246, 266

art associations and councils, 16
Art Galleries of Historic Roswell, 239
Art in the Park, 263
art museums, 16
Art on the Historic Courthouse Square, 190
ART Station, 189
Arts at Emory, 163, 166
Arts Clayton Gallery, 281
Asian Square, 167
Atkins Park Tavern, 105, 231, 260
Atlanta Ambassador Force, 49
Atlanta Audubon Society, 18
Atlanta Ballet, 25, 107
Atlanta Bicycle Campaign, 18
Atlanta Black Arts Festival, 13
Atlanta Book Exchange, 111
Atlanta Botanical Garden, 28, 92–93, 95
Atlanta Braves, 40, 73–74
Atlanta Chinese Dance Company, 163
Atlanta Convention and Visitors Bureau, 30, 49, 117, 279
Atlanta Cyclorama and Civil War Museum, 34, 56–57
Atlanta Decorative Arts Center, 141
Atlanta Dogwood Festival, 26, 95, 113
Atlanta Falcons, 40, 74
Atlanta Falcons Headquarters and Training Facility, 201, 208
Atlanta Festival Ballet, 303
Atlanta Fish Market, 131
Atlanta Gay Men's Chorus, 109
Atlanta Grill, 69
Atlanta Hawks, 40, 74
Atlanta History Center, 28, 34, 123–24, 127
Atlanta Hotel Connections, 147
Atlanta Jazz Festival, 26, 35, 78, 95, 113
Atlanta Link, 81
Atlanta Marriott Alpharetta, 229
Atlanta Memorial Park, 36, 127–28
Atlanta Metropolitan Statiscal Area (MSA), 17
Atlanta Motor Speedway and Gift Store, 17, 300–301, 305
Atlanta Opera, 25, 107
Atlanta Preservation Center Tours, 30, 54, 84, 122
Atlanta Pride Festival, 95
Atlanta Silverbacks, 40, 165

Atlanta South RV Resort, 302–3
Atlanta South Taxi, 304
Atlanta State Farmer's Market, 27, 293
Atlanta Steeplechase, 32
Atlanta Symphony Orchestra, 25, 34, 107, 138
Atlanta Thrashers, 40, 74
Atlanta University, 13
Atlanta West Campground, 274
Atlanta Wind Symphony, 237
Atlanta/Frazier Street Historic District, 247
Atlanta's Chinatown Shopping Square, 167
Atlantic Limousine Service, 40
Atlantic Lyric Theatre, Ballethnic Dance Company, 109
Atlantic Station, 83
AtlanTIX, 25, 49, 117
Atmosphere, 103
attractions: hours of operation, 17, 32; rates, 37; worth driving for, 44–45
Au Pied de Cochon, 131, 137
Austell, 267, 270, 271
auto racing, 17, 198, 300–301, 313
Autrey Mill Nature Preserve and Heritage Center, 226
Autumn Artfest on the Courthouse Square, 191
Autumn Oaks Arts and Crafts Festival and Battle of Jonesboro Civil War Reenactment, 295

B

Babette's, 102
Bacchanalia/Quinones at Bacchanalia, 99, 112
Backstreet Boutique, 142
Baker Woodlands/Hahn Woods/Lullwater/ Wesley Woods Forest, 156–57
Bald Ridge Creek Campground, 229
Balloons Over Georgia, 17, 224
Baraonda Café Italiano, 103
Barrington Hall, 31, 219
Barrow County, 195
Barrow County Chamber of Commerce, 194
Barrow County Museum, 197
Bass Pro Shops Outdoor World, 189
Battle of Atlanta Day, 169
Battle of Jonesboro, 37
Beach at Clayton County International Park, The, 15, 17, 285

Beach Party, 169

beaches, 17

Beacon Dance, 163

Bells Ferry Park, 256

Belly General Store, 105, 113

Beluga, 139

Benjamin Franklin Swanton House, 151

Bennett Park, 225

Bennett Street, Buckhead, 141

Bentley's Bed & Breakfast, 229

Best Gwinnett Taxi and Limo, A, 194

Best Western Granada Suites, 97

Best Western Shenandoah Inn, 317

Beverly Hills Inn, 129

bicycling: Braselton, 199; Buckhead, 125; Decatur, 154; Downtown, 63; East Point, 284–85; Mableton, 275; McDonough, 301; overview, 18, 36; Peachtree City, 285; Powder Springs, 275; Roswell, 222; Smyrna, 252; Stone Mountain, 178; Whitesburg, 313

Biffle Cabin, 151

Big Chicken and Big Chicken KFC, 25, 245, 259

Big Creek Greenway, 226

Big Haynes Creek Nature Center, 184

Biplane Rides Over Atlanta, 14, 154

bird-watching, 18, 90, 154, 178

Bitsy Grant Tennis Center at Atlanta Memorial Park, 41, 127

Black Shoals Park, 184

Black World Music Series, 143–44

Blackburn Tennis Center and Park, 41, 155

Blackfriars of Agnes Scott College, 165

Blind Willie's, 107–8

Blue and Gray Trail, 25

Blue Heron Nature Preserve, 128

Blue Moon Stable, 314

Blue Sky Concerts, 169

Blue Willow Inn, 187

Bluepointe, 131

Board of Trade Fine Consignments, The, 238

boating. See also canoeing, kayaking, tubing, white-water rafting; sailing: Buckhead and Vinings, 125; Buford, 200; Chattahoochee River, 18–19; Decatur, 155; Flowery Branch, 199–200; Lake Lanier Islands, 200; Stone Mountain Park, 179

Bobby Jones Golf Course at Atlanta Memorial Park, 29, 91, 126

Boisfeuillet Jones Atlanta Civic Center, 41, 109

Bolling Way, 122

Bona Allen Mansion, 207

Bone Shakers Bicycle Shop, 275

Bone's, 131–32

Bonsai Trees Intl. Co., 240

books: antiquarian, 15; bird-watching, 18; camping, 21; hiking/walking, 31; mountain biking, 34; set in the city or state, 19, 213

Boxwoods Gardens and Gifts, 142

Brake Pad, The, 290

Braselton, 195, 197, 198, 204, 205–6, 207

Braves Chop House, 56

Braves Clubhouse Store, 56

Braves Stadium Shuttle, 50

Brina Beads, 142

Broadway in Atlanta, 41

Brookhaven, 118

Brookwood Hills, 118–19

Brookwood RV Resort Park, 257

Brumby Chair Company, The, 28, 262

Brunswick U.S. Play, 253

BUC (Buckhead's Uptown Connection), 19, 20

Buckhead and Vinings/Atlanta: dining, 130–37; to do, 125–27; entertainment, 137–40; getting around, 118; getting there, 117–18; green space, 127–28; lodging, 129–30; map, 116; medical emergencies, 118; overview, 115–17; parking, 118; public restrooms, 118; to see, 120–25; shopping, 140–43; special events, 143–44; tourist information/guidance, 117; villages and neighborhoods, 118–20

Buckhead Business Association, 117

Buckhead Coalition, 117

Buckhead Design Center, 141

Buckhead Diner, 132

Buckhead Forest, 119

Buckhead Safety Cab, 118

Buford, 195–96, 200, 202, 205, 207

Buford Highway, 153

Buford Highway Farmer's Market, 27, 168

Buford Trout Hatchery, 217–18

Buggy Shop Museum, 310–11

Bullfrog's Bar and Grille, 206

Bulloch Hall, 31, 219–20, 234

Burdett Tennis Center, 287
bus/rail service, 19–21
Busy Bee Café, 71
Butterfly Festival, 169
Byblos, 234–35
B-52's, 292

C

C. Dickens, 15, 142
Cabbagetown, 50–51, 70–71
Cabernet, 230
Café Alsace, 161
Café at the Ritz-Carlton Buckhead, The, 132
Café Intermezzo, 136
Café Lily, 161
Callanwolde Fine Arts Center, 149–50
Camp Bulloch, 224–25
Camp Yesteryear, 225
campgrounds: Acworth, 257; Astell, 274; Buford,
    205; Conyers, 186; Cumming, 229; Lake
    Lanier Islands, 205; Marietta, 257;
    McDonough, 302–3; Stone Mountain Park,
    186; Whitesburg, 317; Winder, 205
camping, 21
Candler Park and Golf Course, 29, 51, 65, 71, 91
Cannonball Trail, The, 26, 251
Canoe, 132–33
canoeing, kayaking, tubing, white-water rafting,
    21, 125, 155, 222, 253, 313
Capitol City Opera, 25, 137–38
Cappella Books, 76
car rentals, 21–22
carriage tours, 22, 63, 253
Catfish Hollow, 318
Cathedral Bookstore, 142
cemeteries, 22
Centennial Olympic Park, 36, 65–66
Center for Puppetry Arts, 22, 86–87, 109
Center Stage Atlanta, 107
Central Park, 223, 225, 227
Chamblee, 154, 163, 167
Chamblee Antique Dealers Association, 15
Chamblee's Antique Row/Broad Street Antique
    Mall, 167
Champps Americana, 233
Chandlery, The, 240

Charles Wadsworth and Friends Concert, 320
Charleston Park, 227
Chastain Arts and Crafts Center, 121
Chastain Memorial Park and Tennis Center, 36,
    41, 127, 128
Chastain Park Amphitheater, 34, 35, 107, 138
Chastain Park Trail, 31, 125
Chatahoochee-Flint Heritage Highway, 312
Chateau Elan Golf Courses, 201–2
Chateau Elan Summer Concert Series, 34
Chateau Elan Vineyard Fest, 209
Chateau Elan Winery and Resort, 30, 38, 44,
    198, 199
Chattahoochee Handweavers Guild, 24
Chattahoochee Nature Center, 35, 226–27
Chattahoochee River: boating, 18–19, 155, 252;
    fishing, 155, 253; overview, 22, 39, 124, 216
Chattahoochee River National Recreation Area
    (CRNRA): bird-watching, 154, 252;
    Bowman's Island Unit, 224, 226; East and
    West Palisades Unit, 128; hiking, 254–55;
    Island Fort Unit, 157–58; mountain biking,
    34; overview, 35, 39, 124–25; Vickery Creek
    Unit, 221, 223, 228
Chattahoochee River Outfitters, 21, 222, 253
Chattahoochee River Park, 228
Chattahoochee-Oconee National Forests, 33, 35
Cheesecake Factory, The, 136
Cherokee Music Company, 240
Cherokee Run Golf Club, 181
Chick-fil-A Bowl Parade/Chick-fil-A Bowl, 79
Chief Vann House Historic Site, 35
Chieftans Museum and Major Ridge Home, 35
children and families, to see and do: Austell,
    270–71; Braselton, 197; Buford, 201;
    Conyers, 175; Cumming, 217–18; Decatur,
    155; Downtown, 53–54, 63–65; Fayetteville,
    285; Flowery Branch, 201; Jonesboro,
    281–82, 285; Kennesaw, 253; Lake Lanier
    Islands, 201; Lawrenceville, 179–80; Lilburn,
    176; Locust Grove, 299–300; Marietta,
    253–54; McDonough, 301; overview, 22;
    Powder Springs, 271; Roswell, 223, 224–25;
    Stone Mountain Park, 175, 180
Children's at Egleston, 148
Children's Healthcare of Atlanta at Scottish Rite,
    215

Children's Healthcare of Atlanta Children's Christmas Parade, 26, 79

China Cooks, 236

Chris and Merry Carlos Horse Park and Stables at Chastain, 126

Christmas at Callanwolde, 150

Christmas in Roswell, 242

Church Street Market, 262

Church/Cherokee Historic District, 247

Churchill Grounds, 108

City Club Marietta, 254

City Gallery at Chastain Park, 122

City Grill, 69

City of Decatur Walking Tour, 42, 153

City of Stockbridge Municipal Park, 287–88

city parks, 36

City Segway Tours-Atlanta, 30, 54

City Walk, 238

CityPass, 22–23

Civil War sites, 23, 37

Clairmont Historic District, 149

Clark Atlanta University Art Galleries, 52–53

Clark Community Park, 288

Classic Chastain, 138

Clayton County Convention and Visitors Bureau/ Jonesboro Depot Welcome Center, 279

Clayton County Schools Performing Arts Center, 292

climate, 44

Clyde Shepherd Nature Preserve, 157

Coal Mountain Park, 225

Cobb Community Transit, 20, 246, 267

Cobb County Convention and Visitors Bureau, 245, 266

Cobb County Department of Parks, Recreation and Cultural Affairs, 25, 255–56, 271–72

Cobb County Parks, Recreation, and Cultural Affairs, 271, 272

Cobb County parks, Recreation and Cultural Affairs, 256

Cobb Energy Performing Arts Center, 107

Cobb Playhouse and Studio, 261

Cobb Symphony Orchestra, 260

Coca-Cola Café, 124

Coca-Cola Roxy Theater, The, 140

Cochran Ball Park, 288

Cochran Mill Nature Center, 288

Cold Stone Creamery, 162

Cole Town Historic District, 309

Collectors' Corner, 319–20

College Park, 280, 286, 287, 289, 290

College Park Golf Course, 286

College-Temple Historic District, 309

Collier Hills-Ardmore Park, 119

Collins Avenue Historic District, 247

Colonial Homes, 119

Colors Festival of Arts, 241

Columbia Barrow Medical Center, 195

Comfort Inn, 317

Commerce Factory Stores, 26

Community Alliance of Stage and Theater/Whistlestop Players, 275

Conant Performing Arts Center, 140

Concerts by the Springs, 216, 241

Concerts on the Plaza, 276

Concerts on the Square, 169

Concord Covered Bridge Historic District, 24, 248

Confederate Hall Historical and Environmental Education Center at Stone Mountain Park, 177

Confederate Lion statue, 59

Continental Coffee and Sweets, 188

Conyers, 174, 175, 177, 181, 182, 183, 184, 186, 187–88

Conyers Cherry Blossom Festival, 174, 190

Conyers Convention and Visitors Bureau/Conyers Welcome Center, 173

Cookies by Design, 240

Cool Beans Coffee Roasters, 260

Corner Café, 136

counties, 24

Country Inn and Suites, 317

covered bridges, 24, 175, 216, 248

Cowboys Atlanta, 261

Coweta County African American Heritage Museum and Research Center, 311

Coweta County Convention and Visitors Bureau and Welcome Center, 307

Coweta County Fairgrounds, 315

Crabapple, 216

Crash and Burn, 142

Criminal Records, 77
Crossroads at Stone Mountain Park, 180
cruises, 24
Cubihatcha Outdoor Center/Towaliga River
Preserve, 35, 302
Culpepper House Bed and Breakfast, 310, 316
Cultural Arts Center of Douglasville/Douglas
County, 268–69, 275
cultural events: current information, 24–25;
tickets, 25
cultural sites: Buckhead, 121; Buford, 196;
Decatur, 149–50; Douglasville, 268–69;
Downtown, 52–53; Jonesboro, 281;
Kennesaw, 248; Midtown, 84; Roswell, 217;
Sandy Springs, 217
Cumming Playhouse, 237
Cumming-Forsyth County Chamber of
Commerce, 214
curiosities, 25

D
Dabney-Hunter-Simmons Memorial Park, 288
Dahlonega, 221–22
dance, 107, 163, 188, 260, 303
Dante's Down the Hatch, 139
Dave and Buster's, 259
Davidson-Arabia Mountain Nature Preserve and
Heritage Area, 35, 185
Dawsonville, 221
day camps, 125
Daytime Transportation, 173, 246, 266
Decatur: dining, 159–63; to do, 154–56; enter-
tainment, 163–66; getting around, 147; get-
ting there, 147; green space, 156–58; lodging,
158–59; map, 146; medical emergencies,
148; overview, 145; parking, 147; to see,
149–54; shopping, 166–68; special events,
168–70; tourist information/guidance, 145;
villages/neighborhoods, 148–49
Decatur Arts Festival and Garden Tour, 168–69
Decatur Cemetery, 151
Decatur Civic Chorus, 163
Decatur Holiday Candlelight Tour of Homes, 170
DeKalb Choral Guild, 163
DeKalb Convention and Visitors Bureau, 145
DeKalb County Parks and Recreation, 155–56

DeKalb Greenway Trails, 157
DeKalb Medical Center at Decatur, 148
DeKalb Medical Center at Hillandale, 174
DeKalb Symphony Orchestra, 25, 163–64
Delta Airlines Summer Chastain Series, 138
Department of Music/Kennesaw State
University, 260
Department of Theatre and Performance
Studies/Kennesaw State University, 261
di Paolo Cucina, 233
dick and harry's, 232–33
Dick Lane Velodrome, 284–85
Dick's Sporting Goods, 126
Dining Room at the Ritz-Carlton Buckhead, The,
132, 133
dining/restaurants: hours of operation, 17, 26;
overview, 25, 38–39; prices, 25; rates, 37
disc golf, 179, 223
Discover Mills, 189
Discovering Stone Mountain Museum at
Memorial Hall in Stone Mountain Park, 178
Dixieland Fun Park, 14, 285
Dog Days, 142
Don White Memorial Park, 228
Doraville, 167
Dorsey Studios and Theater, 165
DoubleTree Hotel Atlanta/Roswell, 229
Douglas County Local Welcome Center, 265
Douglas County Museum of History and Art, 269
Douglasville, 267, 268–69, 274
Douglasville Convention and Visitors Bureau
and Welcome Center, 265
Down South Treasures Museum Shop, 293
Downtown/Atlanta: dining, 69–72; to do, 63–65;
entertainment, 72–75; getting around,
49–50; getting there, 49; green space,
65–67; lodging, 67–68; map, 48; medical
emergencies, 50; overview, 47; parking, 50;
public restrooms, 50; to see, 52–63; shopping, 75–77; special events, 77–79; tourist
information/guidance, 49; tourist seasons,
50; villages and neighborhoods, 50–52
Dream Gardens of Dunwoody Tour, 169
Dreamland Barbecue, 235
driving, traffic and highway tips, 41–42
driving tours, 25–26
Druid Hills, 54, 148

DUKW amphibious vehicles, 24
Duluth, 196, 197, 207–8, 208–9
Dunaway Gardens, 28, 314
Dunwoody Nature Center and Nature Preserve, 157–58
DuPre's, 262

E

EARL, The, 164
East Atlanta Strut, 169
East Atlanta Village, 148–49, 162, 166
East Point, 280, 284–85, 290, 291
East Roswell Park, 223, 225
Eclipse di Luna, 136
Eddie's Attic, 164
Eddie's Trick Shop, 262
Edible Expressions, 235
1890 King-Keith House Bed and Breakfast, 67
Ellis Hotel, The, 67
Embassy Limousine, 194
Emerald Pointe Golf Club, 202
Emerald Pointe Resort, 30, 38, 206
emergencies, medical, 26
Emory Conference Center Hotel, 158–59
Emory Crawford Long Hospital, 50
Emory Inn Atlanta Bed and Breakfast, 159
Emory University Hospital, 148
Emory-Adventist Hospital, 246, 267
Equestrian Center at Chateau Elan, 197
equestrian events, 197, 217
ESPN Zone, 139
Eternity Limousine Service, 308
Etowah Indian Mounds Historic Site, 35
Euclid Avenue Yacht Club, 73
Eurasia, 159
events. *See* festivals and events
Executive Priority Limousine Service, 40
Express Trolley Tour, 42

F

fab'rik, 111
factory outlets, 26
Fadó Irish Pub, 122, 139
Fair Oaks Park, 256
Fairburn, 280, 283, 292

Fairburn City Hall, 279
Fairlie-Poplar Historic District, 51
Fall Festival, 264
Fall Festival and Chili Cook-Off, 305
fall foliage, 26–27
Falling For Henry Fine Arts Festival, 295
Farmer's Market, Cumming, 240
farmer's markets, 27
Farmhouse at the Inn at Serenbe, The, 289–90
Fashionista Week, 143
Fay Gold Gallery, 141
Fayette County Chamber of Commerce, 279
Fayette-Coweta Family Theatre, 292
Fayetteville, 280, 283, 284, 285, 286, 291–92, 293
Fayetteville Golf Club, 286
Federal Reserve Bank of Atlanta Visitors Center and Monetary Museum, 87
Feed Store, The, 289
Fellini's Pizza, 122
Fernbank Café, 161
Fernbank Museum of Natural History, 34, 151–52
Fernbank Science Center, 152
Ferst Center for the Arts, Georgia Institute of Technology, 109
festivals and events, 26
Fifth Street Bridge, 89
Filene's Basement, 26, 143
Fina, Your Italian Bistro, 290
fire permits, 27
First Impressions, 297
fishing: Cumming, 223; Decatur, 155; guide services, 28; Lawrenceville, 200; Lithia Springs, 270; Midtown, 90–91; overview, 27–28, 126; Roswell, 223; Stone Mountain Park, 179
Fishing at Lake Lanier with Bill Vanderford, 200
Fishing for Kids!, 155
Flat Creek Nature Center, 288
Flatiron, The, 164
Flint River, 39
Floataway Café, 112, 159–60
Flowery Branch, 193, 196, 197, 199–200, 204, 208
Flowery Branch Historic Train Depot Museum and Historic Caboose, 197
Flying Biscuit Café, 71

Fogo de Chao, 133
Folk Art Park, 53
Folk Tales on the Rails, 264
Forest Park, 290–91, 293
Forsyth County Fair, 13, 242
Forsyth County Parks and Recreation, 227
Fort Mountain State Park, 35
Fort Peachtree, 122
Fort Yargo State Park, 21, 23, 24, 36
Fort Yargo State Park and Will-A-Way Recreation
    Area, 202, 203–4, 205
Forty Oaks Nature Preserve, 157
Foster House, The, 231–32
Founders Cemetery, 220
Four Seasons Hotel Atlanta, 97
Fourth in the Park, 263
Fourth of July Golf Cart Parade, 294
Fox Theatre, 31, 41, 54, 109–10
Frabel Art Glass, 28–29
Frabel Gallery, 141–42
Fratelli di Napoli, 235
Frederick Brown Jr. Amphitheater, 291
Freedom Parkway Trail, 31, 63
French/American Brasserie, 133
Fresh Express Trolley Tour, 292
frights, 28, 181, 271, 286, 314
Fritti Restaurant, 105
Frock of Ages, 76
Frogtown Cellars, 44
From Civil War to Civil Rights Tour, 55, 60
Front Page News, 72, 103–4
fruit/berry picking, 28, 301
Fullers Park, 256
Fun Town of Henry County, 14, 301
Funk Heritage Center and Appalachian
    Settlement, 35

G

Galleria Direct, 246, 266
Galleria Specialty Mall, 263
Garden Hills, 119
Garden House Bed and Breakfast, 158
gardens: Buckhead, 127; Conyers, 184; Decatur,
    156; Downtown, 65–67; Loganville, 184;
    Midtown, 92–93; Newnan, 314–15; overview,
    28

Gardner Park, 288
Gaslight Inn Bed & Breakfast, 96–97
Gay, Mary Ann Harris, 151
George's Bar and Restaurant, 106
Georgia Antiques and Design Center, 167
Georgia Aquarium, 15, 53–54
Georgia Association of Agricultural Fairs, 13
Georgia Association of Museums and Galleries,
    16
Georgia Atlas and Gazetteer, 33
Georgia Ballet, 260
Georgia Basketry Association, 24
Georgia Bicycle Federation, 18
Georgia Bikes, 18
Georgia Capitol Museum, 57, 61
Georgia Council for the Arts, 16
Georgia Department of Economic
    Development's Tourism Division, 17, 32, 33
Georgia Department of Natural Resources,
    Environmental Protection Division, 33
Georgia Department of Transportation, 33
Georgia Dome, 55
Georgia Ensemble Theater, 238
Georgia Film, Video & Music Office, 27
Georgia Force, 40, 74
Georgia Grown Visitors Center and Gifts, 293
Georgia Institute of Technology Campus Tours,
    30, 84–85
Georgia International Horse Park, 86, 175, 182,
    183, 186
Georgia Music Hall of Fame at Discover Mills,
    178
Georgia Perimeter Native Plant Garden and
    Wildflower Center of Georgia, 28, 156
Georgia Philharmonic Orchestra, 237
Georgia Public Broadcasting, 29
Georgia Renaissance Festival, 293–94
Georgia Shakespeare Festival, 41, 140
Georgia State Archives/National Archives
    Southeast Region, 286
Georgia State Capitol, 31, 57
Georgia Tech Hotel and Conference Center, 98
Georgia Tech Technology Square Trolley, 19, 20,
    82
Georgia Tennis Hall of Fame, 127
Georgia Thoroughbred Owners and Breeders
    Association, 32

Georgia Wine Council, 44

Georgia Wine Country, 44

Georgia Wine Highway, 44

Georgian Grill, The, 274

Georgian Terrace Hotel, 97–98

Georgia's Antique Trail, 15

Geranium Festival, 305

Ghost Talk-Ghost Walk, 218

ghost tours, 29

Gladys Knight and Ron Winans' Chicken and
   Waffles, 104

Glenn Hotel, The, 67–68

Glenn Hotel Restaurant and Bar, The, 69

Glorious Events, 138

Glover Park Concert Series, 34, 263

Golden's on the Square, 318

golf: Braselton, 201–2; Buckhead, 126; College
   Park, 286; Conyers, 181; Decatur, 155;
   Downtown, 65; Fayetteville, 286; Jonesboro,
   286; Lake Lanier Islands, 201; Marietta, 254;
   Midtown, 91; overview, 29–30; Stockbridge,
   286; Stony Mountain Park, 181–82

Golf Academy at Chateau Elan, 202

Golf Villas at Chateau Elan Winery and Resort,
   The, 205

Gone With the Wind Driving Tour of Homes, 26,
   284

Goodwin Home, 123

Governor's Mansion, 31, 123

Grady Memorial Hospital, 50

Grand Hyatt Atlanta, 129

Grant Park, 36, 51, 54, 66

Grantville, 310, 312, 319

Grantville Day, 321

Grassroots Girls, 209

Gray Line Tours, 30

Great American Cover-Up Annual Quilt Show, 241

Great Barn at Stone Mountain Park, The, 180

Great Decatur Beer Tasting Festival, 170

Great Gatsby's Auction Gallery, 167

Great Georgia Air Show, The, 295

Great Restorations Day Spa, 202

Greater Atlanta Shuttle, 215

Green Market at Piedmont Park, 112

Green Sprout, 104

Greenville Street/LaGrange Historic District,
   309

Greenwood's on Green Street, 235

Greyhound Bus Lines, 19

Grimes Bridge Skate Park, 224

Gritz Family Restaurant, 303

Groove with the Grapes/Chateau Elan Summer
   Concert Series, 209

guidance. See tourist information/guidance

guided tours, 30, 54–56, 84–85, 122, 176, 218,
   282–83

Gumbeaux's-A Cajun Café, 274

Gwinnett Airport Shuttle, 173

Gwinnett Ballet Theatre, 188

Gwinnett Choral Guild, 164

Gwinnett Classic Limousine, 194

Gwinnett Community Symphony Orchestra, 164

Gwinnett Convention and Visitors Bureau, 145,
   193

Gwinnett County, 195

Gwinnett County Transit, 20, 174

Gwinnett Gladiators, 40, 165

Gwinnett Historic Courthouse/Georgia Veterans
   Council War Museum, 176–77

Gwinnett History Museum, 178

Gwinnett Philharmonic, 25, 188

Gwinnett Shuttle, 147

Gwinnett Transit, 194–95

H

Halloween Hayride and Family Festival, 28, 286

Halloween Hikes, 242

Hamilton's, 258

Hammonds House Galleries and Resource
   Center for African American Art, 13, 61–62

Hampton Inn, 317

Hancock and Hartwell, 142–43

handicapped access, 30

Hank Aaron statue, 56

Hapeville, 280–81, 291, 292

Happy Days, 294

Haralson Mill Covered Bridge, 24, 175

Harbor Landing, 33, 200

Harbor Landings Houseboats, 206–7

Hard Rock Café, 71

Harold Nash Lake Lanier Striper and Bass
   Fishing Guide Service, 200

Harrison Park, 256

Harry's Farmer's Market, 27, 240
Hartsfield-Jackson Atlanta International Airport and Visitor Center, 14, 30, 49, 117, 279
Haven Restaurant and Bar, 133
Hawthorn Suites Golf Resort, 186
Haynes Manor, 119
Haynes Manor Park and Memorial Park Trail, 128
Heartfield Manor, 67
Heaven Blue Rose Contemporary Gallery, 239
Hembree Park, 225
Hemingway's Tropical Bar and Grill, 259–60
Henry County Chamber of Commerce, Convention and Visitors Bureau and Welcome Center, 279, 297
Henry Medical Center, 280, 298
Henry Players, The, 304
Henry Singers, The, 304
Heritage Park, 300
Heritage Sandy Springs, 213
Herndon Home, 13, 57–58
Hidden Acres Nature Preserve, 185
HiFi Buys Amphitheatre, 34, 35, 291
High Museum of Art, 16, 22, 87–88
Highland Games, 191
Highland Inn, The, 99
Highland Woodworking, 112
hiking/walking/running. *See also* walking tours: books, 31; Buckhead, 129; Kennesaw, 255; Lithonia, 182; Marietta, 254–55; Midtown, 91; overview, 30–31; Powder Springs, 271–72; Roswell, 223; Smyrna, 255; Stone Mountain Park, 182
Historic Buford/Tannery Row Artist Colony, 196
Historic College Park Arts Festival, 294–95
Historic Complex of the DeKalb Historical Society, 31, 151
Historic Crabapple Antique Village, 238
Historic Downtown Alpharetta, 238
Historic Downtown Atlanta, 54
Historic Fayetteville Walking Tour, 284
Historic Grantville Driving Tour, 26, 312
historic homes and sites: Alpharetta, 220; Buckhead, 122–23; Conyers, 177; Decatur, 151; Downtown, 56–61; Hampton, 300; Jonesboro, 283; Kennesaw, 248–49; Lawrenceville, 176–77; Mableton, 269;

Marietta, 248, 249, 251–52; McDonough, 300; Midtown, 85–86; overview, 31; Roswell, 218–20; Sandy Springs, 220; Stone Mountain Park, 177; Villa Rica, 269
Historic Mansell House and Gardens, 220
Historic Oakland Cemetery, 22, 31, 58–59
Historic Roswell Antique Market, 238
Historic Roswell Convention and Visitors Bureau/Visitor Center, 213
Historic Shops of Crabapple, 216, 238
Historic Site Annual Pass, 36
Historic Sycamore Street, 149
Historic Tours, Roswell, 218
history, 10–11
History Camps, 151
Holiday Bonfire and Marshmallow Roast, 170
Holiday Harbor Marina, Campsites and Resort, 33, 257
Holiday in Lights, 66, 79
Holiday Inn Express, 317
Holiday Marina on Lake Lanier, 33, 200
Holliday-Dorsey-Fife House, 283
Horace W. Sturgis Library Art Gallery/Kennesaw State University Art Gallery, 248
Horizon Theater, 74
Horror Hill Haunted Trail and Vertigo Haunted Trail, 28, 314
horse racing, 32
horseback riding, 32, 125, 126, 182, 202, 224, 314
Horseradish Grill, 133–34
Horsin' Around Summer Horse Camps, 125
Hospitality Highway: Sandy Springs, Roswell, Alpharetta, Cumming, and Points North: dining, 230–37; to do, 222–26; entertainment, 237–38; getting around, 214–15; getting there, 214; green space, 226–29; lodging, 229; map, 212; medical emergencies, 215; overview, 211–13; parking, 215; public restrooms, 215; to see, 216–22; shopping, 238–40; special events, 241–42; tourist information/guidance, 213–14; villages/neighborhoods, 215–16
Hotel Indigo-Atlanta Midtown, 98
Houston Mill House, 160
Howard Johnson, 317
Huey's, 136

Hughes Spalding Children's Hospital, 50
hunting, 32
Hurt Road Park, 256

I

Ice Forum at Town Center, 255
Imagine It! The Children's Museum of Atlanta,
  22, 54
Imperial Fez, 134
In the Fullness of Time, 295
Indian Festival, 191
Inman Park, 51–52, 54, 67
Inman Park Festival and Tour of Homes, 78
Inn at Chateau Elan Winery and Resort, The,
  205–6
Inn at Serenbe, The, 27, 289
Inside CNN Atlanta Studio Tour, 55
InterContinental Buckhead, 129
International Association of Fairs and
  Expositions, 26
International Farmer's Market, Chamblee, 27
International Farmers Market, Norcross, 168
International House of Pancakes, 137
Interstate Airport Jitney, 246
Irby, Henry, 116
Irby's Tavern, 116
It's a Wonderful House, 209
Ivan Allen Jr. Braves Museum and Hall of Fame,
  56, 63–64

J

J. Alexander's, 160
Jam Sessions at the Roswell Visitors Center, 237
Jameson Inn, 317
Japanese Garden, 28
Java Monkey, 162–63
Java Vino, 107
Jennie T. Anderson Theatre, 261
Jewish Theater of the South/Marcus Jewish
  Community Center of Atlanta, 41, 165
Jimmy Carter Presidential Library and Museum,
  28, 34, 62, 65
Joan Glancey Memorial Hospital, 195
Jocada Museum of Jazz History, 269
Joël, 134

Joe's, 162
Joe's on Juniper, 104
John A. Williams Theatre at the Cobb Energy
  Centre for the Performing Arts, 261
John Howell Park, 93
John Ripley Forbes Big Trees Forest Preserve,
  227
Johnny Mercer Collection/Georgia State
  University, 53
Johnny's Hideaway, 139
Jonesboro, 281–84, 285, 286, 292, 293
Jonesboro Depot Welcome Center/Road to Tara
  Museum Gift Shop, 293
July Fourth Festivities and Steam Tractor Parade,
  241
July 4th fireworks, Buckhead, 143
Junkman's Daughter, 77
JW Marriott Buckhead Atlanta, 121, 129–30

K

Kangaroo Conservation Center, 44, 45
kayaking. *See* canoeing, kayaking, tubing, white-
  water rafting
Kedron Fieldhouse and Aquatic Center, 287
Keep Georgia Beautiful, 33
Kennesaw, 245, 247, 248–49, 250, 251, 253, 255,
  259
Kennesaw Fall Antique Festival, 264
Kennesaw Mountain, 34
Kennesaw Mountain National Battlefield Park,
  23, 36, 248–49, 251, 255
Kenny's Alley at Underground Atlanta, 73
King Center for Non-Violent Social Change, 13,
  60
King Plow Arts Center/Actors' Express Theatre
  Company, 75
King Week, 77
Kreature Komforts of Marietta, 262–63
Kudzu Flea Market, 168
Kudzu Playhouse of Roswell, 238
KYMA, 134

L

La Grotta, 134
Lake Acworth, 247, 256

Lake Allatoona, 33, 247

Lake Clara Meer, 90–91

Lake Houses on Lanier, The, 205

Lake Lanier, 33

Lake Lanier Area: dining, 207–8; to do, 198–203; entertainment, 208; getting around, 194–95; getting there, 194; green spaces, 203–4; lodging, 204–7; map, 194; medical emergencies, 195; overview, 193; parking, 195; to see, 196–98; shopping, 208–9; special events, 209; tourist information/guidance, 193–94; villages/neighborhoods, 195–96

Lake Lanier Islands: boating, 200; for children and families, 201; dining, 206, 208; golf, 201–2; lodging, 205, 206–7; spas, 202

Lake Lanier Islands Beach and Water Park, 14, 17, 201

Lake Lanier Islands Campground, 205

Lake Lanier Islands Equestrian Center, 32, 202

Lake Lanier Lodges, Boat Rentals, 200

Lake Spivey Golf Club, 286

lakes, most significant, 33

Landmark Diner, 137

Landmarks Through History Tour, 30, 282

Lanier Flight Center, 201

Lanier National Speedway, 17, 198

Lanier Sailing Academy, 40, 202

LaQuinta Inn, 317

Larry Bell Park, 256

Larry's Lanier Guide Services, 200

Las Americas, 167

Lasershow Spectacular at Stone Mountain Park, 26, 188

Lawrenceville, 174, 176–77, 178, 179–80, 189

Lawrenceville Tourism and Trade Association, 173

Le Clos at Chateau Elan Winery and Resort, 207

Lenox Square and Visitor Center, 117, 140–41

Lenox Towers, 121

Lewis Grizzard Museum, 311–12

Lewis-Vaughn Botanical Garden, 28, 184

"Light Up" Senoia, 321

Lilburn, 174–75

Lilburn Daze Arts and Crafts Festival, 175, 191

Limerick Junction, 108

limousines. *See* shuttles/limousines

Links Golf Club, 286

Lionel Hampton Trail, 31

Lithonia, 179, 182

litter control laws, 33

Little Billie's Strawberry Farm, 301

Little Five Points, 52, 72

Lobby at TWELVE, The, 100

Lodges at Historic Banning Mills Country Inn, Executive Retreat and Spa, The, 317

lodging: bed and breakfasts, 17–18, 27; cottage rentals, 23–24; current inventory, 33; inns, 33; rates, 37; resorts, 38; special, 40

Log Cabin Hour, 151

Lost Mill Workers of Roswell Monument, 220

Lost Mountain Park, 272

Lunch on the Main, 290

Lynne Farris Gallery, 75

M

Mable House, 269

Mable House Barnes Amphitheatre, 35, 274–75

Macy's Great Tree Lighting, 144

Madras Saravan Bhavan, 161

Magical Nights of Lights, 209

Main Street Antique Market, 239

Main Street Stone Mountain Village Self-Guided Walking Tour, 176

M.A.K. Local Historic District, 149

Male Academy Museum, 312

Malibu Grand Prix Family Entertainment Center, 14, 155

Manuel's Tavern, 106

maps, 33

March to the Sea Heritage Trail, 25

Margaret Mitchell House and Museum, 31, 85, 95

Margaret Mitchell Playhouse/Antique Funeral Museum, 281–82

Marietta: dining, 258–60; to do, 252–56; entertainment, 260–62; getting around, 246; getting there, 246; green space, 256; lodging, 257–58; map, 244; medical emergencies, 246; overview, 243–44; parking, 246; public restrooms, 246; to see, 248–52; shopping, 262–63; special events, 263–64; tourist information/guidance, 245; villages/neighborhoods, 247–48

Marietta Antique Street Festival, 263
Marietta Confederate Cemetery/Marietta City
    Cemetery, 22, 251
Marietta Conference Center and Resort, 38,
    257–58
Marietta Fire Museum, 249
Marietta *Gone with the Wind* Movie
    Museum/Scarlett on the Square, 250
Marietta Heritage Passport, 249
Marietta Museum of History, 250
Marietta National Cemetery, 251
Marietta Pilgrimage Christmas Home Tour, 264
Marietta Square/Glover Park, 251–52
Marietta Welcome Center and Visitors Bureau,
    245
Marietta/Cobb Museum of Art, 16, 249
marinas, 33
Marriott Evergreen Conference Resort and Spa,
    186
Marriott Stone Mountain Inn, 186
Martin Luther King Jr. National Historic Site, 13,
    36, 59–60
Mary Gay House, 151
Mary Mac's Tea Room, 71–72
Mary's, 164–65
Masquerade, 73
mass transit. *See* bus/rail service
Matilda Bean, 290
Mayfield Dairy Farms, 197
McDonough, Hampton, Lovejoy and Locust
    Grove: dining, 303; to do, 300–302; enter-
    tainment, 303–4; getting around, 297; get-
    ting there, 297; green space, 302; lodging,
    302–3; map, 298; medical emergencies, 298;
    overview, 296–97; parking, 297; public rest-
    rooms, 297; to see, 299–300; shopping,
    304–5; special events, 305; tourist informa-
    tion/guidance, 297; villages/neighborhoods,
    298–99
McDonough Holiday Tour of Homes, 305
McDonough Hospitality and Tourism
    Bureau/McDonough Welcome Center, 297
McIntosh, Chief William, 315
McIntosh Reserve, 313, 315–16, 317
Medieval Times Dinner and Tournament, 26,
    179–80
Memorial Weekend "Task Force Patriot Salute to
    the Troops," 190
Merry Olde Marietta Christmas, A, 264
Metropolitan Atlanta Rapid Transit Authority
    (MARTA), 19, 20
Mezza a Lebanese Bistro, 161
Miami Circle Market Center, 141
Michael C. Carlos Museum of Emory University,
    16, 152–53
Midtown Art Walking Tour, 42, 95
Midtown/Atlanta: dining, 99–107; to do, 90–92;
    entertainment, 107–10; getting around, 82;
    getting there, 81; green space, 92–95; lodg-
    ing, 96–99; map, 82; medical emergencies,
    82; overview, 81; parking, 82; public rest-
    rooms, 82; to see, 84–90; shopping, 111–13;
    special events, 113; villages/neighborhoods,
    83–84
Midway Park, 225
Milsted 104 *Dinky* Steam Locomotive, 177
Milton Log Cabin, 220
Milton's Restaurant and Bar, 230
miniature golf, 182, 202, 255
Mitchell, Margaret, 85, 87
Mittie's Café, 233–34, 237
Mocha Delites, 291
Monarch Tower, 121
Monastery of the Holy Spirit, 177
Moonlight and Music Concert Series, 34, 190
Moreland, 310, 311–12, 313
Moreland Driving Tour, 313
Moreland Independence Day Barbecue, 321
Morningside/Lenox Park, 83
Morrow, 281, 286, 288, 291
Morrow Tourist Center, 279
Moss Blacksmith Shop, 240
mountain biking, 18, 34, 183
Mountain View Restaurant at the Stone
    Mountain Inn, 188
mountains, 34
Mountasia Family Fun Center, 14, 253–54
Murphy's, 106
Museum of Contemporary Art of Georgia, 16, 89
Museum of Design, 62
museums: Buckhead, 123–24; Decatur, 151–53;
    Douglasville, 269; Downtown, 54, 61–63;
    Duluth, 197; Fairburn, 283; Fayetteville, 283;
    Flowery Branch, 197; Jonesboro, 283–84;

Kennesaw, 250; Lawrenceville, 178; Marietta, 249–50; Midtown, 86–87; Moreland, 311–12; Newnan, 311, 312; overview, 34; Powder Springs, 269; Roswell, 220–21; Senoia, 310–11; Smyrna, 250; Stone Mountain Park, 177–78; Winder, 197

music: Buckhead, 137–38; concert series, 34; Decatur, 163–64; Downtown, 72–73; Fayetteville, 291–92; Kennesaw, 260; Mableton, 274–75; Marietta, 260; McDonough, 304; Midtown, 107; Morrow, 291; Norcross, 188; Peachtree City, 291; Roswell, 237; Stockbridge, 304

Music at Emory, 164

Music in the Park, 294

Music on the Square Summer Concert Series, 34, 305

My Favorite Things Antique Shop, 292

N

NAM, 100

Nan Thai Fine Dining, 100

Nash Farm Battlefield, 300

National Barrel Horse Association, 32

National Black Arts Festival, 26, 78–79, 113

National Museum of Patriotism, 34, 89

national parks, 36

Native American sites, 35

nature preserves and parks: Acworth, 256; Alpharetta, 226, 228; Braselton, 204; Buckhead, 127–28; Conyers, 184; Cumming, 226, 227–28; Decatur, 156–57; Hampton, 302; Lithia Springs, 273; Lithonia, 185; Locust Grove, 302; Marietta, 256, 272; Midtown, 93–95; Morrow, 288; Newnan, 315; overview, 35; Palmetto, 288; Peachtree City, 288; Powder Springs, 272, 273; Roswell, 226–27, 228; Sandy Springs, 227; Stockbridge, 287–88; Stone Mountain, 185; Whitesburg, 315–16; Winder, 203–4; Winston, 272

Nature Trails of Stone Mountain Park, 182

NAVA, 121, 134

Neighborhood Playhouse, 165

New American Shakespeare Tavern, 41, 110

New Echota Cherokee Capital Historic Site, 35

New Senoia Raceway, 313

New World of Coca-Cola, 34, 62–63

New Year's Eve Peach Drop, 79

New York Prime, 134

Newman Wetlands Center, 35, 302

Newnam Historic District, 309

Newnan: dining, 317–18; to do, 313–14; entertainment, 319; getting around, 308; getting there, 308; green space, 314–16; lodging, 316–17; map, 308; medical emergencies, 309; overview, 307; parking, 309; public restrooms, 309; to see, 310–13; shopping, 319–20; special events, 320–21; tourist information/guidance, 307; villages/neighborhoods, 309–10

Newnan Candlelight Tour of Homes, 321

Newnan Driving Tour, 313

Newnan Historic District, 309

Newnan Theatre Company, 319

Newnan-Coweta County Chamber of Commerce, 307

Nickajack Park, 272

nightlife: Buckhead and the Vinings, 139–40; Decatur, 164–65; Downtown, 73; Hapeville, 292; Kennesaw, 261; Midtown, 107–8; Newnan, 319

Nikolai's Roof, 69

Nino's Cucina Italiana, 134–35

Noah's Ark Animal Rehabilitation Center, 45, 299–300

Noodle, 161

Norcross, 149, 155, 160, 162, 164, 167, 168

Norcross Station Cafe, 162

Norman's Landing, 234

North Fulton Golf Course at Chastain Memorial Park, 29, 126

North Fulton Regional Medical Center, 215

North Fulton Tennis Center, 41, 225

North Georgia Premium Outlets, 26

North Georgia State Fair, 13, 252

North Villa Rica Commercial Historic District, 268

Northeast Georgia Medical Center, 195

Northeast Georgia Mountains Travel Association, 193

Northeast Georgia Welcome Center, 193

Northside Hospital, 215

Northside Hospital Forsyth, 195, 215
Northwest Atlanta Trail, 31
Northwest Marietta Historic District, 247
Notoberfest, 169
Nottingham Antiques and Reproductions, 141

O

Oak Grove Plantation and Gardens, 314–15, 316
Oakhurst, 149
Oakhurst Arts and Music Festival, 170
Oakwood Restaurant, 290–91
Oglethorpe University Museum of Art, 121
Old Campbell County Museum, 283
Old Courthouse Art Show/Taste of Fayette, 294
Old Courthouse on the Square/Jim Cherry
    Museum, 153
Old Dixie Highway, 25–26
Old Jail/Clayton County Historical Museum, 283
Old Mill Museum, 312
Old Soldier's Day Parade, 241–42
Old Stockbridge Days, 294
Old Town Beach Party, 190
Old-Fashioned Holiday Celebration, Candlelight
    Tour of Historic Homes, and Kris Kringle
    Market, 276
Olive and Fig, 240
Olmstead Linear Park, 157
Omni Hotel at CNN Center, 68
ONE.midtown kitchen, 104
Onstage Atlanta and Abracadabra Children's
    Theatre, 165
Oregon Park, 256
Orme Park, 93–94

P

Paddy's Irish Pub at Chateau Elan Winery and
    Resort, 207
Paddy's Taxi, 214
Paizano's Pizza and Pasta, 162
Palm Restaurant, The, 135
Palmetto, 281, 286, 288, 289–90, 292
Panola Mountain State Conservation Park, 35,
    36, 288
Pano's & Paul's, 135
Paolo's Gelato Italiano, 106

Pappy Red's Barbecue, 234
Paris on Ponce, 111
Park Café, 207–8
Park Tavern Brewery and Eatery, 95
Park 75 Restaurant, 100–101
parking, 35–36
ParkPass, 35–36
Parks, Recreation and Cultural Affairs of
    Atlanta, 128
Parsons, 240
Pastries a GoGo, 162
PATH Foundation, 30–31, 36
Patrick Cleburne Confederate Memorial
    Cemetery, 22, 283
Peach Festival Outlet Shops, 26
Peachtree Arts and Crafts Association, 24
Peachtree City, 281, 285, 287, 288, 291
Peachtree City Tennis Center, 41, 287
Peachtree Heights, 119–20
Peachtree Heights East, 120
Peachtree Highlands National Historic District,
    120
Peachtree Hills, 120
Peachtree Palisades East, 121
Peachtree Park, 120
Peachtree Peddlers Flea Market, 304
Peachtree Road Race, 95, 143
Peachtree Street, 89–90
Peacock Mansion, 120
Perk Place Coffee Shop, 291
Persepolis, 236
Pet Friendly Travel, 37
Peter Bonner's Historical and Hysterical Tours,
    282–83
pets, 36–37
Phipps Plaza, 141
Piece of Cake, 142
Pied Piper Parade, Concert, and Fireworks, 169
Piedmont Fayette Hospital, 280
Piedmont Hospital, 82, 118
Piedmont Newnan Hospital, 309
Piedmont Park, 36, 89, 90, 91–92, 94–95
Piercing Experience, 75
Pilgreen's on Lake Dow, 303
PineIsle Golf Course, 202
Pinnacle Park, 121, 128
Pittypat's Porch, 69–70

PJ's Café, 303
Platinum Point Historic District, 309
Plaza Fiesta, 166
Ponce de Leon Avenue, 153
Poncey-Highland, 83, 99
Poole's Mill Park and Historic Covered Bridge, 24, 216
population, 37
Powder Springs Park, 272
Powers' Crossroads Country Fair and Art Festival, 321
Pricci, 135
Pride of Dixie Antique Market, 168
Prime, 135
Prime Meridian, 70
Proof of the Pudding, 138
Psycho Sisters, 76
public restrooms, 37
Puckett's Station Arts and Crafts Festival, 321
Pumpkin Festival, 191
Pura Vida, 106–7
Pure Taqueria, 234
PushPush Theater/SmallTall Theater, 166

Q

Queen of Sheba, 160
Quinones at Bacchanalia, 99–100

R

R. Thomas Deluxe Grill, 137
Raiford Gallery, 239
rail service. *See* bus/rail service
railroad excursions and museums, 37
Rainbow Ranch, 223
Rainwater, 230
Rankin M. Smith Sr. IMAX Theatre, 152
Rare Footage, 167
Raven's Nest Artisans Marketplace, 208
Ray's Killer Creek, 230
Ray's on the River, 258
Red Baron's Antiques, 239
Redan Park, 179
Redneck Gourmet Corner Cafe, 318
reenactments, 37
Renaissance Festival, 26

Renaissance Waverly Hotel, 257
Rent a Wreck of Marietta, 246
Restaurant Eugene, 135
Re-Use the Past, 319
Rhodes Hall, 31, 86
Rhyne Park, 256
Rialto Center for the Performing Arts at Georgia State University, 75
Richards and Westbrook Galleries, 109
Ride the Ducks Adventure at Stone Mountain Park, 179
Ridgedale Park, 120
Ritz-Carlton, Atlanta, The, 68
Ritz-Carlton, Buckhead, 130
Riverboat Cruise at Stone Mountain Park, 179
rivers, 39
Riverside Park, 228
Riverside Sounds Concert Series, 34
Road Atlanta and Panoz Racing School, 17, 198
Road to Tara Museum, 283–84
Robert L. Stanton Rose Garden, 28, 152, 156
Robert W. Woodruff Arts Center, 84
Rockdale Medical Center, 174
Room at TWELVE Centennial Park, 70
Root House Museum, The, 31, 249
Roscoe Dunaway Gardens Historic District, 310
Roswell Area Park, 225
Roswell Art Center West, 217
Roswell Arts Festival, 242
Roswell Bicycles, 222
Roswell Bookstore, 239
Roswell Clock and Antique Co., 239
Roswell Cultural Arts Center, 238
Roswell Cultural Arts Center Summer Puppet Plays and Workshops, 241
Roswell Fire and Rescue Museum, 220–21
Roswell Ghost Tour, 29, 218
Roswell Magnolia Storytelling Festival, 241
Roswell Recreation and Parks Department, 227
Roswell Riverside Sounds, 241
Roswell Trail System and River Walk, 43, 223
Roswell Visual Arts Center, 217
Rum Creek Golf Club, 286
Rumi's Kitchen, 236
Ruth's Chris Steak House, 70

S

Sacred Heart Tattoo Parlor, 76

Sage, 230–31

sailing, 40, 202

Sambuca Jazz Cafe, 140

Sanctuary Latin Nightclub, 139

Sandy Ridge Park, 301

Sandy Springs Festival, 216, 242

Sandy Springs Historice Site/Williams-Payne House, 220

Sandy Springs Hospitality Board, 213

Savoy Bar and Grill, The, 98, 101

Sawnee Mountain, 34

Sawnee Mountain Park, 225

Sawnee Mountain Preserve, 35, 227–28

Scarlett O'Hara (paddle wheeler), 24

scenic drives: Fayetteville, 284; Grantville, 312; Jonesboro, 284; Kennesaw, 251; Marietta, 251; Midtown, 89–90; Moreland, 313; Newnan, 312, 313; Senoia, 313

Scenic Railroad and Live Show/Stone Mountain Park, 183–84

Schatten Gallery of the Woodruff Library, 150

Scott's Book Store, 319

Scouts Alley, 56

Screen on the Green film festival, 95

Seasons Brewing Company, 233

Senior Activity Center, Alpharetta, 225

Senoia, 310–11, 313, 316–17

Senoia City Hall, 307

Senoia Driving Tour of Homes, 26, 313

Senoia Historic District, 310

Senoia Tour of Homes and Progressive Dinner, 320

Sevananda, 76–77

Seven Gables Restaurant, 187–88

700 Miami Circle;Rib Ranch, 122

755 Club, 56

Seven Springs Museum, 269

Seven Stages Theater, 75

17th Street Bridge, 89

Several Dancers Core, 163

Sewell Park, 256

Shakerag Arts and Crafts Festival, 295

Shakerag Knoll Skateboard Park, 287

Sharon Springs Park, 225

Sharpsburg, 319–20

Shaw Park, 256

Sheep to Shawl Day, 143

Shellmont Inn, 96

Sheraton Colony Square Hotel, 98–99

Sherwood Shuttle, 279

Shillings on the Square, 260

Shillings Top of the Square, 258

Shoal Creek Campground, 205

shopping: factory outlets, 26; Georgia/Atlanta made, 28–29; Georgia-grown produce, 28; hours of operation, 26; overview, 40

Shops of Historic Roswell, 238

Shucker's Oyster Bar, 274

shuttles/limousines, 40

Silver Comet Depot, 252, 255, 275

Silver Comet Trail, 31, 43, 252, 255, 271

Silver Hill Manor, 185

Silver Leaf Limousine, 194

Six Feet Under, 59, 71

Six Flags American Adventures, 14, 254

Six Flags Over Georgia, 14, 21, 270–71

Six Flags White Water, 14, 254

Skate Escape, 92

skating, 92, 224, 255

Skyride at Stone Mountain Park, 180

Slopes BBQ, 235

Slovakia Restaurant, 258–59

Smith Plantation Home, 31

Smokey Road Scenic Drive, 313

smoking, 40

Smyrna, 247–48, 250, 255, 256, 260

Smyrna Museum, 250

Smyrna Welcome Center/Aunt Fanny's Cabin, 245

Social Circle, 187

Soda Shop, The, 208

Sotto Sotto, 103

South Buckhead, 120

South Candler Street, 149

South City Kitchen, 101

South Decatur Trolley Trail, 31

South Fulton Medical Center, 280

South Fulton Tennis Center, 41, 287

Southeastern Flower Show, 26, 77

Southeastern Railway Museum, 37, 197

Southern Artistry, 189

Southern Crescent: dining, 289–91; to do, 284–87; entertainment, 291–92; getting around, 279; getting there, 279; green space, 287–88; lodging, 289; map, 278; medical emergencies, 280; overview, 277; parking, 280; to see, 281–84; shopping, 292–93; special events, 293–95; tourist information/guidance, 279; villages/neighborhoods, 280–81

Southern Crescent Symphony Orchestra, 25, 304

Southern Hospitality Limo Service, 214

Southern Museum of Civil War and Locomotive History, 37, 250

Southern Regional Medical Center, 280

Southern Skillet, The, 235

Southside Theatre Guild, 292

Spa at Chateau Elan Winery and Resort, The, 203

Spa Suites at Chateau Elan Winery and Resort, 206

Spa Sydell, 126

Space, 112

spas, 126, 202, 203

Spelman College Museum of Fine Arts, 53

Spice, 101

Spice of Life Food and Cultural Celebration, 264

Spivey Hall, 291

sports teams, 40

Sprayberry's Barbecue, 318

Spring Hill Suites, 317

Spring Jonquil Festival, 263

Springvale Park, 66–67

Spruill Center for the Arts, 150

Spruill Center Gallery, 150

Spruill Gallery Community Garden, 150

Spruill Organic Farmers Market, 150

St. Joseph's Hospital, 215

St. Patrick's Day Family Festival, 78, 143

St. Patrick's Day Parade, 78

Stage Door Players, 166

Stan Smith Tennis Center at Chateau Elan Winery and Resort, 41, 203

Stanley House Inn, The, 257

Star Community Bar, 73

Star Provisions, 112

Starbucks, 137

Starbucks Café, 188

Starlight Movie Series, 263

Starr's Mill Scenic Stop, 284

StarTime Entertainment Complex, 14, 223

state parks, 21, 24, 35–36

Stately Oaks Plantation, 284

Steak N Shake, 137

Steeplechase at Callaway, 32

Stefan's Vintage Clothing, 76

Stockbridge, 281, 286, 287–88

Stone Mountain, 34

Stone Mountain Christmas, 191

Stone Mountain General Store, 189

Stone Mountain Golf Club at Stone Mountain Park, 181–82

Stone Mountain Park Antebellum Plantation, 177

Stone Mountain Park Campground, 21, 186

Stone Mountain Park Mini Golf, 182

Stone Mountain Trail, 31

Stone Mountain Village, Stone Mountain Park, and Beyond: dining, 187–88; to do, 178–84; entertainment, 188–89; getting around, 173–74; getting there, 173; green space, 184–85; lodging, 185–86; map, 172; medical emergencies, 174; overview, 171–72; parking, 174; public restrooms, 174; to see, 175–78; shopping, 189; special events, 188, 190–91; tourist information/guidance, 172–73; villages/neighborhoods, 174–75

Stone Mountain Village Visitors Center, 173

Storytelling Tours, 218

Strickland, Alice H., 196

Sugar Britches, 167–68

Sugar Creek Golf and Tennis Center, 155, 156

Sugar Magnolia Bed and Breakfast, 67

Summer Concert Series, 34–35, 263

Summer Film Festival, 110

Sun Dial Restaurant, Bar, and View, The, 70

Sun Valley Beach, 271

Sunday in the Park, 79

Sunset Safaris at Zoo Atlanta, 78

SunTrust Lunch on Broad Concert Series, 34, 72

Super VIP Transportation and Limo Service, 246

Swallow at the Hollow, 235–36

Swan Coach House Restaurant, Gift Shop and Gallery, 124, 136

Swan House, 121, 123–24

Sweat Mountain Park, 256

Sweet Auburn, 52

Sweet Auburn Curb Market, 76

Sweet Auburn SpringFest, 78

Sweetie's Flea Market, 304

Sweetwater Creek Intertribal Powwow, 276

Sweetwater Creek State Conservation Park, 36, 270, 273

Sweetwater Creek Summer Festival, 276

Sweetwater Park, 272

swimming, 92, 155, 225, 272, 287

Sycamore Grill, The, 187

Sycamore House, 158

Szechuan Village Restaurant, 274

T

Tabernacle, 72–73

Table 1280 Restaurant and Tapas Lounge, 101–2

Tall Tales of the South 4-D Theater, 189

Tam's Backstage, 232, 237

Tanger Outlets of Commerce, 26, 305

Tanyard Creek Park, 128

Taste of Alpharetta, 241

Taste of Atlanta, 144

Taste of Britain, 168

Taste of Main Street (East Point), 294

Taste of Marietta, 263

taxis, 40–41

Teaching Museum North, 221

Ted's Montana Grill, 162

Tellabration, 242

temperatures, 44

Ten East Washington, 317–18

Ten Pin Alley, 108

Ten Sites for Reflection: A Walking Tour of the Emory University Campus, 153–54

Ten Thousand Villages, 111–12

tennis, 41; Alpharetta, 225; Austell, 272; Braselton, 203; Buckhead, 127; College Park, 287; Cumming, 225; Decatur, 155–56; Mableton, 272; Marietta, 255–56; Midtown, 92; Peachtree City, 287; Powder Springs, 272; Roswell, 225; Sandy Springs, 225; Smyrna, 256

Terrell Mill Park, 256

"The Little Manse"-Erskine Caldwell Museum, 311

theater: Acworth, 261; Alpharetta, 237; Buckhead, 140; Cumming, 237; Decatur, 165–66; Douglasville, 275; Downtown, 74–75; Fairburn, 292; Fayetteville, 292; Jonesboro, 292; Kennesaw, 261; Marietta, 261–62; McDonough, 304; Midtown, 108–10; Newnan, 319; Roswell, 238; Stone Mountain Park, 189; Stone Mountain Village, 189; summer, 41; tickets, 25; year-round, 41

Theater Emory, 166

Theater of the Stars, 41

Theatre in the Square and Alley Theater, 41, 261–62

Theatrical Outfit, 75

Theo's Brother's Bakery, 236

Thomas A. Dorsey Festival, 276

Thomas Deans Fine Art, 142

Thomas-Barber Cabin, 151

Thompson Mills Forest, 204

Three Sisters Vineyards and Winery, 44

Tierra, 102

Tight Line Charters, 200

Toast, 104

Tom Lowe Trap and Skeet Range, 287

Tongue and Groove, 122, 140

Tour of Homes, Newnan, 321

Tour of Southern Ghosts, 28, 29, 181

tourist information/guidance, 30, 32–33

tourist seasons, 43–44

Tower Place 200, 121

Trackside Grill, The, 259

Trader Vic's, 70

Treehouse Challenge at Stone Mountain Park, 180

trolleys, 42

Truman's, 303

tubing. See canoeing, kayaking, tubing, white-water rafting

Tullie Smith Farm, 124

Turner Beach, 56

Turner Field Tours, 55–56, 63–64

Turner First Thursday Art Walks, 77

Tuxedo Park, 120

Twain's Billiards and Tap, 165

Twelve, 112

TWELVE Centennial Park, 68

TWELVE Hotel and Residences Atlantic Station, 99

Twin Lakes RV Park, 229
Twin Oaks Bed and Breakfast at MelaCari
  Cottages, 273–74
Twist, 135
2 Party Limousine Service, 214

U

Udipi Café, 161
Underground Atlanta, 55, 60
Union City, 281
University Inn at Emory, 159
U.S. Forest Service, 34
U.S. Play, 14

V

Variety Playhouse, 73
Varsity, The, 105
Veni Vidi Vici, 102
Veranda Historic Bed and Breakfast Inn, The,
  310, 316–17
Vickery's Crescent Avenue Bar and Grill, 105
Victory Cab of Marietta, 246
Vietnam War Memorial, 221
Villa Rica Tourism Board, 266
Village Inn Bed and Breakfast, 185–86
Village Tavern, 231
Villages Amphitheater, The, 34, 35, 291–92
Vines Botanical Gardens and Manor House, 28,
  184
Vinings. _See_ Buckhead and Vinings
Vinings Inn, The, 135–36
Vinny's, 231
Vintage Tea, 237
Virginia-Highland, 83–84, 96–97, 102–3,
  105–7
Virginia-Highland Bed and Breakfast, 97
Virginia-Highland Summerfest, 113
Virginia-Highland Tour of Homes, 113
Visitor Center at Lenox Square Mall, 49
Visitor Center at the Georgia World Congress
  Center, 49
Visitor Center at Underground Atlanta,
  49
Vortex Bar and Grill, The, 72

W

W. H. Reynolds Memorial Nature Preserve, 288
W Atlanta at Perimeter Center, 159
Waffle House, 137
Wahoo! Grill, 160
Walking Tour of Emory University Campus,
  42
walking tours, 42, 95, 153–54, 176, 228–29,
  284
Wallace Park, 272
Waller Park Extension, 225
Washington Avenue Historic District, 247
waterfalls, 43, 225–26
Watershed, 160
Waterside Restaurant, 187
Web sites, 43
Webb Bridge Park, 225, 228
WellStar Kennestone Hospital, 246, 267
West Cobb Aquatic Center, 272
West End, 52
West Village, 120
Westin Buckhead Atlanta, The, 121, 130
Westin Peachtree Plaza, 68
Westside: Austell, Douglasville, Lithia Springs,
  Mableton, Powder Springs, Villa Rica: din-
  ing, 274; to do, 270–72; entertainment,
  274–75; getting around, 267; getting there,
  266–67; green space, 272–73; lodging,
  273–74; map, 266; medical emergencies,
  267; overview, 265; to see, 268–69; shop-
  ping, 275; special events, 275–76; tourist
  information/guidance, 265–66; tourist sea-
  sons, 267; villages/neighborhoods, 267–68
Westside Trail, 31
Westview Cemetery, 22, 60–61
Wetlands and Watershed Festival, 302
White Glove Limousine, 40
White House, 136
Whitesburg, 313, 315, 317
white-water rafting. _See_ canoeing, kayaking,
  tubing, white-water rafting
Whitlock Avenue Historic District, 247
Whitlock Inn Bed and Breakfast, The, 257
Whitworth Inn, 204
Wick Tavern, 269
Wild Horse Creek Park, 272, 273

Wild Horse Creek Trail, 43, 271–72
William Bremen Jewish Heritage Museum, 34, 89
William Davis BMX Track, 285
Wills Park, 223, 225, 228
Wills Park Equestrian Center, 217, 228
Willy's Mexicana Grill, 95
Winder, 196, 197, 202, 203–4, 205
Windows Restaurant, 206
Wine Growers Association of Georgia, 44
Wine Tasting Festival, 170
wineries, 44
Wired & Fired, 112–13
Wolf Mountain Vineyards and Winery, 44
Woodfire Grill, 102
Woodruff Park, 67
Wren's Nest House Museum, 34, 61

X

Xperimental Puppetry Theater, 87
Xpress, 20–21

Y

Yellow Daisy Festival, 190
Yellow River Game Ranch, 45, 176
Yellow River Park, 185
Yellow Rose Carriage Service, 22, 30, 253
Young Deer Creek Park, 227
Your DeKalb Farmer's Market, 27, 168

Z

Zoo Atlanta, 45, 64–65
zoos/animal preserves, 45
Zyka, 161